Network Security Technologies:

Design and Applications

Abdelmalek Amine
Tahar Moulay University, Algeria

Otmane Ait Mohamed
Concordia University, Canada

Boualem Benatallah
University of New South Wales, Australia

A volume in the Advances in Information
Security, Privacy, and Ethics (AISPE) Book
Series

Information Science
REFERENCE
An Imprint of IGI Global

Managing Director:	Lindsay Johnston
Production Editor:	Jennifer Yoder
Development Editor:	Austin DeMarco
Acquisitions Editor:	Kayla Wolfe
Typesetter:	John Crodian
Cover Design:	Jason Mull

Published in the United States of America by
Information Science Reference (an imprint of IGI Global)
701 E. Chocolate Avenue
Hershey PA 17033
Tel: 717-533-8845
Fax: 717-533-8661
E-mail: cust@igi-global.com
Web site: http://www.igi-global.com

                    Library of Congress Cataloging-in-Publication Data

Network security technologies : design and applications / Abdelmalek Amine, Otmane Ait Mohamed, and Boualem Benatallah, editors.
     pages cm
  Includes bibliographical references and index.
  ISBN 978-1-4666-4789-3 (hardcover) -- ISBN 978-1-4666-4790-9 (ebook) --ISBN 978-1-4666-4791-6 (print & perpetual access) 1. Computer networks-- Security measures. I. Amine, Abdelmalek, editor of compilation. II. Ait Mohamed, Otmane editor of compilation. III. Benatallah, Boualem, editor of compilation.
  TK5105.59.N3434 2014
  005.8--dc23
                    2013040298

This book is published in the IGI Global book series Advances in Information Security, Privacy, and Ethics (AISPE) (ISSN: 1948-9730; eISSN: 1948-9749)

British Cataloguing in Publication Data
A Cataloguing in Publication record for this book is available from the British Library.

For electronic access to this publication, please contact: eresources@igi-global.com.

Advances in Information Security, Privacy, and Ethics (AISPE) Book Series

ISSN: 1948-9730
EISSN: 1948-9749

MISSION

In the digital age, when everything from municipal power grids to individual mobile telephone locations is all available in electronic form, the implications and protection of this data has never been more important and controversial. As digital technologies become more pervasive in everyday life and the Internet is utilized in ever increasing ways by both private and public entities, the need for more research on securing, regulating, and understanding these areas is growing.

The **Advances in Information Security, Privacy, & Ethics (AISPE) Book Series** is the source for this research, as the series provides only the most cutting-edge research on how information is utilized in the digital age.

COVERAGE

- Access Control
- Device Fingerprinting
- Global Privacy Concerns
- Information Security Standards
- Network Security Services
- Privacy-Enhancing Technologies
- Risk Management
- Security Information Management
- Technoethics
- Tracking Cookies

IGI Global is currently accepting manuscripts for publication within this series. To submit a proposal for a volume in this series, please contact our Acquisition Editors at Acquisitions@igi-global.com or visit: http://www.igi-global.com/publish/.

Titles in this Series

For a list of additional titles in this series, please visit: www.igi-global.com

Information Security in Diverse Computing Environments
Anne Kayem (Department of Computer Science, University of Cape Town, South Africa) and Christoph Meinel (Hasso-Plattner-Institute for IT Systems Engineering, University of Potsdam, Potsdam, Germany)
Information Science Reference • copyright 2014 • 300pp • H/C (ISBN: 9781466661585) • US $245.00 (our price)

Network Topology in Command and Control Organization, Operation, and Evolution
T. J. Grant (R-BAR, The Netherlands) R. H. P. Janssen (Netherlands Defence Academy, The Netherlands) and H. Monsuur (Netherlands Defence Academy, The Netherlands)
Information Science Reference • copyright 2014 • 330pp • H/C (ISBN: 9781466660588) • US $215.00 (our price)

Cases on Research and Knowledge Discovery Homeland Security Centers of Excellence
Cecelia Wright Brown (University of Baltimore, USA) Kevin A. Peters (Morgan State University, USA) and Kofi Adofo Nyarko (Morgan State University, USA)
Information Science Reference • copyright 2014 • 334pp • H/C (ISBN: 9781466659469) • US $215.00 (our price)

Multidisciplinary Perspectives in Cryptology and Information Security
Sattar B. Sadkhan Al Maliky (University of Babylon, Iraq) and Nidaa A. Abbas (University of Babylon, Iraq)
Information Science Reference • copyright 2014 • 334pp • H/C (ISBN: 9781466658080) • US $245.00 (our price)

Analyzing Security, Trust, and Crime in the Digital World
Hamid R. Nemati (The University of North Carolina at Greensboro, USA)
Information Science Reference • copyright 2014 • 281pp • H/C (ISBN: 9781466648562) • US $195.00 (our price)

Research Developments in Biometrics and Video Processing Techniques
Rajeev Srivastava (Indian Institute of Technology (BHU), India) S.K. Singh (Indian Institute of Technology (BHU), India) and K.K. Shukla (Indian Institute of Technology (BHU), India)
Information Science Reference • copyright 2014 • 279pp • H/C (ISBN: 9781466648685) • US $195.00 (our price)

Advances in Secure Computing, Internet Services, and Applications
B.K. Tripathy (VIT University, India) and D.P. Acharjya (VIT University, India)
Information Science Reference • copyright 2014 • 405pp • H/C (ISBN: 9781466649408) • US $195.00 (our price)

Security Engineering Techniques and Solutions for Information Systems Management and Implementation
Noureddine Boudriga (Engineering School of Communications, Tunisia) and Mohamed Hamdi (Engineering School of Communications, Tunisia)
Information Science Reference • copyright 2014 • 359pp • H/C (ISBN: 9781615208036) • US $195.00 (our price)

www.igi-global.com

701 E. Chocolate Ave., Hershey, PA 17033
Order online at www.igi-global.com or call 717-533-8845 x100
To place a standing order for titles released in this series, contact: cust@igi-global.com
Mon-Fri 8:00 am - 5:00 pm (est) or fax 24 hours a day 717-533-8661

Editorial Advisory Board

Table of Contents

Detailed Table of Contents

Mai Abu Baqar, Al-Balqa' Applied University, Jordan

Hamza Aldabbas, Al-Balqa' Applied University, Jordan

Tariq Alwadan, The World Islamic Sciences and Education University, Jordan

Mai Alfawair, Al-Balqa' Applied University, Jordan

Helge Janicke, De Montfort University, UK

Mobile Ad Hoc Network (MANET) and Vehicular Ad Hoc Network (VANET) are autonomous systems connected by wireless communication on a peer-to-peer basis. They are self-organized, self-configured, and self-controlled infrastructure-less networks. These kinds of networks have the advantage of being able to be set-up and deployed anywhere and anytime because it has a simple infrastructure set-up and no central administration. Distributing information between these nodes over long ranges in such networks, however, is a very challenging task, since sharing information always has a risk attached to it, especially when the information is confidential. The disclosure of such information to anyone else other than the intended parties could be extremely damaging. They are explored in this chapter.

Ansam Khraisat, University of Ballarat, Australia

Ammar Alazab, Deakin University, Australia

Michael Hobbs, Deakin University, Australia

Jemal Abawajy, Deakin University, Australia

Ahmad Azab, University of Ballarat, Australia

Cybercriminals continue to target online users of banks. They are improving their techniques and using high levels of skill in their attacks. Their continued search for different methods to commit crime makes the existing protection system less effective. They have developed crime toolkits which have become more accessible and simpler to use, and this has attracted more cybercriminals to cybercrime. In this chapter, the authors study the methods that are used in crime toolkits. They present the development and current trend of crime toolkits and reveal the methods that have been used to commit cybercrime successfully.

Chapter 3

Ahmed Chaouki Lokbani, Taher Moulay University of Saida, Algeria

Ahmed Lehireche, Djillali Liabes University of Sidi Bel Abbes, Algeria

Reda Mohamed Hamou, Taher Moulay University of Saida, Algeria

Abdelmalek Amine, Taher Moulay University of Saida, Algeria

Given the increasing number of users of computer systems and networks, it is difficult to know the profile of the latter, and therefore, intrusion has become a highly prized area of network security. In this chapter, to address the issues mentioned above, the authors use data mining techniques, namely association rules, decision trees, and Bayesian networks. The results obtained on the KDD'99 benchmark have been validated by several evaluation measures and are promising and provide access to other techniques and hybridization to improve the security and confidentiality in the field.

Chapter 4

Mehran Asadi, The Lincoln University, USA

Afrand Agah, West Chester University of Pennsylvania, USA

Christopher Zimmerman, West Chester University of Pennsylvania, USA

In this chapter, the authors examine the impacts of applying game theory on the network throughput, network voltage loss, and accuracy of malicious node detection in wireless sensor networks. Nodes in a wireless sensor network use our proposed protocol when deciding whether or not to forward packets they receive from other sensors in order to conserve power. Wireless sensor network nodes achieve this by optimizing their decision-making based on a framework using game theory. Defining a suitable cost and profit for routing and forwarding incoming packets and keeping a history of past behaviors of non-cooperating nodes gradually forces malicious nodes out of the wireless sensor network.In this chapter, the authors examine the impacts of applying game theory on the network throughput, network voltage loss, and accuracy of malicious node detection in wireless sensor networks. Nodes in a wireless sensor network use our proposed protocol when deciding whether or not to forward packets they receive from other sensors in order to conserve power. Wireless sensor network nodes achieve this by optimizing their decision-making based on a framework using game theory. Defining a suitable cost and profit for routing and forwarding incoming packets and keeping a history of past behaviors of non-cooperating nodes gradually forces malicious nodes out of the wireless sensor network.

Chapter 5

Mekkaoui Kheireddine, Dr Moulay Tahar University, Algeria

Rahmoun Abdellatif, Djillali Liabès University, Algeria

Sensor networks are composed of miniaturized wireless sensor nodes with limited capacity and energy source. Generally, these sensor networks are used, in many applications, to monitor inaccessible environments (battlefields, volcano monitoring, animal tracking...), hence the impossibility to replace or to recharge the batteries. As sensors may be deployed in a large area, radio transceivers are the most energy consuming of sensor nodes, which means that their usage needs to be very efficient in order to maximize node life, which leads us to maximize the network's life. In wireless sensor networks and in order to transmit its data, a node can route its messages towards destination, generally the base station, either by using small or large hops, so optimizing the hop length can extend significantly the lifetime of the network. This chapter provides a simple way to verify, which makes the energy consumption minimal by choosing proper hop length.

There is a need to be able to verify plaintext HTTP content transfers. Common sense dictates authentication and sensitive content should always be protected by SSL/HTTPS, but there is still great exploitation potential in the modification of static content in transit. Pre-computed signatures and client-side verification offers integrity protection of HTTP content in applications where SSL is not feasible. In this chapter, the authors demonstrate a mechanism by which a Web browser or other HTTP client can verify that content transmitted over an untrusted channel has not been modified. Verifiable HTTP is not intended to replace SSL. Rather, it is intended to be used in applications where SSL is not feasible, specifically, when serving high-volume static content and/or content from non-secure sources such as Content Distribution Networks. Finally, the authors find content verification is effective with server-side overhead similar to SSL. With future optimization such as native browser support, content verification could achieve comparable client-side efficiency.

The scientific tumultuous intonation has swept our feet's, of its balance and at the same time wheedled us to reach the take-off arena from where we can march equipped and outfitted into the subsequent century with confidence & self-assurance; by unearthing solutions for all information security related issues (with special emphasis on privacy issues). Examining various outstanding research problems that encompass to be embarked upon for effectively managing and controlling the balance between privacy and utility, the research community is pressurized to propose suitable elucidations. The solution is to engender several Privacy-Preserving Data Publishing (PPDP) techniques like Perturbation, swapping, randomization, cryptographic techniques etc., Amongst the various available techniques k-anonymity is unique in facet of its association with protection techniques that preserve the truthfulness of the data. The principal chip in of this sketch out comprises: 1) Motivation for this exploration for Amelioration Of Anonymity Modus Operandi For Privacy Preserving Data Mining; 2) investigation of well-known research approaches to PPDM; 3) argue solutions to tackle the problems of security threats and attacks in the PPDM in systems; 4) related survey of the various anonymity techniques; 5) exploration of metrics for the diverse anonymity techniques; 6) performance measures for the various anonymity techniques; and 7) contradistinguish the diverse anonymity techniques and algorithms.

The high adoption in daily lives of services offered by the Web 2.0 has opened a wide field for the proliferation of new Web-based services and applications. Social networks, as the main exponent of this new generation of services, require security systems to ensure end user authentication and access control to shared information. Another feature that is becoming increasingly important in these scenarios is the delegation of controlled access between the different API (Application Programming Interfaces) to integrate services and information. The safe use of these Web services requires end user security credentials and different authentication and authorization technologies. This chapter provides an introduction to the most relevant protocols and standards in the area of Web service security, which are able to provide authentication and authorization mechanisms.

Chapter 9

Wireless networks are inherently insecure due to the fact that information on the network can be passively retrieved by an eavesdropper using off-the-shelf network hardware and free software applications. The most common solution for this vulnerability is the Wireless Protected Access (WPA) protocol. This protocol provides data encryption and access control for wireless networks. However, the WPA protocol contains drawbacks in its authentication mechanisms that can cause inconveniences for end users and performance degradation for the network. Furthermore, many of the authentication methods used with WPA are not friendly to small and resource-constrained wireless devices. This chapter presents the design of a new wireless security protocol for privacy and authentication using efficient Identity-Based Encryption (IBE) techniques. This protocol can be used to eliminate the need for a central authentication server for enterprise networks, as well as to provide the new feature of privacy without authentication for public wireless networks. This work also puts forth an analysis and validation of the new protocol, including security strength, storage overhead, communication overhead, and computational efficiency.

Chapter 10

Human Interactive Proof (HIP) systems have been introduced to distinguish between various groups of users. CAPTCHA methods are one of the important branches of HIP systems, which are used to distinguish between human users and computer programs automatically and block automated computer programs form abusing Web services. The goal of these systems is to ask questions, which human users can easily answer but current computer programs cannot. In this chapter, the authors collect different pioneering works, which are done on CAPTCHA systems and create a complete survey of them. They collect more than 100 published works and classify them into 3 categories. This chapter contains different works, which are done for creating CAPTCHA methods and assessing CAPTCHA methods from different aspects, including the attacks done against CAPTCHA methods. This chapter can be used by researchers in CAPTCHA domains to quickly find previous works.

The focus of this chapter is two-fold: It first presents the classical network attacks (such as Session Hijacking, Man-in-the-Middle attack, DNS attacks, Distributed Denial of Service attacks, and other miscellaneous attacks), which have exploited the various vulnerabilities of computer networks in the past, and reviews the solutions that have been implemented since then to mitigate or reduce the chances of these attacks. The authors then present the different network security controls, including the protocols and standards (such as IPSec, Kerberos, Secure Shell, Transport Layer Security, Virtual Private Networks, Firewalls, and S/MIME) that have been adopted in modern day computer networks to control the incidence of attacks in modern day computer networks.

Recent malicious attempts are intended to get financial benefits through a large pool of compromised hosts, which are called software robots or simply bots. A group of bots, referred to as a botnet, is remotely controllable by a server and can be used for sending spam emails, stealing personal information, and launching DDoS attacks. Growing popularity of botnets compels to find proper countermeasures, but existing defense mechanisms hardly catch up with the speed of botnet technologies. Bots are constantly and automatically changing their signatures to successfully avoid the detection. Therefore, it is necessary to analyze the weaknesses of existing defense mechanisms to find the gap and then design new framework of botnet detection that integrates effective approaches. To get a deep insight into the inner-working of botnets and to understand their architecture, the authors analyze some sophisticated sample botnets. In this chapter, they propose a comprehensive botnet analysis and reporting framework that is based on sound theoretical background.

Chapter 13

Reliability analysis of engineering systems has traditionally been done using computationally expensive computer simulations that cannot attain 100% accuracy due to their inherent limitations. The authors conduct a formal reliability analysis using higher-order-logic theorem proving, which is known to be sound, accurate, and exhaustive. For this purpose, they present the higher-order-logic formalization of independent multiple continuous random variables, their verified probabilistic properties, and generalized relations for commonly encountered reliability structures in engineering systems. To illustrate the usefulness of the approach, the authors present the formal reliability analysis of a single stage transmission of an automobile.

Chapter 14

This chapter deals with a challenging issue in intrusion detection research field, which is IDS adaptability. First, it introduces the intrusion detection concepts, then presents with details the two existing generations of IDSs and addresses their major problem: permanent coverage of new attacks patterns in a dynamic changing environment. Thereafter, it evokes the requirement of adaptability in IDS as a mean to remedy this deficiency. Later, it explores the most eminent approaches that are proposed for IDS adaptability. It describes their functional architecture and discusses their strong aspects and weaknesses. At the end, new trends toward the intrusion detection adaptability problematic are mentioned and followed by a conclusion.

Preface

The advances in telecommunication, IT technologies, and security challenges have produced the network security technologies field. This field deals with the art, the knowledge, methodologies, and techniques from diverse area, such as cryptography, network communication, and protocol, etc. It is devoted to solving security problems in a systematic way in order to ensure security of software and communication functionalities at basic, enhanced, integrated, and architectural levels. The scope of the book is to provide the latest knowledge and technologies used and applied in the network security area. In addition, it analyses malicious threats, viruses, and attacks that can compromise network integrity at hardware or software levels.

In Chapter 1, a review of Mobile Ad Hoc Networks (MANET) and Vehicular Ad Hoc Networks (VANET) is proposed. These networks are autonomous systems connected by wireless communication on a peer-to-peer basis. They are self-organized, self-configured, and self-controlled infrastructure-less networks. These kinds of networks have the advantage of being able to be set-up and deployed anywhere and anytime because they have a simple infrastructure set-up and no central administration. Distributing information between these nodes over long ranges in such networks, however, is a very challenging task, since sharing information always has a risk attached to it, especially when the information is confidential. The disclosure of such information to anyone other than the intended parties could be extremely damaging.

Cybercriminals continue to target online users of banks. They are improving their techniques using high levels of skill in their attacks. Their continued search for different methods to commit crime makes the existing protection system less effective. They have developed crime toolkits, which have become more accessible and simpler to use, and this has attracted more cybercriminals to cybercrime. In Chapter 2, a review of the methods that are used in crime toolkits is presented. The new development and the current trend of crime toolkits are presented. In addition, the chapter discusses the methods that have been used to commit cybercrime successfully.

In Chapter 3, the authors addresses the issue of network security using data mining techniques, namely association rules, decision trees, and Bayesian networks. The results obtained on the KDD'99 benchmark have been validated by several evaluation measures and are promising and provide access to other techniques and hybridization to improve the security and confidentiality in the field.

In Chapter 4, the impacts of applying game theory on the network throughput, network voltage loss, and accuracy of malicious node detection in wireless sensor networks are examined. Nodes in a wireless sensor network use our proposed protocol when deciding whether or not to forward packets they receive from other sensors in order to conserve power. Wireless sensor network nodes achieve this by optimizing their decision-making based on a framework using game theory. Defining a suitable cost and profit for routing and forwarding incoming packets and keeping a history of past behaviors of non-cooperating nodes gradually forces malicious nodes out of the wireless sensor network.

Chapter 5 deals with issues of extending battery lifetime in wireless sensors networks. These networks are composed of miniaturized wireless sensor nodes with limited capacity and energy sources. Generally, these sensor networks are used, in many applications, to monitor inaccessible environments (battlefields, volcano monitoring, animal tracking...), hence the impossibility of replacing or to recharging the batteries. As sensors may be deployed in a large area, radio transceivers are the most energy consuming of sensor nodes, which means that their usage needs to be very efficient in order to maximize node life, which leads to maximizing the network life. In wireless sensor networks and in order to transmit its data, a node can route its messages towards destination, generally the base station, either by using small or large hops, so optimizing the hop length can extend the lifetime of the network. This chapter provides an algorithm that makes the energy consumption minimal by choosing proper hop length.

In Chapter 6, the author discusses the need to be able to verify plaintext HTTP content transfers. Common sense dictates authentication and sensitive content should always be protected by SSL/HTTPS, but there is still great exploitation potential in the modification of static content in transit. Pre-computed signatures and client-side verification offers integrity protection of HTTP content in applications where SSL is not feasible. The author demonstrates a mechanism by which a Web browser or other HTTP client can verify that content transmitted over an untrusted channel has not been modified. Verifiable HTTP is not intended to replace SSL. Rather, it is intended to be used in applications where SSL is not feasible, specifically when serving high-volume static content and/or content from non-secure sources such as Content Distribution Networks. It is found that content verification is effective with server-side overhead similar to SSL. With future optimization, such as native browser support, content verification could achieve comparable client-side efficiency.

In Chapter 7, the author presents an abridgment of Amelioration of Perturbation Modus Operandi for Privacy Preserving Data Mining. Examining various outstanding research problems that encompass effective management and control of the balance between privacy and utility, the research community is pressurized to propose a resolution. The solution is to engender several PPDM techniques like perturbation, swapping, randomization, cryptographic techniques, etc. Amongst the various available techniques perturbation is unique in facet of its association with protection techniques that preserve the truthfulness of the data. Perturbation is a property that models the fortification of released data in opposition to possible re-identification of the respondents to which the data refers.

Chapter 8 provides an introduction to the most relevant protocols and standards in the area of Web service security, which are able to provide authentication and authorization mechanisms. The high adoption in the daily lives of services offered by Web 2.0 has opened a wide field for the proliferation of new Web-based services and applications. Social networks, as the main exponent of this new generation of services, require security systems to ensure end user authentication and access control to shared information. Another feature that is becoming increasingly important in these scenarios is the delegation of controlled access between the different Application Programming Interfaces (API) to integrate services and information. The safe use of these Web services requires end user security credentials and different authentication and authorization technologies.

Chapter 9 is interested in developing new security mechanisms in Wireless networks, which are inherently insecure due to the fact that information on the network can be passively retrieved by an eavesdropper using off-the-shelf network hardware and free software applications. The most common solution for this vulnerability is the Wireless Protected Access (WPA) protocol. This protocol provides data encryption and access control for wireless networks. However, the WPA protocol contains drawbacks in its authentication mechanisms that can cause inconveniences for end users and performance degradation for the network. Furthermore, many of the authentication methods used with WPA are not friendly to small and resource-constrained wireless devices. This work presents the design of a new wireless security protocol for privacy and authentication using efficient Identity-Based Encryption (IBE) techniques. This protocol can be used to eliminate the need for a central authentication server for enterprise networks, as well as to provide the new feature of privacy without authentication for public wireless networks. This work also puts forth an analysis and validation of the new protocol, including security strength, storage overhead, communication overhead, and computational efficiency.

In Chapter 10, the authors present a collection of different works, which are done on CAPTCHA systems, and create a complete survey of published works. They categorize more than 100 published works and classify them into 3 categories. This chapter contains different works, which are done for creating CAPTCHA methods and assessing CAPTCHA methods from different aspects, including the attacks done against CAPTCHA methods. Researchers in CAPTCHA domains can use this chapter to quickly find previous works.

A great amount of information is circulated through the Internet. Some of it exclusively belongs to a special group of users and requires protection and safeguarding against unauthorized access. To this end, a category of systems called Human Interactive Proof (HIP) has been introduced to distinguish between various groups of users. Completely Automatic Public Turing Test to Tell Computer and Human Apart (CAPTCHA) methods are one of the important branches of HIP systems that are used to distinguish between human users and computer programs automatically. These methods are based on Artificial Intelligence (AI) topics. The goal of these systems is to ask questions that human users can easily answer but current computer programs cannot. These methods are used to block automated computer programs—software robots or simply bots—form abusing Web services.

The focus of Chapter 11 is two-fold: It first presents the classical network attacks (such as Session Hijacking, Man-in-the-Middle attack, DNS attacks, Distributed Denial of Service attacks, and other miscellaneous attacks) that have exploited the various vulnerabilities of computer networks in the past and review the solutions that have been implemented since then to mitigate or reduce the chances of these attacks. The authors then present the different network security controls including the protocols and standards (such as IPSec, Kerberos, Secure Shell, Transport Layer Security, Virtual Private Networks, Firewalls, and S/MIME) that have been adopted in modern day computer networks to control the incidence of attacks in modern day computer networks.

Chapter 12 provides a deep insight into the inner working of botnets and their architecture by analyzing some sophisticated sample botnets. In this chapter, the author proposes a comprehensive botnet analysis and reporting framework that is based on sound theoretical background. Recent malicious attempts are intended to get financial benefits through a large pool of compromised hosts, which are called software robots or simply bots. A group of bots, referred to as a botnet, is remotely controllable by a server and can be used for sending spam emails, stealing personal information, and launching DDoS attacks. Growing popularity of botnets compels one to find proper countermeasures, but existing defense mechanisms hardly catch up with the speed of botnet technologies. Bots are constantly and automatically changing their signatures to successfully avoid detection. Therefore, it is necessary to analyze the weaknesses of existing defense mechanisms to find the gap and then design new frameworks of botnet detection that integrate effective approaches.

In Chapter 13, the authors conduct a formal reliability analysis using a higher-order-logic theorem, which is known to be sound, accurate, and exhaustive. Reliability analysis of engineering systems has traditionally been done using computationally expensive computer simulations that cannot attain 100%

accuracy due to their inherent limitations. For this purpose, they present the higher-order-logic formalization of independent multiple continuous random variables, their verified probabilistic properties, and generalized relations for commonly encountered reliability structures in engineering systems. To illustrate the usefulness of their approach, they present the formal reliability analysis of a single stage transmission of an automobile.

Finally, Chapter 14 is explores the intrusion detection field that has significantly evolved from a classical ad hoc generation of Intrusion Detection Systems (IDS) to automatic generation, which is more effective. However, the continuous coverage of new attacks remains an unreachable goal. This challenge is closely linked to information technology evolution, which constantly imports changes in network environments and attack strategies. For this reason, the Intrusion Detection System (IDS) must adjust itself, according to every change in its target environment, to be able to handle continuously every attack occurrence and accomplish its everlastingness and effectiveness. This requirement, which is referred to as adaptability, is missing in the two existing generations of IDS. It makes the IDS a learning system in relation to its target environment, practicing an autonomous incremental learning of normal and intrusive behaviour. Most recent research work tends toward IDS adaptability, which is the origin of a new generation of IDS, called adaptive IDS.

Abdelmalek Amine
Tahar Moulay University, Algeria

Otmane Ait Mohamed
Concordia University, Canada

Boualem Benattallah
University of New South Wales, Australia

Chapter 1
Review of Security in VANETs and MANETs

Mai Abu Baqar
Al-Balqa' Applied University, Jordan

Hamza Aldabbas
Al-Balqa' Applied University, Jordan

Tariq Alwadan
The World Islamic Sciences and Education University, Jordan

Mai Alfawair
Al-Balqa' Applied University, Jordan

Helge Janicke
De Montfort University, UK

ABSTRACT

Mobile Ad Hoc Network (MANET) and Vehicular Ad Hoc Network (VANET) are autonomous systems connected by wireless communication on a peer-to-peer basis. They are self-organized, self-configured, and self-controlled infrastructure-less networks. These kinds of networks have the advantage of being able to be set-up and deployed anywhere and anytime because it has a simple infrastructure set-up and no central administration. Distributing information between these nodes over long ranges in such networks, however, is a very challenging task, since sharing information always has a risk attached to it, especially when the information is confidential. The disclosure of such information to anyone else other than the intended parties could be extremely damaging. They are explored in this chapter.

1. INTRODUCTION

Recently, ad hoc networks received extensive attention in both industrial and military applications, because of the striking property of creating a network while moving from one place to another and not requiring any pre-designed infrastructure. This chapter therefore presents an introduction of mobile ad hoc networks (MANETs) in Section 2, with its characteristics described in Section 2.1: constrained resources, infrastructure less, low and variable bandwidth, dynamic topology, multi-hop communications, limited device security, limited physical security, and short range connectivity. These unique characteristics in MANETs present appreciable challenges, therefore Section 2.2 describes the vulnerabilities and challenges of MANET: lack of secure boundaries, restricted power supply, unreliability, lack of centralized management facility, threats from compromised nodes, and scalability.

DOI: 10.4018/978-1-4666-4789-3.ch001

There are many applications of MANETs therefore Section 2.3 presents these applications: home networks, enterprise networks, military applications, emergency response networks, sensor networks, and Vehicular ad hoc Networks (VANETs). Section 3 presents an introduction to VANETs, and describes the modern vehicles' components.

Section 3.1 presents history and background of VANETs by reviewing these projects and consortiums in VANET: PROMETHEUS project (program for European traffic with highest efficiency and unprecedented safety), DRIVE project (dedicated road drive infrastructure for vehicle safety in Europe), C2CCC (car2car communication consortium). Section 3.2 presents an overview of recent wireless communication technologies for VANETs: Wi-Fi, WiMAX and DSRC (Dedicated short range communication). Section 3.3 presents characteristics of VANETs: dynamic topology, random disconnection, mobility modelling, computational power, and variable density. The striking features of these networks raise both challenges and opportunities in achieving security, Section 4 presents these challenges.

Section 5 presents the security requirements: authentication, authorisation, access control, privacy, confidentiality, availability, survivability, data integrity, and non-repudiation. Section 6 presents both types of attacks: passive attacks are hard to detect because they are based on 'snooping' on transmitted packets between entities, whereas in active attacks the attacker tries to change or destroy the data being transmitted within the network. External active attack and internal active attacks are also described in Section 6. Section 7 presents a set of security mechanisms which can be used to enforce the security requirement: cryptography, digital signature, access control, authentication, traffic padding, notarization, and routing control. Section 7.1 presents the access control models: Discretionary Access Control (DAC), Mandatory Access Control (MAC), and Role-Based Access Control (RBAC).

Section 8 presents an overview of the cryptographic background to understand work already done on securing VANETs and MANETs. Two main types of cryptographic algorithms are used in cryptography: symmetric key algorithms presented in Section 8.1 in which sender and receiver both use the same key (secret key) for encryption and decryption, whereas in asymmetric key algorithms presented in Section 8.2, the sender and the receiver uses two different keys for encryption and decryption. Public Key Infrastructure (PKI), Digital signature, and Digital Certificate will also be discussed in detail in Sections 8.2 and 8.3 respectively.

Finally, Section 9 presents a critical review of the security issues in both MANETs and VANETs. It also provides a survey of existing solutions in the field of security to highlight a particular area, not been addressed up to now: controlling the information flow that allows the originator to control the dissemination of data communicated between nodes. This is to ensure that data remains confidential not only during transmission but also after it has been communicated to another peer.

2. MOBILE WIRELESS AD HOC NETWORKS (MANETS)

Mobile ad hoc networks are autonomous systems which consist of a number of mobile nodes that communicate between themselves using wireless transmission. They are thus self-organized, self-configured and self-controlled infrastructure-less. This kind of network has the advantage of being able to be set up and deployed anywhere and anytime because it has a simple infrastructure setup and no central administration. Mobile ad hoc networks (MANETs) are case of wireless ad hoc networks, progressively more popular and successful in the marketplace of wireless technology.

These networks are particularly useful to those mobile users who need to communicate in situations where no fixed wired infrastructures are available. Obvious examples are the military or the emergency services: one clear situation might be a fire fighter who needs to connect to an ambulance. In such situations a collection of mobile nodes with wireless network interface can form a transitory network (Sarkar, Basavaraju & Puttamadappa, 2007). Recently, ad hoc networks received extensive attention in both industrial and military applications, because of the striking property of creating a network while moving from one place to another and it does not require any pre designed infrastructure.

2.1 The Characteristics of MANET

A mobile ad hoc network (MANET) is an independent system of mobile nodes linked by wireless connections. These nodes are free to move arbitrarily; therefore, the topology of wireless networks change swiftly and in an unpredictable manner.

Generally, direct communication in MANETs is possible only between adjacent nodes. Thus, communication between distant nodes is established using multiple-hop. Since the locations may change dynamically, as a consequence the interconnections between the adjacent nodes may change continually. Each mobile node functions as both host and router, relaying data packets from one node to another. MANETs have many characteristics that make them distinguishable from other wireless and wired networks (Al-Jaroodi, 2002; Murthy & Manoj, 2004; Toh, 2001; Chadha & Kant, 2007; Carvalho, 2008) which are in detail:

- **Constrained Resources:** Most MANET devices are small hand-held devices like personal digital assistants (PDAs), laptops and cell phones. These devices have limitations because of their restricted battery-capacity, small processing power and storage facilities. Energy consumption is an important criterion when designing the MANET.

- **Infrastructure-less (Autonomous):** MANETs are based on the teamwork between independent peer-to-peer nodes that communicate with each other. Without any pre-planned arrangement or base station, all nodes have the same role in the network. There are no pre-set roles like router, server or gateways for the nodes participating in the network.

- **Low and Variable Bandwidth:** Wireless links which connect the MANET nodes have much smaller bandwidth than wired links. The effects of interference, congestion and noise are more significant.

- **Dynamic Topology:** MANET nodes can move arbitrarily; thus the nodes can dynamically enter and leave the network, continually change their links and topologies. This leads to frequent changes in the routing information.

- **Multi-hop communications:** The communication in MANET between any two nodes is performed by numerous intermediary nodes whose functions are to relay data-packets from one point to another. Ad hoc networks require multi-hop communications, for example, in Figure 1, nodes A and D must engage the help of nodes B and C to relay data-packets between them in order to communicate.

- **Limited Device Security:** MANETs devices are usually small and can be transported from one place to another. Unfortunately, as a result these devices can be easily lost, stolen or damaged.

- **Limited Physical Security:** MANETs are in general more vulnerable to physical layer's attacks than wired networks; the possibility of spoofing, eavesdropping, jamming and denial of service (DoS) attacks should be carefully considered. However the self-administration nature of MANET makes them more robust against single failure points.

Figure 1. Mobile ad hoc network of four nodes, using the transmission range of nodes B and C in order to communicate between node A and node D

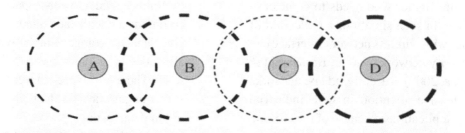

- **Short Range Connectivity:** MANETs rely on radio frequency (RF) technology to connect, which is in general considered to be short range communication. For that reason, the nodes that want to communicate directly need to be in the close frequency range of each other.

2.2 The Vulnerabilities and Challenges of MANET

The key challenges in designing MANETs result from the decentralised nature and lack of central infrastructure like a base station, access point or server. In addition to that, all communications are carried out through the wireless medium. These unique characteristics present appreciable challenges for MANETs as mentioned in (Li & Joshi, 2004; Papadimitratos & Haas, 2003; Mishra & Nadkarni, 2003; Zhang & Lee, 2005):

- **Lack of Secure Boundaries:** In comparison with wired networks where the devices must have a physical access to the network medium, mobile ad hoc networks have no apparent secure boundary. There is no need for attackers to have physical access to the network; once the attackers are in the transmission range of any other devices, then they can join and communicate with other devices.

- **Restricted Power Supply:** In contrast to wired networks where the nodes can get their electrical supply directly from the power points, MANETs nodes are generally operated by small batteries with limited lifetime. Nodes are therefore less likely to be able to operate intensive computations, which makes them vulnerable to a denial-of-service attack (DoS). This can be done by sending additional routing packets to a targeted node, in order to be executed by the targeted node in an attempt to exhaust its battery.

- **Unreliability:** Due to the limited battery supply and mobility in MANETs, the mobile devices cannot be assured as being reliable to serve communication participants; some nodes may behave in a 'selfish' manner when it finds that there is only limited power supply.

- **Lack of Centralized Management Facility:** The lack of centralized management makes the detection of attacks complicated. Mobile ad hoc networks are highly dynamic and large scale therefore they cannot be easily monitored. Also benign (non-malignant) failures in the mobile ad hoc network are fairly common, for example, transmission destructions and packet dropping. As a result, malicious failures will be more difficult to discover.

- **Threats from Compromised Nodes:** Due to the movement of the nodes in ad hoc networks, it can be challenging to detect the malicious attack carried out by a compromised node, particularly in a large scale ad hoc network.

- **Scalability:** In MANETs nodes entering and leaving the network cause frequent changes to the network topology; the network may consist of hundreds to thousands of nodes; the routing protocols configurations and key management services therefore have to be adjusted to fit these new conditions.

2.3 Applications of Mobile Ad Hoc Networks

There are many applications of mobile ad hoc networks; these have been listed in (Sarkar, Basavaraju & Puttamadappa, 2007; Bharathidasan & Ponduru, 2002; Murthy & Manoj, 2004; Yousefi, Bastani & Fathy, 2007; Carcelle, Dangand & Devic, 2006; Yick, Mukherjee & Ghosal, 2008):

1. **Home Network and Enterprise Network:** One use of MANET is in some home environments, such as home wireless networks, smart homes and personal area networks (PAN) which we can make communication between smart household appliances, in comparison with fixed wireless network, wireless ad hoc devices can move in free manner and they organise themselves in an arbitrary type. Roaming can be carried out while the devices are communicating with each other, which is suitable to businesses demand such as in office wireless networks, conferences, meeting rooms and networks at construction areas.

2. **Military Applications:** Mobile ad hoc network can be valuable to soldiers in order to establish communication for tactical campaigns; setting up a fixed infrastructure in enemy areas or in hostile lands may not be possible in such conditions. Whereas, MANETs can offer the required communication promptly and quickly. The coordination of military objects moving at high speeds, such as fleets of airplanes or warships is another application in this area.

3. **Emergency Response Network:** Mobile ad hoc network can be used to supply emergency management services applications, for example in disaster recovery, fire fighting, search and rescue operations where the whole communication infrastructure has been demolished or is unavailable. Deploying MANETs in these places can set up an infrastructure quickly.

4. **Sensor Network:** Wireless sensor networks can be deployed in ad hoc mode to assist monitoring and controlling physical surroundings from distant places with sufficient accuracy. These sensors might be equipped with a selection of components (processor, radio transceiver, actuator, micro-controller, and energy source) in order to measure several physical attributes like motion, temperature, moisture, atmospheric pressure, sound, vibration, pollution and velocity. Sensor networks are used in military applications such as battlefield observation; equipment ammunition; targeting; and nuclear, biological and chemical attack detection and reconnaissance. It is also commonly used in many manufacturing and civilian applications, such as monitoring product quality, controlling machines, healthcare applications, home automation control (smart home), and traffic control.

5. **Vehicular Ad hoc Network (VANET):** It is a subclass of mobile ad hoc networks (MANETs), where the mobile nodes are vehicles; today vehicles are becoming "computer networks on wheels," these vehicles are free to move and organise themselves arbitrarily, which they can exchange information between themselves and Road Side Units (RSUs), in order to increase safety in the roads by warning the drivers about ongoing hazard situations, and increasing the responsiveness of their surroundings and make them more vigilant.

In another aspect inter-vehicle communication(IVC) can be used to enhance passenger comfort and traffic system such as exchanging traffic information, weather information, petrol station, restaurants location and price information, and providing the interactive communication like offering access to the Internet.

3. VEHICULAR AD HOC NETWORKS (VANETS)

Vehicular ad hoc network is a new emerging network technology derived from ad hoc networks, which can provide wireless communication services between vehicles and adjacent road side units; it is a promising technology for future smart vehicle systems and intelligent transportation systems (ITS).

In VANETs, each vehicle in the system as in Figure 2 has a computing device, a short-range wireless interface, event data recorder (EDR), front and rear sensors and a GPS (Global Positioning System) device which is progressively more becoming common in vehicles today, in order to provide vehicles' location, speed, current time and direction.

3.1 History and Background

The idea of inter vehicle communication (IVC) has gained considerable interest in the last few decades, which includes vehicle-to-vehicle (V2V),

Figure 2. A modern vehicle is a network of sensors/actuators on wheels (Olariu & Weigle, 2009)

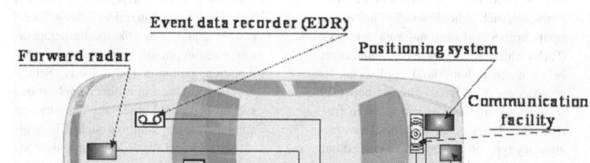

and vehicle-to-infrastructure (V2I) communications. In Europe for examples PROMETHEUS (program for European traffic with highest efficiency and unprecedented safety) project was created during 1987-1995 by eighteen European car manufacturers, incorporating more than forty research institutions in addition to state authorities; the main purpose of the PROMETHEUS project was automated driving (adaptive cruise control) for private cars. The next project DRIVE (dedicated road drive infrastructure for vehicle safety in Europe) was created during 1988-1994; the main purpose of the DRIVE project was to improve traffic efficiency and safety considering road-side infrastructure (Olariu & Weigle, 2009). These projects led substantial progresses in European road transport; however the deployment of inter vehicle communication was not adequate enough to deploy, because of the need of a suitable wireless communication technology.

When new wireless technologies have emerged, to support the revolution of vehicular ad hoc networks, the number of academic and industrial interests in VANETs has increased. and many efforts moved from the pure research stage to the experimental and execution stage. As a result a non-profit organization called C2CCC (car2car communication consortium) was created by Audi, BMW, Daimler Chrysler, Fiat, Renault, and Volkswagen.

After that IEEE 802.11p task group was formed which is focused on providing wireless access technology for vehicular environment; in accordance with the official IEEE 802.11p working group project timelines, the standard is scheduled to be published in December 2010. Recently, Toyota and Microsoft have declared a 12 million dollar joint investment on including Microsoft's Azure cloud platform in upcoming Toyota vehicles for better telematics (Oates, 2011).

The main goal of these projects and consortiums are to increase road safety, increasing transportation efficiency, and reducing the impact of transportation on the environment.

3.2 Wireless Communication Technologies for VANETs

In recent years various wireless network technologies have been developed to offer different services, increased coverage area and data rates. In this introduction we will describe in overview:

3.2.1 Wi-Fi

(Abbreviation of Wireless Fidelity) is a class of wireless (LAN) devices; the technology is based on the IEEE 802.11 standards (Lehr & McKnight, 2003). Today, Wi-Fi devices can be found in many desktop computers, smart phones, printers, and indeed all modern laptops and (PDAs) are equipped with Wi-Fi technology. Wi-Fi's original purpose was mobile computing devices (for example laptops in LANs), but is now progressively more used for more purposes, including VoIP phones, games, and televisions and DVD players. Wi-Fi today is more commonly used to provide an Internet LAN connection to Wi-Fi enabled devices like a computers, smart phones or PDAs. The above functions require the device to be within range of an access point.

The most common Wi-Fi standard IEEE 802.11g has a data transfer rate of around 54 Mbps; the range indoors is a maximum 150 feet (approximately 45 meters) and double that outdoors though, this depends on the conditions, like obstacles, power and weather. In Wi-Fi both 802.11b and 802.11g are using 2.4 GHz under the speed of 11 Mbps and 54 Mbps respectively, while 802.11n operates in both 2.4 and 5 GHz with theoretical speed 600 Mbps (Gast 2005).

In Wi-Fi MAC (Media Access Controller) users are competing when they are connected to Wi-Fi access point, and users therefore have different levels of bandwidth. Wi-Fi however is short range (tens of meters) can be encrypted with WEP(Wired Equivalent Privacy) or WPA and WPA2 (Wi-Fi Protected Access encryption).

3.2.2 WiMAX

(Worldwide Interoperability of Microwave Access) is based on the IEEE 802.16 standard (also called Broadband Wireless Access). WiMax was formed in 2001 by the WiMax Forum, in order to endorse WiMax as a standard (Andrews, Ghosh & Muhamed, 2007).

WiMax was described as a standard based technology for use as "last mile" broadband delivery rather than using wires. WiMax was planned to be used to link Wi-Fi hotspots together. WiMax 802.16 operates at range of 10-66 GHz and is classified as fixed wireless broadband; later, in 2004 802.16a was updated and operates at lower frequency range 2-11 GHz and is classified as fixed wireless broadband as well; finally in 2005 mobile wireless broadband was created under 802.16 e which operates at frequency range of 2-6 GHz (Ghosh, Wolter, Andrews & Chen, 2005).

WiMax technology has an advantage which is not affected by obstacles like buildings. This makes WiMax especially useful and cost-effective for countryside homes where setting a traditional wire would be more difficult and very expensive.

WiMax is equipped with stronger encryption than Wi-Fi, and typically suffers less interference. WiMax speed in theory delivers up to 70 Mbps, and range coverage 112 Km. These numbers changes depends on the conditions, like obstacles, power and weather, expected values is 10 Mbps in 2 Km coverage area.

3.2.3 DSRC

In 1999, Dedicated Short-Range Communication (DSRC) spectrum was allocated by the U.S. Federal Communication Commission (FCC), for intra-vehicle communication at 5.9 GHz. The original goal was to make public safety applications possible in order to rescue lives and increase of quality of traffic flow (Biswas, Tatchikou & Dion, 2006; Bai & Krishnan, 2006), but it is now increasingly used for comfort applications.

In order to decrease the cost and support DSRC development, they permitted the private services as well. DSRC supports vehicle speeds up to 120 mile/hour, and the transmission range is between 300m and up to 1000m. This will enable operations related to the improvement of traffic flow, highway safety, and other intelligent transport system (ITS) applications.

DSRC spectrum is divided into seven 10 MHz wide channels as shown in Figure 3, the Channel 178 (control channel) is confined to safety communications only. The two channels at the edges of the spectrum are kept back for future advanced accident avoidance applications and high-powered public safety usages. The four channels (service channels) are left for both safety and non safety usage (Jiang, Taliwal, Meier, Holfelder & Herrtwich, 2006).

3.3 Characteristics of VANETs

VANETs have similarities with MANETs like low and variable bandwidth, short range connectivity, infrastructure-less, and self-organisation, but can be distinguished from MANETs by the unique characteristics such as high mobility and unreliable channels. These caused research challenges such as routing protocols, data broadcasting, and security issues. Most the routing protocols that have been used in MANETs cannot be applied in VANETs, because they suffered from poor performances caused by the fast movement in vehicles.

The most important differences between them is that vehicles in VANETs can move randomly but still predictably (restricted by geography of roads), even if they move at much higher speeds than traditional MANETs. Vehicles in VANETs are also have much higher power than in MANETs (Misra, Woungang & Misra, 2009; Manui & Kakkasageri, 2008; Olariu & Weigle, 2009). At the end of this section a comparison between the characteristics of MANETs and VANETs is provided as shown in the Table 1.

Figure 3. DSRC channel arrangement (Jiang, Taliwal, Meier, Holfelder & Herrtwich, 2006)

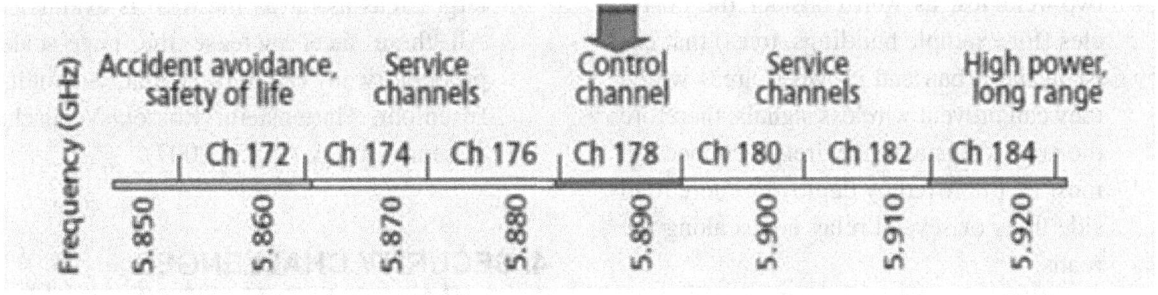

Table 1. Comparison between characteristics of MANETs and VANETs

Characteristic	MANET	VANET
Constrained Resource	✓	×
Topology	Dynamic	More Dynamic than MANET
Mobility Prediction	×	✓
Multi-hop	✓	✓
Limited Device Security	✓	×
Limited Physical Security	✓	✓
Short Range Connectivity	✓	✓
Infrastructure less	✓	✓
Low and Variable Bandwidth	✓	✓

- **High and Dynamic Topology**: Because of the high speed and random of movement in vehicles, the topology of VANETs changes rapidly (Li & Wang, 2008), for instance, assuming that all vehicles have the same transmission range which is 300 meters, a link can be formed between any two vehicles if the distance between them is less than 300 meters. In the worst possible scenario, if there are two vehicles driving in opposite directions, with the speed of 60 miles/hour (26.6 meters/second) consequently, the connection will last only for at most 11.2 seconds.

- **Random disconnection (frequent fragmentation) in network scale**: The vehicles in VANETs are free to move; hence they can dynamically enter or leave the network. Consequently, the connectivity in VANETs would change frequently (Wisitpongphan, Bai, Mudalige & Tonguz, 2007) which it will affect the network structure services, for example, in a low vehicles traffic density case, where there are two vehicles that need to communicate with each other, and there was only one vehicle in between them, if this vehicle changed its direction to another road, this will cause disconnection between these two vehicles, as well consider the obstacles (for example buildings, trees) that exist in the urban and crowded areas which they can prevent wireless signals, therefore the need to sustain the wireless connection must be improved by deploying more road side units or several relay nodes along the roads.

- **Mobility modelling and prediction**: Mobility and prediction model plays a significant role when designing protocols in VANETs, because of the high mobility of vehicles, high speed of vehicles and dynamic topology. Generally, we can predict the future position of vehicles if we know their speed and road maps, because the vehicles are restricted to pre-built high ways, roads, and streets (Fiore, Harri, Filali & Bonnet, 2007).

- **High energy and computational power**: There are a common characteristic in VANETs which make them are distinguished from other networks; vehicles can have large energy, adequate storage, and high processor, powerful wireless transceivers and high data rate because nodes in VANETs are vehicles instead of small handheld devices as in MANETs.

- **Potentially large-scale and variable density**: In traditional wireless network the nodes number can be restricted or can be expected, in VANETs however the nodes number can be much larger and cannot be predicted, for example, assume an urban and crowded area with thousands of vehicles and a plenty of roads and streets, where the vehicles are located close to each other in the same area, and consider the case where vehicles are driving at period in the morning and evening of the greatest burden upon the channels of transportation in the same time (rush hour),

in addition VANETs can be extended in large areas as far as the road is available. All these facts increase the large-scale probability in VANETs (Killat, Schmidt-Eisenlohr, Hartenstein, Rossel, Vortisch, Assenmacher & Busch, 2007).

4. SECURITY CHALLENGES FOR VANETS AND MANETS

Since, security is an essential component in VANETs and MANETs, the striking features of these networks raise both challenges and opportunities in achieving security, unlike other traditional networks (wired) where nodes must have physical access to the network line or communicate through several lines of protection like firewalls and gateways. VANET and MANET use the wireless medium so attacks on a wireless network can come from all directions and target any node. It gives high opportunity to be attacked if does not has certain security measurements. Consequently, link attack ranging from passive attack to active attack, message replay, message leakage, message contamination and message distortion can occur. All these mean that VANETs and MANETs do not have a clear line of defence, and every node must be arranged for the different kind of attacks (Zhang & Lee, 2005).

Therefore, in order to achieve high survivability and scalability, VANETs and MANETs should have a distributed architecture with no central administration, and of course the high mobility nature in these networks should be considered, since prior trust cannot be counted upon in such networks; any intended solution to the security aspects therefore, should be adaptive 'on the fly' to these changes and should have the ability to deal with large networks as in VANET it may consist of hundreds or even thousands of mobile nodes.

The distinctive characteristics of VANETs bring a new set of essential challenges to security design such as open peer-to-peer network architecture, sharing of the wireless medium, large-scale density, the high relevance of vehicle geographic location and dynamic network topology. These challenges noticeably make the looking for security solutions that perform both data protection and applicable network performance are required.

Distributing information between nodes in VANETs and MANETs over long ranges in such networks, however, is a very challenging task, since sharing information always has a risk attached to it especially when the information is confidential.

Normally in addressing network security, three significant issues need to be considered in the system: security requirements, security attacks and security mechanisms. Security requirements take account of the functionality required to provide a secure networking system, whereas the security attacks include the techniques that might be carried out to break these requirements. Finally, the security mechanisms are the fundamental elements used to enforce the security requirements. Section 5 therefore presents the security requirements: authentication, authorisation, access control, privacy, confidentiality, availability, survivability, data integrity, and non-repudiation. Section 7.1 presents the access control models: Discretionary Access Control (DAC), Mandatory Access Control (MAC), and Role-Based Access Control (RBAC).

Attacks on VANETs and MANETs can be divided into two types: passive and active attacks. Section 6 therefore presents both types of attacks: passive attacks are hard to detect because they are based on 'snooping' on transmitted packets between entities, whereas in active attacks the attacker tries to change or destroy the data being transmitted within the network. External active attack and internal active attacks are also described in Section 6. Section 7 presents a set of security mechanisms which can be used to enforce the security requirement: cryptography, digital signature, access control, authentication, traffic padding, notarization, and routing control.

Section 8 presents an overview of the cryptographic background to understand work already done on securing VANETs and MANETs, as well as the recent research. Two main types of cryptographic algorithms are used in cryptography: symmetric key algorithms presented in Section 8.1 in which sender and receiver both use the same key (secret key) for encryption and decryption, whereas in asymmetric key algorithms presented in Section 8.2, the sender and the receiver uses two different keys for encryption and decryption. Public Key Infrastructure (PKI), Digital signature, and Digital Certificate will also be discussed in detail in Sections 8.2 and 8.3 respectively.

Section 9 presents a critical review of the security issues in both MANETs and VANETs. It also provides a survey of existing solutions in the field to highlight a particular area, not been addressed up to now: controlling the information flow in these networks (Janicke, Sarrab & Aldabbas, 2012; Aldabbas, Janicke, Abu Jassar & Alwada'n, 2012; Aldabbas, Alwada'n, Janicke & Al-Bayatti, 2012), aims to provide an architecture that allows the policy-based architecture to control the dissemination of data communicated between nodes. This is to ensure that data remains confidential not only during transmission but also after it has been communicated to another peer.

5. SECURITY REQUIREMENTS

The security requirements are specified by standards of several organisations such as the International Telecommunications Union (ITU-T), which defines the security requirement as a set of services provided by the system which ensures the adequate security level for data communication, by giving specific protection to system resources. ITU-T, in their recommendation X.800 and X.805 defines these requirements as follows (Al-Jaroodi, 2002; Menezes, Van Oorschot & Vanstone, 1997; Li & Joshi, 2004; Stallings USA, 2005; Xing & Wang 2007):

- **Authentication**: Authentication verifies the identity of each node and its eligibility to access the network. This means that nodes in these networks are required to verify the identities of the communicated entities in the network, in order to ensure that they are communicating with the correct entity. This requirement is an essential and difficult requirement to satisfy. If the authentication stage was not fulfilled, no further requirements would be properly implemented. For example, if two entities are using symmetric-key encryption for securing the communication and one of these entities become compromised caused by the lack of authentication, then all encrypted material such as the shared key and the encryption algorithm will be available to that adversary entity.

- **Authorisation and Access Control**: Each node is required to have access to shared resources, services and personal information on the network. In addition, nodes should be capable of restricting each other from accessing their private information. There are many techniques that can be used for access control such as Discretionary Access Control (DAC), Mandatory Access Control (MAC) and Role Based Access Control (RBAC) (to be discussed in Section 7.1). Traditionally authorisation policies are related to auditing techniques to track resource usage and deduce statistics about nodes in the network.

- **Privacy and confidentiality**: Each node has to secure both the information that is exchanged between it and others, and secure the location information and the data stored on these nodes. Privacy means preventing the identity and the location of the node from being disclosed to any other entities, while confidentiality means keeping the secrecy of the exchanged data from being revealed to those who do not have permission to access it. Data confidential-

ity can be applied by using any encryption techniques based on secure key management system. Whereas protecting the users' privacy such as node-id, position, and travelling routes needs something more than encrypting the data, indeed sophisticated mechanisms are required to conceal those users' attributes such as using a pseudonym technique.

- **Availability and survivability**: The network services and applications should be accessible when needed, even in the presence of faults or malicious attack such as denial-of-service attack (DoS), while survivability means the capability of the network to restore its normal services under such these conditions. These two requirements should be supported in any network.

- **Data integrity**: The data transmitted between nodes should be received by the intended entities without been tampered with or changed by unauthorised modification. This requirement is essential especially in military, banking and aircraft control systems, where data modification would cause potential damage.

- **Non-repudiation**: This ensures that nodes when sending or receiving data-packets should not be able to deny their responsibilities of those actions. This requirement is essential especially when disputes are investigated to determine the entity which misbehaved. Digital signature techniques are used to achieve this requirement to prove that the message was received from or sent by the alleged node.

6. SECURITY ATTACKS

Attacks on VANETs can be divided into two types, namely, passive and active attacks (Stallings USA, 2005; Murthy & Manoj, 2004). Passive attack are based on 'snooping' upon transmitted packets between entities; the goal of the attacker is to acquire data that is being sent without modifying it, but not to stop the operation of the network, thus breaching the confidentiality requirement. Passive attacks are hard to detect because the data packets are sent and received normally and neither the sender nor receiver is aware that the attacker has read the packet or has intercepted the traffic pattern. Therefore, it is more important to prevent such this attack rather than to detect it; the prevention mechanisms involved use encryption algorithms to encrypt the data being transmitted, thereby preventing attackers from acquiring any useful information from the data overheard.

Whereas in active attacks the attacker tries to change or destroy the data being transmitted in the network, thereby interrupting the normal operations of the network. Active attacks can be divided into two types, external and internal attacks. External attacks can be executed by nodes from outside the network. This kind of attack can be prevented easily by using authorisation and access control mechanisms. By contrast, internal attacks are very difficult to prevent and can cause severe damage, because they come from malicious nodes who are already authorised inside the network. The security architecture proposed for VANET should therefore provide a comprehensive end-to-end security solution in order to prevent/ detect data leaks. This work identifies the security requirements in VANETs, their objectives, and the methods by which they could be applied to VANETs, therefore a set of security mechanisms needs to be defined. Cryptography is one of the most powerful tools that can be used to achieve most of the security requirements, such as peer entity authentication, data origin authentication, data confidentiality, and data integrity as shown in Table 2. The next section will show some security mechanisms that are needed to understand the work that has been done to manage and secure VANETs.

7. SECURITY MECHANISMS

These are the security mechanisms as they are defined in X.800 (Stallings USA; 2005):

- **Cryptography (Encipherment):** In this mechanism data is transformed or encrypted into a not understandable format at the sender side, by using mathematical algorithms based on one or two encryption keys, and then it is decrypted to readable format again at the receiver side.
- **Digital Signature**: In this mechanism extra data are added to the message to give the receiver a 'guarantee' that the data come from a legitimate sender, and was not altered in transmission (integrity).
- **Access Control**: A mechanism to enforce access rights to resources.
- **Authentication Exchange**: A mechanism destined to ensure the identity of an entity.
- **Traffic Padding**: A mechanism destined to frustrate traffic analysis attempts by adding extra bits into gaps in data packets.
- **Notarization**: A trusted third party (certificate authority) which is trusted by all parties to facilitate interactions to assure certain properties of data exchange.
- **Routing Control**: A mechanism used to select special securing routes for specific data and enable routing changes accordingly, particularly when a break of security is suspected.

7.1 Access Control

Protecting resources and information from unauthorised access is an important cornerstone in any information security system, this can be done by controlling how these resources and information can be accessed, otherwise unauthorized access or disclosure of confidential information especially in military systems would be an extremely damaging and fatal. So the need for access control arose because it is the first line of defence against unauthorized access to network resources and information. The purpose of using access control is to give the ability to control, monitor, restrict, and protect the confidentiality of resources and to define how users (subjects) can interact with other systems or resources and information (objects); the subject can be a user, program, or process that accesses an object, where the object can be a computer, database, or file (Harris, 2007). Access control models had been divided into three models based on the mechanisms of setting the access to these objects; each model type has a different method to control accessing objects by subjects. This section explains these different models as we describe them in below:

1. **Discretionary Access Control**: Each resource (object) in Discretionary Access Control (DAC) has an owner who specifies and controls of which users (subjects) can access his resource (object), and states the permission type the subjects may have on this object. In this kind of access control model the access is restricted to the subjects based on the authorisation granted by the initial owner of this object. The initial owner of an object is the subject who created it (Sandhu & Munawer, 1998). It is called Discretionary Access Control (DAC) because of the access is based on the discretion of the owner (subject); the user in this model is allowed to specify the type of access to his object. Access control lists (ACLs) is a form of Discretionary Access Control (DAC) which has been used in various operating systems such as Microsoft Windows, Linux, and Macintosh systems, the properties of any file in these systems have an options that allow you to control and choose which users can get an access to this resource and what the permissions may they have.

2. **Mandatory Access Control**: Subjects and data owners do not have an option to specify who can access their resources, the administrator makes that instead. Both users (subjects) in Mandatory Access Control (MAC) model have a security clearance (secret, top secret, confidential, and so on), and also data (objects) classified similarly to security clearance, these security clearances are stored in security labels, which are given to subjects and objects (Sandhu & Munawer, 1998). Mandatory Access Control (MAC) model is arranged and stern more than in Discretionary Access Control (DAC) and found on a security label system (sensitivity). For example, a user (subject) may cleared a security level of secret, and the data (object) that been requested to access has a security label of top secret, then the user will be rejected to access this data because his security clearance (secret) is lower than the classification of the data (top secret), in order to get accessed to such this resource the subject must have a security label which is equal or higher than the security label of the object. This type of access control model has been used in applications where classification of information and confidentiality is essential, especially in military system where accessing the information is allowed for a specified set. Mandatory Access Control (MAC) model used in Unix systems, and recently SE Linux which developed by the National Security Agency (NSA) (Peter Loscocco 2001).

3. **Role-Based Access Control**: In role-based access control (RBAC) model the subject will be given an access to the object based on his role or functional position (position assigned to a particular person or thing), this model is also called non-discretionary access control, because allocating a user to a role is obligatory. This means that user does not have the choice to specify what role he will be given. Role-based access control (RBAC) model is more complex than Discretionary

Access Control (DAC), instead of specifying the access control at the object level with Access Control List (ACLs) by the subject, the administrator in (RBAC) is required to transform the policies into permission as soon as setting (ACLs). Using (RBAC) model in such these companies where the members of staff can come and leave the company in a dramatic manner is a paramount system, better than using (DAC) and (MAC) models. For example, if an x is an employee assigned to contractor role after that x left the company, then y become his replacement in this way the new replacement employee can be easily mapped to this role by the system administrator (Ferraiolo, Sandhu, Gavrila, Kuhn & Chandramouli, 2001).

As we see from Table 2 the confidentiality requirement can be solved by using encryption and routing control mechanisms, otherwise disclosing private information by a malicious node (inside the network) to unauthorised nodes will cause a fatal problem and data will be leaked. Therefore, encipherment tools (to be described in Section 8) are widely used in security systems and solve part of the problem by encrypting data exchanged between entities. Using a mechanism based on access control to ensure confidentiality, however, has still not been used, so we recommend any future research in this scope should consider using access control mechanism especially Discretionary Access Control (DAC) to ensure data confidentiality and privacy in such networks.

Most of the previous security solutions used in VANETs and MANETs focused on conventional cryptographic techniques which are the most powerful tools that can be used to achieve most of the security requirements such as authentication, data confidentiality, data integrity and non-repudiation. The next section, therefore, will give an overview of the cryptographic background to understand work already done on securing VANETs and MANETs.

8. CRYPTOGRAPHIC BACKGROUND

Cryptography (Stallings USA, 2005; Menezes, Van Oorschot & Vanstone, 1997) is the science of encoding in cipher using specific mathematics and algorithms to encrypt and decrypt data in order to ensure secrecy and/or authenticity of messages. Using cryptography data are transformed or encrypted to a format incomprehensible to third parties at the sender side by using mathematical algorithms based on one or two encryption keys. It is then decrypted to a readable format again at the receiver side. This enables nodes to transmit secret information through insecure networks, so that it cannot be read by any node except the intended node. The main goals of cryptography

Table 2. Relationship between security requirements and mechanisms (Stallings USA, 2005)

Requirement	Mechanism				
	Encipherment	Digital Signature	Access Control	Data Integrity	Routing Control
Authentication	Y	Y			
Access control			Y		
Confidentiality	Y				Y
Data integrity	Y	Y		Y	

are to ensure confidentiality, integrity, authentication and non-repudiation security requirements.

In cryptography, the input to an encryption algorithm or the output of a decryption algorithm is called plaintext. Before data are sent from one node to another, the plaintext is converted into an unintelligible form which called ciphertext by the process of encryption using certain algorithms or functions. The intended receiver can then decipher/decrypt the ciphertext back into original text (plaintext) by the process of decryption. Mathematically, if M represents the plaintext message and C represents the ciphertext message as shown in Figure 4, we can say then:

The encryption and decryption algorithms are based on keys, which are small amounts of information used by the cryptographic functions. Keys must be distributed and kept secure to ensure security of the system; this is why they are called secret keys. The security of administering the keys in cryptography science is called key management. Two main types of cryptographic algorithms are used in cryptography: symmetric key algorithms, where sender and receiver both use the same key (secret key) for encryption and decryption, whereas in asymmetric key algorithms, sender and receiver uses two different keys for encryption and decryption. These two algorithms will be discussed in the following Section 8.1 and 8.2 respectively. Digital signature, digital certificate, Public Key Infrastructure (PKI) also will be discussed in following Sections 8.2 and 8.3 respectively.

8.1 Symmetric Key Algorithms

Symmetric Key Algorithms (Stallings USA, 2005; Menezes, Van Oorschot & Vanstone, 1997) are those kinds of cryptographic algorithms based on the existence of a shared key (agreed between the participants' nodes) in both the sender and receiver sides. The key used in such symmetric encryption/decryption algorithm is required to be exchanged through a secured channel. Both participants' nodes must share the same key before starting to communicate; this key can be used in both encryption and decryption processes (K) and it must be maintained secret to protect the communication afterwards. Symmetric key cryptography is the process where both sender and the receiver use the same secret key to encrypt and decrypt. An example is depicted in Figure 5 where Alice ciphers the plain text message (m) using the shared secret key (k), as a result the plaintext is changed to a ciphertext (c). Bob wants to receive the message sent from Alice in a readable format, thus he deciphers the received ciphertext (c) using the same secret key (K) which is been used in the encryption algorithm at Alice's side to change it back again to a readable format (m).

Symmetric-key algorithms can be divided into two types: stream ciphers and block ciphers. Stream ciphers encrypt a byte of the plaintext message one at a time, whereas block ciphers encrypt a number of bytes as a single unit. Blocks of 64 bits have been previously used. Currently, however, AES (Advanced Encryption Standard) has

Figure 4. Listing 1

Listing 1: Encryption and decryption formulas

```
Encryption :: E(M)= C
Decryption :: D(C)= M
```

Figure 5. Symmetric key scheme (Stallings USA, 2005)

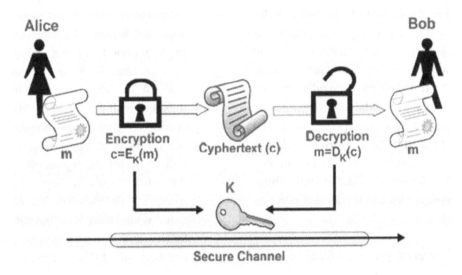

been approved by National Institute of Standards and Technology (NIST) in 2001; it uses 128-bit blocks which replaces the commonly used Data Encryption Standard (DES) (Robles & Choi, 2009, Types of Symmetric algorithms n.d.).

Generally, symmetric cryptography is much faster to execute than asymmetric cryptography. Because symmetric key algorithms require a secret key to be shared between the participants' nodes, however, any other node which 'knows' the shared secret key can decipher the messages sent in the network. The drawback of symmetric-key algorithms is thus that if the shared secret key is compromised, all messages can be deciphered which can make the whole system susceptible to attack. Therefore, the secret key in such a cryptography type needs to be altered frequently and stored securely during the key distribution process. Data integrity and non-repudiation requirements are solved by hash functions and digital signatures respectively. Key-management issues are solved by RSA (Rivest, Shamir and Adleman) encryption and by DH (Diffie-Hellman) key agreement algorithm (Types of Symmetric algorithms n.d.).

8.2 Asymmetric Key Algorithms

Asymmetric Key Algorithms (Stallings USA, 2005; Menezes, Van Oorschot & Vanstone, 1997) are those kinds of cryptographic algorithms in which encryption and decryption are carried out using two different keys, one of which is referred to as the public key and the other is referred to as the private key. Asymmetric key algorithm is also termed a public key cryptography using two keys. One key is used for ciphering and the other one is used for deciphering. The decryption key is kept secret, therefore, it is termed the "private key," whereas the encryption key is known to all participants' nodes to be able to send encrypted messages, therefore it is termed the "public key". Every node that has the public key can send encrypted messages to the node that possesses the private key, but message encrypted with the public key can be decrypted only with the corresponding private key. Both keys are related mathematically; the private key however, cannot be derived from the public key. The key management issue in symmetric key algorithm solved by public key cryptography (asymmetric key) after the idea of asymmetric algorithms was first published in 1976 by Diffie and Hellman (Diffie & Hellman, 1976).

An asymmetric key encryption scheme is depicted in Figure 6. At the start, both Alice and Bob should have an authenticated pair of public and private keys. If Alice wants to send a ciphered message m to Bob, she needs to know Bob's public key (PK[Bob]) in order to encrypt the message m and change it to a ciphertext (c). Bob is able to decrypt this ciphertext (c) using his private key (SK[Bob]) which is secret and known only to him. Public key cryptography can be divided into two subtypes which are:

- **Public key encryption:** A form of cryptographic system in which encryption and decryption are performed using two different keys, one to encrypt the plaintext, and another one to decrypt the ciphertext. Neither key will do both functions. When a message has been encrypted with a receiver's public key, it can be decrypted by only that receiver which has the correspondent private key. In this way the confidentiality requirement can be ensured.

- **Digital signature:** An approach to authenticate the identity of the sender which enables the sender of a message to attach a piece of code that functions as a signature. The signature is created by calculating the hash of the message and encrypting the message with the sender's private key. The sender's signature guarantees the source and integrity of the message sent to other nodes. Therefore, any message signed with the sender's private key can be taken to mean that the message has not been tampered with. In this way the authenticity, integrity and non-repudiation requirements can be ensured (Hunt, 2001).

The main problem when using public-key cryptography is how to prove that a certain public key is genuine (belongs to the claimed node) or not, and has not been tampered with or changed by an unauthorised third party. This problem is solved using a public-key infrastructure (PKI) approach, which is an arrangement that matches public keys with respective nodes identities via a one or more group(s) of third parties, which is termed as certificate authority (CA) to authorise

Figure 6. Asymmetric key scheme

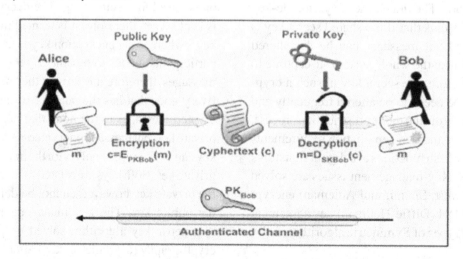

the ownership of key pairs (Palomar, Tapiador, Hernández-Castro & Ribagorda, 2009).

Rivest, Shamir and Adleman (Rivest, Shamir & Adleman, 1978) proposed a novel algorithm for obtaining digital signatures and public-key cryptosystems in 1978 which was termed afterwards as RSA. This is an example of public key cryptography based on the integer factorisation difficulty, in RSA (m) plaintext message can be encrypted or ciphertext can be decrypted using the following formula as shown in Figure 7.

One of the advantages of using public key cryptography (Mollin, 2007; Katz & Lindell, 2008) is to provide a technique for implementing digital signatures. Digital signatures give a guarantee to the receiver of a particular message that it has been sent from a node of authenticated identity, and also to ensure that the content of message is received to the intended node without it having been tampered with or changed by unauthorised modification. Digital signatures thus ensure authentication and data integrity system requirements. A digital signature also ensures non-repudiation requirement, in which the sender should not be able to deny its responsibilities of some actions. This requirement is essential especially when disputes are investigated to determine which node misbehaved. Therefore, digital signature technique is used to achieve this requirement to prove that the message was received from or sent by the alleged node.

A digital signature acts as the traditional handwritten signature. The handwritten signature however, can be imitated, whereas a digital signature is better than handwritten because it is harder to be counterfeited. It also certifies that the content of the message is received intact as well as the identity of the sender is authenticated.

As depicted in Figure 8 as a replacement of encrypting message using the receiver node's public key, digital signature encrypts the message using the sender's node's private key. Therefore, the same message can be decrypted using the sender's public key, so that tells the receiver node that the message originated from that sender. As depicted in Figure 8, if Alice wants to send an encrypted message m to Bob signed by Alice's identity, she calculates the hash digest of the message m using a specified hash function. Alice then encrypts this digest using her private key (SK[Alice]) to produce the signature and sends it with the message to Bob. When the message received at Bob's end, he recalculates the hash digest of the received message using the same hash function which was implemented at Alice's side and compares it with the hash digest generated from decrypting the signature using Alice's public key of (PK[Alice]). If both digests match that means the message m must have been created from Alice and it has not been changed or tampered with during transmission.

8.3 Digital Certificate

The Digital Certificate is an electronic document used for establishing the credentials of a node (i.e. certify the identities of nodes) which combines a digital signature to match between the public key and the nodes' identification to verify the nodes' identities. It is issued and certified by one or more certification authorities (CAs) (Digital Certifi-

Figure 7. Listing 2

```
Listing 2: RSA encryption and decryption formulas

c=m^e mod n
m=c^d mod n
```

Figure 8. Digital signature example

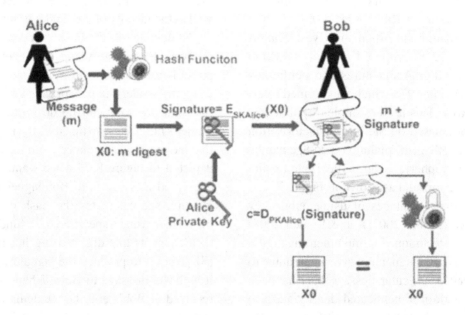

cates n.d.a, Digital Certificates n.d.b). In public cryptographic system nodes need to make sure that they are ciphering to legitimate identities of nodes. The important of digital certificates comes from protecting the network from the man-in-the-middle attack scenario. The man-in-the-middle attack is a potential threat in such environments where keys exchanged between nodes and servers can enable the attacker to insert, read, and modify messages sent among two victim nodes without either node being aware of the connection they have used has been compromised. In this type of attack the attacker makes autonomous links with the victims to play with messages sent between them. Victim nodes believe that they are communicating directly and securely between each other, when in fact the entire connection is managed by the attacker (Stallings USA, 2005).

For instance, if Alice wants to send a message to Bob securely, she will ask for Bob's public key. If Emma (the attacker) can find the public key of Bob and be able to intercept the messages sent between Alice and Bob, the man-in-the-middle attack can be mounted. First, Emma will imper-

sonate the identity of Bob and send her public key to Alice as if it were Bob's public key. This will make Alice believe that it belongs to Bob and she will use it to encrypt the message and then send it back to Bob. This encrypted message will be intercepted by Emma (Almomani, 2007).

This time Emma ciphers the message using her private key, keeps a copy of it and re-ciphers it using the correct public key of Bob. Once the message is received by Bob, he will believe that it was sent by Alice. This scenario shows simply the need for some method of ensuring that Alice and Bob have genuinely used each other's public keys and not the attacker's public key. If not, they will remain vulnerable to such an attack. Digital certificates therefore are used to prevent this kind of attack happening. They are like the traditional identification cards such as passports and drivers' licenses which can verify the identities of their owners'. Similar to traditional identification cards which are issued by identified government authorities, digital Certificates in MANETs and VANETs are also issued by trusted third parties. A digital Certificate verifies the identity of the node but instead of including a photo and a signature of the certificate's owner, digital certificates bind the owner's public key to the owner's private key. Therefore, digital certificates contain node identification, serial number, expiry date, public key, and digital signature of the certification authority (CA) which issued the certificate. This signature in the certificate act as attestation by the certificate's signer that the information of node and the public key belong together (Al-Bayatti, 2009).

In order to make a digital signature, a certification authority (CA) employs its private key to digitally sign each certificate it issues. The CA creates a message digest from the certificate using a specified hash function, and then encrypts this digest with its private key, and inserts the digital signature inside the certificate. When the certificate is received at the node, the node recalculates the hash digest of the received certificate using the same hash function which was implemented by the CA, and then compares it with the hash digest generated from decrypting the certificate using the CA's public key to verify the certificate's integrity. If both digests match, that means the certificate must have been created from the CA and has not been changed or tampered with during transmission. If they do not match then the certificate is not original or has been issued from a non certified authority (Digital Certificates n.d.a).

9. STATE OF THE ART

In comparison with wired networks where the devices must have a physical access to the network medium, mobile ad hoc networks have no apparent secure boundary. There is no need for the attackers to have a physical access to the network; once the attackers are in the transmission range of any other devices, then they can join and communicate with other devices. According to the nature of mobility in ad hoc networks, liberty to join, moving outside and inside the networks

makes MANETs vulnerable to attacks, which can result from any device in the same transmission range (Carvalho, 2008). In comparison with wired networks where the nodes can get electrical supply directly from the power points, in MANETs nodes are generally operated by small batteries with limited lifetime. This makes nodes unable to perform intensive computations over prolonged periods of time. An attacker on the other hand is typically able to provide sufficient power-supply and thus must be assumed to be able to perform intensive computations (Mehul & Limaye, 2009), meaning that attack and defence in these networks is not equally matched. The lack of centralized management in MANETs makes detection of attacks difficult, since they are highly dynamic and large scale therefore they cannot be easily monitored; benign (non-malignant) failures in the MANETs are also fairly common, for example transmission destructions and packet dropping. As a result, malicious failures will be more difficult to discover. Since security is an essential component in a hostile environment, these unique characteristics of MANETs raise challenges that security requirements must address (Yang, Luo, Ye, Lu & Zhang, 2004; Djenouri, Khelladi & Badache, 2005).

There has been appreciable work by the research community (Yang, Luo, Ye, Lu & Zhang, 2004; Burbank, Chimento, Haberman & Kasch, 2006; Zhou & Haas, 1999; Hubaux, Buttyán & Capkun, 2001; Capkun, Buttyán & Hubaux, 2003) in message encryption, digital signature, and key management. Many challenges particularly related to the privacy and data confidentiality of originator, however, remain to be solved. These available approaches which have been used in MANETs such as access control, digital signature, and encryption focused only in securing the channel during the transmission, however how these nodes act after and use this information has been mostly neglected.

Most research on security in VANETs addressed location privacy (Sampigethaya, Li, Huang & Poovendran, 2007; Yan & Chen, 2010) and 'big brother' scenarios (Raya & Hubaux, 2005) where location of nodes can be tracked by an untrusted third party. The CARAVAN scheme (Sampigethaya, Huang, Li, Poovendran, Matsuura & Sezaki, 2005) allows mobile nodes to maintain privacy by forming groups in which the group leader acts as a proxy on behalf of all members of the group with a random silent period to mitigate tracking of nodes. Others (Dotzer, 2006, Gerlach & Guttler Dublin, 2007; Tang & Hong n.d.) addressed the same problem by using pseudonyms to hide the relationship between the identity and the location. Although pseudonyms are significant in overall security of VANETs are advantageous for protecting the identity, these solutions do not provide full security for VANETs in term of data confidentiality, as they cannot control the dissemination of information. Indeed for many application-level services the knowledge of the senders' identity is paramount to their function. Hence, pseudonyms could only be one part of a privacy solution, but the need for more comprehensive solution(s) allowing originators of information control over its dissemination, remains to be solved.

In addition, a few academic papers have been published by Raya's group et al to provide a general survey of crucial security issues, giving an overview of challenges, adversaries, attacks, properties of VANET, and useful security mechanisms to design robust solutions (Raya & Hubaux, 2005; Raya & Hubaux, 2007). In later research (Raya, Papadimitratos & Hubaux, 2006) they proposed a secure architecture in VANET to address these issues.

Existing approaches to security of MANETs include traditional cryptographic solutions using public key certificates (Li & Wang n.d., Wu, Chen, Wu & Cardei, 2007) to maintain trust, in which a Trusted Third Party (TTP) or Certificate Authority (CA) certifies the identity associated

with a public key of each communicated entity, Almomani and Zedan (Almomani & Zedan, 2007) proposed a comprehensive, top-down, end-to-end security solution for MANET based upon a well defined architecture and exploiting two of the ITU-T recommendations: X.800, and X.805. Such approaches can therefore, provide end-to-end secure communication channels. These approaches mainly focused on message confidentiality, integrity and non-repudiation, they do not consider however the trust management of the communicated entities, and how these certified entities act is left to the application layer (Blaze, Feigenbaum & Lacy, 1996). Therefore, Al-Bayatti et al (Al-Bayatti, Zedan & Cau, 2009) proposed behaviour detection algorithm combined with threshold cryptography digital certificates to satisfy prevention and detection to securely manage Mobile Ad hoc Network of Networks (MANoNs), whereas Zhou and Haas (Zhou & Haas, 1999) studied the security threats, vulnerabilities and challenges which faces the ad hoc network. In their work (Zhou & Haas, 1999) they protected the packets sent between nodes by choosing the secure routing path to the destination node based on the redundancies routes between nodes to maintain the availability requirement. This is because all key-based cryptographic approaches such as digital signature need a proper and secure key management scheme to bind between the public and private keys to the nodes in the network; Zhou and Haas subsequently used replication and new cryptographic technique (threshold cryptography) (Desmedt 1994, Desmedt & Frankel, 1990) to build a secure key management process to achieve the trust between a set of servers in ad hoc networks by distributing trust among aggregation of nodes to certify nodes are trustworthy.

Securing the routing in MANETs has also been given much attention by the researchers; many approaches, therefore, have been proposed to deal with external attack. Sirios and Kent (Sirois & Kent, 1997) proposed an approach to protect the packet sent to multi receivers by using keyed one-way hash function supported by windowed sequence number to ensure data integrity.

In an analogous context of commercial and medical environments, individuals also demand that their personal information such as their names, addresses, phone numbers, national insurance numbers, credit card details, passwords, or date of birth (DOB) are transmitted confidentially. In particular they need assurance that these sensitive data have been securely communicated to the appropriate persons or organisations and to no others. Therefore, Pearson and Mont (Pearson & Casassa-Mont, 2011) employed a clever idea of sticking policies with data to control how the personal information should be processed, handled, shared with other specified parties.

10. SUMMARY

This chapter presented a review of wireless ad hoc networks and mobile ad hoc networks (MANETs); it also described the characteristics, challenges, vulnerabilities of mobile ad hoc network, and then numerated the applications of MANET. This chapter also presented an introduction of the vehicle ad hoc networks (VANETs), history and background, also it described the characteristics and challenges of vehicle ad hoc network, this chapter also provided a comparison between characteristics of MANETs and VANETs as described in the Table 1.

Although VANETs and MANETs are interesting for many applications, they nevertheless have several challenges. Each of these challenges can be considered as a separate research area needing intensive investigation. Researchers investigated the security issues in both MANETs and VANETs and they proposed many solutions; this chapter therefore this chapter highlighted the network security concepts: security requirements, security attacks and security mechanisms, it also presented an overview of the cryptography background, and presented the related work in privacy and confidentiality issues in both VANETs and MANETs. Finally, this chapter presented some of the previous work (State of the Art) on securing VANETs and MANETs.

REFERENCES

Al-Bayatti, A., Zedan, H., & Cau, A. (2009). Security solution for mobile ad hoc network of networks (manon). In *Proceedings of Networking and Services* (pp. 255–262). ICNS. doi:10.1109/ICNS.2009.30

Al-Bayatti, A. H. (2009). *Security management for mobile ad hoc network of networks (MANoN)*. (PhD Thesis). De Montfort University, Leicester, UK.

Al-Jaroodi, J. (2002). *Security issues at the network layer in wireless mobile ad hoc networks at the network layer (Technical Report)*. Lincoln, NE: Faculty of Computer Science and Engineering, University of Nebraska-Lincoln.

Aldabbas, H., Alwada'n, T., Janicke, H., & Al-Bayatti, A. (2012). Data confidentiality in mobile ad hoc networks. *International Journal of Wireless and Mobile Networks*, *4*(1), 225–236. doi:10.5121/ijwmn.2012.4117

Aldabbas, H., Janicke, H., AbuJassar, R., & Alwada'n, T. (2012). Ensuring data confidentiality and privacy in mobile ad hoc networks. In *Advances in computer science and information technology: Networks and communications* (pp. 490–499). Berlin: Springer. doi:10.1007/978-3-642-27299-8_51

Almomani, I., & Zedan, H. (2007). *End-to-end security solution for wireless mobile ad hoc network (WMANET)*. Academic Press.

Almomani, I. M. (2007). *Security solutions for wireless mobile ad hoc networks (WMANET)*. (PhD Thesis). De Montfort University, Leicester, UK.

Andrews, J. G., Ghosh, A., & Muhamed, R. (2007). *Fundamentals of WiMAX: Understanding broadband wireless networking*. Upper Saddle River, NJ: Prentice Hall.

Bai, F., & Krishnan, H. (2006). Reliability analysis of DSRC wireless communication for vehicle safety applications. In *Proceedings of Intelligent Transportation Systems Conference*, (pp. 355–362). IEEE.

Bharathidasan, A., & Ponduru, V. (2002). *Sensor networks: An overview (Technical Report)*. Davis, CA: Department of Computer Science, University of California.

Biswas, S., Tatchikou, R., & Dion, F. (2006). Vehicle-to-vehicle wireless communication protocols for enhancing highway traffic safety. *IEEE Communications Magazine, 44*(1), 74–82. doi:10.1109/MCOM.2006.1580935

Blaze, M., Feigenbaum, J., & Lacy, J. (1996). Decentralized trust management. In *Proceedings of the 1996 IEEE Symposium on Security and Privacy*. IEEE Computer Society Press.

Burbank, J., Chimento, P., Haberman, B., & Kasch, W. (2006). Key challenges of military tactical networking and the elusive promise of manet technology. *IEEE Communications Magazine, 44*(11), 39–45. doi:10.1109/COM-M.2006.248156

Capkun, S., Buttyán, L., & Hubaux, J. (2003). Self-organized public-key management for mobile ad hoc networks. *IEEE Transactions on Mobile Computing, 2*(1), 52–64. doi:10.1109/TMC.2003.1195151

Carcelle, X., Dangand, T., & Devic, C. (2006). Ad-hoc networking. In *Proceedings of IFIP International Federation for Information Processing*.

Carvalho, M. (2008). Security in mobile ad hoc networks. *IEEE Security Privacy, 6*(2), 72–75. doi:10.1109/MSP.2008.44

Chadha, R., & Kant, L. (2007). *Policy-driven mobile ad hoc network management*. Hoboken, NJ: Wiley-IEEE Press. doi:10.1002/9780470227718

Desmedt, Y. (1994). Threshold cryptography. *European Transactions on Telecommunications, 5*(4), 449–458. doi:10.1002/ett.4460050407

Desmedt, Y., & Frankel, Y. (1990). Threshold cryptosystems. In *Proceedings of Advances in Cryptology* (CRYPTO'89). Springer.

Diffie, W., & Hellman, M. (1976). New directions in cryptography. *IEEE Transactions on Information Theory, 22*(6), 644–654. doi:10.1109/TIT.1976.1055638

Digital Certificate.s (n.d.a). Retrieved from http://technet.microsoft.com/en-us/library/cc962029.aspx

Digital Certificates. (n.d.b). Retrieved from http://www.webopedia.com/TERM/D/digital_certificate.html

Djenouri, D., Khelladi, L., & Badache, N. (2005). A survey of security issues in mobile ad hoc networks. *IEEE Communications Surveys, 7*(4).

Dotzer, F. (2006). Privacy issues in vehicular ad hoc networks. In *Privacy enhancing technologies*. Springer. doi:10.1007/11767831_13

Ferraiolo, D., Sandhu, R., Gavrila, S., Kuhn, D., & Chandramouli, R. (2001). Proposed NIST standard for role-based access control. *ACM Transactions on Information and System Security, 4*(3), 224–274. doi:10.1145/501978.501980

Fiore, M., Harri, J., Filali, F., & Bonnet, C. (2007). Vehicular mobility simulation for VANETs. In *Proceedings of Simulation Symposium*. IEEE.

Gast, M. (2005). *802.11 wireless networks: The definitive guide*. Sebastopol, CA: O'Reilly Media.

Gerlach, M., & Guttler, F. (2007). Privacy in VANETs using changing pseudonyms-ideal and real. In *Proceedings of Vehicular Technology Conference*. IEEE.

Ghosh, A., Wolter, D., Andrews, J., & Chen, R. (2005). Broadband wireless access with wimax/802.16: Current performance benchmarks and future potential. *IEEE Communications Magazine*, 43(2), 129–136. doi:10.1109/MCOM.2005.1391513

Harris, S. (2007). *CISSP all-in-one exam guide*. New York: McGraw-Hill Osborne Media.

Hubaux, J., Buttyán, L., & Capkun, S. (2001). The quest for security in mobile ad hoc networks. In *Proceedings of the 2nd ACM International Symposium on Mobile Ad Hoc Networking & Computing*. ACM.

Hunt, R. (2001). PKI and digital certification infrastructure. In *Proceedings of Networks*. IEEE.

Janicke, H., Sarrab, M., & Aldabbas, H. (2012). Controlling data dissemination. In *Data privacy management and autonomous spontaneus security*. Springer. doi:10.1007/978-3-642-28879-1_21

Jiang, D., Taliwal, V., Meier, A., Holfelder, W., & Herrtwich, R. (2006). Design of 5.9 GHz DSRC-based vehicular safety communication. *IEEE Wireless Communications*, 13(5), 36–43. doi:10.1109/WC-M.2006.250356

Katz, J., & Lindell, Y. (2008). *Introduction to modern cryptography*. London: Chapman & Hall.

Killat, M., Schmidt-Eisenlohr, F., Hartenstein, H., Rossel, C., Vortisch, P., Assenmacher, S., & Busch, F. (2007). Enabling efficient and accurate large-scale simulations of vanets for vehicular traffic management. In *Proceedings of the Fourth ACM International Workshop on Vehicular Ad Hoc Networks*. ACM. http://doi.acm.org/10.1145/1287748.1287754

Lehr, W., & McKnight, L. (2003). Wireless Internet access: 3G vs. WiFi. *Telecommunications Policy*, 27(5-6), 351–370. doi:10.1016/S0308-5961(03)00004-1

Li, F., & Wang, Y. (2008). Routing in vehicular ad hoc networks: A survey. *IEEE Vehicular Technology Magazine*, 2(2), 12–22. doi:10.1109/MVT.2007.912927

Li, S., & Wang, X. (n.d.). *Enhanced security design for threshold cryptography in ad hoc network*. Academic Press.

Li, W., & Joshi, A. (2004). Security issues in mobile ad hoc networks-a survey. *White House Papers Graduate Research in Informatics at Sussex*, 17, 1–23.

Manui, S., & Kakkasageri, M. (2008). Issues in mobile ad hoc networks for vehicular communication. *IETE Technical Review*, 25(2), 59.

Mehul, E., & Limaye, V. (2009). Security in mobile ad hoc networks. In *Handbook of research in mobile business: Technical, methodological and social perspectives*. Hershey, PA: IGI Global.

Menezes, A., Van Oorschot, P., & Vanstone, S. (1997). *Handbook of applied cryptography*. Boca Raton, FL: CRC.

Mishra, A., & Nadkarni, K. (2003). Security in wireless ad hoc networks. In *The handbook of ad hoc wireless networks*. Boca Raton, FL: CRC Press, Inc.

Misra, S., Woungang, I., & Misra, S. C. (2009). *Guide to wireless ad hoc networks.* New York: Springer-Verlag New York Inc. doi:10.1007/978-1-84800-328-6

Mollin, R. (2007). *An introduction to cryptography.* Boca Raton, FL: CRC Press.

Murthy, C. S. R., & Manoj, B. (2004). *Ad hoc wireless networks: Architectures and protocols.* Upper Saddle River, NJ: Prentice Hall PTR.

Oates, J. (2011). *Toyota and Microsoft ink e-car deal in a cloud of telematics.* Retrieved from http://www.theregister.co.uk/2011/04/07/microsoft_toyota/

Olariu, S., & Weigle, M. (2009). *Vehicular networks from theory to practice.* New York: Chapman & Hall. doi:10.1201/9781420085891

Palomar, E., Tapiador, J., Hernández-Castro, J., & Ribagorda, A. (2009). 17 cooperative security in peer-to-peer and mobile ad hoc networks. In *Cooperative wireless communications.* Academic Press. doi:10.1201/9781420064704.ch17

Papadimitratos, P., & Haas, Z. J. (2003). *Securing mobile ad hoc networks.* Boca Raton, FL: CRC Press, Inc. Retrieved from http://dl.acm.org/citation.cfm?id=989711.989743

Pearson, S., & Casassa-Mont, M. (2011). Sticky policies: An approach for privacy management across multiple parties. *Computers & Society,* *1*(99), 60–68. doi:10.1109/MC.2011.225

Peter Loscocco, N. (2001). Integrating flexible support for security policies into the Linux operating system. In *Proceedings of the FREENIX Track: 2001 USENIX Annual Technical Conference.* Boston: USENIX Association.

Raya, M., & Hubaux, J.-P. (2005). The security of vehicular ad hoc networks. In K. P. Laberteaux, H. Hartenstein, D. B. Johnson & R. Sengupta (Eds.), *Vehicular ad hoc networks,* (pp. 93-94). ACM. Retrieved from http://dblp.uni-trier.de/db/conf/mobicom/vanet2005.html#RayaH05

Raya, M., & Hubaux, J.-P. (2007). Securing vehicular ad hoc networks. *Journal of Computer Security,* *15*(1), 39–68.

Raya, M., Papadimitratos, P., & Hubaux, J.-P. (2006). Securing vehicular communications. *IEEE Wireless Communications,* *13*(5), 8–15. doi:10.1109/WC-M.2006.250352

Rivest, R. L., Shamir, A., & Adleman, L. (1978). A method for obtaining digital signatures and public-key cryptosystems. *Communications of the ACM,* *21,* 120–126. http://doi.acm.org/10.1145/359340.359342 doi:10.1145/359340.359342

Robles, R., & Choi, M. (2009). Symmetric-key encryption for wireless Internet scada. *Security Technology,* 289–297.

Sampigethaya, K., Huang, L., Li, M., Poovendran, R., Matsuura, K., & Sezaki, K. (2005). Caravan: Providing location privacy for vanet. In Embedded security in cars (ESCAR). Citeseer.

Sampigethaya, K., Li, M., Huang, L., & Poovendran, R. (2007). Amoeba: Robust location privacy scheme for vanet. *IEEE Journal on Selected Areas in Communications,* *25*(8), 1569–1589. doi:10.1109/JSAC.2007.071007

Sandhu, R., & Munawer, Q. (1998). How to do discretionary access control using roles. In *Proceedings of the Third ACM Workshop on Role-Based Access Control.* ACM. http://doi.acm.org/10.1145/286884.286893

Sarkar, S. K., Basavaraju, T. G., & Puttamadappa, C. (2007). *Ad hoc mobile wireless networks: Principles, protocols and applications*. Boston: Auerbach Publications. doi:10.1201/9781420062229

Sirois, K., & Kent, S. (1997). Securing the nimrod routing architecture. In *SNDSS*. IEEE.

Stallings, W. (2005). *Cryptography and network security: Principles and practice* (4th ed.). New York: Pearson Education.

Tang, L., & Hong, X. (n.d.). *Protecting location privacy by camouflaging movements*. Academic Press.

Toh, C. (2001). Maximum battery life routing to support ubiquitous mobile computing in wireless ad hoc networks. *IEEE Communications Magazine, 39*(6), 138–147. doi:10.1109/35.925682

Wisitpongphan, N., Bai, F., Mudalige, P., & Tonguz, O. (2007). On the routing problem in disconnected vehicular ad-hoc networks. In *Proceedings of 26th IEEE International Conference on Computer Communications*. IEEE.

Wu, B., Chen, J., Wu, J., & Cardei, M. (2007). A survey of attacks and countermeasures in mobile ad hoc networks. In *Wireless network security* (pp. 103–135). Academic Press. doi:10.1007/978-0-387-33112-6_5

Xing, F., & Wang, W. (2007). Understanding dynamic denial of service attacks in mobile ad hoc networks. In *Proceedings of Military Communications Conference*. IEEE.

Yan, Z., & Chen, Y. (2010). Adcontrep: A privacy enhanced reputation system for MANET content services. In Ubiquitous intelligence and computing (pp. 414–429). Academic Press.

Yang, H., Luo, H., Ye, F., Lu, S., & Zhang, L. (2004). Security in mobile ad hoc networks: Challenges and solutions. *IEEE Wireless Communications, 11*(1), 38–47. doi:10.1109/MWC.2004.1269716

Yick, J., Mukherjee, B., & Ghosal, D. (2008). Wireless sensor network survey. *Computer Networks, 52*(12), 2292–2330. doi:10.1016/j.comnet.2008.04.002

Yousefi, S., Bastani, S., & Fathy, M. (2007). On the performance of safety message dissemination in vehicular ad hoc networks. In *Proceedings of 4th European Conference on Universal Multiservice Networks* (pp. 377–390). ECUMN.

Zhang, Y., & Lee, W. (2005). Security in mobile ad-hoc networks. In *Ad hoc networks* (pp. 249–268). Academic Press. doi:10.1007/0-387-22690-7_9

Zhou, L., & Haas, Z. (1999). Securing ad hoc networks. *IEEE Network, 13*(6), 24–30. doi:10.1109/65.806983

KEY TERMS AND DEFINITIONS

MANET: Mobile ad hoc network (MANET).
VANET: Vehicular ad hoc network (VANET).

Chapter 2
Trends in Crime Toolkit Development

Ansam Khraisat
University of Ballarat, Australia

Michael Hobbs
Deakin University, Australia

Ammar Alazab
Deakin University, Australia

Jemal Abawajy
Deakin University, Australia

Ahmad Azab
University of Ballarat, Australia

ABSTRACT

Cybercriminals continue to target online users of banks. They are improving their techniques and using high levels of skill in their attacks. Their continued search for different methods to commit crime makes the existing protection system less effective. They have developed crime toolkits which have become more accessible and simpler to use, and this has attracted more cybercriminals to cybercrime. In this chapter, the authors study the methods that are used in crime toolkits. They present the development and current trend of crime toolkits and reveal the methods that have been used to commit cybercrime successfully.

INTRODUCTION

Cybercriminals are people who use digital devices to commit crimes in cyberspace. The current prevalence of cybercrime is a major threat to information security. Initially, cybercriminals were hackers (often professional technical coders) who trespassed into the cyber world by implementing simple malware to conduct attacks. These attacks were generally aiming at gaining a reputation in the underground market, or to cause financial loss to a targeted user by deleting system data or stealing personal passwords. While occasionally their actions resulted in significant financial losses to victims it usually brought little or no financial gain to them(Sood & Enbody, 2013).

Currently, users and organizations are using Internet services heavily on their daily transactions because of the ease of attaining high speed Internet connections as Digital Subscriber Line (DSL), third Generation (3G) and others. Such new Internet services as e-commerce, online banking, online advertisements and others which moved the economy online. This economy movement shifted the motivation of Cybercriminals from getting individual reputations in the underground

DOI: 10.4018/978-1-4666-4789-3.ch002

market and working as individuals into working as organized large groups with more money profit driven intentions.

However, Cybercrimes are becoming more serious. The underground market has allowed criminals to achieve cybercrime intentions in different ways. Unlike before, where a Cybercriminal needed to have a strong computer technical background, today the naïve user can conduct Cybercrime using tools which are sold in the underground market. These user friendly tools are called crimeware toolkits and can be used to create sophisticated malware binaries or to propagate these malware binaries. Figure 1 demonstrates a simple underground market scenario (Hogben, Plohmann, Gerhards-Padilla, & Leder, 2011) that reflects how Cybercriminals are using strategy as organized groups which are profit driven. It also demonstrates the ease of being a Cybercriminal or purchasing a Cybercrime service. Malware writers create a Crimeware toolkit that can be used to create malware binaries or to distribute malware with

a simple interface where naïve criminals can use it. After that, the malware distributor distributes and sells the Crimeware toolkit to Cybercriminals. Services and support may be offered with the tool kit where help is required. Finally Cybercriminals can infect devices and distribute attacks using these toolkits. It should also be noted that services may be offered to criminals who are ready to pay for an attack service without the need to buy any type of toolkit.

Different studies and reports demonstrate the distribution and losses caused by Cybercrime. Symantec stated that, on average, 42 billion spam messages a day are sent around the world (Symantec, 2011). In 2012, $110 billion worldwide was lost to cybercrime, with Australia recording $2 billion in losses (Norton, 2012). HP Enterprise Security, showed different losses for different countries, in which US scored highest loss with $8.9 million in just 2012 (Ponemon, 2012). Finally, 13% of North America home networks were

Figure 1. Underground market

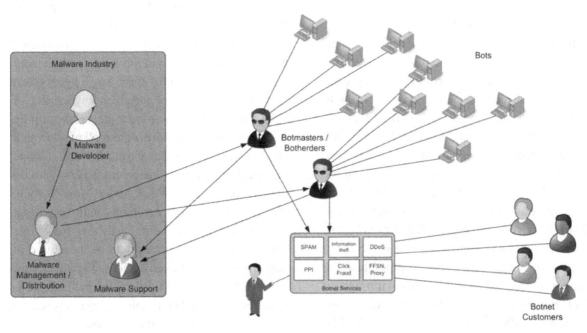

infected and compromised with malware during 2012 (Kindsight, 2012)

This chapter explores cybercrime trends, future threats, and the persistent development of the cybercrime threat landscape. It also presents Cybercrime evolution through time in malware propagation approaches and attack types.

This chapter is organized as follows. In Section 2, we present the crime toolkits development. In Section 3, we study crime toolkits trends. In Section 4, we discuss the existing protection mechanism. Section 5 provides the conclusion to this chapter.

THE EVOLUTION OF MALWARE SOFTWARE DEVELOPMENT KITS

This section studies the development of crimeware toolkits that can be bought from underground markets and used by non-technical or technical Cybercriminals. Crimeware toolkits have accelerated the process by which a new exploit can spread throughout the threat landscape, and this has been made possible, in part, by the various innovations that attack toolkit developers have integrated into their products.

In the past, malicious writers had to create their own malicious code from scratch, so a successful attack was dominated by criminals with greater technical knowledge. However, criminals rapidly started developing user-friendly crime toolkits. In the 1980s, hacking and Internet crime started gradually because Internet users did not believe hackers were serious in trying to take down the Internet(Steven Malby, 2013). In the 1990s, Internet crime was beginning to become serious; the aim of this crime was script kiddies (Steven Malby, 2013). In the 2000s, Internet crime is not about hackers, or script kiddies, but money. Thus, the numbers of targeted attacks have risen throughout 2011 from the usual 77 per day in 2010 to an average of 82 per day in 2011 (Symantec 2011). The reason for the growth of malware on the Internet

is the development of new methods that make it harder for the existing detection system to detect.

Attackers have benefited from crime toolkits that make it easier to create widespread malicious attacks. For the naïve attacker, crime kits mean that they can launch sophisticated attacks without having any technical knowledge. Malware developers for these crime toolkits are proposing regular updates, different features, new tool modules, discussion groups, tutorials, and service to customers before, during and after purchase. The success of the kit lies in its straightforward user interface, sophisticated design, encryption, and seemingly successful marketing model. In Table 1, we provide an overview of the malware evolution for the period 1980s until the present. As time progresses, so does the complexity, sophistication, malice and automation of malware.

Crimeware toolkits expose a widespread number of attack vectors. Different toolkits employ different exploits and techniques. Much of this variation comes from the different origins, skills, and goals of the authors. Table 2 summarizes some of the features and techniques used by present-day malware. Some features regularly appear, such as phishing and keystroke logging. These are often the "normal" actions performed by malware. Other features, such as the ability to take screenshots, are becoming more common as websites implement methods for overcoming basic key loggers (such as visual passwords or onscreen keyboards). A Web injection feature is used to create fake pop-up menus, usually in the form of a small window that suddenly appears in the victim's browser. Online service features allow naïve customers, who do not have any technical background, to ask for help via instant messages or emails with installing, customizing and updating malware. Real time capability allows the attacks to be monitored in real time for the infected devices. The attacks are automated and do not need any manual intervention from the attacker. Finally, encryption is used to hide the presence of the malware.

Table 1. Malware evolution

Features	1980s	1990s	2000s	Present
Spread method	Floppy disk	Floppy disk, Email and same network	Email	Drive-by downloads
Users become victims	Insert desk	Open email	Open email	Browser website
Examples	Brain Morris Worm	Vandoies	Code Red	Zeus
Detection mechanism	Signature Based Intrusion Detection System (SIDS)	SIDS and Email filter	SIDS	SIDS, Anomaly based Intrusion Detection System (AIDS)

Table 2. Malware features

Malware Name	Propagation Method				Attack Methods and Attack Capabilities							
	Phishing	Drive-by download	Malicious email	Malicious Web link	Web Injection	Browser redirect	Keystroke logging	Online service	Real time	Auto	Screen capture	Encryption
Zeus	✓	✓	✓	✓	✓	✓	✓	✓	✓	✓	✓	✓
SpyEye	✓	✓	✓	✓	✓	✓	✓	✓	✓	✓	✓	✓
InfoStear	✓	✓	✓	✓	✓		✓	✓		✗	✓	✓
Silent Banker	✓	✓	✓	✓	✓	✓	✓	✓	✓	✗	✓	✓
URL Zone	✓	✓	✓	✓	✓	✗	✓	✓	✓	✓	✓	✓
Carberp	✓	✓	✓	✓	✓	✗	✓	✗	✗	✗	✗	✓
Haxdoor	✓	✓	✓	✓	✓	✗	✓	✗	✗	✗	✗	✓
Limbo	✓	✓	✓	✓	✓	✗	✓	✗	✗	✗	✗	✓

The malicious writer can take advantage of a Web application vulnerability to launch an attack (A. Alazab, Alazab, Abawajy, & Hobbs, 2011). It can be seen in Table 2, that most of malware can take screenshots. These malware can target the financial sector and the non-financial sector, such as Facebook, Twitter, Gmail, and Yahoo, and cloud applications, such as Salesforce and Google Apps. However, this new generation of crime toolkits has the ability to evade existing detection using Polymorphism and Dynamic injection into Web pages.

Different types of attacks exist aside from those previous mentioned that can be implemented using Crimeware toolkits (Lashkari, Ghalebandi, & Reza Moradhaseli, 2011). Denial of Service (DoS) attack aims to make a system unavailable. This attack aims to exhaust the system resources either at Network level, by exhausting network resources (routers and switches) and bandwidth, or at non-network level, by exhausting the system resources and keeping them busy, through memory and CPU utilization. Some popular attacks for DoS are the "smurf" attack and SYN flood attack.

Crime toolkits are developing rapidly, with new features added frequently. Table 2 details the features of some of the more prolific malware types. There has been a clear transition from using phishing e-mails to directly modifying banking webpages using JavaScript and injecting HTML straight into the webpage (although phishing still occurs at a high rate).

Malicious writers have the ability to control a naïve user's DNS server and entice them to connect to a fake website (FBI, 2012). In 2012, malicious writers developed malware called DNS Changer (FBI, 2012), which modifies the Internet client's

DNS server settings to change the Internet service provider's legitimate DNS servers.

In terms of architecture evolution, Botnets are the main malware platform threat used by cybercriminals and the root cause of Internet security threats (Binsalleeh et al., 2010; Saad et al., 2011). Botnets are a collection of compromised devices (zombies, bots) that are remotely controlled by a cybercriminal, called a Botmaster, by installing Bot malware on the infected device, in which it creates a backdoor for full remote access for Botmaster without the user's knowledge. The main difference between Botnets and other malware types is the use of Command and Control (C&C) entity/server. The Cybercriminal communicates with the infected devices remotely through C&C entity which allows the cybercriminal to initiate and update an attack, obtain the status for the compromised devices and manage the large number of infected devices.

The use of a C&C server helps the attacker in both managing the infected devices and concealing their identity from lawful agencies. The use of C&C usually has two architectures, either centralized or decentralized. Centralized architecture allows the attacker to control and communicate with infected devices through a central server or a few centralized servers. This approach uses either Internet Relay Chat (IRC) or Hyper Text Transfer Protocol (HTTP). IRC uses clear text or encrypted text to communicate with Botnet groups using simple commands. The attacker may join an unlimited number of zombies to a specific channel and communicate them in parallel, which makes it easy to implement and customize. The malware author contacts zombies by "pushing" commands toward zombies which may be encrypted through private channels. HTTP is preferred by a lot of malware authors as it can be encrypted, it is allowed by firewall settings in most organizations and is easy to use. Zombies contact C&C servers by using a "pull" mechanism to retrieve commands, b the malware author upload commands into server and the infected device contacts this server from time to time using GET and POST commands. Symantec reported that the number of centralized servers used by malware authors for IRC reached 31% and 69% for HTTP in 2009 (Corp, 2010). Unlike centralized architecture, P2P architecture distributes information about Botnet through its participating peers, therefore. Commands to peers are injected to get information.

Exploit Crimeware Toolkits

Exploits are programs and, in many cases, scripts that exploit vulnerabilities in other applications. The most widespread type are browser exploits, which enable the download of malicious files to achieve a number of cyber activities on a victim's computer. It is important to distinguish between exploit toolkits and other toolkits like Botnets. The main aim of an exploit toolkit is to exploit vulnerabilities in general applications (M. Alazab, Monsamy, Batten, Lantz, & Tian, 2012)in order to deliver, download and install the malware (Payload) at the targeted devices. However, Botnets toolkits, such as Zeus, are used to implement malware binaries to communicate with C&C server and to conduct an attack such as stealing online bank accounts.

Exploit toolkits look for weaknesses in a system in order to use them to download malicious binaries without user consent or knowledge. This is known as "drive-by download". These vulnerabilities are widespread throughout different applications that are used by users while surfing the Internet such as, but not limited to, JAVA, Adobe reader, Adobe flash player and Internet browsers as Firefox.

Exploit toolkits are sold in the underground market with an easy, user friendly interface. Prices range from free, with very limited features, to thousands of dollars with sophisticated features such as updates and support. Toolkits can also be rented. Table 4 below lists some of the most popular toolkits and their prices (Jones, 2012).

Blackhole crime toolkit emerged in 2010 and is still being used to exploit vulnerabilities to spread malware. It exploits vulnerabilities for Adobe flash player, Internet explorer and most importantly Java for all platforms. It must be stated that java vulnerabilities had a success that reached 80% for Blackhole according to (Jones, 2012). To avoid detection, Blackhole uses obfuscation in order not to be identified at a network level. A Blackhole kit can be rented for different prices ranging from up to $1500 annually if the customer use his server, or $200 a week - $500 a month if the hosting are to be rented as well (Howard, 2012). Phoenix is another exploit kit that emerged in 2007 which aims to exploit vulnerabilities in Java, Adobe reader and flash and Internet explorer with base price $2200 (MalwareIntelligence, 2010). As Blackhole, Phoenix uses obfuscation to hide its attack.

Sweet orange kit is a brand new threat emerged in 2012. According to bluecoat website (Larsen, 2012), this toolkit guarantees 10% to 15% successful infection rate if a user landed on a compromised website by exploiting vulnerabilities as Java, PDF, Internet Explorer and Firefox. This new toolkit is still unknown since the creators of this toolkit ensure that the code could not be leaked to anybody. Another kit, Nuclear pack, first emerged in 2009 and, after disappearing for some time reemerged in 2012 (Jones, 2012) in where it exploit different kind of vulnerabilities.

Whitehole crime toolkit emerged in 2013 and it uses the same code as Blackhole toolkit. Even though it is still under testing release, this toolkit is sold at underground markets with a price range of $200 – $1800 (Chua, 2013). This toolkit mainly attacks java vulnerabilities, as micro trend experiments revealed (Chua, 2013). According to the trend micro, this toolkit can evade antivirus detection which makes browsers such as Google safe not effective. Cool exploit kit was first noticed in 2012 from "ransomware" malware attacks. This toolkit used windows vulnerability (CVE-2012-5076) and JAVA vulnerability (CVE-2012-5076) to deliver malware. Kafeine, a French researcher, noticed that these vulnerabilities were used by Blackhole exploit tool kit after a small time when Cool exploit kit used them, in which he believes that these two toolkits are related to either the same author or the same group (Kafeine, 2012). The price to rent this toolkit can reach $ 10,000 a month (Krebsonsecurity, 2013). Other Exploit kits exist such as Sakura, Redkit and others with different exploits and different bypass techniques in order not to be identified.

In general, exploit toolkits aims to lure victims to visit the malicious website in order to exploit vulnerabilities and install malware binaries. The malicious writer can create a phishing website and hope that enough unsuspecting visitors are fooled. The malicious writer can also produce a poster that indicates his particular exploit toolkit server, and then allows the poster to spread over the Internet. However, the most effective method is to control a legitimate website, which allows the malicious writer ready access to a large number of Internet users. The malware author has numerous preferences to approach and control legitimate websites, such as obtaining right of entry authorizations to legitimate websites and achieving access to the site through malicious code (DVLabs., 2010). This may be achieved by compromising a trusted website, as illustrated in Figure 2. Cybercriminals first compromise a legitimate website by using code injection. After being compromised, the legitimate server is be connected to the malicious site. As soon as the user visits the legitimate site, they will be redirected to the malicious website where it will install the Malware binaries through drive by download.

Some Cybercriminals use servers called bullet proof servers as malicious servers to install malware binaries. As the name implies, these servers cannot be taken down, even if they identified as malicious. These servers reside mainly in countries without international agreements or collaborations with other countries that aim to fight cybercriminals. Furthermore, there are no lawful agencies or laws in these countries which prohibit the use of malicious servers to harm other devices.

Figure 2. Attack scenario

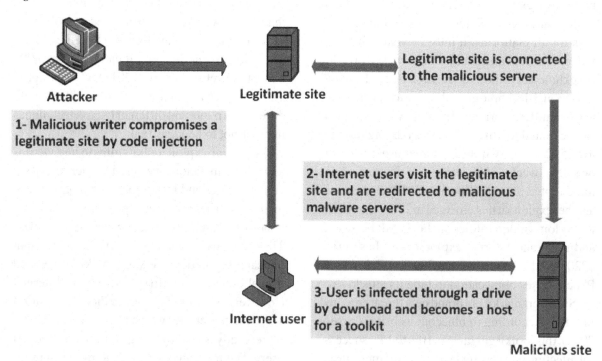

Modern toolkits ask for small payments to download version updates. The procedure of setting up zero-day exploits on toolkits has been modularized so retailers can simply generate and trade their own exploits, guaranteeing their offerings are compatible with the toolkits. This type of association increases the structure and strengths available to the toolkit by enabling third parties to add the original capabilities, thus increasing the number of exploits the toolkit can perform.

Web based attacks to deliver malware binaries through exploiting vulnerabilities have increased dramatically. According to Kaspersky 2012 report (Kaspersky, 2012), Web-infections have increased by 1.7 fold from 2011 to 2012.. Since Java nowadays can be installed on different operating systems, it became very popular to be used by users. This lures Cybercriminals to exploit vulnerabilities for Java in order to infect devices with a malware instead of other vulnerabilities. The Kaspersky report reflects this fact by demonstrating that half

of exploit vulnerabilities attacks targeted Java vulnerabilities in 2012. Adobe reader scored 28% of exploit vulnerabilities attacks.

Aside from using exploit toolkits to deliver and install malware binaries, there are different approaches that can be used to distribute the implemented malware (Lashkari et al., 2011). The Social engineering approach aims to convince the user to install Bot malware by tricking them into believing it is coming from a legitimate source. Spam email is a popular approach to send emails containing links or attachments that contain malware. Also, a traditional approach, such as USB flash that may contain the malware, can be used.

Crime Tool Kit Components

Crime tool kits have components to add extra features to an attack. One or more of the following components could be included: exploit library; browser detection engine; command-and-control servers; user interface, updatability feature; customization feature; and obfuscation feature. An attack kit may also include script code generators to allow a hacker to inject legitimate websites and force Internet users to an illegitimate website. Attack kits are usually programmed by server-side scripting languages, such as PHP. Most kits are programmed by using PHP because it provides dynamic programming which allows a combination of HTML to display dynamic elements on the Web page, and because of the simplicity of development. Most Web hosting offers essential components for clients to execute PHP commands in their hosting, and as a consequence, malware authors compromise the Web hosting.

Exploit Library

Since crime toolkits use exploit codes to spread an attack, the exploits library is an important feature in the crime toolkit. The achievement rate of a specific exploit toolkit deployment relies on the kind of exploits used. In other words, old-fashioned, well-known vulnerabilities could be inefficient to attack. As the antivirus finds protection against these vulnerabilities over time, the capability to change and update these kits with new vulnerabilities make the kits difficult to detect. Thus, malicious writers frequently supply exploit codes for new vulnerabilities to be added to crime toolkits. This permits malware authors to compromise victims before the user solves the vulnerabilities, such as CRiMEPACK, Phoenix, and Eleonore (Symantec, 2010).

Browser Detection Engine

Browser Detection Engines_assist the malware author in identifying which exploits will be used by the crime toolkit. The browser detector helps to detect the vulnerability of Internet users.

Command-and-Control Servers

The main functionality of a command-and-control server is to control the successfully compromised users. Once the botnet is successfully installed, the controller of a botnet is capable of directing the activities of these compromised computers to get critical information.

User Interface

Most crime toolkits provide an administrative panel as a graphical user interface for watching all victim activity, simplifying configuration settings, determining the botnet and arranging attacks.

Updatability Mechanisms

Most of the attacks from crime toolkits permit updates with a new version of kit components. These features enable the crime toolkit user to use the new arsenal.

Obfuscation Techniques

The term obfuscation means changing the program code which then makes the code harder to understand (M. Alazab, Venkataraman, & Watters, 2010).There is a range of different obfuscation techniques employed by attack kit developers and users to evade detection and increase the survivability of their toolkits. Code obfuscation is successfully used by malware writers to avoid antivirus detection.

JavaScript

A primary way to help malicious codes evade detection is via obfuscated JavaScript, which can be achieved by the JavaScript interpreter of the Web browser. These methods can be used in malicious files that act as payloads for these attacks. The aim of the attack toolkit developer is to make the content resistant to reverse engineering, and create a dynamic to avoid detection.

Drive-By Download

A drive-by download attack is a popular method used in crime toolkits. It occurs when a user browses a malicious site, which compromises the user and infects him with malware. Drive-by downloads have become the number one infection vector of malware. A drive-by download is a code that is automatically downloaded to the Internet user without his knowledge. Drive-by downloads are achieved by taking advantage of weaknesses in Web browsers. The malicious code or unwanted download from the Internet can be achieved by the following. First, a person authorizes a download but does not understand the consequences of it (e.g., downloads that install an unknown or counterfeit executable program, ActiveX component, or Java applet). Second, the download can occur through any transfer the user is not aware of. Third, malware can be downloaded without a user's information.

Many reasons exist that make drive-by-download attacks very efficient. First, weaknesses in Web applications are prevalent (Corporation., 2012), and vulnerable Web applications are frequently used as well. Second, crime toolkits that intend to exploit Web application vulnerabilities are available in underground forums (Cova, Kruegel, & Vigna, 2010). Third, highly skilled techniques from malicious writers complicate the exploit code, and send it to Internet users, such as NeoSploit, and LuckySploit.

Web Injection

A Web injection attack is a recent method used by the crime toolkit to compromise a victim through phishing attacks (Stone-Gross et al., 2009). The purpose of a Web injection attack is to inject and perform instructions identified by the malware author in the Web page. It is usually supplementary to Zeus and SpyEye toolkits.

The writer of the crime toolkit who desires to use the Web injection utility of Zeus and SpyEye toolkits, attaches a file for that purpose when generating the malware with the builder component (M. Alazab et al., 2010). For instance, a hacker can add malicious HTML code to an injected website page after the page has completed loading. However, many crime toolkits have the functionality of HTML injection capability. The malware author can modify these crime toolkits to create a fake website with a new additional field. The fake injected website appears like the original website to a user's Web browsers.

A Web injection file is mostly a script file from JavaScript and a HTML tag. This file allows cybercriminals to attack any particular organization, such as a bank. This is done by injecting specific code into victims' browsers so they can change the Web pages user's access in real time. Web injection file users can simply create fake pop-ups, usually a small window that suddenly appears in the forefront of a victim's Web browser. Pop-ups can be launched by a single or double mouse click that requests extra information such as identification number, PIN, password and user name. Web injection files have all of the scripts required to convince victims that the pop-ups are real. They use HTML scripts to make Web pages look original using different parameters.

Automatic Transfer System (ATS)

Cyber criminals use an automated system to silently steal bank accounts without having to be online at the same time. This new method, known as automatic transfer system (ATS), is being used in combination with common crimeware kits to launch attacks through Web browsers that bypass online banking security protection. TrendMicro researchers revealed how two popular crimeware kits, Zeus and SpyEye, used these features to silently transfer money from one account to another (Trustwave, 2012).

Earlier styles of crimeware captured account authorizations via Web injections on the Web page for the duration of a victim's browsing session. Clients could insert extra information in these fields, such as identification numbers and passwords, without realizing the bank was not the one requesting the data. With the data gathered, a malware author may possibly log in independently to steal money from the client.

CRIME TOOLKITS TRENDS

In this section we discuss crime toolkits trends. The damage of attack and impact with new crime toolkits would be increased with the new crime tool kits. The development of new crime toolkits are extremely targeted and organized by cyber-criminals. Figure 3 shows the crime toolkit trends

Advances from targeted attacks will create their way into massive attacks as shown in Figure 3. Malicious writers have used methods to evade detection systems and,o create many forms of threats with the new style. They have moved gradually to the next generation of cybercrime and exploited vulnerabilities in other applications. This new generation of cybercrime has a high degree of stealth over a long duration of operation in order to be effective, and compromised computer systems remain to be of service even after key systems have been penetrated and original goals achieved (Wall, 2007). It also capitalizes on organizational data available on social networking sites to create 'phishing' emails and malware targeted at the types of applications and operating systems (with all their vulnerabilities) typical in particular industries.

Figure 4 shows the comparison between traditional crime toolkits versus advanced crime toolkits. Advanced toolkits are persistent, stealthy, target and zero day. Crime toolkits are becoming

Figure 3. Crime toolkits trends

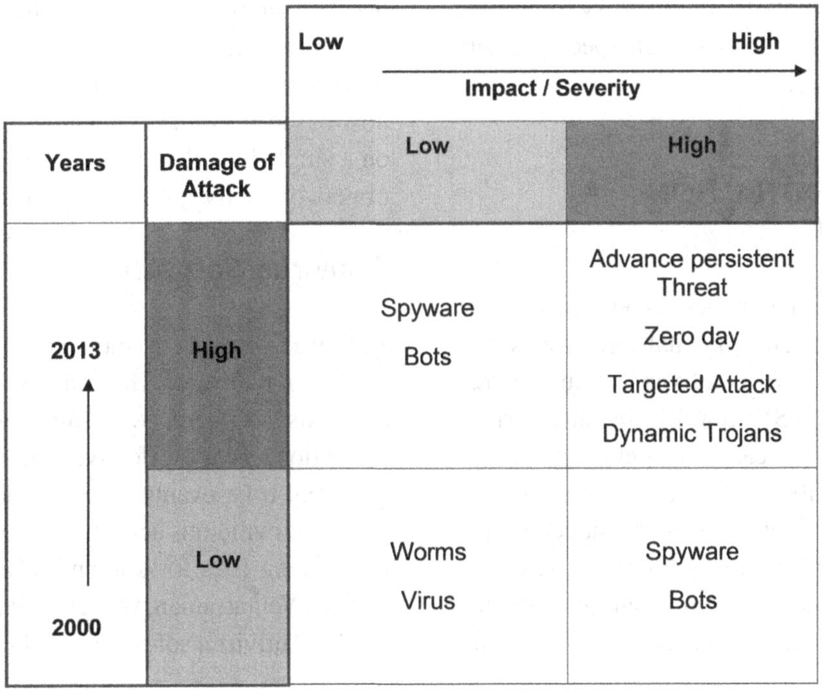

Figure 4. Traditional crime toolkits versus advance toolkits

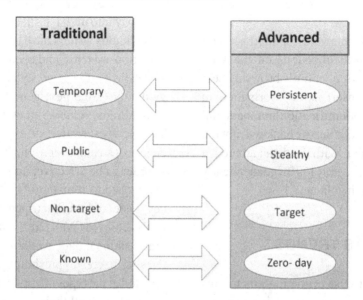

gradually more complex due to many reasons. There are notably more kinds of malware being created in the wild that exploit zero-day vulnerabilities. Crime toolkits have also now been created with polymorphic and stealthy abilities. The polymorphic feature changes certain characteristics of malware for each time of infection. Also, the crime toolkits are now easy to update, which permits a malicious writer to speedily insert codes for new vulnerabilities.

EXISTING PROTECTION MECHANISM

This section describes numerous types of security mechanisms that can make malware threats less severe, such as antivirus software, intrusion prevention systems (IPS), firewalls, content filtering/inspection and application whitelisting. In this section we describe the typical features for each category, the types of malware and attack vector tool addresses, and the methods used to detect and stop malware. Recommendations and guidance for implementing, configuring, and maintaining the

tools are also provided, as well as explanations of the shortcomings of the tools in each catergory and the ways in which they complement other tools.

Firewalls

Firewalls can be software or hardware-built. A network firewall is hardware installed between networks to limit what sort of traffic flow can be authorized from one network to another. A host-based firewall is typically software running on a single host that can limit the entry and exit of network activity for the specific host.

Antivirus Software

Antivirus software is most commonly used for detecting malware. There are several types of antivirus software, with most giving similar protection. To be effective, the software must scan real-time events on a computer system to check for malicious activity. A common example is scanning files for known malware (Mamoun Alazab, Ventatraman, Watters, Alazab, & Alazab, 2011). Antivirus software should be configured to scan all files to achieve maximum protection. Computer users should also be able to perform a scan manually if they want. Antivirus software should also have the ability to disinfect files. This refers to eliminating malware from an infected file or isolating files for future analysis. Antivirus software must perform host-based and network-based antivirus scanning. Administrators of antivirus software advise installing antivirus software on all user computers quickly after the operating system has been installed and regularly updating the software. To ensure the efficiency of the antivirus software signatures should also be kept up to date...

Intrusion Detection Approach

There are two approaches to analysing events using IDSs intrusion detection techniques and these can be categorized into two classes: signature based detection and anomaly based detection. This section provides an overview of both approaches and discusses the advantages and disadvantages of the two ISDs.

Signature Based Intrusion Detection System (SIDS)

SIDS is similar to traditional Anti-virus detection. Often called a misuse detection system, SIDS is based on pattern matching techniques to find a known attack. By examining certain patterns, the SIDS compares incoming data to the database of signatures which are malicious. Once the intrusion matches with a malicious string database, an alert is raised. SIDS commonly provides good detection results for specified, well-known attacks. However, SIDS cannot detect zero-day attacks because the signature does not exist in the database until the signature database is updated. Another disadvantage is that the SIDS must have a pattern to express all of the malicious code that a malicious writer may create which requires regular signature updates. The main advantage

of SIDS is that it is very efficient in detecting known attacks without raising false alarms and can quickly detect an attack.

However, SIDS has the disadvantage that a signature must be created for every attack, and zero day attacks cannot be detected. A SIDS is also prone to false positives since they are commonly based on regular expressions and string matching. While signatures work well against attacks with a fixed behavioural pattern, they do not work well against the multitude of attack patterns created by a human or self-modifying behavioural characteristic. The SIDS has been implemented in many different approach, as well as popular tools, such as Snort.

Anomaly Based Intrusion Detection System (AIDS)

AIDS has attracted the interest of many researchers to overcome the disadvantage of SIDS. Anomaly detectors detect activities that are not the usual behaviour on a computer network. According to this approach, the assumption is that attacker behaviour deviates from normal user behaviour. Accordingly, AIDS involves the training stage and a testing stage. In the training stage, the normal traffic profile is labelled by using data that is accepted as normal behaviour; in the latter, the testing stage is applied to new data sets. The result from this is that the AIDS has the ability to monitor the activities of new users and compares the new data with the obtained profile and tries to detect deviations. Those different from normal behaviour are then flagged as attacks.

AIDS are categorized into many sub-kinds in the literature such as statistical techniques, data mining, artificial neural networks, and genetic algorithms and so on. The main benefit of an anomaly-based scheme is the power to detect zero days malware, thus the unusual user profile is not dependent on the signatures database. Moreover ABD has many advantages. First, they have the ability to find insider attacks. Second, the ABD

Table 3. Explanation of crime toolkits

Name	Year of Appearance	Explanation
Zeus	2007	Uses traditional e-mail phishing methods to infect Internet users.
Limbo	2007	Steals sensitive data. Has ability to inject user's Web page.
Torpig	2008	Steal credit cards and online bank accounts
InfoStear	2009	Has a very specific payload goal. Has ability to collect confidential information from the victim and redirects him to a predetermined website.
Waledac	2009	sends 7000 Spam/day
Silent Banker		Exists by users clicking links on a malicious link
URL Zone	2009	Modifies bank pages to trick victims into transferring funds
SpyEye	2010	Web browser observer and Sniffing of network protocol such as HTTP, FTP, and POP.
Zeus 2.0	2010	Contains the aptitude to overcome the uninstall routine. Novel abilities, containing events to simplify several installations on similar PC.
Haxdoor	2011	Redirects the infected user's URL connection requests.
Carberp	2012	Carberp has the functionality to use general and targeted attacks. It also has new abilities, making it stronger than Zeus.
Cridex	2012	Embedded URL links or HTML attachments that trick the user into browsing the compromised websites

relies on the users profiles. Thus it is extremely hard for an attacker to identify what is normal user activity without generation an alarm (Patcha & Park, 2007). ABD uses machine learning techniques in order to build user profiles. Unfortunately, making a user profiles is a challenging task because ABD looks for unusual activity rather than actual malicious activity (Patcha & Park, 2007). Another major disadvantage of ABD is the possibility of detecting a known attack, with the result being a high rate of false positives (mistake to determine non-attack). Table 3 shows a comparison between signature based detection and anomaly based detection. However, anomaly detection has an advantage over signature-based engines in that a new attack for which a signature does not exist can be detected if it falls out of the normal traffic patterns.

Therefore, AIDS has been the subject matter of a number of studies. We explore a number of various approaches for AIDS. These consist of statistical anomaly detection, data-mining based methods, and machine learning based techniques.

Awareness

Usually, this method is associated with other techniques to achieve effective protection. This means any guidance for computer users on malware prevention supports a decrease in the rate and threat of malware. Users, who are the first protection layer, need to know the methods in which malware compromises the computer, the

Table 4. Exploit toolkits

Kit Name	Year Emerged	Vulnerabilities
Phoenix	2007	Java, Adobe player and reader and Microsoft Internet explorer
Nuclear Pack	2009	Java, Adobe player and reader Microsoft Internet explorer
Blackhole	2010	Java in all OS, Adobe flash player and Microsoft Internet explorer
Sweet Orange	2012	Java, PDF, Internet Explorer and Firefox.
Cool pack	2012	Java and Windows
Whitehole	2013	Java

dangers that malware causes, the lack of ability for other methods to stop all occurrences of malware, and the significance of users in preventing incidents through awareness of avoiding social engineering attacks. Therefore, users must be educated on attack techniques that are targeted to foil users from stealing personal information. Technologies include suspicious emails that try to lead users to reveal personal information and unknown attachments or hyperlinks in e-mails. By studying the crime toolkit, we have recognized that awareness contributes to a reduction in the occurrence of cybercrime as anti-vendors have a very low rate of detection.

Website Checking Tools

Web site checking tools enable databases to look up potentially malicious websites that may be compromised by cybercriminals to deliver malicious binaries. Some tools are based on previous information, while for others; the URL needs to be looked up in real time to detect threats.

CONCLUSION

The availability and effectiveness of crime toolkits has promoted their increased use in cybercrime, these crime toolkits are currently being employed by the malware writers. Attack kits allow a naïve user to enter the cybercrime world with powerful tools which are easy to use through a graphical user interface. Thus, these crime toolkits require a good security model that can protect against zero day attack. Due to the increasing availability of crime toolkits in underground markets, criminal activity can now be carried out by Internet users without much criminal knowledge. These toolkits allow the naïve user to be a creative hacker without much skill.

Antivirus software and firewalls are not enough protection for computers from the latest challenges, and hackers are always trying different and new techniques to hack into computers. Security awareness and user education are important steps that help to prevent most online attacks. Web application protection is still necessary to protect against advanced zero-day threats as such threats emerge via crime toolkits.

REFERENCES

Alazab, A., Alazab, M., Abawajy, J., & Hobbs, M. (2011). Web application protection against SQL injection attack. In *Proceedings of the 7th International Conference on Information Technology and Applications.* Academic Press.

Alazab, M., Monsamy, V., Batten, L., Lantz, P., & Tian, R. (2012). *Analysis of malicious and benign android applications.* Paper presented at the Distributed Computing Systems Workshops (ICDCSW). New York, NY.

Alazab, M., Venkataraman, S., & Watters, P. (2010). *Towards understanding malware behaviour by the extraction of API calls.* Paper presented at the Cybercrime and Trustworthy Computing Workshop (CTC). New York, NY.

Alazab, M., Ventatraman, S., Watters, P., Alazab, M., & Alazab, A. (2011). *Cybercrime: The case of obuscated malware.* Paper presented at the 7th International Conference on Global Security, Safety & Sustainability. Thessaloniki, Greece.

Binsalleeh, H., Ormerod, T., Boukhtouta, A., Sinha, P., Youssef, A., Debbabi, M., & Wang, L. (2010). *On the analysis of the zeus botnet crimeware toolkit.* Paper presented at the Privacy Security and Trust (PST). New York, NY.

Chua, J. P. (2013). *Whitehole exploit kit emerges.* Retrieved from http://blog.trendmicro.com/trendlabs-security-intelligence/whitehole-exploit-kit-emerges/

Corp, S. (2010). *Symantec global Internet security threat report: Trends for 2009.* Academic Press.

Corporation., M. (2012). *Common vulnerabilities and exposures.* Retrieved from http://cve.mitre.org/

Cova, M., Kruegel, C., & Vigna, G. (2010). *Detection and analysis of drive-by-download attacks and malicious JavaScript code.* Academic Press. doi:10.1145/1772690.1772720

DVLabs. H. (2010). 2010 full year top cyber security risks report. Author.

FBI. (2012). *DNSChanger malware.* Retrieved July, 2012, 2012, from http://www.fbi.gov/news/stories/2011/november/malware_110911/DNS-changer-malware.pdf

Hogben, G., Plohmann, D., Gerhards-Padilla, E., & Leder, F. (2011). *Botnets: Detection, measurement, disinfection and defence. European Network and Information Security Agency.* ENISA.

Howard, F. (2012). *Exploring the blackhole exploit kit.* Retrieved from http://nakedsecurity.sophos.com/exploring-the-blackhole-exploit-kit-3/

Jones, J. (2012). *State of web exploit kits.* Paper presented at the BlackHat USA 2012. Las Vegas, NV. Retrieved from http://media.blackhat.com/bh-us-12/Briefings/Jones/BH_US_12_Jones_State_Web_Exploits_WP.pdf

Kafeine. (2012). *Cool exploit kit - A new browser exploit pack on the battlefield with a Duqu like font drop.* Retrieved from http://malware.dontneedcoffee.com/2012/10/newcoolek.html

Kaspersky. (2012). *Kaspersky security bulletin 2012: The overall statistics for 2012.* Retrieved 21 June, 2012, from https://www.securelist.com/en/analysis/204792255/Kaspersky_Security_Bulletin_2012_The_overall_statistics_for_2012

Kindsight. (2012). *Malware report.* Author.

Krebsonsecurity. (2013). *Crimeware author funds exploit buying spree.* Retrieved from http://krebsonsecurity.com/2013/01/crimeware-author-funds-exploit-buying-spree/

Larsen, C. (2012). *Forbidden fruit: The sweet orange exploit kit.* Retrieved from http://www.bluecoat.com/security-blog/2012-12-17/forbidden-fruit-sweet-orange-exploit-kit

Lashkari, A. H., Ghalebandi, S. G., & Reza Moradhaseli, M. (2011). A wide survey on botnet. In *Digital information and communication technology and its applications* (pp. 445–454). Academic Press. doi:10.1007/978-3-642-21984-9_38

MalwareIntelligence. (2010). *Phoenix exploit's kit from the mythology to a criminal business.* Author.

Norton. (2012). *2012 Norton cybercrime report.* Norton.

Patcha, A., & Park, J. M. (2007). An overview of anomaly detection techniques: Existing solutions and latest technological trends. *Computer Networks*, *51*(12), 3448–3470. doi:10.1016/j.comnet.2007.02.001

Ponemon, I. (2012). *Cost of cyber crime study.* United States: Academic Press.

Saad, S., Traore, I., Ghorbani, A., Sayed, B., Zhao, D., Lu, W., & Hakimian, P. (2011). *Detecting P2P botnets through network behavior analysis and machine learning.* Paper presented at the Privacy, Security and Trust (PST). New York, NY.

Sood, A. K., & Enbody, R. J. (2013). Crimeware-as-a-service—A survey of commoditized crimeware in the underground market. *International Journal of Critical Infrastructure Protection, 6*(1), 28-38. doi: http://dx.doi.org/10.1016/j.ijcip.2013.01.002

Steven Malby, R. M. Holterhof, Brown, Kascherus, & Ignatuschtschenko. (2013). Comprehensive study on cybercrime. Academic Press.

Stone-Gross, B., Cova, M., Cavallaro, L., Gilbert, B., Szydlowski, M., Kemmerer, R., & Vigna, G. (2009). *Your botnet is my botnet: Analysis of a botnet takeover.* Academic Press. doi:10.1145/1653662.1653738

Symantec. (2010). *Symantec report on attack kits and malicious websites.* Author.

Symantec. (2011). *Internet security threat report.* Author.

Trustwave. (2012). *Simple solutions to your complex security and compliance challenges.* Retrieved November, 2012, from https://www.trustwave.com/

Wall, D. (2007). *Cybercrime: The transformation of crime in the information age* (Vol. 4). Cambridge, MA: Polity.

KEY TERMS AND DEFINITIONS

A Zero-Day Attack: A cyber-attack utilizing a vulnerability that has not been patched. There is practically no security against a zero-day attack and intrusion detection system cannot detect the attack via signature-based matching.

Botnet: A collection of compromised computers communicating with other similar programs in order to perform tasks, usually installed via malware, under a common command & control infrastructure, controlled by a single person.

Cybercrimes: Criminal or risky events that are informational, global and networked and are to be differentiated from crimes that basically use computers. They are the utilized of transmission media that have create a new style of crime.

Exploit: A weakness or vulnerability in a program or the application that malware writers use to compromise a computer system.

Phishing: The criminally fraudulent method of attempting to acquire information such as usernames, passwords, and credit card details, by masquerading as a trustworthy entity in an electronic transmission media.

Propagation: A type of attack on a Web application which occurs when an attacker inputs malicious strings as parameters in legitimate SQL statement. The SQLIA allows the hacker to gain complete access to the database server a serious threat to the Web application.

Chapter 3
Synthesis of Supervised Approaches for Intrusion Detection Systems

Ahmed Chaouki Lokbani
Taher Moulay University of Saida, Algeria

Ahmed Lehireche
Djillali Liabes University of Sidi Bel Abbes, Algeria

Reda Mohamed Hamou
Taher Moulay University of Saida, Algeria

Abdelmalek Amine
Taher Moulay University of Saida, Algeria

ABSTRACT

Given the increasing number of users of computer systems and networks, it is difficult to know the profile of the latter, and therefore, intrusion has become a highly prized area of network security. In this chapter, to address the issues mentioned above, the authors use data mining techniques, namely association rules, decision trees, and Bayesian networks. The results obtained on the KDD'99 benchmark have been validated by several evaluation measures and are promising and provide access to other techniques and hybridization to improve the security and confidentiality in the field.

INTRODUCTION AND PROBLEMATIC

Currently computers and the Internet in particular play an increasingly important role in our society. Networks and computer systems have become today an indispensable tool for the proper functioning and development of most companies. Thus, computer systems and networks are deployed in various fields such as banking, medicine or the military. The increasing interconnection of these various systems and networks has made them accessible to a diverse population of users that continues to increase. These users, known or unknown, not necessarily full of good intentions to these networks. In fact, they may be trying to access sensitive information to read, modify or

DOI: 10.4018/978-1-4666-4789-3.ch003

destroy them or simply to infringe the proper functioning of the system. Since these networks have emerged as potential targets of attacks, the security has become an essential problem and an unavoidable issue.

Intrusion detection consists in discover or identify the use of a computer system for purposes other than those intended. Many mechanisms have been developed to ensure the security of computer systems and particularly to prevent intrusions, unfortunately, these mechanisms have limitations. In fact, computer systems have vulnerabilities that allow attackers to bypass prevention mechanisms. For this, a second line of defense is necessary: intrusion detection. For each system, a security policy must be defined to guarantee the security properties that must be made by the latter. This policy is expressed by rules, setting three distinct objectives:

The confidentiality-that is to say, the non-occurrence of unauthorized disclosure of information;

- Integrity that is to say, the non-occurrence of improper alterations of information;
- The availability is to say being ready to use.

In this study, we define intrusion, a violation of one of these three objectives. Several approaches have been developed to ensure that the security policy defined for a computer system is respected. It can indeed be circumvented by a malicious user or simply a lack of design can be the source of a breach of it. Artificial intelligence has seen many methods such as data mining and its various techniques that will be used for intrusion detection.

In this article we are experiencing some data mining techniques namely association rules, Bayesian networks and decision trees in the area of intrusion detection. The intrusion detection system designed and will be tested on a benchmark called KDD'99 which is a structured database that will be detailed later.

STATE OF THE ART

Intrusion detection is another procedure used by security personnel to protect the company against attacks. In his concept, intrusion detection tries to detect hackers trying to penetrate a system. Theoretically, detection systems trigger an alarm only when an attack succeeds. Intrusion detection can also help to proactively identify threats, because it provides guidance and gives warning of the threat of an attack is intercepted.

The concept of intrusion detection system was introduced in 1980 by James Anderson. But the subject has not been very successful. It was not until the publication of an intrusion detection model by Denning in 1987 to mark, really the start of the field.

The research in the field is then developed, the number of prototypes has increased enormously. A lot of money has been invested in this type of research in order to increase the safety of its machines. Intrusion detection has become an industry mature and proven technology: almost all the simple problems have been solved, and no major progress has been made in this area in recent years, software vendor's focus more improves the existing detection techniques.

Some tracks remain relatively unexplored:

- Mechanisms to respond to attacks,
- The architecture for intrusion detection systems distributed
- Standards for interoperability between different systems, intrusion detection,
- The search for new paradigms to perform intrusion detection.

One approach to computer security is to create a completely secure system is prevention. But it is rarely possible to make a completely watertight for several reasons.

- Most computer systems have security flaws that make them vulnerable to intrusions. Find and repair all is not possible for technical and economic reasons. (Balasubramaniyan, 1998)
- Existing systems with known vulnerabilities are not easily replaced by safer systems, mainly because they have interesting features that do not have the systems safer, or because they can not be replaced for economic reasons.
- Deploy systems without faults is very hard or impossible because of the faults are unknown or unavoidable.
- Even the most secure systems are vulnerable to abuse by legitimate users who take advantage of their privileges, or suffer from neglect of safety rules.

In response to these difficulties to develop secure systems, a new model of security management systems has emerged (Figure 1).

In this more realistic approach, prevention is one of the four parts of the security management. The detection part is looking for the exploitation of new loopholes. Part investigation tries to determine what happened, based on information provided by the detection part. Part autopsy is to look how to prevent similar intrusions in the future.

In the past almost all the attention of researchers has focused on the prevention part. Detection is now much taken into account, but the other two parties have not yet received the attention they deserve.

As previous work related to the field of intrusion detection and operational safety we find in the literature two major approaches to intrusion detection: the approach by signature and behavioral approach described respectively in Figures 2 and 3.

In this chapter we are particularly interested in the detection part we try to solve by data mining techniques already revealed.

Before describing our approach in the next section, we wish to disclose in Figure 4, the architecture of an intrusion detection system.

Figure 1. A model of security management in an IT system

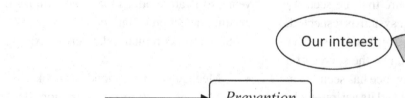

Figure 2. The different stages of a selection procedure of attributes

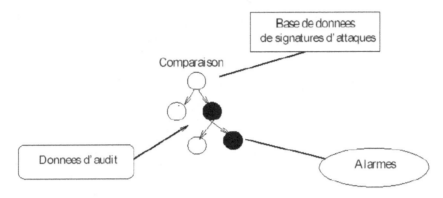

Figure 3. Behavior intrusion detection

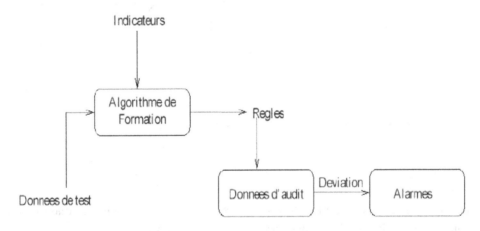

Networks Bayesian

Bayesian Networks are graphical models that represent the relationships probabilized between a set of variables. In recent years, Bayesian networks have become a popular tool for representing and manipulating knowledge. Nowadays Bayesian Networks are used much more because they have huge advantages over other techniques. These networks can intuitively represent an area of knowledge; many experiments show that it is often easier to formalize knowledge as a causal graph that in the form a system based on rules. In addition, they can handle all the data incomplete and can learn the causal relationship can help us make decisions.

A Bayesian network can be formally defined by:

- A directed acyclic graph G, G = G (V, E) where V is the set of nodes of G, and E the set of edges of G.
- A finite probability space (Ω, p).
- A set of random variables associated with the nodes of the graph defined on $[\Omega, p]$ such

$$p\left(v_1, v_{\acute{e}}, \ldots, v_n\right) = \prod_{i=1..n} p(v_i | C\left(v_i\right))$$

with C (Vi) is the set of parents of Vi in the graph.

A Bayesian network is therefore a causal graph, which was associated with a probabilistic repre-

Figure 4. Architecture of intrusion detection system

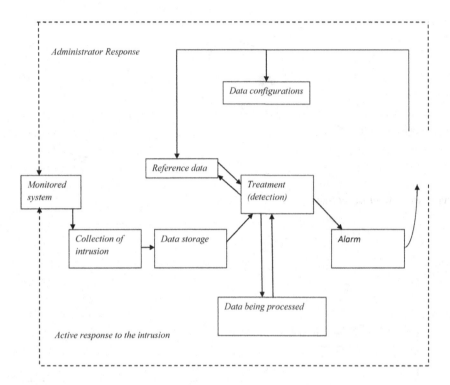

sentation underlying. This representation allows rendering quantitative reasoning about causality that can be done inside the graph.

The use of Bayesian networks is essential to compute the conditional probabilities of events connected to each other by relations of cause and effect. This use is called inference.

If the graph is composed of n nodes, denoted $X=\{X1, X2,..., Xn\}$. The general problem of inference is to compute $p(X \mid Y)$, where $Y \subset X$ and $Xi \notin Y$.

Learning

A Bayesian network is made up of both of a graph and a set of conditional probabilities. Learning of Bayesian network must meet the following two questions:

- How to estimate the conditional probabilities laws?
- How to find the Bayesian network structure?

We'll separate the learning problem into two parts:

- Learning parameters, we assume that the network structure is fixed, and where it is necessary to estimate the conditional probabilities for each node.
- Learning the structure, where the goal is to find the best graph representing the task to solve.

Decision Trees

Decision trees (Quinlan, 1986) (Quinlan, 1993) represent one of the most widely known and used in classification. Their success is partly due to their ability to deal with complex problems of classification. In fact, they offer an easily understood and interpreted, and an ability to produce logical rules of classification.

A decision tree is composed of:

- Decision nodes each containing a test on an attribute.
- Branches generally corresponding to one of the possible values of the selected attribute;
- Sheets comprising the objects that belong to the same class.
- The use of decision trees in classification problems is done in two steps:
- The construction of a decision tree from a training database.
- Classification or inference of classifying a new instance from the decision tree built in the previous step.

The construction of a decision tree is based on a given training set. It is to select a decision node, the appropriate test attribute and then define the class on each leaf of the induced tree.

To build a decision tree, an attribute selection measure is needed. A good measure should help to limit the size of the tree and give coherence to semantic nodes that compose it.

In our study, the attribute is the number 37 (A37) KDD'99's benchmark that will be detailed later.

Rules of Association

To formalize the principles of association rules, we assume that the data D (a set of objects or transactions) to explore are binary, ie each transaction that can be described by a finite set of attributes I = $\{i1, \ldots, im\}$, also called items. Each transaction t will be a subset of I. In addition, it assigns to each transaction identifier (TID for "Transaction IDentifier"): D = $\{t1, \ldots, tn\}$. Table 1 illustrates this type of data, for a total of 10 transactions $\{\{t1, \ldots, t10\}$ described by seven items $\{i1, \ldots, i7\}$. We will use throughout this section illustration of the example described by Table 1 to understand the formalism of association rules.

For a set X of items (called itemsets typically) of I, we say that a transaction T contains X if and only if $X \subseteq t$. For example, the itemset $\{i3, i4\}$ is contained in the transaction t1.

We call, support of an itemset X is the ratio between the number of transactions containing X and the total number of transactions in D. This proportion is denoted Sup.

$$\sup(x) = \frac{\{t \epsilon D : X \subseteq t\}}{D}$$

In other words, the support of an itemset corresponds to the frequency of appearance thereof in the data. In the data listed above, we have for example:

$$\sup(i_1) = \frac{\{t_2, t_3, t_5, t_6, t_8\}}{10} = \frac{5}{10} = 50\%$$

Table 1. Sample illustration

t1	i3 i4 i5
t2	i1 i3 i5 i6
t3	i1 i3 i4 i7
t4	i2 i4 i6
t5	i1 i2 i4 i5 i7
t6	i1 i2 i3 i4 i5 i7
t7	i2 i4 i5 i6
t8	i1 i4 i6
t9	i3 i4 i6
t10	i2 i3 i5 i6

$$\sup\left(i_3, i_4\right) = \frac{\left\{t_2, t_3, t_6, t_9\right\}}{10} = \frac{4}{10} = 40\%$$

By the definition of an itemset, we have the following property:

Property 1: (Anti monotonicity) Given two itemsets X and Y, we have:

$$X \subseteq Y \Rightarrow \sup\left(x\right) \geq \sup\left(y\right)$$

Property 2: Less intuitively, also note that:

$$\sup\left(x \cup y\right) \leq \min\left(\sup\left(x\right), \sup\left(y\right)\right) \leq$$
$$\max\left(\sup\left(x\right), \sup\left(y\right)\right) \leq \sup\left(x \cap y\right)$$

We say that an itemset X is frequent if its support is greater than or equal to a given threshold σ. An itemset not having sufficient support is said, not frequent.

Thus, choosing a threshold σ = 30% is obtained on the previous data that {i1} and {i3, i4} are frequent, but {i1, i3, i4} is not. However, choosing a threshold of 10%, the three itemsets are frequent.

Property 3: Given a fixed reference threshold σ,
Any subset of a frequent itemset is frequent,
Any superset of an infrequent itemset is not frequent.
An association rule is a pair (A, B), where A and B are itemsets nonempty disjoint, ie A ≠ ∅ and B ≠ ∅ and A ∩ B ≠ ∅.

Classically We denote such a couple as A → B.
We define the support of an association rule as the support of the itemset A ∪ B (ie the percentage of transactions that contain both A and B):

$$\sup\left(A \, et \, B\right) = \sup\left(A \cup B\right) \frac{\left\{t \epsilon D : A \subseteq t \, et \, B \subseteq t\right\}}{D}$$

We also define the confidence of a rule A and B, denoted by Conf (A ∧ B), as the ratio between the support of the itemset A ∪ B and A's:

$$CONF\left(A \wedge B\right) = \frac{\sup\left(A \cup B\right)}{\sup\left(A\right)}$$

Provided to approximate the probability px to observe an event X by its frequency fx = Sup (X) in D, the support and confidence of an association rule A ∧ B is read, then respectively as the probability joint to observe events A and B, and the conditional probability of observing B, knowing A.

The generation of association rules is performed directly, without accessing the context of extraction, and the cost of this phase in execution time is therefore small compared to the cost of mining of frequent itemsets. The general principle of the generation of association rules is as follows.

For each frequent itemset l1 in F (the set of frequent itemsets), all subsets l1, of l2 are determined and the value of the support (l1) / support (l2) is calculated. If this value is greater than or equal to a confidence level minconfiance then the association rule l2-> {l1 — l2} is generated.

The problem of the relevance and the usefulness of extracted association rules is one of the major practical problems of mining association rules. The increase in minimum thresholds of support and confidence in order to reduce the number of rules Generated, is not a satisfactory solution because it removes redundant rules. We adapt bases to reduce the time of the extraction of association rules and the memory space used during the extraction.

Elimination of attributes that contains redundant data association is based on the use of the taxonomy of attributes.

The presentation to the user of a set of rules covering all attributes of the database.

EXPERIMENTATION AND RESULTS

Corpus Used

Data base KDD'99' s are oriented intrusion detection, they represent lines of TCP / IP dump where each line is a connection characterized by 41 attributes (detailed in Table 2), as the duration of the connection, the protocol type, etc.. Taking into account the values of its attributes, each connection in KDD'99' s is considered a normal connection or an attack.

In our study we chose a method based on the selection of attributes that can select a subset of relevant attributes from the original set of attributes according to a performance criterion. These methods allowing to characterize data more quickly and therefore cost in computation time will be minimized. The selection of attributes does not change the original data representation: selected attributes keep their semantic departure and can then be more easily interpreted by the user. In our study, the choice fell on the attribute A37.

According Dash [1997], a procedure for selection of attributes is generally composed of four steps (Figure 5).

Contingency Table and Evaluation Measure

Contingency table (or table of co-occurrence) is a tool often used when it is desired to study the relationship between two variables that take discrete values (or categories). In our case, the variables are in the columns, actual (also known as "Gold Standard") and in the lines, the result of the filter. The sum of each column gives the actual number of elements in each class and of each line gives the number of elements seen by the classifier in each class. The following table shows the shape of the contingency table (Table 3).

Error Rate by Class

(False positives and false negatives): it is the fraction of the number of objects in a category erroneously classified in another class.

$$FPR = \frac{FP}{VN + FP}$$

$$FNR = \frac{FN}{VP + FN}$$

Rate of Good Ranking

(True positives and true negatives or sensitivity and specificity)

$$VPR = \frac{VP}{VP + FN} = 1 - FNR$$

$$VNR = \frac{VN}{VN + FP} = 1 - FPR$$

Precision and Recall

The precision indicates the proportion of spam messages among detected as spam, while the recall is the ratio between the number of detected spam rightly and the total number of spams.

Table 2. List of attributes based connections KDD'99' s

Attributs basiques
A1 connection time (number of seconds)
A2 protocol type, e.g. tcp, udp, etc..
A3 Network Service (destination) ex. http, telnet
A4 connection status (normal or error)
A5 nb data (in bytes) from the source to the destination
A6 nb data (in bytes) from the destination to the source
A7 1 if connection is from / to the same host / port 0 otherwise
A8 nb fraguements "erroneous"
A9 # of urgent packets

Attributs relatifs au contenu
A10 nb indicators "hot"
A11 number of tests failed login
A12 1 if the login success, 0 otherwise
A13 nb conditions "compromise"
A14 1 if root shell is obtained; 0 otherwise
A15 1 if the command was the command "su root", 0 otherwise
A16 # of access to the "root"
A17 nb creations operations _chiers
A18 nb shell prompt
A19 nb _chiers operations on access control
A20 # of outbound commands in an ftp session
A21 1 if the login belongs to the list of "hot", 0 otherwise
A22 1 if the login is username "guest", 0 otherwise

Attributs basés sur le temps utilisant des fenêtres de temps de deux secondes
A23 # of conn. for the same host
A24 # of conn. for the same service
A25% of conn. for the same host with the error "SYN"
A26% of conn. for the same service with the error "SYN"
A27% of conn. for the same host with the error "REJ"
A28% of conn. for the same service with the error "REJ"
A29% of conn. for the same host using the same service
A30% of conn. for the same host using di_érents services
A31% of conn. for the same service using di_érents hosts

Attributs basés sur le temps utilisant des fenêtres de temps de 100 connex.
A32 # of conn. for the same host
A33 # of conn. for the same host using the same service
A34% of conn. for the same host using the same service
A35% of conn. for the same host using di_érents services
A36% of conn. for the same host with src port
A37% of conn. for the same host and the same service using different hosts
A38% of conn. for the same host with the error "SYN"
A39% of conn. for the same host and the same service with the error "SYN"
A40% of conn. for the same host with the error "REJ"
A41% of conn. for the same host and the same service with the error "REJ"

Figure 5. The different stages of a selection procedure of attributes

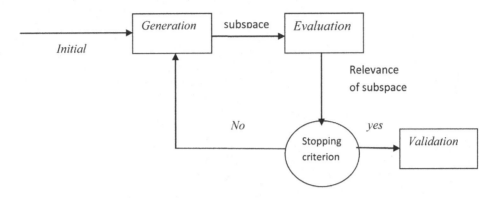

Table 3. Form of the contingency table

	True « Abnormal »	**True « Normal »**
Classement « Abnormal »	VP	FP
Classement « Normal »	FN	VN

Where

VN: True negatives: Normal seen by the filter as Normal or Normal correctly classified.

FN: False negative: Abnormal seen as Normal or Abnormal not correctly classified.

VP: True positives: Abnormal seen as Abnormal or Abnormal correctly classified.

FP: False positive: Normal seen as Abnormal or Normal not correctly classified.

$$Precision = \frac{VP}{VP + FP}$$

$$Recall = \frac{VP}{VP + FN} = VPR$$

Accuracy

This is the total error rate, the two classes combined.

$$Accuracy = \frac{\left(VP + VN\right)}{\left(VP + FN + VN + FP\right)}$$

RESULTS

Table 4 shows the results of different classifiers used in our study (see also Figure 6). The results are excellent and give an ascendancy over decision trees. Bayesian networks are powerful tools for reasoning and decision under uncertainty as decision trees are most commonly used in classification problems.

In terms of time complexity, Bayesian networks have polynomial complexity and are less expensive

Table 4. Results of learning by naïve bayes with data cleaning

Approach	# Con.	Precision	Recall	F-Measure	Accuracy	Kappa Statistic	Confusion Matrix	
							Abnormal	**Normal**
Bayesian networks	25192	89.60%	89.60%	89.60%	89.59%	79.06%	12272	1177
							1445	10298
Décision Trees	25192	99.60%	99.60%	99.60%	99.55%	99.11%	13389	60
							51	11692
Association rules	25192	96.30%	96.20%	96.20%	96.20%	99.11%	12652	797
							159	11584

Figure 6. Synthesis of the results of classification for the different approaches

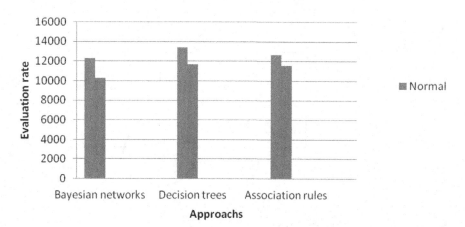

than the decision trees that have a non-polynomial complexity.

Association rules are easy to interpret and use. The model based on association rules is simple unequivocal because the calculations are elementary (it only calculates the frequency of occurrence) but the method is expensive in computation time. Clustering and minimum support method can reduce the calculation time but can inadvertently remove important rules. Regarding the quality of the rules, the method can produce rules trivial or useless. Trivial rules are rules obvious, therefore, do not provide information. Unnecessary rules are rules difficult to interpret.

Figures 7 and 8 give an overview on the ancestry of decision trees relative to Bayesian networks and association rules.

CONCLUSION AND PERSPECTIVES

We experimented three approaches supervised for intrusion detection for known benchmark namely KDD'99. Approaches tested gave good results for each with advantages and disadvantages. The tests were carried out on 10% of existing connections of KDD'99. 10% of the test database thus found has been a learning base. Attribute selection was made on the attribute A37 of KDD'99.

As future work, we plan to develop a meta-classifier based on supervised approaches give good results to improve the intrusion detection system, exploiting the complementarily of supervised namely decision trees, networks Bayesian and association rules and explore other data mining techniques.

Figure 7. Connections properly classified for the different approaches

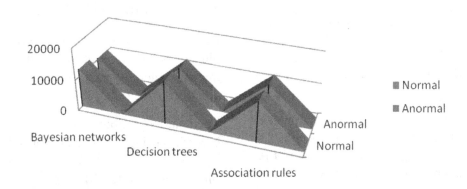

Figure 8. Connections not properly classified for the different approaches

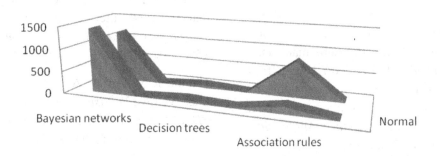

	Bayesian networks	Decision trees	Association rules
▪ Normal	1445	51	159
▪ Anormal	1177	60	797

REFERENCES

Amine, A., Hamou, R. M., & Simonet, M. (2013). Detecting opinions in tweets. *International Journal of Data Mining and Emerging Technologies*, *3*(1), 30–39. doi:10.5958/j.2249-3220.3.1.004

Axelsson, S. (2000). *Intrusion detection systems: A survey and taxonomy (Technical Report)*. Academic Press.

Cooper, G. F. (1990). The computational complexity of probabilistic inference using Bayesian belief networks. *Artificial Intelligence*, *42*(2), 393–405. doi:10.1016/0004-3702(90)90060-D

Debar, H., Dacier, M., & Wespi, A. (1999). Towards a taxonomy of intrusion-detection systems. *Computer Networks*, *31*(8), 805–822. doi:10.1016/S1389-1286(98)00017-6

Denning, D. E., & Neumann, P. G. (1985). *Requirements and model for IDES—A real-time intrusion detection expert system* (Document A005). SRI International. Balasubramaniyan, J. S., Garcia-Fernandez, J. O., Isacoff, D., Spafford, E., & Zamboni, D. (1998). An architecture for intrusion detection using autonomous agents. In *Proceedings of Computer Security Applications Conference*, (pp. 13-24). IEEE.

Dougherty, J., Kohavi, R., & Sahami, M. (1995). Supervised and unsupervised discretization of continuous features. In *Proceedings of ICML* (pp. 194-202). ICML.

Duda, R. O., Hart, P. E., & Stork, D. G. (2000). *Pattern classification and scene analysis: Pattern classification*. Academic Press.

Esposito, F., Malerba, D., Semeraro, G., & Kay, J. (1997). A comparative analysis of methods for pruning decision trees. *IEEE Transactions on Pattern Analysis and Machine Intelligence*, *19*(5), 476–491. doi:10.1109/34.589207

Fayyad, U. M., & Irani, K. B. (1992). On the handling of continuous-valued attributes in decision tree generation. *Machine Learning*, *8*(1), 87–102. doi:10.1007/BF00994007

Friedman, N., & Goldszmidt, M. (1996). Building classifiers using Bayesian networks. In *Proceedings of the National Conference on Artificial Intelligence* (pp. 1277-1284). Academic Press.

Fürnkranz, J. (1997). Pruning algorithms for rule learning. *Machine Learning*, *27*(2), 139–172. doi:10.1023/A:1007329424533

Hamou, R. M., Amine, A., & Boudia, A. (2013). A new meta-heuristic based on social bees for detection and filtering of spam. *International Journal of Applied Metaheuristic Computing*, *4*(3), 15–33. doi:10.4018/ijamc.2013070102

Hamou, R. M., Amine, A., Lokbani, A. C., & Simonet, M. (2012). *Visualization and clustering by 3D cellular automata: Application to unstructured data*. arXiv preprint arXiv:1211.5766

Hamou, R. M., Amine, A., & Rahmani, M. (2012). A new biomimetic approach based on social spiders for clustering of text. In *Proceedings of Software Engineering Research, Management and Applications 2012* (pp. 17–30). Berlin: Springer. doi:10.1007/978-3-642-30460-6_2

Hamou, R. M., Lehireche, A., Lokbani, A. C., & Rahmani, M. (2010). Representation of textual documents by the approach wordnet and n-grams for the unsupervised classification (clustering) with 2D cellular automata: A comparative study. *Computer and Information Science, 3*(3), 240–255.

Ilgun, K., Kemmerer, R. A., & Porras, P. A. (1995). Probability propagation. *IEEE Transactions on Software Engineering, 21*(3), 181–199. doi:10.1109/32.372146

Lunt, T. F., Javitz, H., Tamaru, A., & Valdes, A. (1995). *Detecting unusual program behavior using the statistical component of the next-generation intrusion detection expert system (NIDES). SRI International.* Computer Science Laboratory.

Chapter 4
Applying Game Theory in Securing Wireless Sensor Networks by Minimizing Battery Usage

Mehran Asadi
The Lincoln University, USA

Afrand Agah
West Chester University of Pennsylvania, USA

Christopher Zimmerman
West Chester University of Pennsylvania, USA

ABSTRACT

In this chapter, the authors examine the impacts of applying game theory on the network throughput, network voltage loss, and accuracy of malicious node detection in wireless sensor networks. Nodes in a wireless sensor network use our proposed protocol when deciding whether or not to forward packets they receive from other sensors in order to conserve power. Wireless sensor network nodes achieve this by optimizing their decision-making based on a framework using game theory. Defining a suitable cost and profit for routing and forwarding incoming packets and keeping a history of past behaviors of non-cooperating nodes gradually forces malicious nodes out of the wireless sensor network.In this chapter, the authors examine the impacts of applying game theory on the network throughput, network voltage loss, and accuracy of malicious node detection in wireless sensor networks. Nodes in a wireless sensor network use our proposed protocol when deciding whether or not to forward packets they receive from other sensors in order to conserve power. Wireless sensor network nodes achieve this by optimizing their decision-making based on a framework using game theory. Defining a suitable cost and profit for routing and forwarding incoming packets and keeping a history of past behaviors of non-cooperating nodes gradually forces malicious nodes out of the wireless sensor network.

DOI: 10.4018/978-1-4666-4789-3.ch004

1. INTRODUCTION

A Wireless Sensor Network (WSN) consists of wireless sensors, small devices that collect data readings such as light or temperature from an environment. The sensors then send the data to a base station, a central location for data to congregate (Akyldiz, Sankarasubramaniam, Su, and Cayirci (2002)). Wireless sensor networks have potential to revolutionize the way in which the real world is monitored and controlled. Wireless Sensor networks impose a series of security challenges for network designers (Chong & Kumar, 2003). Among these security problems, Denial of Service (DoS) attacks, defined as any event that diminishes or eliminates a network's capacity to perform its expected function, degrade networks' intended services to its users. One simple form of a DoS attack is arbitrarily neglecting to forward some messages (Malekzadeh, Abdul Ghani, Subramaniam, and Desa (2011)).

A malicious node can drops messages on a random or arbitrary basis, but still participate in lower-level protocols, and may even acknowledge reception of data to the sender, Such a node is neglectful. The dynamic source routing protocol is susceptible to this attack (Eidenbenz, Kumar, and Zust (2006)). Because the network caches routes, communications from a region may all use the same route to a destination, and a malicious node can degrade or block traffic from a region to a base station (Karlof & Wagner, 2003).

Game theory has been used in various fields such as economics, politics and biology; it is a field of study that attempts to model decision-making (Osborne & Rubinstein, 1994). Game theory has previously been applied within the context of modeling multiple nodes in a wireless sensor network attempting to share a shared medium: their radio communication channels (Felegyhazi & Hubaux, 2007).

We incorporate game theory for the purpose of extending a sensor's battery life. This is accomplished by helping the sensors optimize their

decision making process about whether or not to forward any data packets they may receive (Agah, Asadi, and Zimmerman 2011) and (Agah, Das, and Basu 2005). On one hand, if a node decides to never forward any packets, it conserves its available battery power, but no data flows through the network from that particular node. However, if a node forwards every packet that it receives, then node demonstrates its reliability and traffic flows through the network but the node will run out of battery power much faster than if the node were to not forward any of the incoming packets. By use of game theory, we attempt to extend a node's battery life while allowing it to forward an acceptable amount of packets through the network to have an optimum configuration (Asadi, Zimmerman, and Agah 2012).

We investigate how selfish behavior of individual players may affect the performance of the network as a whole. In a wireless sensor network, each node generates its own data and forwards incoming packets for others. Forwarding packets can consume a considerable amount of battery life. In this chapter we include the following features:

- **Game theory:** Game theory can provide insight into approaches for optimization. Often node decisions at a particular layer are made with the objective of optimizing performance at some other layer of the network. Game theory allows us to investigate the existence, uniqueness and convergence to a steady state point when network nodes perform independent adaptations. Using game theory helps us to design incentive schemes that lead to independent, self-interested participants towards outcomes that are desirable from a system-wide point of view (Machado & Tekinay, 2008).

- **Cooperation:** Nodes in a sensor wireless network have to economize on their resources. There is a trade-off between good cooperation and resource consumption. At the same time, if they do not forward messages, others might not forward either, thereby denying service in the whole network. Non-cooperation with other nodes and only exploiting their readiness to cooperate is one of several boycotting behavior patterns. Therefore, there has to be an incentive for a node to forward messages that are not destined to itself (Eidenbenz, Anderegg, and Wattenhofer, 2007) and (Eidenbenz, Kumar, and Zust, 2006), (Eidenbenz, Resrta, and Santi, 2008) and (Levin, 2006).

- **Reputation:** The network's performance can reach an undesirable state due to the selfish or malicious behavior of individual wireless network nodes. Incentives are proposed to steer nodes towards desirable operational equilibrium of the network behavior. We use a reputation system for incentivizing nodes. Each node gains reputation by providing services (forwarding incoming packets) to others (Michiardi & Molva, 2002). Each node builds a positive reputation for itself by cooperating with others and is tagged as a selfish or a malicious node otherwise. Reputation is maintained as a probabilistic distribution, enabling the node to have full freedom and not get constrained by some discrete levels of reputation as used in eBay, Yahoo auctions (Resnick, Kuwabarra, Zeckauser, and Friedman (2000). Note that reputation is not a physical quantity but it is a belief; it can only be used to statistically predict the future behavior of other nodes and cannot define deterministically the actual action performed by them (Ganeriwl & Srivastava, 2004).
- **Battery:** A major challenge is maximizing the lifetime of these battery-powered wireless sensors to support such transmissions. If we do not carefully schedule and budget discharging, the battery-powered sensors might waste a huge amount of energy (Chi & Yang, 2006) and (Nurmi, 2006).

2. GAME FORMULATION

We analyze the mathematical modeling of battery discharge behavior in a wireless sensor network. As in any game, each player tries to maximize its own benefit, which is the available battery for each individual sensor node. However if a node forwards all incoming packets then over time the node would retrench its own energy reserves. Therefore, nodes have a tendency of not forwarding packets and acting selfishly to conserve energy. Our goal (Zimmerman, Agah, and Asadi, 2011) and (Asadi, Zimmerman, and Agah, 2013) is to give incentives to those nodes that participate in the network activities by forwarding incoming packets. Defining this as a game theoretic framework gives as the opportunity to find Nash equilibrium for the network. Solving this problem means finding a Nash equilibrium (Owen, 2001) for the whole network, whereas each node is preprogrammed with a set of rules, and maximizing the payoff for the entire network (Crosby, Hester, and Pissinou, 2011) and (Felegyhazi, Buttyan, and Hubaux, 2007) is the solution for the game.

Each node has a discrete representation for its remaining energy, and the incentive for each node is to have a better reputation in the network, where each node can be positively or negatively affected by its reputation. Therefore, there is a trade-off between saving energy resources and maintaining reputation. Gradually, nodes with low reputation will be isolated and labeled as selfish or malicious nodes, and at each node,

A game is formulated as $G = <N, A, \{u_i\}>$ where N is the set of players (decision makers), A_i is the action set of player i, $A = A_1 * A_2 * ... * A_n$ is the Cartesian product of the sets of actions available to each player, and $\{u_i\}$ is the set of utility functions that each player i wishes to maximize, where $u_i : A \to R$.

Our framework enforces cooperation among nodes and provides punishment for non-cooperative behavior. Since all players are rational and rational players always optimize their profits over time, the key to solve this problem is when nodes of a network use resources, they have to contribute to the network life in order to be entitled to use resources in the future. To keep track of the behavior of other nodes, the base station keep tracks of past behavior of each node and as they contribute to common network operation, their reputation increases (the base station updates it). Our task is in solving a game by predicting the strategy of each player, considering the information that the game offers and assuming that the players are rational.

Authors in (Sengupta, Chatterjee, and Kwiat, 2010) have proposed a game theoretic framework for power control in wireless sensor networks, but the results only show the transmitting power versus the utility. Authors in (Campos-Nanez, Garcia, and Li, 2008) proposed an efficient power management in wireless sensor networks but they have only presented the average coverage. However, we demonstrate the actual voltage loss of the network in the presence of malicious nodes as well as utility and the accuracy of malicious node detection.

2.1 Equilibrium

Let us assume two bargainers have the opportunity to reach agreement on an outcome in some set X and perceive that if they fail to do so then the outcome will be some fixed event D. Here the set X is the set of feasible divisions of positive reputation and D may be the event in which neither party receives any positive reputation. The set of Nash equilibrium of a bargaining game of alternating offers is very large. One such equilibrium is that in which both players always proposes x^* and always accept a proposal x if and only if $x = x^*$. For any agreement x and period t, there is a Nash equilibrium for which the outcome is the acceptance of x in period t. One such equilibrium is that in which through period $t - 1$, each player demands the maximum reputation and rejects all proposals, and from period t on proposes x and accepts only x (Osborne and Rubinstein, 1994). We assume players alternate their offers in periods of the game; each period t represents one round of bargaining. The first move of the game occurs in period 0, when the first player makes a proposal (forward my incoming packet), which second player then either accepts or rejects. Consider the Nash equilibrium in which both players always propose x^* and player i accepts a proposal x in period t if and only if $U_i(x, t) > U_i(x^*, t)$. In the equilibrium second player's strategy dictates that in any period he rejects such a proposal x, this threat induces the first player to propose x^*. Second player's threat is incredible, given first player's strategy: the best outcome that can occur if second player carries out his threat to reject x is that there is agreement on x^* in the next period, an outcome that second player likes less than agreement on x in period 0, which he can achieve by accepting x.

The base station increments the reputation of nodes at periodic intervals. If a node rejects a proposal (forwarding a packet) neither party receives a positive reputation from the base station. Acceptance ends the game, while rejection leads to the next period, in which second player makes a proposal (increase my reputation), which first player has to accept or reject. Again, acceptance ends the game; rejection leads to the next period, in which it is once again first player's turn to make a proposal. There is no limit on the number of rounds of negotiations (Osborne & Rubinstein, 1994). The fact that some offer is rejected places no restrictions on the offers that may subsequently be made. In particular, a player who rejects a proposal x may subsequently make a proposal that is worse for him than x. If no offer is ever accepted then the outcome is the disagreement event (Osborne & Rubinstein, 1994).

Our assumption is that each player cares only about whether an agreement is reached and the time and content of the agreement, not about the path of proposals that preceded the agreement. We will define a bargaining game between nodes of wireless sensor network, and by finding the solution; we mathematically guarantee the best strategy for forwarding incoming packets, while keeping a good reputation and saving battery life of each node.

Maximizing cooperation between nodes and minimizing battery usage at each node are the two main goals that we investigate in the above game theoretic framework. Any breach of cooperation results in packets being dropped; therefore, partial cooperative strategy never leads to an equilibrium point. Meanwhile boundary conditions can be set to achieve cooperation in a network of selfish nodes. Our goal is to propose a strategy that is more adaptive to full cooperation after a node's misbehavior. It is important to realize that an attacker carries out even malicious attacks after seeking the cooperation (unknowingly) of other non-malicious nodes in the network.

To use network services, we motivate nodes to contribute to the network operations, where nodes receive incentives for their cooperation. We minimize battery usage; the decrease in available battery level must discourage nodes from overloading the network but not to the limit that they do not cooperate with the rest of the network for their selfish act of energy utilization. Therefore we need to design a cooperative security mechanism that enforces cooperation and shows that when no countermeasures are taken against misbehaving nodes, network operation can be heavily jeopardized. Also we capture and describe battery usage behavior at each node, and based on this battery model we present a battery-aware strategy for each node to avoid energy loss but gain better reputation over the course of the game.

2.2 Payoff and Reputation

Each node i has a von Neumann-Morgenstern utility function defined over the outcomes of the stage game G, as $u_i : A \rightarrow R$, where A is the space of action profiles (Owen, 2001). A's action profile space is listed as:

$$A = \begin{cases} Forward & packets & A_1 \\ DonotForward & packets & A_2 \end{cases}$$

Let G be played several times and let us award each node a payoff, which is the sum of the payoffs, it received in each period from playing G. Here, $u_i^t = \alpha r_i^t - \beta c_i^t$ where r_i^t is the node i's reputation, c_i^t is the cost of sending or forwarding a packet of the node as energy loss, and α and β are weight parameters. We assume that measurement data can be included in a single message that we call a packet, where packets all have the same size. The transmission cost for a single packet is a function of the transmission distance (Rappaport, 2002).

At time t, each node calculates the utility to be gained for each of the two actions available. For forwarding a packet, the utility is calculated as:

$$u_{A_1}^t = T * r_i^{t+1} - B * (c_s + c_r)$$

where r_i^{t+1} is the predicted gain of node i's reputation. For sending a packet, c_i^t is broken down into two constant values: c_s and c_r. c_s is the voltage cost to send a packet and c_r is the voltage cost to receive a packet. B is the weight parameter for cost, and represents the importance of being conservative about sending packets when a node has a low battery leave. At a node's highest battery level, B will be 1. As the node's battery level decreases and crosses designated thresholds, B will increase. T is the weight parameter for the gain component of the equation and represents the number of units of time since node i has last forwarded a packet. T starts at 1 for each node i and increments every time a node i decides to not forward a packet. When a node sends a packet, T is reset back to 1. If a node has recently sent a packet, it may not be important to send another packet right away, which is why T starts at a low value. But as time passes without forwarding any packets, it is important that a node sends data through the network, which leads T to increase. The utility for not forwarding a packet is calculated as: $u^t_{A_2} = T * 0 - B * c_s$.

Since there is no gain in reputation when not sending a packet, the gain is 0. However, receiving a packet from another node still costs energy. After calculating the utility for each of these actions, the node will perform the action that yields the greater utility. The strategy for each node i at time t is described as:

$$s_i(h^t) = \begin{cases} Forward & u^{t+1}_{A_1} > u^{t+1}_{A_2} \\ DonotForward & otherwise \end{cases}$$

In order to compute the values of a node's gain, we turn our attention to the work proposed in (Michiardi & Molva, 2002). In this work the authors proposed the concept of subjective reputation, which reflects the reputation calculated directly from the subject's observation. In order to compute each node's reputation at time t, we use the following formula:

$$r_i^t = \sum_{k=1}^{t-1} \rho_i(k)$$

where $\rho_i(k)$ represents the ratings that the base station has given to node i, and $\rho_i \in [-1, 1]$. If the number of observations collected since time t is not sufficient, the final value of the subjective reputation takes the value 0. The base station increments the ratings of nodes on all actively used paths at periodic intervals. An actively used path is one on which the node has sent a packet within the previous rate increment interval. Recall that reputation is the perception that a person has of another's intentions. When facing uncertainty, individuals tend to trust those who have a reputa-

tion for being trustworthy. Since reputation is not a physical quantity and only a belief, it can be used to statistically predict the future behavior of other nodes and cannot define deterministically the actual action performed by them. Table 1 depicts the notations that were used throughout this paper.

3. CONFIGURATIONS

We use three major network configurations. The first configuration, named case1, consists of a network of wireless sensors, which broadcast packets to any nodes within range. Since the nodes in our experiment are located within a small distance of each other, all nodes in the network are capable of broadcasting directly to every other node in the network. Whenever a node receives a packet from another node and forwards the packet, that packet is re-broadcast to every node within range. For networks of a large size, this generates a large amount of traffic. In an attempt to remedy this, another network configuration was developed.

Table 1. Parameters and notations

Cost of forwarding packet at node i	c_i
History at node i	h_i
Rating of node i	ρ_i
Reputation at node i	r_i
Utility at node i	u_i
Voltage cost of sending	c_s
Voltage cost of receiving	c_r
Weight Parameters	α_i, β_i, B, T

The second configuration (case2) utilizes a neighbor system. Each node has a neighbor table that holds the IDs of several neighbors, which are determined by a handshaking process that occurs after the nodes boot up and send an initial voltage reading to the base station. The neighbor relationship is bi-directional. Whenever a node receives a packet, it checks the data. This gives the ID number of the node that just sent the packet. If the ID found in path of the packet is not found in the neighbor table of the receiving node, the node ignores the packet and no further action is taken. However, if the ID of the node that just forwarded the packet matches an ID in the neighbor table, then the node's number of packets received is incremented and the node will take the appropriate action with the packet. Since we did not have access to a large testing area where we could spread the nodes out further, this is an attempt to emulate a less dense, less traffic-heavy network than what is found in case1.

The third network configuration utilizes cluster networking. The network consists of groups of sensors called clusters, where the sensors in a cluster report to a sensor in the network that is designated as the cluster-head of the network. All non cluster-heads within a cluster, known as members of a cluster, only communicate directly with their respective cluster-heads. Cluster-heads transfer data to the base station where the data is to be collected and stored (Bandyopadhyay & Coyle, 2003). In our simulations, the process of determining which cluster-head a sensor reports to, is based on the sensor's battery level. If a member receives a packet broadcast by a cluster-head within range, the member will forward that packet directly to its cluster-head.

For each configuration, simulations are run both with and without using game theory. By doing so, we can compare average network throughput, as well as voltage loss, and see under which scenario using one would be favorable over the other. The sensor programs for the game theory and non game theory configurations are identical except that the game theory program implements the strategy of whether or not to forward a packet that it receives. For the first two configurations, the networks are either entirely comprised of nodes that implement game theory or entirely of nodes that do not implement game theory. When we implement game theory in the cluster-networking configuration, only the cluster-heads implement game theory.

For the first two network configurations, the sizes of the test networks start at 5 nodes, then increase by 5 up to 30 nodes. This allows us to observe what trends occur in reputation, voltage loss, and utility as the size of the network increases considerably. For the cluster-networking configuration, all tests are run with a network size of 30 nodes.

3.1 Malicious Node Detection

For each game theory and non game theory configuration, simulations of networks consisting of entirely normal nodes were run, as well as simulations of networks containing varying percentages of malicious nodes. A node that acts maliciously is one that randomly drops packets in order to conserve its energy. For malicious non game theory nodes, before forwarding a packet the node randomly decides whether or not it wants to not forward the packet. For malicious game theory nodes, the node randomly decides whether or not it wants to not forward the packet before the strategy is applied.

In our simulations, we introduce malicious nodes into the network to see how they affect the network and if there is a way to detect and neutralize such nodes. Malicious nodes randomly drop packets, reducing the throughput of the network and they also consume additional power when randomly deciding whether or not to drop packets.

Since we are assuming that the base station has unlimited memory comparing to individual nodes, it keeps track of the reputation of each node in the network. Periodically, the base station checks the throughput and will decide whether or not a node is acting maliciously based on its throughput. The base station takes the current reputation of each node in the network and calculates the average, as well as the standard deviation. If a node's reputation is lower than the average minus the standard deviation, that node is deemed malicious. The base station sends a packet to that node ordering the node to turn its radio off and shut down.

4. PERFORMANCE EVALUATION

In the broadcast scenarios, the simulation starts with an initial voltage reading from each sensor. In this work we have used MICAZ sensors (MEMSIC Inc.), which run on TinyOs (TinyOS). Next, a packet is broadcast once every 200 milliseconds for 300 seconds. Then a final voltage reading is sent to the base station. In the neighboring system scenarios, after the initial voltage reading, the neighbor handshaking phase takes place. After the neighbor handshaking process, each node broadcasts data once every 200 milliseconds for 300 seconds. Lastly, a final voltage reading is sent to the base station. In the cluster networking scenarios, an initial voltage reading is sent from each sensor. Next, cluster membership is established for each non cluster-head node in the network. After that, a packet is broadcast once every 200 milliseconds for 300 seconds. Afterward, a final voltage reading is sent to the base station.

During the simulation, if a node receives a packet it will forward it or apply the game theory strategy, depending on the scenario. After sending the packets, each node turns its radio off for 10 seconds to get rid of the traffic in the network. Then, every node turns their radio on and sends one final voltage packet to the base station. This gave us a clear start and end voltage for calculating voltage loss. For malicious node detection, the base station checks to see if any nodes are malicious after 60 seconds into the simulation, and then once every 30 seconds after that. Any

nodes that are deemed as malicious are turned off via radio.

As shown in Figure 1, reputations for simulations using game theory have a lower reputation, than simulations not using game theory, regardless of network size. By implementing game theory, the average throughput of the network drops, but this is to be expected since the sensors are dropping packets based on a set of rules in order to save power.

Figure 2 shows that for case1, implementing game theory results in a lower voltage loss for smaller networks, but results in a greater voltage loss for larger networks. As the size of a network increases, so does the traffic. Since deciding whether or not to forward a packet by using a strategy also consumes power, there is a point where the frequency of deciding whether or not to forward an incoming packet is so high that the energy used for implementing the strategy is greater than the amount of energy the node tries to save by not forwarding packets. For case2, implementing game theory consistently results in a lower network voltage loss. The neighbor system helps reduce the amount of traffic in the network, which prevents the voltage loss that happens with larger networks in case1.

As indicated by Figure 3, our procedure for detecting malicious nodes works best for networks containing small amounts of malicious nodes. Since malicious nodes usually have a lower reputation, if there are a small number of them present in the network, it is easier to detect them. However, if normal nodes in a network typically have low reputations, or if many nodes in the network have lowered reputations, it is difficult to detect malicious nodes because they don't stand out.

Figure 4 shows that our procedure for detecting malicious nodes raises a low percentage of false positives. For the most part, a small amount of false positives are raised, aside from case1 game theory scenarios. Since the nodes in the case1 game theory scenarios typically have a low reputation and there are less normal nodes in the network

Figure 1. Average network throughput for normal nodes

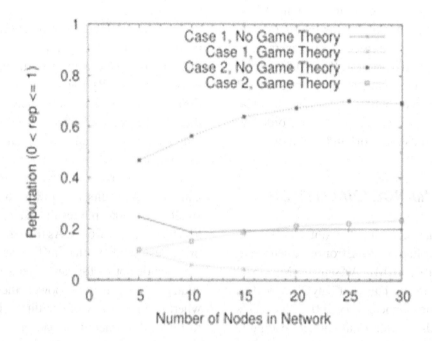

Figure 2. Average network voltage loss for normal node

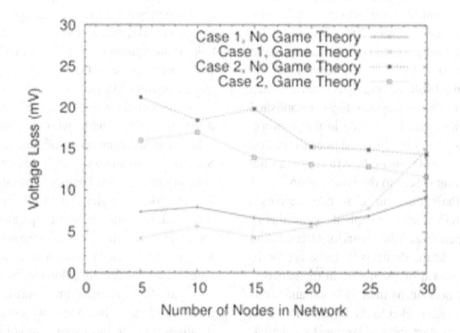

Figure 3. Average percentage of malicious nodes correctly removed from network

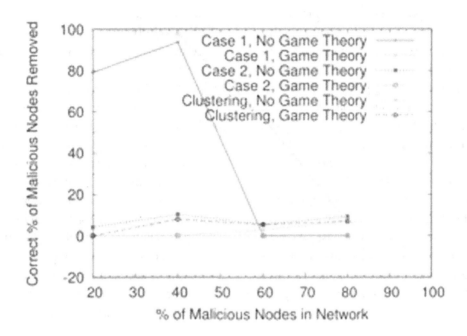

Figure 4. Average percentage of normal nodes incorrectly removed from network

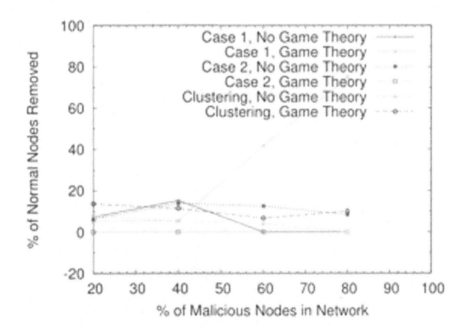

as the number of malicious nodes increases, the percentage of false positives detected increases.

As seen in Figure 5, average reputations for game theory cases are lower than non-game theory cases, except for the clustering scenarios, where reputation is higher by using game theory in networks with a larger percentage of malicious nodes.

As seen in Figure 6, in most cases, voltage loss is lower with game theory implemented than if not, even with the presence of malicious nodes.

Due to how we model utility in our project, utility is bound to decrease. Therefore, a better utility is not defined by how quickly it can rise, but rather how slowly it can decrease. As seen in Figure 7, for our case1 scenarios, utility for networks implementing game theory have a lower utility than those, which do not implement game

theory. However, this is caused by the high amount of traffic in a larger network.

As seen in Figure 8, for our case2 scenarios, utility for networks implementing game theory have a higher utility than those, which do not implement game theory. Despite the large network size, the neighbor system reduces the amount of traffic that flows through the network.

Figure 9 shows that, by implementing game theory, the average utility is higher than when game theory is not implemented in cluster networks.

Our results indicate that, under most cases, implementing game theory in a wireless sensor network is beneficial, as it helps reduce the amount of voltage consumption throughout the network. By adding a decision making process, such as when to send and not to send packets, the sensors conserve energy while maintaining the throughput.

Figure 5. Average network throughput for malicious nodes

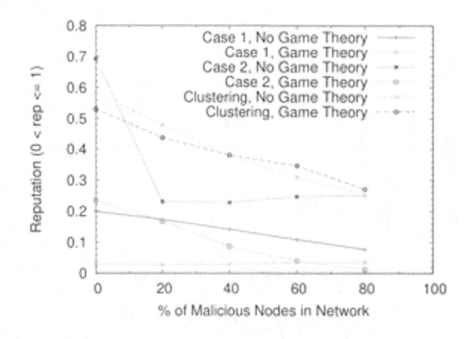

Figure 6. Average network voltage loss for malicious nodes. Broadcast (case1), hop-by-hop (case2)

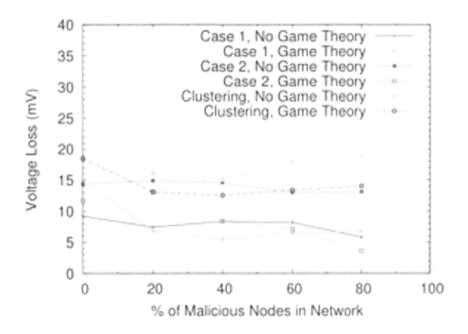

Figure 7. Average network utility for Broadcast (case 1) and scenario (Network size-30 nodes)

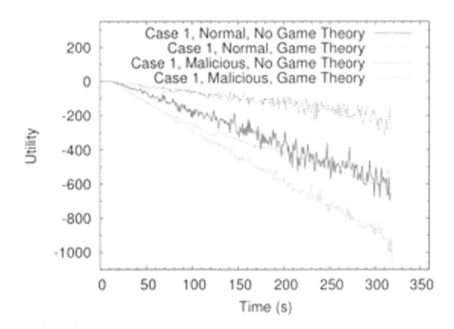

Figure 8. Average network utility for hop-by-hop (case 2) scenario (network size - 30 nodes)

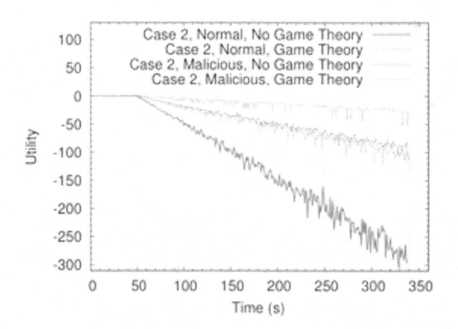

Figure 9. Average network utility for clustering scenarios (Network size - 30 nodes)

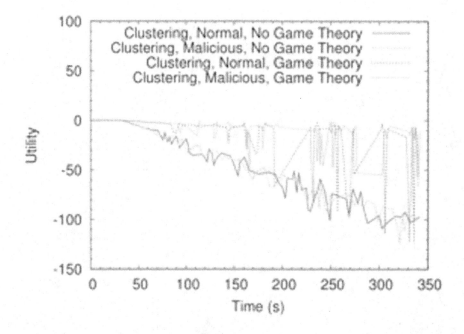

Experimenting with different strategies in order to save power, as well as improving the accuracy of the malicious node detection procedure can extend this work. Other possible extensions of this work would be to experiment with packets of different priorities and also implementing different mechanisms for selection of cluster heads.

ACKNOWLEDGMENT

This work is supported by the National Science Foundation under grant number 1054492.

REFERENCES

Agah, A., Asadi, M., & Zimmerman, C. (2011). *Maximizing battery life: Applying game theory to wireless sensor networks*. The West Chester Research Consortium.

Agah, A., Das, S. K., & Basu, K. (2005). Enforcing security for prevention of DOS attack in wireless sensor networks using economical modeling. In *Proceedings of the 2nd IEEE International Conference on Mobile Ad-Hoc and Sensor Systems (MASS)*. IEEE.

Agah, A., Das, S. K., & Basu, K. (2005). Preventing DOS attack in sensor and actor networks: A game theoretic approach. In *Proceedings of IEEE International Conferences on Communications (ICC)*. IEEE.

Akyldiz, I. F., Sankarasubramaniam, Y., Su, W., & Cayirci, E. (2002). Wireless sensor networks: A survey. *Journal of Computer Networks, 38*.

Asadi, M., Zimmerman, C., & Agah, A. (2012). A quest for security in wireless sensor networks: A game theoretic model. In *Proceedings of the International Conference on Wireless Networks (ICWN)*. ICWN.

Asadi, M., Zimmerman, C., & Agah, A. (2013). A game-theoretic approach to security and power conservation in wireless sensor networks. *International Journal of Network Security, 15*(1), 50–58.

Bandyopadhyay, S., & Coyle, E. (2003). *An energy efficient hierarchical clustering algorithm for wireless sensor networks*. INFOCOM.

Buchegger, S., & Boudec, J. L. (2002). Nodes bearing grudges: Toward routing security fairness and robustness in mobile ad hoc network. In *Proceedings of the 10th Euronicro Workshop on Parallel, Distributed and Network-Based Processing*. Academic Press.

Campos-Nanez, E., Garcia, A., & Li, C. (2008). A game-theoretic approach to efficient power management in sensor networks. *Operations Research, 56*(3), 552–561. doi:10.1287/opre.1070.0435

Chang, L., Zhan, J., & Matwin, S. (2005). Privacy preserving k-nearest neighbor classification. *International Journal of Network Security, 1*(1), 46–51.

Chau, C., Wahab, M. H., Qin, F., Wang, Y., & Tang, Y. (2009). *Battery recovery aware sensor networks*. Paper presented at the 7th International Symposium on Modeling and Optimization in Mobile, Ad Hoc and Wireless Networks (WiOpt). New York, NY.

Chi, M., & Yang, Y. (2006). *Battery-aware routing for streaming data transmissions in wireless sensor networks*. Berlin: Springer Science and Business Media, LLC.

Chong, C., & Kumar, S. P. (2003). Sensor networks: Evolution, opportunities and challenge. *Proceedings of the IEEE, 91*(8).

Crosby, G. V., Hester, L., & Pissinou, N. (2011). Location aware, trust-based detection and isolation of compromised nodes in wireless sensor networks. *International Journal of Network Security, 12*(2), 107–117.

Eidenbenz, S., Anderegg, L., & Wattenhofer, R. (2007). Incentives-compatible, energy-optimal, and efficient ad hoc networking in a selfish milieu. In *Proceedings of the 40th Hawaii International Conference on System Science* (HICSS). ACM.

Eidenbenz, S., Kumar, V. S., & Zust, S. (2006). Topology control game for ad hoc networks. *ACM Mobile Networks and Application, 11*(2).

Eidenbenz, S., Resrta, G., & Santi, P. (2008). The commit protocol for truthful and cost-efficient routing in ad hoc networks with selfish nodes. *IEEE Transactions on Mobile Computing, 7*(1). doi:10.1109/TMC.2007.1069

Felegyhazi, M., Buttyan, L., & Hubaux, J. P. (2003). Equilibrium analysis of packet forwarding strategies in wireless ad hoc networks: The static case. In *Proceedings of Personal Wireless Communications*. Academic Press. doi:10.1007/978-3-540-39867-7_70

Felegyhazi, M., & Hubaux, J. P. (2007). *Game theory in wireless networks: A tutorial*. EPFL-Switzerland. LCA-REPORT.

Ganeriwl, S., & Srivastava, M. B. (2004). *Reputation based framework for high integrity sensor networks*. Paper presented at the ACM Workshop on Security of Ad hoc and Sensor Networks. New York, NY.

Heidemann, J., Ye, W., & Estrin, D. (2002). *An energy efficient mac protocol for wireless sensor networks*. Paper presented at IEEE INFOCOM. New York, NY.

Karlof, C., & Wagner, D. (2003). *Secure routing in wireless sensor networks: Attacks and countermeasures*. Paper presented at the 1st IEEE International Workshop on Sensor Network Protocols and Applications (SPNA). New York, NY.

Levin, D. (2006). *Punishment in selfish wireless networks: A game theoretic analysis*. Paper presented at the Workshop on the Economics of Networked Systems. New York, NY.

Liu, Y., & Yang, Y. R. (2003). Reputation propagation and agreement in mobile ad-hoc networks. In *Proceedings of IEEE Wireless Communications and Networking Conference* (WCNC). IEEE.

Machado, R., & Tekinay, S. (2008). A survey of game theoretic approaches in wireless sensor networks. *Elsevier Computer Networks Journal, 52*.

Malekzadeh, M., Abdul Ghani, A. A., Subramaniam, S., & Desa, J. (2011). Validating reliability of omnet++ in wireless networks DOS attacks: Simulation vs. test-bed. *International Journal of Network Security, 123*(1), 13–21.

MEMSIC Inc. (n.d.). *Micaz wireless measurement system*. Retrieved from http://www.memsic.com

Michiardi, P., & Molva, R. (2002)a. *Core: A collaborative reputation mechanism to enforce node cooperation in mobile ad hoc networks*. Paper presented at the Communications and Multimedia Security Conference. New York, NY.

Michiardi, P., & Molva, R. (2002b). *Game theoretic analysis of security in mobile ad hoc networks (Research Report)*. Institute Eurecom.

Michiardi, P., & Molva, R. (2002c). *Prevention of denial of service attack and selfishness in mobile ad hoc networks (Research Report)*. Institute Eurecom.

Michiardi, P., & Molva, R. (2002d). *Simulation based analysis of security exposures in mobile ad hoc networks*. Paper presented at the European Wireless 2002: Next Generation Wireless Networks: Technologies, Protocols, Services and Applications. New York, NY.

Nurmi, P. (2006). *Modeling energy constrained routing in selfish ad hoc networks*. Paper presented at the International Conference on Game Theory for Networks (GameNets). New York, NY.

Osborne, M., & Rubinstein, A. (1994). *A course in game theory*. Cambridge, MA: The MIT Press.

Owen, G. (2001). *Game theory*. New York: Academic Press.

Park, C., Lahiri, K., & Raghunathan, A. (2005). *Battery discharge characteristic of wireless sensor nodes: An experimental analysis*. IEEE SECON.

Rappaport, T. S. (2002). *Wireless communications: Principles and practice*. Upper Saddle River, NJ: Prentice Hall.

Resnick, P., Kuwabarra, K., Zeckauser, R., & Friedman, E. (2000). Reputation systems: Facilitating trust in e-commerce systems. *Communications of the ACM*, *43*(12). doi:10.1145/355112.355122

Sengupta, S., Chatterjee, M., & Kwiat, K. (2010). A game theoretic framework for power control in wireless sensor networks. *IEEE Transactions on Computers*, *59*(2). doi:10.1109/TC.2009.82

Tiny, O. S. (n.d.). *Tinyos documentation*. Retrieved from http://docs.tinyos.net

Zimmerman, C., Agah, A., & Asadi, M. (2011). *Applying economical modeling to wireless sensor networks for maximizing the battery life*. Paper presented at the 26th Pennsylvania Computer and Information Science Educators (PACISE) Conference. Philadelphia, PA.

Zimmerman, C., Agah, A., & Asadi, M. (2011). *Incorporating economical modeling to extend battery life in wireless sensor networks*. Paper presented at the Graduate Research and Creative Projects Symposium. New York, NY.

Chapter 5

Short–Hops vs. Long–Hops:
Energy–Efficiency Analysis in Wireless Sensor Networks

Mekkaoui Kheireddine
Dr Moulay Tahar University, Algeria

Rahmoun Abdellatif
Djillali Liabès University, Algeria

ABSTRACT

Sensor networks are composed of miniaturized wireless sensor nodes with limited capacity and energy source. Generally, these sensor networks are used, in many applications, to monitor inaccessible environments (battlefields, volcano monitoring, animal tracking…), hence the impossibility to replace or to recharge the batteries. As sensors may be deployed in a large area, radio transceivers are the most energy consuming of sensor nodes, which means that their usage needs to be very efficient in order to maximize node life, which leads us to maximize the network's life. In wireless sensor networks and in order to transmit its data, a node can route its messages towards destination, generally the base station, either by using small or large hops, so optimizing the hop length can extend significantly the lifetime of the network. This chapter provides a simple way to verify, which makes the energy consumption minimal by choosing proper hop length.

INTRODUCTION

Recent development in Micro-Electro-Mechanical Systems (*MEMS*) technology, wireless communications and digital electronics have allowed the development of low-cost, low-power, multifunctional sensor nodes that are small in size and communicate un-tethered in short and long distances. These sensors, also known as motes, are generally composed of a power source (battery), a processing unit with limited capacity and a communication component (transceiver) (Gerard, 2008).The deployment of sensor nodes for the monitoring and the detection of different events in the environment is known as Wireless Sensor Network (WSN).

In these last years, wireless sensor networks have been deployed in many applications, to

DOI: 10.4018/978-1-4666-4789-3.ch005

perform the monitoring tasks, like military surveillance, disaster management (Simon, Maroti, Lèdeczi & Balogh, 2004), forest fire detection, seismic detection (Werner-Allen and all, 2006), habitat monitoring, biomedical health monitoring (Lorincz and al, 2004), inventory tracking, animal tracking, hazardous environment sensing and smart spaces, general engineering, commercial applications, home applications (Akyildiz & Vuran, 2010; Sohraby, Minoli & Znati, 2007), Indeed, Business 2.0 lists wireless sensor networks as one of the top six technologies that will change the world, and Technology Review at MIT and Globalfuture identify WSNs as one of the 10 new technologies that will change our life (Imad & Mohammed, 2005).

A wireless sensor network consists of hundreds to myriads of sensor nodes, which appear to be deployed randomly by a car, airplane or a rocket launcher. Each node has a strict limitation in the usage of its electric power as well as computation and memory resources. They typically utilize intermittent wireless communication. Therefore, sensor networks should be well-formed to achieve its purposes and to extend the network life's; indeed how well the network is formed determines the life of the whole network as well as the quality of data transmission, also the manner to reduce channel contention.

Sensor nodes are, always, endowed by a limited battery power and, generally, deployed randomly in inaccessible fields; which make it almost the time impossible to recharge or to replace the dead battery. So, battery power in WSN is considered as scarce resource and must be used efficiently. Sensor node consumes battery in sensing data, receiving data, sending data and processing data. The most energy-consuming component is the Radio Frequency module that provides wireless communications (Akyildiz, & Vuran, 2010). Consequently, Out of all sensor node operation, sending and receiving data consumes more energy than any other operation. The energy consumption

when transmitting 1 bit of data, by a sensor, on the wireless channel is equivalent to the energy required to execute thousands of cycles of CPU instructions (Yick, Mukherjee & Ghosal, 2008). Therefore, the energy efficiency of the wireless communication protocol largely affects the energy consumption and network lifetime of wireless sensor networks.

In the most times, sensor nodes in WSN do not have the necessary power and the communication range to directly send its collected data from the environment to the base station. So, the multi-hops mode of communication, is generally, used to forward data and to reach the base station (Akyildiz & Vuran, 2010), this multi-hop protocol consists to send the data from each sensor to its neighbors, which, in their turns send the data to their neighbors, and so on, until the base station is reached. Hence, a typical sensor node will not only sense and forwards its own data but also have to play the role of a router, i.e. forward the data of its neighbors in the base station's direction, and as discussed above, the two operations of sending and receiving data consume more energy than any other operation. It can be inferred that data gathering and routing are the nucleus area in WSN, where good protocols should be developed in order to achieve optimal energy consumption.

Currently, all modern radio transceivers can adjust their transmitting power (Pesovie, Mohorko & Karl, 2010), in order to reach their closer or their farthest neighbors or relays, so, in WSNs, the base station could be reached with either large number of smaller hops or small number of larger hops both by using multi-hops protocol. Energy efficiency, of these two approaches, is based on:

- The path loss between the transmitter and the receiver,
- The power consumption of the radio transceiver in the two operating modes, receiving and sending data.

The idea, over the number of required hops to reach the base station, comes from the fact that each strategy (long-hops and short-hops routing) has its own advantages, i.e. forwarding data to the base station over several short hops minimizes the transmission energy which increases with the communication distance. However, sending data, over long distance between relays, reduces the reception cost (as the number of nodes involved in data routing decreases) which is ignored in many works in the literature.

Effectively, in many works, the reception power in WSNs is neglected (Singh, Woo & Raghavendra, 1998; Pesovie, Mohorko & Karl, 2010), this makes routing over short-hops is always preferable, because it decrease the energy used in transmitting data, by using small hops, i.e. low transmission energy. However, this is not realistic, because in many other works (Heinzelman, Chandrakasan & Balakrishnan, 2000, Mario, Joern & Klaus, 2006; Boukerche, 2008; Akylidiz, 2010), the authors showed that the reception power cannot be ignored, and thus it must be included to compute the energy transmission, when using nodes as relays in multi-hop routing scheme.

Based on the comparison between the two strategies, in this paper, we will provide a simple condition on the length of the hop that, if respected, leads us to extend the wireless sensors networks life's, by optimizing the energy consumption. The rest of this paper is organized as follows; related works are presented in section II, in section III the propagation model is presented. The short-hops vs. the long-hops analysis is presented in section IV followed by a comparison between short-hops and long-hops in section IV, result validation is presented in section V and the conclusion in section VI.

RELATED WORKS

The problem of routing packets over long-hops or short-hops has been treated by many authors in recent years and their conclusions are varied depending on the criteria considered and the approach taken (Fedor & Collier, 2007).

Some theoretical works (Mario, Joern & Klaus, 2006; Fedor & Collier, 2007) shows that multi-hop routing is more efficient than single-hop routing. This is in an opposite to observations in some real world WSN, which shows that single-hop routing, can be much more energy efficient than multi-hop routing (Haenggi & Puccinelli, 2005; Haenggi, 2004). Besides energy efficiency, single-hop routing can also have advantages for other network parameters, such as end-to-end delay, lower packet loss, etc (Pesovie, Mohorko & Karl, 2010).

Yin, Shi & Shang (2005) presented two strategy of control; one of the methods consists of decreasing the transmission range of each node. According to the authors, this scheme will reduce the overall power consumption of the network, as a route with many short hops is generally more energy-efficient than one with a few long hops.

Haenggi (2004) specified many reasons why long-hop routing is more advantageous. One of them is the power efficiency. The author claimed that although the transmitted energy drops significantly with distance, the reduction of radiated power does not yield a decrease in the total energy consumption.

In this paper, we provide the optimal length for hops that make energy consumption optimal. For this end, we need to use the model, of the energy consumption, defined for the wireless sensor networks.

PROPAGATION MODEL

Radio channel between transmitter and receiver can be established only when strength of the received radio signal is greater than receiver's sensitivity threshold (Pesovie, Mohorko & Karl, 2010). The reduction in signal power density, on the path between transmitter and receiver, is called path loss. In our study we use the log-distance path loss model, so the power received by a remote node by d meters from the sender can be expressed as follows (Pesovie, Mohorko & Karl, 2010; Fedor & Collier, 2007; Theodore, 2009):

$$P(d) = P_0 \times \left(\frac{d_0}{d}\right)^{\alpha} \tag{1}$$

where P_0 represents the power of the signal received at distance d_0 from a transmitter and α is the path loss exponent, which is empirically measured under different propagation scenarios (Theodore, 2009; Fedor & Collier, 2007). Typical values of path loss exponent in such scenarios are presented in Table 1.

In this paper, we use Equation (1) to express the minimum power required to communicate over a given distance and we compare the two routing strategies (long-hops and short-hops routing). Every node is transmitting with the minimum

Table 1. Typical values of path loss exponent

Environment	α
Free-space	2
Urban area LOS	2,7 to 3,5
Urban area no LOS	3 to 5
Indoor LOS	1,6 to 1,8
Factories no LOS	2 to 3
Buildings no LOS	4 to 6

power, required to guarantee the signal at the receiver, is equal to the sensitivity threshold P_t of the receiver (Mario, Joern & Klaus, 2006; Fedor & Collier, 2006). According to the Figure 1 we can therefore write:

$$P_t = P_x \times \left(\frac{d_0}{x}\right)^{\alpha} \tag{2}$$

From which, we can get the energy required to reach the destination:

$$P_x = P_t \times \left(\frac{x}{d_0}\right)^{\alpha} \tag{3}$$

In some pure theoretical models of wireless transmission, authors assume that all consumed energy is radiated into the air by a transmitter, and a receiver doesn't spend any energy during a reception (Pesovie, Mohorko & Karl, 2010). According to them, if we consider only the total power transmitted over the path, then the short-hop strategy would be the most energy efficient, but since the reception cost should not be neglected (Akyildiz & Vuran, 2010; Boukerche, 2008; Marion, Joern & Klaus, 2006), we will show in this paper that the use of long-hop strategy between two nodes (source and destination) is an optimal alternative. This is due to the fact that the savings in transmission power by the multi-hop scheme does not compensate for the resulting additional reception energy cost. The energy cost of the reception P_r can be equivalent to transmitting over a distant t (Mario, Joern & Klaus, 2006). Thus, it can be expressed by the formula:

$$P_r = P_t \times \left(\frac{t}{d_0}\right)^{\alpha} \tag{4}$$

Figure 1. Transmission distance for one hop

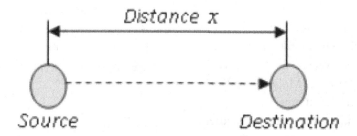

SHORT-HOPS VS. LONG-HOPS ANALYSIS

Figure 2 represents two topologies of multi-hop routing between two distant nodes, a source A and a destination B, with a distance d. The first topology uses n hops to transmit data from A to B (using short-hops of distance x); while the second uses m hops (using long-hops of distance y); with $n = 2m$ (i.e. $y = 2x$), so we can write:

$$P_t = P_x \times \left(\frac{d_0}{x}\right)^{\alpha} = P_y \times \left(\frac{d_0}{y}\right)^{\alpha} \qquad (5)$$

Since $y = 2x$, Equation (5) becomes:

$$P_y = P_x 2^{\alpha} \qquad (6)$$

Using Equation (3) and Equation (4), we can now compute the energy required to transmit a message between A and B. For the first topology, we have a path with n hops. Thus we can express the power required to transmit data from A to B, using n hops, P_{nh}, as:

Figure 2. Transmission distance for: (1) n-hops - (2) m-hops

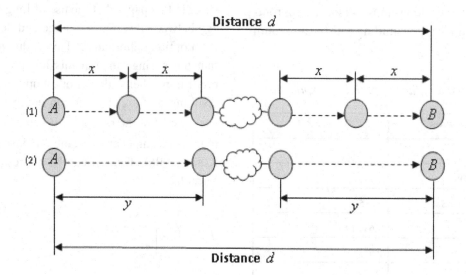

$$P_{nh} =$$

$$\overbrace{\left(0P_r + P_x\right)}^{A} + \overbrace{\left(P_r + P_x\right) + ... + \left(P_r + P_x\right)}^{(n-1)nodes} + \overbrace{\left(P_r + P_x\right)}^{B} \tag{7}$$

And it can be expressed, also as:

$$P_{nh} = nP_x + nP_r \tag{8}$$

which can be written as:

$$P_{nh} = 2m \times P_x + 2m \times P_r \tag{9}$$

We know from Equation (6), that

$$P_x = \frac{P_y}{2^\alpha},$$

therefore Equation (9) becomes:

$$P_{nh} = m \times P_y \left[\frac{1}{2^{\alpha-1}} + 2\frac{P_r}{P_x}\right] \tag{10}$$

With the same way, we can get the power required to transmit data from A to B using m hops:

$$P_{mh} = mP_y + mP_r \tag{11}$$

which equal to:

$$P_{mh} = m \times P_y \left[1 + \frac{P_r}{P_y}\right] \tag{12}$$

SHORT-HOPS VS. LONG-HOPS COMPARAISON

In this section we present our main result. Lets compute, now, $P_{nh} - P_{mh}$:

$$P_{nh} - P_{mh} =$$

$$m \times P_y \left[\frac{1}{2^{\alpha-1}} + 2\frac{P_r}{P_y}\right] - m \times P_y \left[1 + \frac{P_r}{P_y}\right] \tag{13}$$

This is equal to:

$$P_{nh} - P_{mh} = m \times P_y \left[\frac{1}{2^{\alpha-1}} - 1 + \frac{P_r}{P_y}\right] \tag{14}$$

Since $m \times P_y \succ 0$, therefore, $P_{nh} - P_{mh} \succ 0$, if and if only:

$$\frac{1}{2^{\alpha-1}} - 1 + \frac{P_r}{P_y} \succ 0 \tag{15}$$

Therefore:

$$\frac{P_r}{P_y} \succ 1 - \frac{1}{2^{\alpha-1}} \tag{16}$$

This means:

$$y \prec \frac{t}{\sqrt[\alpha]{1 - \frac{1}{2^{\alpha-1}}}} \tag{17}$$

And since $y = 2x$, Equation (17) becomes:

$$x \prec \frac{t}{2 \times \sqrt[\alpha]{1 - \frac{1}{2^{\alpha-1}}}} \tag{18}$$

And since $y \succ x$, inequalities (17) and (18) means that optimal energy consumption can be achieved when the lengths of the hops are included in the interval:

$$\left] \frac{t}{2 \times \sqrt[\alpha]{1 - \dfrac{1}{2^{\alpha-1}}}}, \frac{t}{\sqrt[\alpha]{1 - \dfrac{1}{2^{\alpha-1}}}} \right[$$

SIMULATION AND RESULTS VALIDATION

In Order to validate this condition, we perform, in this section, the experiments with two wireless sensor networks to verify the condition deduced from the theoretical analysis, the first-one of these networks is composed of *Mica2* sensors and the second-one is composed of *Mica2dot* sensors.

We use, in our simulation, the experimental characteristics of these two sensors, so in order to evaluate the power consumed by *Mica2* and *Mica2dot* to transmit data from a node to another one, we will use the physical characteristics presented in (Anastasi, Falchi, Passarella, Conti & Gregori, 2004) and described in Table 2.

Table 2. Experimental characteristic of mica2 and mica2dot motes

	Mica2	Mica2dot
Reception	16 mW	12 mW
Transmission	18mW	14 mW
Transmission range	55 m	135 m
With maximum t_x power	70 m	230 m

First Case Study

To simulate the behavior of *Mica2* sensors, we assume that the networks are composed of aligned *Mica2* nodes (Transmitter-Relays-Sink) with a length of 760 meters (distance between Transmitter and Sink), and we compute the energy consumed by these networks with different number of hops, which means different hop lengths, which means also, different number of relays.

Computing the total consumed power for these different aligned networks, with different hops length (i.e. different number of relays), gives the results in Table 3.

We conclude from the Table 3, that the optimal number of hops, that provide the minimum energy consumption, is 16 hops (i.e. hop length is 47.5 meter), which is verified by our condition that limits the length of hops that offer minimum energy consumption in: $]36.6678, 73.3357[$. For easier reading, we present the results in the Figure 3.

Table 3. Mica2-Power consumption Vs hops length

Hops Number	Hop Length	Total Power Consumed mW
6	126.6666	662.7732
8	95.0	557.59
10	76.0	503.672
11	69.0909	488.4290
12	63.3333	475.3866
14	54.2857	466.9028
16	47.5	466.2968
18	42.2222	476.9244
20	38.0	491.836
21	36.1904	499.6533
22	34.5454	503.3204
24	31.6666	521.2308
26	29.2307	546.1027
28	27.1428	569.4514
30	25.3333	591.5625

Figure 3. Mica2: Energy consumption vs. hops length

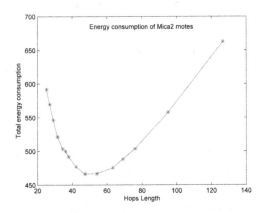

Second Case Study

With the same way, we simulate the behavior of *Mica2dot* sensors; we compute the consumed power for different aligned networks, with different hops length. We got the results presented in Table 4.

Table 4. Mica2dot-Power consumption vs. hops length

Hops Number	Hop Length	Total Power Consumed mW
5	152.0	148.7193
6	126.6666	145.1566
8	95.0	151.4496
10	76.0	164.3596
11	69.0909	172.3269
12	63.3333	180.5783
14	54.2857	199.3528
16	47.5	219.1441
18	42.2222	240.3855
20	38.0	262.1798
22	34.5454	283.5317
24	31.6666	305.7131
26	29.2307	328.7930
28	27.1428	351.6764
30	25.3333	374.4000

From Table 4 we can get the number of hops that makes the energy consumption minimum, which equals to 6 hops (i.e. length hop = 126.6666). This result is verified, also, by our condition which limits the length of hops that ensure the minimum energy consumption in $]88.3883, 176.7766[$. For easier reading, we present the results in the Figure 4.

CONCLUSION

We have analyzed the problem of hopping distance strategy in WSN and simulation results show the impact of the choice of the hops length. We showed, also, that the condition expressed in this paper, guarantee more energy efficiency, and help us to extend the network's life. Moreover, using the minimum hop length can be more efficient in the case of transmission failures that require retransmission. In futures works we will focus on the problem of routing data by the less costly path in terms of energy, using the condition presented in this paper.

Figure 4. Mica2dot: Energy consumption vs. hops length

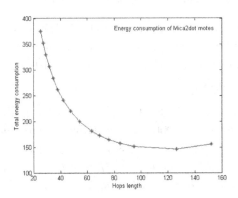

REFERENCES

Akyildiz, I. F., & Vuran, M. C. (2010). *Wireless sensor networks*. Hoboken, NJ: John Wiley and Sons. doi:10.1002/9780470515181

Añastasi, G., Falchi, A., Passarella, A., Conti, M., & Gregori, E. (2004). Performance measurements of motes sensor networks. In *Proceedings of the 7th ACM International Symposium on Modeling, Analysis and Simulation of Wireless and Mobile Systems* (pp. 174-181). New York, NY: ACM Press.

Boukerche, A. (2008). Algorithms and protocols for wireless sensor networks. Hoboken, NJ: A John Wiley and Sons.

Fedor, S., & Collier, M. (2007). On the problem of energy efficiency of multi-hop vs one-hop routing in wireless sensor networks. In *Proceedings of the 21st International Conference on Advanced Information Networking and Applications Workshops* (pp. 380-385). Washington, DC: IEEE Computer Society.

Gerard, M. (2008). *Smart sensor systems*. Hoboken, NJ: John Wiley & Sons Inc.

Haenggi, M. (2004). Twelve reasons not to route over many short hops. In *Proceedings of 60th Vehicular Technology Conference* (pp. 3130-3134). Piscataway, NJ: IEEE Computer Society.

Haenggi, M., & Puccinelli, D. (2005). Routing in ad hoc networks: A case for long hops. *IEEE Communications Magazine*, 93–101. doi:10.1109/MCOM.2005.1522131

Heinzelman, W. R., Chandrakasan, A., & Balakrishnan, H. (2000). Energy-efficient communication protocol for wireless microsensor networks. In *Proceedings of the 33rd Hawaii International Conference on System Sciences* (pp. 3005-3014). Washington, DC: IEEE Computer Society.

Imad, M., & Mohammed, I. (2005). *Handbook of sensor networks: Compact wireless and wired sensing systems*. New York, NY: CRC Press.

Lorincz, K. et al. (2004). Sensor networks for emergency response: Challenges and opportunities. *IEEE Pervasive Computing / IEEE Computer Society [and] IEEE Communications Society*, *3*(4), 16–23. doi:10.1109/MPRV.2004.18

Mario, N., Joern, P., & Klaus, K. (2006). Evaluation of energy costs for single hop vs. multi hop with respect to topology parameters. In *Proceedings of IEEE International Workshop on Factory Communication Systems*, (pp. 175-182). IEEE.

Pesovie, U. M., Mohorko, J. J., & Karl, B. Z. F. (2010). Single-hop vs. multi-hop energy efficiency analysis in wireless sensor networks. In *Proceedings of Telekomunikacioni forum TELFOR, Srbija*, (pp. 23-25). TELFOR.

Simon, G., Maroti, M., Lèdeczi, A., & Balogh, G. (2004). Sensor network-based countersniper system. In *Proceedings of the 2nd International Conference on Embedded Networked Sensor Systems* (pp. 1-12). New York, NY: ACM Press.

Singh, S., Woo, M., & Raghavendra, C. S. (1998). Power-aware routing in mobile ad hoc networks. In *Proceedings of the 4th Annual ACM/IEEE International Conference on Mobile Computing and Networking* (pp. 181-190). ACM/IEEE. doi:10.1145/288235.288286

Sohraby, K., Minoli, D., & Znati, T. F. (2007). *Wireless sensor networks: Technology, protocols, and applications*. Hoboken, NJ: Wiley-Interscience. doi:10.1002/047011276X

Theodore, S. (2009). *Wireless communications: Principles and practice* (18th ed., Vol. 2, p. 707). Upper Saddle River, NJ: Prentice Hall PTR.

Werner-Allen, G., Lorincz, K., Welsh, M., Marcillo, O., Johnson, J., Ruiz, M., & Lees, J. (2006). *Deploying a wireless sensor network on an active volcano* (2nd ed., Vol. 10, pp. 18–25). Piscataway, NJ: IEEE Educational Activities Department.

Yick, J., Mukherjee, B., & Ghosal, D. (2008). Wireless sensor network survey. *Computer Networks*, *52*(12), 2292–2330. doi:10.1016/j.comnet.2008.04.002

Yin, B., Shi, H., & Shang, Y. (2005). A two-level strategy for topology control in wireless sensor networks. In *Proceedings of the 11th International Conference on Parallel and Distributed Systems – Workshops* (pp. 358-362). Washington, DC: IEEE Computer Society.

KEY TERMS AND DEFINITIONS

Energy Efficiency: As sensors are endowed with limited source of energy, this make the battery the most critical resource and it use must be very efficient.

Hop Length: Each strategy (long-hops and short-hops) has its advantages and its inconvenient, thus choosing the ideal hop length increase significantly the network life's time.

Long-Hop: Using long-hops in routing protocols, means use more energy to transmit data between the source and the destination but it reduce also the number of the node used as relays.

Multi-Hops Routing: Usually, sensors (data collector) don't have the capacity to transmit its data directly to the base station, so multi-hop routing protocols are used.

Network's Lifetime: Network's lifetime has a strong dependence on the nodes' battery capacity, it is the time wherein the network can perform the environment monitoring and ensures the delivery of the collected data to the end user.

Short-Hop: The most modern sensors can adjust their transmitting power of their transceivers to reach it neighbors. Using short-hops means involve more nodes to transmit data from the source to the destination.

Wireless Sensor Network: Wireless sensor network consists of sensors, with limited capacities, that are deployed in a field in order to perform the monitoring. In addition to the monitoring, these sensors cooperate between them to route data from a node (data collector) to the sink.

Chapter 6
HTTP^V:
Verifiable HTTP across an Untrusted Channel

Subrata Acharya
Towson University, USA

ABSTRACT

There is a need to be able to verify plaintext HTTP content transfers. Common sense dictates authentication and sensitive content should always be protected by SSL/HTTPS, but there is still great exploitation potential in the modification of static content in transit. Pre-computed signatures and client-side verification offers integrity protection of HTTP content in applications where SSL is not feasible. In this chapter, the authors demonstrate a mechanism by which a Web browser or other HTTP client can verify that content transmitted over an untrusted channel has not been modified. Verifiable HTTP is not intended to replace SSL. Rather, it is intended to be used in applications where SSL is not feasible, specifically, when serving high-volume static content and/or content from non-secure sources such as Content Distribution Networks. Finally, the authors find content verification is effective with server-side overhead similar to SSL. With future optimization such as native browser support, content verification could achieve comparable client-side efficiency.

1. INTRODUCTION

Recent events indicate malicious modification of static HTTP content does occur. For example, the Tunisian government successfully compromised the Facebook, Yahoo, and Gmail accounts of protesters by injecting JavaScript into the front pages of these services Ragen (2011). Even though the authentication was sent over HTTPS and therefore not susceptible to eavesdropping, the injected script sent a copy of the username and password

to a government-controlled destination. This attack could have been prevented if the browser could have detected the page was modified in transit before enabling active content such as JavaScript.

Less intrusive modification of pages is also possible: for example, a government controlled Internet Service Providers (ISPs) may censor information by on-the-fly rewriting of HTML containing certain keywords. While such censorship can easily be detected by comparing content from an uncensored source, or by word-of-mouth,

DOI: 10.4018/978-1-4666-4789-3.ch006

this takes time and a way to access the content in an uncensored fashion. If HTTP content can be verified, the user can immediately know something is amiss.

Censorship and spying issues aside, ISPs have in the past been known to modify HTTP traffic in-transit for revenue purposes (Odvarko, 2008). Two competing technologies, *Phorm* and *NebuAd*, both have the ability to track browsing behavior and add or replace advertisement content on webpages with "targeted" advertising designed to generate revenue stream for these ISPs Topolski (2008). This type of activity is not necessarily harmful to end-users, but deprives websites of advertisement revenue. To this effect, Verifiable HTTP could inform sites of the occurrence of this event.

1.1 Dynamic vs. Static Content

For the purposes of this research work, we will place web content into two broad categories: *dynamic* and *static*. Dynamic content is generated specifically by the server for the client, and will vary between clients and between sessions. Static content is generated once and does not change. In a website with mostly or entirely public content, much of the content is likely to be static. Examples of such a site would be a website for a restaurant, featuring menus, daily and weekly specials, hours and directions. This information changes infrequently, at most once per day, and often not at all. Even a website with majority user-generated content, such as a blog, forum or social networking, has many static elements.

A user's home page on any generic user-generated site pulls content from many sources, from dynamic to entirely static. The main content of the page is entirely dynamic, generated specifically by or for the users and changes whenever there is any activity on the site. The profile pictures (representing friends, forum posters, blog commenters, etc.) displayed will vary based on the generated page content, but the individual pictures will only change when a user changes his or her picture. If there is advertising on the site, the ads displayed will change with each page fetched, but all users will get the ads currently in rotation, and the content of each ad does not change. The site's logo, graphics, navigation menus plus the non-displayed elements such as style-sheets and scripts are the same for all users and do not change. If a visitor to the site is not logged in, they will be directed to a public page asking them to log in or create an account. This serves to illustrate even sites with dynamic content have static pages or page content.

1.2 Static Content vs. Dynamic Delivery Systems

Many sites optimize the serving of static content. This may range from using separate web servers for static content to using the services of a Content Distribution Network (CDN). A CDN is a service that delivers content from a source more optimal to serve multiple clients. This may mean the CDN source is closer to the client in terms of network topology (and therefore often geography), or has higher bandwidth. CDNs often serve multiple customers from the same set of distributed physical resources. In addition to content provider a system, many organizations and ISPs operate caching proxies to locally mirror frequently accessed static content (Davidson, 2008).

1.3 SSL Overview

HTTPS, or HTTP over SSL/TLS, is a mechanism to provide end to end security of the HTTP session. SSL (renamed TLS in more recent versions) is a general purpose protocol for encapsulating application-layer data to provide confidentiality, integrity, and authenticity services (Magnini, 2005). Encryption and message authentication codes provide the former two services, while public-key cryptography and certificate verification provider the latter.

SSL operates by first authenticating the server to the client (and optionally authenticating the client to the server.) This is accomplished by exchanging certificates. Certificates contain a public key and are signed by the issuing certificate authority (a trusted third party.) Once the server has been authenticated to the client, the client can generate random data and use an asymmetric crypto-algorithm such as RSA to encrypt it with the server's public key, and send it to the server. Only the server's private key will be able to decrypt this data, ensuring only the client and the server will have the shared secret. This shared secret functions as a session key for the symmetric crypto-algorithm selected to protect the remainder of the SSL session. Application data carried over SSL is segmented into records, which are protected by a Message Authentication Code (MAC) appended to the record. A MAC is a keyed hash of the record data, and ensures the data has not been corrupted or altered in transit. If the application data carried over the SSL session is HTTP, the protocol is referred to as HTTPS (Wikipedia, 2010).

1.4 SSL Limitations

The key strength of HTTPS is that it offers a high level of trust for individual web sessions. However, there are situations in which SSL is not well suited to provide the required security: for example, when the same public static content must be served to all clients, possibly from a Content Distribution Network. For performance and trust reasons, SSL is not used. Additionally, SSL adds significant overhead to the HTTP session, and is often deemed overkill for content that is not personal or sensitive. Historically, SSL has not been usable when several websites or domains are served from the same IP address. This is commonly the case with CDNs. More recent implementations of SSL work around this limitation via extensions to the SSL/TLS protocol. However, a potential vulner-

ability exists when using SSL with CDNs. Even if a CDN supports SSL, if a site wishes to protect CDN-served content, the site must trust the CDN with their SSL certificate and private key.

1.5 Challenges

When serving public content, in contract to confidentiality integrity is very important. When content is served from a CDN, the requirements for authenticity are modified. The authenticity of the server is not important, but the authenticity of the content is very pertinent. Content can be reasonably protected against modification by using SSL/HTTPS, but the overhead required may not be feasible for some sites, especially for high-volume static content.

Many sites host static, publicly-accessible content on content distribution networks (CDNs) that are not under their direct control. An HTTPS channel for CDN-hosted content would be resource-intensive and potentially risky. HTTPS content from a third-party would have to either be signed by a third-party certificate, or a third party would have to be in possession of the site's SSL certificate. Client-side implementation needs to be able to reliably detect if verification is in use. If content is being modified in transit, an attempt may be made to disable content verification and it should also be detected.

1.6 Goals

To this effect the goals of this research are to:

- Enable the client to verify content that has not been modified in transit or modified on the server since the last authorized update of the content. The verification should be accomplished by client-site computation, a request based on this computation, and further computation based on the returned result.

- Perform verification without any server-side computation per request in a manner compatible with CDNs and other third-party hosting.
- Enable signatures to be cryptographically strong and not easily forged.
- Provide a method for detecting verification is in use and to indicate what content can be verified. A secure channel should be optionally supported for this method in order to provide resistance against modifications that would attempt to disable verification.
- Implement client-side verification in the form of a browser extension. Verification should occur automatically for supported content. If verification succeeds, a small indication should be presented. If verification fails, a noticeable warning should be given and all active content on the page should be disabled.

2. METHODOLOGY

Content verification can be performed by securely signing the content, and implementing signature verification on the client. A secure hashing algorithm combined with RSA cryptography should provide a suitable signing mechanism.

2.1 Server-Side Signing

Initially a private/public RSA key pair is obtained. While a key pair may be generated solely for content signing purposes, it would be beneficial to use the existing SSL certificate and associated private key. This will allow the client to further verify that the content has been signed by an authentic source, as the certificate, and therefore the public key, has been signed by a certifying authority. Additionally, the client would already have the public key if an HTTPS connection has been made. A configuration file listing the verifiable content types, verifiable content paths and wildcards, and the location of the content signatures is generated. It is highly recommended a secure channel such as HTTPS be supported for this information, since a secure way of providing the verified content list is crucial to ensure that verification occurs. For all verifiable content, a hash of the content is generated using a suitable secure hashing algorithm and the hash value is encrypted with the appropriate private key to generate a signature of the content. The resulting signature is published at the URL based on the content signature path and the unencrypted hash value (Mogul, & Van Hoff, 2002).

If content is hosted on a CDN, the URL of the content may not directly reference the domain of the site providing the content. An example of this would be content served from an *akamai.net* URL. Additionally, CDNs may move content around to optimize their network or balance load using HTTP redirects to point clients to the new location. Therefore, the verifiable content paths should be augmented by regular expressions (regexes) to which the full content URL will be compared. As content signatures are normally hosted with signed content, the path to the content signature will then be relative to the current content path.

It is feasible that a collection of related sites (for example, various domain names of a single organization) would want to share static content amongst them. Each domain name would have a different SSL certificate and public key; therefore the content would have to be signed by each private key. If the URL of the content signature is based solely on the content hash, there can only be one signature. To facilitate this, the path to the content signature should also include a fingerprint of the public key used to sign the content. This will allow shared content to have multiple signatures.

Furthermore, there are many sites that leverage external content. For example there are scripts to fetch advertising, site statistics providers, and public APIs from external sources. While a site has no direct control over external content, it would still be important to ensure that the content hasn't been tampered with during transit. Content signatures are normally hosted with signed content and it is not possible to place a content signature with external content. Therefore, it should be possible to retrieve, sign, and publish a signature of external content at an alternate location.

2.2 Client-Side Verification

The client retrieves the verifier configuration from the site and caches this information for a reasonable period of time. When verifiable content is requested, the client hashes the content received using an identical secure hashing function. The client makes a request for the signature based on the verification path plus the generated hash value. If the content has not been modified, the request should be made to the proper URL of the content's signature. The retrieved signature value, when verified with the appropriate public key, should return a value identical to the generated hash value.

2.3 Security Analysis

Simple content tampering will generate a different hash value and hence leads to an URL that does not have a valid verification path. An attacker can prevent access to such known content signature URL paths. If the verifier configuration has been fetched, this will cause the content to fail verification in the same way as modifying the content. An attacker can intercept requests based on the hash value of the modified content and generate replies. However, a correct signature cannot be generated based on the hash of the modified content without knowledge of the private key used to sign the content.

Preventing a request for the verifier configuration will prevent content verification from being attempted. For this reason, it is recommended that the configuration be made available and fetched via a secure channel such as SSL. Except an SSL Man-in-the-Middle attack (which can be mitigated

by certificate verification, and is beyond the scope of this work), the only way an attacker can interfere with SSL is to block SSL connections. This is likely to interfere with the functionality of the site (such as preventing login) and raise the level of attack suspicion.

There is one obvious method by which an attacker can transparently defeat verification: by allowing tampered content to positively verify by intercepting an unsecured request for the verifier configuration and then returning a configuration (and content signatures) based on an attacker-controlled key pair. Hence it is important that the configuration be always transferred over a secure channel.

2.4 Server Configuration

Content signing is performed when content is modified, or when a private key used to sign content is changed or added. This is accomplished by executing a server-side script as an administrative user. The script reads a configuration XML file formatted as follows: *keypair* indicates the certificate and matching private key used to sign content. The fingerprint of the public key will be used along with the *SHA-1* hash of the content to build the filename of the signature. *clientconfig* indicates the path and filename to generate the XML file the client will fetch to determine if content verification is in use. This should point to the root of the site, and be at a location accessible via HTTPS. A content tag defines a content set to verify. Multiple content tags can be specified to process multiple content paths. All content found under the *basepath* with a full path and filename matching regex will be processed. *baseurl* is the URL path at which *basepath* is served. The client will check the content URL against *baseurl* and perform a regex match to determine if the content should be verified. For serving content from a CDN, *baseurl* should be the static part of the CDN URL (not including the CDN domain information).

The content is signed with the private key, using the cryptographic parameters specified by the certificate (or by default *SHA-1* with *RSA* encryption). The filename is generated from the MD5-fingerprint of the public key and the *SHA-1* hash of the content. The signature is base64 encoded and saved using the generated filename in *signaturepath*. *signaturepath* is an absolute filesystem path if prefixed with "/" and appended to the path of the content being signed if it is not. In some cases, when content is external to the site or is served from a CDN, the URL to the signature may not be relative to the content URL. In this case *signatureurl* is used to indicate to the client the location for fetching the URL and will be treated by the client as relative or absolute in the same manner as *signaturepath*. If *signatureurl* is not present, the value in *signaturepath* will be used for *signatureurl*.

As presented in Figure 1, content located at */home/username/public_html/* and served from *http://localhost/~username/<content_path>/ content.ext* will have the signature files placed in */home/username/public_html/contentverify/*. The client will expect this to be served from *http:// localhost/~username/<content_path>/content- verify/*. The example is also signing content that is not being served from the site. This content has been fetched from www.externalsite.com/path/to/ external-content/ and placed in */home/username/ copy-of-external-content/*. The signatures of this content will be placed in */var/www/html/con- tentverify/*, which is served from the URL http:// localhost/contentverify/.

Figure 1. Server configuration

```
<?xml version='1.0' ?>
<verifycontent>
    <keypair>
            <certificate>file:///etc/ssl/
certs/ssl-cert-snakeoil.pem</certificate>
            <privatekey>file:///etc/ssl/
private/ssl-cert-snakeoil.key</privatekey>
        </keypair>
    <clientconfig>/home/tparker/public_html/
contentverify.xml</clientconfig>
        <content>
            <basepath>/home/tparker/
public_html</basepath>
            <baseurl>/~tparker/</baseurl>
            <regex>/content\/.*(htm|jpg|jpeg|
gif|css|js)/</regex>
            <signaturepath>contentverify/</
signaturepath>
        </content>
        <content>
            <basepath>/home/tparker/copy-of-
external-content/</basepath>
            <baseurl>www.externalsite.com/
path/to/external-content/</baseurl>
            <regex>/*\.js/</regex>
            <signaturepath>/var/www/html/
contentverify/</signaturepath>
            <signatureurl>/contentverify/</
signatureurl>
        </content>
</verifycontent>
```

2.5 Server Side Implementation

Server-side signing is accomplished by a PHP script, designed to be accessed as an administrative web page, or alternatively invoked from the shell. Command line invocation is important if, for security, the web server is allowed to read but not write to the web content. In the case, the script would be run as a privileged user using the syntax: *php -f sign.php <config.xml>*

2.6 Client Configuration

Verification-enabled web clients expect to find a configuration XML at a default location, and at-tempt to fetch this configuration via HTTPS. If a valid configuration is found, it should be cached for the domain of the URL in the address bar (the domain of the content URL may not match the address bar). The *publickey* used to sign the content, if present in the XML, is superseded by the public key of the site SSL certificate. If HTTPS is not available, HTTP can be used as a fallback. This is not optimal, as there is no integrity protection of the configuration. Furthermore, if HTTP is used, an SSL certificate is not available, and the *publickey* in the configuration XML must be used. The client configuration XML is in the following format as depicted in Figure 2.

Figure 2. Client configuration

```
<?xml version="1.0"?>
<verifyconfig>
        <publickey>


<fingerprint>5e1887471be913bbfe5442553868
8997</fingerprint>
                <n>7FRTBdhcT/
A07VraPQI3MjgxaR5omtyRMkgSY2VaYCzyDdWwRXM
nkzxnSO62VGSDeaNE0ComT/fv/9IKTvYhmSo/
mc7uTnZfZQlUmelJ/
lJNsaEIokZp3tHz3UwAU1QUvmk87ZgjbuMQ9dU2Vp
F4JxzrXP1VjWCrwRwBEVd8Fc8=</n>
                <e>AQAB</e>
        </publickey>
        <content>
                <baseurl>/</baseurl>
                <regex>content\/.*(html|jpg|
jpeg|gif|css|js)</regex>

        <signatureurl>contentverify/</
signatureurl>
        </content>
</verifyconfig>
```

Publickey is the fingerprint, modulus and public exponent of the public key used to sign the content. This should be taken from the public key of the site SSL certificate if SSL is in use. If client-side code has access to the server SSL certificate, the server certificate data should be preferred over the *publickey* data.

A content tag indicates a set of signed content. All content fetched from a path starting with *baseurl* (optionally including the hostname of externally content) with a full URL matching regex will be verified. The signature will be fetched from *signatureurl*, which is absolute from the site domain if prefixed by "/" and relative to the content path otherwise. The signature filename is composed of the fingerprint of the public key and the SHA-1 hash of the content being verified.

2.7 Client-Side Implementation

Client-side implementation in the simplest form would be a standalone application that would function in the same manner as the server-side verification script. This has limited use, as most often HTTP content is viewed in a web browser. For this reason, extending the functionality of a web browser to verify content is our choice for client-side verification. The Firefox 4.0 browser was chosen as the platform for client-side development as it provides a robust API for examining HTTP requests and responses.

2.8 Firefox Extension Details

The Firefox XUL API provides a mechanism for intercepting HTTP requests and responses. This is referred to as the observer service. Our code registers as a listener for events, and when an event of interest occurs, a method in our code is called. When we receive an event with the http-on-modify-request topic, this indicates an HTTP request has been initiated, but a connection to the server has not yet been established. If the request is an Initial Document (a request for an HTML page vs. a request for content such as images on the page), we examine the full host and domain of the site to determine if we have already have a Verifier object for this site. If not, we instantiate a new Verifier, which will attempt to fetch the configuration from https://site/contentverify.xml. The triggering HTTP request remains suspended until the configuration is fetched and parsed, or it is determined that a configuration does not exist.

The other event we get notified about is http-on-examine-response. This event occurs when the response from an HTTP request begins to arrive. When we receive this event, we check to see if we have a configured Verifier for the site. If so, we attach a *TracingListener-like StreamGrabber* to the request. The *StreamGrabber* copies the HTTP response content and calls back to the Verifier when the entire content is available. The Verifier hashes the content and tries to fetch a signature based on the configuration, the public key fingerprint, and the hash value. If a signature can be found, and decryption of the signature with the public key yields a value matching the hash of the content, the verification status of the content is set to true. JavaScript implementation of RSA cryptography Wu (2009) is extended to provide decryption using the public key and is used to decrypt the signature. The client-side extension presents a single user interface button to the user. When this buttons is activated, the status of all content for which verification has been attempted is involved as depicted in Figure 3.

3. PERFORMANCE

Performance testing was performed on an Ubuntu Linux 10.10 virtual server with 512 MB RAM, Apache 2.2.16, PHP 5.3.3. 1000 unique images were generated by using *pnmtext* to generate images consisting of digits from "000" through "999" inclusive. The bitmap images were converted to GIF images of approximately 100 bytes each. As

Figure 3. User interface

each image is created an *<IMG src='nnn.gif'>* HTML tag is generated and added to index.html.

The signing script is then executed to hash, sign, and write signature files for each of the 1000 images and the index page, with the time to execute the script measured by invoking it from the time command. This was repeated several times to determine an average run time of 6.115 seconds as depicted in Figure 4. Client side network overhead per signature fetch is approximately 900 bytes, and consists of an HTTP request of approximately 450 bytes, HTTP response headers of approximately 300 bytes, and a fixed 172 bytes of digital signature.

In comparison, SSL overhead varies by implementation. An estimated 6.5K is required to establish a new SSL session (this can vary substantially base on the certificate chain and ciphers negotiated) and resuming an established SSL session requires ~330 bytes. Each application data record incurs approximately 40 bytes of overhead. A signature fetch by the client involves no additional server resources other than what is required to return a small amount of content in response to an HTTP request. Client-side performance and comparison to SSL is beyond the scope of this work. The goal of content signing is primarily to reduce server load. Firefox extension API limitations require sub-optimal implementation choices such as performing RSA cryptography in JavaScript.

4. RELATED WORK

In our literature survey we have found a dearth of efforts to support resource constrained verifiability of HTTP request to ensure the security of distributed information systems. The effort that aligns closest is the HTTP response signing using DSSEC Dumitru, Giurgiu, Kleef, & Timmers (2010). *HTTPsig* uses public key cryptography for signing HTTP responses. It relies on a DNSSEC infrastructure to store and authenticate public keys without key material stored at a third party. However, the approach is not suited for resource constrained environments.

5. CONCLUSION

Cryptographic signing and verification of content is a proven method of detecting content tampering in transit. Signing is performed offline, not per-request, therefore is compatible with content distribution mechanisms and is suitable for resource-constrained or third-party distribution environments where SSL may not be suitable. The proposed approach has been verified as a browser extension for content verification on Mozilla Firefox 4.0 (Mozilla, 2011).

5.1 Future Work

Presently content signatures data is stored in a single signature per file. This requires the client to make multiple HTTP requests, each returning a small amount of data. If content is not expected to change frequently, it may be advantageous to place all content signatures by a specific *keypair* in one file. The client can retrieve and cache all

Figure 4. Content signing performance

Run		
1	real	0m 6s 152ms
	user	0m 5s 676ms
	sys	0m 0s 184ms
2	real	0m 6s 139ms
	user	0m 5s 752ms
	sys	0m 0s 200ms
3	real	0m 6s 146ms
	user	0m 5s 676ms
	sys	0m 0s 248ms
4	real	0m 6s 56ms
	user	0m 5s 720ms
	sys	0m 0s 212ms
5	real	0m 6s 73ms
	user	0m 5s 640ms
	sys	0m 0s 292ms
6	real	0m 6s 116ms
	user	0m 5s 612ms
	sys	0m 0s 256ms
7	real	0m 6s 142ms
	user	0m 5s 740ms
	sys	0m 0s 232ms
8	real	0m 6s 79ms
	user	0m 5s 580ms
	sys	0m 0s 252ms
9	real	0m 6s 41ms
	user	0m 5s 704ms
	sys	0m 0s 224ms
10	real	0m 6s 207ms
	user	0m 5s 788ms
	sys	0m 0s 216ms
Average		0m 6s 115ms
		0m 5s 689ms
		0m 0s 232ms

content signatures the first time a signature is required, refreshing all signatures when content newer than the current signature set is encountered. If content is expected to change frequently, one signature per file is likely more efficient. Moreover, client side implementation of signature verification is inefficient and limited by the Firefox extension API. Functionality such as active blocking of content failing verification cannot be reliably implemented. Additionally, SSL server certificate details are not available to the extension, necessitating a fallback to the public-key in the configuration XML. Adding support in the native code of the browser engine is required to fully implement content verification.

REFERENCES

Davidson, B. (2008, November). *Web caching and content delivery resources*. Retrieved June 2013 from http://www.web-caching.com

Dumitru, C., Giurgiu, A., Kleef, A., & Timmers, N. (2010). *HTTPsig: HTTP response signing using DNSSEC*. Retrieved June 2013 from http://tnc2010.terena.org/schedule/posters/pdf/100511170332niek_tnc2010_poster.pdf

Magnini, G. (2005, September). *Introduction to SSL*. Retrieved June 2013 from https://developer.mozilla.org/en/Introduction_to_SSL

Mogul, J., & Van Hoff, A. (2002, January). *Instance digests in HTTP*. Retrieved June 2013 from http://tools.ietf.org/html/rfc3230

Mozilla. (2011, February). *Intercepting page loads - MDC docs*. Retrieved June 2013 from https://developer.mozilla.org/en/XUL_School/Intercepting_Page_Loads

Odvarko, J. (2008, September). *NsITraceableChannel intercept HTTP traffic*. Retrieved June 2013 from http://www.softwareishard.com/blog/firebug/nsitraceablechannel-intercept-http-traffic

Ragen, S. (2011, January). *Tunisian government harvesting usernames and passwords*. Retrieved June 2013 from http://www.thetechherald.com/article.php/201101/6651/Tunisian-government-harvesting-usernames-and-passwords

Topolski, R. M. (2008, June). *NebuAd and partner ISPs: Wiretapping, forgery and browser hijacking*. Retrieved June 2013 from http://www.freepress.net/files/NebuAd_Report.pdf

Wikipedia. (2010, December). *SSL with virtual hosts using SNI*. Retrieved June 2013 from https://wiki.apache.org/httpd/NameBasedSSLVHostsWithSNI

Wu, T. (2009, September). *RSA and ECC in JavaScript*. Retrieved June 2013 from http://www-cs-students.stanford.edu/~tjw/jsbn/

KEY TERMS AND DEFINITIONS

HTTPSig: HTTP Response Signing Using DNSSEC.

Hypertext Transfer Protocol (HTTP): An application protocol for distributed, collaborative, hypermedia information systems. HTTP is the foundation of data communication for the World Wide Web.

Mozilla Firefox: A free and open source[1] web browser developed for Microsoft Windows, Mac OS X, and Linux coordinated by Mozilla Corporation and Mozilla Foundation. Firefox uses the Gecko layout engine to render web pages, which implements current and anticipated web standards.

PHP: PHP is a server-side scripting language designed for web development but also used as a general-purpose programming language. PHP is now installed on more than 244 million websites and 2.1 million web servers. Originally created by Rasmus Lerdorf in 1995, the reference implementation of PHP is now produced by The PHP Group. While PHP originally stood for *Personal

Home Page, it now stands for *PHP: Hypertext Preprocessor*, a recursive acronym.

Private Key Encryption: In cryptography, a private or secret key is an encryption/decryption key known only to the party or parties that exchange secret messages.

Public Key Encryption: A cryptographic system that uses two keys -- a *public key* known to everyone and a *private* or *secret key* known only to the recipient of the message.

Secure Sockets Layer (SSL): A cryptographic protocols that provide communication security over the Internet. TLS and SSL encrypt the seg-ments of network connections at the Application Layer for the Transport Layer, using asymmetric cryptography for key exchange, symmetric encryption for privacy, and message authentication codes for message integrity.

XML: Extensible Markup Language (XML) is a markup language that defines a set of rules for encoding documents in a format that is both human-readable and machine-readable. It is defined in the XML 1.0 Specification produced by the W3C, and several other related specifications, all gratis open standards.

Chapter 7
Amelioration of Anonymity Modus Operandi for Privacy Preserving Data Publishing

J. Indumathi
Anna University, India

ABSTRACT

The scientific tumultuous intonation has swept our feet's, of its balance and at the same time wheedled us to reach the take-off arena from where we can march equipped and outfitted into the subsequent century with confidence & self-assurance; by unearthing solutions for all information security related issues (with special emphasis on privacy issues). Examining various outstanding research problems that encompass to be embarked upon for effectively managing and controlling the balance between privacy and utility, the research community is pressurized to propose suitable elucidations. The solution is to engender several Privacy-Preserving Data Publishing (PPDP) techniques like Perturbation, swapping, randomization, cryptographic techniques etc., Amongst the various available techniques k-anonymity is unique in facet of its association with protection techniques that preserve the truthfulness of the data. The principal chip in of this sketch out comprises: 1) Motivation for this exploration for Amelioration Of Anonymity Modus Operandi For Privacy Preserving Data Mining; 2) investigation of well-known research approaches to PPDM; 3) argue solutions to tackle the problems of security threats and attacks in the PPDM in systems; 4) related survey of the various anonymity techniques; 5) exploration of metrics for the diverse anonymity techniques; 6) performance measures for the various anonymity techniques; and 7) contradistinguish the diverse anonymity techniques and algorithms.

DOI: 10.4018/978-1-4666-4789-3.ch007

Everyone designs who devises courses of action aimed atchanging existing situations into preferred ones — Herbert Simon (1996)

1. INTRODUCTION

Knowledge-based decision making is growing leaps and bounds owing to the fabulous escalation in technology development for collection of digital information by governments, corporations, and individuals. There is an incessant stipulation for data mining and data publishing. For example, licensed hospitals in California are mandatory to put forward detailed demographic data on every patient discharged from their facility (Carlisle et al. 2007). In June 2004, the Information Technology Advisory Committee released a report entitled *Revolutionizing Health Care through Information Technology* (President Information Technology Advisory Committee 2004). This pointed out the sharing of a nation-wide medical knowledge database through computer-assisted clinical decision support. Data publishing is equally omnipresent in other domains. For example, Netflix, a popular online movie rental service, recently published a data set containing movie ratings of 500,000 subscribers, in a drive to improve the accuracy of movie recommendations based on personal preferences (New York Times, Oct. 2, 2006); AOL published a release of query logs but quickly removed it due to the re-identification of a searcher (Barbaro and Zeller 2006).

2. IMPETUS FOR PPDP

Currently, the so-called privacy fortification modus operandi is deficient in privacy protection. They simply remove the explicit identifier of the record holders before releasing the data. L.Sweeney (2002) performed to show a privacy attack on William Weld, who is a former governor of the state of Massachusetts. By linking a voter list with some publicly available medical data on some shared quasi-identifier namely zip code, date of birth, and sex together with his medical information like diagnosis and medication he easily identified Weld's name. Weld's case is not an unexpected occurrence because L.Sweeney (2002) additionally pointed out that 87% of the U.S. population had reported characteristics that likely made them unique based on only such quasi-identifier.

This type of attack is called the *linking attack*, where the attacker needs two pieces of a priori knowledge: (1) the record holder is (likely to be) involved in the released data, and (2) the quasi-identifier of the record holder. By simple observation and common sense we can obtain this priori knowledge. For example, knowing his boss was absent for staying in a hospital, the attacker knew that his boss' medical information would appear in the released medical data from that hospital. For example, Maclean's (2005) was able to purchase months of phone logs of Jennifer Stoddart, who is the privacy commissioner of the federal government of Canada, from a U.S. data broker for US$200. The requested information returned within several hours and it even included an updated monthly statement which Stoddart herself had not received yet.

The current practice of privacy protection first and foremost focuses on policies and guidelines to confine the types of publishable data and on concords on the use and storage of sensitive data. This has *serious limitations* like either it deforms data excessively or requires a trust level that is impractically high in many data-sharing scenarios.

The need of the hour is to press the research communities into service to devise methods of privacy protection, which, simultaneously publishes the data in hostile environments and preserves it. We already have two approaches PPDM and PPDP. We will start to discuss the assumptions and desirable properties for PPDP, clarify the differences and requirements that distinguish PPDP from other related problems, and systematically summarize and evaluate different approaches to PPDP. *Privacy-preserving data publishing* (PPDP) provides methods and tools for publishing useful information while preserving data privacy and is focused on preventing this kind of linking attack.

3. PRIVACY-PRESERVING DATA PUBLISHING (PPDP)

The data and information collected from citizens under various schemes of the government can be classified as *sensitive and insensitive*. The sensitive data and information collected can be further subdivided into top secret, secret, confidential and restricted. The data collected is normalized, then subjected to analysis and modeling. Further this data and information which is stored for future purposes is called the *static data*. Sometimes data and information might be are collected over a period of time either continuously or discretely and this type is called the *dynamic data stream*. For example, the heart beat, pulse, temperature of an elderly person collected via embedded sensors. In this type of investigations, data mining has a broad sense, not essentially constrained to pattern mining or model building. For example, a sanatorium might collect data from patients and promulgates the patient records to an external AID's/T.B sanatorium center. The data mining conducted at the sanatorium center could be anything from a simple count of the number of men with AID's/T.B to a sophisticated cluster analysis.

There are two models of data publishers (Gehrke 2006). In the *untrusted* model, the data publisher is not trusted and may attempt to identify sensitive information from record owners. Various cryptographic solutions (Yang et al. 2005); anonymous communications (Chaum 1981; Jakobsson et al. 2002); and statistical methods (Warner 1965) were proposed to collect records anonymously from their owners without revealing the owners' identity.

In the *trusted* model, the data publisher is trustworthy and people are forced to provide their personal information to the data publisher; however, the trust is not transitive to the data beneficiary. In this research work, we assume the trusted model of data publishers and consider privacy issues cropping up in the data promulgating phase.

The following are several *desirable assumptions and properties* in practical data publishing:

We intend to classify the publishers as the proletarian *data publisher* and non proletarian *data publishers*. The proletarian *data* publisher is bothered only about the data collection and does not know who will be the data users. For example, the hospitals in California publish patient records on the Web (Carlisle et al. 2007). The hospitals do not know who the recipients are and how the recipients will use the data. The hospital publishes patient records because it is required by regulations (Carlisle et al. 2007) or because it supports general medical research, not because the hospital needs the result of data mining. Consequently, it is irrational to expect the data publisher to do more than anonymize the data for publication in such a state of affairs.

In other state of affairs, the data publisher who outsources the data to external data miners, where he could release a customized data set that preserves specific types of patterns for such a data mining task.

Non proletarian *data* publisher *can be an attacker*. For example, the data recipient, say remedy research companies, is a trustworthy entity; however, it is not easy to guarantee that all its employees are trustworthy as well. This assumption makes the PPDP problems and solutions very challenging.

Publish data, not the data mining result. PPDP emphasizes publishing data records about individuals (i.e., micro data). Clearly, this requirement is more stringent than publishing data mining results, such as classifiers, association rules, or statistics about groups of individuals.

For example, in the case of the Netflix data release, useful information may be some type of associations of movie ratings. However, Netflix decided to publish data records instead of such associations because the participants, with data records, have greater flexibility in performing the required analysis and data exploration, such as mining patterns in one partition but not in other partitions; visualizing the transactions containing a specific pattern; trying different modeling methods and parameters, and so forth. The assumption for publishing data and not the data mining results, is also closely related to the assumption of a non-expert data publisher. For example, Netflix does not know in advance how the interested parties might analyze the data. In this case, some basic "information nuggets" should be retained in the published data, but the nuggets cannot replace the data. The pharmaceutical researcher may need to examine the actual patient records to discover some previously unknown side effects of the tested drug (Emam 2006). If a promulgated record does not match to an existing patient in real life, it is difficult to deploy data mining results in the real world. In such state of affairs we have to think about an approach to preserve privacy and offer utility orthogonally.

Klosgen(1995) attempts Data anonymization to categorize data into fixed or variable intervals. The utility and privacy factor of the mystified data are reliant on the choice of the interval. The data is less useful for a large interval, while an interval that is too small does not provide enough privacy protection of the data. Sweeney (2002) proposes a generalization and suppression approach to attaining the required anonymity level: generalization substitutes a value with a less specific value, while suppression does not liberate a value at all. This pledges that each data item will communicate to at least k other entries, even if the records are unswervingly linked to external information. He categorizes sets of k similar records by a process of suppression and generalization, can preserve statistical information for small values of k, but

fail to preserve the original clusters because of the process of suppression and generalization. Data anonymization (k-anonymity) uses a generalization/suppression approach for data mystification. Generalization is the process of making the data less precise but still consistent.

Sweeney (2002) developed the *k-anonymity* framework in which the original data is altered so that the information for any entity cannot be distinguished from (k − 1) others. A diversity of fine-tuning of this framework has been projected since its preliminary manifestation. A few of the exertion (*e.g.*, (Sweeney (2002), K. LeFevre et al.(2005)) start from the original dataset and methodically or avariciously generalize it into one that is k-anonymous. A few begin with a wholly generalized dataset and methodically concentrate the dataset into one that is austerely k-anonymous. The predicament of k-anonymization is not merely to uncover any k-anonymization, but to, in its place, find one that is "good" or even "best" according to some proven cost metric. Each one of the preceding efforts provides its own unique cost metrics for sculpting advantageous anonymization. Cost metrics characteristically tally the information loss resulting from the suppression or generalizations applied.

4. THE ANONYMIZATION APPROACH

Anonymization is accomplished by suppressing (deleting) individual values from data records (*e.g.*, name and PAN numbers are removed), and/or reinstating each occasion of certain attribute values with a more general value (*e.g.*, the zip codes 600-025 might be replaced with 600*).

In the most basic form of PPDP(Benjamin et al., 2010), the data publisher has a table of the form *D*(Explicit Identifier, Quasi Identifier, Sensitive Attributes, Non-Sensitive Attributes), where Explicit Identifier is a set of attributes, such as name and social security number (SSN), containing information that explicitly identifies record owners; Quasi Identifier (QID) is a set of attributes that could potentially identify record owners; Sensitive Attributes consists of sensitive person-specific information such as disease, salary, and disability status; and Non-Sensitive Attributes contains all attributes that do not fall into the previous three categories (Burnett et al. 2003). The four sets of attributes are disjoint. Most works assume that each record in the table represents a distinct record owner.

(Benjamin et al., 2010), *Anonymization* (Cox 1980; Dalenius 1986) refers to the PPDP approach that seeks to hide the identity and/or the sensitive data of record owners, assuming that sensitive data must be retained for data analysis. Clearly, explicit identifiers of record owners must be removed. Even with all explicit identifiers being removed, Sweeney (2002a) showed a real-life privacy threat to William Weld, former governor of the state of Massachusetts. In Sweeney's example, an individual's name in a public voter list was linked with his record in a published medical database through the combination of zip code, date of birth, and sex. Each of these attributes does not uniquely identify a record owner, but their combination, called the *quasi-identifier* (Dalenius 1986), often singles out a unique or a small number of record owners. According to Sweeney (2002a), 87% of the U.S. population had reported characteristics that likely made them unique based on only such quasi-identifiers. In the above example, the owner of a record is re-identified by linking his quasi-identifier. To perform such *linking attacks*, the attacker needs two pieces of prior knowledge: the victim's record in the released data and the quasi-identifier of the victim. By simple observation and common sense we can obtain this priori knowledge.

To prevent linking attacks, the data publisher provides an anonymous table(Benjamin et al., 2010),*T*(*QID*', Sensitive Attributes, Non-Sensitive Attributes), *QID*' is an *anonymous* version of the original *QID* obtained by applying *anonymization operations* to the attributes in *QID* in the original table *D*. Anonymization operations hide some detailed information so that several records become indistinguishable with respect to *QID*'. Consequently, if a person is linked to a record through *QID*', that person is also linked to all other records that have the same value for *QID*', making the linking ambiguous. Alternatively, anonymization operations could generate synthetic data table *T* based on the statistical properties of the original table *D*, or add noise to the original table *D*. The *anonymization problem* is to produce an anonymous *T* that satisfies a given privacy requirement determined by the chosen privacy model and to retain as much data utility as possible. An *information metric* is used to measure the utility of an anonymous table. Note that the Non-Sensitive Attributes are published if they are important to the data mining task.

5. RELATED WORK

A closely related research area is *privacy-preserving data mining* (Aggarwal and Yu 2008c). The term, privacy-preserving data mining (PPDM), emerged in 2000 (Agrawal and Srikant 2000). The initial idea of PPDM *was* to extend traditional data mining techniques to work with the data modified to mask sensitive information. The key issues were how to modify the data and how to recover the data mining result from the modified data. The solutions were often tightly coupled with the data mining algorithms under consideration. In contrast, PPDP may not necessarily be tied to a specific data mining task, and the data mining task may be unknown at the time of data publishing. Furthermore, some PPDP solutions(Benjamin et al., 2010), emphasize preserving the data truthfulness at the record level as discussed earlier, but often PPDM solutions do not preserve such a property. In recent years, the term "PPDM" has evolved to cover many other privacy research problems, even though some of them may not directly relate to data mining.

In this survey, we do not aim to provide a comprehensive exposure of the official statistics methods because some well-brought-up surveys already exist (Adam and Wortman 1989; Domingo-Ferrer 2001; Moore 1996; Zayatz 2007).

In this survey, we review recent work on Anonymization approaches to privacy preserving data promulgating (PPDP) and provide our own insights into this topic as shown in Table 1 and 2. There are several fundamental differences between the recent work on PPDP and the previous work proposed by the official statistics community. Recent work (Benjamin et al., 2010), on PPDP considers background attacks, inference of sensitive attributes, generalization, and various notions of data utility measures, but the work of the official statistics community does not.

6. ARCHITECTURE OF THE PROPOSED SYSTEM

As depicted in Figure 1, our framework encompasses a transactional database (modelled into a text database), a set of algorithms used for flustering data from the database, a transaction retrieval engine for fast retrieval. We bring out a diagrammatic representation of the architecture as shown in Figure 1 and 2 involved in the proposed architecture.

Data concealing is used to limit the revelation of data by applying a mystification process to the originally collected data and publishing it the public. We refer synonymously the Mystification process of the original data as data befuddling; the terms concealed data set represents the output of such mystification; the concealed data set refers both to the published data and the information provided to the users about the mystification.

Data collectors collects data from data providers. These heterogeneous data can be protected by limiting the data access using password, firewalls etc., Owing to the versatility of the data mining tasks, any one best suitable technique can be selected from a family of privacy-preserving data mining (PPDM) methods using the technique selector. This technique is used for protecting privacy before data are shared. The technique selector can either use the PPDM Ontology to select the desired technique. The algorithms are

Table 1. Amelioration of anonymity algorithms for privacy preserving data publishing

Author/ Year	Name of the Algorithm	Mechanism Involved
Hundepool and Willenborg/1996	μ-argus	Sub tree Generation, Cell Suppression
Sweeney/1998	Data fly	Full-Domain Generation, Record Suppression
Samarati/2001	Binary search algorithm	Full-Domain Generation, Record Suppression
Sweeney/2002	MinGen algorithm	Full-Domain Generation, Record Suppression
Iyengar/2002	Genetic Algorithm	Sub tree Generation, Cell Suppression
Wang/2004	Bottom-Up Generalization	Sub tree Generalization
Fung/2005	Top down specialization(TDS)	sub tree generalization, value suppression
LeFevre/2005	Incognito	Full-Domain Generation, Record Suppression
Bayardo and Agrawal/2005	K-Optimize algorithm	sub tree generalization, record suppression
LeFevre/2006	Mondrian Multidimensional	Multidimensional Generation
Xu/2006	Bottom-up and Down Greedy	Cell generalization
Aggarwal/2006	Gather Clustering	Clustering
Aggarwal and Yu/2008	Condensation algorithm	Condensation

Table 2. Amelioration of anonymity modus operandi for privacy preserving data publishing

Name of the Privacy Preserving Modus Operandi /Year/ Authors	Characteristics/ Features	Advantages	Disadavantages
k-anonymity(1998) Samarati and L.sweeney	• if one record in the table has some QID, at least k-1 other record also have the value QID • QID should have at least k minimum group size value	individual record hidden in a crowd of size k	• Identifying a proper QID is a hard problem. • Finding a k-anonymity solution with suppressing fewest cells
l-diversity(2006) Machanavajjhala	An equivalence class is said to have l-diversity if there are at least l"well-represented" values for the sensitive attribute. i.e. l-diversity requires every QID group to contain atleast l "well represented" sensitive values	it prevents homogeneity and background knowledge attack.	• l-diversity may be difficult and unnecessary to achieve. • l-diversity is insufficient to prevent attribute disclosure(i.e.it tends to skewness and similarity attack). • Distinct l-diversity does not prevent probabilistic attack.
Confidence bounding(2006) Kewang	quasi-identifier(QID → s, h) bounds the attacker's confidence of inferring the sensitive value s in any group on QID to the maximum h, where s is sensitive attribute and h is the threshold	it allows the flexibility for the data publisher to specify a different threshold h for each combination of QID and s according to the perceived sensitivity of inferring s from a group on QID.	It does not prevent attribute linkage attack.
(α, k)-Anonymity(2006) Raymond Chi-Wing Wong	it protects both identifications and relationships to sensitive information in data and to limit the confidence of the implications from the quasi-identifier to a sensitive value (attribute) to within α	it avoids the sensitive information which is inferred by strong implications.	
(X,Y)-Privacy(2006) Ke Wang	(X,Y)-anonymity states that each group on X has at least k distinct values on Y. However, if some Y values occur more frequently than others, the probability of inferring a particular Y value can be higher than 1/k. To address this issue (X,Y)-Privacy comes, which combines both (X,Y)-anonymity and confidence bounding. X and Y are disjoint set of attributes.		
Personalized privacy(2006) Xiao and Tao	• It allows each record to specify there one privacy level. • Each sensitive attribute have taxonomy tree and each record owner specifies guarding node in this tree	Guarding node is specified by each record by its owner to his own tolerance of sensitivity.	
Multi R k-anonymity(2007) M. Ercan Nergiz	it focus on multi relational tables whereas k-anonymity satisfies only on single tables	Multi R k-anonymity emphasize that the k-anonymization is applied at record owner level.	While converting the private data to multi-dimensional data it fails to prevent individual identity.
(k, e)-Anonymity(2007) Zhang	It address the numerical sensitive attributes		It leads to proximity attack
t-closeness(2007) Tiancheng Li	An equivalence class is said to have t-closeness if the distance between the distribution of a sensitive attribute in this class and the distribution of the attribute in the whole table is no more than a threshold t.	• It prevents skewness attack. • It provides efficient closeness by using earth mover distance.	• It lacks in flexibility specifying different protect levels for different sensitive value. • EMD function is not suitable for preventing attribute linkage on numerical sensitive attribute • It greatly degrades the data utility because it requires the distribution of sensitive attributes to be the same in all QID groups.

used for modifying the unique facts by some means, with the intention that the private data and private knowledge linger private even subsequent to the mining process. Metrics is used to find the measure of these techniques. The input to this block is unpreserved data whereas its output is privacy preserved and befuddled data. This is given as an input and is subject to any of the data mining techniques.

Figure 1. The PPDP Framework: High-level

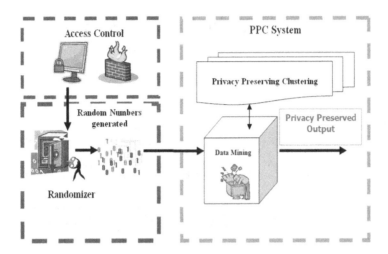

Figure 2. Modus operandi for selecting the best anonymity PPDP technique for an application-high level diagram

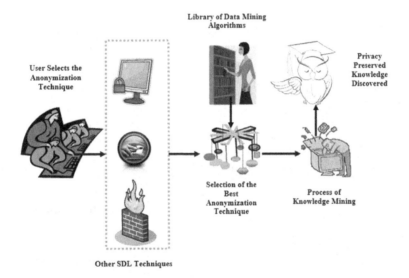

7. EVALUATION AND EXPERIMENTAL RESULTS

- **Data Utility:** The percentage of similarity between the data mined results from original data and randomized data.
- **Data Privacy:** For quantifying privacy provided by a method, we use a measure based on how closely the original values of a modified attribute can be estimated.

If it can be estimated with c % confidence that a value x lies in the interval $(X_1; X_2)$, then the interval width $(X_2 - X_1)$ defines the amount of privacy at c % confidence level.

The graphs in Figure 3, Figure 4, Figure 5, and Figure 6 show all the recordings of all the various anonymity approaches that have been implemented.

Figure 3. Elapsed time vs. quasi-identifier size

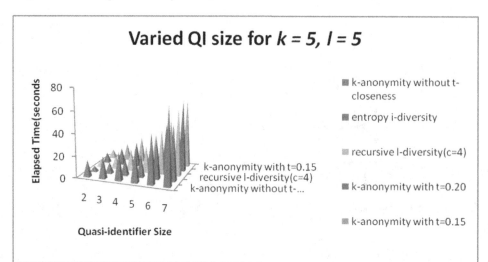

Figure 4. Elapsed time vs. parameter

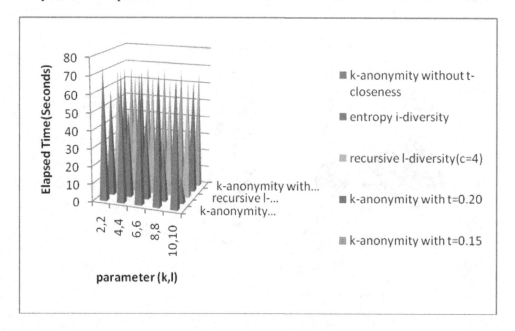

8. CONCLUSION AND FUTURE WORK

We will be able to understand the potential impact of the various anonymity PPDM Techniques only when we model in full-scale applications. We do deem, nonetheless that our argument should make others vigilant to the perils intrinsic to heuristic approaches to anonymity PPDM Limitations. Heuristic methods are based on assumptions which are tacit and not implicit. If for a given data anonymity PPDM limitation problem, the

Figure 5. Min Average vs. parameter(k,l)

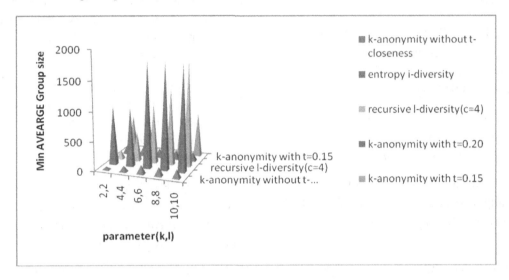

Figure 6. Utility vs. privacy

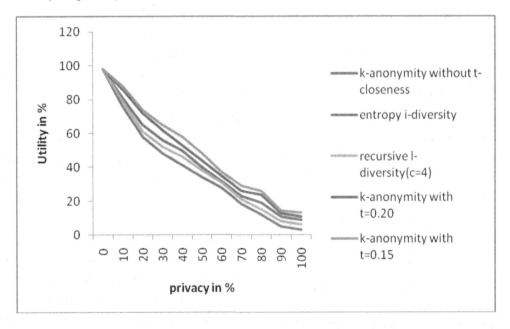

execution of model-based solutions emerges to be too complicated or too costly to carry out, heuristic approaches need to be incorporated with a meticulous analysis aimed at probing the extent to which the approach formalizes rational group inclination structures and/or data user behaviors. This will escort logically to such issues as the incorporation of priors and utilities which need special attention.

REFERENCES

Adam, N. R., & Wortman, J. C. (1989). Security control methods for statistical databases. *ACM Computing Surveys, 21*(4), 515–556. doi:10.1145/76894.76895

Aggarwal, C. C., & Yu, P. S. (2008). Privacy preserving data mining: Models and algorithms. *Advances in Database Systems, 34*(22), 513.

Agrawal & Srikant. (2000). Privacy preserving data mining. *Proceedings of the ACM SIGMOD Conference on Management of Data, 15* (3), 439–450.

Barbaro & Zeller. (2006). A face is exposed for AOL searcher no. 4417749. *New York Times, 42* (4), 248–263.

Carlisle, D. M., Rodrian, M. L., & Diamond, C. L. (2007). *California inpatient data reporting manual, medical information reporting for California* (5th ed.). Office of Statewide Health Planning and Development.

Clark, C. F. (1978). The introduction of statistical noise to utility company data on a micro data tape with that data matched annual housing survey data. *Draft Project Report. Bureau of Census, 13*, 321–327.

Dalenius, T. (1986). Finding a needle in a haystack - Or identifying anonymous census record. *Journal of Official Statistics, 2*(3), 329–336.

Domingo-Ferrer, J., & Torra, V. (2001). Confidentiality, disclosure and data access: Theory and practical applications for statistical agencies. *Pre-Proceedings of ETK-NTTS, 179*(11), 1663–1677.

Fuller. (1993). Masking procedures for microdata disclosure limitation. *Journal of Official Statistics, 9*(2), 383–406.

Fung, Wang, Chen, & Yu. (2010). Privacy-preserving data publishing: A survey of recent developments. *ACM Computing Surveys, 42*(4). doi:10.1145/1749603.1749605

Gitanjali, J., Banu, Mary, Indumathi, & Uma, G.V. (2007). An agent based burgeoning framework for privacy preserving information harvesting systems. *Computer Science and Network Security, 7*(11), 268–276.

Greenberg, B. (1990). Disclosure avoidance research at the census bureau. In *Proceedings of Census Bureau Annual Research Conference.* Washington, DC: US Government.

Indumathi, J., & Uma, G. V. (2007a). Customized privacy preservation using unknowns to stymie unearthing of association rules. *Journal of Computer Science, 3*(12), 874–881.

Indumathi, J., & Uma, G. V. (2007b). Using privacy preserving techniques to accomplish a secure accord. *Computer Science and Network Security, 7*(8), 258–266.

Indumathi, J., & Uma, G. V. (2008a). An aggrandized framework for genetic privacy preserving pattern analysis using cryptography and contravening-conscious knowledge management systems. *Molecular Medicine and Advance Sciences, 4*(1), 33–40.

Indumathi, J., & Uma, G. V. (2008b). A new flustering approach for privacy preserving data fishing in tele-health care systems. *International Journal of Healthcare Technology and Management, 9*(5), 495–516. doi:10.1504/IJHTM.2008.020201

Indumathi, J., & Uma, G.V. (2008c). A novel framework for optimized privacy preserving data mining using the innovative desultory technique. *International Journal of Computer Applications in Technology, 35*(2/3/4), 194 – 203.

Indumathi, J., & Uma, G. V. (2008d). A Panglossian solitary-skim sanitization for privacy preserving data archaeology. *International Journal of Electrical and Power Engineering, 2*(3), 154–165.

Kim & Winkler. (1995). Masking microdata files. In *Survey Research Methods Section* (pp. 114–119). American Statistical Association.

Klosgen, W. (1995). Anonymization techniques for knowledge discovery in databases. In *Proceedings of the First International Conference on Knowledge and Discovery in Data Mining*, (pp. 186-191). Academic Press.

LeFevre. DeWitt, & Ramakrishnan. (2005). Incognito: Efficient full-domain k-anonymity. In *Proceedings of the 2005 ACM SIGMOD International Conference on Management of Data (SIGMOD'05)*. Baltimore, MD: ACM.

Maclean's J. Gatehouse V. (2005). *You are exposed* (*Canadian Ed.*, pp. 26–29). Maclean's.

Moore, R. A. Jr. (1996). *Controlled data-swapping techniques for masking public use microdata sets*. Washington, DC: US Bureau of Census.

President Information Technology Advisory Committee. (2004). *Revolutionizing health care through information technology*. Washington, DC: Executive Office of the President of the United States.

Simon, H. A. (1996). *The sciences of the artificial*. Cambridge, MA: MIT Press.

Sweeney. (2002). k-Anonymity: A model for protecting privacy. International Journal on Uncertainty, Fuzziness and Knowledge-Based Systems, 10(5), 557-570.

Zayatz, L. (2007). Disclosure avoidance practices and research at the U.S. census bureau: An update. *Journal of Official Statistics, 23*(2), 253–265.

Chapter 8
Web Service Security:
Authentication and Authorization Technologies

Elena M. Torroglosa García
University of Murcia, Spain

Gabriel López Millán
University of Murcia, Spain

ABSTRACT

The high adoption in daily lives of services offered by the Web 2.0 has opened a wide field for the prolif-eration of new Web-based services and applications. Social networks, as the main exponent of this new generation of services, require security systems to ensure end user authentication and access control to shared information. Another feature that is becoming increasingly important in these scenarios is the delegation of controlled access between the different API (Application Programming Interfaces) to inte-grate services and information. The safe use of these Web services requires end user security credentials and different authentication and authorization technologies. This chapter provides an introduction to the most relevant protocols and standards in the area of Web service security, which are able to provide authentication and authorization mechanisms.

INTRODUCTION

Today, end users make use of a wide variety of Internet services. For each, a registration process is required in order to define an end user's service profile. This implies the management of new usernames and passwords, and a large amount of, usually, private information.

The Cambridge Dictionary Cambridge University Press (Cambridge University Press, 2012)

defines identity as "who a person is, or the qualities of a person or group which make them different from others". The reality is that anyone who wants to make use of an Internet service usually needs to share some private information with the service provider, be it a real need (in the case of address and billing information) or a requirement of the business model (for example, in the case of being asked for gender and age). These users need tools to make the management of their mul-

DOI: 10.4018/978-1-4666-4789-3.ch008

tiple identities in the network easier. An identity management system ought to provide end users with these mechanisms, from the management of simple service accounts, to offering value-added functions such as ensuring privacy, advanced access control or Single Sign On (SSO).

When organizations wish to share their resources among their registered end users, the concept of identity federations appears. Identity federations define how, making use of trust relationships, end users of any of the involved organizations are able to request access to the services offered by the rest. Some identity management systems like Higgins (The Eclipse Foundation, 2012) and Shibboleth ("Shibboleth Project," 2012) provide end users the ability to homogenize the use of authentication credentials (typically username and password) to deal with identity federations.

When an end user wants to access a Web service, the service provider needs to confirm that she is a valid end user (and usually identified as such) on its system. To carry out the authentication process, the service provider usually makes use of an identity management system, which is responsible for retrieving the end user's required information and verifying the authenticity of her identity. Examples of those authentication mechanisms are HTTP Basic and Digest (Franks et al., 1999), Forms Based (Oracle Group, 2010), digital certificates (TLS) (Tim Dierks, 2008), etc. If the authentication is successful, it generates an authentication proof, also called authentication token, to the service provider. With this token, the service provider will be sure that the end user has been authenticated in the system and can access the protected resource. Another relevant concept is the Single Sign-On (SSO) (Määttänen, 2002). SSO allows end users to access different service providers within an identity federation, with authentication only required the first time they access during a session lifetime. This mechanism

provides significant advantages, such as saving re-authentication time and improving the user experience.

The access control system of a service provider may require, beside end user authentication, an authorization process. Authorization makes use of additional information in order to decide whether the end user meets the requirements imposed by the service or not. By definition, authorization is the process that determines to what resources of a service provider the end user has permission to access. Furthermore, access control (Damiani, Vimercati, & Samarati, 2005) is the process of gathering information and taking decisions about service delivery. For this, the service provider must contact the identity management system and request end user attributes. In this case, the amount of information gathered depends on the data the end user has added to her identity profile, and the available attributes disclosure policies.

This section has introduced the existence of different types of entities: A service provider is an organization willing to offer Internet services, including Web, email, multimedia data, e-commerce or network access; providers dealing with end user's identity are known identity providers, which can be classified depending on the specific role they perform. For example, an authentication provider is responsible for demonstrating that an end user is really who she claims to be, offering an authentication token as proof of the successful authentication. Beside, the attribute provider is the responsible for dealing with additional end user information (attributes).

The following sections introduce some of the most relevant technologies that can be used today to deploy identity management systems and identity federations for Web services, providing frameworks to manage end user's authentication and authorization requirements for fine grain access control scenarios.

MECHANISMS TO ENSURE SECURITY AT WEB SERVICES

This section provides a survey of the most important protocols and standards in the area of authentication and authorization security mechanisms for Web services. In order to facilitate the establishment of similarities and differences between those mechanisms, we propose a running example: a traditional end user of Web services (Alice) is registered in an identity provider (www.idp.com). She wants to buy the latest CD of her favourite music group in a digital music store (www.music-store.com), and to receive it at home.

It is worth noting that, in order to ensure the confidentiality of communications between those entities, Web technologies delegate on the security transport layer that protects the communication channel with protocols such as TLS 1.0 (T. Dierks & Allen, 1999) or SSL3.0 (Freier, Karlton, & Kocher, 2011).

SAML (Security Assertion Markup Language)

SAML is an open standard (Hal Lockhart & Campbell, 2008) developed and approved by the OASIS SSTC ("OASIS Security Services (SAML) Technical Committee," 2012). It makes use of the XML language (Bray, Paoli, Sperberg-McQueen, Maler, & Yergeau, 2008) to exchange authentication and authorization data between security domains, usually between an identity provider and a service provider. SAML dates from January 2001, when the OASIS SSTC met for first time with the aim of defining an XML framework for exchanging authentication and authorization information. The current version (v2.0) was released in March 2005. As said before, the specification recommends, and in some cases requires, a variety of security mechanisms such as the use of SSL 3.0 or TLS 1.0 for security at the transport level.

SAML defines three main entities, Figure 1. The User is the one who wants to access a resource or Web service, and therefore needs to be authenticated and, optionally, authorized. The Service Provider (SP) is responsible for offering the service to the User, and relies on the Identity Provider (IdP) for the task of her identification and authentication. Besides the authentication process, the Identity Provider could provide service providers additional information (role, age, etc.) about the User in the form of attribute statements. Following the running example, Alice plays the User's role, the Identity Provider represents the www.idp.com entity and the Service Provider represents the music store service (www.music-store.com).

SAML defines the exchange of authentication, attributes and authorization decisions statements between the entities involved. Authentication statements, issued by Identity Providers, inform the Service Provider that the end user has, by means of a specific authentication method, been successfully authenticated. Attribute statements provide name-value pairs with information associated with the subject (User) that can be used by the Service Provider to take the final access control decision. Authorization decision statements (deprecated in v2.0) assert that the subject has been authorized to perform a certain action on a specific resource based on some kind of evidences.

Figure 1. Relations between SAML entities

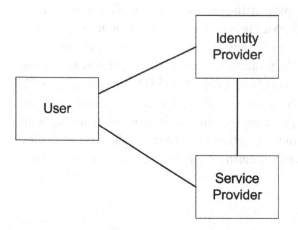

To request these statements, the standard defines several protocols (Scott Cantor, Kemp, Philpott, & Maler, 2005) based on a request-response scheme, such as the *Assertion Query and Request Protocol*, the *Artifact Resolution Protocol* or the *Single Logout Protocol*, which is the most relevant is the *Authentication Request Protocol*.

In addition, SAML defines several bindings (Hughes et al., 2005) which describe how to transport a SAML message on a standard format message using several communication protocols. Specifically, the *HTTP Redirect POST binding* defines the message exchange in base64-encoded format over HTTP redirections.

Finally, SAML defines several profiles (S. Cantor, Hirsch, Kemp, Philpott, & Maler, 2005), by defining specific sets of rules and syntax restrictions to solve specific business problems, such as the definition of constraints on the contents of SAML statements, protocols, and bindings; for example, the *Web Browser SSO Profile*, the *Assertion Query/Request Profile* and the *Artifact Resolution Profile*.

The authentication flow described in Figure 2 represents the *SAML Web Browser SSO Profile*. It starts when the User (Alice) wants to access (1) through her User Agent (for example, a Web browser) to the Service Provider (SP) (www. music-store.com). Alice is not authenticated, so SP initiates a discovery process (2) in order to ascertain know which her Identity Provider (IdP) is. This process is usually based on a MetaData service (S. Cantor, Moreh, Philpott, & Maler, 2005), known by the entities involved. Once SP knows about the Identity Provider, it issues (3) an explicit SAML authentication request, *AuthnRequest* (Figure 3) to the IdP, making use of a Web redirection, which includes some relevant information such as the request's issuer (*<saml:Issuer>*). The IdP (4) authenticates Alice (the method is out of the scope of the standard), and responds (5) to the SP using a XHTML form inside a Web redirection

Figure 2. SAML web browser SSO profile

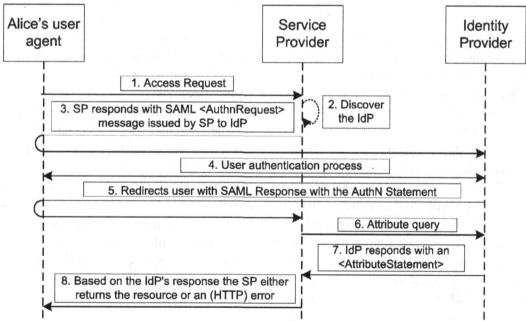

Figure 3. SAML authentication request

```
<samlp:AuthnRequest
    xmlns:samlp="urn:oasis:names:tc:SAML:2.0:protocol"
    xmlns:saml="urn:oasis:names:tc:SAML:2.0:assertion"
    ID="identifier_1"
    Version="2.0"
    IssueInstant="2012-04-05T110:05:31Z"
    AssertionConsumerServiceIndex="1">
    <saml:Issuer>https://www.music-store.com/SAML2</saml:Issuer>
    <samlp:NameIDPolicy
      AllowCreate="true"
      Format="urn:oasis:names:tc:SAML:2.0:nameid-format:transient"/>
</samlp:AuthnRequest>
```

that contains the SAML authentication statement (*AuthnStatement*).

Figure 4 shows an example of an Authentication Response that includes the *Subject* inside the authentication statement. It is worth noting that the *NameID* field, that represents the end user identifier, is a transient pseudonym and not the real identity for privacy reasons. It is digitally signed by IdP and validated by SP, so a trust relationship must exist between both entities. It algo contains the SP destination URI (www.music-store.com), the assertion's issuer (in this case: Alice's IdP) and the successful status of the authentication process, among other things.

The SP requests (6) additional User attributes (i.e. Alice's preferred language, age, entitlement, or postal address) from the IdP in order to take an access authorization decision. The IdP checks who is making the request and who is the subject (Alice's pseudonym). Then, it prepares the requested attributes and responds to the SP with a SAML *AttributeStatement* sentence (7). Using this information, the SP responds to Alice, allowing or denying her access to the desired service.

In SAML, the concept of SSO is managed with the help of HTTP (Barth, 2011). From the point of view of the IdP, if further authentication requests from the same user are received during the validity period of the authentication statement previously generated, she is not asked for a new authentication process. HTTP-cookies are used to manage an HTTP session between the IdP and the User.

This standard is widely used in federated environments of universities and research networks like Cisco Networking Academy (Cisco, 2012), or in large Web applications providers like Google (Google Developers, 2012). In addition, there are multiple implementations of this mature standard, such as the Shibboleth package ("Shibboleth Project," 2012).

WS-Security and WS-Trust

WS-* is a family of Web services specifications developed by the OASIS WSS TC ("OASIS Web Services Security (WSS) TC," 2006). The aim of this specification is to provide a flexible set of mechanisms that can be used to construct a range of security protocols. The WS-Security specification (Lawrence & Kaler, 2006d) defines a flexible and feature-rich extension to SOAP (Gudgin et al., 2007), specifying how integrity and confidentiality on Web messages can be enforced and the communication of different kind of security tokens. The standard mainly focuses on the use of XML Signature (Eastlake, Reagle, Solo, Hirsch, & Roessler, 2008) and XML Encryption (Eastlake & Reagle, 2002) to provide end-to-end security, but by itself, it does not provide a complete security solution for Web services. So it is complemented with specifications like WS-Trust (Nadalin, 2009), WS-SecureConversation (Lawrence & Kaler, 2007a) and WS-SecurityPolicy

Figure 4. SAML authentication response

```
<samlp:Response
  xmlns:samlp="urn:oasis:names:tc:SAML:2.0:protocol"
  xmlns:saml="urn:oasis:names:tc:SAML:2.0:assertion"
  ID="identifier_2" InResponseTo="identifier_1" Version="2.0"
  IssueInstant="2012-04-05T10:05:381Z"
  Destination="https://www.music-store.com/SAML2/SSO/POST">
  <saml:Issuer>https://wwww.idp.com/SAML2</saml:Issuer>
  <samlp:Status>
    <samlp:StatusCode Value="urn:oasis:names:tc:SAML:2.0:status:Success"/>
  </samlp:Status>
  <saml:Assertion
    xmlns:saml="urn:oasis:names:tc:SAML:2.0:assertion"
    ID="identifier_3" Version="2.0" IssueInstant="2012-04-05T10:05:381Z">
    <saml:Issuer>https://www.idp.com/SAML2</saml:Issuer>
    <ds:Signature xmlns:ds="http://www.w3.org/2000/09/xmldsig#">...</ds:Signature>
    <saml:Subject>
      <saml:NameID format="urn:oasis:names:tc:SAML:2.0:nameid-format:transient">
        3f7b3dcf-1674-4ecd-92c8-1544f346baf8
      </saml:NameID>
      <saml:SubjectConfirmation Method="urn:oasis:names:tc:SAML:2.0:cm:bearer">
        <saml:SubjectConfirmationData
          InResponseTo="identifier_1"
          Recipient="https://www.music-store.com/SAML2/SSO/POST"
          NotOnOrAfter="2012-04-05T110:15:381Z"/>
      </saml:SubjectConfirmation>
    </saml:Subject>
    <saml:Conditions
      NotBefore="2012-04-05T10:05:381Z" NotOnOrAfter="2012-04-05T10:15:381Z">
      <saml:AudienceRestriction>
        <saml:Audience>https://www.music-store.com/SAML2</saml:Audience>
      </saml:AudienceRestriction>
    </saml:Conditions>
    <saml:AuthnStatement AuthnInstant="2012-04-05T10:03:381Z"
     SessionIndex="identifier_3">
     <saml:AuthnContext>
        <saml:AuthnContextClassRef>
          urn:oasis:names:tc:SAML:2.0:ac:classes:PasswordProtectedTransport
        </saml:AuthnContextClassRef>
      </saml:AuthnContext>
    </saml:AuthnStatement>
  </saml:Assertion>
</samlp:Response>
```

(Lawrence & Kaler, 2007b). This section focuses on WS-Security and WS-Trust.

WS-Trust specification defines a Web service security model (Figure 5) that allows security tokens to be exchanged in order to enable the issuance and dissemination of credentials within different trusted organizations. The main entity of this model is the Security Token Service (STS), which is responsible for issuing, renewing and validating security tokens based on evidences in which the STS trusts. The use of different kinds of security tokens such as SAML sentences (Lawrence & Kaler, 2006a), Kerberos tickets (Lawrence & Kaler, 2006b), or X.509 certificates (Lawrence & Kaler, 2006c) are defined in the WS-Security specification.

Figure 5 shows the main entities in this specification. In order to establish a trusted communication between a Web Service and STS, the Web Service requires some, proof such as a signature, or the proof of possession of a security token (or a set of them). The token generation process is usually carried out by the STS. The Requestor entity represents a service or client that wants to access a Web Service. This Web Service can require the incoming request message to prove the possession

Figure 5. WS-Trust security token service scheme

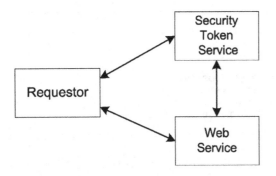

of a set of claims or statements. If the Requestor does not have the necessary token to prove the claims required by the Web Service, it contacts the appropriate authority (STS) and requests the specific token. The message formats to request and reply for the issuance, the validation and the renewing of security tokens are defined by the WS-Trust specification.

In this case, the comparison with the running example is not so immediate. Alice (Requestor) wants to access www.music-store.com (Web Service). This service requires a specific access or authentication token that Alice does not have. Alice accesses the www.idp.com (STS), in order to obtain the appropriate token. Alice can then provide www.music-store.com with the proof needed to gain the service access.

The STS issuance token process, Figure 6 - A, uses the *RequestSecurityToken* (*RST*) request (1) that includes details (Figure 7) about the type of the required token (*mySpecialToken*), the type of request *(Issue)* and other information that might be needed. Besides, the STS may require the authentication of the end users, so the request can include end user credentials (i.e. username and password) or another authentication information at SOAP Security Header, depending on the specific STS policies (outside of the scope of the specification). The *RequestSecurityTokenResponse* (*RSTR*) message (2) provides the security token and other related information such as the type (*TokenType*) and the request context as is shown in Figure 8.

The second part of Figure 6 - B shows how token is used to gain access to the Web Service (WS). The Requestor sends a *HTTP Request* (3) to the service including the new token. Now, the WS can send it to the STS in order to check whether it is valid or not (4). The validation binding has a similar pattern to the previous messages. In this case (Figure 9), the RST request includes the specific *RequestType* and the *ValidateTarget* element that the reference to the token typically contains. After being evaluated by the STS, it replies (5) to the WS with the RSTR indicating the token status (Figure 10), including a specific code (*valid* or *invalid*) and, optionally, the reason as a human-readable text.

Figure 6. WS-Trust STS detailed interaction flow

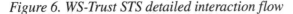

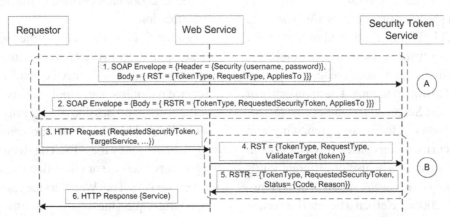

Figure 7. Request Security Token for a new token

```
<S11:Envelope xmlns:S11="..." xmlns:wsu="..." xmlns:wsse="..."
        xmlns:xenc="..." xmlns:wst="...">
    <S11:Header>
        ...
        <wsse:Security>
            <xenc:ReferenceList>...</xenc:ReferenceList>
            <xenc:EncryptedData Id="encUsername">...</xenc:EncryptedData>
            <ds:Signature xmlns:ds="...">
                ...
             <ds:KeyInfo>
                <wsse:SecurityTokenReference>
                    <wsse:Reference URI="#myToken"/>
                </wsse:SecurityTokenReference>
             </ds:KeyInfo>
            </ds:Signature>
        </wsse:Security>
        ...
    </S11:Header>
    <S11:Body wsu:Id="req">
        <wst:RequestSecurityToken>
            <wst:TokenType>
                http://www.idp.com/mySpecialToken
            </wst:TokenType>
            <wst:RequestType>
                http://docs.oasis-open.org/ws-sx/ws-trust/200512/Issue
            </wst:RequestType>
        </wst:RequestSecurityToken>
    </S11:Body>
</S11:Envelope>
```

Figure 8. Request Security Token response

```
<wst:RequestSecurityTokenResponse xmlns:wst="...">
    <wst:TokenType>http://example.org/mySpecialToken</wst:TokenType>
    <wst:RequestedSecurityToken>...token value...</wst:RequestedSecurityToken>
    <wst:Lifetime>...</wst:Lifetime>
    ...
</wst:RequestSecurityTokenResponse>
```

Figure 9. Request Security Token for validation

```
<wst:RequestSecurityToken xmlns:wst="...">
    <wst:TokenType>...</wst:TokenType>
    <wst:RequestType>
        http://docs.oasis-open.org/ws-sx/ws-trust/200512/Validate
    </wst:RequestType>
    <wst:ValidateTarget>... </wst:ValidateTarget>
    ...
</wst:RequestSecurityToken>
```

The proposed WS-Trust architecture does not consider the request for additional data (attribute). However, it is open to the use of access control policies in order to manage the different aspects to determine the requirements to be satisfied by the Requestor. Moreover, to make use of SSO mechanisms in federations, it is necessary to incorporate the WS-Federation (H. Lockhart, Andersen, Bohren, & others, 2006) specification, which extends the functionality of the STS and

Figure 10. Request Security Token response for validation

```
<wst:RequestSecurityTokenResponse xmlns:wst="..."  >
    <wst:TokenType>...</wst:TokenType>
    <wst:RequestedSecurityToken>...</wst:RequestedSecurityToken>
    ...
    <wst:Status>
        <wst:Code>...</wst:Code>
        <wst:Reason>...</wst:Reason>
    </wst:Status>
</wst:RequestSecurityTokenResponse>
```

outlines how to carry out the interactions when more than one STS are involved.

WS-Trust and WS-Security are implemented within Web services libraries, provided by vendors or by open source collaborative efforts. Web services frameworks that implement the WS-* family protocols include: GlassFish Metro Project ("GlassFish Metro Project," 2012), Apache's Rampart (part of axis2) (Apache Foundation, 2012), Microsoft's WCF ("Windows Communication Foundation Security Benefits," 2012) and WIF ("Windows Identity Foundation," 2012).

OpenID

OpenID ("OpenID Authentication 2.0," 2007) is an open and free standard for authentication that provides end users with mechanisms to authenticate at a Web service in a decentralized environment making use of an URL (Berners–Lee, Fielding, & Masinter, 2005) or XRI (Davis, Sakimura, Lindelsee, & Wachob, 2005), like end user identifiers, which can be verified by any target service. It is also a personal data management system, in such a way that when an end user authenticates in a new service for registration, she is requested to indicate the data she wants to share with the new site.

The main advantage of a decentralized authentication system like OpenID is that the end user uses only one username/password credential to request access to hundreds of Web services without having to remember access passwords and names for each different site. In services supporting this standard, end users do not have to create a specific account to gain access to them. Instead, they only need an OpenID identifier, created at an OpenID Provider (OP), which allows the identity of the end user to be verified for any service compatible with the protocol.

OpenID specification defines three main entities, as shown in Figure 11. The User Agent is the entity acting in place of the end user (i.e. Web browser) when she wants to access a resource or Web service, and needs to be authenticated. The Relaying Party (RP) offers a Web service to the end user, and relies on the OP the task of the authentication process. Following the running example, the User Agent represents Alice's Web browser, the OpenID Provider is Alice's Identity Provider (www.idp.com) and the Relaying Party represents www.music-store.com.

Figure 11 describes the message flow for the OpenID authentication. First, Alice starts the authentication process by sending her identifier (e.g. http://www.idp.com/alice/) to the RP (www.music-store.com) through the Web browser (1). The RP normalizes Alice's identifier and discovers the OpenID Provider (www.idp.com) associated to the identifier. Using this information, the RP can, optionally, establish an association with the OP (2). The association process calculates a shared secret (usually based on a Diffie-Hellman exchange (Diffie & Hellman, 1976)) between the RP and the OP, which is used by the OP to sign subsequent messages and by the RP to verify those messages. If they avoid the shared secret generation step, the RP will need to do direct requests after

Figure 11. OpenID interaction flow schema

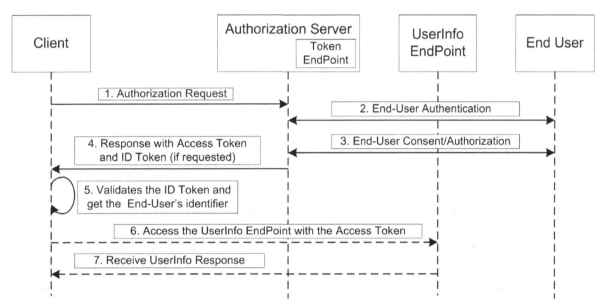

each authentication request/response in order to verify the signatures. After that, the RP redirects Alice with an OpenID authentication request to the OP (3). An example of this request is shown in Figure 12. It includes several fields, some related to the end user (such as *opened.claimed_id* and *opened.identity*), some related to the RP, like the *opened.realm* or *opened_return_to*. The authentication process (4) carried out by the OP is outside the scope of the OpenID specification.

Once Alice has been authenticated, she is redirected again (5) from the OP to the RP with the result of the authentication process, using the URI indicated at *opened.return_to*. This response (Figure 13) includes the end user authentication information such as the end user identifier (*openid.*

identity), the OP Endpoint URL (*openid.op_endpoint*), the list of signed fields (*openid.signed*) and a digital signature (*opened.sig*).

RP verifies (6) the received statement using either the shared key established during the previous association (2) or by sending a direct request to the OP. If the verification is correct RP allows (7) Alice access to the store.

OpenID does not specify which authentication mechanism must be used, so, the security depends on the trust in the OP. If it does not offer enough trust and the authentication mechanism is unreliable, the authentication will not be appropriate for services requiring strong security. Nevertheless, one popular advantage of OpenID, is to allow any end user to set up their own authentication service,

Figure 12. OpenID authentication request example

```
https://www.idp.com/accounts/o8/id
?openid.ns=http://specs.openid.net/auth/2.0
&openid.claimed_id=http://specs.openid.net/auth/2.0/identifier_select
&openid.identity=http://specs.openid.net/auth/2.0/identifier_select
&openid.return_to=http://www.music-store.com/checkauth
&openid.realm=http://www.music-store.com/
&openid.assoc_handle=ABSmpf6DNMw
&openid.mode=checkid_setup
```

Figure 13. OpenID redirect example after a successful user log-in and confirmation

```
http://www.music-store.com/checkauth
?openid.ns=http://specs.openid.net/auth/2.0
&openid.mode=id_res
&openid.op_endpoint=https://www.idp.com/accounts/o8/ud
&openid.response_nonce=2012-05-18T04:14:41Zt6shNlcz-MBdaw
&openid.return_to=http://www.music-store.com:8080/checkauth
&openid.assoc_handle=ABSmpf6DNMw
&openid.signed=op_endpoint,claimed_id,identity,return_to,response_nonce,assoc_hand
le
&openid.sig=sgfiWSVLBQcmkjvsKvbIShczH2NOisjzBLZOsfizkI=
&openid.identity=https://www.idp.com/accounts/o8/id/id=ACyQatix......AY983DpW4UQV_U
&openid.claimed_id=https://www.idp.com/accounts/o8/id/id=ACyQat....AY983DpW4UQV_U
```

which would offer more confidence because they have the service and personal data control.

The OpenID standard has been widely criticized for security and privacy reasons. On the one hand, the unification of all the end user identities in one OpenID entity entails high risks, because all the end user related information is protected by a single authentication process. On the other hand, the OP is the central point of authentication through which OpenID services must pass, so the OP knows the end user's information about sites and services visited. Besides, if the OpenID Provider or end user's credentials are compromised, the entire digital life of the end user will be disclosed.

OpenID allows federated SSO login based on the use of the OpenID Identifier. The protocol enables Relaying Parties to validate the identity of an OpenID user at the OpenID Provider, including the optional ability to request end user's attributes by means of an extension to the standard named OpenID Attribute Exchange 1.0 (Hardt, Bufu, & Hoyt, 2007).

This authentication protocol is offered by some of the most important Internet companies such as Google (Google, 2012), Yahoo (Yahoo, 2012), MySpace ("MySpace Developer Team," 2012) or Paypal (X.commerce, 2012).

OAuth (Open Authorization)

OAuth is an open standard (Hammer, 2010) for authentication and authorization that allows end users to share limited access to their protected resources with third-party applications, orchestrating the approval interaction between a resource owner (end user) and a resource provider (service provider). Its functionality is based on the exchange of authorization codes and security tokens to manage the access control. The standard allows Clients (consumers such as Web services and applications) to access to protected resources stored at Web services (Resource Servers) through an API, without the end users (Resource Owners) having to reveal their access credentials stored in the Resource Servers to the Clients.

Although version 2.0 has been recently approved as RFC standard, it has been widely used since its first drafts by the main social networks, such as Twitter (Twitter Developers, 2012) and Facebook (Facebook Developers, 2012), with the support and adoption by companies such as Google or Microsoft.

In November 2006, during the development of the OpenID implementation for Twitter, there emerged the need for a solution that allows end users to authorize certain applications access to their resources by delegating the access to them. The OAuth discussion group was created in April 2007 and soon had the support of Google. In October 2007, the final draft of the OAuth Core 1.0

was presented, and one year later, a minor revision called "OAuth 1.0 Revision A" (Atwood, 2009) was published. Finally, in April 2010, RFC 5849 (Hammer-Lahav, 2010) was published with the title "The OAuth 1.0 Protocol". Only three months later, Twitter began to require of all third party applications to use OAuth to access to Twitter's APIs. In late April 2010, OAuth IETF Working Group published the first draft of OAuth 2.0 protocol (Hardt, 2012), whose standardization was completed in October 2012. This new version focuses on simplifying the development of clients, at the same time as providing specific authorization flows for Web services, desktop applications, mobile phones and home devices.

The OAuth architecture defines four types of roles that interact through the exchange of messages as shown in Figure 14. First, the Resource Owner (RO) is the entity that can grant the access to the protected resource stored at the Resource Server (RS). The RS is responsible for answering protected resource requests. The Client represents the application that requests access to the protected resource on behalf of the Resource Owner through an authorization grant. Finally, the Authorization Server (AS) is responsible for issuing access tokens to the Client, authenticating the Resource Owner and requesting her authorization.

OAuth 2.0 completely redefines the architecture of the previous versions to the point of not maintaining compatibility with them. Among the new features, the protocol defines three profiles

by client type (Web application, user-agent and native application), four types of authorization grants used for request access tokens, it provides a new mechanism called bearer token that relaxes the cryptography requirements and allows greater interoperability. In general, it simplifies cryptography mechanisms and requirements for cryptographic signing of statements and tokens.

The OAuth architecture implies a change of perspective from the previous models. In this case, the Client represents www.music-store.com, that needs to access to Alice's postal address to be able to send the CD to her home after the purchase has been completed. Alice is represented by the role of the RO, and her identity provider (www.idp.com) would play the role of the Authorization Server. Finally, to cover all the roles, we assume that Alice's home postal address is stored in her identity provider's profile; so in this case, the www.idp.com would play the role of Resource Server too.

In more detail, Figure 15 shows the messages exchanged in the *authorization code grant* scenario. This scenario introduces the User Agent role, which consists of a public client application (e.g. Web browser) that is responsible for downloading and executing on the Alice's device (the Resource Owner) the Client code from a Web server.

The Authorization Code Grant flow (Figure 15) shows the scenario in which the Client (www.music-store.com) requests access to the protected resource (Alice's personal information) by making use of an authorization code grant to carry out the sale. In first place (1), the Client has to request authorization (Figure 16) from Alice (Resource Owner) by asking indirectly through the Authorization Server (www.idp.com), which receives the Client's identifier (*client_id*) and the redirection URI (*redirect_uri*) used to send back the response to Client. All messages are exchanged using HTTP protocol and protected by TLS. An example of a *HTTP Request* for the authorization request as is shown below:

Figure 14. OAuth entities

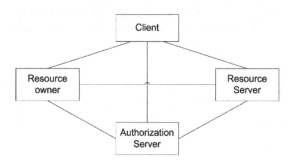

Figure 15. OAuth authorization code flow

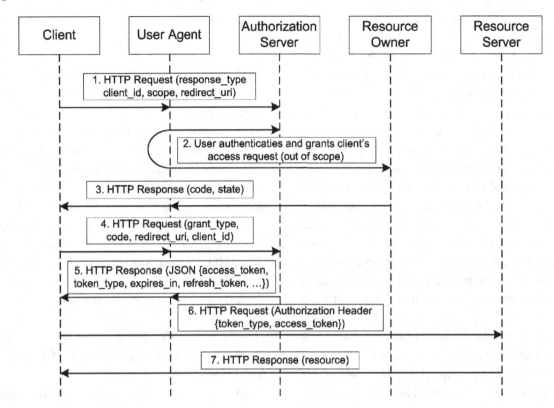

Figure 16. OAuth authorization request example

```
GET /authorize?response_type=code&client_id=A2nJpRkay7&state=cba
     &redirect_uri=http%3A%2F%2Fwww.music-store.com%0A HTTP/1.1
Host: authzserver.idp.com
```

The Authorization Server (Alice's IdP) has to authenticate (2) Alice and asks whether she grants or denies the access request to her personal information. If Alice agrees, Client receives (3) an authorization code grant (*code*) as a proof of her authorization and any local state (*state*) provided by the Client's request, as shown at Figure 17.

Using this credential, Client (4) requests an *access token* from the Authorization Server (Figure 18). The Authorization Server authenticates the Client (*Authorization Header*), validates the

Figure 17. OAuth authorization response

```
HTTP/1.1 302 Found
Location: https://www.music-store.com/ep?code=pKc3jkFoVnfCYkaybORrmdql
     &state=cba
```

Figure 18. OAuth access token request example

```
POST /token HTTP/1.1
Host: authzserver.test.com
Authorization: Basic JQSzdZs0z2WJpmMpntEFn3S0zmCa
Content-Type: application/x-www-form-urlencoded;charset=UTF-8
    grant_type=authorization_code&code=pKc3jkFoVnfCYkaybORrmdql
    &redirect_uri=http%3A%2F%2Fwww.music-store.com%0A
```

authorization code, and makes sure that the redirection URI (Berners–Lee et al., 2005) matches with the one received in the previous message. If the validation is correct, the Client receives (5) the access token (*access_token*) and, in some cases, a refresh token (*refresh_token*) as depicted in the example (Figure 19).

Now, the Client (www.music-store.com) requests access (6) to Alice's personal information (the protected resource), using the access token as proof of the access grant. As result of a correct process, the Client retrieves (7) Alice's attributes (e.g. her postal address) and completes the sale by sending the music CD to Alice's home. The access tokens can have different formats and structures based on the resource server security requirements, and can contain diverse end user attributes, but these details are beyond the scope of the OAuth specification and are not considered in the scenario.

In other scenarios, it is not always necessary to perform all the previously described steps. For example, in the Implicit Grant flow, the Client directly obtains the access token as the result of the authorization request, instead of the authorization code, so reducing the number of interactions

required. In this case, the Client is not authenticated and the security checks fall on the redirection address used by the Client, which may be previously agreed on between the Client and the AS. Besides, OAuth defines an extension grant type based on bearer tokens (Jones, 2012). The possession of a token of this type allows Clients to request an access token (and access to the associated resource) without the need to demonstrate possession of a cryptographic key. All these features and the specific use of the bearer tokens are described in the RFC 6750 (Jones & Hardt, 2012).

Although OAuth was designed as an authorization protocol, its use as authentication mechanism is widely extended. OAuth allows Clients to perform a Resource Owner pseudo-authentication based on the authentication made by the AS, before the authorization request. If the Client obtains the authorization grant, it is means that the end user has been successfully authenticated. This mechanism offers an alternative to as the Single Sign On delegating the authentication process on the AS.

The OAuth protocol has been well received among the top companies of Internet and, in particular, the most popular social networks. Its architecture design and its approach toward Web

Figure 19. OAuth access token response example

```
HTTP/1.1 200 OK
Content-Type: application/json;charset=UTF-8
Cache-Control: no-store
Pragma: no-cache
{
    "access_token":"oic2ZFsaXG3nMzYWpEjrFA,"
    "token_type":"test_type,"
    "expires_in":3600,
    "refresh_token":"IkueF2Tt0Qj9J1vGzhxPew"
}
```

services make it a lightweight authorization protocol and it facilitates the development of client applications. Besides, it seems to be the perfect complement for other protocols widely used in these scenarios, such as OpenID. For these reasons, companies like Google (Google, 2012), Microsoft ("OAuth 2.0," 2012), Facebook or Twitter already use it in their services.

OpenID Connect

This new protocol (Sakimura, Bradley, Jones, Medeiros, & Jay, 2013)makes use of the OpenID concepts to add an identity layer on top of the OAuth 2.0 protocol. The framework, that follows the OAuth concept, allows clients of all types (including browser-based, mobile, and JavaScript clients) to verify the identity of an end user based on the authentication made by the (OAuth) Authorization Server (AS), before requesting the end user's authorization, and it provides mechanisms to obtain basic information about her profile.

OpenID Connect offers a set of specifications that provides a lightweight framework for identity interactions through the REST APIs (Richardson & Ruby, 2007). The specification set is extensible, allowing the optional encryption of identity data, the discovery of OpenID providers, and advanced session management.

The objective of OpenID Connect is to integrate all the OpenID's features with OAuth protocol. In this sense, OpenID Connect incorporates into its specification the *authorization codes* and the *access tokens* defined in OAuth, adding a new third type of token, named *ID token*, which contains authentication information and can be used later to request additional end user information. The specification incorporates the new endpoint called *UserInfo EndPoint*, which corresponds with a protected resource that returns claims (attributes) about end user information. The Client can request access by submitting the respective access token. In the running example, this new role is performed by Alice's identity provider (www.

idp.com), since it is responsible for protecting and providing Alice's private information. The answers provided by the *UserInfo EndPoint* can include three different types of claims: normal, aggregated (from other sources but provided by the OpenID Provider) and distributed (references are provided so that the Client can retrieve them).

Figure 20 depicts the OpenID Connect implicit authorization flow (Sakimura, Bradley, Jones, Medeiros, Mortimore, et al., 2013a) that consists of a scenario in which the Client (www.music-store. com) requests access to Alice's *UserInfo EndPoint* (www.idp.com) that contains her personal information (e.g. her postal address). First, the Client prepares an Authorization Request (1) and sends it to the AS. The request (Figure 21) contains parameters such as *reponse_type* (fixed to *"token id_token"* for requesting both *access token* and *ID token*) and *scope* (set to *openid*, that informs the AS that it is a OpenID Connect request, and *profile* that request the default profile claims of the *UserInfor EndPoint*). Other relevant parameters included in the request are the Client's ID (*client_id*) and the redirection URI (*redirect_uri*) used by the AS.

Once the request has been received, the AS has to authenticate Alice (2) and to obtain her consent/authorization (3) for the Client access. Both authentication and authorization mechanisms are outside the scope of the OpenID Connect standard. If Alice is successfully authenticated and consents to the Client grant, the AS sends (4) the End User back to the Client with the *access token* and the *ID token* as it was requested in the *response_type* field of authorization request from Figure 21; a response example is shown in Figure 22.

The Client verifies (5) the ID token itself by checking the validity of several fields, such as the Client's ID (*client_id*) and the audience restriction (*aud*), as detailed at OpenID Connect Message specification (Sakimura, Bradley, Jones, Medeiros, Mortimore, et al., 2013b). After successful validation, the Client (www.music-store. com) may send (6) a *UserInfo requests* (Figure

Figure 20. OpenID Connect implicit code flow

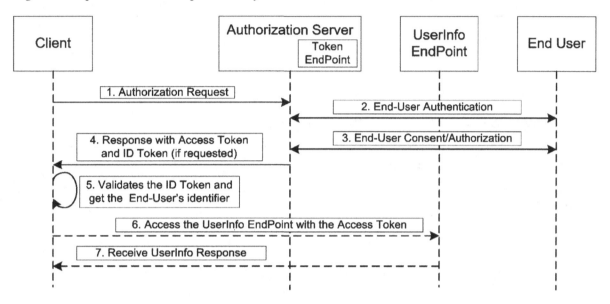

Figure 21. OpenID Connect authorization request example to the Authorization Server

```
HTTP/1.1 302 Found
Location: https://server.example.com/authorize?
response_type=token%20id_token
&client_id=s6BhdRkqt3
&redirect_uri=https%3A%2F%2Fclient.example.org%2Fcb
&scope=openid%20profile
&state=af0ifjsldkj
```

Figure 22. OpenID Connect response example

```
HTTP/1.1 200 OK
Content-Type: application/json;charset=UTF-8
Cache-Control: no-store
Pragma: no-cache
{
  "access_token":"SlAV32hkKG,"
  "token_type":"bearer,"
  "expires_in":3600,
  "refresh_token":"tGzv3JOkF0XG5Qx2TlKWIA,"
  "id_token":"eyJ0NiJ9.eyJlc ... I6IjIifX0.DeWt4Qu ... ZXso"
}
```

23) with the ID token to the *UserInfo Endpoint* to obtain (7) further information (Figure 24) about Alice, such as her postal address, which is needed to complete the sale. For federated login scenarios, in which the Authorization Services are federated, it is sufficient for Clients to use the ID token obtained from authorization requests, to obtain the SSO features.

As can be seen, OpenID Connect raises a complete and fully functional solution that promises a very interesting future. Although currently its use is not yet common, companies like Google, Twitter or Microsoft are collaborating in the development of the final specification of the protocol, which is still under review.

Figure 23. OpenID Connect UserInfo request

```
GET /userinfo?schema=openid HTTP/1.1
Host: www.idp.com
Authorization: Bearer "eyJ0NiJ9.eyJ1c ... I6IjIifX0.DeWt4Qu ... ZXso"
```

Figure 24. OpenID Connect UserInfo EndPoint's response

```
HTTP/1.1 200 OK
Content-Type: application/json;charset=UTF-8
Cache-Control: no-store
{
 "user_id": "248289761001,"
 "name": "Alice Smith,"
 "given_name": "Alice,"
 "family_name": "Smith,"
 "address": "211B Baker Street, London,"
 "email": "alicesmith@idp.com,"
 "picture": "http://www.idp.com/alicesmith/me.jpg"
}
```

FUTURE RESEARCH DIRECTIONS

Once identity management systems have been consolidated to provide authentication and authorization frameworks for Web services, new challenges emerge in order to ensure a better user experience, strong security and privacy.

The management of several digital identities and the use of identity federations can confuse end users about what kind of personal information is being revealed and to whom. The definition of tools to manage attribute reveal policies and the use of standard languages to define those policies (like XACML (Moses, 2005)) are topics that should be managed by Web services and identity providers.

Strong end user authentication also has to be taken into account. Although it could worsen the user experience, strong cryptography, like digital public key certificates, would improve end user security considerably.

In contrast, some users are requesting more privacy. Concepts like anonymity and pseudonymity are always present in the proposed solutions, but today there is no clear solution for that.

CONCLUSION

This chapter introduces the reader to some of the most relevant standards and protocols currently used by Internet organizations to ensure end users' identity for Web services. We have covered generic frameworks, like WS-Security and WS-Trust, providing extensible mechanisms and high degree of flexibility for deployment and specific and rigid proposals, like OpenID. In between, we can find solutions such as SAML and OAuth, providing different profiles and bindings and able to offer enough flexibility to be very attractive for Web services developers. In fact, the latter are the most common solutions adopted today by Internet Web services. We have to take into account that these are not independent proposals. For example, OpenID Connect has been born from the combination of OpenID and OAuth, seeking to take the advantages of each. WS-* was designed with SAML in mind as the security sentences definition language, and OAuth defines new profiles in combination with SAML.

Furthermore, for each of these solutions, we have presented the main use case, offering a brief description of the entities involved and the information flow. Additionally, we have provided a running example in order to offer a clear view of involved roles and entities.

Finally, because of the analysis performed in this chapter, we have noticed an increasing trend to provide, as far as possible, interoperability between the different existing technologies. Emerging services, like social networks, demand the ability of exchanging authentication and authorization information to provide end users with a homogeneous view of their identity information across services.

REFERENCES

Apache Foundation. (2012). *Apache rampart.* Apache Software Foundation. Retrieved May 2013 May 2013 from https://axis.apache.org/axis2/java/rampart/

Atwood, M. (2009). *OAuth core 1.0 revision A.* Retrieved May 2013 May 2013 from http://oauth.net/core/1.0a/

Barth, A. (2011). *RFC 6265 - HTTP state management mechanism.* Internet Engineering Task Force (IETF). Retrieved May 2013 May 2013 from https://tools.ietf.org/html/rfc6265

Berners–Lee, T., Fielding, R., & Masinter, L. (2005). *RFC 3986 - Uniform resource identifier (URI), generic syntax.* Network Working Group. Internet Engineering Task Force (IETF). Retrieved May 2013 from https://tools.ietf.org/html/rfc3986

Bray, T., Paoli, J., Sperberg-McQueen, C. M., Maler, E., & Yergeau, F. (2008). Extensible markup language (XML) 1.0 (5th ed.). W3C Recommendation.

Cambridge University Press. (2012, June). *Cambridge dictionary online.* Retrieved May 2013 from http://dictionary.cambridge.org/

Cantor, S., Hirsch, F., Kemp, J., Philpott, R., & Maler, E. (2005). *Profiles for the OASIS security assertion markup language (SAML) V2.0.* OASIS Standard.

Cantor, S., Kemp, J., Philpott, R., & Maler, E. (2005). *Assertions and protocols for the OASIS security assertion markup language (SAML) V2.0 (SAML core).* OASIS Standard. Retrieved May 2013 from http://docs.oasis-open.org/security/saml/v2.0/saml-core-2.0-os.pdf

Cantor, S., Moreh, J., Philpott, R., & Maler, E. (2005). *Metadata for the OASIS security assertion markup language (SAML) V2.0.* OASIS Standard.

Cisco. (2012). *Cisco networking academy.* Retrieved May 2013 from http://www.cisco.com/Web/learning/netacad/index.htm

Damiani, E., di Vimercati, S. D. C., & Samarati, P. (2005). *New paradigms for access control in open environments.* Paper presented at the Fifth IEEE International Symposium on Signal Processing and Information Technology. New York, NY.

Davis, P., Sakimura, N., Lindelsee, M., & Wachob, G. (2005). *Extensible resource identifier (XRI) syntax V2.0.* OASIS Committee Specification. Retrieved May 2013 from http://docs.oasis-open.org/xri/V2.0

Dierks, T. (2008). *RFC 5246: The transport layer security (TLS) protocol version 1.2.* Retrieved May 2013 from http://tools.ietf.org/html/rfc5246

Dierks, T., & Allen, C. (1999). *TLS protocol (version 1.0) – RFC 2246.* Network Working Group. Retrieved May 2013 from http://www.ietf.org/rfc/rfc2246.txt

Diffie, W., & Hellman, M. (1976). New directions in cryptography. *IEEE Transactions on Information Theory, 22*(6), 644–654. doi:10.1109/TIT.1976.1055638

Eastlake, D., & Reagle, J. (2002). *XML encryption syntax and processing*. W3C Recommendation.

Eastlake, D., Reagle, J., Solo, D., Hirsch, F., & Roessler, T. (2008). XML signature syntax and processing (2nd ed.). W3C Recommendation.

Eclipse Foundation. (2012). *Higgins project - Personal data service*. Retrieved May 2013 from http://eclipse.org/higgins/

Facebook Developers. (2012). *Core concepts: Authentication*. Facebook Developers. Retrieved May 2013 from https://developers.facebook.com/docs/authentication/

Franks, J., Hallam-Baker, P., Hostetler, J., Lawrence, S., Leach, P., Luotonen, A., & Stewart, L. (1999). *HTTP authentication: Basic and digest access authentication*. RFC 2617.

Freier, A., Karlton, P., & Kocher, P. (2011). *Secure socket layer (SSL) protocol version 3.0 – RFC 6101*. Intenert Engineering Task Force (IETF). Retrieved May 2013 from http://tools.ietf.org/html/rfc6101

GlassFish Metro Project. (2012). Retrieved May 2013 from http://metro.java.net/

Google. (2012). *Federated login for Google account users*. Google Developers. Retrieved May 2013 from https://developers.google.com/accounts/docs/OpenID

Google Developers. (2012). *SAML single sign-on (SSO) service for Google Apps*. Retrieved May 2013 from https://developers.google.com/google-apps/sso/saml_reference_implementation

Gudgin, M., Hadley, M., Mendelsohn, N., Moreau, J., Frystyk, H., Karmarkar, A., & Lafon, Y. (2007). SOAP version 1.2 part 1: Messaging framework (2nd ed.). W3C Recommendation.

Hammer, E. (2010). *Introducing OAuth 2.0*. Hueniverse Blog. Retrieved May 2013 from http://hueniverse.com/2010/05/introducing-oauth-2-0

Hammer-Lahav, E. (2010). *RFC 5849 - The OAuth 1.0 protocol*. Internet Engineering Task Force (IETF). Retrieved May 2013 from http://tools.ietf.org/html/rfc5849

Hardt, D. (2012). *The OAuth 2.0 authorization framework*. Internet Engineering Task Force (IETF). Retrieved May 2013 from http://tools.ietf.org/html/rfc6749

Hardt, D., Bufu, J., & Hoyt, J. (2007). *OpenID attribute exchange 1.0*. OpenID.net. Retrieved May 2013 from https://openid.net/specs/openid-attribute-exchange-1_0.html

Hughes, J., Cantor, S., Hirsch, F., Mishra, P., Philpott, R., & Maler, E. (2005). *Bindings for the OASIS security assertion markup language (SAML) V2.0*. OASIS Standard. Retrieved May 2013 from ttp://docs.oasis-open.org/security/saml/v2.0/saml-profiles-2.0-os.pdf

Jones, M., & Hardt, D. (2012). *The OAuth 2.0 authorization protocol: Bearer tokens usage*. Internet Engineering Task Force (IETF). Retrieved May 2013 from http://tools.ietf.org/html/rfc6750

Lawrence, K., & Kaler, C. (2006a). *Web services security: SAML token profile 1.1*. OASIS Web Services Security (WSS) TC. Retrieved May 2013 from http://docs.oasis-open.org/wss/v1.1/wss-v1.1-spec-errata-os-SAMLTokenProfile.pdf

Lawrence, K., & Kaler, C. (2006b). *Web services security: Kerberos token profile 1.1*. Web Services Security (WSS). Retrieved May 2013 from http://docs.oasis-open.org/wss/v1.1/wss-v1.1-spec-errata-os-KerberosTokenProfile.pdf

Lawrence, K., & Kaler, C. (2006c). *Web services security: X.509 certificate token profile 1.1*. Web Services Security (WSS). Retrieved May 2013 from http://docs.oasis-open.org/wss/v1.1/wss-v1.1-spec-errata-os-x509TokenProfile.pdf

Lawrence, K., & Kaler, C. (2007a). *WS-Secure-Conversation 1.3*. OASIS Web Services Secure Exchange TC. Retrieved May 2013 from http://docs.oasis-open.org/ws-sx/ws-secureconversation/200512/ws-secureconversation-1.3-os.html

Lawrence, K., & Kaler, C. (2007b). *WS-SecurityPolicy 1.2*. OASIS Web Services Secure Exchange TC. Retrieved May 2013 from http://docs.oasis-open.org/ws-sx/ws-securitypolicy/200702/ws-securitypolicy-1.2-spec-os.html

Lawrence, K., & Kaler, K. (2006d). *Web services security: SOAP message security 1.1 (WS-Security 2004)*. OASIS Standard. Retrieved May 2013 from http://docs.oasis-open.org/wss/v1.1/wss-v1.1-spec-errata-os-SOAPMessageSecurity.pdf

Lockhart, H., Andersen, S., Bohren, J., et al. (2006). *Web services federation language (WSFederation)*. OASIS Standard. Retrieved May 2013 from http://download.boulder.ibm.com/ibmdl/pub/software/dw/specs/ws-fed/WS-Federation-V1-1B.pdf

Lockhart, H., & Campbell, B. (2008). *Security assertion markup language (SAML) V2.0 technical overview*. OASIS Committee Draft. Retrieved May 2013 from https://www.oasis-open.org/committees/download.php/27819/sstc-saml-tech-overview-2.0-cd-02.pdf

Määttänen, T. (2002). *Single sign-on systems*. Helsinki University of Technology.

Moses, T. (2005). *eXtensible access control markup language (XACML) version 2.0*. OASIS Standard. Retrieved May 2013 from http://docs.oasis-open.org/xacml/2.0/access_control-xacml-2.0-core-spec-os.pdf

MySpace Developer Team. (2012). *MySpace developers platform*. Author.

Nadalin, A. (2009). *WS-trust 1.4*. OASIS Standard. Retrieved May 2013 from http://docs.oasis-open.org/ws-sx/ws-trust/v1.4/os/ws-trust-1.4-spec-os.pdf

OASIS Security Services (SAML) Technical Committee. (2012). Retrieved May 2013 from https://www.oasis-open.org/committees/tc_home.php?wg_abbrev=security

OASIS Web Services Security (WSS) TC. (2006). Retrieved May 2013 from https://www.oasis-open.org/committees/tc_home.php?wg_abbrev=wss

OAuth 2.0. (2012). *Microsoft MSDN*. Retrieved May 2013 from http://msdn.microsoft.com/en-us/library/live/hh243647.aspx

OpenID Authentication 2.0. (2007). Retrieved from OpenID.net

Oracle Group. (2010). *Understanding login authentication*. Retrieved May 2013 from http://docs.oracle.com/javaee/1.4/tutorial/doc/Security5.html

Richardson, L., & Ruby, S. (2007). *RESTful web services: Web services for the real world*. Sebastopol, CA: O'Reilly Media.

Sakimura, N., Bradley, J., Jones, M., de Medeiros, B., & Jay, E. (2013, June). *OpenID connect standard 1.0 - draft 21*. OpenID.net Working Group.

Sakimura, N., Bradley, J., Jones, M., de Medeiros, B., Mortimore, C., & Jay, E. (2013a, June). *OpenID connect implicit client profile 1.0 - Draft 11*. OpenID.net Working Group.

Sakimura, N., Bradley, J., Jones, M., de Medeiros, B., Mortimore, C., & Jay, E. (2013b, June). *OpenID connect messages 1.0 - draft 20*. OpenID.net Working Group.

Twitter Developers. (2012). *Authentication & authorization*. Twitter Developers. Retrieved May 2013 from https://dev.twitter.com/docs/auth

Windows Communication Foundation Security Benefits. (2012). *MSDN Microsoft*. Retrieved May 2013 from http://msdn.microsoft.com/en-us/library/ms735093.aspx

Windows Identity Foundation. (2012). *MSDN Microsoft*. Retrieved May 2013 from http://msdn.microsoft.com/en-us/library/ee517276.aspx

X.commerce. (2012). *Standard OpenID integration for PayPal access getting started guide*. Author.

Yahoo. (2012). *Yahoo! meets OpenID*. Yahoo Inc. Retrieved May 2013 from http://openid.yahoo.com/

Chapter 9
Identity–Based Encryption Protocol for Privacy and Authentication in Wireless Networks

Clifton Mulkey
Texas A&M University – Corpus Christi, USA

Dulal C. Kar
Texas A&M University – Corpus Christi, USA

ABSTRACT

Wireless networks are inherently insecure due to the fact that information on the network can be passively retrieved by an eavesdropper using off-the-shelf network hardware and free software applications. The most common solution for this vulnerability is the Wireless Protected Access (WPA) protocol. This protocol provides data encryption and access control for wireless networks. However, the WPA protocol contains drawbacks in its authentication mechanisms that can cause inconveniences for end users and performance degradation for the network. Furthermore, many of the authentication methods used with WPA are not friendly to small and resource-constrained wireless devices. This chapter presents the design of a new wireless security protocol for privacy and authentication using efficient Identity-Based Encryption (IBE) techniques. This protocol can be used to eliminate the need for a central authentication server for enterprise networks, as well as to provide the new feature of privacy without authentication for public wireless networks. This work also puts forth an analysis and validation of the new protocol, including security strength, storage overhead, communication overhead, and computational efficiency.

DOI: 10.4018/978-1-4666-4789-3.ch009

1. INTRODUCTION

From large corporations to street-corner coffee shops, wireless networks provide an important means of connectivity in today's world. However, security in wireless communications is hindered by the fact that wireless media is by nature a broadcast media. Since wireless signals are carried on radio waves, any receiver within range can potentially intercept a message passed between a wireless access point and a client. In fact, free tools exist that allow users to listen to traffic in promiscuous mode, capturing any data that happens to come to the wireless network card ("Wireshark," n.d.). Furthermore, this type of network sniffing is passive, and cannot be detected by intrusion detection systems that may be operating on the network.

Without encryption, a wireless eavesdropper can capture potentially sensitive information from other clients on the wireless network. Although some traffic is protected using application or session layer security protocols, there are still many plaintext messages that are sent across the wireless media. For example, email, instant message programs, and HTTP often send messages in plain text which can be captured easily. This inherent security risk on wireless networks is often mitigated today by using the Wireless Protected Access (WPA) protocol (Eaton, n.d.). WPA and its second revision, WPA2, both operate in the same manner, but with a different security strength (MacMichael, n.d.). The WPA protocol includes two authentication modes, WPA Pre-Shared Key (WPA-PSK) and WPA Extensible Authentication Protocol (WPA-EAP). Using WPA-PSK, a pre-shared key is required to gain access to the network, so that only authenticated users can connect to the access point. Though WPA-PSK has greatly improved wireless security, it still may not be a good solution for all scenarios. Since the WPA-PSK key is a symmetric key, it must be distributed to all users of the network. This may be infeasible for very large wireless networks. In addition, this creates a problem for networks that expect to have a large number of temporary users. Furthermore, any user that obtains the WPA-PSK network key may still be able to sniff traffic from other users on the network (MacMichael, n.d.). WPA-EAP provides a much stronger authentication method and does not require a pre-shared key among the access point and all clients. However, WPA-EAP requires a central authentication server and a persistent database with all authorized user credentials (MacMichael, n.d.). For this reason, it may not be suitable for small or single access point wireless networks. The reliance on a central server can also create a bottleneck or single point of failure for the network. In addition, WPA-EAP uses higher level public key protocols that may require certificate storage and exchange, as well as expensive encryption. Finally, for some wireless networks, such as in a coffee shop or airport, it may be desirable to have traffic confidentiality but not client authentication.

To address the issues with the WPA protocol, a novel protocol using a form of asymmetric cryptography known as Identity Based Encryption (IBE) is proposed. Asymmetric cryptography is needed to avoid the requirement for shared keys. More specifically, IBE is used because it eliminates the need for public key storage and certificate infrastructure. IBE can be used to securely share symmetric keys, which can later be used by AES symmetric encryption to establish secure channels. IBE key exchange methods can also be formulated in such a way to authenticate both the access point and the client. IBE uses Elliptic Curve Cryptography (ECC), which provides high cryptographic strength with a smaller amount of computation and smaller key size in comparison to traditional public key methods (Anoop, 2012; Kar, Ngo, & Mulkey, 2011). This provides for a smaller communication, computation, and storage overheads for the protocol, and opens the door for the protocol to be used on resource-constricted devices. Because of these characteristics of IBE, this protocol can be managed by individual access points without the need for a central server. This allows the work of network authentication to be distributed and removes a single point of failure.

The overall contribution of this work is the design of such a protocol for wireless network privacy and authentication. This protocol design includes the case for networks requiring privacy and authentication and for networks without a need for authentication. The design also considers key management and authentication for both single and multiple access point networks. Finally, this design also specifies the mathematics and cryptographic techniques necessary to achieve the protocol functionality, as well as the communication steps and link-layer frame specifications needed for practical operation.

This work also consists of an analysis and validation of security strength and overheads of the new protocol. The security analysis discusses the cryptographic strength of the protocol in relation to NIST standards (NIST, 2007). It also defines several possible attacks to the protocol and proofs of resistance to these attacks. For the analysis of protocol overheads, this work considers the storage, communication, and computation overheads that are associated with clients and wireless access points participating in the protocol.

The remainder of the chapter is structured as follows. Section 2 provides a review of previous research and background information in fields relating to IBE and wireless network security. Section 3 gives the design and details of the new wireless security protocol contributed by this work. Section 4 contains the security and overhead analysis of the new protocol. Finally, Section 5 is the conclusion of this work and gives some topics that may be considered for future research in the area.

2. LITERATURE REVIEW

2.1 Identity Based Encryption

The concept of identity based encryption was first introduced by Shamir in 1984 (Shamir, 1984). IBE is a form of asymmetric or public key cryptography. However, instead of using pseudo-random public keys derived through mathematical functions, common identity strings are used. The example proposed by Shamir involves using email addresses as public keys. In our case, we will use MAC addresses as public keys since the wireless security protocol will operate on the link layer. Another significant difference between IBE and traditional public key systems is that clients cannot generate their own private keys. Instead, an IBE system requires some authoritative server with a master secret key. This server is the only one that can generate and distribute private keys based on identity strings. This requirement stems from the fact that public keys are not mathematically derived. If clients had the ability to generate the private key for their own identity string, they could also generate the private key for any other client's identity string. It should be noted, however, that the infrastructure required for an IBE key generating authority is still minimal compared to the requirements of the certificate system used in traditional public key cryptosystems (MarKovic, 2007). In the case of a wireless network, the function of IBE key generation and authentication could be performed by the access point itself.

Though the basic process is similar to traditional public key cryptosystems, less overhead is required for IBE because there is no need to communicate public keys. At the time of its introduction there were no mathematical systems that could provide the properties required for the functioning of an IBE cryptosystem (Shamir, 1984). It was the invention of elliptic curve cryptography and pairing functions on elliptic curves that later made IBE possible.

2.2 Pairing Based Cryptography for IBE

Pairing based cryptography (PBC) is the mathematical mechanism that makes modern IBE implementations possible. The first practical IBE cryptosystem using PBC was developed by Boneh and Franklin in 2003 (Boneh & Franklin, 2003). The Boneh and Franklin scheme uses a pairing function known as the Weil pairing. This pairing performs the mapping, $G1 \times G1 \rightarrow G2$ where $G1$ is an additive group of elliptic curve points, and $G2$ is a finite field. In general terms, a pairing function maps two elliptic curve points to an element in a finite field, known as the extension field. This function is usually represented by e, with $e(P, R) = k$, where P and R are points on an elliptic curve and k is an element of the extension field. In order for PBC and IBE to work, the pairing function e must have the bilinear property: $e(sP, tR) = e(P, R)^{st}$, where s and t are scalars.

The following example from Kar, et al. shows how this property may be used to share an encrypted message using IBE (Kar, Ngo, & Mulkey, 2011). First let us assume that we have a trusted party holding a secret s. The trusted party computes $R = sP$ and publishes R and P which are points on an elliptic curve. Also assume that each party has already retrieved its private key from the trusted server. The private key is sQ_x, where Q_x is an elliptic curve point representing that party's ID. Let us suppose Alice wants to generate an encryption key for sending data to Bob. She first determines Q_{Bob} using Bob's identity string and some known hash-to-point function. Next, she generates an elliptic curve point $U = kP$, where k is a random scalar. Finally, Alice generates a key using $e(kR, Q_{Bob})$ and sends this along with U to Bob. Assuming Bob has already retrieved his private key sQ_{Bob} from the trusted server, he can now determine the key generated by Alice calculating $e(U, sQ_{Bob})$. The following

equation shows how Bob can retrieve the shared key using the bilinearity property.

$$e(U, sQ_{Bob}) = e(kP, sQ_{Bob}) = e(P, Q_{Bob})^{ks} = e(ksP, Q_{Bob}) = e(kR, Q_{Bob})$$

(1)

Using similar methods, IBE and pairing functions can also be used to achieve authentication using signatures.

The security of pairing based IBE systems relies on the difficulty of either the Bilinear Diffie Hellman Problem (BDHP) or the Gap Diffie-Hellman Problem (GDHP) ("Pairing," n.d.). The definition of the BDPH is to find $e(P, P)^{abc}$ given $\{P, aP, bP, cP\}$ where P is a point on an elliptic curve and a, b, and c are scalars. The definition of the GDHP is to find abP given $\{P, aP, bP\}$. One or both of these problems should be infeasible in order for an IBE cryptosystem to be secure. In addition, the pairing function in an IBE system has the side effect of allowing the Elliptic Curve Discrete Logarithm Problem (ECDLP) in $G1$ to be converted to a Discrete Logarithm Problem (DLP) in $G2$ (Szczechowiak et al, 2009). For this reason, both of these problems must also be sufficiently hard to maintain security. The order of the extension field $G2$ is q^k, where q is the order of the field on which the elliptic curve is defined (Freeman, Scott, & Teske, 2009). The value k is known as the embedding degree and is a property of the elliptic curve. It is desirable to maximize the embedding degree in order to achieve a difficult DLP in $G2$ while keeping the order of $G1$ relatively small. For example, Barreto and Naehrig provide a detailed description of the construction of pairing friendly elliptic curves over F_p, where p is a 256 bit prime (Barreto & Naehrig, 2006). These curves are specially constructed to have an embedding degree of 12. This creates an extension field of order $256 \times 12 = 3072$, which meets the DLP hardness standards to achieve 128 bit security

(NIST, 2007). Besides the Weil pairing used in the Boneh and Franklin scheme, another pairing function known as the Tate pairing can also be used. The Tate pairing is often more computationally efficient than the Weil pairing ("Pairing," n.d.).

2.3 Recent Developments in IBE for Wireless Sensor Networks

Due to the small key sizes of ECC and the fact that IBE does not need a public key infrastructure to operate, IBE has become a popular candidate for encryption and authentication in Wireless Sensor Networks (WSNs) (Oliveira et al., 2007; Szczechowiak & Collier, 2009; Xiong & Wong, 2010). Since the computing devices involved in WSNs are severely limited in terms of computation power and energy, much research has been done in this field for further increasing the efficiency of IBE. One of the significant advances that has been achieved in some recent implementations of IBE for WSNs is the reduced Tate (ηT) pairing (Kar, Ngo, & Mulkey, 2011). The ηT pairing algorithm operates over special types of elliptic curves, known as supersingular curves. Using this type of pairing, IBE has been implemented efficiently for small wireless devices (Szczechowiak & Collier, 2009). The IBE scheme outlined in (Szczechowiak & Collier, 2009) even leverages properties of supersingular curves to eliminate the need for hash-to-point operations and reduce the number of pairing operations necessary. Due to the efficiency achieved for IBE on WSNs, it is likely that IBE can also provide great performance on the more powerful devices, such as access points and laptop PCs, that are involved in a traditional wireless LAN. Furthermore, this shows that IBE security for wireless LANs can also be efficient enough for use with the growing number of mobile and hand-held devices.

2.4 Wireless Protected Access

The WPA addition to wireless Ethernet protocol was originally specified in the IEEE 802.11i revision (Eaton, n.d.). WPA was designed to overcome serious security vulnerabilities found in the previous Wired Equivalent Privacy (WEP) standard, as well as add advanced authentication methods.

2.4.1 Privacy

The privacy specifications for the WPA protocol can be divided into two revisions. This first is WPA Temporal Key Integrity Protocol (WPA-TKIP) (Eaton, n.d.). WPA-TKIP was designed to be fully compatible with existing WEP hardware. For this reason, TKIP uses the same RC4 stream encryption algorithm as WEP. This algorithm encrypts data using a 104 bit key and a 24 bit initialization vector. WPA-TKIP overcomes the cryptographic weakness of WEP by using an Initialization Vector (IV) and an Extended Initialization Vector (EIV) field to create a stronger initialization vector for the cipher algorithm. By mixing the first 2 bytes of the IV field and all 4 bytes of the EIV field, a 48 TKIP sequence number (TSC) is created and is different for each frame. This 48 bit TSC could theoretically be used over 100 years without overlapping at the maximum transmission rate of wireless Ethernet (Eaton, n.d.). Along with the TSC, TKIP uses a temporal key for encrypting frames. The temporal key is derived from the master network key in WPA-PSK mode, or is established by other means in WPA-EAP. Each frame in a WPA-TKIP session is encrypted with a different key. The 128 bit packet key, (24 bit initialization vector plus 104 bit RC4 key) is derived from the 48 TSC, the temporal key, and the sender's MAC address.

The second mode of privacy specified by the 802.11i standard is WPA Counter Mode CBC Protocol (WPA-CCMP or WPA2) (Stallings,

2005). This form of WPA is more computationally intensive and is not compatible with older WEP based hardware. However, the protocol is much more cryptographically secure as it uses the 128 bit AES algorithm in Cipher Block Chaining (CBC) mode. The IV and EIV are again used as a 48 bit initialization vector to seed the AES algorithm. The 128 bit AES session key is derived in a similar manner to that in TKIP. The MIC field is also calculated using the Michael hash function as in TKIP. The major difference in the CCMP frame format is the omission of the ICV field, which is no longer needed since backward compatibility is not a goal of WPA-CCMP.

2.4.2 Authentication

WPA provides two different modes of authentication that can be used for wireless networks (Eaton, n.d.). The two modes are known as Pre Shared Key (WPA-PSK) and Extensible Authentication Protocol (WPA-EAP). It should also be noted that WPA does not provide privacy without authentication. At least one of these authentication modes is used on any WPA network.

The simpler and more commonly used of the two is PSK mode. In PSK mode, network authentication is controlled by a master key. Any client that wishes to join the network is required to have this master key. As mentioned above, this master key is used to derive the session key used to encrypt frames between the access point and the client. This authentication mode is convenient for home and small office networks with a limited number of users. No central authentication server is required and a single access point can enforce access to the network. However, WPA-PSK does not scale well because of the need for every client to have knowledge of the same master password.

For larger networks involving multiple access points, WPA-EAP can be used. WPA-EAP requires a central authentication server with a database of credentials for authorized users. EAP uses upper layer protocols to create a secure connection to the authentication server. In some EAP systems, digitally signed certificates are used to verify the access point, authentication server, or clients. WPA-EAP can be further divided into four major types, all using different specific authentication mechanisms (Eaton, n.d.).

Each client of an EAP network has its own set of credentials, so the system scales much better than PSK mode. Key management is also effective because user credentials can easily be added, removed, or modified by the system administrator on the authentication server. However, the central authentication server can also be a single point of failure or a performance bottleneck for the wireless network.

3. PROTOCOL DESIGN

3.1 Preliminaries

Before describing the design and functionality of the new protocol for wireless network security, the necessary preliminaries for defining and understanding the protocol will be discussed. As mentioned in Section 1, identity based encryption techniques will be used to provide authentication and key setup. Although many different IBE pairing methods exist, this protocol uses IBE over supersingular elliptic curves. Many definitions of supersingular exist for elliptic curves (Freeman, Scott, & Teske, 2010). However, the specific property of supersingular curves that we are interested in for this work is the existence of efficient distortion maps. Pairing over many elliptic curves breaks down when the two points being paired are linearly dependent (Freeman, Scott, & Teske, 2010). For this reason the second argument to the pairing function must be a point on some variation of the original elliptic curve over a larger finite field (Grabher, Groszschaedl, & Page, 2008). With supersingular curves, the distortion map gives an easy way to transform a point on an elliptic curve to a second point that is in a different cyclic sub-group, essentially removing linear dependence (Freeman, Scott, & Teske, 2010). The result is that the pairing over supersingular curves can operate on two points from the same elliptic curve. This allows for simpler IBE protocols that can be used to eliminate the need for a hash-to-point function. The specific pairing algorithm used in this work is the ηT pairing, which is the fastest known pairing over supersingular curves (Xiong, Wong, & Deng, 2010).

To analyze this protocol, we use a supersinglar curve defined over the ternary field $F_{3^{509}}$, given in (Beuchat et al., 2009). The curve over this field is defined by $y^2 = x^3 - x + b$, where b is between -1 and 1. The modulus used for the field is the polynomial $x^{509} - x^{318} - x^{191} + x^{127} + 1$. This curve has an embedding degree of 6, which results in the extension field $F_{3^{509 \times 6}}$. The order of the curve and the size of the extension field is large enough to provide 128 bit security, or about the same security level as 3054 bit RSA (Beuchat et al., 2009; NIST, 2007). A curve at this security level is chosen in order to match the standards of WPA-CCMP and the NIST standards for the foreseeable future beyond 2030 (NIST, 2007). More curves are available that can provide this level of security. This protocol provides a method for choosing to use different curves within some pre-defined set that is known beforehand by clients and access points.

To ensure privacy on the network once a secure connection is established, the WPA-CCMP encryption standard and packet format will be used. This provides for 128 bit security and message integrity. The WPA-CCMP privacy standard is chosen because the protocol is widely accepted and supported by most modern devices.

The following list defines the specific parameters that are involved in the design of the protocol and give the notations that will be used for the remainder of this work:

- E : This is the notation for the elliptic curve being used. The specific curve used in this work is defined over $F_{3^{509}}$. Points in on the elliptic curve are denoted as being in the group $E(F_{3^{509}})$. For functionality of this protocol, E will be an index referring to a pre-defined set of elliptic curve parameters that are known beforehand.

- e : This denotes the pairing function, which gives the following mapping:

$$E(F_{3^{509}}) \times E(F_{3^{509}}) \to F_{3^{509 \times 6}} \qquad (2)$$

- s : This is the IBE master secret key that is known only to the access point. s is a 128 bit integer.

- P : This is a random point on the elliptic curve. P is chosen by the AP and is part of the public parameters of the IBE system.

- Q : This is another point on the elliptic curve and is calculated by $Q = sP$ on the AP. Q is also a public parameter.

- g : This is calculated by $e(P,P)$ on the AP. g is another public parameter of the system.

- $H1$: This is a hash function that converts a binary MAC address to a 128 bit integer, which is suitable for elliptic curve scalar multiplication. MD5 might be used for $H1$. However, a simpler and faster hash function could be used because the security of the protocol does not rely on $H1$ being one-way.

- $H2$: This is a hash function that converts an element of the extension field $E(F_{3^{509 \times 6}})$ to a 128 bit integer. This hash should be one-way. MD5 could also be used in this case despite its weaknesses. Possible birthday attacks are not an issue for the usage of this hash.

- **Public Keys:** The public key of each node involved in the protocol is a 128 bit integer calculated by $H1$ (node MAC address). The MAC address for each node works well for the public key since MAC addresses are unique. MAC addresses are already required for communication at the link layer, so no overhead is incurred to share public keys. The public key for the access point will be denoted as a. The public key for each network client will be denoted as c_i.

- **Private Keys:** The private key of each device is an elliptic curve point calculated by the AP as

$$\tfrac{1}{s+h} P,$$

where h is the node public key. The value $\tfrac{1}{s+h}$ is calculated over the finite field Z_p where p is a 128 bit or larger prime integer. The private key for the AP will be denoted as A, ($A = \tfrac{1}{s+a} P$). The private keys for each client will be denoted as C_i, ($C_i = \tfrac{1}{s+c_i} P$).

3.2 Functionality Without Authentication

One of the main features of this protocol is the option to provide privacy without authentication. As mentioned in Section 1, this feature could be used for public wireless networks to eliminate the security risk of passive traffic sniffing. In this protocol, an IBE method adapted from (Sakai & Kasahara, 2003; Szczechoiak & Collier, 2009) is used to establish a shared session key between each wireless client and the AP. This method is not as concise as some other IBE protocols, but it has the advantage that the client does not have to perform a costly pairing calculation for key setup. The client does not need to hold any IBE parameters or network secrets prior to connecting to the

AP. Since the 802.11 wireless protocol already provides for the exchange of node information via probe requests, we will use this mechanism to retrieve IBE parameters from the AP. Once a session key has been established and shared, the remainder of the communication between the AP and the client is encrypted using the method of WPA-CCMP. The following steps describe the steps taken in the protocol to provide privacy without authentication.

1. The AP periodically sends a beacon frame as specified in 802.11 protocol to make clients aware of its existence and security requirements.

2. A client wishes to connect to the AP. If the client does not have the parameters for the AP cached, it sends a probe request to retrieve the IBE parameters for the network.

3. The AP responds with a probe response containing the necessary IBE parameters: $\langle E, P, Q, g \rangle$.

4. The client now begins the connection process. It sends an association request to the AP, indicating that it wishes to connect using the supported unauthenticated privacy method.

5. The AP sends an association response to the client, indicating the client can go ahead with session key generation.

6. The client generates two random 128 bit integers, w and t where t is the eventual session key. The client also calculates the AP public key, $a = H1$ (AP MAC address). It is to be noted that the client already possesses the MAC address of the AP from the initial beacon frame.

7. The client then generates two more values: $M1 = w(Q + aP)$ and $M2 = t \oplus H2(g^w)$ ($\oplus$ denotes the xor operation). $M1$ and $M2$ are sent to the AP in an authentication management frame.

8. The AP retrieves the session key t by calculating $t = H2(e(A, M1)) \oplus M2$.

9. AP sends an authentication successful message back to the client. Although the client is not actually authenticated in a cryptographic sense, authentication frames are used to signal that the client has permission to join the network with the secure channel.

10. The client and AP are now ready to commence normal data communication. The remainder of the communication is encrypted using the shared session key and WPA-CCMP.

It is to be noted that the AP is able to successfully retrieve t because of the bilinearity property of the IBE pairing function:

$$e(A, M1) = e(\tfrac{1}{s+a} P, w(Q + aP)) =$$
$$e(P, Q + aP)^{\frac{w}{s+a}} = e(P, (s + a)P)^{\frac{w}{s+a}} = e(P, P)^w = g^w \tag{3}$$

and

$$H2(g^w) \oplus M2 = t \tag{4}$$

Figure 1 illustrates the protocol steps and the messages that must be sent between the AP and the wireless client.

In this way, a client is able to generate and share a random session key with the AP without having any prior keys or parameters from the AP. This session key is then used to derive the values needed to encrypt packets with AES for WPA-CCMP privacy. Since each client generates its own random key per session, the data sent over the encrypted channel can only be read by that client and the AP. The security of this key establishment protocol without authentication is discussed further in Section 4.1.1.

Figure 1. Sequence diagram of protocol without authentication

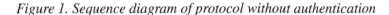
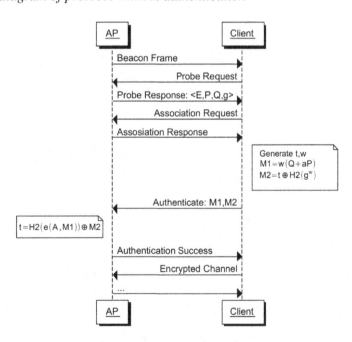

3.3 Functionality With Authentication

If authentication is required by the network, it can also be achieved by the IBE protocol without the reliance on upper layer methods. It is undesirable to use a master network password that is shared among users as in WPA-PSK. Instead, we want each client authentication to be independent of other clients. Independent authentication is also a part of WPA-EAP. However, the proposed IBE protocol has the advantage of not requiring a user database and authentication server. To provide this functionality, IBE private keys will be generated for each network client and connections will be authenticated using this private key. IBE has the feature that private keys have an inherent authenticity in that the AP generates the private keys using the IBE master secret. In contrast, clients generate their own private keys in traditional public key cryptography systems, resulting in the need for certificate verification by trusted outside authorities (Marcovic, 2007).

3.3.1 Initial Connection

Though IBE private keys provide an effective means for authentication, we must still have a way for each client to make an initial connection to the AP and securely retrieve its private key for the future. For this step we must involve a system administrator or some outside system to provide temporary user IDs and random passwords for the first connection by each client. These user ID and password pairs can be stored on the AP until the client connects and receives its private key for the first time. Neither the temporary passwords nor the IBE private keys need to be stored permanently on the AP. Figure 2 shows the steps taken when a client connects and authenticates to an AP for the first time, after the temporary id/password pair has been set up and issued to the client.

Figure 2. Sequence diagram for first-time client connection and authentication

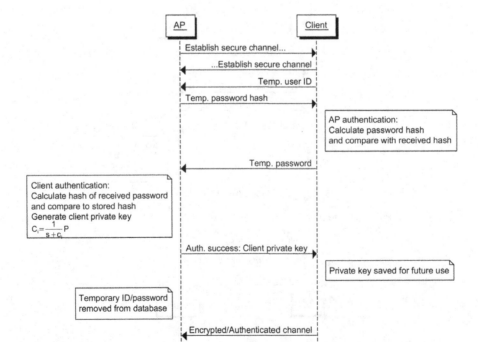

The following steps are involved in the first-time connection.

1. The client and AP establish a secure connection in the same way as the unauthenticated protocol above.
2. The client sends the temporary user ID to the AP.
3. The AP looks up the user ID and password hash in its table. It then sends the password hash to the client. This step is performed in order to authenticate the AP to the client.
4. The client authenticates the AP by calculating the hash of its password and comparing it to the hash received from the AP. If the hashes match, the client proceeds to send the temporary password to the AP. If the hashes do not match, the client sends a disassociation frame to terminate the connection.
5. The AP receives the temporary password from the client and calculates the hash. If the hash matches what is stored in its database, the AP proceeds. Otherwise, the AP sends a disassociation frame to terminate the connection.
6. The client and AP have now been authenticated. The AP calculates the new client private key: $C_i = \frac{1}{s+c_i} P$. The AP sends the private key to the client in an authentication success frame. The temporary user ID and the password are also deleted from the database.
7. The client receives and saves its private key for future connections. The client also saves the public IBE parameters for the AP in order to avoid the need for another parameter probe request in the future. Normal data communication can now begin and is encrypted over the authenticated secure channel.

3.3.2 Subsequent Connections

Once the client has performed the initial connection and authentication, all subsequent connections will be authenticated using the IBE private key. Since the IBE private keys are generated using the master secret that is held by the AP, both the client and AP can be authenticated to each other. In this protocol, a key exchange similar to the Diffie-Hellman method is used (Schneier, 1996). Unlike a traditional Diffie-Hellman exchange, the properties of IBE ensure that keys can only be agreed upon between an authentic AP and an authentic client. Once the key setup steps are completed, a challenge and response mechanism is used to authenticate the client and allow it to connect. The security of this key exchange and authentication mechanism is studied further in Section 4.1.2. Figure 3 shows the protocol steps for client connection and authentication after the client has obtained its private key.

The steps involved in the protocol are as follows:

1. The AP periodically sends beacon frames to make clients aware of its existence.
2. The client sends an association request to the AP, indicating that it already possesses its private key.
3. The AP sends an association response indicating that the client can go ahead with authentication.
4. The client generates a random 128 bit number p and calculates $p(Q + aP)$. The client sends $p(Q + aP)$ to the AP in an authentication request frame.
5. The AP receives the authentication request, generates a random 128 bit r, and calculates $r(Q + c_iP)$. The AP sends $r(Q + c_iP)$ back to the client.
6. The AP and the client simultaneously calculate the session key:

Figure 3. Sequence diagram for subsequent client connection and authentication

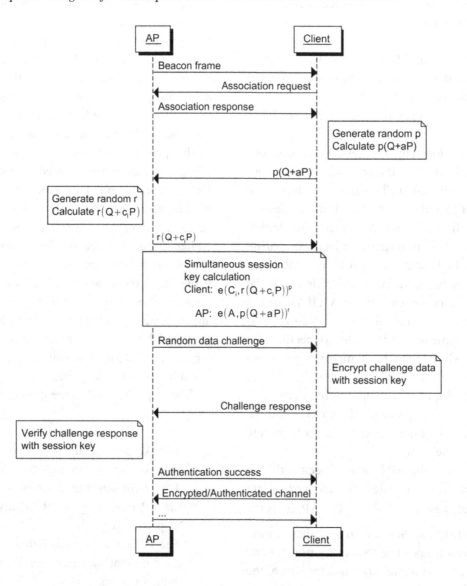

a. The client calculates

$$H2(e(C_i, r(Q + c_i P))^p).$$

b. The AP calculates

$$H2(e(A, p(Q + aP))^r).$$

Both the client and the AP are able to securely share the 128 bit session key because of the relation:

$$e(C_i, r(Q + c_i P))^p = e(\tfrac{1}{s+c_i} P, r(sP + c_i P))^p$$

$$= e(P, (sP + c_i P))^{\frac{rp}{s+c_i}}$$

$$= e(P, P)^{rp} \qquad (5)$$

and

$$e(A, p(Q + aP))^r = e(\tfrac{1}{s+a} P, p(sP + aP))^r$$

$$= e(P, (sP + aP))^{\frac{rp}{s+a}}$$

$$= e(P, P)^{rp} \qquad (6)$$

7. Once the session key is calculated, the AP sends a random data payload to the client as a challenge.
8. The client receives the random challenge, encrypts it using the session key and WPA-CCMP, and returns it to the AP.
9. The AP also performs encryption on the challenge data using the session key. It compares the result to the challenge response received from the client to determine if the client has arrived at the correct session key. If the client does have the correct session key, it is authenticated and the AP sends an authentication success frame. Otherwise, the AP sends a disassociation frame to terminate the connection.
10. The client and AP can now commence normal data communication. All further traffic is encrypted using WPA-CCMP standards and the shared session key.

In this way, a client can achieve authentication while establishing a secure channel to the network. In this scenario, little or no user interaction is required on the client or AP side. The only requirement is that the client possesses the private IBE key that it was given during the initial connection. It should also be noted that no previous information about the client needs to be stored on the AP. All client information needed by the AP for this protocol can be calculated from the MAC address of the client.

3.4 Key Management and Changes

3.4.1 New Clients

As mentioned above, adding new clients to an authenticated network will require some form of initial interaction. In the simplest case, a system administrator could be charged with generating user ID and random password combinations for each new client. The user ID numbers may be random or may be an employee or student ID. For added security, the MAC address of the new client could also be obtained and stored along with the user ID/password. The AP could then check whether the temporary password is being used with the correct MAC before allowing first-time authentication. However, this would of course increase the difficulty of the initial setup. Temporary passwords should be stored as a SHA-224 hash in keeping with the NIST standard for 128 bit security (NIST, 2007). The password hashes and IDs will be uploaded to the AP via some secure channel. Since the temporary passwords are no longer needed after the first-time client connection and authentication, they can be automatically deleted to free up space on the AP. In this way, no central user database or authentication server is needed beyond the AP. For larger wireless networks, it may be desirable to have some kind of automated system for the setup and distribution of the initial temporary keys. The design of such a system is beyond the scope of this work, however it is important to note that this system would not have to be working at all times for the network to function.

3.4.2 IBE Parameter Changes

For security reasons, it will likely be desirable to generate new master keys and IBE parameters on a periodic basis. A change in either the master key or the public parameters will invalidate the private keys and make clients unable to authenticate. It would be infeasible to treat all clients as new users and redo the first-time authentication steps after each key change. In order to facilitate key changes and parameter changes more efficiently a key timestamp mechanism is added to the protocol. With this mechanism, the AP stores one or more sets of old parameters. For each old set, only $< E, s, P >$ need to be stored. During the initial authentication, the AP attaches a timestamp to the client private key. The client stores this timestamp along with its private key. Then, every time the client wishes to join the network, it sends its timestamp to the AP in the association request. The AP can use this timestamp to determine whether the requesting client possesses a private key generated with current parameters or with an old set. If the client's private key is current, the authentication steps proceed normally. If the timestamp shows that the private key was generated with an older set of parameters stored on the AP, the client will be allowed to authenticate using the old set of parameters. Once authentication is complete and a secure channel is established, the AP generates a new timestamp and a client private key and sends them to the client. The client must then remove its old private key and store the new one. The client must also request and store the new set of parameters from the AP. The lifetime of each set of IBE master key and parameters and the time period during which the old parameters are valid should be dictated by the company or network policy. If a client possesses a private key that is older than any set of parameters on the AP, it simply must be treated as a new user and go through the first-time authentication process.

3.5 Operation on Multiple Access Point Networks

Many wireless networks that use authentication will involve more than just a single access point. As discussed in the literature review, many access points can be joined together over a wired network to form an Extended Service Set (ESS). To the user, the ESS appears as a single wireless network even though multiple access points are involved. For this type of network, the authentication should behave the same from the user perspective regardless of the specific AP the client is associating with. In addition, clients should be able to migrate between different access points on the ESS as seamlessly as possible. WPA-EAP provides this functionality by storing all authentication information on a central server. When a client sends an authentication request to a particular AP, the AP contacts the central server over a secure wired channel to get the client authentication information. On a large network with many users moving on and off the network, the central server may become a bottleneck since it must handle authentication requests from all APs. Furthermore, the authentication server becomes a single point of failure for the network.

Due to the small storage requirements of IBE parameters, the protocol in this work can achieve multi-AP network functionality simply by replicating the IBE parameters over all access points. Here it is assumed that the access points are connected by a secure wired backbone. A single AP or a system administrator can be tasked with generating IBE parameters and distributing them to all other access points across the wired backbone. In the same way, temporary user IDs and passwords for new clients can be replicated to all access points. In this case, the AP that performs the initial authentication for a new client must send a message to all other access points to delete the temporary password from their own new client database. With this setup, all access points will be able to perform their own authentication functions for clients that connect directly to them. This removes the bottleneck and the single point of failure created by the reliance on a central authentication server. Since all access points possess the same IBE parameters, client migration will still be able to function as normal. When a client moves from one AP to another in the same ESS, the same basic authentication steps are taken as in normal connections. The only difference is that reassociation management frames are used when connecting to the new access point. This causes the new AP to retrieve any frames that are buffered for the client at the old AP after authentication is successful. This functionality is already included as a part of the 802.11 wireless protocol (Stallings, 2005). In order for migration to be seamless for the user, the IBE authentication steps must be able to complete quickly. An analysis of the time involved in the IBE computations can be found in Section 4.4. An interesting feature that could be explored for extra security would be the use of a secure splitting scheme to store the master secret among all access points. This would make the network resistant to a compromised AP since the master secret is not known by any single AP. However, performance would be decreased because many or all access points would need to participate in order to authenticate each client.

3.6 Frame Format

All messages in key establishment and authentication will be passed using 802.11 management frames. For the development of the protocol, we assume a maximum transmission unit of 1500 bytes in keeping with the common Ethernet MTU (Kurose & Ross, 2008). The communication analysis in Section 4.3 shows that this payload size is more than sufficient for all protocol messages that must be passed. In order to facilitate this IBE protocol, a 4 bit control code is added at the beginning of the data payload. The management frame type along with the control code is used to determine the protocol message type. Figure 4 shows the diagram for the frame format.

Beside the 4 bit control code, a 4 bit pad is added to the frame in order to achieve byte alignment. These 4 bits can also be used for other protocol fields in the future if needed. This concludes the design specifications for the IBE protocol for wireless network security. The remaining portion of this chapter discusses and analyzes the performance and security of this new protocol.

4. PROTOCOL ANALYSIS

In order to validate the new IBE wireless security protocol designed in this work, this section provides an analysis of protocol performance. The cryptographic security of the protocol is covered first, considering both the authenticated and unauthenticated versions of the protocol as well as resistance to some possible attacks. Secondly, the overhead of the protocol is discussed. The overhead analysis consists of storage, communication, and computation overheads. The results of the overhead analysis show that this protocol is a viable solution for wireless security and is also suitable for hand-held and limited-resource wireless devices.

4.1 Security

It should first be noted that an attacker may have access to a portion of the network and protocol

Figure 4. IBE protocol frame layout

Bytes	≤ 30	4 bits	4 bits	≤ 1499	4
	802.11 Header	Control Code	Padding	Protocol Payload	FCS

information due to the nature of wireless networks. To discuss possible attacks on the protocol, it is assumed that the attacker has obtained or is able to obtain all information that is passed across the network. For any wireless network, this includes the MAC address of the AP and the MAC addresses of all clients. It is also important to realize that an attacker can easily spoof the MAC address of any client. From the protocol designed here, the attacker can easily obtain this set of information: $\langle E, P, Q, g, a, c_i \rangle$. However, these parameters are already considered public to the protocol and, as shown below, will not aid an attacker in capturing a session key or feigning authentication.

4.1.1 Protocol Without Authentication

For the functionality of the protocol without authentication, we are not concerned with the authenticity of either the client or the AP. However, we do wish to maintain privacy for each client connected to the network. To this end, the session key t must be unavailable to any other party beside the AP and the respective client. In the communications necessary for this protocol, $M1 = w(Q + aP)$ and $M2 = t \oplus H2(g^w)$ can be captured from the network by an attacker. In addition, the attacker could easily calculate $(Q + aP)$. The exclusive-or of t with $H2(g^w)$ is essentially a one-time pad. In order for an attacker to obtain t, he must obtain g^w, or just w since g is already public. Now the attacker does know $w(Q + aP)$ and $(Q + aP)$, but w cannot be obtained from these values due to the ECDLP. As mentioned in the literature review, this ECDLP could be converted to a DLP in the extension field $F_{3^{509 \times 6}}$. However, the size of the extension field still makes the DLP sufficiently infeasible to solve. g^w could also be obtained by $e(A, w(Q + aP))$, but this would require access to

$$A = \tfrac{1}{s+a} P.$$

Although the attacker does know a and P, he cannot obtain A because the master secret s is known only to the AP. Furthermore, s, t and w have 2^{128} possible values, making a brute force attack infeasible. In conclusion, an attacker cannot likely obtain t from any information communicated across the network in this protocol.

Assuming that an access point can only allow one instance of a particular MAC address to be connected to the network at a time, it may be possible for an attacker to perform a denial of service attack against a particular client. As mentioned previously, an attacker can obtain the MAC of another client and log on to the unauthenticated network using the stolen MAC. This creates a denial of service because the legitimate client cannot log on or establish a session key with the AP as long as the attacker remains connected. However, privacy is not breached in this scenario due to the fact that session keys are randomly generated by the client per association.

4.1.2 Protocol With Authentication

When discussing the security of this IBE protocol on networks where authentication is desired, we must consider both AP authentication and client authentication. Furthermore, both the initial authentication with temporary passwords and subsequent authentications using IBE private keys must be taken into account.

The network access point must be able to authenticate itself to the client in order to prevent an attacker from pretending to be an AP and establishing a fake secure channel with clients. This is especially true for the initial client connection and authentication because an unauthenticated AP could trick a client into sending its temporary initial password, thus giving an attacker a means to access the legitimate network. It is for this reason that the AP must first send the temporary password hash stored in its database to the client upon an initial connection. This is seen in step 3 of the first-time connection protocol described in Section 3. By doing this, the client can verify that the AP does possess the correct temporary password that was created by the system administrator or other outside system. Only an authentic AP on the network could possess this information, and the client will not send the temporary password to the AP unless this verification is successful. For subsequent connections, the AP is authenticated to the client by its possession of the IBE master secret s. Without s, an AP will not be able to generate its own private key or retrieve the session key calculated in the protocol steps for subsequent authentication. The reasons for this are shown below in the discussion of possible attacks. If the AP is not able to calculate the session key, no data from the client can be decrypted, so no information will be leaked.

Client authentication is also achieved on the first connection using the temporary, first-time password. Once the client has determined that the AP is authentic, it will send the temporary password to the AP over the encrypted connection that has already been established. The AP can then compare the received password with its database to determine if the client is authentic. This of course relies on some outside secure method for distributing temporary passwords to first-time clients. Subsequent authentications require the client to possess a valid IBE private key and the MAC address corresponding to that key. The authentication of clients is validated by using the challenge-response mechanism described in the subsequent authentication protocol. Using this method, the AP can determine whether the client has been able to calculate the correct session key, thus proving the authentication of the client. Once again, the validity of an IBE private key is contingent on the master secret s.

Many possible attacks exist for which this IBE protocol must be able to resist. Below is a description of likely attacks to the network and how this protocol proves to be resilient to these attacks.

- **Rogue AP:** As mentioned previously, an attacker could insert an AP that claims to be a part of the legitimate ESS. In this case, the attacker can easily obtain the public parameters $\langle E, P, Q, g \rangle$, and the IBE public keys corresponding to any MAC address. However, the rogue AP cannot obtain the master secret s, which is known only to authentic access points. Furthermore, the rogue AP does not have the database of temporary password hashes used for first-time authentication, so it will not be able to authenticate to itself to any first-time clients. For subsequent connection authentication, let us assume that the rogue AP possesses its own secret $k \neq s$, with which it has generated its own private key A_k. During the key generation phase of subsequent authentication, the client calculates:

$$e(C_i, r(Q + c_i P))^p = e(P, P)^{\frac{rp(s+c_i)}{s+c_i}} \qquad (7)$$

However, the AP calculates:

$$e(A_k, p(Q + aP))^r = e(P, P)^{\frac{rp(s+a)}{k+a}} \qquad (8)$$

Therefore, the rogue AP is unable to retrieve the correct session key. Even if the AP falsely tells the client that the authentication is successful, it will not be able to retrieve any data encrypted by the client with the session key.

- **Authentic client private key used with wrong MAC address:** If an attacker somehow manages to steal the private key, C_i, from a client without obtaining the client's MAC address, the IBE protocol will not allow the attacker to authenticate with the network. In this case, the MAC address used by the attacker will correspond to some public key $c_i' = H1$(attacker MAC address). During session key generation, the AP will calculate:

$$e(A, p(Q + aP))^r = e(P,P)^{\frac{rp(s+a)}{s+a}} \qquad (9)$$

However, the client calculates:

$$e(C_i, r(Q + c_i'P))^p = e(P,P)^{\frac{rp(s+c_i')}{s+c_i}} \qquad (10)$$

which does not result in the correct session key. Consequently, the client will not be able to correctly respond to the challenge from the AP and will be disassociated from the network.

- **MAC of an authentic client with an invalid private key**: In order for an IBE private key to authenticate correctly with the network, it must have been generated with the correct master secret s. Even if an attacker possesses the MAC of an authentic client, it cannot connect to the network with an invalid private key. Let us assume that the attacker has generated its own IBE private key, C_i' using the public parameters and some secret key $k \neq s$. During the session key generation phase, the AP calculates the same value shown in Equation 9. However, the client calculates:

$$e(C_i, r(Q + c_iP))^p = e(P,P)^{\frac{rp(s+c_i)}{k+c_i}} \qquad (11)$$

which does not result in the correct session key. Again, the client will not be able to successfully respond to the authentication challenge from the AP.

- **Invalid MAC address and invalid private key:** The proof of security in this case clearly follows from the previous two cases.

- **Rogue/Hijacked Client:** In some cases, an attacker may be able to capture a client that possesses an authentic IBE private key. Another scenario resulting in the same situation is an inside attack, where a previously authenticated user decides to attack the network using an authenticated client. In this case, the client will still be able to access the network, but will not be able to sniff traffic from any other clients of the network due to the randomly generated session keys. Furthermore, even an authentic client cannot obtain private keys from other clients without obtaining the master secret s. Even though an authentic client does possess C_i, c_i, and P, it will not be able to obtain $\frac{1}{s+c_i}$ or s due to the ECDLP.

- **Hijacked AP:** In the event that an AP is physically hijacked by an attacker, it may be possible for the attacker to retrieve s and any saved temporary password hashes, breaching the security of the network. The method for secure storage of secrets on the access point is beyond the scope of this chapter. However, it is likely that such a hijacking would be easily detected on a single AP network. On a multiple AP network, a secure splitting scheme could be used to store s and the temporary hashes among all the access points. If a splitting scheme is used, the compromise of an AP would not result in a security breach as the secrets cannot be obtained from any one AP.

4.1.3 WPA-CCMP Secure Channel

In order to provide security once the secure channel between the AP and client has been established, the widely accepted WPA-CCMP (WPA2) protocol is used. The 128 bit AES encryption algorithm in cipher block chaining mode used for this protocol provides a security level recommended by NIST through the 2030 (NIST, 2007). Furthermore, the 48 bit IV used in encrypting each packet has a theoretical lifetime of 100 years at the maximum wireless transmission rate (Eaton, n.d.). The use of this IV effectively provides a unique encryption key for every frame transmitted on the network. More details on WPA-CCMP can be found in Section 2. Further analysis of WPA security mechanisms can be found in (Eaton, n.d.; Lashkari, Danesh, and Samadi, 2009).

4.2 Storage Overhead

In order for this protocol to be carried out entirely on access points and clients without help from outside servers, it should require only a small amount of storage space. Here, we analyze the data storage requirements for this IBE protocol on both access points and clients. The storage requirements of the programming needed for this protocol is not analyzed in this work.

4.2.1 Access Point

We will first discuss the storage requirements for access points. Each access point must store the elliptic curve attributes for multiple different curves that are to be used in the protocol. As given by the index, E, in the protocol, there can be a total of 256 different elliptic curves stored and chosen from. However, there will likely be a much small number of stored curves in practical use. The following list shows the attributes that must be stored for each elliptic curve (Brown, 2010):

- The elliptic curve equation
- $f(x)$: The polynomial field modulus
- a, b : Coefficients of the curve equation
- G : The base generator point on the curve

- n : The order of G
- h : Cofactor of n. $n \times h =$ total order of the curve
- e : Embedding degree

The size of each of these attributes can vary depending on the type and security level of each elliptic curve. It is likely that the largest element of these attributes is G, which is an element of the base field and a point on the elliptic curve.

Once a particular curve is chosen the access point must also store IBE parameters for the operation of a specific instance of the protocol. Here we use storage sizes specific to the elliptic curve over $F_{3^{509}}$ used throughout this work. It is first important to discuss the storage of points on the elliptic curve. Since the curve is defined over a ternary field, each of the 509 ternary digits in the field is represented with 2 bits. Therefore, an element of $F_{3^{509}}$ is stored with 1018 bits. Furthermore, a point on an elliptic curve consists of (x, y), where x and y are both elements of the base field. To avoid the need for two field elements to be stored for each curve point, we can take advantage of the fact that an elliptic curve has two possible y values for a given x value. Using this information, we can simply store an extra bit that is used to choose between the two y values (Xiong, Wong, & Dong, 2010). Using this method, an elliptic curve point can be stored with $1018 + 1$ bits, which rounds to 128 bytes. g, which is an element of $F_{3^{509 \times 6}}$ also requires 2 bits for each of its 3054 ternary digits. This results in a space requirement of 6108 bits which rounds to 764 bytes. Table 1 shows the parameters that must be stored on the AP.

In addition to the IBE parameters, the AP must also store the database of temporary user IDs and passwords for new clients. We assume that each user ID is 10 characters long. Along with the SHA-224 hash used to store passwords, a single ID/password combination requires 38 bytes. How-

Table 1. AP parameter storage requirements

Parameter	Bytes
E	1
s	16
P, Q	128 each
g	764
A	128
Total	1165

ever, since these combinations are removed from the database after first-time authentication, there should never be a considerably large number of ID/passwords stored on the AP.

All other values needed in the operation of the protocol can be calculated on the fly by the access point. However, it would improve speed to cache some parameters that are commonly used. The first value that should likely be cached is the IBE private key for the AP, $\frac{1}{s+a}P$.

This is simply a point on the elliptic curve, which requires 128 bytes. Another value to aid in computation is $(Q + c_i P)$ corresponding to recent or frequent clients. This is also an elliptic curve point.

If storage is severely constrained, a method given in (Xiong, Wong, & Deng, 2010) can be used to further reduce the size of elliptic curve points. Consider a string of 5 ternary digits. These digits can represent the decimal values 0 through 242, which can also be represented by 8 bits. Therefore, every 5 ternary digits can be mapped to 8 bits. Using this method, the storage requirement for an elliptic curve point can be reduced from 128 bytes to 102 bytes. The parameter g can also be reduced from 764 bytes to 611 bytes. This does, however, incur an extra computation overhead. For now, we assume that storage space is not limited to the point of justifying this compression method.

4.2.2 Client

As in the AP, the client must also store curve attributes for each available elliptic curve in the protocol. Beyond this, the client only needs to store its own private key, C_i, which is an elliptic curve point. All other values needed in the protocol can either be retrieved from the AP or calculated. However, to avoid excess communication, the client should also cache $\langle E, P, Q \rangle$. This is also necessary for functionality of the IBE parameter changing protocol described in Section 3.4.2. Furthermore, the client should store the point $(Q + aP)$ to reduce computation on future authentications. Table 2 gives a summary of parameters that need to be stored on the client.

4.3 Communication Overhead

The IBE security protocol in this work has a relatively small communication overhead. Each protocol frame contains a control field that constitutes 1 byte, including padding. Only some of the protocol frames contain additional payloads, as described below. Since no upper layer protocols are used, there is no need for many frames to be transferred in order to establish upper layer sessions, such as TCP. The only point in the protocol in which a significant overhead is incurred is during connection setup.

Table 2. Client parameter storage requirements

Parameter	Bytes
C_i	128
E	1
P, Q	128 each
$(Q + aP)$	128
Total	513

The largest portion of data that must be transferred is the IBE public parameters, $\langle E, P, Q, g \rangle$. As shown in the above storage analysis, this constitutes a total of 1021 bytes, which can easily fit in one frame. These parameters are only sent when requested by the client via a probe request frame. In addition, clients can cache the parameters to reduce communication during subsequent connections.

4.3.1 Protocol Without Authentication

After the exchange of public parameters, the protocol without authentication requires an exchange of four frames, as seen in Figure 1. The only frame that contains a payload during this exchange is the transmission of $M1$ and $M2$. Since $M1$ is a curve point and $M2$ is a 128 bit integer, the total payload is 144 bytes. All other frames exchanged during this protocol are control frames and contain no payload.

4.3.2 Protocol with Authentication

The IBE protocol with authentication contains two phases: the initial authentication and subsequent authentications. The initial authentication includes the encrypted channel setup from the protocol without authentication, as well as 4 additional frames. These frames include payloads of the user ID, temporary password hash, temporary password, and the IBE client private key, as shown in Figure 2. The most significant payload in this set is the IBE private key, which is an 128 byte curve point. All other payloads will contain only a small number of bytes.

The authenticated key setup for subsequent connections requires a total of 7 frames to be exchanged, as shown in Figure 3. Of these 7, only 4 contain payloads: the 2 key setup frames and the 2 challenge-response frames. The key setup frames each contain a 128 byte elliptic curve points. The size of the challenge-response payload can vary,

but needs to be at least 16 bytes in keeping with the 128 bit security level. All other frames contain only the control field.

Whether using the protocol with or without authentication, the exchanges described above only take place once per connection. After the session key is established, all following messages transferred via WPA2-CCMP, which incurs 12 bytes of overhead per frame over unsecured 802.11 wireless Ethernet.

4.4 Computation Overhead

Due to the small amount of communication required, computation will likely be the limiting factor on the speed of the IBE protocol. Access points will likely have limited computation power, although they do have a persistent power source. Mobile devices may have limited computing power and often do not have a persistent power source. Elliptic curve and IBE computations have been shown to perform efficiently enough for devices with very limited computing power (Szczechowiak & Collier, 2009; Xiong, Wong, & Deng, 2010). In order to analyze and justify the efficiency of this IBE protocol, the basic computations required for each phase of the protocol are described. In addition, benchmark tests are conducted to estimate the timings of basic ECC and IBE operations. For the overall summary of computation overhead, only elliptic curve and IBE operations are considered, since these operations will easily dominate the computation requirements.

4.4.1 Benchmarks

In order to estimate the time requirements of various computations used throughout this protocol, benchmark tests were conducted using IBE pairing code adapted from (Beuchat et al., 2009, "Tate Pairing," 2009). This code is written in C++, with some inline assembly instructions included. The benchmark tests were conducted on a 32-bit Intel Core2 Duo processor at 3.00

GHz. The code was built and run under Windows 7 with Microsoft Visual C++ 2008. Though the processor used is dual core, the benchmarking program was forced to run in a single thread, so no parallelism is used. The elliptic curve and pairing algorithm benchmarked here is the same curve over $F_{3^{509}}$ and ηT pairing used throughout the development of this work. In order to achieve accurate timings, each basic operation was iterated multiple times and the average computation time was calculated from these iterations. Though the original source code from ("Tate Pairing," 2009) was only used to estimate the calculation time of the ηT pairing, it was adapted for this work to time other primitive operations involved in the overall IBE protocol. Table 3 shows the results of this benchmark.

The processor clock of 3.0 GHz is likely higher than most mobile devices that use wireless networks. In order to obtain timings for a slower processor speed, which is more representative of the limited-resource devices that should be accommodated by the IBE protocol, the CPU scaling feature of the benchmarking computer was used. With the help of this feature, another set of benchmarks was conducted using the lowest configurable processor frequency of 656 MHz. The results of the same benchmarks conducted at this processor speed are shown in Table 4.

Beside the ηT pairing, elliptic curve scalar multiplication and exponentiation over $F_{3^{509}}$ are the two other operations that play a large role the computation required for this IBE protocol. Using the benchmarks of the basic operations, the upper bounds for these two operations can be determined. The traditional method for efficiently computing elliptic curve scalar multiplication is the binary method (Liu & Ning, 2008). Since an efficient method for point tripling is given for the particular curve used in this work, a similar ternary method can be used for efficiently calculating xP. With this method, a 128-bit scalar multiplication requires at most 80 point triples and 81 point additions, assuming $2P$ has been pre-computed. As shown in the benchmarks, an efficient function for cubing over $F_{3^{509}}$ is also given. Therefore, a similar method can be used to perform exponentiation in this field. Since this IBE protocol requires an exponentiation by a 128 bit number, at most 80 cubes and 81 multiplications are required, assuming the square of the base element is pre-computed. Table 5 shows the resulting upper bounds for elliptic curve scalar multiplication and exponentiation over $F_{3^{509}}$. It should also be noted that some speed can be gained in both calculations by using the sliding window method as described in (Liu & Ning, 2008). However, the use of this method requires additional memory to store pre-computed values.

Table 3. IBE computation benchmarks at 3.0 GHz

Operation	Iterations	Average Time (sec)
EC Addition	100000	2.34×10^{-5}
EC Point Triple	100000	1.60×10^{-6}
Multiplication over $F_{3^{509 \times 6}}$	10000	2.81×10^{-5}
Cube over $F_{3^{509 \times 6}}$	100000	2.34×10^{-6}
ηT Pairing	1000	6.879×10^{-3}

Table 4. IBE computation benchmarks at 656 MHz

Operation	Iterations	Average Time (sec)
EC Addition	100000	3.791×10^{-4}
EC Point Triple	100000	2.34×10^{-5}
Multiplication over $F_{3^{509 \times 6}}$	10000	4.165×10^{-4}
Cube over $F_{3^{509 \times 6}}$	100000	3.603×10^{-5}
ηT Pairing	1000	1.07297×10^{-1}

Table 5. Upper bounds for computing EC scalar multiplication and exponentiation

Operation	Time (3.0 GHz)	Time (656 MHz)
EC Scalar Multiplication	2.023×10^{-3} sec	3.258×10^{-2} sec
Exponentiation over $F_{3^{509 \times 6}}$	2.463×10^{-3} sec	3.662×10^{-2} sec

4.4.2 Parameter Generation

Before the IBE protocol is operational, the access point must generate the IBE public parameters and the master secret for the network. These parameters must also be regenerated when a system administrator determines that a key or parameter change needs to be made. The time needed to generate these parameters is generally not a concern since the AP has a persistent power source, and parameter generation is only done occasionally. However, it is shown that parameter generation can still be achieved quite fast in comparison with other common public key systems. The steps involved in parameter generation require a total of 3 elliptic curve scalar multiplications and 1 pairing computation.

4.4.3 Protocol without Authentication

When functioning in the unauthenticated mode, the IBE protocol designed here has the advantage that the client does not have to calculate a pairing. This is important to save as much energy as possible for resource-limited devices. The client steps require a total of 2 elliptic curve scalar multiplications, 1 elliptic curve addition, and 1 exponentiation over $F_{3^{509 \times 6}}$. After the first connection, a and $(Q + aP)$ can be cached for future connections. Therefore, subsequent connections only require 1 elliptic curve multiplication and 1 exponentiation. The total time required for these operations is less than a single pairing calculation. As for the access point, 1 pairing calculation and 1 128-bit exclusive-or operation must be calculated.

4.4.4 Protocol With Authentication

The computation requirements for the protocol with authentication are different between the initial connection and the subsequent connections. For the initial connection, all computations from the protocol without authentication must be done by both the client and the AP. Beyond this, the client is not required to perform any more elliptic curve or IBE operations. The AP must perform one more elliptic curve scalar multiplication in order to compute the private key for the new client.

The subsequent connections with authentication require the most computation overhead of any phase of the protocol. This is due to the fact that IBE methods are used to authenticate both the AP and the client. Here we assume that the client has already cached $(Q + aP)$, since the first-time connection must have already taken place. Therefore, the client process involves a total of 1 elliptic curve scalar multiplication, 1 pairing calculation, and 1 exponentiation over $F_{3^{509 \times 6}}$. For the access point, we assume that neither the public key of the client nor the value $(Q + c_i P)$ is cached, since there is no guarantee that the AP has calculated these values before this point. Therefore, the AP process involves 2 elliptic curve scalar multiplications, 1 elliptic curve addition, 1 pairing calculation and 1 exponentiation over $F_{3^{509 \times 6}}$.

4.4.5 Summary

The total estimated upper bounds for each phase of the protocol are calculated using the benchmark results and the basic operations outlined above. Tables 6 and 7 show these results for the client and the access point, respectively. In order to provide a reference point for these time estimations, benchmarks were performed on the same machine for the commonly used RSA public key encryption method (Schneier, 1996). These benchmarks were performed using a 3072 bit modulus, which provides approximately the same security strength as the parameters used for this IBE protocol. The code for these benchmarks was developed from scratch and utilizes the standard OpenSSL library. Encryption and decryption is performed using a plaintext that is a random 128 bit number to simulate a session key. It should also be noted that RSA encryption turns the 16 byte plaintext into a 384 byte ciphertext. The operations were iterated multiple times, and the average time per iteration is reported. Table 8 summarizes these results. The performance of the IBE protocol surpasses that of RSA in all areas except encryption. Furthermore, the RSA operations shown are only sufficient to share a session key. Further operations would have to take place in order to provide authentication. On the other hand, the IBE protocol is able to provide authentication within the same operations of key generation. These results show promise that

Table 6. Summary of client computation time bounds

Protocol Phase	Basic Ops.	Time (3.0 GHz)	Time (656 MHz)
Unauthenticated Protocol	2 EC mult., 1 EC add., 1 exp.	6.532×10^{-3} sec	1.022×10^{-1} sec
Auth. Protocol (First-time)	2 EC mult., 1 EC add., 1 exp.	6.532×10^{-3} sec	1.022×10^{-1} sec
Auth. Protocol (Subsequent)	1 EC mult., 1 pairing, 1 exp.	1.136×10^{-2} sec	1.765×10^{-1} sec

Table 7. Summary of AP computation time bounds

Protocol Phase	Basic Ops.	Time (3.0 GHz)	Time (656 MHz)
Parameter Generation	3 EC mult., 1 pairing	1.295×10^{-2} sec	2.050×10^{-1}
Unauthenticated Protocol	1 pairing	6.879×10^{-3} sec	1.073×10^{-1} sec
Auth. Protocol (First-time)	1 pairing, 1 EC mult.	8.902×10^{-3} sec	1.399×10^{-1} sec
Auth. Protocol (Subsequent)	2 EC mult., 1 EC add, 1 pairing, 1 exp.	1.341×10^{-2} sec	2.094×10^{-1} sec

Table 8. Summary of RSA computation times (3072 bit modulus)}

Operation	Iterations	Avg. Time (3.0 GHz)	Avg. Time (656 MHz)
Key Generation	60	1.842 sec	23.82 sec
Encryption	6000	1.408×10^{-4} sec	2.259×10^{-3} sec
Decryption	600	8.738×10^{-2} sec	1.296 sec

this IBE protocol will be able to computationally outperform WPA-EAP protocols, which rely on upper layer encryptions mechanisms such as RSA.

5. CONCLUSION

Wireless networks are vulnerable by nature, and the growing use of these networks makes security increasingly important. Though the WPA wireless security protocol already exists and is widely used, improvements on this protocol can be made using more recent cryptographic techniques. With this in mind, this work provides the design and analysis of a new wireless security protocol using identity based encryption methods to provide privacy and authentication. This new protocol also provides a novel feature in which privacy can be achieved on networks where authentication is not desired. This may prove useful for the growing number of public networks in coffee shops, airports, hotels, and so on. For networks that do require authentication, this new IBE protocol provides improvements over

current WPA-PSK and WPA-EAP authentication mechanisms. More specifically, this protocol does not require a master key to be shared among all clients of the network as in WPA-PSK. In regard to WPA-EAP, this protocol eliminates the need for a central authentication server. This simplifies the setup for small, single access point networks and removes the single point of failure created by the authentication server on larger networks. Furthermore, this protocol distributes authentication among the access points of a large network, removing a possible performance bottleneck and ensuring that clients can always authenticate over only 1 hop.

This protocol has also been developed with smaller, resource-limited mobile device in mind, since IBE techniques are widely researched for use in wireless sensor networks. The IBE methods in this protocol use relatively small parameters, in comparison with traditional public key systems, while still providing a high level of security. It can be seen that these IBE techniques are more lightweight and computationally efficient than the commonly used RSA methods. Furthermore, this protocol does not rely on upper layer network protocols, so frame transmission is kept to a minimum during key set up and authentication.

The protocol designed here also provides a 128 bit security level throughout key setup and authentication. The security level is also maintained during data communications by the use of the WPA-CCMP privacy standard. This level of security is recommended for use by the NIST through the year 2030 (NIST, 2007). Higher or lower security levels can also be used if desired with minor adjustments to the protocol.

One interesting study to extend this work would be the consideration of different pairing algorithms over different types of elliptic curves. On example would be curves over prime-order fields, F_p. The authors of (Barreto & Naehrig, 2006) show that curves can be constructed over a 256 bit prime order field with an embedding degree of 12. This work results in curves with 128 bit security and small base fields. The work in (Beuchat et al., 2009) shows that pairings can be calculated even faster in this field than the field that has been used in this thesis. The disadvantage of these curves, however, is that they are not supersingular and require the use of the Ate pairing algorithm (Grabher, Groszschaedl, and Page, 2008). This would in turn require a more complicated overall protocol. Benchmark results of many different security levels are also shown in (Beauchat et al., 2009). If a lower level of security is acceptable for a particular network, the use elliptic curves over smaller finite fields can further increase the speed of this protocol.

REFERENCES

Anoop, M. (2007, May). *Elliptic curve cryptography: An implementation tutorial*. Retrieved August 30, 2012, from http://www.infosecwriters.com/ text_resources/pdf/Elliptic_Curve_AnnopMS.pdf

Barreto, P., & Naehrig, M. (2006). Pairing-friendly elliptic curves of prime order. In *Proceedings of Selected Areas in Cryptography – SAC 2005* (pp. 319–331). Berlin: Springer.

Beuchat, J.-L., López-Trejo, E., Martínez-Ramos, L., Mitsunari, S., & Rodríguez-Henríquez, F. (2009, December). Multi-core implementation of the tate pairing over supersingular elliptic curves. In *Proceedings of the 8th International Conference in Cryptology and Network Security*, (pp. 12-14). Academic Press.

Boneh, D., & Franklin, M. (2003). Identity-based encryption from the Weil pairing. *SIAM Journal on Computing*, *32*(3), 586–615. doi:10.1137/ S0097539701398521

Brown, D. R. (2010, January). *Sec 2: Recommended elliptic curve domain parameters*. Retrieved from www.secg.org/collateral/sec2_final.pdf

Eaton, D. (n. d.). Diving into the 802.11i spec: A tutorial. *EETimes News and Analysis*. Retrieved August 30, 2012, from http://www.eetimes.com/ electronics-news/4143367/Diving-into-the-802-11i-Spec-A-Tutorial

Freeman, D., Scott, M., & Teske, E. (2010). A taxonomy of pairing-friendly elliptic curves. *Journal of Cryptology*, *22*(2), 224–280. doi:10.1007/ s00145-009-9048-z

Grabher, P., Groszschaedl, J., & Page, D. (2008). On software parallel implementation of cryptographic pairing. In *Selected areas in cryptology* (pp. 35–50). Berlin: Springer-Verlag.

Kar, D. C., Ngo, H. L., & Mulkey, C. J. (2011). Applied cryptography in wireless sensor networks. In Nemati & Yang (Eds.), Applied cryptography for cyber security and defense: Information encryption and cyphering, (pp. 146-167). Hershey, PA: IGI Global.

Kurose, J. F., & Ross, K. W. (2008). The link layer and local area networks. In *Computer networking: A top-down approach* (4th ed.). Upper Saddle River, NJ: Pearson Education Inc.

Lashkari, A., Danesh, M., & Samadi, B. (2009). A survey on wireless security protocols (WEP, WPA, and WPA2/802.11i). In *Proceedings of Second IEEE International Conference on, Computer Science and Information Technology (ICCSIT)*, (pp. 48-52). IEEE.

Liu, A., & Ning, P. (2008). TinyECC: A configurable library for elliptic curve cryptography in wireless sensor networks. In *Proceedings of the 7th International Conference on Information Processing in Sensor Networks*, (pp. 245-256). Academic Press.

MacMichael, J. L. (n.d.). Auditing wi-fi protected access (WPA) pre-shared key mode. *Linux Journal, 137*.

Markovic, M. (2007). Data protection techniques, cryptographic protocols and PKI systems in modern computer networks. In *Proceedings of 14th International Workshop on Systems, Signals, and Image Processing and 6th EURASIP Conference focused on Speech and Image Processing, Multimedia Communications, and Services*, (pp. 13-24). EURASIP.

NIST. (2007, March). *Recommendation for key management - Part 1: General*. National Institute of Standards and Technology (NIST). Retrieved August 30, 2012, from http://csrc.nist.gov/publications/nistpubs/800-57/sp800-57-Part1-revised2_Mar08-2007.pdf

Oliveira, L., Aranha, D., Morais, E., Daguano, F., Lopez, J., & Dahab, R. (2007). Tinytate: Computing the tate pairing in resource-constrained sensor nodes. In *Proceedings of Sixth IEEE International Symposium on Network Computing and Applications (NCA)*, (pp. 318 -323). IEEE.

Pairing. (n.d.). *The pairing based crypto lounge*. Retrieved August 30, 2012, from http://www.larc.usp.br/~pbarreto/pblounge.html

Sakai, R., & Kasahara, M. (2003). Id based cryptosystems with pairing on elliptic curve. *Cryptology ePrint Archive, Report 2003/054*. Retrieved August 8, 2012, from http://eprint.iacr.org/2003/054

Schneier, B. (1996). *Applied cryptography* (2nd ed.). Hoboken, NJ: John Wiley and Sons.

Shamir, A. (1984). Identity based cryptosystems and signatures. In *Proceedings of Cryptology* (pp. 47–53). Berlin: Springer-Verlag.

Stallings, W. (2005). *Wireless communications and networks* (2nd ed.). Upper Saddle River, NJ: Pearson Education Inc.

Szczechowiak, P., & Collier, M. (2009). Tinyibe: Identity-based encryption for heterogeneous sensor networks. In *Proceedings of Fifth International Conference on Intelligent Sensors, Sensor Networks, and Information Processing (ISSNIP)* (pp. 319-354). ISSNIP.

Szczechowiak, P., Kargl, A., Scott, M., & Collier, M. (2009). On the application of pairing based cryptography to wireless sensor networks. In *Proceedings of the Second ACM Conference on Wireless Network Security*. ACM.

Tate Pairing. (2009). *Multi-core implementation of the tate pairing over supersingular elliptic curves (source code)*. Retrieved May 7, 2011, from: http://delta.cs.cinvestav.mx/~francisco/temp/Page-TatePairing2009/TatePairing-2009.html

Wireshirk. (n.d.). *Wireshark network protocol analyzer*. Retrieved August 30, 2012, from www.wireshark.org

Xiong, X., Wong, D., & Deng, X. (2010). Tinypairing: A fast and lightweight pairing-based cryptographic library for wireless sensor networks. In *Proceedings of IEEE Wireless Communications and Networking Conference (WCNC)*. IEEE.

Chapter 10
Distinguishing Human Users from Bots:
Methods and Assessments

M. Hassan Shirali-Shahreza
Amirkabir University of Technology, Iran

Sajad Shirali-Shahreza
University of Toronto, Canada

ABSTRACT

Human Interactive Proof (HIP) systems have been introduced to distinguish between various groups of users. CAPTCHA methods are one of the important branches of HIP systems, which are used to distinguish between human users and computer programs automatically and block automated computer programs form abusing Web services. The goal of these systems is to ask questions, which human users can easily answer but current computer programs cannot. In this chapter, the authors collect different pioneering works, which are done on CAPTCHA systems and create a complete survey of them. They collect more than 100 published works and classify them into 3 categories. This chapter contains different works, which are done for creating CAPTCHA methods and assessing CAPTCHA methods from different aspects, including the attacks done against CAPTCHA methods. This chapter can be used by researchers in CAPTCHA domains to quickly find previous works.

INTRODUCTION

Many aspects of human life are affected by the expansion of the World-Wide Web (WWW). In particular, in developed countries, many daily affairs from daily shopping to education and commerce can be done using the Internet. A common action which is done in most websites, especially those belonging to commercial and administrative

applications, is to fill out registration forms for certain purposes. After filling out the forms by entering the required information, the individuals are allowed to login into that website and carry out certain jobs.

Unfortunately, there are persons who abuse Web services by writing programs which do automatic false registration in websites. These programs automatically fill out forms with incor-

DOI: 10.4018/978-1-4666-4789-3.ch010

rect information in order to enroll in the site. This wastes a large volume of the resources of the site in favor of the profit-seeking programmers and reduces the performance of the system.

Various methods have been presented in order to prevent such attacks, aiming at distinguishing between human users and computer programs. The main characteristic of these methods should be their automaticity so as to be run only by using the computer; because examination of a large bulk of registration on the Internet Web sites by human forces requires a great deal of time and expense and in some cases, such as email services Web sites, using human force for examining the registration forms is practically impossible. Therefore, it is necessary to use automatic systems to distinguish human users from computer programs.

In the discussions of artificial intelligence (AI), a test known as the Turing test (Turing, 1950) is proposed for testing the intelligence of a computer. In this test, a human person and a computer are put in two different rooms and a human interrogator in a third room asks them questions. If the interrogator cannot recognize which room the computer is in and which room the human, it is said that the computer has passed the Turing test.

A similar method to the Turing test can be used to distinguish human users from computer programs with the difference that the human interrogator is replaced with a computer. The computer interrogator asks questions from the applicant to distinguish between the human user and the computer program. These methods are known as CAPTCHA (Completely Automated Public Turing test to tell Computers and Human Apart), after the CAPTCHA project which is done at Carnegie Mellon University (von Ahn et al., 2004). Therefore, the main focus of these methods is on questions that the human user can easily answer but the present computer programs are hardly likely to be able to answer.

The CAPTCHA methods were successful in blocking automated programs from abusing Web services. The developers of first known CAPT-CHA method, which is developed in AltaVista, said that their method could successfully block more than 95% of spam URL's added to AltaVista search engine during its first year usage in 1997 (Baird & Popat, 2002). With the increase of spammers during past years, more websites are using CAPTCHA in their Web services to protect their services from abusing by spammers.

Nowadays, we are facing CAPTCHA on many websites: whenever we want to register for an account in a website, when we want to post a comment to a blog, when we are reporting a bug for a product, or even if we are using a service more than usual, such as when we are sending too much search queries to a website or trying more than 3 times to enter our email password. Their success made this field an attractive field for researchers and many works are done for designing CAPTCHA methods and assessing their robustness to attacks.

The aim of this chapter is to provide a complete survey of works done on CAPTCHA. As we will see in section 2, there are a number of surveys of CAPTCHA methods, but they are not broad. This survey tries to be comprehensive, which it means that we are collecting nearly all of the published works done on CAPTCHA including different papers reporting a work and also technical reports which are describing the work in more details. A shorter version of this survey is presented in Shirali-Shahreza & Shirali-Shahreza (2008d). This chapter is an expanded version which covers more methods with more detail discussion. We are also adding a new section for covering methods which are especially designed for disabled people, because we think that it is an important topic and is an open field for further research.

The structure of this chapter is as follows: In section 2 we will mention the history of CAPTCHA methods and provide a classification for different types of CAPTCHA methods. We divided the CAPTCHA methods into three categories: OCR-Based, Visual Non-OCR-Based and Non Visual. Methods of each type are reviewed in sections 3, 4 and 5 respectively. A number of CAPTCHA methods are designed especially for disabled people. We review them in section 6. Then we will review the works done on assessing robustness of CAPTCHA methods and breaking them in section 7. In the last section, we will provide some directions for further research on CAPTCHA and then we conclude the chapter.

CAPTCHA METHODS

In this section we provide a brief history of CAPTCHA methods. We also describe how we categorize the proposed CAPTCHA methods.

It was first in 1997 when Andrei Broder and his colleagues devised a system to distinguish between human users and computer programs. In the same year, the AltaVista website used this method to prevent automatic URL submission in its search engine. In this method, a distorted English word was shown to the user and the user was asked to type it. Distortion was so that OCR systems could not recognize the word (Baird & Popat, 2002). This method which is designed in AltaVista in 1997 is known as one of the first CAPTCHA methods (Baird & Popat, 2002; Broder, 2002).

von Ahn defined CAPTCHA methods formally in von Ahn et al. (2003). His paper in Communication of ACM (CACM) (von Ahn et al., 2004) has a brief description of methods created in the CAPTCHA project. In the CMU CAPTCHA project, a number of methods are designed including Gimpy, EZGimpy and PIX. The EZGimpy method which is one of the early methods developed in CAPTCHA project was used in Yahoo website till 2004. More information1 about CAPTCHA project at CMU can be found on their project website (Blum et al., 2000) and also in the von Ahn (2005) PhD dissertation.

CAPTCHA Surveys

Baird has a survey of some CAPTCHA methods in Baird (2006). His paper in HIP 2002 workshop is one of the first papers which introduce the CAPTCHA problem (Baird, 2002). He has another paper describing the problem in more details (Baird & Popat, 2002). His preface on the HIP 2005 workshop proceedings also describes the status of CAPTCHA methods at that time (Baird & Lopresti, 2005). Pope & Kaur (2005) is another survey of CAPTCHA which reviews a number of famous CAPTCHA methods and their application in E-Commerce. It must be mentioned that all of these surveys are not broad and mention a small number of methods. The survey we will provide in this chapter tries to cover different methods have been proposed and automated attacks against them.

CAPTCHA Categorization

We can divide the CAPTCHA methods into three groups: OCR-Based, Visual Non-OCR-Based and Non Visual. Our classification is similar to the classification used in Yan & Ahmad (2008b) which divides the CAPTCHA methods into three categories: Text-Based, Sound-Based and Image-Based. Their Text-Based methods are similar to our OCR-Based methods, their Image-Based methods are similar to our Visual Non-OCR-Based methods, and their Sound-Based methods are part of our Non Visual methods. A number of methods we will review in the Non Visual methods such as Text-Domain methods cannot be categorized in one of the categories proposed in Yan & Ahmad (2008b).

Optical Character Recognition (OCR) programs are used for automatically reading the texts, but they have difficulty reading texts printed with a low quality (Baird et al., 2003) and can only recognize high-quality typed texts that use common standard formats. However, this defect of the OCR systems can be taken as an advantage by changing the picture of a word so that it can only be recognized by a human user but not by any OCR system.

In OCR-Based methods, the image of a word with distortion and various pictorial effects is shown to the user and he/she asked to type that word. Due to presence of various pictorial effects, a computer program will encounter problems in the recognition of the word and only a human user can recognize the word. EZGimpy is an example of OCR-Based methods. We will explain these methods in section 3. But these methods usually result in dissatisfaction of users which initiates effort to design easier CAPTCHA which are usually Non-OCR-Based. On the other hand, efforts have been made for breaking these methods such as Mori & Malik (2003). In section 7 we will discuss some of these attacks.

In contrast, we can talk about Visual Non-OCR-Based and Non Visual methods which are easier to pass for users than OCR-based ones and are not using OCR systems problems. These methods will be studied in sections 4 and 5 respectively. For example, in Collage CAPTCHA method (Shirali-Shahreza & Shirali-Shahreza, 2007b), the image of some objects with distortion is shown to the user and he/she is asked to click on a certain object.

One of the reasons that Non-OCR-Based methods are designed is the problems that disabled people have in using OCR-Based methods. This problem is also addressed by World Wide Web Consortium (W3C). They have a note published in 2005 which discusses the inaccessibility of CAPTCHA (W3C, 2005). These are the guidelines proposed in Web Content Accessibility Guidelines (WCAG) 2.0 for CAPTCHA accessibility (W3C, 2008):

- "If the purposed non-text content is to confirm that content is being accessed by a person rather than a computer, then text alternatives that identify and describe the purpose of the non-text content are provided.
- Alternative forms of CAPTCHA using output modes for different types of sensory perception are provided to accommodate different disabilities."

Non-OCR-Based methods such as sound-based CAPTCHA are usually used as an accessible alternative to OCR-Based methods in Web services. Because of the importance of this problem, we will review the methods designed for disabled people in a separate section (section 6).

OCR-BASED METHODS

Early OCR-Based CAPTCHAs

The Gimpy method and its easier version named EZGimpy which was used by Yahoo from 2000 to 2004 are among the famous OCR-Based methods. They are developed in the CAPTCHA project at CMU and described in details in von Ahn (2005). Gimpy uses distortions such as color backgrounds, salt and pepper noise, non-linear transformation, and foreground grids.

Pessimal Print (Baird et al., 2003; Coates et al., 2001) is another example of early OCR-Based methods which tries to reduce the quality of the image of a word (e.g. by removing some parts of characters) in order to make it difficult for OCR systems to recognize it. Another early work on OCR-Based CAPTCHA methods is Xu et al. (2000) which is done in the Georgia Institute of Technology in 2000.

BaffleText is another OCR-Based method (Baird & Luk, 2003; Chew & Baird, 2003) which focuses on generating meaningless pronounceable words. The authors claim that such words are easier for human users to recognize, while could not be predicted in OCR system using language models. ScatterType (Baird et al., 2005a; Baird et al. 2005b; Baird & Riopka, 2005) is another method created by authors of BaffleText method. Its main motivation is to break a character into a number of small parts and move each part slightly in a random direction to make it more difficult for the computer to recognize the characters. Bentley & Mallows (2006) discuss how to generate random words which are easier for human users. Another similar paper is Wang & Bentley (2006).

A special method for using OCR-Based methods in console applications such as remote login protocols like Secure Shell (SSH) is presented by Dailey & Namprempre (2004).

A different kind of OCR-Based CAPTCHA is presented in Baird & Bentley (2005) under the name "Single-Click CAPTCHAs". This method shows a series of words, which have various pictorial effects, in random places on the screen and asking the user to click on a particular word. Although this method is also using OCR limitations and can be categorized as an OCR-based method, it is different from previous methods. In those methods, the user must type the word while here the user must simply click on the concerned word. So, this method is easier for human users. Another hybrid method which has both OCR-Based and Non-OCR-Based parts is described in Lopresti (2005).

Handwritten Words

Rusu proposed Handwritten CAPTCHA, which uses scanned handwritten words for generating CAPTCHA images (Rusu, 2006 ;Rusu & Govindaraju, 2004 ;Rusu & Govindaraju, 2005a ;Rusu & Govindaraju, 2005b). This method relies on the fact that recognizing the handwritten words is more difficult than printed words. Liao & Chang (2004) method uses visual patterns as foreground and background for displaying the text which the user must type. Another similar OCR-Based method is proposed by Ferzli et al. (2006).

New Generation of OCR-Based CAPTCHAs

The method which is currently used by Microsoft Web services is described in Chellapilla et al. (2005a), Chellapilla et al. (2005b), Chellapilla et al. (2005c), Chellapilla & Simard (2004), and Simard et al. (2003). This method is designed after assessing different OCR-Based methods and unlike the earlier works that tries to make recognition more difficult - for example by adding noise -, tries to make the segmentation more difficult, similar to ScatterType.

reCAPTCHA (von Ahn et al., 2008) is another new OCR-Based CAPTCHA which is designed by von Ahn, the designer of Gimpy in the CMU CAPTCHA project. The reCAPTCHA goal is using human processing and recognition power to help digitalize scanned books.

In this method, at first a collection of words which the OCR programs cannot recognize is created. Then each of these words is shown with another control word to the user and he must type both words. If the user correctly recognizes the control word, then his answer for the other word is used as the correct recognition for the word which the OCR programs cannot recognize. So this method is helping OCR systems to better digitalize the scanned words. After finding the correct answer for words which OCR failed on them, they select the more difficult terms as new control terms and used in future tests.

CAPTCHA for Other Languages

The majority of works done on CAPTCHA are for English CAPTCHA methods. There are a few CAPTCHA methods for other languages such as

(Shirali-Shahreza & Shirali-Shahreza, 2006b; Shirali-Shahreza & Shirali-Shahreza, 2006c; Shirali-Shahreza & Shirali-Shahreza, 2007f; Shirali-Shahreza & Shirali-Shahreza, 2007g; Xu et al., 2005; Yang, 2002). Each language has its own advantages and disadvantages for designing OCR-Based CAPTCHA methods (Shirali-Shahreza & Shirali-Shahreza, 2006c; Yang, 2002).

For example, in the Persian and Arabic languages, the dot is used in many characters and is very important in recognition of characters. So methods such as adding noise cannot be done easily for Persian and Arabic OCR-Based methods. On the other hand, the characters are connected to each other in Persian and Arabic words, similar to cursive English writing. So the segmentation of words is more difficult in Persian and Arabic languages which made these languages more difficult for OCR systems. This is an advantage in designing OCR-Based CAPTCHA methods (Shirali-Shahreza & Shirali-Shahreza, 2006c). In addition special writing styles in different languages such as calligraphy is also used to create OCR-Based CAPTCHA methods for non-English languages (Shirali-Shahreza & Shirali-Shahreza, 2007g; Xu et al., 2005).

OCR-Based Methods Comparison

To better compare the different aspects of the OCR-Based CAPTCHA methods, we compare a number of methods reviewed in this section in Table 1. This table is an expanded version of the table in Shirali-Shahreza & Shirali-Shahreza (2006c).

Using OCR-Based CAPTCHA methods is difficult for disabled and elderly people. Current CAPTCHA methods used in most of websites such as Google, MSN and Yahoo are successful in detecting automatic programs, but it is gained at the cost of user dissatisfactory. Solving these CAPTCHA requires good eyesight and also the ability to read degraded text, so elderly people who usually suffer from eyesight problems and disabled people such as blind people cannot pass these tests easily. To solve these problems, the researchers designed a number of CAPTCHA methods which are easier than OCR-Based methods for human users. We will review these methods in next sections.

Table 1. A comparison between OCR-based CAPTCHAs (Expanded version of table in Shirali-Shahreza & Shirali-Shahreza (2006c))

Method Name	Meaningful Words	Rotation	Non-Linear Deformation	Background	Two Color Only	Various Fonts	Use Numbers
Old AltaVista	No	Yes	No	No	Yes	Yes	Yes
Gimpy	Yes	No	Yes	Yes	No	Yes	No
Pessimal Print	Yes	No	No	No	Yes	Yes	No
BaffleText	Yes	No	No	No	Yes	Yes	No
Dynamic Visuals	No	No	No	Yes	No	Yes	Yes
Yahoo Method	No	Yes	Yes	No	Yes	Yes	Yes
Handwritten	Yes	Yes	Yes	Yes	No	Yes	No
Scatter Type	No	No	No	No	Yes	Yes	No
MSN Hotmail	No	Yes	Yes	No	Yes	No	Yes
Persian BaffleText	No	No	No	Yes	No	Yes	No

VISUAL NON-OCR-BASED METHODS

In addition to OCR-Based methods, there are other visual methods which do not use OCR software weaknesses. These methods usually use the drawbacks of computer vision systems such as their difficulties in identifying the type of an object in an image.

Object Recognition Methods

Non-OCR-Based methods that are based on object recognition can be divided into two main groups: object identification and object localization.

Object Identification

In the first group, the user must recognize the answer and then either enters the name of the object or selects it from a list of possible options.

PIX method (von Ahn, 2005) is one of the first Non-OCR-Based methods. In PIX, a number of images, for example 4 images that have a similar subject are selected and shown to the user and the user is asked to select the subject of the images among a list of subjects. More information about PIX and EPS-Game which is designed for creating the required image database can be found in (von Ahn, 2005). Bongo which is another Visual Non-OCR-Based method created in the CMU CAPTCHA project in 2001 (Blank, 2001).

Three similar methods are proposed in Chew & Tygar (2004): Naming CAPTCHA, Distinguishing CAPTCHA and Anomaly CAPTCHA. The Naming CAPTCHA is very similar to PIX method (von Ahn, 2005). The only difference between PIX and Naming CAPTCHA is that in Naming CAPTCHA, the user must type the object's name which is common between six images while in the PIX method the user select the name from a list. In Distinguishing CAPTCHA, two set of images, each contains three images of the same object are shown to the user. The user must determine whether the two sets have the same subject or not. In Anomaly CAPTCHA, six images are shown to the user. Five images have the same subject and the user must select the image which has different subject.

In the ASIRRA method (Elson et al., 2007; Microsoft, 2007) - which is developed at Microsoft Research with the help of Petfinder.com - a number of different images (for example 12 images) of cats and dogs are shown to the user and the user is asked to select the images of cats.

Object Localization

The second group of Non-OCR-Based methods is based on object recognition and focuses on locating an object in an image. In these methods, the user is asked to identify and locate (by clicking) on a specific object in an image containing multiple objects.

The "Single-Click CAPTCHA" method proposed in Baird & Bentley (2005) is one example of this group. In this method, an image is shown to the user and he/she is asked to click on a particular place on the screen. For example, a scene of a mountain is shown and the user is asked to click on the mountain's top. In this method the concerned points must be determined manually.

Datta & Wang (2005) who are working on Content Based Image Retrieval (CBIR) systems, proposed a method which uses the problems of CBIR methods. They provide techniques to combine a number of images and create a composite image. This composite image is shown to the user and he/she is asked to click on a certain part of the image. The idea of Liao (2006) method is to exchange a number of blocks in an image and ask the user to click on that blocks. Another example of Non-OCR-Based methods which is based on object recognition is ASIRRA (Elson et al., 2007).

In the Collage CAPTCHA method (Shirali-Shahreza & Shirali-Shahreza, 2007b), the images of some different objects (for example six objects such as airplane, car, apple, orange, pineapple and ball) are chosen. Then some effects such as rotating are done on the images and then they are merged to create a single image. This image is shown to the user and he/she is asked to click on a certain object.

Instead of using images, we can use movies in the CAPTCHA methods. In Athanasopoulos & Antonatos (2006) an animated CAPTCHA method is proposed which is similar to Online Collage CAPTCHA method (Shirali-Shahreza & Shirali-Shahreza, 2007c) requires to click on the named object. Its difference with Online Collage CAPTCHA method (Shirali-Shahreza & Shirali-Shahreza, 2007c) is that the images of objects are moving in the movie and the user must click on the image while it is moving. Another method which uses small movies is Motion CAPTCHA (Shirali-Shahreza & Shirali-Shahreza, 2008c). In Motion CAPTCHA, the user must selects the sentence which is better describes the shown movie. This method uses a bank of small movies which have a small textual description.

Face Recognition Methods

A group of researchers uses face recognition problems to design CAPTCHA methods. The face recognition method proposed by Misra & Gaj (2006) is showing a set of face images and asked the user to find the two face images which are representing the same person. In this method, a number of effects such as blurring and mirroring are done on images. ARTiFACIAL (Rui & Liu, 2003a; Rui & Liu, 2003b; Rui et al., 2005) is another similar method developed at Microsoft Research. It asks the user to find the complete human face among a number of imperfect faces.

Labeled Image Database Creation

Most of visual Non-OCR-Based methods require a database of labeled images. Creating a database of labeled images is costly and time consuming, so a number of techniques are proposed to

solve this problem. An approach for solving this problem is creating games such as EPS-Game (von Ahn, 2005). Another idea is using image search engines for this purpose (Shirali-Shahreza & Shirali-Shahreza, 2008a; Shirali-Shahreza & Shirali-Shahreza, 2007c). Hoque et al. (2006) use another idea for this problem: they render 3D scenes from 2D images for creating CAPTCHA images instead of using a bank of images.

CAPTCHA methods are usually designed for using with computers and are not suitable for other devices such as mobile phones and PDAs. A number of methods are designed especially for devices such as mobile phones (Shirali-Shahreza, 2008; Shirali-Shahreza & Shirali-Shahreza, 2006a). These methods are designed for devices using stylus like PDA (Personal Digital Assistant). In the Drawing CAPTCHA method (Shirali-Shahreza & Shirali-Shahreza, 2006a), numerous dots are drawn on a noisy background and the user is asked to connect certain dots to each other. The Highlighting CAPTCHA (Shirali-Shahreza, 2008) method asks the user to highlight the shown word on the screen.

NON VISUAL METHODS

Audio CAPTCHA

One of the main categories of non visual methods are sound based CAPTCHA methods. In these methods, instead of showing an image, a sound clip is played for the user and the user is asked to recognize and type the word. The sound clip is created by converting text to speech by Text-To-Speech (TTS) engines. Moreover, to make it more difficult for computer programs to recognize the word, some effects are applied on the sound, such as adding noise and background sounds. These systems are usually used beside other CAPTCHA methods, especially OCR-Based methods, as an accessibility option for disabled people. One of the first examples of these methods is Chan (2002).

Other examples are Chan (2003), Kochanski et al. (2002), Lopresti & Shih (2002), and Tam et al. (2008). We will review a number of these methods in more detail in the next section (section 6).

Text Domain CAPTCHA

CAPTCHA in text domain was desired from the beginning, such as Godfrey (2002), but there are few works done in this field (Bergmair & Katzenbeisser, 2004; Ximenes et al., 2006; Przydatek, 2002). As the authors of these papers said, designing a Text Domain CAPTCHA is very difficult and currently there is no text based CAPTCHA that can be used practically in real world websites. It seems that it is not possible to design a text domain CAPTCHA method that can be used practically.

Other Types of CAPTCHA Methods

A new type of CAPTCHA methods are proposed in Chew & Tygar (2005) in which there is no specific answer to the question asked from the user. The answers of different users are collected and used to decide whether the new user answering the test is a human or computer. For example they are asking questions like "Pick the best joke among the shown jokes".

Another group of methods uses questions which need reasoning to be answered such as Shirali-Shahreza & Shirali-Shahreza (2007d). These methods usually use simple mathematics questions which the user must solve. But they are using some techniques to be robust against attacks, such as using different patterns for questions or using the images of some words (Shirali-Shahreza & Shirali-Shahreza, 2007d). This idea can be extended to create HIP systems which can distinguish between different groups of people, such as method explained in Shirali-Shahreza et al. (2007).

CAPTCHA METHODS FOR DISABLED PEOPLE

Disabled people usually have problems with CAPTCHA methods; because most of CAPTCHA methods are designed for and tested by non-disabled persons (e.g. see the test group description in Chellapilla et al. (2005a)). So special CAPTCHA methods are designed for disabled persons including Holman et al. (2007), Markkola & Lindqvist (2008), Sauer et al. (2008), Shirali-Shahreza & Shirali-Shahreza (2007a), Shirali-Shahreza & Shirali-Shahreza (2008f), and Yan & Ahmad (2008b).

Shirali-Shahreza & Shirali-Shahreza (2008f) method is designed for deaf persons. In this method, a small movie showing a word in sign language is displayed to the user and he/she is asked to type the word. This method is designed to distinguish deaf users from other users.

The methods described in Shirali-Shahreza & Shirali-Shahreza (2007a) and Holman et al. (2007) use different ideas. Shirali-Shahreza & Shirali-Shahreza (2007a) use the computer limitations in understanding and answering descriptive questions. In this method, a simple mathematical question is created and converted to an audio file using a Text-To-Speech (TTS) system. Then the audio file is played for the user and he/she is asked to type the answer of the question. Instead of relying on computer weaknesses in recognizing noisy speech, this method relies on computer weaknesses in reasoning and understanding. This method is similar to Shirali-Shahreza & Shirali-Shahreza (2007d), but it uses speech instead of image to ask the question.

In the method proposed by Holman et al. (2007), and the developed version in Sauer et al. (2008), the system selects an object, such as a bird. Then it plays a sound file which can represents that object for the user, such as the bird sound and then the user must select the name of the object from a list of names. Although using this method is easier than a method like PIX (von Ahn, 2005), creating a large dataset of images and corresponding sounds is a hard task as mentioned in Sauer et al. (2008).

The above mentioned methods are designed for people with one disability, such as blind people. The problem of designing CAPTCHA methods for people with multiple disabilities is analyzed in Shirali-Shahreza & Shirali-Shahreza (2008b) and a number of recommendations for designing such systems are proposed. In addition to methods designed for disabled people, a number of methods are designed for a special group of people such as children (Shirali-Shahreza & Shirali-Shahreza, 2008e) or non-English users (Shirali-Shahreza & Shirali-Shahreza, 2007e).

ASSESSING CAPTCHA METHODS

Attacks to Solve CAPTCHA Automatically

The main goal of CAPTCHA methods is preventing automatic computer programs (named bots) from abusing Web services, so it is important to assess their robustness to attacks. During recent years, there are a series of works done on assessing the robustness of CAPTCHA methods. To do this, researchers try to design a program which can pass the test. Since the majority of the CAPTCHA works are based on the weaknesses of OCR systems, the conducted attacks are mostly in the form of recognition of words with inappropriate shape.

One of the first and well known attacks to CAPTCHA methods (which is done to break Gimpy method) is Mori & Malik (2003). In this method, the EZ-Gimpy method and the Gimpy method have been correctly recognized in 92% and 33% of the times respectively. Other attacks on Gimpy method are He & Liu (2005), Moy et al. (2004), Mori et al. (2005), and Thayananthan

et al. (2003). For example the method reported by Moy et al. (2004) can pass the EZ-Gimpy method in 99% of the situations. In addition, it can recognize the Gimpy-r method, which is a newer improvement of the Gimpy methods, at 78% of the situations.

A series of in depth works on analysis of CAPTCHA methods are done in Microsoft Research labs. Chellapilla et al. (2005b) show that computers are more successful than human users in some parts of solving OCR-Based CAPTCHA methods. They also reported their result on attacking a number of OCR-Based methods which are used in websites such as Yahoo and Google in Chellapilla et al. (2005a) and Chellapilla & Simard (2004).

The conclusion of the Chellapilla & Simard (2004) notes that the majority of existing techniques are based on making the recognition of the characters difficult, while the character segmentation which is required for breaking these systems is more difficult. The method they proposed in this paper can recognize the method of Yahoo in 45% of the cases and the method used by Google in GMail service in 5% of the tests. Meanwhile, in the Yahoo method, the precision rate of the character segmentation is 58% and the accuracy rate of the character recognition is 95%. In Google's method, the character segmentation and recognition precision rate are 10% and 89% respectively.

Ponec (2006) described two attacks on two OCR-Based CAPTCHA methods and discuss about the security which CAPTCHA methods can provide. There are also attempts to break certain CAPTCHA methods such as Aboufadel et al. (2005) and Zhang et al. (2004).

More recent attack on OCR-Based CAPTCHA methods are reported in Yan & Ahmad (2007) and Yan & Ahmad (2008a). Yan & Ahmad (2008a) attacks use novel techniques to solve the CAPTCHA methods which are currently used in Web services such as Microsoft and Google. They can recognize the Microsoft CAPTCHA with success rate 61% and the Google method with success rate 8.7%.

As we mentioned at the beginning of this section, most of the attacks are done on OCR-Based methods. But there are some works which try to break other major types of CAPTCHA methods such as sound based methods. Tam et al. (2008) report the results of an attack to sound based CAPTCHA methods. They can achieve 96.8% recognition rate for digits and can pass the test in 58% of times.

There is also an attack on the ASIRRA method (Elson et al., 2007) by Golle (2008). They are using SVM (Support Vector Machines) to distinguish between cats and dogs images based on color and texture features. They can correctly classify images with 82.7% accuracy and pass the ASIRRA CAPTCHA tests in 10.3% of tests.

Usability Evaluation of CAPTCHA

There are also other works on assessing CAPTCHA methods which do not try to break CAPTCHA methods and instead assess them from a special aspect. von Ahn et al. (2003) have a formal definition of CAPTCHA methods and further analysis. Another paper which analyses the limits and security of CAPTCHA method is Bentley & Mallows (2005). There are a number of papers presented in the HIP 2002 workshop which analyzed different aspects of CAPTCHA systems (Hopper, 2002; Jueles, 2002; Spitz, 2002). Although these papers are written when there were a few proposed CAPTCHA methods, but some of their concerns are still valid. There are also some short papers which analyses the CAPTCHA systems and their overall efficiency such as Brelstaff & Chessa (2005), Kolupaev & Ogijenko (2008), and Voth (2003). There is a detailed discussion on the spam problem and using CAPTCHA methods to stop spams in Goodman & Rounthwaite (2004).

There are also a number of studies about usability and accessibility of CAPTCHA methods for disabled people (Sauer et al., 2008; Yan & Ahmad, 2008b). Sauer et al. (2008) test a sound based CAPTCHA method by visually impaired users in different situations such as using a word document to type the numbers as they hear it or only memorizing it. Their results show that it took about 1 minute in average for participants to answer a test, while their success rate is only 46%, which is very low in comparison to the desired 90% success rate proposed in Chellapilla et al. (2005c).

Yan & Ahmad (2008b) develop a simple framework for assessing the usability of CAPTCHA systems. They analyzed three types of CAPTCHA systems: text-based (OCR-Based methods in our classification), sound-based (Non Visual methods in our classification) and image-based (Visual Non-OCR-Based methods in our classification). They are also providing some tips for improving usability of available methods.

CONCLUSION AND FURTHER RESEARCHES

Today, various services are offered through the Internet. Most of these services are designed for human users, but can be abused with automated computer programs (software robots or simply bots). In this chapter, we provide a complete survey of proposed CAPTCHA methods. This survey tries to be complete and we do our best to collect all of the published works and provide their citation in this chapter. So this chapter can be used as a complete bibliography of the proposed CAPTCHA methods during recent years.

In this chapter, at the first section we define the problem that CAPTCHA systems aim to solve. Then we present the history of CAPTCHA methods in section 2 and also describe how we categorize various CAPTCHA methods. We divide the available CAPTCHA methods into three categories: OCR-Based methods (section 3), Visual Non-OCR-Based methods (section 4) and Non Visual methods (section 5).

The majority of proposed CAPTCHA methods, especially the CAPTCHA methods which are used in common websites, are OCR-Based CAPTCHA methods which request the user to enter the shown word. Disabled people have some problems in using these methods, so special methods are designed for them. Due to the importance of this topic, we reviewed the methods which are designed for disabled people in a separate section (section 6).

Finally, we survey the works which are done for assessing the CAPTCHA methods from different aspects, especially their robustness to attacks and their usability in section 7.

Nowadays, the Internet is used to offer different services to human users. An important concern is to offer good services to human users. One of the requirements of this is preventing automated computer programs (bots) from abusing these services. This is the reason that many researches had done on this topic during recent years and it seems that this field need more works.

A look at the history of proposed methods shows that the main concern in designing most of the methods, especially the methods which are designed for real world usage, is to be robust against computer attacks. But recent results, including new attacks and usability studies, show that while human users have some problems with current methods, these methods can be broken. Furthermore, we can see that usability and accessibility aspects are becoming more important. So we think that designing more accessible CAPTCHA is still an open field for further researches. In addition, newer attacks show that current approaches such as using OCR problems or speech recognition problems cannot be survive for long time and new ideas must be used.

REFERENCES

Aboufadel, E., Olsen, J., & Windle, J. (2005). Breaking the holiday inn priority club CAPTCHA. *The College Mathematics Journal, 36*(2), 101–108. doi:10.2307/30044832

Athanasopoulos, E., & Antonatos, S. (2006). Enhanced CAPTCHAs: Using animation to tell humans and computers apart. In *Proceedings of 10th IFIP International Conference on Communications and Multimedia Security (CMS 2006)* (pp. 97–108). IFIP.

Baird, H. S. (2002). The ability gap between human & machine reading systems. In *Proceedings of First Workshop on Human Interactive Proofs (HIP 2002)*. HIP.

Baird, H. S. (2006). Data complexity in pattern recognition. In M. Basu, & T. K. Ho (Eds.), *Complex image recognition and web security*. London: Springer-Verlag London Ltd.

Baird, H. S., & Bentley, J. L. (2005). Implicit CAPTCHAs. In *Proceedings of SPIE/IS&T Electronic Imaging, Document Recognition and Retrieval XII* (Vol. 5676, pp. 191–196). IEEE.

Baird, H. S., Coates, A. L., & Fateman, R. J. (2003). Pessimalprint: A reverse turing test. *International Journal on Document Analysis and Recognition, 5*(2–3), 158–163. doi:10.1007/s10032-002-0089-1

Baird, H. S., & Lopresti, D. P. (2005). Second international workshop on human interactive proofs - Preface. In *Proceedings of Second International Workshop on Human Interactive Proofs (HIP 2005)*. HIP.

Baird, H. S., & Luk, M. (2003). Protecting websites with reading-based CAPTCHAs. In *Proceedings of Second International Workshop on Web Document Analysis (WDA2003)*. WDA.

Baird, H. S., Moll, M. A., & Wang, S. Y. (2005a). A highly legible CAPTCHA that resists segmentation attacks. In *Proceedings of Second International Workshop on Human Interactive Proofs (HIP 2005)* (pp. 27–41). HIP.

Baird, H. S., Moll, M. A., & Wang, S. Y. (2005b). Scattertype: A legible but hard-to-segment CAPTCHA. In *Proceedings of the 8th International Conference on Document Analysis and Recognition (ICDAR 05)* (Vol. 2, pp. 935–939). ICDAR.

Baird, H. S., & Popat, K. (2002). Human interactive proofs and document image analysis. In *Proceedings of 5th IAPR International Workshop on Document Analysis Systems* (pp. 507–518). IAPR.

Baird, H. S., & Riopka, T. P. (2005). Scattertype: A reading CAPTCHA resistant to segmentation attack. In *Proceedings of SPIE/IS&T Electronic Imaging, Document Recognition and Retrieval XII* (pp. 197–207). SPIE.

Bentley, J., & Mallows, C. (2005). How much assurance does a PIN provide? In *Proceedings of Second International Workshop on Human Interactive Proofs (HIP 2005)* (pp. 111–126). HIP.

Bentley, J., & Mallows, C. (2006). CAPTCHA challenge strings: Problems and improvements. In *Proceedings of 18th SPIE/IS&T Electronic Imaging, Document Recognition and Retrieval XIII*. SPIE.

Bergmair, R., & Katzenbeisser, S. (2004). Towards human interactive proofs in the text-domain: Using the problem of sense-ambiguity for security. In *Proceedings of 7th International Information Security Conference (ISC 2004)* (pp. 257–267). ISC.

Blank, D. (2001). A practical turing test for detecting adbots. *Intelligence, 12*(4), 6–7. doi:10.1145/376451.376458

Blum, M., von Ahn, L., & Langford, J. (2000). *The CAPTCHA project.* Retrieved from http://www.captcha.net/

Brelstaff, G., & Chessa, F. (2005). Practical application of visual illusions: Errare humanum est. In *Proceedings of the 2nd Symposium on Applied Perception in Graphics and Visualization (APGV 05)* (pp. 161). APGV.

Broder, A. (2002). Preventing bulk URL submission by robots in altavista. In *Proceedings of First Workshop on Human Interactive Proofs (HIP 2002)*. HIP.

Chan, N. (2002). Sound oriented CAPTCHA. In *Proceedings of First Workshop on Human Interactive Proofs (HIP 2002)*. HIP.

Chan, T. Y. (2003). Using a text-to-speech synthesizer to generate a reverse Turing test. In *Proceedings of the 15th IEEE International Conference on Tools with Artificial Intelligence (ICTAI 03)* (pp. 226–232). IEEE.

Chellapilla, K., Larson, K., Simard, P., & Czerwinski, M. (2005a). Building segmentation based human-friendly human interaction proofs (HIPs). In *Proceedings of Second International Workshop on Human Interactive Proofs (HIP 2005)* (pp. 1–26). HIP.

Chellapilla, K., Larson, K., Simard, P., & Czerwinski, M. (2005b). Computers beat humans at single character recognition in reading based human interaction proofs (HIPs). In *Proceedings of Second Conference on Email and Anti-Spam (CEAS 2005)*. CEAS.

Chellapilla, K., Larson, K., Simard, P., & Czerwinski, M. (2005c). Designing human friendly human interaction proofs (HIPs). In *Proceedings of the SIGCHI Conference on Human Factors in Computing Systems (CHI 05)* (pp. 711–720). ACM.

Chellapilla, K., & Simard, P. (2004). Using machine learning to break visual human interaction proofs (HIPs). In *Proceedings of Advances in Neural Information Processing Systems (NIPS 2004)*. NIPS.

Chew, M., & Baird, H. S. (2003). Baffletext: A human interactive proof. In *Proceedings of SPIE/IS&T Electronic Imaging, Document Recognition and Retrieval X* (pp. 305–316). SPIE.

Chew, M., & Tygar, J. (2004). Image recognition CAPTCHAs. In *Proceedings of the 7th International Information Security Conference (ISC 2004)* (pp. 268–279). ISC.

Chew, M., & Tygar, J. (2005). Collaborative filtering CAPTCHAs. In *Proceedings of Second International Workshop on Human Interactive Proofs (HIP 2005)* (pp. 66–81). HIP.

Coates, A. L., Baird, H. S., & Fateman, R. J. (2001). Pessimal print: A reverse Turing test. In *Proceedings of the 6th International Conference on Document Analysis and Recognition (ICDAR 2001)* (pp. 1154–1158). ICDAR.

Dailey, M., & Namprempre, C. (2004). A text-graphics character CAPTCHA for password authentication. In *Proceedings of 2004 IEEE Region 10 Conference (TENCON 2004)* (Vol. 2, pp. 45–48). IEEE.

Datta, R., Li, J., & Wang, J. Z. (2005). IMAGINATION: A robust image-based CAPTCHA generation system. In *Proceedings of the 13th Annual ACM International Conference on Multimedia (MULTIMEDIA 05)* (pp. 331–334). ACM.

Elson, J., Douceur, J. R., Howell, J., & Saul, J. (2007). ASIRRA: A CAPTCHA that exploits interest-aligned manual image categorization. In *Proceedings of the 14th ACM Conference on Computer and Communications Security (CCS 2007)* (pp. 366–374). ACM.

Ferzli, R., Bazzi, R., & Karam, L. J. (2006). A CAPTCHA based on the human visual systems masking characteristics. In *Proceedings of 2006 IEEE International Conference on Multimedia and Expo (ICME 06)* (pp. 517–520). IEEE.

Godfrey, P. B. (2002). Text-based CAPTCHA algorithms. In *Proceedings of First Workshop on Human Interactiv Proofs (HIP 2002)*. HIP.

Golle, P. (2008). Machine learning attacks against the ASIRRA CAPTCHA. In *Proceedings of the 15th ACM Conference on Computer and Communications Security (CCS '08)* (pp. 535–542). ACM.

Goodman, J., & Rounthwaite, R. (2004). Stopping outgoing spam. In *Proceedings of the 5th ACM Conference on Electronic Commerce* (pp. 30–39). ACM.

He, L., & Liu, H. (2005). Shape context for image understanding. In *Proceedings of the 5th WSEAS International Conference on Signal, Speech and Image Processing* (pp. 276–281). WSEAS.

Holman, J., Lazar, J., Feng, J. H., & D'Arcy, J. (2007). Developing usable captchas for blind users. In *Proceedings of the 9th International ACM SIGACCESS Conference on Computers and Accessibility (ASSETS '07)* (pp. 245–246). ACM.

Hopper, N. (2002). Security and complexity aspects of human interactive proofs. In *Proceedings of First Workshop on Human Interactive Proofs (HIP 2002)*. HIP.

Hoque, M. E., Russomanno, D. J., & Yeasin, M. (2006). 2D CAPTCHAs from 3D models. [IEEE.]. *Proceedings of the IEEE SouthEastCon, 2006*, 165–170.

Jueles, A. (2002). At the juncture of cryptography and humanity. In *Proceedings of First Workshop on Human Interactive Proofs (HIP 2002)*. HIP.

Kochanski, G., Lopresti, D., & Shih, C. (2002). A reverse turing test using speech. In *Proceedings of the 7th International Conference on Spoken Language Processing (ICSLP 2002)* (pp. 1357–1360). ICSLP.

Kolupaev, A., & Ogijenko, J. (2008). CAPTCHAs: Humans vs. bots. *IEEE Security & Privacy, 6*(1), 68–70. doi:10.1109/MSP.2008.6

Liao, W. H. (2006). A CAPTCHA mechanism by exchange image blocks. In *Proceedings of the 18ᵗʰ International Conference on Pattern Recognition (ICPR 06)* (pp. 1179–1183). ICPR.

Liao, W. H., & Chang, C. C. (2004). Embedding information within dynamic visual patterns. In *Proceedings of the 2004 IEEE International Conference on Multimedia and Expo (ICME 04)* (Vol. 2, pp. 895–898). IEEE.

Lopresti, D. (2005). Leveraging the CAPTCHA problem. In *Proceedings of Second International Workshop on Human Interactive Proofs (HIP 2005)* (pp. 97–110). HIP.

Lopresti, D., & Shih, C. (2002). Human interactive proofs for spoken language interface. In *Proceedings of First Workshop on Human Interactive Proofs (HIP 2002)*. HIP.

Markkola, A., & Lindqvist, J. (2008). Accessible voice captchas for internet telephony. In *Proceedings of the 4ᵗʰ Symposium on Usable Privacy and Security (SOUPS '08)*. SOUPS.

Microsoft. (2007). *ASIRRA (animal species image recognition for restricting access)*. Retrieved from http://research.microsoft.com/asirra/

Misra, D., & Gaj, K. (2006). Face recognition CAPTCHAs. In *Proceedings of the Advanced International Conference on Telecommunications and International Conference on Internet and Web Applications and Services (AICT-ICIW 06)* (pp. 122). AICT-ICIW.

Mori, G., Belongie, S., & Malik, J. (2005). Efficient shape matching using shape contexts. *IEEE Transactions on Pattern Analysis and Machine Intelligence, 27*(11), 1832–1837. doi:10.1109/TPAMI.2005.220 PMID:16285381

Mori, G., & Malik, J. (2003). Recognizing objects in adversarial clutter: Breaking a visual CAPTCHA. In *Proceedings of 2003 IEEE Conference on Computer Vision and Pattern Recognition (CVPR 03)* (Vol. 1, pp. 134–141). IEEE.

Moy, G., Jones, N., Harkless, C., & Potter, R. (2004). Distortion estimation techniques in solving visual CAPTCHAs. In *Proceedings of 2004 IEEE Conference on Computer Vision and Pattern Recognition (CVPR 04)* (Vol. 2, pp. 23–28). IEEE.

Ponec, M. (2006). Visual reverse turing tests: A false sense of security. In *Proceedings of the 2006 IEEE Workshop on Information Assurance* (pp. 305–311). IEEE.

Pope, C., & Kaur, K. (2005). Is it human or computer? Defending e-commerce with captchas. *IT Professional, 7*(2), 43–49. doi:10.1109/MITP.2005.37

Przydatek, B. (2002). On the (im)possibility of a text-only CAPTCHA. In *Proceedings of First Workshop on Human Interactive Proofs (HIP 2002)*. Palo Alto, CA: HIP.

Rui, Y., & Liu, Z. (2003a). *ARTIFACIAL: Automated reverse turing test using facial features* (Tech. Rep. No. MSR-TR-2003-48). Microsoft.

Rui, Y., & Liu, Z. (2003b). Excuse me, but are you human? In *Proceedings of the 11ᵗʰ ACM International Conference on Multimedia (MULTIMEDIA 03)* (pp. 462–463). ACM.

Rui, Y., Liu, Z., Kallin, S., Janke, G., & Paya, C. (2005). Characters or faces: A user study on ease of use for HIPs. In *Proceedings of Second International Workshop on Human Interactive Proofs (HIP 2005)* (pp. 53–65). HIP.

Rusu, A. (2006). *Exploiting the gap in human and machine abilities in handwriting recognition for web security applications*. (Doctoral dissertation). University of New York at Buffalo, Buffalo, NY.

Rusu, A., & Govindaraju, V. (2004). Handwritten CAPTCHA: Using the difference in the abilities of humans and machines in reading handwritten words. In *Proceedings of the 9ᵗʰ International Workshop on Frontiers in Handwriting Recognition (IWFHR 04)* (pp. 226–231). IWFHR.

Rusu, A., & Govindaraju, V. (2005a). A human interactive proof algorithm using handwriting recognition. In *Proceedings of the 8ᵗʰ International Conference on Document Analysis and Recognition (ICDAR 05)* (Vol. 2, pp. 967–971). ICDAR.

Rusu, A., & Govindaraju, V. (2005b). Visual CAPTCHA with handwritten image analysis. In *Proceedings of Second International Workshop on Human Interactive Proofs (HIP 2005)* (pp. 42–52). HIP.

Sauer, G., Hochheiser, H., Feng, J., & Lazar, J. (2008). Towards a universally usable captcha. In *Proceedings of the 4ᵗʰ Symposium on Usable Privacy and Security (SOUPS'08)*. SOUPS.

Shirali-Shahreza, M. (2008). Highlighting CAPTCHA. In *Proceedings of the Conference on Human System Interaction (HSI2008)* (pp. 247–250). HSI.

Shirali-Shahreza, M., & Shirali-Shahreza, M. H. (2008a). Online PIX CAPTCHA. In *Proceedings of the IEEE International Conference on Signal Processing, Communications and Networking (ICSCN 2008)* (pp. 582–585). IEEE.

Shirali-Shahreza, M., & Shirali-Shahreza, S. (2006a). Drawing CAPTCHA. In *Proceedings of 28ᵗʰ International Conference on Information Technology Interfaces (ITI 2006)* (pp. 475–480). ITI.

Shirali-Shahreza, M., & Shirali-Shahreza, S. (2007a). CAPTCHA for blind people. In *Proceedings of the 7ᵗʰ IEEE International Symposium on Signal Processing and Information Technology (ISSPIT 2007)* (pp. 995–998). IEEE.

Shirali-Shahreza, M., & Shirali-Shahreza, S. (2007b). Collage CAPTCHA. In *Proceedings of the 20ᵗʰ IEEE International Symposium Signal Processing and Application (ISSPA 2007)*. IEEE.

Shirali-Shahreza, M., & Shirali-Shahreza, S. (2007c). Online collage CAPTCHA. In *Proceedings of the 8ᵗʰ International Workshop on Image Analysis for Multimedia Interactive Services (WIAMIS 2007)* (pp. 58). WIAMIS.

Shirali-Shahreza, M., & Shirali-Shahreza, S. (2007d). Question-based CAPTCHA. In *Proceedings of the International Conference on Computational Intelligence and Multimedia Applications (ICCIMA 2007)* (Vol. 4, pp. 54–58). ICCIMA.

Shirali-Shahreza, M., & Shirali-Shahreza, S. (2008b). CAPTCHA systems for disabled people. In *Proceedings of the IEEE Intelligent Computer Communication and Processing 2008 (ICCP 2008)* (pp. 319-322). IEEE.

Shirali-Shahreza, M., & Shirali-Shahreza, S. (2008c). Motion CAPTCHA. In *Proceedings of the Conference on Human System Interaction (HSI 2008)* (pp. 1042–1044). HSI.

Shirali-Shahreza, M. H., & Shirali-Shahreza, M. (2006b). Persian/Arabic baffletext CAPTCHA. *Journal of Universal Computer Science, 12*(12), 1783–1796.

Shirali-Shahreza, M. H., & Shirali-Shahreza, M. (2006c). Persian/Arabic CAPTCHA. *IADIS International Journal on Computer Science and Information Systems, 1*(2), 63–75.

Shirali-Shahreza, M. H., & Shirali-Shahreza, M. (2007e). Localized CAPTCHA for illiterate people. In *Proceedings of the International Conference on Intelligent & Advanced Systems (ICIAS 2007)*. ICIAS.

Shirali-Shahreza, M. H., & Shirali-Shahreza, M. (2007f). Multilingual CAPTCHA. In *Proceedings of 5th IEEE International Conference on Computational Cybernetics (ICCC 2007)* (pp. 135–139). IEEE.

Shirali-Shahreza, M. H., & Shirali-Shahreza, M. (2007g). Nastaliq CAPTCHA. *Iranian Journal of Electrical and Computer Engineering, 5*(2), 109–114.

Shirali-Shahreza, S., & Shirali-Shahreza, M. (2008d). Bibliography of works done on CAPTCHA. In *Proceedings of the 3rd International Conference on Intelligent System & Knowledge Engineering (ISKE 2008)*. ISKE.

Shirali-Shahreza, S., & Shirali-Shahreza, M. (2008e). CAPTCHA for children. In *Proceedings of 3rd International Conference on System of Systems Engineering (SoSE 2008)*. SoSE.

Shirali-Shahreza, S., & Shirali-Shahreza, M. (2008f). A new human interactive proofs system for deaf persons. In *Proceedings of the 5th International Conference on Information Technology: New Generations (ITNG 2008)* (pp. 807–810). ITNG.

Shirali-Shahreza, S., Shirali-Shahreza, M., & Movaghar, A. (2007). Exam HIP. In *Proceedings of the 2007 IEEE International Workshop on Anti-Counterfeiting, Security, Identification (ASID 2007)* (pp. 415–418). IEEE.

Simard, P. Y., Szeliski, R., Benaloh, J., Couvreur, J., & Calinov, I. (2003). Using character recognition and segmentation to tell computer from humans. In *Proceedings of the 7th International Conference on Document Analysis and Recognition (ICDAR 03)* (Vol. 1, pp. 418–423). ICDAR.

Spitz, A. L. (2002). A feeble classifier relying on strong context. In *Proceedings of First Workshop on Human Interactive Proofs (HIP 2002)*. HIP.

Tam, J., Simsa, J., Huggins-Daines, D., von Ahn, L., & Blum, M. (2008). Improving audio CAPTCHAs. In *Proceedings of the 4th Symposium on Usability, Privacy and Security (SOUPS '08)*. SOUPS.

Thayananthan, A., Stenger, B., Torr, P., & Cipolla, R. (2003). Shape context and chamfer matching in cluttered scenes. In *Proceedings of 2003 IEEE Conference on Computer Vision and Pattern Recognition (CVPR 03)* (Vol. 1, pp. 127–133). IEEE.

Turing, A. M. (1950). Computing machinery and intelligence. *Mind, 59*(236), 433–460. doi:10.1093/mind/LIX.236.433

von Ahn, L. (2005). *Human computation.* (Doctoral dissertation). Carnegie Mellon University, Pittsburgh, PA.

von Ahn, L., Blum, M., Hopper, N. J., & Langford, J. (2003). CAPTCHA: Using hard AI problems for security. In *Proceedings of International Conference on the Theory and Applications of Cryptographic Techniques (EUROCRYPT 2003)* (pp. 294–311). Springer.

von Ahn, L., Blum, M., & Langford, J. (2004). Telling humans and computers apart automatically. *Communications of the ACM, 47*(2), 56–60. doi:10.1145/966389.966390

von Ahn, L., Maurer, B., McMillen, C., Abraham, D., & Blum, M. (2008). reCAPTCHA: Human-based character recognition via web security measures. *Science, 321*(5895), 1465–1468. doi:10.1126/science.1160379 PMID:18703711

Voth, D. (2003). The paradox of CAPTCHAs. *IEEE Intelligent Systems, 18*(2), 6–7. doi:10.1109/MIS.2003.1234761

W3C. (2005). *Inaccessibility of CAPTCHA* (W3C Working Group Note No. 23 November 2005). Retrieved from http://www.w3.org/TR/2005/NOTE-turingtest-20051123/

W3C. (2008). *Web content accessibility guidelines (WCAG) 2.0* (W3C Proposed Recommendation). Retrieved from http://www.w3.org/TR/2008/PR-WCAG20-20081103/

Wang, S. Y., & Bentley, J. L. (2006). CAPTCHA challenge tradeoffs: Familiarity of strings versus degradation of images. In *Proceedings of the 18th International Conference on Pattern Recognition (ICPR 06)* (pp. 164–167). ICPR.

Ximenes, P., dos Santos, A., Fernandez, M., & Celestino, J. (2006). A CAPTCHA in the text domain. In *Proceedings of Workshops on the Move to Meaningful Internet Systems 2006 (OTM 2006)* (pp. 605–615). OTM.

Xu, J., Essa, I. A., & Lipton, R. J. (2000). *Hello, are you human?* (Tech. Rep. No. GIT-CC-00-28). Atlanta, GA: Georgia Institute of Technology.

Xu, S., Lau, F. C. M., Cheung, W. K., & Pan, Y. (2005). Automatic generation of artistic Chinese calligraphy. *IEEE Intelligent Systems*, *20*(3), 32–39. doi:10.1109/MIS.2005.41

Yan, J., & Ahmad, A. S. E. (2007). Breaking visual CAPTCHAs with naive pattern recognition algorithms. In *Proceedings of 23rd Annual Computer Security Applications Conference (ACSAC 2007)* (pp. 279–291). ACSAC.

Yan, J., & Ahmad, A. S. E. (2008a). A low-cost attack on a Microsoft CAPTCHA. In *Proceedings of the 15th ACM Conference on Computer and Communications Security (CCS '08)* (pp. 543–554). ACM.

Yan, J., & Ahmad, A. S. E. (2008b). Usability of CAPTCHA or usability issues in CAPTCHA design. In *Proceedings of the 4th Symposium on Usable Privacy and Security (SOUPS '08)*. SOUPS.

Yang, K. (2002). Issues for Chinese CAPTCHA. In *Proceedings of First Workshop on Human Interactive Proofs (HIP 2002)*. HIP.

Zhang, Z., Rui, Y., Huang, T., & Paya, C. (2004). Breaking the clock face HIP. In *Proceedings of 2004 IEEE International Conference on Multimedia and Expo (ICME 04)* (Vol. 3, pp. 2167–2170). IEEE.

KEY TERMS AND DEFINITIONS

Accessibility: The capability of being available and reachable to a wide range of people.

CAPTCHA (Completely Automated Public Turing test to tell Computers and Human Apart): A challenge-response test that verifies whether the user who interacts with the system is human.

HIP (Human Interactive Proof): Interactive challenges that determines whether or not the user belongs to a specific group

Image Processing: A set of signal processing techniques to either enhance an image or extract information from it.

Objection Recognition: Automatic detection of different objects in a scene and identifying their type.

OCR (Optical Character Recognition): Process of converting scanned documents into computer encoded digital documents.

Turing Test: A machine's intelligibility test in which a judge tries to distinguish between the human and computer contestants.

Chapter 11
Network Security:
Attacks and Controls

Natarajan Meghanathan
Jackson State University, USA

ABSTRACT

The focus of this chapter is two-fold: It first presents the classical network attacks (such as Session Hijacking, Man-in-the-Middle attack, DNS attacks, Distributed Denial of Service attacks, and other miscellaneous attacks), which have exploited the various vulnerabilities of computer networks in the past, and reviews the solutions that have been implemented since then to mitigate or reduce the chances of these attacks. The authors then present the different network security controls, including the protocols and standards (such as IPSec, Kerberos, Secure Shell, Transport Layer Security, Virtual Private Networks, Firewalls, and S/MIME) that have been adopted in modern day computer networks to control the incidence of attacks in modern day computer networks.

INTRODUCTION TO COMPUTER NETWORKS

With the phenomenal growth in the Internet, network security has become an integral part of computer and information security. Network security comprises of the measures adopted to protect the resources and integrity of a computer network. This section reviews the basics of computer networks and Internet in order to lay a strong foundation for the reader to understand the rest of this chapter on network security.

ISO-OSI Reference Model

The communication problem in computer networks can be defined as the task of transferring data entered by an application user in one system to an application user in another system through one or more intermediate networks (Comer, 2008). The communication problem is solved using a layered approach through a collection of protocols forming the so-called protocol suite. Each layer, dealing with a particular aspect of the communication problem, is implemented with a particular protocol and the protocols co-operate with each other to solve the entire communication problem. The Open Systems Interconnection (OSI) model

DOI: 10.4018/978-1-4666-4789-3.ch011

(Zimmermann, 1980) is an abstract representation of the basic layers (as stated below and also shown in Figure 1, in top to bottom order) involved to solve the communication problem: Application, Presentation, Session, Transport, Network, Data-link and Physical layers.

The application layer specifies how one particular application uses a network and contacts the application program running on a remote machine. The presentation layer deals with the translation and/or representation of data at the two end hosts of the communication. The session layer is responsible for establishing a communication session with a remote system and it also handles security issues like password authentication before the application user can connect to the remote system. The transport layer provides end-to-end, reliable or best-effort, in-order data packet delivery along with support for flow control and congestion control. The network layer deals with forwarding data packets from the source to the destination nodes of the communication. The data-link layer deals with the organization of data into frames and provides reliable data delivery over the physical medium. The physical layer provides the encoding/decoding schemes and the

Figure 1. OSI model

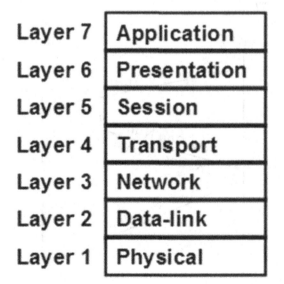

Layer 7	Application
Layer 6	Presentation
Layer 5	Session
Layer 4	Transport
Layer 3	Network
Layer 2	Data-link
Layer 1	Physical

modulation/demodulation schemes for the actual transmission of data, over the physical medium, as a sequence of bits of 1s and 0s.

TCP/IP Protocol Stack

The seven-layer OSI model is conceptual: it shows the different activities required for communication between application programs running in two different hosts. Its full implementation will result in excessive overhead and will lead to huge delays in data delivery at the destination (Comer, 2008). The TCP/IP (Transmission Control Protocol/ Internet Protocol) protocol stack (Stevens, 1994), shown in Figure 2, is the commonly used model for wide area communications, like the Internet. The TCP/IP protocol stack is composed of the Application, Transport, Internet and the Link layers (from top to bottom). The application layer of the TCP/IP model is in-charge of the responsibilities of the application, presentation and session layers of the OSI model. The transport layer of the TCP/IP model is similar to the transport layer of the OSI model. The Internet layer takes care of addressing and routing the data packets across different heterogeneous networks. Each machine and router in the Internet has a unique IP address. The link layer of the TCP/IP model combines the functionalities of the data-link layer and physical layer of the OSI model. The link layer supports the organization of data into frames and their encoding/decoding mechanisms. The structure and transmission of the frames depends on the topology and hardware technology (like Ethernet, Token Ring and etc) used for the network. A data packet is referred to as segment, datagram and frame at the transport, Internet and the link layers respectively.

TCP Connection Establishment

The two commonly used transport layer protocols in the TCP/IP protocol stack (Stevens, 1994) are the Transmission Control Protocol (TCP) and the User Datagram Protocol (UDP). TCP is a con-

Figure 2. TCP/IP protocol stack and the structure of a data packet

			Data	Layer 4	Application
Segment		TCP or UDP Header	Data	Layer 3	Transport
Datagram	IP Header	TCP or UDP Header	Data	Layer 2	Internet
Frame	Frame Header	IP Header	TCP or UDP Header	Data	Layer 1	Link

nection-oriented, byte-stream based protocol and provides reliable, in-order data delivery. UDP is a connectionless, message-based protocol and provides only best-effort service for end-to-end data delivery. Processes running TCP have to establish a connection before exchanging any data packet. During this connection establishment mechanism, the two processes exchange information about the capabilities and resources available at their respective hosts for the particular communication session that is about to begin. This will help the TCP process running in one host to adjust its data sending rate according to the resources (like the memory buffer space) available for the TCP process at the receiving host. In order to avoid replay errors, the two processes pick an arbitrary starting sequence number for the data packets sent by them. Each byte of data is given a unique, monotonically increasing sequence number. The sequence number of a data packet sent using TCP represents the sequence number of the first byte of the data transmitted in that packet.

The TCP connection-establishment process (shown in Figure 3) is a three-way handshake mechanism (Comer, 2008) and is explained as follows through this example: Let a process running in host A initiate a session with a process at host B by sending a Synchronization (SYN)

packet to host B with the initial sequence number set to X. The process at host A will include information about the memory resources available (through the 'Advertised Window' field of the TCP header) in the SYN packet. If the process at host B is willing to establish a communication session with the process at host A, then it sends back a SYN/ACK packet that will indicate the memory resources available at host B for this communication, the starting sequence number of

Figure 3. TCP connection establishment mechanism

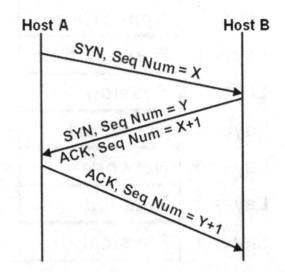

the data packets coming from the process at host B and an acknowledgment for receiving the SYN packet from the process at host A. The process at host A will respond back with an ACK packet if it accepts to the advertised window value of host B and is willing to tune down its data sending rate accordingly. Note that the acknowledgment sent to a process/host for receiving a packet with a particular sequence number (say X) indicates the sequence number (X+1) of the next packet expected from the process/host. Typically, host A could be a client and host B could be a server.

Internet Control Message Protocol (ICMP)

IP provides best-effort service in delivering datagrams from one host to another host through one or more intermediate networks. The TCP/IP protocol suite provides an error-reporting protocol called the Internet Control Message Protocol (ICMP) that operates in tandem with IP. IP uses ICMP to report errors and certain critical information to the end hosts. Each ICMP message is identified by an 8-bit type field in the IP header. One of the commonly used ICMP message is ECHO Request/Reply (Postel, 1981). An ECHO request message is sent to the ICMP process running on a host computer to check whether the host is alive. If the host is alive, the host sends a response using the ECHO Reply message.

CLASSICAL NETWORK SECURITY ATTACKS

In this section, we describe some of the classical attacks that have exploited the typical vulnerabilities of computer networks and the solutions deployed to combat or reduce the chances of some of these attacks.

Threats in Transit

The network interface card (NIC) of each host in a network is uniquely identified with a hardware address. The NIC will be programmed to pick up only the packets addressed to: (i) The unicast hardware address corresponding to the host, (ii) The multicast hardware address corresponding to the multicast group in which the host is a member of and (iii) The broadcast hardware address. A capable intruder can reprogram the NIC with the hardware address of another host and accept packets addressed to that host. To avoid being caught, the intruder can put a copy of the packet back to the network.

Wiretapping is the process of extracting information as it flows through a wire (Pfleeger, 2006). The process of wiretapping differs depending on the communication medium used. In cables, wiretapping can be done through the use of a packet sniffer or through inductance. A packet sniffer is a computer software or hardware that can intercept the traffic passing through a local area network (LAN) cable (Connolly, 2003). A packet sniffer can be used for both beneficial and malicious purposes: (i) To analyze network problems and monitor network usage, (ii) To filter suspect content from network traffic, (iii) To study the structure of the packet headers of the different protocols used over the network, (iv) To detect network intrusion attempts and (v) To gather information for effecting a network intrusion. As an ordinary wire emits radiation during the propagation of electrical signals through it, an intruder can tap the wire and read radiated signals through inductance without making physical contact with the cable. An intruder intercepting the signals on a broadband cable has to separate the targeted signal from all the multiplexed signals.

Wireless signals are broadcast through the open space and are more susceptible for tapping.

For example, the signal path of microwave signals has to be fairly wide to make sure the antenna of the receiver will be hit by the transmitted signal. But, the wider the signal path, the more it is easy for an intruder to interfere with the line of sight of transmission between the sender and the receiver and also to pick up the entire transmission from an antenna located closely to the receiver. Similarly, with satellite communication, there is a tradeoff between coverage and secure communication. A footprint is defined as the pattern produced on the surface of the earth from the satellite's transmitter (Pfleeger, 2006). A broader footprint is needed to maximize coverage because the signals can be picked up over a huge region. On the other hand, a smaller footprint is desirable to reduce the risk of interception. The angle of dispersion of a satellite transponder is a parameter that could be controlled to adjust the spread of a footprint.

An optical fiber, made of thin glass strands, can carry light pulses over long distances without being much affected by electrical interference (Pfleeger, 2006). Optical fibers are more secure than any other transmission media because of the following two reasons: (i) Optical fibers are fine tuned to achieve total internal reflection. So, the entire network should be retuned to facilitate tapping and interception and (ii) Optical fibers carry light energy and not electrical signals. So, inductance based tapping would not be possible.

TCP Session Hijacking

TCP session hijacking refers to the act of taking over an already established TCP session and injecting packets into the stream that are processed by the receiver as if the packets are coming from the authentic owner of the session (Russell et. al., 2002). A TCP session is identified by the quadruple: client IP address, client port number, server IP address and server port number. Any packet that reaches either machine with the above identifiers is considered to be part of the existing session. If attackers can spoof these items, they can pass TCP packets to the client or server and have those packets processed as coming from the other machine.

To successfully hijack an existing TCP session, an attacker has to first desynchronize the session and then inject the intended commands. To desynchronize an existing TCP session (refer Figure 4) between a client and server, the attacker has to first predict the sequence number that is about to be used by a client (or server) and use that sequence number before the client (or server) gets a chance to use. If the attacker has access to the network, a packet sniffer can be used to look into the packets belonging to the TCP session and one can accurately predict the expected sequence number from the ACK packets exchanged. If the attacker cannot sniff the TCP session between the client and server, then the attacker has to try all possible options and guess the expected sequence number. When the attacker successfully hijacks the TCP session and injects own spoofed data packets (as if the data packets are coming from the original client), the server will acknowledge the receipt of the data packet to the original client by sending it an ACK packet. As this ACK packet will most likely bear a sequence number that is not expected by it, the original client will attempt to resynchronize with the server by sending it an ACK packet with the sequence number that it is expecting. This ACK packet will in turn contain a sequence number that the server is not expecting and so the server will resend its last ACK packet. This cycle will continue and the rapid passing back and forth of the ACK packets creates the TCP ACK storm (refer Figure 5). As the attacker injects more and more data packets, the size of the ACK storm increases and can quickly bring down performance of the network. After a certain number of unsuccessful resynchronization attempts, the original client eventually gets exhausted and closes the connection with the server.

Figure 4. Desynchronizing a TCP session

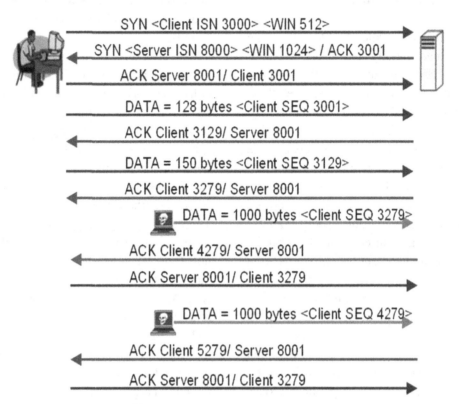

Figure 5. Creating a TCP ACK storm

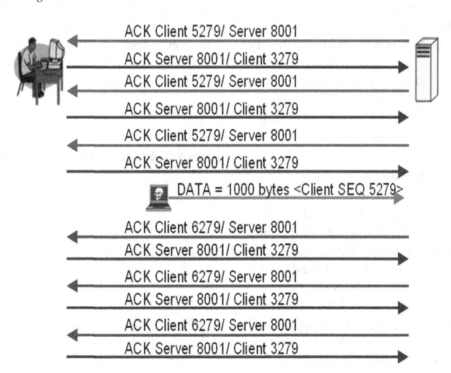

Man in the Middle Attack

With a Man-In-The-Middle (MITM) attack, an attacker can read, modify and insert messages between two communicating parties, without either party knowing that the link between them has been compromised (Russell et. al., 2002). To successfully carry out this attack, one must be able to observe and intercept messages between the two victims. We describe below an example for an MITM attack on public-key cryptography: Let A and B be the two communicating parties and let M be the attacker who wants to deliver a false message to B. To get started, B sends its public key to A. If M can intercept the communication channel between A and B, then M gets access to the public key of B. Then, M sends A, a spoofed message that claims to have come from B. In this message, M sends its own public key, but A thinks it has received the public key of B. When A sends a data packet to B, it encrypts the packet with (what A considers as) the public key of B and inserts the encrypted message in the channel. M intercepts the message and decrypts it with its own private key to extract the actual message sent by A to B. M then encrypts the message with the public key of B. Note that M could even modify the message before encrypting it again. M inserts the new encrypted message back in the channel so that the message can go to B. B decrypts the message using its own private key and reads the message assuming it came from A.

Echo-Chargen Attack

Chargen (Character Generator) is a protocol of the TCP/IP protocol stack and is used for testing and performance measurement purposes (Postel, 1983). Chargen runs on TCP port 19 and also on UDP port 19. When a client opens a TCP connection with a server on TCP port 19, the server starts sending arbitrary characters back to the client, until the TCP connection is closed. Whenever a host sends a UDP message to a server on UDP port 19,

the server responds back with an arbitrary message and the number of characters in the message will be in the range [0…512].

An attacker can trigger the Echo-Chargen attack by spoofing a conversation between the Echo Request/Reply service and the Chargen service and then redirecting the output of each service to the other, creating a rapidly expanding spiral of traffic in the network. In Figure 6, we see an attacker triggering the attack by sending a spoofed message to one of the targeted hosts (host A) running the Chargen service at UDP port 19. The message is spoofed in such a way that it appears to have originated from the other targeted host (host B) and UDP port 7, which is the port number used for Echo-Request/Reply messaging. Host A now sends a UDP message from port 19 to port 7 of host B. Host B will consider this as an Echo Request message and sends back a Reply message to UDP port 19 of host A. Host A will treat the Reply message as a message received for the Chargen service and sends back a new arbitrary UDP message to port 7 of host B. This cycle of message exchange between the two services will continue and generate excessive traffic in the network. Eventually, the attack consumes memory and processor power at the targeted hosts (A and B) making them become non-responsive to user commands.

Figure 6. A typical Echo-Chargen attack

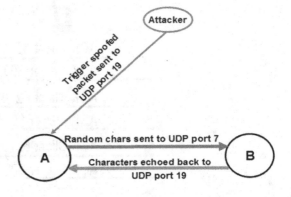

Smurf Attack

A perpetrator can launch the Smurf attack (Russell et. al., 2002) by sending a spoofed Echo-Request message to a network's broadcast IP address. The spoofed Echo-Request message has the victim's IP address as the source IP address. Hence, each host receiving the broadcast Echo-Request message will send an Echo-Reply message to the victim. The victim will be overwhelmed with a flood of Echo-Reply messages. Thus, the Smurf attack is a kind of Denial-of-Service (DoS) attack. Two solutions have been currently adopted in the Internet to prevent a Smurf attack (Senie, 1999): (i) Routers do not forward datagrams having the destination address as a broadcast IP address and (ii) Hosts are configured not to reply for Echo-Request messages that were received as a broadcast message.

Traffic Redirection Attack

A compromised router can send out route update messages to all its neighboring routers informing them that it lies on the shortest path to every network in the Internet (Thing et. al., 2005). The neighboring routers forward all of their incoming data packets to this compromised router, which will get eventually flooded with the data packets and starts dropping them. The data packets do not make it to the destination.

Attacks on Domain Name Service (DNS)

A DNS server is a machine that holds a table (called the DNS cache) mapping the domain names to IP addresses (Austein, 2007). The server queries other DNS servers higher up in the domain name hierarchy to resolve domain names for which it does not have an IP address entry in its DNS cache and updates its cache with the mapping learnt. DNS cache poisoning is an attack using which the DNS server is made to believe a domain name-IP address mapping as authentic, while, in reality, it is not (Pfleeger, 2006). Once the DNS cache is poisoned, the entry stays for a while in the cache and affects the clients who use the DNS server in the mean time. For example, an attacker can replace the IP address information for a target file server with the IP address of a compromised file server which the attacker controls. The attacker creates fake entries in the compromised server with file names matching those on the target server. These files could contain malicious contents such as a worm or virus. Users who want to download files from the target file server may end up unknowingly downloading files with malicious content from the compromised file server.

Distributed Denial of Service (DDoS) Attacks

DDoS attacks involve breaking into hundreds or thousands of machines all over the Internet (Russell et. al., 2002). The attacker installs malicious software on all these compromised machines (called zombies) and controls them to launch coordinated attacks on victim sites. DDoS attacks are normally aimed at exhausting the network bandwidth, overwhelming a router's processing capacity and breaking network connectivity to the victims. The attacker uses any convenient method (like exploiting the buffer overflow attack (Pfleeger, 2006) or tricking the victim to open and install an unknown code from an email attachment) to plant a Trojan Horse (Pfleeger, 2006) on a target machine and transform it into a zombie by also installing a rootkit software. The rootkit helps to conceal the presence of the Trojan Horse and hide its malicious activities. After forming sufficient number of zombies, the attacker sends a signal to all the zombies to launch the DDoS attack on a chosen victim machine. Each zombie may launch the same or a different type of attack on the victim.

DDoS attacks involve breaking into hundreds or thousands of machines all over the Internet (Russell et. al., 2002). The attacker installs malicious software on all these compromised machines (called zombies) and controls them to launch coordinated attacks on victim sites. DDoS attacks are normally aimed at exhausting the network bandwidth, overwhelming a router's processing capacity and breaking network connectivity to the victims. The attacker uses any convenient method (like exploiting the buffer overflow attack (Pfleeger, 2006) or tricking the victim to open and install an unknown code from an email attachment) to plant a Trojan Horse (Pfleeger, 2006) on a target machine and transform it into a zombie by also installing a rootkit software. The rootkit helps to conceal the presence of the Trojan Horse and hide its malicious activities. After forming sufficient number of zombies, the attacker sends a signal to all the zombies to launch the DDoS attack on a chosen victim machine. Each zombie may launch the same or a different type of attack on the victim.

SYN Flood Attack

During the TCP connection establishment process, the server maintains a SYN_RECV queue to keep track of the connection requests for which it has allocated the resources and responded back with a SYN/ACK message, but the corresponding ACK from the client has not yet been received. The server eventually times out waiting for the ACK packet and removes the incomplete connection request from its queue. An attacker can launch a DDOS attack by sending several SYN connection request messages using spoofed non-existing IP addresses and never respond back with the ACK messages (Russell et. al., 2002). The SYN_RECV queue of the server gets filled up with incomplete connection request messages. Even though these incomplete connection requests are discarded after the timeout, if a genuine client attempts to establish a TCP connection with the server in the mean time, the server discards the SYN request from that client.

NETWORK SECURITY CONTROLS

This section describes several network security controls that have been adopted in modern day computer networks to combat the threats and prevent or reduce the chances of an attack.

Link Encryption vs. End-to-End Encryption

Encryption applied between every pair of hosts connected by a link is called link-to-link encryption (Pfleeger, 2006). Link encryption is preferred when all the hosts in the network are secure, but the communication medium is shared among several users and is not secure. Almost all the components of a data frame (except the source and destination hardware addresses in the frame header) are encrypted before the frame is inserted onto the physical communications link. As the frame reaches the next hop receiver (could be a router or the end host), the frame is decrypted at the bottom protocol layer and sent to the higher layers for further processing and forwarding. Since encryption is at the bottom protocol layer, the message is exposed in plaintext at all the other layers of the sender and receiver and at the link and Internet layers of the intermediate hosts for hardware addressing and routing. Thus, link encryption protects the message in transit between two computers, but the message is in plaintext inside the end hosts and the intermediate hosts. One or more of the intermediate hosts may not be credible.

Encryption applied between two application programs running at the end hosts of a communication is called end-to-end encryption (Pfleeger, 2006). Here, only the data portion of the packet is encrypted at the highest level (i.e. the application layer) and the packet is transmitted with the data in encrypted form throughout the Internet. Thus, end-to-end encryption protects the data against disclosure while in transit, but the data packet could go through potentially insecure intermediate hosts. Table 1 (Pfleeger, 2006) compares the pros and cons of link encryption and end-to-end encryption.

Virtual Private Networks

There are two types of IP addresses: public and private. A public IP address (Comer, 2008) is globally unique and only one machine connected to the public Internet can have a public IP address. Private IP addresses are one of the solutions to reduce the exhaustion of IP address space (Comer, 2008). A private IP address has to be unique only within the set of networks of a particular organization. Larger organizations have sites at different locations in the world. The hosts in the different sites of the organization may be identified with a unique private IP address. But the same set of private IP addresses can be used in the networks of different organizations. Hence, a packet with a private IP address as the destination IP address cannot be used to route packets from one site to another site of an organization through the public Internet.

The virtual private network (VPN) technology uses IP-in-IP tunneling (Simpson, 1995) to encrypt and encapsulate the IP datagram that has the private IP addresses of the two end hosts with another IP header that has the source and destination IP addresses as the public IP address of the gateway routers for these two private networks. Each organization is required to have one or more gateway routers with a public IP address in order to facilitate communication over the public Internet. As the original IP datagram is encrypted, no intermediate forwarding host in the public Internet can look at the contents of the message. Figure 7 illustrates the notion of a VPN and Figure 8 displays the structure of an IP datagram as it goes through the different phases of IP-in-IP tunneling.

Secure Shell

Secure Shell (SSH) is a network protocol that allows a user to securely interact with remote machines by establishing a secure channel for data exchange (Simpson, 1995). SSH replaced TELNET (Postel & Reynolds, 1983) and other insecure remote shell programs that were used in the past to send information in plaintext, including passwords, to remote systems. SSH encrypts the information sent over the insecure Internet and thus provides both confidentiality and integrity of

Table 1. Comparison of link encryption and end-to-end encryption

Link Encryption	End-to-End Encryption
End hosts of every link should share a key and should be able to do encryption and decryption	The intermediate hosts of a transmission path do not need to have cryptographic facilities.
If there are N hosts and n users in a network ($N << n$), the number of keys needed would be $N(N-1)/2$	The number of keys needed for symmetric encryption and public-key encryption would be $n(n-1)/2$ and $2n$ respectively.
All message transmissions have to be encrypted and decrypted at every link.	Encryption is application and message specific and need not be done for all messages.
One encryption algorithm may be used for all users in all links	Each application user can deploy an encryption algorithm of choice.
Data is exposed at the end hosts and the intermediate hosts	Except the application layer, data is encrypted at both the end hosts and the intermediate hosts

Figure 7. Virtual Private Network

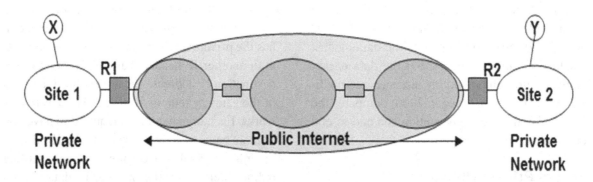

Figure 8. Structure of an IP datagram during different phases of IP-in-IP tunneling

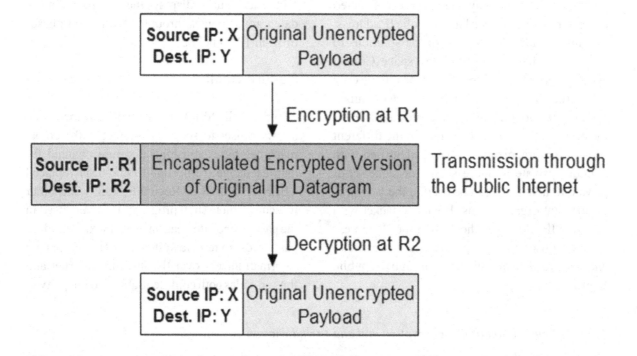

data. SSH operates over a sequence of three phases as illustrated by the timeline diagram shown in Figure 9. The three phases are described below:

Step 1: Host Identification

The client machine needs to ensure that it is communicating with the remote machine it has been asked to by the application program, and not with another machine that is spoofing it. The server machine on the remote side also has the option to ensure that the user is connecting from the machine as it appears to be, and not from another machine that is spoofing it. This step is accomplished as outlined below:

Figure 9. Steps to establish a Secure Shell (SSH) connection

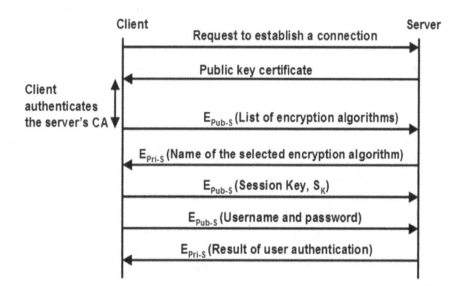

- The client contacts the server and requests for its public-key certificate.

- The client maintains a list of public keys for server machines available to it. If it is asked to contact a machine for which it does not have a public key locally held, it will warn the user with a message telling that the public key reported by the server is not in the list of known hosts and ask the user whether the user wants to continue connecting.

- If the user agrees to continue connecting, the client verifies the authenticity of the Certifying Authority (CA) that issued the public key certificate for the server and if satisfied, accepts the public keys. The machine then adds the server's public keys to its personal list of host public keys.

- When the administrator has included the public key for the client machine in the per-machine list of known host public keys on the server machine, the server may want the client machine to prove that it is what it claims to be.

- The server will create a "challenge" encrypted with the client's host public key and send it to the client. Only a genuine client machine will be able to decrypt this message with its private key. The client then sends the same challenge encrypted with the public key of the server. If the server when decrypting the message gets the same challenge it sent, the client is genuine.

Step 2: Encryption

The objective of this step is to establish a secure end-to-end link that supports encryption of the data transferred. Even the password and other authentication information are encrypted and are not transmitted in plaintext. This step is accomplished as outlined below:

- Once the host identification step is successfully done, the client sends a list of encryption algorithms it could use and their corresponding keys. This is sent encrypted with the public key of the server.

- The server decrypts the list with its private key and chooses the strongest encryption algorithm that it could handle from the list sent by the client.
- The server then notifies the selected encryption algorithm to the client by encrypting the notification using its private key.
- The client generates the appropriate secret session key for the encryption algorithm selected and notifies the session key to the server by encrypting the notification with the public key of the server.
- The server decrypts the notification with its private key and extracts the secret session key.

Step 3: User Authentication

In this step, the user proves to the server that he/she has the right to perform operations as a particular user on the server machine. This is accomplished as outlined below:

- The client asks for the username and password from the user, encrypts them with the server's public key and sends to the server.

- The server checks the validity of the username and password and if everything is fine, accepts the connection request by sending the confirmation encrypted with its private key.
- The client decrypts the confirmation with the server's public key and the client and server are all set to exchange data securely using the encryption algorithm selected and the secret session key agreed.

Transport Layer Security (TLS)

Transport Layer Security (TLS; Dierks & Rescorla, 2008) is the successor of the Secure Sockets Layer (SSL; Freir et. al., 1996) cryptographic protocol and it provides secure communication of the datagrams of the transport layer protocols as part of an end-to-end connection across the network. TLS has been used for a wide-variety of applications like Web browsing, electronic mail, voice-over-IP, instant messaging and etc.

We now explain the sequence of steps to be followed to establish a TLS connection between a client and a server and it is pictorially illustrated in Figure 10:

Figure 10. TLS connection establishment mechanism

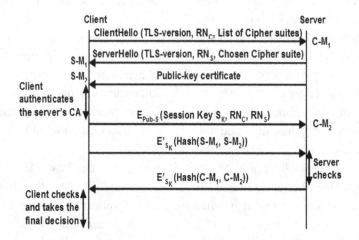

- The client initiates the connection request by sending a *ClientHello* message to the server. This message has the following information: (i) The latest TLS-version supported by the client; (ii) A random number arbitrarily chosen by the client and (iii) A list of suggested cipher suites (i.e., the encryption algorithms to be used, the key exchange and authentication algorithms, as well as the hashing algorithms to generate message authentication codes).

- The server responds back with a *ServerHello* message that includes the following information: (i) The TLS version chosen by the server based on the version information submitted by the client; (ii) A random number arbitrarily chosen by the server and (iii) The cipher-suite chosen from the list of choices offered by the client.

- The server also sends its public-key certificate to the client. The client may contact the CA that issued the certificate and confirm that the certificate is authentic before proceeding. The server also has the option of asking for the client's public-key certificate by sending a *CertificateRequest* message, so that the connection can be mutually authenticated.

- The client generates a shared session key and sends it along with the client-side and server-side random numbers, all encrypted with the public key of the server. The client-side and server-side random numbers are merely sent to enhance each other's authentication.

- The server decrypts the message received with its private key and extracts the shared session key.

- The client then computes a hash of the messages received so far from the server using the hashing algorithm agreed upon, encrypts the hash value with the shared session key using the encryption algorithm selected and sends it to the server.

- The server decrypts the client's message with the shared session key using the decryption algorithm selected. The server then independently calculates the hash of all its messages to the client using the hashing algorithm agreed upon. If the hash value matches with the hash value in the message sent by the client, the server basically accepts the connection request from its direction. The server then computes a hash of all the messages it has received so far from the client and then sends it to the client by encrypting the hash value with the shared session key.

- The client decrypts the message with the shared session key and independently computes a hash of the messages sent to the server. If the computed hash value matches with the hash value sent by the server, then the client has basically authenticated the server. Thus, a TLS connection is established.

IP Security (IPSec)

The IP Security Protocol suite (IPSec; Kent & Atkinson, 1998a) is implemented at the IP layer, so it does not require any change to existing transport layer and application layer protocols. IPSec is primarily designed to address the fundamental shortcomings of the IP layer such as IP address spoofing, wiretapping and session hijacking. The following two protocols are used to provide packet-level security for both IPv4 and IPv6:

- IP Authentication Header, AH (Next Header protocol ID: 51) provides integrity, authentication and non-repudiation (Kent & Atkinson, 1998b).

- IP Encapsulating Security Payload, ESP (Next Header protocol ID: 50) provides confidentiality, along with authentication and integrity protection (Kent & Atkinson, 1998c).

Security Association

The basis of IPSec is a Security Association (SA), characterized by the set of security parameters agreed upon for a secure communication channel between two communicating hosts (Maughan et. al., 1998). Each host can have several SAs in effect for communication with different remote hosts. A SA is identified using a Security Parameter Index (SPI) – a 32-bit identifier and the IP address of the partner host on the other side of the SA. The SPI and the partner IP address are used to index to the Security Association Database (SADB) that has information about the characteristics of different SAs. A SA is characterized by the following parameters: Encryption algorithm, Encryption key, Encryption parameters like the Initialization Vector, Integrity/Authentication algorithms (keyed-HMAC algorithms and the key; Bellare et. al., 1996) and Lifespan of the SA.

SAs are uni-directional. For two hosts to communicate in either direction, SAs have to be established separately in both directions. For host A to securely send data packets to host B, and make host B to believe that the data packet did come from host A, it should establish a SA with host B. Such a SA is said to be "outbound" at A and "inbound" at B. An IPSec header of a datagram sent from host A to host B, should have the secure features of the SA that is "inbound" at B and similarly the IPSec header of a datagram sent from host B to host A should have the secure features of the SA that is "inbound" at A.

Prior to establishing an IPSec SA, the two end hosts need to exchange their public-key certificates digitally certified by a trusted third-party certificate authority (CA). This is done through the Internet Key Exchange (IKE) protocol (Harkins & Carrel, 1998). Once the two hosts have exchanged each other's public-key certificates, then they are said to have established an IKE Security Association (IKE SA). Establishing an IKE SA is a pre-requisite to establish an IPSec SA. The procedure to establish an IPSec SA is explained as follows:

- Host A wishing to send data packets to host B needs to establish an "inbound SA" with host B.
- Host A picks a SPI that has not been yet chosen for communication with B and sends a "SA Establishment Request" message to B which contains the following:
  - SPI for the inbound SA channel at host A (i.e., the outbound SA channel at host B)
  - Lifespan of the association – negotiable by host B
  - The packet-level security protocol chosen (AH or ESP) – negotiable by host B
    - If AH is chosen, then the list of keyed-HMAC algorithms that could be used is specified. Host B will choose one from this list if it wishes to receive packets from host A.
    - If ESP is chosen, then the list of keyed-HMAC algorithms along with the list of encryption algorithms and key-derivation functions that could be used will be sent.
- All negotiation messages (including the SA Establishment Request) are encrypted at the sender side using the receiver's public key and decrypted with the receiver's private key at the receiver side.
- Hosts A and B agree on a shared session key using the Diffie-Hellman exchange algorithm (Diffie & Hellman, 1976).
- The shared session key would be used for the keyed-HMAC algorithm.
- Each host uses the shared session key and the key-derivation function agreed upon to derive the secret key to be used for encryption and decryption of the data at hosts A and B respectively.

Authentication Header (AH)

AH provides integrity and data origin authentication for IP datagrams. AH operates on the top of IP, using the IP protocol number 51. The different fields in an AH are described below (also refer Figure 11). The structure of an original IPv4 datagram and IPv4 datagram with AH is shown in Figure 12.

- **Next Header:** Identifies the transport layer protocol
- **Payload Length (AH Length):** Indicates the length of the whole AH in 32-bit words
- **Reserved:** Indicates that this field is reserved for future use and it must be set to zero
- **SPI:** Identifies the security association
- **Sequence Number:** Identifies the datagrams sent as part of a SA. This field is a monotonically increasing identifier and is used to assist in anti-replay protection
- **Authentication Data:** Contains the integrity/authentication check value (keyed-HMAC) calculated over the entire packet, including the header fields that do not change at the intermediate hosts. The size of the keyed-HMAC may vary with each SA and may not be exactly multiple of 32 bits. If this is the case, the HMAC will be padded.

- **Encapsulated Security Payload (ESP):** ESP provides origin authentication, integrity and confidentiality protection for the IP datagrams. The different fields in an ESP header are described below (Figure 13). The structure of an original IPv4 datagram and IPv4 datagram with ESP header is shown in Figure 14.
- **SPI:** Identifies the security association
  - **Sequence Number:** Identifies the datagrams sent as part of a SA. This field is a monotonically increasing identifier and is used to assist in anti-replay protection
  - **Payload data:** Indicates the data to be transferred
  - **Padding:** Used with certain block ciphers for padding the payload data to a full block length.
  - **Pad length:** Indicates the size of the padding in bytes

Figure 11. Structure of an Authentication Header (AH)

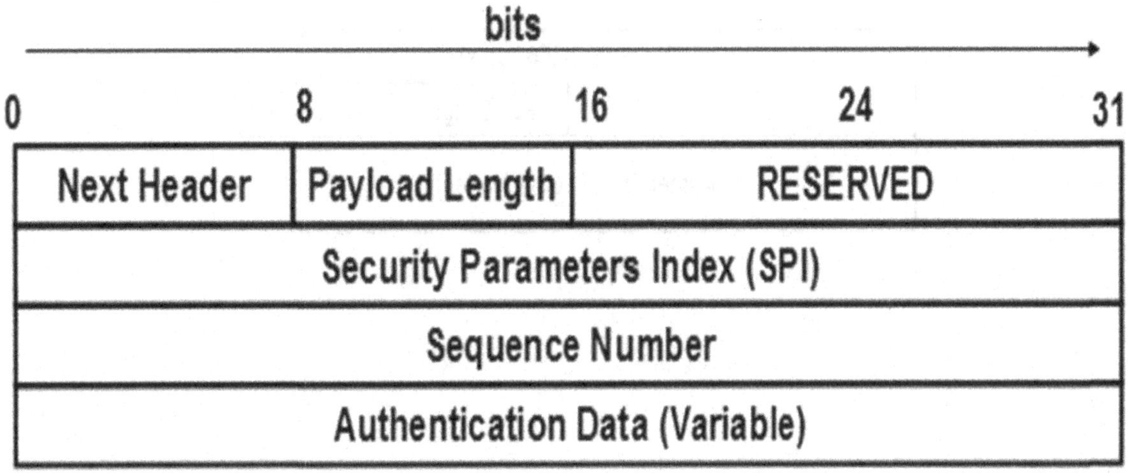

Figure 12. Incorporating AH header in an IPv4 datagram

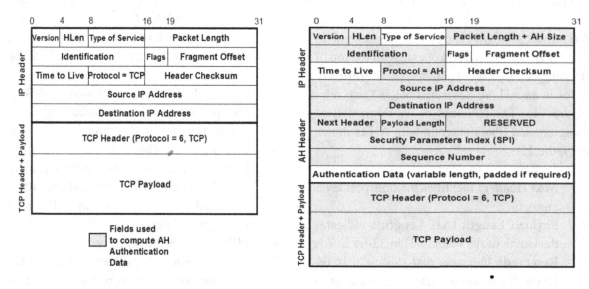

(i) *Original IPv4 Datagram*   (ii) *IPv4 Datagram with AH Header*

Figure 13. Structure of an Encapsulated Security Payload (ESP) header

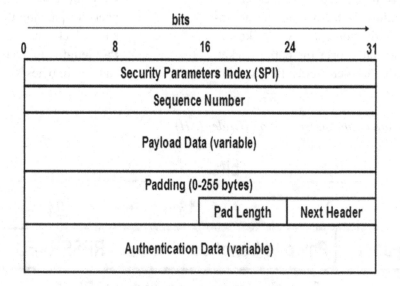

Figure 14. Incorporating ESP header in an IPv4 datagram

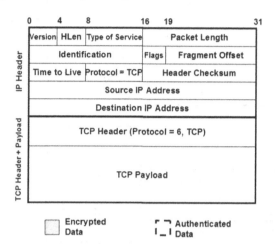

(i) *Original IPv4 Datagram*

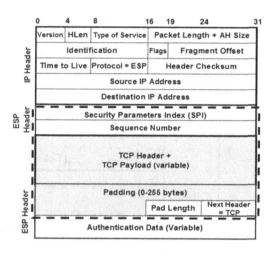

(ii) *IPv4 Datagram with ESP Header*

- ○ **Next Header:** Identifies the transport layer protocol
- ○ **Authentication Data:** This is the integrity/ authentication check value (keyed-HMAC) calculated over only the SPI, Sequence Number in the ESP header, the actual data, padding data, pad length and the Next Header field.

Kerberos

Kerberos (Neuman & Tso, 1994) is an authentication protocol used by processes/hosts communicating over an insecure network to verify each other's identity in a secure manner. It is based on the idea that a central server provides authenticated tokens called "tickets" to requesting applications. A ticket is an unforgeable, non-replayable, authenticated object. The security of the protocol depends on the assumption that the participating machines maintain loosely synchronized time. The four entities involved in Kerberos are: (i) Authentication Server, AS; (ii) Ticket Granting Server, TGS; (iii) Service Server; SS and (iv) Ticket Granting Ticket, TGT. A client authenticates itself to the AS once and obtains a ticket that can be used

to obtain additional tickets from the SS without requiring the client to re-authenticate itself for every service requested. The sequence of steps of the protocol is described below (also shown in Figure 15):

Kerberos Protocol Steps

The following are the steps of the Kerberos protocol:

- **Step 1- User Client-based Logon:** The user submits the username and password information to the client machine. The client machine uses a one-way function on the entered password to compute the secret key for the user.
- **Step 2- Client Authentication:** The client sends the username in plaintext to the Kerberos AS. The AS checks the username in its database, and if an entry exists, the AS sends back two messages:
  - ○ **Message A:** Contains the Client/ TGS session key encrypted with the secret key for the user (derived from the user's password at the AS).

Figure 15. Kerberos protocol steps

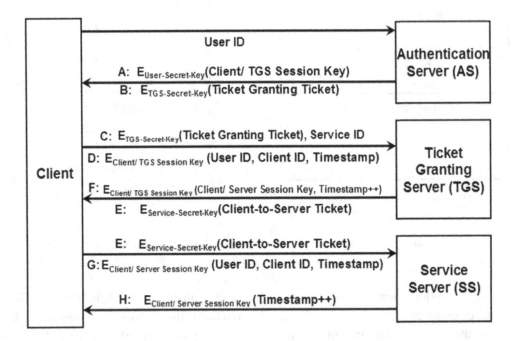

- ◦ **Message B:** Contains the Ticket-Granting Ticket, TGT, which includes the following:
- ◦ username,
- ◦ network address of the user's client machine,
- ◦ validity period of the TGT and
- ◦ Client/ TGS session key. The TGT is encrypted using the secret key of the TGS.

Once the client receives messages A and B, the client decrypts message A with the secret key of the user and extracts the Client/ TGS session key.

- • **Step 3- Client Service Authorization:** The client sends the following two messages to the TGS:
  - ◦ **Message C:** Contains the TGT from message B and identification for the requested service.

- ◦ **Message D:** Contains the authentication information for the user/client. The authentication information submitted includes the username, the network address of the user/client machine and a timestamp. All of this information is encrypted using the Client/ TGS session key. After receiving message C, the TGS decrypts the message with its secret key and extracts the Client/TGS session key. The TGS then decrypts message D using the Client/ TGS session key and sends back the following two messages to the client:
- ◦ **Message E:** Contains the Client-to-Server Ticket, which includes the username, the network address of the user/client machine, the validity period the ticket and the Client/Server session key. The ticket is encrypted

with the secret key of the server for the service requested.

○ **Message F:** Contains the Client/ Server session key and the timestamp of message D incremented by 1. Both the key and the timestamp are encrypted with the Client/ TGS session key. After the client receives messages E and F, it uses the Client/ TGS session key to decrypt message F to extract the Client/ Server session key.

- **Step 4- Client Service Request:** The client sends the following two messages to the SS: (i) message E (received from the TGS) and (ii) message G, containing the username, the network address of the user/ client machine and the timestamp, all encrypted with the Client/Server session key. The SS decrypts message E using its secret key and extracts the Client-to-Server ticket and the Client/Server session key. The SS decrypts message G using the Client/Server session key and extracts the user/client identification information. If the user/client identification information in message G matches with the user/client information in the Client-to-Server ticket, the SS increments the timestamp information in message G by 1. The incremented timestamp is encrypted using the Client/ Server session key and sent back to the client (as message H). The client on receiving message H decrypts the message with the Client/Server session key. If the timestamp value in message H is the value expected by the client, the client trusts the server and start sending service requests to the server.

Strengths of Kerberos

Following are the strengths of the Kerberos protocol:

- A user's password is not sent on the wire (either in plaintext or ciphertext) during session initiation.
- Kerberos provides cryptographic protection against spoofing. Each service access request is mediated by the TGS, which knows that the identity of the user/client is authenticated by the Kerberos AS and processes the user/client request encrypted with the Client/TGS session key
- As each ticket has a limited validity period, long-term cryptanalytic attacks cannot be launched.
- Kerberos assumes that the clocks across all the clients and the servers are synchronized. A host responds back only if the request messages have timestamp value close to the current time at the host.
- Kerberos provides mutual authentication. The TGS and SS can respectively get access to the Client/TGS session key and the Client/Server session key only after they can decrypt the messages containing these keys with their appropriate secret keys. The client uses this approach to indirectly authenticate the servers.

Weaknesses of Kerberos

Following are the weaknesses of the Kerberos protocol:

- Kerberos requires continuous availability of a trusted ticket-granting server for all access control and authentication checks.
- Authenticity of servers requires a trusted relationship between the TGS and every service server.
- Timely transactions are required to reduce chances of a user with genuine ticket being denied service.

- Password guessing could still work to get the valid secret key for a user. The whole system is still dependent on the user password.

- Kerberos does not scale well as the number of service servers is increased. The TGS has to maintain a trustworthy relationship and maintain the secret key for each SS. Adding backup service servers further complicates the situation.

- Network services cannot be accessed without obtaining Kerberos authentication. All applications run by the users in the network need to go through Kerberos authentication.

Firewalls

A firewall is a device that filters traffic between a "less trustworthy" outside network and a "protected" inside network (Pfleeger, 2006). A firewall is often implemented in software and is basically a code running on a dedicated computer located in the periphery of the network to be protected. All traffic exiting and entering the network should go through the firewall. Hence, the firewall is often a kind of bottleneck for network performance. This is also the reason why non-firewall functions are not normally performed at a computer running the firewall and hence it becomes hard for an attacker to get access to the firewall code by making use of the program vulnerabilities in the non-firewall code, if any exists.

Firewall design often makes use of either "default-deny" or "default-allow" approach (Pfleeger, 2006). In the default-deny approach, the firewall will be configured to allow only explicitly stated network connections. Any network traffic that does not match with the firewall ruleset will be denied access. In the default-allow approach, a firewall will be configured with the set of rules that describe what network traffic should be specifically blocked. Network traffic that does not match with the firewall ruleset will be allowed

access. The security policies implemented at a firewall depend on the specific threats against which the inside network needs to be protected. Firewalls can be classified into four different categories: Packet filters (ii) Stateful inspection firewall (iii) Application proxy firewall and (iv) Personal firewall

Packet Filters

A packet filtering firewall (Pfleeger, 2006) controls access to packets based on the network address (representing the network of the source or the destination) or IP address (source or destination IP address) or port numbers (representing specific transport layer protocols). Packet filter firewalls can be of two types: (i) Egress filter – packets will be sent out (or not sent out) only to specific networks and/or belonging to specific transport layer protocols; (ii) Ingress filter – packets belonging to (or not belonging to) certain specific networks or specific transport layer protocols could be let in. In order to combat IP spoofing, packet filter firewalls are often configured not to let inside a packet that has an IP address corresponding to the internal network being protected. As we increase the number of specific networks, IP addresses and transport layer protocols whose traffic needs to be blocked, the code for a packet filter firewall becomes lengthy.

Stateful Inspection Firewall

A packet filter firewall is stateless: it operates on packets on an individual basis and does not store or apply the state information pertaining to the action taken on packets processed earlier. Stateful firewalls examine each packet with regards to their overall placement in the packet series belonging to a specific connection. A stateful firewall (Pfleeger, 2006) maintains records of all connections passing through it and will be able to determine whether a packet is part of any existing connection or a new connection. The connection state will be used to trigger specific rules for the firewall. Some of these could be: (i) The firewall can stop packets belonging to an already terminated TCP connection from getting inside the network or to a TCP connection that has been not yet established. (ii) The firewall may not let more than a specific amount of data to be transferred from the protected network to a specific network or an outside IP address. (iii) The firewall may not allow beyond a maximum number of TCP connections per IP address.

Application Proxy Firewall

The packet filters and the stateful inspection firewalls take actions by only looking at the headers of the data packets. An application proxy firewall acts as an intermediate gateway attempting to look not only at the packet headers but also at the data inside the packets entering or leaving the network to be protected. All communication between the users of the internal protected network and the Internet has to pass through the proxy server instead of allowing users to directly communicate with servers on the Internet.

An application proxy firewall (Pfleeger, 2006) is dual homed (refer Figure 16): for client applications running inside the protected network, the application proxy firewall acts as a proxy server and for server applications in the outside network, the application proxy firewall acts as a proxy client. The request generated by an internal user (client) to connect to an external service goes through the application proxy firewall that runs a proxy server for the particular service being requested. The proxy server evaluates the connection request and decides to permit or deny the request based on a set of rules that are managed for the individual network service. Only packets that comply with the services of the application protocols are allowed by the proxy server, which forwards the accepted request to the proxy client. The proxy client then contacts the real server in the Internet on behalf of the real client in the protected network and proceeds to relay requests from the proxy server to the real server and the responses from the real server to the proxy server. The proxy server relays requests and responses between the proxy client and the real client in the protected network.

The application firewall could also act as the proxy server for a real client in the outside network and as a proxy client for a real server inside the protected network. In this case, the real client contacts the proxy server, which evaluates the request and forwards the request to the proxy client. The proxy client contacts the real server

Figure 16. Application proxy firewall

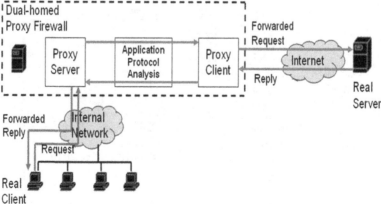

running in the internal network and forwards the response from the real server to the proxy server. The proxy server forwards the response to the real client in the outside network.

Personal Firewall

Personal firewalls (Pfleeger, 2006) are very much needed for standalone machines connected to the Internet through various means like dial-ups, cable modems or DSL connections. Having a separate firewall computer to protect a single computer system can be too expensive and complex. A personal firewall is an application program running on a specific computer system. The firewall screens the incoming and outgoing traffic for the computer system and blocks the unwanted traffic from entering or leaving the system. The user could configure the personal firewall to accept traffic only from certain sites or not from specific sites and to generate logs of the past activities. The personal firewall can also be configured to function as a virus scanner so that any incoming data to the system will be first scanned for any potential virus infection.

What Firewalls Can and Cannot Block

A firewall can be held responsible if and only if it is the only means for traffic to leave or enter the inside network being protected. If the inside network has a host that is connected to the outside network through a modem, then the whole of the inside network is exposed to the outside network through the modem and the host. The firewall cannot be held responsible if certain malicious traffic manages to get into the network through the modem and the host (Pfleeger, 2006). A firewall is often a single point of failure for the network being protected. Modern day networks have layered firewall architecture (refer Figure 17) comprising multiple firewalls: a screening router implemented with the packet filter, followed by a proxy firewall and then followed by a personal firewall at every host in the network. The security policies of a firewall must be constantly updated to take into account the latest intrusion attempts and potentially harmful application software that come into existence.

Figure 17. A layered firewall architecture

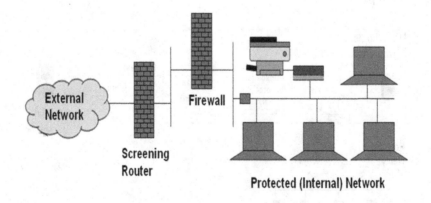

Secure E-Mail

Electronic mail (e-mail) has become a common communication method for both business and ordinary users. An e-mail, while propagating in the network channels, is very public and is exposed in plaintext at every point from the sender's system to the recipient's screen. This section analyzes the key requirements for a secure e-mail and explores two designs that satisfy one or more of these key requirements.

Key Requirements for Secure E-Mail

Any design for secure e-mail should take into consideration that the protection measures should be enforced within the body of the message as the existing e-mail network in the Internet should not be changed in order to provide e-mail security. The key requirements (Pfleeger, 2006) for secure e-mail are as follows:

- **Confidentiality:** E-mail contents should not be exposed on the path from the sender to the receiver.
- **Integrity:** The receiver should see in the e-mail, the same content which the sender sent.

- **Authenticity:** Receiver should be able to verify that the e-mail message indeed came from the sender.
- **Non-repudiation:** The sender of the e-mail cannot deny having sent the message.

Secure E-Mail Design for Confidentiality, Non-Repudiation and Sender Authenticity

One could provide confidentiality by encrypting the message (before transmission) so that the message gets transmitted in ciphertext in the network channels and can be seen in plaintext only at the receiver after a successful decryption. In addition to ensuring confidentiality during transmission, it is essential for the receiver to verify the authenticity of the sender and also use the e-mail as a proof that the sender did send the message and cannot deny sending such a message. A plausible design to achieve all of this is explained below and it is also pictorially represented in Figure 18. This is also the basic idea behind the Pretty Good Privacy (PGP) secure e-mail software (Garfinkel, 1994) used for sending text messages in secured fashion.

The payload portion of the e-mail contains the encrypted version of the sender's public key certificate and the encrypted version of the

Figure 18. Secure e-mail design for confidentiality, non-repudiation and sender authenticity

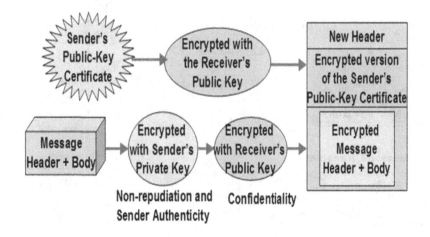

original e-mail header and the e-mail message. The sender's public key certificate is encrypted with the receiver's public key and included in the payload portion. The original message and the e-mail header are first encrypted with the sender's private key (provides non-repudiation and sender authenticity) and the ciphertext resulting from this encryption is further encrypted with the receiver's public key (provides confidentiality) and the resulting ciphertext is included in the payload portion of the e-mail transmitted in the network channels. The header of this e-mail is a plaintext copy of the e-mail header enclosed in the encrypted format in the payload portion.

Secure E-Mail Design for S/MIME

S/MIME (Secure/ Multi-purpose Internet Mail Extensions; Ramsdell, 1999) is a secure e-mail standard commonly used in the Internet. It satisfies all the four requirements for secure e-mail design. The basic idea behind the design of S/MIME is pictorially represented in Figure 19 and is discussed below. The payload of the e-mail sent from the sender to a receiver has four components:

1. **The encrypted version of the original plaintext (e-mail message header and body):** A random session key is generated at the sender side and is used as the secret key for this symmetric encryption. This component satisfies the requirement of providing confidentiality.

2. **The encrypted version of the random session key used for the symmetric encryption of the original message header and body:** The session key is encrypted with the receiver's public key. This approach of generating a random session key to encrypt every message sent and also sending the session key along with the message avoids the offline use of a key distribution algorithm (Diffie & Hellman, 1976) between the sender and the receiver. This component satisfies the requirement of providing confidentiality.

3. **The encrypted version of the hash of the original e-mail message header and body:** A hash value of the original e-mail message header and body is computed using a standard hashing algorithm like SHA1 (Eastlake & Jones, 2001). This hash value is

Figure 19. Secure e-mail design for S/MIME

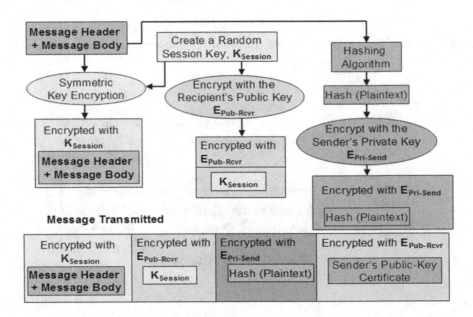

encrypted with the private key of the sender. This component satisfies the requirement of providing message integrity.

4. **The encrypted version of the public-key certificate of the sender:** The public-key certificate of the sender is encrypted with the public key of receiver so that it can be decrypted only by the receiver and used for extracting the hash value of the plaintext message header and body. This component satisfies the requirement of providing sender authenticity and non-repudiation.

CONCLUSION

The crux behind network security is to ensure access to the network and its data for authorized hosts/users and deny access to unauthorized hosts/users. A secure network needs to have tamper-proof communication media and resilient protocol mechanisms that can avoid or reduce the chances of an attack. A close look at the classical network attacks described in Section 2 reveals that IP spoofing has been behind the success of most of these attacks. Hence, it has become a design requirement that in addition to authenticating the application users, it is also essential to authenticate the networks and hosts from which the application users are communicating in the Internet. Protocol mechanisms like SSH, TLS, IPSec and Kerberos ensure that the above requirement is being taken care of and reduce the chances of spoofing-based attacks. A single security control mechanism cannot combat all kinds of network attacks. The security control mechanism(s) chosen for a network should be based on the specific threats that currently exist for the network. There is always a tradeoff between using security control mechanisms as mere plug-in modules and making them more embedded with the core functionality of the protocols in the TCP/IP stack. It would be better for a security control mechanism to require changes to be made only in one particular layer of the Internet protocol stack rather than all the layers.

ACKNOWLEDGMENT

This work was partly funded through the U. S. National Science Foundation (NSF) CCLI/TUES grant (DUE-0941959) on "Incorporating Systems Security and Software Security in Senior Projects." The views and conclusions contained in this document are those of the authors and should not be interpreted as necessarily representing the official policies, either expressed or implied, of the funding agency.

REFERENCES

Austein, R. (2007). *DNS name server identifier (NSID) option*. IETF RFC 5001.

Bellare, M., Canetti, R., & Krawczyk, H. (1996). Keying hash functions for message authentication. In *Proceedings of the 16th Annual International Cryptology Conference* (pp. 1-15). Santa Barbara, CA: Springer.

Comer, D. E. (2008). *Computer networks and internets* (5th ed.). Upper Saddle River, NJ: Prentice Hall.

Connolly, K. J. (2003). *Law of internet security and privacy*. Alphen aan den Rijn, The Netherlands: Aspen Publishers.

Dierks, T., & Rescorla, E. (2008). *The transport layer security (TLS) protocol, v. 1.2*. IETF RFC 5246.

Diffie, W., & Hellman, M. E. (1976). New directions in cryptography. *IEEE Transactions on Information Theory, 22*, 644–654. doi:10.1109/TIT.1976.1055638

Eastlake, D., & Jones, P. (2001). *US secure hash algorithm 1 (SHA1)*. IETF RFC 3174.

Freir, A. O., Karlton, P., & Kocher, P. C. (1996). *The SSL protocol version 3.0*. Netscape's Final SSL 3.0 Draft.

Garfinkel, S. (1994). *PGP: Pretty good privacy.* Sebastopol, CA: O'Reilly.

Harkins, D., & Carrel, D. (1998). *The internet key exchange (IKE).* IETF RFC 2409.

Kent, S., & Atkinson, R. (1998a). *Security architecture for the internet protocol.* IETF RFC 2401.

Kent, S., & Atkinson, R. (1998b). *IP authentication header.* IETF RFC 2402.

Kent, S., & Atkinson, R. (1998c). *IP encapsulating security (ESP).* IETF RFC 2406.

Maughan, D., Schertler, M., Schneider, M., & Turner, J. (1998). *Internet security association and key management protocol (ISAKMP).* IETF RFC 2408.

Neuman, B. C., & Tso, T. (1994). Kerberos: An authentication service for computer networks. *IEEE Communications, 32*(9), 33–38. doi:10.1109/35.312841

Pfleeger, C. (2006). *Security in computing* (4th ed.). Upper Saddle River, NJ: Prentice Hall.

Postel, J. (1981). *Internet control message protocol.* IETF RFC 792.

Postel, J. (1983). *Character generator protocol.* IETF RFC 864.

Postel, J., & Reynolds, J. (1983). *TELNET protocol specification.* IETD RFC 854.

Ramsdell, B. (1999). *S/MIME version 3 message specification.* IETF RFC 2633.

Russell, R., Kaminsky, D., Puppy, R. F., Grand, J., Ahmad, D., & Flynn, H. … Permeh, R. (2002). *Hack proofing your network* (2nd Ed.). Amsterdam: Syngress.

Senie, D. (1999). *Changing the default for directed broadcasts in routers.* IETF RFC 2644.

Simpson, W. (1995). *IP in IP tunneling.* IETF RFC 1853.

Stevens, W. R. (1994). *TCP/IP illustrated: The protocols* (Vol. 1). Boston: Addison-Wesley Professional.

Thing, V., Lee, H., & Sloman, M. (2005). Traffic redirection attack protection system. In *Proceedings of the 20th International Information Security Conference* (pp. 309-325). Chiba, Japan: IFIP.

Ylonen, T. (2006). *The secure shell (SSH) authentication protocol.* IETF RFC 4252.

Zimmermann, H. (1980). OSI reference model - The ISO model of architecture for open systems interconnection. *IEEE Transactions on Communications, 28*(4), 425–432. doi:10.1109/TCOM.1980.1094702

ADDITIONAL READING

Beecroft, A. J., & Michael, J. B. (2009). Passive Fingerprinting of Network Reconnaissance Tools. *Computer, 41*(12), 91–93. doi:10.1109/MC.2009.405

Blum, J. J., & Eskandarian, A. (2007). A Reliable Link-Layer Protocol for Robust and Scalable Intervehicle Communications. *IEEE Transactions on Intelligent Transportation Systems, 8*(1), 4–13. doi:10.1109/TITS.2006.889441

Chandrasekhar, S., Chakrabarti, S., & Singhal, M. (2012). A Trapdoor HAsh-based Mechanism for Stream Authentication. *IEEE Transactions on Dependable and Secure Computing, 9*(5), 699–713.

Chasaki, D., & Wolf, T. (2012). Attacks and Defenses in the Data Plane of Networks. *IEEE Transactions on Dependable and Secure Computing, 9*(6), 798–810. doi:10.1109/TDSC.2012.50

Cheminod, M., Durante, L., & Valenzano, A. (2013). Review of Security ISsues in Industrial Networks. *IEEE Transactions on Industrial Informatics, 9*(1), 277–293. doi:10.1109/TII.2012.2198666

Chen, R., Park, J.-M., & Marchany, R. (2007). A Divide-and-Conquer Strategy for Thwarting Distributed Denial-of-Service Attacks. (2007). *IEEE Transactions on Parallel and Distributed Systems*, *18*(5), 577–588. doi:10.1109/TPDS.2007.1014

Chen, S., & Ranka, S. (2005). Detecting Internet Worms at Early Stage. *IEEE Journal on Selected Areas in Communications*, *23*(10), 2003–2012. doi:10.1109/JSAC.2005.854124

Chung, C.-J., Khatkar, P., Xing, T., Lee, J., & Huang, D. (2013). NICE: Network Intrusion Detection and Countermeasure Selection in Virtual Network Systems. *IEEE Transactions on Dependable and Secure Computing*, *10*(4), 198–211. doi:10.1109/TDSC.2013.8

Coates, G. M., Hopkinson, K. M., Graham, S. R., & Kurkowski, S. H. (2008). Collaborative Trust-Based Security Mechanisms for a Regional Utility Intranet. *IEEE Transactions on Power Systems*, *23*(3), 831–844. doi:10.1109/TPWRS.2008.926456

Du, W. (2011). SEED: Hands-on Lab Exercises for Computer Security Education. *IEEE SEcurity & Privacy*, *9*(5), 70–73. doi:10.1109/MSP.2011.139

Hashim, F., Munasinghe, K. S., & Jamalipour, A. (2010). Biologically Inspired Anomaly Detection and Security Control Frameworks for Complex Heterogeneous Networks. *IEEE Transactions on Network and Service Management*, *7*(4), 268–281. doi:10.1109/TNSM.2010.1012.0360

Huang, F., Yang, Y., & He, L. (2007). A Flow-based Network Monitoring Framework for Wireless Mesh Networks. *IEEE Wireless Communications*, *14*(5), 48–55. doi:10.1109/MWC.2007.4396942

Leckie, T., & Yasnisac, A. (2004). Metadata for Anomaly-based Security Protocol Attack Deduction. *IEEE Transactions on Knowledge and Data Engineering*, *16*(9), 1157–1168. doi:10.1109/TKDE.2004.43

Li, C.-T. (2013). A New Password Authentication and User Anonymity Scheme based on Elliptic Curve Cryptography and Smart Card. *IET Information Security*, *7*(1), 3–10. doi:10.1049/iet-ifs.2012.0058

Liu, A. X., Torng, E., & Meiners, C. R. (2011). Compressing Network Access Control Lists. *IEEE Transactions on Parallel and Distributed Systems*, *22*(12), 1969–1977. doi:10.1109/TPDS.2011.114

Liu, N., Zhang, J., Zhang, H., & Liu, W. (2010). Security Assessment for Communication Networks of Power Control Systems using Attack Graph and MCDM. *IEEE Transactions on Power Delivery*, *25*(3), 1492–1500. doi:10.1109/TPWRD.2009.2033930

Mahmud, S. M., & Shanker, S. (2006). In-vehicle Secure Wireless Personal Area Network (SWPAN). *IEEE Transactions on Vehicular Technology*, *55*(3), 1051–1061. doi:10.1109/TVT.2005.863341

Nichols, E. A., & Peterson, G. (2007). A Metrics Framework to Drive Application Security Improvement. *IEEE Security & Privacy*, *5*(2), 88–91. doi:10.1109/MSP.2007.26

Nogueira, M., Silva, E., Santos, A., & Albini, L. C. P. (2011). Survivable Key Management on WANETs. *IEEE Wireless Communications*, *18*(6), 82–88. doi:10.1109/MWC.2011.6108337

O'Mahony, D. (1994). Security Considerations in a Network Management Environment. *IEEE Network*, *8*(3), 12–17. doi:10.1109/65.283929

Pang, Z.-H., & Liu, G.-P. (2012). Design and Implementation of Secure Networked Predictive Control Systems under Deception Attacks. *IEEE Transactions on Control Systems Technology*, *20*(5), 1334–1342. doi:10.1109/TCST.2011.2160543

Rasheed, A., & Mahapatra, R. N. (2012). The Three-Tier Security Scheme in Wireless Sensor Networks with Mobile Sinks. *IEEE Transactions on Parallel and Distributed Systems*, *23*(5), 958–965. doi:10.1109/TPDS.2010.185

Ten, C.-W., Manimaran, G., & Liu, C.-C. (2010). Cybersecurity for Critical Infrastructures: Attack and Defense Modeling. *IEEE Transactions on Systems, Man, and Cybernetics*, *40*(4), 853–865. doi:10.1109/TSMCA.2010.2048028

Teng, J., & Wu, C. (2012). A Provable Authenticated Certificateless Group Key Agreement with Constant Rounds. *Journal of Communications and Networks*, *14*(1), 104–110. doi:10.1109/JCN.2012.6184555

Younis, M., Ghumman, K., & Eltoweissy, M. (2006). Location-Aware Combinatorial Key Management Scheme for Clustered Sensor Networks. *IEEE Transactions on Parallel and Distributed Systems*, *17*(8), 865–882. doi:10.1109/TPDS.2006.106

KEY TERMS AND DEFINITIONS

Confidentiality: A security characteristic that requires information transmitted over a network be not read by unauthorized users.

Firewall: A hardware or software-based network security system that monitors packets leaving and entering a network and uses a rule set to decide whether or not the packets should be allowed through.

Integrity: A security characteristic that requires information transmitted over a network be not modified and that the receiver sees exactly what the sender sent.

IP-in-IP Tunneling: The mechanism of encapsulating an IP datagram in another IP datagram, typically used to establish a virtual communica-tion link between two machines over a sequence of networks that cannot directly route the inner encapsulated datagram.

IPSec: It is a protocol suite to secure IP com-munications by facilitating the end hosts and/or the gateway routers to agree (at the beginning of the communication session) and use (for each IP packet) the encryption and hashing algorithms to provide confidentiality, integrity and authen-tication.

IP Spoofing: Refers to sending IP packets that appears to come from an IP address that does not actually correspond to the sender.

Kerberos: It is an authentication protocol that works on the basis of a "ticket" issued by a Ticket Granting Server to authenticated clients/users who submit it to a server (to prove their identity) at which a service is requested.

Man-in-the-Middle Attack: An attack by which a third party can read, modify and insert messages between two communicating parties, without either party knowing that the link between them has been compromised.

Message Authentication: A security charac-teristic that requires a receiver be able to validate whether the message was indeed sent by a sender who claims to have sent it.

Non-Repudiation: A security characteristic that enforces a sender to be not able to deny send-ing the message once s/he sent it.

Secure Shell (SSH): SSH is a cryptographic protocol (running at the Internet layer of the TCP/IP protocol stack) that facilitates two machines to establish a secure communication channel across a sequence of one or more insecure networks.

Session Hijacking: A security attack by which an attacker desynchronizes a communication ses-sion (by typically corrupting the sequence number from the client expected at the server) that is in progress between a client and server and manages to take control of the session (with the server) for the rest of its duration.

Transport Layer Security (TLS): TLS is a cryptographic protocol (running at a lower sub layer of the application layer above the transport layer, according to the TCP/IP protocol stack) that uses the X.509 certificates and asymmetric encryption algorithms to facilitate two communicating parties to agree on a session key that can be further use to encrypt the data exchanged between the two parties.

Chapter 12
Botnets:
Analysis, Detection, and Mitigation

Hamad Binsalleeh
Concordia University, USA

ABSTRACT

Recent malicious attempts are intended to get financial benefits through a large pool of compromised hosts, which are called software robots or simply bots. A group of bots, referred to as a botnet, is remotely controllable by a server and can be used for sending spam emails, stealing personal information, and launching DDoS attacks. Growing popularity of botnets compels to find proper countermeasures, but existing defense mechanisms hardly catch up with the speed of botnet technologies. Bots are constantly and automatically changing their signatures to successfully avoid the detection. Therefore, it is necessary to analyze the weaknesses of existing defense mechanisms to find the gap and then design new framework of botnet detection that integrates effective approaches. To get a deep insight into the inner-working of botnets and to understand their architecture, the authors analyze some sophisticated sample botnets. In this chapter, they propose a comprehensive botnet analysis and reporting framework that is based on sound theoretical background.

1. INTRODUCTION

The tremendous growth in the use of Internet technologies in different walks of life has molded the living habits of most people. The traditional ways of trading and marketing, training and education, communication and broadcasting are replaced by the innovative Web-based applications and online systems. However, the same Internet applications are abused by perpetrators and hackers for committing different kinds of crimes including spamming, phishing, drug trafficking, cyber bullying, child

pornography, and distributed denial of service (DDoS) attacks. In the majority of Internet mediated cybercrimes, the victimization tactics used vary from simple anonymity to identity theft and impersonation. Therefore, Internet security has become the focus of most research studies during the last couple of decades.

Malicious software including viruses, worms, spyware, Trojan horses, and botnets are considered as vehicles for different kinds of Internet attacks. Such malware has risen to become the primary source of most scanning (Staniford, Hoagland,

DOI: 10.4018/978-1-4666-4789-3.ch012

& McAlerney, 2002), DDoS attacks (D. Moore, Shannon, Brown, Voelker, & Savage, 2006), direct attacks (Anagnostakis et al., 2005), and fraudulent activities (Evan, Farnam, & Danny, 2005; Lee, 2008; Ramachandran & Feamster, 2006) over the Internet. To avoid being detected, most Internet malware evolve in their forms and properties, e.g., from worms to botnets. Recent studies indicate that botnets are proved to be the primary 'platform'(Lee, 2008) where the cyber criminals create global cooperative networks that are instrumental in most cybercriminal attacks. Although the existence of botnets has been noticed since very long, the recent growth in botnets mediated cybercrimes has attracted the attention of the mainstream Internet communities.

Unlike worms, which are arguably fun-oriented, botnets are truly profit-oriented. Due to the development of more smarter botnets and lack of efficient detection mechanism the botmasters are controlling a good portion of the Internet resources. In early 2007, Vint Cerf, 'the father of the Internet', speculated that up to one quarter of all the computers connected to the Internet are believed to participate in botnet-related activities (Weber, 2007) . The alarming increase in both the power of botnets and its infectious effects has turned botnets to be the biggest threat to Internet security (Lee, 2008). Currently, botnets are the root cause of many of Internet attacks and malicious activities (Paul Bcher, 2008; Evan et al., 2005; Ramachandran & Feamster, 2006) as listed below:

- **Information theft:** Most of the botnets designed to steal sensitive information (e.g. identities, credit card numbers, passwords, or product keys) from a victim's local machine. This can be achieved by employing keyloggers or screen or video capturing utilities. In 2005, the FBI estimated that botnets caused 20 million dollars in losses and theft out of which one of the scam bilked a Midwest financial institution out of millions (Bohn, 2007).

- **Spam production:** According to Cisco 2008 annual report, more than 90% of the email exchanged over the Internet is spam (Ward, 2006). Most of these spam messages are actually sent from botnets. Some of the popular botnets including Bobax (Stewart, 2007) and Storm worm (Grizzard, Sharma, Nunnery, Kang, & Dagon, 2007; Holz, Steiner, Dahl, Biersack, & Freiling, 2008) were designed especially for flooding spam only.

- **Phishing:** Botnets are primarily developed to host phishing sites. Attackers usually send out spam messages to trick users, through social engineering techniques, to visit phishing sites in order to get their sensitive information. The independent research and advisory firm Financial Insights (Financial Insights Evaluates Impact of Phishing on Retail Fi- nancial Institutions Worldwide, 2004) estimated that in 2004, global financial institutions experienced more than $400 million in financial losses due to phishing only. It is estimated the U.S. businesses lose an around $2 billion a year as their clients become victims of email phishing. (Daswani & Stoppelman, 2007)

- **Click fraud:** In this case, the attacker gets profit by directing the botnet to click on specific ads links. For instance, Clickbot.A was known to have controlled over more than 100,000 machines to execute a low noise click fraud attack through syndicated search ads (Daswani & Stoppelman, 2007). According to ClickForensics (Click Fraud Index, 2009), click fraud alone amounted to 12.7% of all pay- per-click advertisements in the second quarter of 2009.

- **Distributing unwanted software:** Botnets normally used to distribute mal- ware and other harmful software. According to a recent reports (Vijayan, 2008), one botnet illegally installed adware on hundreds of thousands of computers in the U.S. including some belonging to the military.

- **DDoS attacks:** Botnets are commanded to launch a targeted or Distributed Denial-of-Service (DDoS) attack against any Internet system/service. The accumulated bandwidth of the botnet is the main source of achieving DDoS. Nowadays, most of DDoS attacks are launched from botnet platforms and are hard to detect. For example, in May 2007, a DDoS attack was launched against the Estonian government and commercial websites (Davi, 2007).

A botnet is generally considered as a generic platform for online criminal attacks. A detailed analysis of the impacts of malware, particularly bot- nets, on the Internet economy can be found in a recent report (Malicious software (malware): A security threat to the Internet economy, 2008) published by OECD (Organization for Economic Co-operation and Development) and APEC (Asia Pacific Economic Co-operation).

The rest of this chapter is organized as follows: In Section 2, we give an overview of botnets by describing the constituent parts of most common botnets and the inner working of these components. In Section 3, state-of-the-art research for botnet detection, mitigation and recovery measures are presented.

2. BOTNET OVERVIEW

A bot is a software robot or a malware instance that runs autonomously and automatically on a compromised machine without being noticed by the victim user. The bot code is often written by professional programmers and usually supports several kinds of malicious functionalities (Barford & Yegneswaran,2007) that are instrumental in a variety of attacks and malicious activities. The term botnet, derived from the word bot, is a

network of bots that are controlled by an attacker called a botmaster or botherder.

In general, a bot typically uses a combination of existing advanced malware victimizing. For example, a bot can use keylogger techniques and rootkit techniques. Analogous to worms, a bot has the potential capability of increasing its size and propagating over the Internet. Moreover, it can spread by employing the existing social engineering techniques and systems such as instant messaging and email communication system. Recently, bots have adopted the phishing techniques to trick the victim to download specified malware (Niels, Panayiotis, Abu, & Fabian, 2008). As a result of these multiple propagation vectors, the attacker gets control over many victim machines within a short span of time. Currently, the regular of size of most botnets ranges from tens to hundreds of thousands of bots including exceptionally large botnets comprising of several millions of bots (Krebs, 2007). Compared to other intrusion systems, botnets are distinct in two ways: first, bots are goal-directed, e.g., the purpose of most attacks (such as spamming and DDoS attacks) to gain financial profits (Financial Insights Evaluates Impact of Phishing on Retail Financial Institutions Worldwide, 2004); second, the botmaster (the owner of botnet) can interact with his/her bots via Command-and-Control (C&C) servers.

2.1 Botnet Life Cycle

As depicted in Figure 1, the life cycle of typical botnet starts with an ordinary personal computer that is initially get infected by some propagation vectors. The infected system first launches malicious activities locally and then attempts to communicate with the botnet infrastructure. From the botnet infrastructure, the infected machine will have an opportunity to update itself with the latest malware binaries. The acquired binaries, instruct the infected system to communicate with the rest of the botnet infrastructure, in addition to other modules. Generally, the infected system is directed to download the updates through a variety of file transfer protocols (e.g. FTP, HTTP). At specific point of time, the botmaster tries to instruct its botnet infrastructure (C&C) with all the necessary information to launch an attack. After a successful attack, the botnet may lose some of its systems due to the presence of detection and mitigation systems inside the networks. To fill the gap, the botnet attempts to recruit more systems to be used in future attacks.

2.2 Bot Propagation and Infection Techniques

To avoid being detected by various deployed detection systems, bots are designed in such a way that enables them to change their propagation mechanisms over the passages of time. For instance, an infected bot may apply scanning to all possible ranges of IP space for computers running exploitable services. These exploitable services allow the previous infected hosts to inject a small amount of shellcode into the victim machine. Unlike worms, botnets are difficult to be classified merely on the basis of their scanning

Figure 1. Botnet life cycle

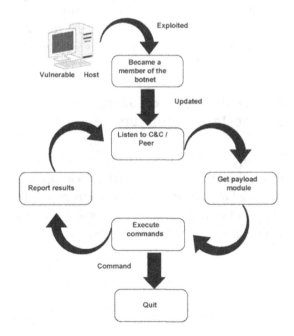

techniques. Botnets are adopting those behaviors and the existence of human controller (botmaster), allow them to cause stealthier and targeted attacks.

With the development of more sophisticated protection and detection techniques, the way of botnets attack is now more similar to that of a Trojan horse. Trojans tricks victims to install malware believing them as useful and beneficial software. Similarly, bot infection is spread by transmitting binaries as email attachments. Once received, the naive user may open malware executable and thus is infected. These infection scenarios are comparatively less alarming, as they require some action on the part of a user prior to complete the infection cycle. Another effective infection technique is called the Web drive by downloads, a technique where the user visits a Web site that can exploit targeted Web browsers and then infects the system. In addition to that, P2P file sharing technologies is successfully exploited by the botmasters to distribute malware binaries.

2.3 Botnet C&C Architecture

Every new generation of bots introduce themselves by exploring different C&C techniques, through which they can be updated and directed by the botmaster. A botmaster can use different kinds of command and control mechanisms in terms of communication protocols and network structures. One of the good choices would be to employ the Internet Relay Chat (IRC) protocol, which is widely used nowadays. Moreover, HTTP is another good choice for the attackers as it hardens the detection process because the HTTP traffic is mostly allowed in network polices. More advanced botnets do not rely on centralized command and control mechanisms and instead are using distributed control techniques to avoid the single point of failure problem; such as, the usage of peer-to-peer networks to organize and control botnet more consistently (Grizzard et al., 2007; Holz, Steiner, et al., 2008; Lemos, 2006; Vogt, Aycock, & Michael J. Jacobson, 2007).

3. STATE-OF-THE-ART

The literature in the domain of botnet detection is enormous and is not limited to one research area. Our objective is to combine the innovative contributions in the area of traffic classification, encrypted traffic classification, and malware analysis and then propose an integrated approach, which will pave the way for developing a detection and mitigation system for botnets. Some techniques have shown considerable success in identifying or categorizing anomalies in the network or system behaviors (Livadas, Walsh, Lapsley, & Strayer, 2006; W. T. Strayer, Walsh, Livadas, & Lapsley, 2006). Others demonstrated the power of machine learning tools for spam filtering and intrusion detection (Zhuang, Dunagan, Simon, Wang, & Tygar, 2008; Xie et al., 2008). On the other hand, traffic analysis and correlation analysis were also used as the basis of many successful approaches in detecting suspicious application behaviors (Gu, Porras, Yegneswaran, Fong, & Lee, 2007; Guofei, Roberto, Junjie, & Wenke, 2008; Gu, Zhang, & Lee, 2008; W. Strayer, Lapsely, Walsh, & Livadas, 2008; Yen & Reiter, 2008). As a result of the increase usage of encrypted traffic in botnet communications, encrypted traffic classification may prove to be a valuable tool for the detection of botnet communications (Ramsbrock, Wang, & Jiang, 2008; Wu & Wolthusen, 2007). Finally, malware analysis feeds the whole process with valuable insights, predicted behaviors, and expected communication patterns.

3.1 Features/Observations of Botnets

Botnets have behavioral features that can help us to detect their existence. Akiyama et al. (2007) explained three behavioral features of botnets which have been used in many detection approaches: relationship, response, and synchronization.

- **Relationship:** Within any botnet, the botmaster keeps a one-to-many relationship between him/her and the botnet. This observation assumes that we can utilize the structure of the relationship between the botnet components in order to detect it. So, it is important to extract the relationships in a botnet from the collected traffic and then identify suspicious groups that hold a certain relationship to be a botnet.
- **Synchronization:** Generally in any botnet, the botmaster triggers a command to instruct the botnet to lunch preprogrammed activities. In this context, all bots that receive this command may be synchronized with each other to take some actions such as DDoS attacks, reporting their activities, sharing information, or sending emails. Therefore, there will be an observed amount of traffic at specific points of time which can be correlated to receiving commands.
- **Response:** When bots receive any command from their master, they usually respond immediately and accurately. On the other hand, when a human operator receives a message, he/she responds after variable thinking time with wide variety of possible actions. This observation can be used to track bots based on the response time of hosts upon receiving specific messages.

3.2 Taxonomy of Existing Botnet Detection Systems

Recently, several papers have proposed various approaches for detecting botnets. Each approach tries to address the botnet detection from specific angle. In the following, we categorize the botnet literature into eight different categories.

3.2.1 Network-Based

Network-based detection techniques attempt to detect botnets based on several network traffic anomalies such as high network latency, high volumes of traffic, traffic on unusual ports, and unusual system behavior that could indicate the presence of malicious bots in the network.

Statistical analysis can be considered as the basis of many intrusion detection systems. For instance, Binkleyand and Singh (2006) proposed a technique that combines both IRC statistics and TCP anomalies to detect IRC-based botnets. Their approach is useful only for detecting certain botnet instances which perform noticeable scanning activity. On the other hand, the usage of DNS anomalies has also been proposed to detect botnets. For example, Ramachandran, Feamster, and Dagon (2006) introduced a method using DNS blacklist (DNSBL) to locate botnet members that generate spam. The basic assumption of this approach is that the botmasters may use DNSBL to query the status of their bots, so the machine that generates many queries that are rarely queried by others is declared as suspicious. This approach is limited to specific instances of spam botnets, which can result in many false positives.

Another commonly used approach is signature-based detection. Rishi (Jan & Thorsten, 2007) is considered as a signature-based IRC botnet detection system that matches known nickname patterns of IRC bots. Similar to a typical signature-based Anti-Virus (AV) tool or Intrusion Detection System (IDS), this approach is accurate only if its complete and exact signature base is available which an inherent weakness of signature-based solutions is. Some approaches apply flow analysis to network traffic to detect malicious behaviors. For example, Anestis, Brian, and David (2007) introduced network flow level detection for IRC botnet controllers in backbone networks. Their approach utilize suspicious host activity reports to identify flows for analysis, then use IRC data flow profiles to detect IRC-based botnets.

Machine learning and data mining algorithms are usually used to improve the overall accuracy of various detection methods. In this context, Livadas et al. (2006); W. T. Strayer et al. (2006) proposed a machine learning based approach for bot-net detection using network-level traffic features (e.g. inter-arrival timing, packet size) of the IRC protocol. They adopt a two stage process which first distinguishes IRC flows and then identifies botnet C&C traffic from normal IRC flows. Although these techniques are effective in detecting some botnets, they are specific to IRC-based botnets. In addition, for accurate analysis and detection, these techniques require access to payload content. Thus, it cannot detect encrypted C&C traffic. Moreover, their approach de-pends on the accuracy of the training phase to classify normal and abnormal activities which is a challenging task with the presence of dynamic botnets. Using traffic classification techniques, Lu, Tavallaee, Ram-midi, and Ghorbani (2009) proposed an online bot-net traffic classification system, called BotCop, in which the network traffic are fully classified into different application communities by using payload signatures and a decision tree model. Then for each classified application community, they apply the characteristic of flows to differentiate the botnet communication traffic from normal traffic. The usage of payload content specific signature can be evaded by the adversary through changing the structure of the content or the use of encryption.

Correlation approaches are used to group many infection events or symptoms to declare or detect malicious activity. This approach has been introduced recently in botnet detection. Gu et al. (2007) introduced the BotHunter as an IDS dialog correlation technique that associates IDS events to a user-defined bot infection dialog model. Their approach is based on the vertical correlation techniques which analyze each host inbound and out-bound events. Stealthy bots can avoid BotHunter by evading event timing correlation. Moreover, Shirley and Mano (2008) presented a model to evade BotHunter by eliminating any suspicious external events that participate in their bot infection dialog model. To complement the BotHunter, Gu et al. (2008) presented the BotSniffer which is based on horizontal correlation to detect and find similarities in C&C traffic inside network traces. However, it is used mainly for detecting centralized C&C activities. To overcome this limitation, Guofei et al. (2008) also proposed a solution that is independent of the protocol and the structure used by botnets. Also, it is based on horizontal correlation techniques but, it clusters similar communication and similar malicious traffic, and then cross-correlate them to find infected systems. Similar to BotMiner, Yen and Reiter (2008) proposed Traffic Aggregation for Malware Detection (TAMD) which aggregates hosts based on their characteristics (destination, payload, and OS platform). They apply three layers of aggregation functions to identify infected hosts. First, they aggregate internal hosts that accessed certain external IP addresses. Then, they extract any communication that caries similar payloads based on edit distance technique. Finally, they identify the common platforms. Recently, Yen, Huang, Monrose, and Reiter (2009) introduced new characteristic to add another aggregation layer to identify the browser platform of the infected systems. Generally, horizontal correlation approaches cannot detect individual infected systems. On the other side, vertical correlation approaches require prior knowledge about C&C channels and the propagation methods of any targeted botnet.

When an individual bot receives specific command, it responds to the C&C in very short time accordingly. Wurzinger et al. (2009) take advantage of this characteristic and develop an approach to detect the existence of individual bots. Simply, their technique takes a bot binary and then collects its network traces in a controlled environment. As soon as they notice any response activity, they correlate the network traces to model received commands and generated response within specific time window. Finally, they use these models as signatures to detect different bot variants. Like other approaches, this technique suffers from analyzing network traces when it is encrypted because their approach uses content-based analysis to locate command strings. Another limitation is the timing window which affects many approaches that rely on the command and response time feature.

Addressing the detection problem with the same characteristic (command and response time) but with the help of traffic classification, Lu, Tavallaee, and Ghorbani (2009) introduced a hierarchical approach to classify network traffic into known network applications and then within those applications they use frequent characteristics techniques to identify botnet communities. This approach shares the same limitations with Wurzinger et al. (2009) approach.

3.2.2 Attack-Behavior

One direction to detect botnet is using their attack behavior. For example, botnets are responsible for most of the spam emails. Giving these facts, researchers studied the spamming behavior of botnets and introduced many approaches to analyze and detect spamming botnets. John, Moshchuk, Gribble, and Krishnamurthy (2009) studied the spamming botnets using their Botlab framework. Using a real-time monitoring system, they collected spams and then manage to download the related bot binaries (URL signatures) which they run in a controlled environment and then analyze the outgoing traffic. Another work focusing on embedded URLs in spam messages was presented in AutoRE by Xie et al. (2008) where they analyzed the sending behaviors and email content patterns. Their approach intended to produce URL signatures based on regular expressions to identify botnet campaigns. As any signature or content based systems, malware designers have the upper hand to change the behavior or the content to evade detection.

An important attack that can be caused by botnets is the so called DDoS attacks. Freiling, Holz, and Wicher- ski (2005) proposed a prevention approach for DDoS attacks. They rely on the fact that many bots receive such a command from a controller to launch the DDoS attack on a specific target. Their approach requires understanding the structure of the botnet in order to implement customized bot agent to spy on the network and receive commands. By analyzing all the activities of the collected traffic, the bot controller can be revealed, tracked and then taken down.

Recently, Web-account abuse attacks targeted Web email service providers. Zhao et al. (2009) implemented the BotGraph which is a more specific detection system to detect Web account abuse attack. Their approach is based on the observation that bot user accounts share IP addresses in the login or the sending procedure. They address this attack by two behavior analysis components: history based change detection to identify aggressive signup activities and graph-based to detect stealthy login activities.

3.2.3 Operation-Behavior

Botherders are constantly developing more sophisticated techniques to achieve their goals. When a botherder directs large botnet, he requires a reliable hosting infrastructure to command the botnet effectively. Traditionally, C&C servers have been located by their bots using their IP addresses, DNS names, or their node IDs in Peer-to-Peer (P2P) overlays. Recently, botnet designers have developed several ways to make these schemes more flexible and robust against take-down actions, e.g., by using IP fast-flux techniques. Criminals introduce Fast-Flux Service Networks (FFSNs) which are simply hosting a service by many different IP addresses, i.e., they construct a proxy network on top of compromised machines that are used to build resilient hosting infrastructure using public DNS (Know Your Enemy: Fast-Flux

Service Networks, 2007). Generally, FFSNs can be classified as single fast-flux and double fast-flux. Single fast-flux technique is known by frequently changing the mapping of *A* records (Mockapetris, 1987) of domain names to IP addresses of compromised systems in the botnet. The double fast-flux technique is similar to the single fast-flux but it has an additional layer of redundancy that keeps changing the authoritative *NS* records (Know Your Enemy: Fast-Flux Service Networks, 2007; Mockapetris, 1987).

Fast-Flux technique has captured the attention of some researchers to study and analyze botnets that are using this mechanism. For example, Holz, Gorecki, Rieck, and Freiling (2008) introduced a complete study and analysis of FFSNs that are used by spamming botnets. They presented different metrics which can be used to identify malicious fast-flux activities. Furthermore, they studied the characteristics of FFSNs and developed detection algorithms that first extract URL links inside spam emails and then, using a linear classifier, they identify FFSNs based on the number of unique IP addresses in DNS queries, the number of unique AS (Mockapetris, 1987) numbers of those IP addresses, and the number of *NS* records in a single lookup. In another work, Nazario and Holz (2008) continued the analysis with live network traces which reveal botnet memberships and domain names. They extended the heuristic features of FFSNs that are used by botnets. Passerini, Paleari, Martignoni, and Bruschi (2008) introduced a set of features to characterize FFSNs. Their approach, called FluXOR, collects suspected domain names from different sources, monitors their DNS response messages over specific period of time and then uses a trained Naive Bayesian classifier to classify these domain names as either benign or malicious FFSNs. Similarly, Caglayan, Toothaker, Drapeau, Burke, and Eaton (2009) presented a distributed architecture of Web services to detect FFSNs activities using active and passive monitoring of DNS properties.

There are many challenges associated with botnet detection systems based on FFSNs behavior such as monitoring rapid changes to DNS records, classification of historical behavior, real time detection, and differentiation from legitimate behavior of FFSNs.

Stone-Gross et al. (2009) reported their experience to take control of the Torbig botnet for ten days. This botnet reveals the new concept of locating C&C servers by introducing a domain flux technique. Using this technique, each bot generates domain name lists periodically and then contacts them to resolve C&C IP addresses. In their work, they take advantage of the deterministic domains generation algorithm and the fact that the botherders are not controlling all future generated domains. So, they get control of future domain names and then wait for bots to communicate with their monitored C&C servers. The collected data and network communications brought valuable insights about the inner details of botnet management and their huge threats to the user data privacy.

Hu, Knysz, and Shin (2009) presented a cooperative system for detecting redirection botnet (fast-flux networks). Like previous approaches, they collect domain names from spamming emails and they also extract domains from the network traces. These data sources get probed to collect botnet redirections features such as DNS record behavior, flow characteristics, and connection patterns. Finally, their approach classified domain names into malicious or benign using some advanced classification techniques.

3.2.4 Host-Based

Host-based botnet detection approaches try to detect malicious activities that can be observed on a local host. This can be achieved by monitoring the system behavior, modeling user interaction, and tracing the network data flow inside the system.

Taint-propagation analysis is one of the commonly used techniques in host-based botnet detection systems. As an example, Stinson and Mitchell proposed, the BotSwat (Stinson & Mitchell, 2007), a host-based tracking system to identify processes that manipulate the network traces from untrustworthy external sources, and then identify the possibility of remote control behavior of the monitored systems. This technique may cause many false positives because of many programs manipulate data from network conversations. Moreover, taint propagation analysis turns out to be very heavy for detection purposes which affect the performance of the detection system. Furthermore, when data encryption is used, this approach would not work.

Takemori, Fujinaga, Sayama, and Nishigaki (2009) proposed a claim driven-scheme for botnet detection and cooperative scheme for C&C tracking. Their system operates in enterprise-like networks where every host is equipped with attack monitoring and a reporter system that reports to a coordinated tracking center. When a system detects any attack behavior, it reports that incident to the coordinator which then provides it with a list of infected machines. When the victim machine finds any access record that involves connection with any infected machine, then it is considered to be infected. After that, it sends its access records to the coordinator in order to construct the topology of the botnet. To detect any malicious activities on the system, they keep monitoring specific symptoms in the communication patterns such as bot code downloading through HTTP protocol, control messages by IRC protocol, exploits in famous vulnerabilities, DNS messages, and SMTP messages. Their approach relies on the user system to claim any bot process which may introduce many false positives and reduce the performance of the tracking coordinator. Another drawback is that they assume the only way to download bot updates is through HTTP protocol that can be achieved by other protocols such as FTP or P2P. Their solution is limited to IRC botnets or centralized C&C servers.

One of the facts of bot behavior is that they need to communicate regularly and stealthy with their C&C server. Giroire, Chandrashekar, Taft, Schooler, and Papagiannaki (2009) used this feature to develop a new temporal measure of connection regularity to a set of destinations. They target the end-points to detect the C&C communications using the fact that infected bots have to be synchronized with their C&C servers. Their approach aggregates destination end-points and then based on that it checks the persistence in the host communications. In order to differentiate legitimate application from malicious activities, the system needs to construct a whitelist within a specific training period. After that and based on a predefined persistence threshold, the system can track the new persistence of destinations and then detect and determine any C&C communications. This method suffers from the whitelist creation problem and defining concise persistence threshold which depends on the network setup and policies. Furthermore, it can be defeated by decentralized C&C techniques.

Behavior analysis techniques have been applied to detect malicious activities in the host machine. Martignoni, Stinson, Fredrikson, Jha, and Mitchell (2008) developed a behavior-based approach to model malware high-level actions. They consider and model possible bot actions such as proxying, key logging, information harvesting, program downloading and program executing. Using action behavior specifications and sequence of events for process execution, their system is able to detect any monitored actions with the help of hierarchical behavior graphs. This method is based on data-flow analysis of program execution and system calls which may introduce an open door to evade the detection process. Malware can use non-standard techniques to achieve its goals and evade the whole detection process. Similarly, Liu, Chen, Yan, and Zhang (2008) participated to

host-based systems by introducing the BotTracer which detects bot existence by monitoring three bot features: automatic startup, C&C channels establishment, and information harvesting. Their model employs a virtual machine solution to detect and monitor automatic communication attempts to the C&C and then classifies them according to event model. Lastly, the BotTracer monitors local system activities to detect any attack preparation stages and raise an infection alarm. The main drawback of this approach is that any bot behavior that comes with user interaction will evade the whole detection. Also, their mechanism based on the sequence of events which the bot can eliminate them by following alterative techniques. Like the BotSwat, the white listing requirements can introduce many false positives to the detection process.

3.2.5 Human-Behavior

There are intrinsic differences between the human interaction and the bot interaction with computer applications. These behavior differences were considered by several researchers to improve the detection of infected hosts. For instance, Gummadi, Balakrishnan, Maniatis, and Ratnasamy (2009) studied the identification of human-generated traffic to classify normal activities using an attestation technique. They introduce the usage of attester to certify and verify any keyboard or mouse clicks of specific system for emails and Web requests. Using a verifier module, anyone (server) can know who is behind any traffic generated forming any host (client) and whether it is a user or a bot action. The verification process results in good detection rates against email spams, DDoS, and click fraud attacks. Similarly, Deian Stefan and Xu (2009) designed a host-based cryptographic verification approach. Such a technique in this field has to deal with legitimate actions of trusted applications which cannot be verified by the identification system.

3.2.6 Log-Correlation

Log files are considered as a valuable resource for network, system, execution, and application events. There are limited numbers of works that are using these resources for botnet detection. This is because of the huge number of events and information that are stored inside log files. Recently, Masud, Al-khaleeb, Khan, Thuraisinghatn, and Hamlcn (2008) proposed robust and effective flow-based botnet traffic detection by mining multiple log files. They introduced multiple log correlation for C&C traffic detection. They correlate specific characteristics that are based on the observation about bot response time upon receiving commands. This method does not impose any restriction on the botnet communication protocol and is therefore applicable to non-IRC botnets. Furthermore, this method does not require access to payload content. Hence, it is effective even if the C&C payload is encrypted or is not available (Masud et al., 2008). Similarly, Al-Hammadi and Aickelin (2006) presented an approach to track the changes in the log file sizes of various computers where similar changes in the log files of different machines indicate potential bot-coordinated activity.

3.2.7 Honeypot-Based

In order to get a full understanding of botnets behavior, honeypots are widely deployed in order to capture, track, and analyze different malware. Although honeypots are effective tools for collecting and tracking botnets, they have several limitations. First, low-interaction honeypots such as Nepenthes (Baecher, Koetter, Holz, Dornseif, & Freiling, 2006) can capture attacks from only a limited number of known exploits that they faithfully emulate, and high-interaction honeypots can neither implement all services nor deal with the scalability problem. Second, honeypots are mainly designed to capture malware that propagates via scanning for remote vulnerabilities, so they cannot easily capture malware using other propagation methods such as email and Web drive-by-download, which is probably two of the most widely, used propagation vectors (Niels et al., 2008). Third, there is no control on the frequency or the volume of malware captured using this approach because a honeypot can only wait and hope for the malware to contact it. Fourth, malware may avoid scanning the networks with "know" honeypots (Bethencourt, Franklin, & Vernon, 2005). Furthermore, it can detect the virtual machine environments that are commonly used by honeypots (Holz & Raynal, 2005) and alter its behavior to evade analysis. Finally, honeypots report infections on only their decoy machines; they generally cannot directly tell which non-decoy machines in the enterprise network are members of a botnet. These weaknesses limit the capability of honeypots as effective detection systems.

3.2.8 Botnet Tracking

In the traceback field, there are two main areas of interest. The first one is network layer (IP) traceback and the second is tracing approaches that are resilient to stepping stone hosts. The first category was used earlier in the era of fast-spreading worms when there was no stepping stone hosts were involved. Savage, Wetherall, Karlin, and Anderson (2000) introduced the packet marking technique by embedding tracing information inside the IP header fields. Goodrich (2002) extended this idea by introducing "randomize-and-link" which scales for more datasets. A different technique for IP traceback is the log/hash-based which was introduced by Snoeren et al. (2001), and enhanced by Li, Sung, Xu, and Li (2004), and enhanced by Li et al. [72]. Recently many techniques have been proposed to trace attackers who use stepping stone hosts under various conditions. Inter-packet timing has been used to correlate encrypted traffic across the stepping stone hosts and/or low-latency anonymity systems. Most timing-based correlation schemes are passive with the exception of active methods (Yoda & Etoh, 2000; Y. Zhang & Paxson, 2000; Donoho et al., 2002; X. Wang, Reeves, & Wu, 2002; X. Wang & Reeves, 2003; Blum, Song, & Venkataraman, 2004; X. Wang, Chen, & Jajodia, 2005, 2007) . Ramsbrock et al. (2008) proposed a method with similar concept using active watermarking principle. Their method uses the packet length as extra parameters in addition to the packet timing, to encode the watermark. As a result, they require much fewer packets than other methods (X. Wang & Reeves, 2003; X. Wang et al.,2005, 2007).

3.3 Botnet Measurement and Size Estimation

Measurement studies provide better understanding for the botnet phenomenon and its characteristics. The majority of the research works in the area of botnet measurement devote their efforts to estimate the populations of various kinds of botnets in today's Internet. Dagon, Gu, and Lee (2008) measured three botnets topologies (centralized, peer-to-peer, and random) using three metrics (effectiveness, efficiency, and robustness). Abu Rajab, Zarfoss, Mon- rose, and Terzis (2006) observed the botnet phenomenon from three different perspectives (DNS, IRC, passive). Rajab, Zarfoss, Monrose, and Terzis (2007) considered the discrepancies in botnet size estimation and suggested that botnet size should be a qualified term that is relevant only within the context of the counting method used to generate the result.

3.4 Next-Generation Botnet Architectures

Several researchers started to design new botnet architectures to help in developing techniques against these kinds of botnets before they appear in the wild. The main theme in this area is to analyze the current botnet vulnerabilities and then propose new methods to enhance the capabilities of the botnet.

P. Wang, Sparks, and Zou (2007) presented a design of an advanced hybird-P2P botnet that is resilient against current detection and mitigation systems. Some of their new botnet designs utilize encrypted communications, high connectivity, scalability, and less information leakage about the botnet inside each bot. On the other hand, Vogt et al. (2007) introduced another new botnet design based on smaller botnets. A collection of smaller botnets, called supper-botnets, can be coordinated to launch different attacks. Each botnet can have different infrastructure than the others, but they can communicate with each other to propagate commands from the botmaster. These kinds of botnets are harder to be taken down by the current detection systems because of their distributed nature and since there is no single C&C channel. Another idea for new botnet was introduced by Starnberger et al. [85] which concentrated on designing stealthy botnet communication and minimizing any information disclosure from captured bot. Recently, Z. Zhang, Ando, and Kadobayashi (2009) improve the super-botnet idea (Vogt et al., 2007) and proposed bot-enclave design which enhanced the C&C servers and protected their communication. Their proposal emphasizes on how the botmaster can propagate, manage, operate, and protect the botnet.

3.5 Botnet Reverse Engineering

Reverse Code Engineering (RCE) is the process of analyzing the disassembly of an executable, with the purpose of recreating the actual source code, or just a pseudo-code representation of the executable behavior. RCE can disclose every decision taken and every algorithm used in a program, but the process can be very time consuming. Compilation of an executable will strip most of the meaningful information from comments, variable names, and so forth. Furthermore, the use of optimization by compilers will also diffuse the structure of the disassembly compared to the source code. For this reason, RCE is often used as an addition to the behavioral analysis by only investigating the interesting section of the disassembly. These sections can be found, for example, by looking for the use of strings appearing in the bots network communication or by finding sections where API calls behind some interesting behavior are made.

Debugging software is the process of running the code with a debugger attached, permitting the use of breakpoints and variable inspection at any point in the code. Debugging is a very helpful addition to inspect the disassembly. It provides good clues to functions implementation, if the actual input and output to the functions are traced.

3.5.1 Case Studies

Bot reverse engineering can be considered as one of the primary factors that feed the learning curve about the underground community. Valuable information can be obtained by analyzing the malware binaries, network traces, and infected system behavior. In the literature of botnet, researcher's provided some case studies of famous botnet variants. Their studies aimed to gain some knowledge about botnet behaviors and then develop some methods to evade them. There are three main categories of botnets based on their C&C architecture: IRC, HTTP, and P2P. For IRC botnets, Barford and Yegneswaran (2007) evaluated four different instances of IRC botnets. This comprehensive study reveals a lot of knowledge about botnet capabilities in controlling the infected system, C&C, propagation, attacks, updates delivery, obfuscation, and deception mechanisms. During this work, they determine possible infection interactions of IRC botnets and their command strings.

With the rise of HTTP botnets, researchers studied couple of instances to understand the inner details of these new botnet behaviors. Nazario (2007) introduced one of the first HTTP botnet analysis studies about BlackEnergy which is considered as a Web-based bot tool. This analysis provided the research community with complete information about the botnet architecture, commands, and communication patterns. Like any Web-based bot tool, there was a PHP based C&C which collects some statistics about the botnet and the bot binaries were built by a customizable malware builder program. The main threat behind this botnet was DDoS, but there no significant attacks have been noticed. Another analysis was presented by Chiang and Lloyd (2007) for Rustock rootkit which contains a spam bot module. They noticed from the network traces that the communication was encrypted by the RC4 algorithm which makes it difficult for the detection systems. Moreover, the rootkit and the advanced and multiple levels of obfuscation gave hard time for AV systems. Generally, this rootkit was mainly used for spamming purposes which can be updated through C&C servers. In their analysis, they were able to extract the encryption key of the C&C communication patterns. Recently, HTTP-based botnets were involved in many click frauds. One of the famous botnets that are responsible for click fraud attacks is the *Clickbot.A*. Daswani and Stoppelman (2007) presented a detailed case study about *Clickbot.A* instance which reveals new techniques for click fraud activities. Their analysis uncovered the main components of this botnet and their management techniques, commands, and configuration.

Botnet herders realized very clearly the challenges to hide their existence with centralized control approaches. In contrast, they shifted to decentralized techniques, P2P communication protocol, which provided them with huge scalability and became more resilient against traditional detection and tracking techniques. Recently, there were some contributions to understand and analyze the existing P2P based botnet instances. For example, Porras, Sadi, and Yegneswaran (2007) reverse engineered Storm botnet variant to uncover its capabilities to control bots, hide binary distribution, and obfuscation techniques. From their analysis, Storm botnet manage its C&C communication by the Overnet protocol with some customized communication patterns. Generally, the Storm botnet is used for sending spam and has capabilities for DDoS attacks. From other perspective, Grizzard et al. (2007); Holz, Steiner, et al. (2008) reported on Storm botnet by exploring the encryption key generation algorithm that is used by each Storm variant to establish secure communication with other peers in the botnet.

Another example of P2P-based botnets was Nugache which controls its army by a customized P2P protocol architecture. Dittrich and Dietrich (2008) reported some information about their analysis for Nugache instance. They analyzed the communication patterns which involved the key exchange process (Rijndael algorithm) to encrypt the C&C communications. Using an encrypted P2P network, the botherder instructs the botnet to listen to a specific IRC channel for DDoS commands. Nugache has been updated later to use P2P networks for all its communications. Again, Dittrich and Dietrich (2008) addressed extra aspects of analysis and investigated the size estimation of the Nugache botnet using a customized bot client crawler.

3.6 Conclusion

While a variety of anti-botnets techniques have been developed, none of them is a silver bullet. One can draw the conclusion that none of the available botnet detection methods can provide a solution that is good enough on its own. A practical alternative is to integrate the appropriate techniques together for constituting an in-depth defense boundary.

REFERENCES

Abu Rajab, M., Zarfoss, J., Monrose, F., & Terzis, A. (2006). A multifaceted approach to understanding the botnet phenomenon. In IMC'06: Proceedings of the 6th ACM SIGCOMM Conference on internetInternet Measurement (pp. 41–52). New York, NY, USA: ACM.

Akiyama, M., Kawamoto, T., Shimamura, M., Yokoyama, T., Kadobayashi, Y., & Yamaguchi, S. (2007). A proposal of metrics for botnet detection based on its cooperative behavior. In Saint '07: Proceedings of the 2007 International Symposium on Applications and the internetInternet Workshops. Washington, DC, USA: IEEE Computer Society.

Al-Hammadi, Y., & Aickelin, U. (2006). Detecting botnets through log correlation. Paper presented at In the Workshop on Monitoring, Attack Detection and Mitigation. New York, NY.

Anagnostakis, K. G., Sidiroglou, S., Akritidis, P., Xinidis, K., Markatos, E., & Keromytis, A. D. (2005). Detecting targeted attacks using shadow honeypots. In SSYM'05: Proceedings of the 14th Conference on USENIX Security Symposium. Berkeley, CA, USA: USENIX Association.

Anestis, K., Brian, R., & David, H. (2007). Wide-scale botnet detection and characterization. In Hotbots'07: Proceedings of the First Conference on First Workshop on Hot Topics in Understanding Botnets. Berkeley, CA, USA: USENIX Association.

Baecher, P., Koetter, M., Holz, T., Dornseif, M., & Freiling, F. (2006). The nepenthes platform: An efficient approach to collect malware. Recent Advances in Intrusion Detection, 165–184.

Barford, P., & Yegneswaran, V. (2007). *An inside look at botnets*. Academic Press.

Bethencourt, J., Franklin, J., & Vernon, M. (2005). Mapping internetinternet sensors with probe response attacks. In SSYM'05: Proceedings of the 14th Conference on USENIX Security Symposium. Berkeley, CA, USA: USENIX Association.

Binkleyand, J. R., & Singh, S. (2006, 7 July 2006). An algorithm for anomaly- based botnet detection. In In Proceedings of 2nd Workshop on Steps to Reducing Unwanted Traffic on the internetInternet (p. (pp. 43-48). Berkeley, CA, USA: USENIX Association.

Bohn, K. (2007). Teen questioned in computer hacking probe. Retrieved from http://www.cnn.com/2007/TECH/11/29/fbi.botnets/ index.html

Botgraph: Large scale spamming botnet detection. In Nsdi'09: Pro- ceedings of the 6th USENIX Symposium on Networked Systems Design and Implementation (pp. 321–334). Berkeley, CA, USA: USENIX Association.

Caglayan, A., Toothaker, M., Drapeau, D., Burke, D., & Eaton, G. (2009). Real-time detection of fast flux service networks. In Proceedings Cybersecurity Applications and Technology Conference for Homeland Security, CATCH 2009, (pp. 285-– 292). Academic Press.

Chiang, K., & Lloyd, L. (2007). A case study of the rustock rootkit and spam bot. In Hotbots'07: Proceedings of the First Conference on First Workshop on Hot Topics in Understanding Botnets. Berkeley, CA, USA: USENIX Association.

Click Fraud Index. (2014). Retrieved from http://www.clickforensics.com/resources/click-fraud-index.html

Dagon, D., Gu, G., & Lee, C. (2008). A taxonomy of botnet structures. Botnet Detection, , 143–164.

Daswani, N., & Stoppelman, M. (2007). The anatomy of Clickbot.A. In Hotbots'07: Proceedings of the First Conference on First Workshop on Hot Topics in Understanding Botnets. Berkeley, CA, USA: USENIX Association.

Davi, J. (2014). Hackers take down the most wired country in Europe. Retrieved from http://www.wired.com/politics/security/ magazine/15-09/ff estonia

Deian Stefan, D. Y. Chehai Wu, & Xu, G. (2009). A cryptographic provenance verification approach for host-based malware detection (Tech. Rep.). Rutgers University.

Dittrich, D., & Dietrich, S. (2008). P2P as botnet command and control: A deeper insight. In In Proceedings of 3rd International Conference on Malicious and Unwanted Software (Malware) (p. (pp. 41-48). Piscataway, NJ: Academic Press., USA

Donoho, D. L., Flesia, A. G., Shankar, U., Paxson, V., Coit, J., & Staniford, S. (2002). Multiscale stepping-stone detection: Detecting pairs of jittered interactive streams by exploiting maximum tolerable delay. In Proceedings (p. (pp. 17-35). Berlin, Germany: Springer- Verlag.

Evan, C., Farnam, J., & Danny, M. (2005). The zombie roundup: Understanding, detecting, and disrupting botnets. In Sruti'05: Proceedings of the Steps to Reducing Unwanted Traffic on the internetInternet on Steps to Re-ducing Unwanted Traffic on the internetInternet Workshop. Berkeley, CA, USA: USENIX Association.

Financial Insights Evaluates Impact of Phishing on Retail Financial Institutions Worldwide. (2014). Retrieved from http://www.crm2day.com/ content/t6 librarynews 1.php?news id=EplAlZlEVFjAwhYlkt

Freiling, F. C., Holz, T., & Wicherski, G. (2005). Botnet tracking: Exploring a root-cause methodology to prevent distributed denial-of- service attacks. In In Proceedings of 10th European Symposium on Research in Computer Security (LNCS), esorics 2005, september 12,2005 - september 14 (Vol. 3679 LNCS, pp. 319-335). Milan, Italy: Springer Verlag.

Giroire, F., Chandrashekar, J., Taft, N., Schooler, E., & Papagiannaki, D. (2009). Exploiting temporal persistence to detect covert botnet channels. In In Proceedings of the 12th International Symposium on Recent Advances in Intrusion Detection (RAID'09). RAID.

Goodrich, M. T. (2002). Efficient packet marking for large-scale IP traceback. In Proceedings of the 9th ACM Conference on Computer and Communications Security, November 18,2002 - November 22 (p.(pp. 117-126). Washington, DC, United states: Association for Computing Ma- chinery.

Grizzard, J. B., Sharma, V., Nunnery, C., Kang, B. B., & Dagon, D. (2007). Peer-to-peer botnets: Overview and case study. In Hotbots'07: Proceedings of the First Conference on First Workshop on Hot Topics in Understanding Botnets. Berkeley, CA, USA: USENIX Association.

Gu, G., Porras, P., Yegneswaran, V., Fong, M., & Lee, W. (2007). Bothunter: Detecting malware infection through ids-driven dialog correlation. In SS'07: Proceedings of 16th USENIX Security Symposium on USENIX Security symposium (pp. 1–16). Berkeley, CA, USA: USENIX Association.

Gu, G., Zhang, J., & Lee, W. (2008, February). Botsniffer: Detecting botnet command and control channels in network traffic. In Proceedings of the 15th Annual Network and Distributed System Security Symposium (NDSS'08). NDSS.

GummadiR.BalakrishnanH.ManiatisP.RatnasamyS. (2009).

Guofei, G., Roberto, P., Junjie, Z., & Wenke, L. (2008). Botminer: Clustering analysis of network traffic for protocol and structure-independent botnet detection. In SS'08: Proceedings of the 17th Conference on Security Symposium (p. (pp. 139-154). Berkeley, CA, USA: USENIX Association.

Holz, T., Gorecki, C., Rieck, K., & Freiling, F. C. (2008). Measuring and detecting fast-flux service networks. In Proceedings of the 15th Annual Network and Distributed System Security Symposium (NDSS'08). NDSS.

Holz, T., & Raynal, F. (2005). Detecting honeypots and other suspicious environments. In (Vol. 2005, p. 29 - 36). West Point, NY: United statesAcademic Press.

Holz, T., Steiner, M., Dahl, F., Biersack, E., & Freiling, F. (2008). Measurements and mitigation of peer-to-peer-based botnets: A case study on storm worm. In LEET'08: Proceedings of the 1st USENIX Workshop on Large-Scale Exploits and Emergent Threats (pp. 1–9). Berkeley, CA, USA: USENIX Association.

http://news.bbc.co.uk/1/hi/business/6298641.stm

http://news.bbc.co.uk/2/hi/technology/5219554. stm

Hu, X., Knysz, M., & Shin, K. G. (2009). RBseeker auto-detection of redirection botnets. In In Proceedings of 16th Annual Network & Distributed System Security Symposium (NDSS'09). NDSS.

Jan, G., & Thorsten, H. (2007). Rishi: Identify bot contaminated hosts by IRC nickname evaluation. In Hotbots'07: Proceedings of the First Conference on First Workshop on Hot Topics in Understanding Botnets. Berkeley, CA, USA: USENIX Association.

John, J. P., Moshchuk, A., Gribble, S. D., & Krishnamurthy, A. (2009). Studying spamming botnets using botlab. In NSDI'09: Proceedings of the 6th USENIX Symposium on Networked Systems Design and Implementation (pp. 291–306). Berkeley, CA, USA: USENIX Association.

Know Your Enemy. (2014). *Fast-Flux Service Networks*. Retrieved from. http://www.honeynet. org/papers/ff/

Krebs, B. (2014). Storm worm dwarfs world's top supercomputers. Retrieved from http://blog. washingtonpost.com/securityfix/2007/08/storm worm dwarfs worlds top s 1.html

Lee, C. D. D. Wenke; & Wang. (Ed.). (2008). Botnet detection: Countering the largest security threat (Vol. 36). New York: Springer-Verlag New York.

Lemos, R. (2014). *Bot software looks to improve peerage*. Retrieved from. http://www.securityfocus.com/news/11390

Li, J., Sung, M., Xu, J., & Li, L. (2004). Large-scale IP traceback in high-speed internetinternet: Practical techniques and theoretical foundation. In Proceedings - 2004 IEEE Symposium on Security and Privacy, May 09,2004 - May 12 (pVol. 2004, p. 115-129). Berkeley, CA, United states: IEEE Computer Society.

Liu, L., Chen, S., Yan, G., & Zhang, Z. (2008). Bottracer: Execution-based bot-like malware detection. Information Security, , 97–113.

Livadas, C., Walsh, R., Lapsley, D., & Strayer, W. T. (2006). Using ma- chine learning techniques to identify botnet traffic. In In Proceedings of 31st Annual IEEE Conference on Local Computer Networks, November 14,2006 - November 16 (p.(pp. 967-974). Tampa, FL, United states: IEEE Computer Society.

Lu, W., Tavallaee, M., & Ghorbani, A. (2009). Automatic discovery of botnet communities on large-scale communication networks. In Asia CCS'09: Proceedings of the 4th International Symposium on Information, Computer, and Communications Security (pp. 1–10). New York, NY, USA: ACM.

Lu, W., Tavallaee, M., Rammidi, G., & Ghorbani, A. (2009). Botcop: An online botnet traffic classifier. In CNSR '09: Proceedings of the 2009 Seventh Annual Communication Networks and Services Research Conference (pp. 70–77). Washington, DC, USA: IEEE Computer Society.

Martignoni, L., Stinson, E., Fredrikson, M., Jha, S., & Mitchell, J. (2008). A layered architecture for detecting malicious behaviors. Recent Advances in Intrusion Detection, , 78–97.

Masud, M. M., Al-Khaleeb, T., Khan, L., Thuraisinghatn, B., & Hamlcn, K. W. (2008). Flow-based identification of botnet traffic by mining multiple log files. In (p.In Proceedings (pp. 200 - 206). Penang, Malaysia: Academic Press.

Mockapetris, P. (1987, November). Domain names - Implementation and specification (Tech. Rep.). RFC 1035.

Moore, D., Shannon, C., Brown, D. J., Voelker, G. M., & Savage, S. (2006). Inferring internetinternet denial-of-service activity. *ACM Transactions on Computer Systems, 24*(2), 115–139. doi:10.1145/1132026.1132027

Nazario, J. (2007). *Blackenergy ddos bot analysis (Tech. Rep.)*. Arbor Networks.

Nazario, J., & Holz, T. (2008). As the net churns: Fast-flux botnet observations. In In Proceedings of MALWARE 2008. 3rd International Conference on In Malicious and Unwanted Software, (pp. 24-31)., Alexandria, VA: Academic Press, United states.

Niels, P., Panayiotis, M., Abu, R. M., & Fabian, M. (2008). All your iframes point to us. In SS'08: Proceedings of the 17th Conference on Security Symposium (p. (pp. 1-15). Berkeley, CA, USA: USENIX Association.

Not-a-bot (NAB):), improving service availability in the face of botnet attacks. In Paper presented at NSDI 2009. Boston, MA.

OECD. (2014). Malicious software (malware):): A security threat to the internetinternet economy (Tech. Rep.). (2014). Organization for economic cooperation and development (OECD). Retrieved from http://www.oecd.org/dataoecd/53/34/40724457.pdf

Passerini, E., Paleari, R., Martignoni, L., & Bruschi, D. (2008, July). FluXOR. Detecting and monitoring fast-flux service networks. In Proceedings of the 5th Conference on Detection of Intrusions and Malware & Vulnerability Assessment., DIMVA, Paris, France. Springer.

Paul Bcher, M. K. G. W. Thorsten & Holz. (2014). Know your enemy: Tracking botnets. Retrieved from http://www.honeynet.org/papers/ bots/

Porras, P., Sadi, H., & Yegneswaran, V. (2007). A multi-perspective analysis of the storm (peacomm) worm (Tech. Rep.). Computer Science Laboratory, SRI International.

Rajab, M. A., Zarfoss, J., Monrose, F., & Terzis, A. (2007). My botnet is bigger than yours (maybe, better than yours):), why size estimates remain challenging. In Hotbots'07: Proceedings of the First Conference on First Workshop on Hot Topics in Understanding Botnets. Berkeley, CA, USA: USENIX Association.

Ramachandran, A., & Feamster, N. (2006). Understanding the network-level behavior of spammers. *SIGCOMM Comput. Commun. Rev., 36*(4), 291–302. doi:10.1145/1151659.1159947

Ramachandran, A., Feamster, N., & Dagon, D. (2006). Revealing botnet membership using DNSBL counter-intelligence. In In Proceedings of 2nd Workshop on Steps to Reducing Unwanted Traffic on the internetInternet (p. (pp. 49-54). Berkeley, CA, USA: USENIX Association.

Ramsbrock, D., Wang, X., & Jiang, X. (2008). A first step towards live botmaster traceback. In In Proceedings of Recent Advances in Intrusion Detection - 11th International Symposium (LNCS), raid 2008, proceedings, september 15,2008 - september 17 (Vol. 5230 LNCS, pp. 59-77). Cambridge, MA, United states: Springer Verlag.

Savage, S., Wetherall, D., Karlin, A., & Anderson, T. (2000). Practical network support for IP traceback. SIGCOMM Comput. Commun. Rev30(4), 295–306.

Shirley, B., & Mano, C. (2008). A model for covert botnet communication in a private subnet. In Proceedings of NETWORKING 2008 Ad Hoc and Sensor Networks, Wireless Networks, Next Generation Internet, (pp. 624–632). Academic Press.

Snoeren, A. C., Partridge, C., Sanchez, L. A., Jones, C. E., Tchakountio, F., Kent, S. T., & Strayer, W. T. (2001). 10). Hash-based IP traceback. In *Applications, technologies, architectures, and protocols for computer communications* (Vol. 31, pp. 3–14). USA: ACM.

Staniford, S., Hoagland, J. A., & McAlerney, J. M. (2002). Practical auomated detection of stealthy portscans. *J. Comput. Secur., 10*(1-2), 105–136.

Starnberger, G., Kruegel, C., & Kirda, E. (2008). Overbot: A botnet protocol based on kademlia. In Securecomm '08: Proceedings of the 4th International Conference on Security and Privacy in Communication NetowrksNetworks (pp. 1–9). New York, NY, USA: ACM.

Stewart, J. (2014). Bobax trojan analysis. Retrieved from http www.secureworks.com/research/ threats/bobax/?threat=bobax

Stinson, E., & Mitchell, J. C. (2007). Characterizing bots' remote control behavior. In In Proceedings of 4th GI International Conference on Detection of Intrusions and Malware, and Vulnerability Assessment (LNCS), DIMVA 2007, July 12,2007 - July 13 (Vol. 4579 LNCS, pp. 89-108). Lucerne, Switzerland: Springer Verlag.

Stone-Gross, B., Cova, M., Cavallaro, L., Gilbert, B., Szydlowski, M., Kemmerer, R., & Vigna, G. (2009). *Your botnet is my botnet: Analysis of a botnet takeover (Tech. Rep.).* UC Santa Barbara. doi:10.1145/1653662.1653738

Strayer, W., Lapsely, D., Walsh, R., & Livadas, C. (2008). Botnet detection based on network behavior. Botnet Detection, , 1–24.

Strayer, W. T., Walsh, R., Livadas, C., & Lapsley, D. (2006). Detecting botnets with tight command and control. In In Proceedings of 31st Annual IEEE Conference on Local Computer Networks, LCN 2006, november 14,2006 - november 16 (p.(pp. 195-202). Tampa, FL, United states: IEEE Computer Society.

Takemori, K., Fujinaga, M., Sayama, T., & Nishigaki, M. (2009). Host-based traceback; tracking bot and C&C server. In Icuimc '09: Proceedings of the 3rd International Conference on Ubiquitous Information Management and Communication (pp. 400–405). New York, NY, USA: ACM.

Vijayan, J. (2014). Teen used botnets to push adware to hundreds of thousands of pcs. Retrieved from http://www.computerworld.com/s/article/9062839/Teen used botnets to push adware to hundreds of thousands of PCs

Vogt, R., Aycock, J., Michael, J., & Jacobson, J. (2007). Army of bot- nets. In In Proceedings of 14th Annual Network and Distributed System Security Symposium (p. (pp. 111-123). Academic Press.

Wang, P., Sparks, S., & Zou, C. C. (2007). An advanced hybrid peer-to-peer botnet. In Hotbots'07: Proceedings of the First Conference on First Workshop on Hot Topics in Understanding Botnets. Berkeley, CA, USA: USENIX Association.

Wang, X., Chen, S., & Jajodia, S. (2005). Tracking anonymous peer- to-peer VoIP on the internetinternet. In CCS 2005 -In Proceedings of 12th ACM Conference on Computer and Communications Security, November 07,2005 – November 11 (p.(pp. 81-91). Alexandria, VA, United states: Association for Computing Machinery.

Wang, X., Chen, S., & Jajodia, S. (2007). Network flow watermarking attack on low-latency anonymous communication systems. In Proceedings of IEEE Symposium on Security and Privacy, SP'07, May 20,2007 - May 23 (p.(pp. 116-130). Berkeley, CA, United states: Institute of Electrical and Electronics Engineers Inc.

Wang, X., & Reeves, D. S. (2003). Robust correlation of encrypted attack traffic through stepping stones by manipulation of interpacket delays. In Proceedings of the 10th ACM Conference on Computer and Communications Security, ccs 2003, October 27,2003 - October 31 (p.(pp. 20-29). Washington, DC, United states: Association for Computing Machinery.

Wang, X., Reeves, D. S., & Wu, S. F. (2002, 14-16 Oct. 2002). Inter-packet delay based correlation for tracing encrypted connections through step- ping stones. In Proceedings (p. (pp. 244-263). Berlin, Germany: Springer- Verlag.

Ward, M. (2014). *More than 95% of e-mail is ''junk*. Retrieved from.

Weber, T. (2014). *Criminals 'may overwhelm the webweb*. Retrieved from.

Wright, C. V., Monrose, F., & Masson, G. M. (2006). On inferring application protocol behaviors in encrypted network traffic. *Journal of Machine Learning Research, 7*, 2745–2769.

Wurzinger, P., Bilge, L., Holz, T., Goebel, J., Kruegel, C., & Kirda, E. (2009). Automatically generating models for botnet detection. In *Proceedings of Computer Security ESORICS 2009* (pp. 232–249). Academic Press. doi:10.1007/978-3-642-04444-1_15

Xie Y. Yu F. Achan K. Panigrahy R. Hulten G. Osipkov I. (2008). Spamming botnets: Signatures and characteristics. SIGCOMM Com- put. Communication Review, 38(4), 171–182.

Yen, T.-F., Huang, X., Monrose, F., & Reiter, M. (2009). Browser fingerprinting from coarse traffic summaries: Techniques and implications. In *Detection of intrusions and malware, and vulnerability assessment* (pp. 157–175). Academic Press. doi:10.1007/978-3-642-02918-9_10

Yen, T.-F., & Reiter, M. K. (2008). Traffic aggregation for malware detection. In In Proceedings of 5th International Conference on Detection of Intrusions and Malware, and Vulnerability Assessment (LNCS), DIMVA 2008, July 10,2008 - July 11 (Vol. 5137 LNCS, pp. 207-227). Paris, France: Springer-Verlag.

Yoda, K., & Etoh, H. (2000). Finding a connection chain for tracing intruders. In In Proceedings of 6th European Symposium on Research in Computer Security (p. (pp. 191-205). Berlin, Germany: Springer-Verlag.

Zhang, Y., & Paxson, V. (2000, 14-17 Aug. 2000). Detecting stepping stones. In Proceedings of 9th USENIX Security Symposium (p. (pp. 171-183). Berkeley, CA, USA: USENIX Assoc.

Zhang, Z., Ando, R., & Kadobayashi, Y. (2009). Hardening botnet by a rational botmaster. In *Information security and cryptology* (pp. 348–369). Academic Press. doi:10.1007/978-3-642-01440-6_27

Zhao Y. Xie Y. Yu F. Ke Q. Yu Y. Chen Y. Gillum E. (2009).

Zhuang, L., Dunagan, J., Simon, D. R., Wang, H. J., & Tygar, J. D. (2008). Characterizing botnets from email spam records. In Leet'08: Proceedings of the 1st USENIX Workshop on Large-Scale Exploits and Emergent Threats (pp. 1–9). Berkeley, CA, USA: USENIX Association.

Chapter 13
Formal Reliability Analysis of Engineering Systems

Naeem Abbasi
Concordia University, Canada

Osman Hasan
Concordia University, Canada

Sofiène Tahar
Concordia University, Canada

ABSTRACT

Reliability analysis of engineering systems has traditionally been done using computationally expensive computer simulations that cannot attain 100% accuracy due to their inherent limitations. The authors conduct a formal reliability analysis using higher-order-logic theorem proving, which is known to be sound, accurate, and exhaustive. For this purpose, they present the higher-order-logic formalization of independent multiple continuous random variables, their verified probabilistic properties, and generalized relations for commonly encountered reliability structures in engineering systems. To illustrate the usefulness of the approach, the authors present the formal reliability analysis of a single stage transmission of an automobile.

1. INTRODUCTION

The reliability of an engineering system is very important as an unreliable system usually translates to loss of both money and time and a considerable amount of inconvenience. Such reliability analysis is conducted using probabilistic techniques while considering the individual reliabilities of sub-components of the given engineering systems. This analysis usually involves building a model of the given engineering system using random variables and various continuous physical parameters. Computer simulations have traditionally been used for the reliability analysis of engineering systems. Computer simulations are automatic and thus user friendly and can be used to analyze analytically complex systems including the ones that cannot be modeled in a closed mathematical form. However, they cannot guarantee 100% accurate results, because 1)

DOI: 10.4018/978-1-4666-4789-3.ch013

infinite precision real numbers, corresponding to the physical parameters of the system, cannot be precisely modelled in computer memory, 2) due to the enormous size of the present-age engineering systems, e.g., a modern power plant is composed of over a million components, exhaustive testing of all possible input scenarios is not possible due to limited computational resources, and 3) random variables are usually approximated using pseudo random number generators that are not truly random. The accuracy of reliability analysis of engineering systems has become a dire need these days due to their extensive usage in safety-critical applications where an incorrect reliability estimate may lead to disastrous situations including the loss of innocent lives.

Formal methods based techniques such as probabilistic model checking (Baier, Haverkort, Hermanns, & Katoen, 2003) and probabilistic theorem proving (Hasan, 2008) can alleviate some of the inaccuracy limitations of computer simulations. Model checking based techniques can handle finite sized systems or finite models of infinite systems. Some basic probabilistic and statistical

reliability properties of an engineering system can be verified using this technique. However, such results cannot be considered truly formal as the decision procedures used in this process depend on numerical computations.

Theorem proving based techniques, on the other hand, do not suffer from these limitations, however, they lack the foundational formalization required for the reliability analysis of engineering systems. This includes formal reasoning support for multiple independent continuous random variables and relations that describe the reliability of engineering systems in terms of their sub-components.

This paper is targeted towards developing these foundations to facilitate formal reliability analysis using theorem proving. The proposed reliability analysis framework is shown in Figure 1. The reliability modeling and analysis process begins with the construction of a formal model of the system and its environment. The functional and reliability requirements of the system are then formally stated. The proposed reliability analysis framework then facilitates verification, computa-

Figure 1. Formal reliability analysis framework

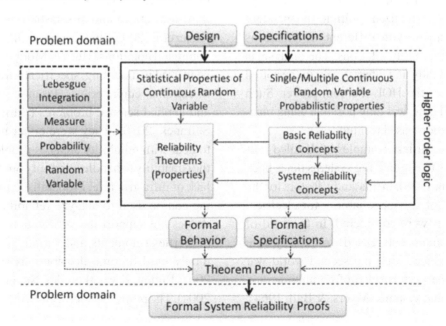

tion, reasoning, and documentation of the reliability proofs in the sound environment of the HOL theorem prover. Finally, the formal functional and reliability analysis results are unformalized and interpreted and stated in an appropriate language in the problem domain.

The two main contributions of this paper are that: 1) it presents the formalization of multiple independent continuous random variables, and the verification of the standard cumulative distribution function properties of multiple continuous random variables in the sound core of the HOL theorem prover; 2) it presents the formalization of various commonly used reliability structures such as series, parallel, series-parallel and parallel-series in higher-order logic. These contributions play a vital role in conducting formal reliability analysis as the multiple continuous random variables can be used to model the randomness associated with each sub component of an engineering system while the reliability structure related formalization can be utilized to construct formal models of the given system using its sub-components as modules and reasoning about its associated properties.

To illustrate the usefulness of our work, we present the formal reliability analysis of a single stage transmission of an automobile. In our analysis, we utilize formalized multiple independent random variables with different distributions and verified reliability relations. The analysis is done mechanically and interactively in the sound environment of the HOL theorem prover. Such analysis, until now, was only possible using inaccurate simulation based techniques.

One of the earliest examples of detailed reliability studies in engineering systems dates back to 1938 (Dean, 1938). In this study, factors for the improvement of service reliability for electrical power systems were considered. In the field of electronics, the concepts related to reliability were initially introduced after the second world war to improve the performance of communication and navigational systems (Myers, & Ball, 1964).

In order to predict reliability, one must model a system and its constituent components in a way that captures failure mechanisms. For example, in the case of electronic systems, a method called the part failure method has been shown to be very accurate (US Department of Defense, 1991). This method has been extensively used by military engineers to predict useful lifetimes of systems and to develop highly reliable systems and equipments. This method is based on calculating failure rates of individual components of the system and then using appropriate formulas to determine the reliability of the whole system. Standards such as MIL-HDBK-2173 (US Department of Defense, 1998), FIDES (FIDES, 2012), and IEEE-1332 (Institute of Electrical & Engineers, 1998) are some of the examples which specify adequate performance requirements and environmental conditions for reliability modeling, analysis, and risk assessment.

Many formal methods based techniques have been extended to analyze reliability of systems during the last two decades. Many expressive formalisms such as stochastic petri nets (Labadi, Saggadi, & Amodeo, 2009) and process algebras (Ciocchetta & Hillston, 2009) along with various probabilistic (Kwiatkowska, Norman, Segala, & Sproston, 2002) and stochastic temporal logics (Baier et al., 2003), and compositional and guarded command notations (Hurd & Morgan, 2005) have been used in modeling, specification and analysis of complex engineering (Hasan & Tahar, 2008) and applied science problems (Barnat, Brim, & Safranek, 2010). They were either not designed to deal with reliability analysis problems or lack the capability to handle reliability problems due to lack of infrastructure. Probabilistic model checking can be used to analyze reliability; however, it does not support the verification of statistical properties (moments and variance) of the commonly used lifetime distributions (Baier et al., 2003; Rutten, Kwaiatkowska, Normal, & Parker, 2004). The proposed approach on the other hand is capable of handling these and other probabilistic and statistical properties.

The accuracy of reliability analysis depends on both the field data gathering and the methods and tools used for analysis. In this paper, we do not address the problem of field data gathering. Our focus is on the higher-order-logic formalization of fundamental concepts of the reliability theory. Until recently it was only possible to reason about reliability problems that involved discrete random variables in a theorem proving environment (Hasan, 2008). Hurd (Hurd, 2002) formalized a probability theory along with discrete random variables in the HOL theorem prover (Gordon & Melham, 1993).

Building upon Hurd's work (Hurd, 2002), Hasan (Hasan, 2008) formalized statistical properties of single and multiple discrete random variables. Hasan (Hasan, 2008) also formalized a class of continuous random variables for which the inverse CDF functions can be expressed in a closed form. Hasan et al. (Hasan, Tahar, & Abbasi, 2010) presented higher-order-logic formalizations of some core reliability theory concepts and successfully formalized and verified the conditions for consistent repairability for reconfigurable memory arrays in the presence of stuck-at and coupling faults. However, all these existing works do not support reasoning about multiple continuous random variables and reliability structures, which is the main scope of the present paper.

The rest of the chapter is organized as follows. The formalization of multiple continuous random variables is described in Section 2. Section 3 presents the formalization of the relations for various reliability structures. Section 4 presents the reliability analysis of an automotive transmission as an illustrative example and Section 5 concludes the paper.

2. PROBABILITY DISTRIBUTION PROPERTIES OF MULTIPLE RANDOM VARIABLES

Hurd (Hurd, 2002) formalized discrete random variables as independent probabilistic algorithms in HOL. Hasan (Hasan, 2008) defined a standard uniform continuous random variable as a probabilistic algorithm with a standard uniform probability mass function utilizing a very large number of random bits (Hasan, 2008). Using this approach, it is possible to model multiple discrete random variables and a maximum of a single continuous random variable as this method exhausts the complete sequence of random bits in the standard continuous random variable. We build on these foundations; we, first, split the random Boolean sequence into a number of disjoint random Boolean sequences, then using Hasan's formalization of continuous random variables, formalize multiple continuous random variables. In our formalization, each random variable receives a disjoint segment of the random Boolean sequence, which ensures that the resulting random variables will be independent.

In the rest of this section, we describe the formalization of multiple random variables as lists of random variables. We verify their CDF properties. Moreover, we formalize the notion of independence of multiple random variables.

2.1 Formal Specification of CDF of Lists of Random Variables

In order to formally specify the CDF of a list of random variables in higher-order logic, we first define two list functions. They are rv_val and rv_lf. The higher-order logic recursive definitions of the two functions rv_val and rv_lf are as follows:

Definition 1: Random Variable Value Function

⊢ ∀s. rv_val [] s = [] ∧

∀ h X s. rv_val (h:: X) s = h s:: rv_val X s

Definition 2: Random Variable Logical Formula Function

⊢ (rv_lf [] [] = T) ∧

(rv_lf (h1:: t1) (h2:: t2) = h1 ≤ h2 ∧ rv_lf t1 t2)

The function rv_val takes a list of random variables, X, and the random Boolean sequence, s, and returns a list of real values. The function rv_lf takes two real lists as input and returns a Boolean expression consisting of conjunction of several terms formed from the corresponding elements of the two input lists.

Each inequality in this Boolean expression is of the form ((EL X i) s ≤ (EL x i)). The function EL takes a list and a natural number as input arguments (for example, EL X i) and returns the corresponding element of the list as output (in this case it would return the ith element of the list X).

Now using Definitions 1 and 2, we formally specify the joint CDF of a list of random variables in Definition 3.

Definition 3: Joint CDF of a List of Random Variables

⊢ ∀X x. mcrv_cdf X x = prob bern {s | rv_lf (rv_val X s) x}

where X is a list of random variables of type (((num→bool)→real) list), and x is a list of real numbers of type (real list).

2.2 Formal Verification of CDF Properties of Lists of CRVs

Using the formal specification of the CDF function for a list of random variables, we formally verify the classical properties of the CDF of a list of random variables, given in Table 1.

We verify these properties under the assumption that the set {s | X s x}, where X represents a list of random variables under consideration, is measurable for all values of the list. The formal proof of these properties was mainly based on reasoning from probability and set theories in HOL and real analysis. The details can be found in (Abbasi, 2012). The formal proofs of these properties not only confirm our formal specifications of the CDF but also can be used to reason about probability distribution properties of multiple random variables.

2.3 Independent Random Variables

The notion of independence for a list of random variables $X = [X_0; X_1; X_2; ... ; X_{N-1}]$ is defined as:

$$P\left(X_0 \leq x_0 \wedge X_1 \leq x_1 \wedge ... \wedge X_{N-1} \leq x_{N-1}\right) = \prod_{i=0}^{i=N-1} P\left(X_i \leq x_i\right)$$

where $x = [x_0; x_1; x_2; ... ; x_{N-1}]$ is a list of real numbers. The subscript in the above equation represents the index of the random variable in the list. N represents the length of the list of random variables X. In order to formalize a list of independent continuous random variables, we first define the notion of a list of disjoint random Boolean sequences using higher-order logic functions s_arb and s_split in Definitions 4 and 5, respectively.

Table 1. Formally verified joint CDF properties in HOL

Description	Joint CDF Property
CDF Bounded	$0 \leq F_{X_1,\ldots,X_n}\left(x_1,\ldots,x_n\right) \leq 1,\ \forall x_1,\ldots,x_n \in R$
CDF Monotonic-Non decreasing	$F_{X_1,\ldots,X_n}\left(x_1,\ldots,a,\ldots,x_n\right) \leq F_{X_1,\ldots,X_n}\left(x_1,\ldots,b,\ldots,x_n\right), a \leq b;$ $\forall x_1,\ldots,x_n,a,b \in R$
Marginal CDF	$\lim_{x_i \to \infty} F_{X_1,\ldots,X_{i-1},X_i,X_{i+1},\ldots,X_n}\left(x_1,\ldots,x_{i-1},x_i,x_{i+1},\ldots,x_n\right) \leq$ $F_{X_1,\ldots,X_{i-1},X_{i+1},\ldots,X_n}\left(x_1,\ldots,x_{i-1},x_{i+1},\ldots,x_n\right)$ $\forall x_1,\ldots,x_n \in R$
CDF at positive Infinity	$\lim_{x_1 \to \infty},\ldots,\lim_{x_n \to \infty} F_{X_1,\ldots,X_n}\left(x_1,\ldots,x_n\right) \leq F_{X_1,\ldots,X_n}\left(\infty,\ldots,\infty\right) = 1,$ $\forall x_1,\ldots,x_n \in R$
CDF at Negative Infinity	$\lim_{x_i \to -\infty} F_{X_1,\ldots,X_i,X_n}\left(x_1,\ldots,x_i,\ldots,x_n\right) \leq F_{X_1,\ldots,X_n}\left(x_1,\ldots,-\infty,\ldots,x_n\right) = 0,$ $\forall x_1,\ldots,x_n \in R$

Definition 4: Boolean Sequence Split Function

⊢ (∀ s M i. s_arb M i 0 = s i) ∧

∀ s n M i. s_arb s M i (SUC n) = s (M*SUC n + i)

The function s_arb takes three arguments. The first argument is a Boolean sequence s. The second and third arguments are natural numbers M and i. The function s_arb can split the input Boolean sequence s into M disjoint Boolean sequences. The third argument i is used to pick every ith element from the input infinite Boolean sequence and the function s_arb returns that Boolean sequence as output. This way we can provide each random variable in the list of random variables with a different infinite random Boolean sequence. This fact also guarantees independence of random variables in the list (Williams, 1991).

Definition 5: List of Disjoint Boolean Sequences

⊢ ∀ M s. s_split 0 M s = [(λx. s_arb s x M) 0] ∧

∀ N M s. s_split (SUC N) M s = (λx. s_arb s x M) (SUC N):: s_split N M s

The function s_split takes a Boolean sequence as input and returns a list consisting of M+1 disjoint Boolean sequences. For example, s_split 2 2 s would return a list of three disjoint Boolean sequences given by [s_arb s 2 2; s_arb s 1 2; s_arb s 0 2].

In order to define the notion of independence of a list of random variables, we first define a list function that we call rv_val indep. This function merges two lists element by element and generates a list. The first list argument of this function is a list of random variables of type ((num->bool)->real) list) and the second list argument is a list consisting of random boolean sequences of type ((num->bool) list). The function merges the two lists element by element and returns a list of real independent random variables.

Definition 6: List Function rv_val_indep

⊢ (rv_val_indep [] [] = []) ∧

(rv_val_indep (h1::t1) (h2::t2) = h1 h2::rv_val_indep t1 t2)

Finally, the HOL formalization of the notion of independence is given in Definition 7.

Definition 7: Independent Random Variable List

⊢ ∀ X x. indep_rv_list X x =

(prob bern {s ∣ rv_lf (rv_val_indep X (s_split (PRE (LENGTH X)) (LENGTH X) s)) x} =

prod1 (0, LENGTH X)

(λi. prob bern {s ∣ EL i (rv_val_indep X (s_split (PRE (LENGTH X)) (LENGTH X) s) ≤ EL i x})) ∧

{s ∣ rv_lf (rv_val_indep X (s_split (PRE (LENGTH X)) (LENGTH X) s)) x} IN events bern ∧

∀ i. {s ∣ EL i (rv_val_indep X (s_split (PRE (LENGTH X)) (LENGTH X) s)) <= EL i x} IN events bern

where X and x are of types (((num -> bool) -> real) list) and (real list), respectively. prod1 is a product of a sequence function and represents the big pi operator ($\prod$). The function s split splits the random Boolean sequence s and returns a list of disjoint random boolean sequences. PRE is a function of type (num->num) and is defined as: ∀m. PRE m = (if m = 0 then 0 else @n. m = SUC n), where @ is the hilbert's choice operator. The

list function EL takes two arguments, a natural number i and a list and returns the ith element of the list.

The second and the third logical terms in Definition 7 state that the respective events are measurable in the probability space. The higher-order logic formalization presented in this section facilitates the verification of expressions for various reliability structures and the reliability analysis of automotive transmission described in Sections 3 and 4, respectively.

3. RELIABILITY ANALYSIS OF COMPLEX SYSTEMS

The reliability structure of an engineering systems is determined by its functional and non-functional requirements. We have verified relations for series, parallel, series-parallel, and parallel-series reliability structures in HOL.

In the following, we briefly describe these results. Formalization and detailed proof descriptions of these results can be found in (Abbasi, 2012).

3.1 Series Connected Systems

In a series connected system (Figure 2) with N components, the system functions as long as all its components are functioning. As soon as any of the system component fails, the system fails as well. The reliability of such a system is mathematically described as:

$$R_S(t) = \prod_{i=1}^{N} R_i(t) \quad (1)$$

In Definition 8, we define a series system structure that consists of N components. These components are modeled using a list of random variables of type ((num->bool)->real) list).

Figure 2. Reliability structure of series connected systems

Definition 8: N Series System Structure Function

⊢ ∀ X x s t N. N_series_system X x s t N =

list_conj_gt (rv_val_indep X (s_split (PRE N) N s)) (FILL_LIST_R x t)

The function rv_val_indep takes two lists as arguments and constructs a single list. The first argument of this function is the list of random variables X. The second argument is another list generated by the function s split. This generated list consists of disjoint segments of the random boolean sequence s.

The function list_conj_gt constructs a conjunction of logical terms, each of which is a greater than inequality and consists of corresponding terms from its two list arguments. Both list arguments of list_conj_gt are real lists. The second argument of list_conj_gt is constructed by the list function LIST_FILL_R, which fills the list x with a real value t.

We define the survival function (the probability of failure at a certain time) of a series connected system with N components in Definition 9.

Definition 9: N Series System Survival Function

⊢ ∀ X x N. N_series_survival_function X x N =

(λt. prob bern {s| list_conj_gt (rv_val_indep X (s_split (PRE N) N s)) (FILL_LIST_ R x t)})

In Theorem 1, we verify the N series system reliability property (Equation 1).

Theorem 1: N Series System Reliability

⊢ ∀ X x t N. indep_rv_list X (FILL_LIST_R x t) ==>

(N_series_survival_function X x N t =

(λt. prod1 (0,N) (λi. prob bern {s| t < EL i (rv_ val_indep X (s_split (PRE N) N s))})) t)

The proof of this theorem follows from the definitions of the series survival function and the independence of a list of random variables and involves reasoning from real, measure, probability, and set theories in the HOL theorem prover.

3.2 Parallel Connected Systems

If N components of a system are connected in parallel (as shown in Figure 3), the system will function properly as long as at least one of the components is functioning. Such a system stops functioning when all the system components fail. The reliability of such a system is mathematically described as:

$$R_P\left(t\right) = 1 - \prod_{i=1}^{N}\left(1 - R_i\left(t\right)\right) \qquad (2)$$

In Definition 10 the parallel system structure function is formalized.

Figure 3. Reliability structure of parallel connected systems

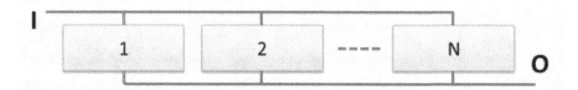

Definition 10: N Parallel System Structure Function

⊢ ∀ X x s t N. N_parallel_system X x s t N =

list_disj_gt (rv_val_indep X (s_split (PRE N) N s)) (FILL_LIST_R x t)

In this definition, rv_val_indep constructs a list of independent random variables as described in the case of series connected systems. The function list_disj_gt constructs a disjunction of logical terms, each of which is a greater than inequality and consists of corresponding terms from its two list arguments.

In Definition 11, we define a parallel connected system with N elements.

Definition 11: N Parallel System Survival Function

⊢ ∀ X x N. N_parallel_survival_function X x N =

(λt. prob bern { s| list_disj_gt (rv_val_indep X (s_split (PRE N) N s)) (FILL_LIST_R x t)})

The first argument is a list of random variables of type ((num->bool)->real) list). The function list_disj_gt takes two lists as arguments and creates a logical expression that consists of disjunction of greater than inequalities involving the corresponding terms of the two input lists. The first list (rv_val_indep X (s split (PRE (LENGTH X)) (LENGTH X) s)) argument of list_disj_gt is a list of real random variables constructed in a similar manner as explained in Definition 8. The function FILL_LIST_R returns the list x after filling it with the variable t. The third argument N represents the number of components in the parallel reliability structure.

The reliability expression for a N parallel connected system (Equation 2) is verified in Theorem 2.

Theorem 2: N Parallel System Reliability

⊢ ∀ t X x. indep_rv_list X (FILL_LIST_R x t) ==>

(N_parallel_survival_function X x N t =

1- prod1 (0,N) (λi. 1 – prob bern {s|t < EL i (rv_val_indep X (s_split (PRE N) N s))}))

3.3 Series Parallel Connected Systems

If a system consists of N components in parallel, where each of such parallel connected component has M components connected in series then such a system is called a series-parallel system. One such example is shown in Figure 4 and the reliability of such a system is given by:

Figure 4. Reliability structure of parallel-series connected systems

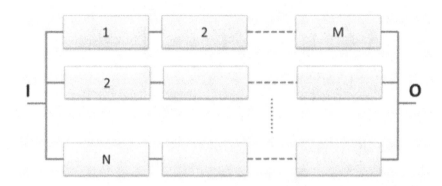

$$R_{SP}(t) = 1 - \prod_{i=1}^{N}\left(1 - \prod_{j=1}^{M} R_{ij}(t)\right) \qquad (3)$$

where R_{ij} is the reliability of the j-th component in the i-th branch of the system. Such a system configuration is typically used to enhance the reliability at the system level.

An N x M series parallel structure has N components connected in parallel such that each of these components has M sub components connected in series. Definition 12 shows how such a system structure function can be formally specified.

Definition 12: NxM Series Parallel System Structure Function

⊢ ∀ N M X s. NxM_series_parallel_system N M X s =

LIST_SPLIT (FILL_LIST_NM M N) (rv_val_indep (FLAT X) (s_split (PRE (N*M)) (N*M) s))

Definition 13 formally describes the series parallel survival function of a N x M system.

Definition 13: NxM Series Parallel System Survival Function

⊢ ∀ X N M. NxM_series_parallel_survival_function X N M =

(λt. prob bern {s| series_parallel_system (LIST_SPLIT (FILL_LIST_NM M N) (rv_val_indep (FLAT X) (s_split (PRE (LENGTH (FLAT X))) (LENGTH (FLAT X)) s))) t s })

The reliability expression for a N x M parallel series system is verified in Theorem 3.

Theorem 3: Series Parallel System Reliability

⊢ ∀ t x. (∀ X x t. indep_rv_list (FLAT X) (FILL_LIST_R x t)) ==>

NxM_series_parallel_survival_function L N M t = 1 − prod1 (0,N) (λi. 1 − prod1 (0,M) (λj. prob bern {s|t < ELEL i j (LIST_SPLIT (FILL_LIST_NM M N) (rv_val_indep (FLAT X) (s_split (PRE (N*M)) (N*M) s)))}))

3.4 Parallel Series Connected Systems

If a system consists of M components connected in series such that each of the series component consists of N sub components connected in parallel. Such a system is called a parallel-series system and is shown in Figure 5. The reliability of such a system is given by:

Figure 5. Reliability structure of series-parallel connected systems

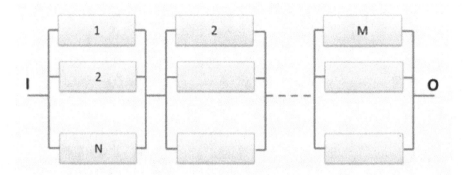

$$R_{PS}(t) = \prod_{j=1}^{M}\left[1 - \prod_{i=1}^{N}\left(1 - R_{ij}(t)\right)\right] \qquad (4)$$

where Rij is the reliability of the ij th component of the system.

Parallel-series connections can be considered as introducing component level redundancy. It can be shown mathematically that such a redundancy improves the reliability of the system more than the system level redundancy [9].

An N x M parallel series structure has been formally described in Definition 14.

Definition 14: NxM Parallel Series System Structure Function

⊢ ∀ N M X s. NxM_parallel_series_system N M X s = LIST_SPLIT (FILL_LIST_NM M N) (rv_val_indep (FLAT X) (s_split (PRE (N*M)) (N*M) s))

Definition 15 formally describes the parallel series survival function of a N x M system.

Definition 15: NxM Parallel Series System Survival Function

⊢ ∀ X N M. NxM_parallel_series_survival_function X N M = (λt. prob bern {s | parallel_series_system (LIST_SPLIT (FILL_LIST_NM M N) (rv_val_indep (FLAT X) (s_split (PRE (LENGTH (FLAT X))) (LENGTH (FLAT X)) s))) t s})

The reliability expression for a N x M parallel series system is verified in Theorem 4.

Theorem 4: NxM Parallel Series System Reliability

⊢ ∀ t x a. (∀ X x t. indep_rv_list (FLAT X) (FILL_LIST_R x t)) ==>

NxM_parallel_series_survival_function X N M t =

prod1 (0,M) (λj. 1-prod1 (0,N) (λi. 1 −prob bern {s | t < ELEL i j (LIST_SPLIT (FILL_LIST_NM M N) (rv_val_indep (FLAT X) (s_split (PRE (N*M)) (N*M) s)))}))

The proofs of theorems 1 through 4 are primarily based on reasoning from the probability, set, measure, Boolean, and real theories in HOL. Such analysis has traditionally been done using simulation based techniques and suffers from accuracy problems and their inability to model true independent random behavior. The higher-order logic formalization presented in this section enables analysis of reliability behavior of many simple and complex engineering systems as will be demonstrated in the next section.

4. AUTOMOBILE TRANSMISSION

The automobile transmission transfers mechanical power from the input shaft to the output shaft using a pair of gears. The power is transmitted from a larger gear on the input shaft to a smaller gear on the output shaft. The reliability of the automobile transmission is very important and is usually determined using three main steps. The first step identifies the reliability relevant components and determines their reliability. The second step determines the reliability structure of the system. Finally, based on the reliability structure of the system, we calculate the overall reliability of the system.

ABC (Naunheimer, Bertsche, Ryborz, Novak, & Kuchle, 2010) and FMEA (Langford, 2006) analysis are qualitative analysis methods commonly used to separate reliability relevant components from reliability neutral components. In this application, the ABC analysis suggests that out of the 27 parts in the automotive transmission only twelve are reliability relevant components of the system (Bertsche & Ingenieure, 2008). These components include the shafts, the bearings, the gears, the fitting keys and the seals. Moreover, the mechanical transmission has a pure serial reliability structure as shown in Figure 6. Therefore, the system reliability R_{TRAN} is given by the product of the reliability of the individual components.

$$R_{TRAN} =$$
$$R_{IS}.R_{OS}.R_{G1B}.R_{G2B}.R_{RB1}.R_{RB2}.R_{FK}.R_{G12P}.R_{RB3}.R_{RB4}.R_{SS1}.R_{SS2}$$
$$(5)$$

4.1 Formal Reliability Analysis of the Automotive Transmission

In this analysis, we assume that Weibull random variable (Bertsche & Ingenieure, 2008) is used to model the reliability behavior of various components of the automotive transmission.

The Weibull distribution is commonly used in such analysis. We first construct a list of N independent Weibull random variables to model the automotive transmission as given in Definition 16.

Definition 16: Automotive Transmission Reliability Model

⊢ ∀ a b N s. auto_rv_list a b N s = rv_val_indep (WB_RV_LIST a b) (s_split (PRE N) N s)

In Definition 16, a and b are lists that contain shape and scale parameters of the Weibull random variables in the WB_RV_LIST. x is a real list, N represents the number of components in the series reliability structure and t is a positive real value. Each element of this list represents the lifetime of a component of the transmission.

Figure 6. Reliability structure of the automobile transmission

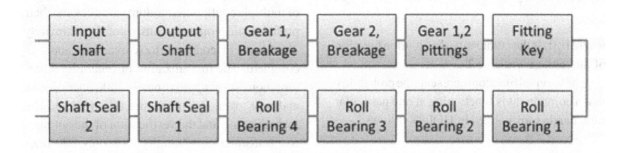

Definitions 17 shows our formalization of list of random variables with weibull distribution.

Definition 17: List of Weibull Random Variables

⊢ (WB_RV_LIST [] [] = []) ∧

(WB_RV_LIST (ah::at) (bh::bt) = [(λa b s. weibull_rv a b s) ah bh] ++ WB_RV_LIST at bt)

The function WB_RV_LIST takes two real lists as arguments and returns a list of independent Weibull random variables. The two real lists contain the corresponding scale and shape parameters of the Weilbull distributions of the random variables in the returned list.

Definition 18 formally describes the reliability model of the automotive transmission. The series reliability structure is modeled using the series reliability structure definition (N series survival function).

Definition 18: Automotive Transmission Reliability Model

⊢ ∀ a b x N t. auto_trans_rel_model_N a b x N t = N_series_survival_function (WB_RV_LIST a b) x N t

4.2 Lifetime Reliability Analysis in HOL

The survival function $S_T(t)$ is defined as:

$$S_T\left(t\right) = 1 - F_T\left(t\right) \qquad (6)$$

where $F_T(t)$ is the cumulative distribution function of the random variable T.

The survival function represents the probability that a component is functioning at one particular time t and is formalized in HOL as follows:

Definition 19: Survival Function

⊢ ∀ rv. survival_function rv = (λt. 1 – CDF rv t)

where CDF is the cumulative distribution function of random variable rv. Both survival function and CDF in HOL are of type (((num → bool) → real) → real → real).

Theorem 5: Automotive Transmission System Reliability

⊢ ∀ a b t. (∀ a b t. indep_rv_list (WB_RV_LIST a b) (FILL_LIST_R x t)) ∧

(∀ i. 0 < (EL i a)) ∧ (∀ i. 0 < (EL i b)) ∧ (0 ≤ t) ∧ (LENGTH (WB_RV_LIST a b) = 12) ==>

(auto_trans_rel_model_N a b x 12 t = prod1 (0,12) (λi. survival_function (EL i (WB_RV_LIST a b)) t))

Theorem 5 formally states that for an automotive transmission, consisting of 12 critical reliability relevant components, the overall system reliability is given by the product of reliability of its individual components (Equation 5), provided the components of the transmission fail independent of each other.

The proof of Theorem 5 required rewriting with Definition 17 and reasoning from Theorem 1 for the series connected system. Theorem 5 provides a formal proof of correctness of the reliability specification of an automotive transmission.

The HOL code describing our formalization of multiple continuous random variables and their probabilistic properties consists of approximately 2000 lines of code and took over 240 hours to complete. The formalization of reliability structures consists of approximately 2500 lines of code and took over 160 manhours to complete. The formalization and the verification of the automotive transmission reliability took only 300 lines of HOL code and only 30 hours to complete. As can be seen that, the automotive transmission reliability analysis results took an order of magnitude less effort to prove than the infrastructure development work. This shows the strength of our work and that it will be very useful for engineers building on this work to attempt larger and more involved hardware and embedded system software reliability analysis problems.

The reliability expressions we presented are guaranteed to be accurate, unlike the simulation based analysis, and are generic due to the universally quantified variables. Such analysis was not possible in the HOL theorem prover earlier.

5. CONCLUSION

In this paper, we presented an approach for formal reliability analysis of engineering systems using higher-order-logic theorem proving. In this context, we also presented the formalization of multiple continuous random variables and verified their classical Cumulative Distribution Function properties. Then building on these foundations, we described the formalization and analysis of commonly used reliability structures. The proposed formalization is general and can facilitate performance and reliability analysis of problems in many domains of engineering and applied sciences. It does not have any theoretical limitations as far as the number of system components and the modeling of complexity of structure is concerned. The results presented are guaranteed to be accurate, unlike simulation based analysis, and are generic due to the universally quantified variables in the proven reliability properties. For illustration purposes, we presented the analysis of an automobile transmission system. The formal reasoning about this system was straightforward and required very little user intervention, which demonstrates the usefulness of our work.

We are currently working on several interesting and large reliability analysis applications. In one such application we are analyzing the reliability of a multiprocessor system consisting of various types of processing units, such as field programmable gate arrays, general purpose processors and memories. In many real-world applications correlated random variables are required. In order to be able to tackle the formal analysis of these applications, we plan to develop formal reasoning support for multiple correlated random variables (Snedecor & Cochran, 1989). Other related future directions of research include the formalization of availability and maintainability theories (Ebeling, 1997) in HOL.

REFERENCES

Abbasi, N. (2012). *Formal reliability analysis using theorem proving*. (PhD Thesis). Concordia University, Montreal, Canada.

Baier, C., Haverkort, B., Hermanns, H., & Katoen, J. (2003). Model checking algorithms for continuous time Markov chains. *IEEE Transactions on Software Engineering, 29*(4), 524–541. doi:10.1109/TSE.2003.1205180

Barnat, J., Brim, L., & Safranek, D. (2010). 05). High-performance analysis of biological systems dynamics with the DiVinE model checker. *Briefings in Bioinformatics, 11*(3), 301–312. doi:10.1093/bib/bbp074 PMID:20478855

Bertsche, B., & Ingenieure, V. D. (2008). *Reliability in automotive and mechanical engineering: Determination of component and system reliability*. Berlin: Springer.

Ciocchetta, F., & Hillston, J. (2009). Bio-PEPA: A framework for the modelling and analysis of biological systems. *Theoretical Computer Science, 410*(33), 3065–3084. doi:10.1016/j.tcs.2009.02.037

Dean, S. (1938). Considerations involved in making system investments for improved service reliability. *EEI Bulletin*, (6), 491-496.

Ebeling, C. (1997). *An introduction to reliability and maintainability engineering*. Hoboken, NJ: McGraw Hill.

FIDES. (2012, April 30). *The FIDES methodology*. Retrieved from http://tinyurl.com/d5a2bn6

Gordon, M., & Melham, T. (1993). *Introduction to HOL: A theorem proving environment for higher-order logic*. Cambridge, UK: Cambridge University Press.

Govil, A. (1983). *Reliability engineering*. Hoboken, NJ: TATA McGraw-Hill Publishing Company.

Hasan, O. (2008). *Formal probabilistic analysis using theorem proving*. (PhD Thesis). Concordia University, Montreal, Canada.

Hasan, O., & Tahar, S. (2008). Performance analysis of ARQ protocols using a theorem prover. In *Proceedings of the International Symposium on Performance Analysis of Systems and Software* (pp. 85-94). IEEE Computer Society.

Hasan, O., Tahar, S., & Abbasi, N. (2010). Formal reliability analysis using theorem proving. *IEEE Transactions on Computers*, *59*(5), 579–592. doi:10.1109/TC.2009.165

Hurd, J. (2002). *Formal verification of probabilistic algorithms*. (PhD Thesis). University of Cambridge, Cambridge, UK.

Hurd, J., McIver, A., & Morgan, C. (2005). Probabilistic guarded commands mechanized in HOL. *Theoretical Computer Science*, *346*(1), 96–112. doi:10.1016/j.tcs.2005.08.005

Institute of Electrical and Electronics Engineers. (1998). *IEEE standard reliability program for the development and production of electronic systems and equipment*. IEEE.

Kwiatkowska, M., Norman, G., Segala, R., & Sproston, J. (2002). Automatic verification of real-time systems with discrete probability distributions. *Theoretical Computer Science*, *282*(1), 101–150. doi:10.1016/S0304-3975(01)00046-9

Labadi, K., Saggadi, S., & Amodeo, L. (2009). PSA-SPN - A parameter sensitivity analysis method using stochastic petri nets: Application to a production line system. *AIP Conference Proceedings*, *1107*(1), 263–268. doi:10.1063/1.3106483

Langford, J. (2006). *Logistics: Principles and applications*. Hoboken, NJ: SOLE Press/McGraw-Hill.

Myers, R. H., & Ball, L. W. (1964). *Reliability engineering for electronic systems*. Hoboken, NJ: J. Wiley.

Naunheimer, H., Bertsche, B., Ryborz, J., Novak, W., & Kuchle, A. (2010). *Automotive transmissions: Fundamentals, selection, design and application*. Berlin: Springer.

Rutten, J., Kwaiatkowska, M., Normal, G., & Parker, D. (2004). *Mathematical techniques for analyzing concurrent and probabilisitc systems* (Vol. 23). American Mathematical Society.

Snedecor, G. W., & Cochran, W. (1989). Statistical methods (No. v. 276). Iowa State University Press.

US Department of Defence. (1991). *Reliability prediction of electronic equipment, military handbook (MIL-HDBK-217F)*. Washington, DC: US Department of Defence.

US Department of Defense. (1998). *Reliability-centered maintenance (RCM) requirements for naval aircraft, weapon systems, and support equipment (MIL-HDBK-2173)*. Washington, DC: US Department of Defense.

Williams, D. (1991). *Probability with martingales*. Cambridge, UK: Cambridge University Press. doi:10.1017/CBO9780511813658

Chapter 14
Adaptive Intrusion Detection Systems:
The Next Generation of IDSs

Hassina Bensefia
Mohamed El Bachir El Ibrahimi University, Algeria

Nassira Ghoualmi-Zine
Badji Mokhtar University, Algeria

ABSTRACT

This chapter deals with a challenging issue in intrusion detection research field, which is IDS adaptability. First, it introduces the intrusion detection concepts, then presents with details the two existing generations of IDSs and addresses their major problem: permanent coverage of new attacks patterns in a dynamic changing environment. Thereafter, it evokes the requirement of adaptability in IDS as a mean to remedy this deficiency. Later, it explores the most eminent approaches that are proposed for IDS adaptability. It describes their functional architecture and discusses their strong aspects and weaknesses. At the end, new trends toward the intrusion detection adaptability problematic are mentioned and followed by a conclusion.

1. INTRODUCTION

The intrusion detection field is characterized by two generations of Intrusion Detection Systems (IDSs). The first IDSs generation is conceived by an ad hoc manner and depends on human expertise. This classical generation presents limited performance related to the IDS target environment which is becoming increasingly changing and complex with growing amount of traffic. As a result, new attack patterns arise and remain undetected. In

order to remedy these deficiencies and remove the ad hoc and manual elements from intrusion detection system design, intrusion detection research is oriented toward the data mining approaches. This attractive paradigm, notably machine learning approaches leads the intrusion detection to a second generation of IDSs called data mining based IDSs. This generation provides more effective intrusion detection models which are automatically built by using learning algorithms. They are endowed with a generalization capacity which covers the

DOI: 10.4018/978-1-4666-4789-3.ch014

new unknown patterns of attacks. However the generalization power reaches its limits through time because of the new attack methods and the emerging attacks which differ significantly from already learned attacks. Then permanent coverage of new attack patterns remains an unreachable goal for the existing IDSs which become progressively inefficient through time. This challenge is closely related to information technology evolution which brings permanent variations in network environments and attacks strategies.

The current network environments are dynamic and changing so that the intrusions occur constantly. For this reason, the IDS must adapt itself to every change in its target environment to be able to detect any new attack pattern and improve its detection performance. The IDS adaptability refers to the ability of continuous automatic incremental learning of the intrusive and normal behaviours. Then the IDS becomes a learning system in relation to its target environment.

2. GENERALITIES AND BASIC CONCEPTS

2.1 Intrusion Detection Concept

The intrusion detection concept was founded by James Anderson in 1980(Anderson, 1980). In his report entitled "Computer Security Threat Monitoring and Surveillance," Anderson states that it is possible to characterize normal use of a computer system thanks to statistical parameters in the records of users' habitual activities, called audit trials. He demonstrates that the audit trials contain the relevant information to reconstitute user's activities. Their analysis enables retracing and understanding the user's behaviour. It identifies the abusive use of the computing resources, the privilege abuse, the excessive use of computer, and may reveal the ongoing and completed attacks.

In this way, Anderson plants the original idea of intrusion detection, which was firstly focused on the mainframe environments. In 1986, Dorothy Denning concretised the ideas of Anderson by developing a prototype for Stanford Research Institute which was baptized « Intrusion Detection Expert System (IDES) ». It was destined to analyze audit trials of government systems and inspect user's activity. In 1987, Denning published the foundations of IDES prototype in a paper entitled « An Intrusion Detection Model » (Denning, 1987). This publication was the beginning of the intrusion detection era. By the IDES, Denning proposed not only the first IDS but a methodological model revealing the necessary knowledge for the intrusion detection. This concept reaches thereafter a blossoming in research field and technology, thanks to the American government considerateness and financing granted to the research projects.

The intrusion detection is closely linked to the audit mechanism which is an ubiquitous functioning option in the modern operating systems (Mé, 1997). that records the events occurring in a computing system. An event may be any undertaken action in a computer system such as logging session, program execution or file access (An Introduction, 1995) (Noel et al., 2002). The recording of events is performed chronologically and takes the form of a file which includes the date and the time of the occurring event, the identifier of the user who initiates the event, the application employed to execute the event as well as the result of the event progress (success or failure). Audit trial is a chronological sequence of event records. It represents the full history of any user activity, system process or application process (An Introduction, 1995) (Mé, 1997). Audit trials analysis enables reconstructing the complete activity, determining its duration, the user who accomplished it, the involved system resources and the results of its achievement (success or failure).

2.2 Intrusion Detection Definition

Intrusion detection is the permanent process of monitoring, collecting and analyzing the occurring events in a protected host/network environment in order to make decision if the undertaken actions are legitimate activities or abnormal behaviours symptomatic to intrusions (Base & Mell, 2001) (Debar et al., 1999). The permanent monitoring and collection of events are guaranteed by the audit mechanism. The processes of event analysis and intrusion identification are carried out after the attack penetration in the host/network environment. The objective of intrusion detection is to identify all intrusive attempts targeting the protected host/network environment and react consequently by establishing an appropriate response plan before the environment is damaged.

The intrusion detection process is composed of three consecutive functional components that are cited below (Base & Mell, 2001) (Labib, 2004):

1. **Collection:** It gathers data related to the occurring events from the audit source of the host/network environment. The collected audit data are huge and in a raw format. Only the relevant data should be selected and organized in an appropriated format.
2. **Analysis:** It inspects the relevant collected audit data in order to classify the occurring events as normal or abnormal activity (intrusion). Two classification errors may be generated:
   a. **False positive**: It is a situation where an activity is classified as intrusion but in reality it is normal activity. It means the detection of an intrusion when no intrusion is present.
   b. **False negative**: It is a situation where an activity is classified as normal activity but in reality it is an intrusion. It means

the absence of intrusion detection when an intrusion is present.
3. **Response:** It is the reaction that should be carried out just after the identification of an intrusion. Two exclusive responses are considered:
   a. Alerting the security administrator through a report related to the detected intrusion.
   b. Initiating defensive measures to prevent the intrusion or attenuate its effect.

2.3 Intrusion Detection Methods

Two main directions dominate the intrusion detection field: the anomaly based detection and the signature based detection.

2.3.1 Anomaly Based Detection

The anomaly based detection method was proposed by James Anderson in 1980 (Anderson, 1980). It was taken back and extended by Dorothy Denning in 1987 (Denning, 1987). This method is based on the assumption that a user has regular usual behaviour, called normal behavior. An intrusion is defined as unusual and abnormal behaviour which is noticed as significant deviation from the usual behaviour and it is called anomaly (Anderson, 1980) (Denning, 1987). Anomaly based detection involves two important phases: a training phase and recognition phase (Lazarevic et al., 2005). The training phase consists in establishing a model of normal behavior by using a set of quantitative parameters to define a statistical behaviour or a set of qualitative parameters to define a characteristic behaviour. The recognition phase consists in analyzing the collected audit data and comparing the users' behaviours to the established normal profile. Any significant deviation from the normal profile is indicated as intrusion. As a consequence, a response to this intrusion should be initiated.

- **Main advantages:**
  - Basing on the principle that any deviation from the established normal profile is an intrusion, anomaly based detection has the ability to detect new unknown attack patterns without requiring prior knowledge about attacks or vulnerabilities. So it partially contributes to the automatic discovery of new attacks.
  - Anomaly based detection method enables the detection of privileges abuse initiated by legitimate users.
- **Limitations:** Despite of its major advantage which is detection of new attack patterns, anomaly based detection presents the following limitations:
  - The establishment of the normal profile model depends on security expert intuition and experience.
  - From one side, the user's behaviour is unforeseeable. From another side, irregular users' behaviour is very dynamic. So it is unfeasible to determine the extent of all the possible variations of the normal behaviour. Therefore, the coverage of the normal behaviour remains incomplete.
  - Anomaly based detection generates a high rate of false positive. A significant deviation from the normal profile may be a new legitimate normal behaviour due to the evolution of the host/network environment or the change of user's function within the organization.
  - Anomaly based detection requires a periodic updating of the preset profile because the normal behaviour may change through time. However, a ma-

licious user can exploit this situation to initiate an intrusion by changing gradually his behaviour in order to make the system habituating this undetected intrusive behaviour.
  - Anomaly based detection is limited in attacks classification. It is unable to predict the attack type of the detected attack. The attack type is very important information during intrusion response.

To palliate the limitations of the anomaly based intrusion detection method, and instead of projecting the analysis towards the normal behaviour, it is directed towards the intrusive behaviour. As a result, the idea of signature based detection emerges.

2.3.2 Signature Based Detection Method

A signature is a predefined pattern composed of one event or a sequence of events and it corresponds to a known attack (Base & Mell, 2001) (Lacasse, 2006). The signatures can be formulated by hand coding the attack manifestation or acquired by the automatic learning of labelled data sets (Hugh et al., 2000). Signature based detection method is founded on the assumption that each attack has its own signature and it can be identified thanks to this signature. For this reason, the signature based method requires a data base of the known attacks signatures. It analyzes the collected audit data by establishing their matching with the attack signatures listed in the data base. Each matching is indicated as intrusion. Then a response is generated.

- **Main advantages:** Signature based detection method has the following strong points:

○ Since the signature based detection employs a data base of the attacks signatures:

- It generates a low rate of false positive.
- The detection of known attacks or attack patterns that are adjacent to known attacks is characterized by high precision and accurateness.

○ Signature based detection is expressive in predicting attacks type. This character facilitates analyzing and understanding the detected attack patterns and helps in responding to any detected intrusion.

- **Limitations:** Signature based detection method admit the following weaknesses:

  ○ Attacks signatures must be coded manually. This coding is delicate and requires human expertise.

  ○ Signature based detection has a limited predictive ability. It detects only the known attacks which their signatures are listed in the attacks signatures data base. It is fundamentally incapable to detect the known attack variants and the new patterns of unknown emerging attacks that do not have corresponding signatures in attacks signatures data base.

  ○ The detection of privilege abuse is difficult because this attack category does not exploit vulnerabilities and does not have known attacks signatures.

  ○ The attacks signatures base must be regularly updated at each discovery of new attack type. This task is tedious because new attacks occur frequently.

The two intrusion detection methods are distinct but they present reciprocal complementarity links. It is recommended to create cooperation between these two methods in the aim to accumulate their strengths and eliminate their weaknesses (Base & Mell, 2001) (Lacasse, 2006) (Lazarevic et al., 2005) (Mé et al., 2001).

2.4 Intrusion Detection Systems (IDSs)

2.4.1 Intrusion Detection System Definition

The Intrusion Detection System (IDS) is the technical mean that automates the intrusion detection process. It may be a software application or an appliance integrating hardware and software components, which is endowed with the functions of collection, analysis and response.

The Intrusion Detection System (IDS) can employ the signature based detection method or the anomaly based detection method or the two methods at once. In practice and particularly in commercial field, the IDSs use signature based detection method. The use of anomaly based detection method is very restricted. It is integrated as a complement for the signature based detection method and it is limited to the detection of network or ports scan such as the case of Cisco IDS (Base & Mell, 2001) (Lacasse, 2006).

2.4.2 Main Types of IDS

2.4.2.1 Host-Based Intrusion Detection System (HIDS)

The intrusion detection beginning was marked by the predominance of central environments (mainframes) and workstations. All the users were local to the system and outside interaction was uncommon. Thus host based IDS was the first type of IDSs. The work of Denning, in 1987, "Intrusion Detection Expert System, IDES," was the first IDS and the first HIDS in the same time.

The HIDS is a software application that can be installed on a host. It is destined to inspect this host and analyze audit trials reporting its activities in the aim to detect the intrusions that threatened it. The HIDS function consists in:

- The inspection of all incoming and outgoing host traffic.
- The inspection of user's behaviour like access to folders, files and privileged services as well as attempts of installing new softwares.
- The integrity control of system files.
- The inspection of system processes and applications.

The inspection of the HIDS is limited to the host environment. For this reason, the HIDS should reside on critical network servers or systems. This will reduce the deployment cost and allow the security administrator to focus on the alarms will be generated by critical systems.

2.4.2.2 Network-Based Intrusion Detection System (NIDS)

The migration to networks environments enabled the communication between hosts and introduced new emerging attacks that target the networks themselves. The HIDSs are not accommodated to inspect a whole network or a network segment. For this reason, the conception of IDSs was adjusted to handle networks environments features and their requirements. Then, the Network based IDSs (NIDS) emerge. NSM (Network Security Monitor), developed, in 1990, for the headquarters of the American government, was the first NIDS.

The NIDS can have two forms. The first form is a software application which should be installed and configured on a dedicated computer. The second form is an appliance which integrates an intrusion detection application. The conception of the NIDS often consists of one or many sensors to capture the traffic on the network segments and an engine which performs the analysis of the captured traffic accordingly to the adopted

intrusion detection method. When an intrusion is noticed, the NIDS triggers a response.

The NIDS can inspect only one network segment. For this reason, it should be placed on the strategic points of the network. The NIDS location depends on the network topology and which attacks types should be detected: internal attacks or external attacks or the both.

NIDS and HIDS differ significantly from each other. Each one has its advantages on the other but they admit complementarity links. The NIDS should be deployed in conjunction with the HIDS. The coexistence of the NIDS with the HIDS in the same environment enables a high security level.

2.4.2.3 Hybrid IDSs

These IDSs are systems that combine HIDS and NIDS modules while offering a central management of the intrusion detection process. They are destined to multi-hosts environments which are composed of workstation networks. An example of hybrid IDSs is DIDS (Distributed Intrusion Detection) (Debar et al, 1999) (Lacasse, 2006). It integrates two IDS modules:

- A HIDS module, called Haystack, which is deployed on every host in the aim to detect local attacks.
- A NIDS module, called NSM (Network Security Monitoring), which is deployed to inspect the network traffic.

Haystack and NSM send their analysis results to another module called Director which performs the final analysis by using the received results.

3. FIRST GENERATION OF IDSS: CLASSICAL IDSS

IDES (Intrusion Detection Expert System), which is developed by Denning (Denning, 1987), was the first IDS. Its design is based on expert system.

Statistical metrics are used to make up the model of the normal profile of the subjects with regard to the computer system objects such as files access, applications execution and sessions logging. IDES allows the detection, in real time, of a large interval of intrusions varying between external penetration and internal abuse. It represents a generic model which is independent of each system, application environment, vulnerabilities or particular types of intrusions. It is regarded as the inspiration source of IDSs development.

The approaches applied to develop the first generation of IDS depend on the adopted intrusion detection method: anomaly based detection or signature based detection.

3.1 Main Approaches Applied to Anomaly Based Detection Method

The main approaches applied to anomaly based detection method are: statistical approach, expert system, artificial neural networks and immunology.

3.1.1 Statistical Approach

It is the most applied approach and the best documented one for the anomaly based detection method (Debar et al., 1999) (Lacasse, 2006) (Mé et al., 2001). It consists of measuring the users behaviour by using a set of variables sampled at regular time intervals (minute, hour, day or week). In a classical environment, the sampled variables may be the beginning session time, ending session time, processor time, disk space, memory space, number of accessed files and the session duration. To define the normal profile, a threshold or an interval of values is associated to each variable (Nobelis, 2004). The current estimated variables are compared to the profile variables in order to evaluate the deviation rate between the past behaviour and the current one. Each significant deviation is considered as intrusion and an alarm is generated.

The major advantage of this approach is the learning of the users' behaviour. But the IDS may be trained progressively by a malicious user to handle an intrusive behaviour as normal one.

3.1.2 Expert System

In this approach, the expert system represents the IDS. The rules base is conceived by two ways (Lacasse, 2006) (Noel et al., 2002):

1. The rules are created by the security administrator from the established security policy. Thus, the rules base reflects the wanted behaviour of the user and it is the means to impose the established security policy.
2. The profile of the normal behaviour is established as rules. These rules are generated from audit records (Kumar & Spafford, 1994) (Labib, 2004). So a learning phase is required to deduce the user normal profile.

The major advantage of this approach is the use of the expert system as IDS. However, the evolution of the rules base makes this latter difficult to manage and maintain. This will affect negatively the IDS performance.

3.1.3 Artificial Neural Networks

The objective of applying artificial neural networks was the prediction of users' behaviour (Mé, 1997) (Nobelis, 2004). The neural network is trained with a representative set of usual commands sequence for each user in the aim to define the user normal profile. In this way, after each command executed by the user, the neural network will predict the following command while taking into account the previous commands. If the current command deviates from the predicted command, then it reflects abnormal behaviour. As a result, an alarm is generated.

This approach enables the adaptation of the neural network to new community of users but it presents the following weaknesses:

- The necessity of appropriated data for the neural network training.
- The neural network does not provide explanation on its reasoning and that doesn't facilitate the decision making to respond to the detected intrusions.

3.1.4 Immunology

This approach makes an analogy with the biologic immunology. Its application in anomaly based detection method is based on the model of the normal behaviour of the services instead of the users' behaviour (Debar et al., 1999) (Mé et al., 2001). This model is established by using the normal execution of system calls sequences of well determined services. Then the training phase consists of observing a service, during a period of time, in the aim to build the base of normal calls sequences called reference table. The recognition phase verifies if the generated sequences are listed in the reference table. Each no listed sequence is considered as intrusion and an alarm is triggered. This approach cannot detect the attacks that exploit the configuration errors of the services.

3.2 Main Approaches Applied to Signature Based Detection Method

The main approaches applied to signature based detection method are: experts system, pattern matching, state transition analysis, colored petri nets and genetic algorithms.

3.2.1 Expert System

This approach describes the known attacks using rules. These rules are manually defined by human expert (Debar et al., 1999) (Noel et al., 2002). The audit events are translated to facts. Using the presented facts and the defined rules, the inference engine undertakes a reasoning to conclude the presence or the absence of intrusions.

This approach offers the following advantages:

- The rules present a natural means to model the experience of human expert in describing attacks.
- The expert system is used as IDS.
- Thanks to the expert system reasoning, the intrusion detection process is comprehensible.

However, the rules base is built manually. It depends completely on human expert experience.

3.2.2 Pattern-Matching

The pattern matching refers to the verification procedure of the presence of the elements forming a given pattern. The simplest form of the pattern matching is the text matching. In intrusion detection, this approach considers every attack signature as a letter belonging to an alphabet which is the set of audit data (Noel et al., 2002). To localize the attack signatures, the audit data is compared to the attack signatures, by using the text matching. If there is similarity, an alert is triggered.

Intrusion detection based on the pattern matching requires a description language and a pattern matching algorithm.

3.2.3 Transition State Analysis

A diagram of state transition is a diagram used to represent automatons. This approach is adopted in intrusion detection to describe the attacks under the form of state transition diagrams (Debar et al., 1999) (Lacasse, 2006). The starting state represents a primitive system. The intermediate states represent the system changes that happen when the attack occurs. The final state represents a compromised system. During the audit data analysis, the system makes transitions from one state to another. If the system starts from a non-compromised state and arrives to one or several compromised states, an intrusion is indicated and an alarm is triggered.

This approach enables the detection of many variations of one attack because the IDS inspects the state changes of the system which are symptomatic to intrusion attempts. However the IDS should maintain the data of each intermediary state of any potential attack. This situation may generate progressively the combinatorial explosion of the quantity of the information maintained by the system as long as the attacks number and the inspected attacks states are increasing.

3.2.4 Colored Petri Nets

Colored petri nets are characterized by their generality, design simplicity and the possibility to be represented as graphs. They represent a better alternative for intrusion detection than the state transition diagrams approach (Noel et al., 2002). They enable the attacks coding into graphs so that the progression of an attack steps is more flexible than the rigid order imposed by the state transition diagrams approach. Instead of maintaining the data to indicate all precedent and actual states of potential attacks, boundaries are used to define the situations corresponding to attacks signatures.

Thanks to colored petri nets, complex signatures attacks may be easily described. Unfortu-

nately, the matching between a complex signature and an audit trial takes a lot of time (Brown et al., 2001).

3.2.5 Genetic Algorithms

Genetic algorithms are applied in intrusion detection in the aim to search the predefined attacks signatures in the audit trials (Mé, 1997) (Nobelis, 2004). This approach optimizes the research of attacks signatures in audit files. It selects the best elements in the attacks signatures population. It allows getting the subset of the attacks which are potentially present in the audit trials, in a reasonable processing time.

Table 1 illustrates the approaches which are involved in the design of the first generation of the most known classical IDSs. We ascertain that:

- The majority of the classical IDSs combine two or more than two approaches.
- The statistical approach and the expert system approach dominate the design of the first generation of IDSs.

Most of the classical IDSs follow the IDES model of Denning such as AudES, Computer Watch, DIDS, HAYSTACK, ISOA, MIDAS, NADIR, NIDX and W&S.

3.3 Limitations of the First Generation of IDSs

Despite of the detection strategy (anomaly based detection, signature based detection or both of them), the first generation of IDSs faces the following problems:

- **Ad hoc manual design:** The majority of the IDSs are designed by ad hoc manual means. They require experience and intuition of the security experts in audit data analysis, normal profile constitution and

Table 1. Approaches used in the first generation of IDSs (Bondi, 2001) (Mé, 1997)

Approach / IDS Name	Statistical Method	Expert System	Artificial Neural Nets	Pattern Matching	Genetic Algorithms	State Transition Analysis	Colored Petri Nets
NIDES	X	X					
AudES		X					
Computer Watch		X					
DIDS	X	X					
HAYSTACK	X	X					
ISOA	X	X					
MIDAS	X						
NADIR	X	X					
NIDX	X	X					
W&S	X						
Hyperview	X	X	X				
ASAX		X		X			
IDIOT				X			X
GASSATA					X		
USTAT		X				X	

attacks signatures coding and understanding. These IDSs depend on the experience of their developers related to the deep knowledge and understanding of computer systems and known intrusions.

- **Specificity to the environment:** Each IDS has its own design and operation principle and uses its own audit data (Kumar & Spafford, 1994). So each IDS is customized and designated for its target environment. An IDS which is developed for a given environment is difficult to deploy it in other environments having similar security policy to its target environment..

- **Evaluation problem:** There is no known standard for IDS experimentation and performance evaluation (Kumar & Spafford, 1994). The lack of a common format of audit trials prevents the experimentation and the effectiveness comparison of the first generation of IDSs in relation to a common attack scenario. So each IDS is efficient in relation to its target environment.

- **Performance limitation:** The effectiveness of the first generation of IDSs is limited in relation to a non-stationary environment. While the environment evolves gradually, the traffic increases quickly in volume and complexity. Also the attacks interval expands more and more. Although this varied traffic is plentiful of events; it is difficult to process and analyze by the first IDSs which are devoid of the capacity of handling a large audit data volume. Besides, the extraction of attacks signatures, normal profile or intrusion detection rules becomes a tedious task which requires time and efforts for the security experts.

- **Inaptitude of detecting new attacks:** Host and network environments are not stationary; in addition, the computer systems become increasingly complex. So the first IDSs can not detect the new unknown attacks. Anomaly based detection is promising in detecting new attacks but it is dismissed out in practice and used only in academic field and research laboratories (Brugger, 2004). Indeed, the coverage of normality is incomplete and the false positive rate is high. The IDSs that are most used and available on the market are signature based IDSs (Honig, 2002). They are designated for detecting only the known attacks. The detection rules which are defined by security experts depend on fixed features or signatures of existing attacks. Then the signature based IDSs are devoid of the capacity that allows the detection of the modified attacks or completely new attacks that are not described by signatures. The detection of only known attacks variations presents a challenge for the first IDSs.

Because of these limitations, the first generation of IDS is qualified as traditional and classical IDSs.

4. SECOND GENERATION OF IDSS: DATA MINING BASED IDSS

Data mining is a paradigm situated at the junction of several disciplines such as statistics, pattern recognition, machine learning and data bases (Lee & Stolfo, 1998). It benefits from the progress in these disciplines and offers several approaches that proved their performance in several domains particularly in intrusion detection field.

Data mining refers to the process of automatic extraction of models from a large data warehouse. The research in intrusion detection moves to data mining approaches to satisfy the following requirements (Lee & Stolfo, 1998) (Lee et al., 2000) (Xu, 2006):

- Remove the ad hoc and manual elements from the design of intrusion detection systems.

- Remedy the difficultness of processing a large amount of audit data.

As anomaly based detection aims to determine the patterns of normal usage from audit data, and the detection based signature refers to the coding and the correspondence of intrusion patterns by using audit data. The distinction between the normal and intrusive activities is visible in audit data which trace the behavioural events of the users and the systems. Then the intrusion detection becomes an analysis process of audit data. So the automation of this process involves the data mining approaches.

4.1 Principles of Data Mining Based Intrusion Detection

It consists of applying data mining algorithms to a large set of audit data in order to automatically build intrusion detection models (Honig et al., 2002). This procedure is called learning phase. It requires the availability of a large set of data called learning data set. The preparation of the data set for the learning phase is an obligatory step. The intrusion detection based on data mining approaches follows and adopts the two main orientations: anomaly based detection and signature based detection.

- Anomaly based detection by data mining: Every instance in the data set must specify a normal activity. For this reason, the data set should be purified from any attack instance. This purification is a manual process which requires an expert's intervention. The training phase consists of applying an algorithm to learn the model of the normal activity from purified data set. Thanks to the learned model, it is possible to subsequently identify each activity that deviates from the learned normal model as an attack.

- Signature based detection by data mining: Each instance in the data set should be labelled as normal or attack type. An algorithm is applied to learn the attack patterns and generate classification rules by using the labelled data set. These rules enable to characterize a normal activity or an attack type and subsequently classifying the audit data.

Data set labeling is a manual process which should be accomplished by an expert according to the nature of the data (normal or abnormal activities). The labeling of abnormal activities is limited to the known attacks types.

4.2 Main Data Mining Approaches Applied to Intrusion Detection

Among the main data mining approaches applied to intrusion detection, statistical approaches and the approaches derived from the machine learning. These approaches are involved in intrusion detection under several facets. As follows, we give concise explanation of the application of each approach in intrusion detection.

4.2.1 Statistical Approaches

The statistical data mining approaches are applied to the anomaly based detection method. In the publication of IDES, Denning described five statistical models that may be adopted to detect the abnormal behavior (Denning, 1987). A statistical model enables to determine from n observations $x_1, x_2, ..., x_n$ performed on a giving variable x, if the value x_{n+1} of the (n+1) observation is normal or abnormal. Denning proposed the following models:

1. **Fixed limit model:** It consists of comparing the new observation of x to already fixed value. In this case, the previous observations of x do not intervene.

2. **Model of the mean and standard deviation:** The observation x_{n+1} is considered as abnormal if it does not belong to the confidence interval defined by the standard deviation and the mean.

3. **Model of covariance:** It adopts the same principle of the model of mean and standard deviation. But it combines several variables to characterize the user behaviour.

4. **Model of markov process:** It consists of defining the probability of passage of a state to another. Every state is defined by the content of an audit recording. A state is judged abnormal if the probability of apparition of the state is low by comparison to the previous states.

5. **Model of time series:** A new observation is judged abnormal if its probability of apparition, at the moment of its apparition, is low.

Denning affirmed that the model of time series is the most effective in terms of accurateness (Denning, 1987). The statistical models were difficult to construct. But currently, the availability of data warehouse and the increase of computational power of the computer systems facilitate their construction and their use. Other statistical approaches have been applied to anomaly based detection like Bayes estimators and decision trees (Brugger, 2004).

4.2.2 Machine Learning Approaches

Machine learning is an artificial intelligence field which consists of developing techniques of learning, reasoning and prediction upon situations that were not previously encountered. The most remarkable machine learning approaches that are applied to intrusion detection: generation by rules induction, genetic algorithms, fuzzy logic, immunology, artificial neural networks, clustering and support vector machines (Brugger, 2004) (Lapas & Pelechrinis, 2007) (Lee & Stolfo, 1998).

1. **Generation by rules induction:** It consists of the generation of rules in the form "IF THEN," from data, by using statistics. This technique is used in intrusion detection to classify the traffic as normal activity or as different intrusive activities. The rules are expressive and comprehensible by a security expert. The most used and effective algorithm for the generation by rules induction is RIPPER (Brugger, 2004). The research works in intrusion detection field show that generation by rules induction is a simple approach but moderately effective for attacks classification (Brugger, 2004).

2. **Genetic algorithms:** The genetic algorithms are used in the intrusion detection field to generate rules. In an identical manner to generation by rules induction, a genetic algorithm is automatically applied by using a system such as REGAL to generate the classification rules for the traffic whether normal activity or attack type (Brugger, 2004).

3. **Fuzzy logic:** The fuzzy logic is a generalization of the classic Boolean logic in which the veracity of a proposition is a real number in the interval [0, 1] where the Boolean false is 0 and the Boolean true is 1. The fuzzy logic is employed in intrusion detection field in combination with statistical metrics (Brugger, 2004). A set of statistical metrics are used to classify data. Fuzzy logic rules are created and applied in the goal to classify the traffic whether it represents a normal activity or a particular type of attack. This approach has proved its effectiveness in the classification of the scan intrusive traffic (Brugger, 2004).

4. **Immunology:** This approach defines the normal traffic as « self » (Brugger, 2004). Abnormal connection examples are generated from the abnormal traffic in a system. Each example is defined as « no-self ». All the system incoming connections are compared with the predefined examples. If there is correspondence between a connection and one example, this connection is considered as « no-self » and therefore it is classified as abnormal activity.

5. **Artificial Neural Networks (ANN):** An Artificial Neural Network (ANN) acquires the knowledge through the training from an appropriate learning data set which should be representative. After being well trained, the ANN will be endowed with a generalization capacity. Thanks to this feature, the ANNs such as Elman neural networks, recurrent neural networks, Hoppfield neural networks, the Radial Basis Functions (RBF) neural networks and Self Organizing Maps (SOM) of Kohonen represent an attractive approach for the intrusion detection field. The artificial neural networks have been used especially in the classification of the traffic (normal or intrusive) and the identification of the attacks classes to which belongs the intrusive traffic (classification of the intrusive traffic). The capacity of generalization of a neural network enables the detection of new unknown attacks patterns and their classification to the appropriate type of attack.

6. **Clustering:** The clustering consists of the partitioning of a set of objects to subsets called clusters (Lapas & Pelechrinis, 2007) (Singhal & Jajodia, 2006). The objects belonging to the same cluster are sharing common properties; they have high level of similarity. The clustering is used in intrusion detection for separating the malicious activities and gathering the instances for each distinct group. The advantage of the clustering in relation to machine learning classification approaches is the no requirement of a labelled data set.

7. **Support Vector Machines (SVMs):** The support vector machines are generalized linear classifiers that separate the data in two classes by using an hyperplane. They

represent learning methods used for the classification and the regression. In intrusion detection, the SVMs are used to classify the traffic as normal or abnormal. They are also used for attacks classification. They have proved more performance than the clustering (Lapas & Pelechrinis, 2007). In classification of the traffic whether normal or intrusive and the classification of the attacks, the SVMs show more performance than the artificial neural networks (Lapas & Pelechrinis, 2007) (Mukkamala et al., 2005). They are trained by using a large data set. They take less time for training and execution than the neural networks. Their prediction accurateness is better than the neural networks.

To improve the effectiveness of intrusion detection, multiple data mining approaches may be used while establishing a correlation between their results. The combination of several data mining approaches is known as "ensemble approach". If one approach fails in the detection of an attack, the other approaches can detect it.

4.3 Examples of Data Mining Based IDSs

- An example of a data mining based IDS employing the signature based detection method is the system MADAM/ID (Mining Audit Data for Automated Models for Intrusion Detection) which is developed in the University of Columbia in USA (Lazarevic et al., 2005) (Singhal & Jajodia, 2006). It was the first project applying the data mining techniques in intrusion detection. This project has proved that the data mining techniques ensure the construction of IDSs by automatic and systematic manner.

- An example of a data mining based IDS employing the anomaly based detection method is MINDS (Minnesota Intrusion Detection System), which is developed in the University of Minnesota in USA (Lapas & Pelechrinis, 2007) (Singhal & Jajodia, 2006). The experimental results of MINDS have proved its performance in the detection of new unknown attacks.

- An example of commercialized IDS using a data mining approach is RealSecure SiteProtector (Lapas & Pelechrinis, 2007). This hybrid IDS is capable to analyse, in a centralized manner, a network infrastructure that includes sub networks, servers and workstations.

4.4 Advantages of the Data Mining Based IDSs

Data mining based IDSs are the second generation of IDSs. They have proved their effectiveness and they present the following advantages compared to the first generation of IDSs which is called traditional IDSs:

- **Analysis ability of large audit data volume:** The use of the data mining approaches in intrusion detection enables to extract useful patterns of the normal and intrusive behaviour from large volumes of audit data. The relevant features in these patterns are used to generate automatically and quickly intrusion detection models capable to identify the known intrusions and the anomalies.

- **Exclusion of the human subjectivity:** The data mining approaches remove the subjectivity associated to the human factor that characterizes the design of the first generation of IDSs. They reduced significantly the dependence of the IDS design on the human expertise. The IDS becomes autonomous thanks to the automatic extraction of the normal behaviour profiles and the attacks signatures from the data sets.

- **Automatic and fast generation of intrusion detection models:** The data mining approaches remove the ad hoc and manual characters from the intrusion detection design process thanks to the automatic construction of intrusion detection models. Indeed, classification rules substitute the profiles and the signatures of attacks coded manually. Also, the statistical models substitute the features and the measures of the system. The data mining approaches enable the generation of intrusion detection models in an automatic and fast manner compared to the traditional IDSs models which are hand-coded and require a very difficult and costly analysis of the audit data by the human experts.

- **Optimization of the detection performance:** The data mining based IDS has the advantage to detect the new attacks that cannot be detected by the traditional signature based IDSs which depends on a static set of signatures. Thanks to the data mining approaches, the IDS evolved from the memorization towards the generalization. The detection models are created automatically. They can do generalization from the patterns of the known attacks and the normal profile to detect the new unknown attacks patterns. The false positive rate generated by data mining based IDSs is less than the one generated by the classical signature based IDSs. The major advantage of data mining based IDSs is their high degree of accuracy in detecting known attacks and their variations.

4.5 Limitations of the Data Mining Based IDSs

Compared to the classical IDSs, the data mining based IDSs are automatically and quickly designed. They are also more effective. However, they are more complex because of the difficulties they encounter and that are cited below:

- **Construction of the data set:** Data mining approaches require an appropriate and representative data set in the aim to train intrusion detection models (Singhal & Jajodia, 2006). The data set must be collected from the raw audit trials and converted in a form suitable for the training process. In the case of signature based detection, each instance in the data set must be labelled as normal activity or a particular type of attack. In the case of anomaly based detection, the data set must be purified and each instance should be labelled as normal activity. The network environments generate very large volumes of network traffic raw data. The procedures of labelling and purification are manually accomplished by an expert. This process is tedious and time consuming.

- **Deployment:** The data mining based IDS is specific to the environment from which the data set is collected. An intrusion detection model which is trained with a dated set collected from a given environment cannot operate properly in other environments. The data mining based IDSs are difficult to deploy because the process of collection and processing of data set must be repeated at each deployment. Indeed; the cost associated to data collection and processing (labelling, purification) is engendered in every deployment of the IDS. To obtain an intrusion detection model that adapts itself to several environments, the data set must be collected from all the environments in which the IDS will be deployed. The creation of such data set is difficult and costly.

- **Updating:** When changes occur in IDS environment or new attacks arise, the intrusion detection models need to be updated through a complete retraining using an updated data set. This retraining will take time whereas it should be done immediately to guarantee the environment protection. In a changing dynamic environment, the updates are frequent. As a consequence, the data mining based IDSs become ineffective (Dass et al., 2003) (Lee et al., 2001).

5. VALIDATION OF INTRUSION DETECTION APPROACHES

To estimate the effectiveness of the approaches applied to intrusion detection and compare their performance, standard datasets are publicly available like DARPA 98, KDD-Cup 99 and NSL-KDD. These datasets are dedicated to off-line evaluation of intrusion detection research works.

The DARPA 98 was the first dataset (Mit, 2003). It is captured and collected by the Lincoln Laboratory of Massachusetts Institute of Technology (MIT) from a simulated military heterogeneous network environment created by Defence Advanced Research Project Agency (DARPA) in 1998. This dataset consists of network connections raw data organized as records. It includes a training set around 5 million connection records and a testing set around 2 million connection records. Each connection record is labelled as normal connection or specific attack type. The attack type fall in one of the four categories: Denial of Service Attack (DoS), User to Root (U2R), Remote to Local (R2L) and Probe (Kayacik et al.,2005) (Mukkamala et al., 2005) (Noel et al., 2002) (Tavallaee et al., 2009).

The KDD-Cup 99 (Knowledge Discovery and Data mining) (Kdd, 2013) is a processed version of DARPA 98 dataset where each connection record is represented by a vector of 41 features and labelled as normal connection or attack type. Since 1999, the KDD-cup 99 was the most widely used dataset for the evaluation of intrusion detection research works. But it includes some inherent problems like the high huge number of redundant records which causes the learning algorithms to be biased toward the frequent records and prevent them from leaning infrequent records (Tavallaee et al., 2009). These redundant records are present in the test set and affect the evaluation results to be biased by the methods which have better detection rates on the frequent records.

The NSL-KDD is an improved version of the KDD-Cup 99 that has solved the inherent problems related to the KDD-Cup 99 (Nsl, 2013) (Tavallaee et al., 2009). It consists of selected records of the KDD-Cup 99 without redundancies and duplications in both the training set and the data set. This new dataset ensures an accurate evaluation of intrusion detection approaches; it becomes the most effective dataset and it is more used than the KDD-Cup 99.

In intrusion detection, the evaluation metrics are Detection Rate (DR) and the False Positive Rate (FPR). An IDS is effective if it has a high Detection Rate (DR) and a low False Positive Rate (FPR).

$$DR = \frac{Number\ of\ the\ Detected\ Intrusions}{Total\ Number\ of\ the\ Intrusions\ in\ the\ Data\ Set}$$

$$FPR = \frac{Number\ of\ the\ normal\ INSTANCES\ Detected\ as\ Intrusions}{Total\ Number\ of\ the\ normal\ INSTANCES\ in\ the\ Dataset}$$

Thanks to the availability of the standards datasets DARPA 98, KDD-Cup 99 and NSL-KDD, the validation of the approaches applied to the intrusion detection has contributed meaningfully in the intrusion detection research field by orienting the research efforts and comparing the different approaches and their results. However they are criticized to be ancient and incomplete by intrusion detection community (McHugh, 2000) (Mukkamala et al., 2005) (Nsl, 2013) (Tavallaee et al., 2009). Their relevance with regard to the new emerging attacks is put in question. In spite of the satisfactory results, the validation of the approaches in intrusion detection is empiric. The construction of a data set which is completely real and representative is extremely difficult and remains an open problem (Brown et al., 2001) (Eskin et al., 2000) (Lee & Stolfo, 1998) (Singhal & Jajodia, 2006).

6. THE CHALLENGING PROBLEM OF DETECTING NEW ATTACKS

The existing IDSs are limited to cover permanently the new attacks patterns. A new attack pattern, without its own corresponding signature listed in the base of signatures, could not be detected by a classical signature based IDS which is devoid of generalization power. The data mining based IDSs are based on learning algorithms. They are endowed with a generalization power enabling the detection of new attacks which have similar patterns to already learned attacks. But this capacity of generalization will decrease through time face to the new methods of attacks or the emerging attacks which may change significantly from already learned attacks.

The signature based intrusion detection covers only the known attacks and their adjacent attacks which are similar to known attacks or slightly different. However, it is incapable to detect completely new attacks. The anomaly based intrusion detection can detect new attacks but the false positive rate is often high because the coverage of the normality is incomplete. The optimization of the detection capacity of an anomaly based IDS by maintaining a low rate of false positive remains an open problem in intrusion detection (Labib, 2004) (Xu, 2006).

The existing IDSs which may belong to the first generation of IDSs (classical IDSs) or to the second generation of IDSs (data mining based IDSs) face difficulties to improve their capacity of detecting new patterns of attacks. These difficulties are due to the following opposing factors:

- The lack of systematic method for the IDS design (Lee et al., 2000) (Lee et al., 1998).
- The lack of an audit standard mechanism and a standard audit format that may be specific for the intrusion detection field.
- The non-stationarity and the complexity of the computer systems which increase the number of threats and exploited vulnerabilities.
- The continuous development of technologies which imports new vulnerabilities.
- The exponential growth of Internet.
- The changing nature of the network environment.
- The individual and evolutionary creativity of attackers which allows the evolution and the permanent presence of new attacks.
- The constantly changing nature in attack strategies.

7. THE REQUIREMENT OF ADAPTABILITY IN INTRUSION DETECTION

The current network environments are dynamic changing, the intrusions occur constantly. The set of detection rules which is generated automatically or coded manually must not be static during a long period of time. The new patterns of attacks must be continuously discovered and the IDS should be frequently updated by an automatic mode. It is not the case of the existing IDSs. At the occurrence of new attack pattern, the signatures base of classical IDS is updated manually; and the data mining based IDS undergoes a complete retraining with an updated set. This retraining is difficult and expensive (Cannady, 2000a).

To reduce the cost of frequent updating of IDSs, the IDS must adjust itself to any change in the environment in which it is deployed. It must be able to learn autonomously the new attacks patterns and initiate its incremental updating without undergoing a manual updating or a retraining. The learning capacity is the means with which the IDS can adjust itself to its target environment and improve its detection effectiveness. The efforts of research in intrusion detection were oriented towards the development of effective IDSs by applying various paradigms as the artificial intelligence, data mining and the pattern recognition (Dass et al., 2003). The capacity of autonomous incremental learning was not addressed. Therefore the existing IDSs are not adaptive to their environments and become progressively inefficient through time. The generic architectural model of the IDS includes specific modules for generic functionalities which are:

- Audit data collection
- Audit data analysis
- Control of the IDS functioning
- Response to detected intrusions

These functionalities do not enable the IDS to adjust itself to the environment and learn new patterns of attacks. Therefore the adaptability is a missing functionality in the design of the existing IDSs. It is a relevant feature that guarantees the everlastingness of the IDS in a dynamic changing environment. It improves, in an incremental manner, its efficiency, through time, thanks to acontinuous and automatic learning of new patterns of attacks and normal behaviour. This characteristic is the beginning of a new generation of IDSs called adaptive IDSs.

8. PRESENTATION AND EVALUATION OF THE EXISTING EMINENT ADAPTIVE INTRUSION DETECTION APPROACHES

Data mining approaches descended of learning machine particularly artificial neural networks have contributed for building learning intrusion detection models. Thanks to their generalization power, they can detect a large variety of unknown attacks which are similar, sufficiently close or comparable to already learned known attacks. New attacks that completely differ from learned attacks remain undetected. Therefore the adaptability of data mining IDS is restricted. In (Eskin et al., 2000) (Honig et al., 2002) (Lee et al., 2000) (Lee et al., 1998) (Magnus & Erland, 2004), various approaches have been adopted to build adaptive intrusion detection models. But these models are devoid of continuous automatic learning capacity. So their adaptability is limited or oriented toward a given objective. Few research works succeeded in developing efficient adaptive intrusion detection IDSs.

The most prominent approach that converges toward continuous adaptive learning is based on Cerebellar Model Articulation Controller (CMAC) neural network and uses reinforcement learning.

8.1 CMAC-Based Online Learning Approach

This approach (Cannady, 2000a) (Cannady, 2000b) applies a Cerebellar Model Articulation Controller (CMAC) neural network. It employs reinforcement learning by using a modified version of the Least Mean Square (LMS) as a learning algorithm. The input vector of the CMAC neural network consists in the network traffic features and a parameter "s" called the feedback back of the network environment of the IDS. This feedback represents the environment performance state resulting of the traffic effect. Figure 1 gives a preview of the structure of the adopted CMAC. The adopted weights updating rule is: $w_{i+1}=w_i +b(o_d-o_a)$, as:

- o_d is the expected output
- o_a is the current output
- b is the learning factor.

After deducing that o_d is inversely proportional to « **s** » what implies that: o_d =1-s . Then the updating rule is modified and becomes w_{i+1}

= $w_i+b((1-s)-o_a)$. After experimentation, it is concluded that the learning factor « b » should not be constant. It must be a variable which changes according to the network environment conditions. Then the learning factor b becomes a function that has the feedback « s » as a variable « **b=1-s** ». The adopted LMS algorithm is modified to handle efficiently a changing network environment so that the weights updating rule becomes: $\mathbf{w_{i+1}=w_i+(1-s)[(1-s)-o_a]}$

Experimentation was conducted in order to test the ability of the CMAC approach to learn and identify new patterns of attacks (Cannady, 2000a). Several tests were performed to estimate the most accurate learning factor that can generate a low error rate. After that, five new (a priori) attacks data vectors that represent dissimilar UDP Packet Storm attacks of varying severity are used to provide an accurate evaluation of the on-line learning ability of the CMAC. These vectors were employed to obtain the state of the protected system which is needed to represent the feedback input in the CMAC. Then the five new attack vectors with the corresponding feedbacks are used as input for

Figure 1. Preview of CMAC structure

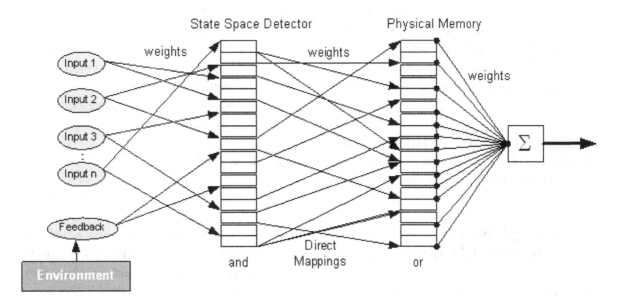

the CMAC. The experimentation shows that the CMAC response is accurate to the desired expected response for the five events which represent five new attack patterns. The response represents the attack probability.

8.1.1 Discussion

We deduce that this approach presents effectiveness in:

- The detection of known attacks.
- The detection of new patterns of attacks.
- The continuous autonomous learning of new patterns of attacks.
- The adaptation to the environment changes.

However, we deduce the following limitations:

- This approach is specific only to denial of service attacks which is a main attack class among the four main attack classes defined in the attacks classification in intrusion detection: Denial of Service (DOS), User to Root (U2R), Remote to Local (R2L) and Probe.
- The denial of service attack class includes several attack subclasses. The proposed approach does not predict the subclass of the detected DOS attack. The prediction of the subclass attack is important during the decision making to respond to the detected intrusion.

There are four models that integrate automatic learning capacity. These models are all network based IDSs and cover the four main classes of attacks.

8.2 Learning Intrusion Detection System, LIDS)

The conception of LIDS (Dass et al., 2003) is based on the idea that the rules base system lacks the flexibility to identify new attacks and must be frequently updated to follow the attacks evolution. Thus, a learning agent is designated to interact with the rules base in the aim to maintain it by incorporating new rules in the case of new attack occurrence or by deleting the rules that can generate false alerts.

Figure 2 illustrates the architecture of LIDS which consists in eight autonomous agents using a blackboard for their communication. The traffic network is collected by agent A1 then analyzed by agent A2 which uses a rules base to identify the abnormal network sessions and predict the type of attack. If there is a probable attack, the agent A3 sends a first alert to the security administrator. The agent A4 collects the information related to the probable attack from the environment such as: the size of the available transmission band of the network and the rate of the CPU and the memory use. This information will be used by agent A5 to verify the presence or the absence of the predicted attack. Agent A6 has a set of four classifiers; each classifier is specific to a main class of attack among the four attack main attack classes defined in intrusion detection. Thanks to these classifiers, A6 can confirm the presence or the absence of the specified attack. Depending on this result, the agent A7, called the learning agent, is designated for interacting with the rules base hosted by the agent A2, to delete the rule corresponding to a false alert or to insert a new rule corresponding to the confirmed attack. In this last case, the agent A8 sends an alert report to the security administrator.

8.2.1 Discussion

We deduce the following advantageous aspects:

- The intrusion detection process establishes a correlation between the network traffic features and the environment parameters. This correlation enables the LIDS to detect the intrusions (the successful attacks) and

Figure 2. Architecture of LIDS

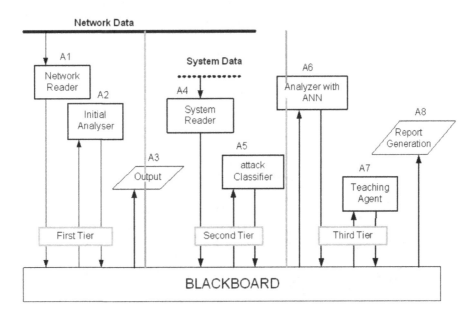

to verify the neutral effect of a potential attack in the network environment.

- The flexibility of LIDS which is expressed by an incremental updating that allows the insertion and the deletion of a rule according to the averification of the presence or the absence of the attack in the environment.

- The learning of new normal behaviour patterns by deleting the rules corresponding to false alerts.

However, we deduce the following weaknesses:

- The adopted detection strategy is not clearly defined. According to the role of agent A2, the rules base is used to identify the abnormal traffic and predict the type of the attack which is present in this traffic. Does the detection strategy combine anomaly based detection with signature based detection? How this combination is made?

- Sending a first alert before the end of the detection process implies the reaction of the security administrator who may un-

dertake actions that can disrupt the productivity of the organization whereas the announced probable attack may be a false alert after the diagnosis of the environment and the affirmation of the absence of the announced attack.

- The coexistence of contradictory rules in the rules base so that the new introduced rule has the priority. However, a rule base must be optimized and coherent without contradictions and redundancies.

8.3 Parallel Hierarchical Intrusion Detection System (PHIDS)

Figure 3 illustrates the architecture of PHIDS (Zhang et al., 2005) which consists in a hierarchy including three levels:

- The first level is an anomaly classifier to identify the abnormal network connections.

- The second level is a signature classifier to identify the main attack class of the detected anomaly among the four attack main classes.

Figure 3. Architecture of PHIDS

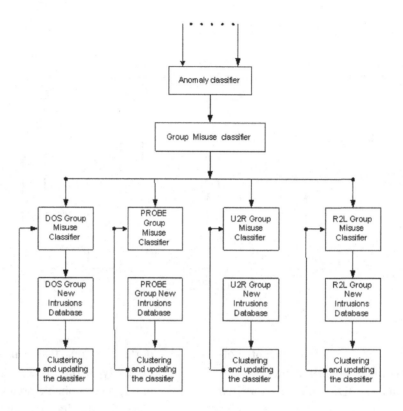

- The third level consists of four signature classifiers. Each one corresponds to a main attack class (DOS, PROBE, U2R and R2L). These classifiers are connected in parallel to the second level of the hierarchy.

When a network connection is classified as anomaly at the first level, it will be classified in one of the four main classes of attack (DOS, PROBE, R2L, U2R) in the second level thanks to the similarity features of the same class. If the attack pattern is not recognized by the classifier corresponding to the predicted attack main class of the third level, then it is considered as new pattern of attack. In this case, its signature will be stored in a data base where it will be submitted thereafter to the clustering.

The clustering creates a set of groups, called clusters, and puts the new patterns of attacks with common properties in a same group. The group designates one attack subclass belonging to an attack main class. If the number of elements in one of the clusters reaches a threshold value which is already fixed, then the classifier corresponding to the main class of attack in the third level will undergo an automatic retraining while including in the data set the signatures of the cluster that reached the threshold. Thus, the classifier will learn the new patterns of attack belonging to a particular attack subclass.

The PHIDS was evaluated using the KDD-Cup 99. Table 2 shows its high performance and ability to identify new attack patterns.

8.3.1 Discussion

The robustness of PHIDS resides in the following factors:

Table 2. Experimental results of PHIDS (Zhang et al., 2005)

	Normal	**SMURF**	**GUESS_PASSWD**	**BUFFER_OVERFLOW**	**IPSWEEP**
DR	99.8	99	99.7	98.8	99.5
FPR	1.2	0.8	4	3. 3	0.8

DR: Detection Rate. FPR: False Positive Rate. Normal: normal connection SMURF: a DOS attack subclass. GUESS_PASSWD: an R2L attack subclass. BUFFER_OVERFLOW: an U2R attack subclass. IPSWEEP: a Probe attack subclass.

- The combination of the two strategies of intrusion detection: the anomaly based detection and the signature based detection. This combination is promising and improves the detection performance.
- The decomposition of the complex process of intrusion detection in a hierarchy of less complex processes so that each process contributes to the detection process.

Despite this robustness, PHIDS admits some weak features:

- Abnormal connection may be an attack as it may be a new pattern of normal connection. This case is not taken into consideration by PHIDS. In addition, the learning of new normal behaviour patterns is a missing functionality in PHIDS.
- During the retraining, the classifier concerned by the retraining will be out of order. Therefore, the PHIDS will be unable to detect the attacks belonging to the main class of attacks corresponding to the classifier which is undergoing retraining.
- The learning is periodic (not incremental) and depends on already fixed threshold which may be reached after a long period of time.
- As retraining the classifier corresponding to main classes of attack, the learning data sets will increase progressively though time. The classifiers can undergo an over training that affects negatively their generalization power.

8.4 Principal Component Analysis Neural Network Intrusion Detection System (PCANN-IDS)

PCANN-IDS (Liu et al., 2007) uses a neural version of Principal Component Analysis (PCA) to reduce the dimension of the features vector of the network connection. The architecture of PCANN-IDS is described in Figure 4. It consists in a hierarchy of three levels.

- The first level of PCANN-IDS is an anomaly classifier to make a distinction between the normal and abnormal connections.
- The second level consists in three signature classifiers so that each classifier corresponds to a main class of attack (U2R, R2L, PROBE).
- The third level consists in three sets of classifiers so that every set is connected to one classifier of the second level. These classifiers correspond to different attack subclasses belonging to the main class of attack which corresponds to the classifier of the second level to which this set of classifiers is connected.

If a current connection is identified by the first level as abnormal, then its features vector is submitted to the second level in order to identify the type of attack. Three cases may occur:

- **First case:** The second level can not identify the main attack class of the connection. Then it is a new unknown main attack

Figure 4. Architecture of PCANN-IDS

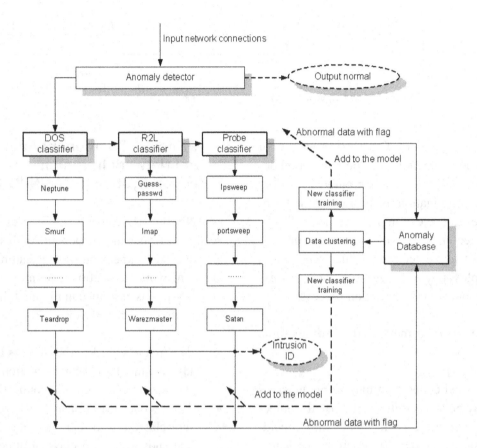

class. The system initializes its flag field by new main attack class.

- **Second case:** The attack is identified by one of the three classifiers of the second level which corresponds to one main attack class. Then, it is identified by one of the classifiers of the third level. As the attack is completely identified, it is a known attack or a variation of a known attack (already learned attack).

- **Third case:** The attack is identified by one of the classifiers of the second level but none of the classifiers of the third level could identify this attack. It is a new unknown subclass of attack. Then the system initializes the flag field of the connection by new subclass of attack.

The new attack signatures that satisfy the first case and the third case are stored in a data base called the anomalies data base. When the number of records reaches a threshold which is already fixed, the system triggers the clustering of these records, according to the content of the flag field. Then it initiates the automatic training of a new signature classifier using as data set the records in the appropriate cluster. The content of the flag field will indicate the level of the hierarchy to which the new classifier will be connected:

- In the case of a new main class of attack, the new classifier will be connected to the second level, in parallel to the classifiers corresponding to the main classes of attacks.

- In the case of a new subclass of attack, the new classifier will be connected to the low-level, in series of the classifiers corresponding to the attack subclasses belonging to the appropriate main attack class.

PCANN-IDS was evaluated using the KDD-Cup 99. The experimental results in Table 3 prove its high performance in detecting known and new attacks.

8.4.1 Discussion

PCANN-IDS presents the following advantages:

- Like PHIDS, PCANN-IDS combines the two strategies of intrusion detection and decomposes the complex process of intrusion detection but this decomposition is more granular in PCANN-IDS than PHIDS.
- The detailed classification of attacks which allows the identification of the attack subclass in addition to the main class of attack.
- The extension of PCANN-IDS to include new main attacks classes and attacks subclasses by adjusting automatically its structure to add new signature classifiers at the second level and the third level of the hierarchy.

But PCANN-IDS presents the following limitations:

Table 3. Experimental results of PCANN-IDS (Liu et al., 2007)

	Normal	DOS	PROBE	R2L
DR	97.1	100	100	97.2
FPR	2.8	0.7	0.5	0.6

DR: Detection Rate. FPR: False Positive Rate.

- Like PHIDS, leaning new patterns of normal behaviour is a missing functionality in PCANN-IDS.
- Like PHIDS, the learning of new attacks is periodic (not incremental) and depends on threshold which is already fixed.
- To apply the Principal Component Analysis (PCA) which is a method of numeric data analysis, PCANN-IDS eliminates the three symbolic features from the features vector of the network connection: protocol, flag and service. However, these three features are more important than other network connection features. This affirmation is proved by the research work that studied the network connection features and classified their importance according to their relevance (Zhang & Zulkernine, 2005).

A critical and comparative study of LIDS, PHIDS and PCANN-IDS is developed in (Bensefia & Ahmed-Nacer, 2008).

8.5 Adaptive Rule-based Intrusion Detection Architecture (ARIDA)

Figure 5 gives an integral preview of the ARIDA which consists in two main components (Shafi et al., 2006).

1. A network agent includes two modules; the packet handler and the rule base. The packet handler extracts the relevant features from the network traffic and sends them to the rule base. This latter contains two sets of rules; normal signatures and attack signatures. The network traffic features are matched against both the rule sets. If the features match any attack rule, an alert is generated and sent to the security console. If there is no matching, the features network traffic is considered as potentially malicious.

Figure 5. Preview of ARIDA

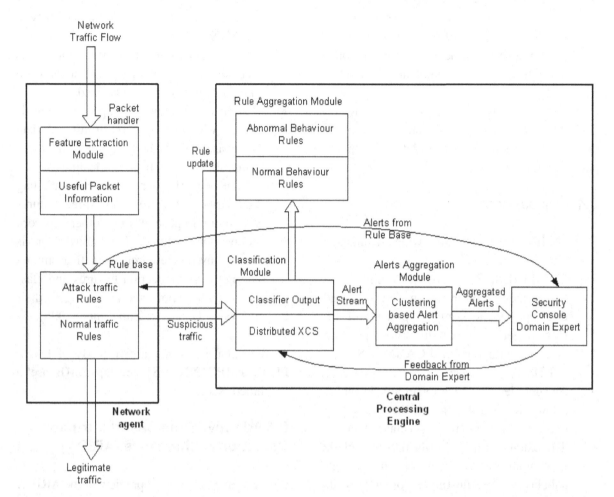

2. A central processing engine includes three modules; a classification module, an alert aggregation module and a rule aggregation module. The classification module is a Learning Classifier System (LCS) which learns dynamically rules. It classifies the malicious network traffic features as normal or malicious and the predicted output is sent to the security supervisor who returns a feedback by ignoring the alert if the event is normal or by affirming an attack if the event is malicious. The alert aggregation module establishes the clustering of the alerts in the aim to reduce the load on the security supervisor. When an alert is sent by the LCS to the alert aggregation module, this module will verify if similar alerts have been sent to the security advisor and are waiting for response. If the alert does not match with any of the existing clusters, a new cluster is created and the alert is sent to the security supervisor. According to the LCS principles, at the reception of the feedback from the security supervisor, the LCS updates its rule base by increasing the fitness of the correct rules and decreasing the fitness of the bad rules in order to delete them from the rule base. The rule aggregation module will process the most accurate rules of the LCS in order to update the signature rule base in the network agent by adding the useful rules.

8.5.1 Discussion

The strong aspects of ARIDA are:

- This architecture integrates an LCS which is a promising approach for building adaptive systems that interact with a dynamic changing environment. Indeed, the LCS is a reactive and an evolving rule base. It represents a complementary module for the signatures rule base that provides accurate new signatures of normal behaviour and attacks to update it in real time.
- This architecture allows incremental learning of new attack patterns and new normal behaviour patterns.
- The learning is undertaken by interacting with the security supervisor who is an element of the IDS environment. So this learning is adaptive to the IDS environment

The weak aspects of ARIDA are summarized as follows:

- Although the learning is adaptive to the IDS environment, it is subjective. Besides the IDS remains depending on the human expertise. This feature was criticized in the first classical generation of IDSs.
- The security supervisor must be seasoned and skilled in security field to be able to recognize an attack and to distinguish between a normal activity and an intrusive one.
- The identification of new patterns of attacks and normal behaviour by the security supervisor may require an investigating time which can influence negatively the response time and the performance of the IDS.

No experiment was carried out on LIDS or ARIDA. The PHIDS and PCANN-IDS are learning IDSs but they are independent of their environments. The CMAC-based online learning approach, the LIDS and the ARIDA models represent adaptive learning IDSs. They demonstrate that the environment is a promising component which favours the IDS adaptability in a dynamic changing environment. So the environment is a relevant dimension that should be considered as a reference for building adaptive intrusion detection systems. The traffic features represent the form and the cause of attack but the effect of the attack will exist in the environment. The state of the environment may reflect the presence or the absence of the attack (Ye et al., 2006).

9. NEW TRENDS FOR ADAPTIVE INTRUSION DETECTION SYSTEMS

The proposed approaches in (Cannady, 2000a) (Cannady, 2000b) (Dass et al., 2003) (Liu et al., 2007) (Shafi et al., 2006) (Zhang et al., 2005) are progress towards the IDSs adaptability. But the feasibility of this adaptability is submitted to methodological and conceptual constraints. Actually, research work on intrusion detection is oriented towards the adaptability. Promising paradigms are explored but the most of proposed approaches are focussed on proposing new learning algorithms to improve the detection rate and reduce the false positive rate. The aspects of incremental continuous learning and adaptation in relation to the environment are not realized.

To plant the feature of adaptability as a native functionality in IDS, research in adaptive intrusion detection should explore other promising paradigms that combine learning, adaptation and evolution aspects such as Learning Classifier Systems (LCS), Evolving Connectionist Systems (ECoS), artificial immune systems, swarm intelligence and game theory. These paradigms can offer the necessary foundations for IDSs adaptability.

10. CONCLUSION

Despite the fact that the intrusion detection is a fertile research area, the adaptability remains a challenging relevant deep problem. It corresponds to the manner of which the IDS adjusts itself to the continuous variations of its target environment in the aim to maintain or improve its effectiveness. The adaptability is strictly associated to the sustainability of the IDS in the current and future host/network environments becoming, more and more, evolutionary and dynamic. It refers to the capacity of automatic continuous incremental learning of the intrusive and normal behaviour. This feature is absent in the two existing generations of IDSs because it was not investigated by the research community and the leaders of IDS technology. Actually, the adaptability imposes itself in the intrusion detection research as an important issue. More focussed research is oriented toward the IDS adaptability which is the origin of a new generation of IDSs, called adaptive IDSs. This new generation constitutes a qualitative jump, in intrusion detection field, in terms of performance, efficiency and sustainability.

REFERENCES

Anderson, J. P. (1980). *Computer security threat monitoring and surveillance (Technical Report)*. Washington, PA: Academic Press.

Bace, R., & Mell, P. (2001). *NIST special publication on intrusion detection. NIST Computer Security Division, National Institute of Standards and Technology*. NIST.

Bensefia, H., & Ahmed-Nacer, M. (2008). Towards an adaptive intrusion detection system: A critical and comparative study. In *Proceedings of International Conference on Computational Intelligence and Security*, (pp. 246-251). Academic Press.

Biondi, P. (2001). *Architecture expérimentale pour la détection d'intrusions dans un système informatique*.

Brown, D. J., Suckow, B., & Wang, T. (2001). *A survey of intrusion detection systems*. San Diego, CA: Department of Computer Science, University of California.

Brugger, S. T. (2004). *Data mining methods for network intrusion detection* (UC Davis Dissertation Proposal). Davis, CA: Department of Computer Science, University of California.

Cannady, J. (2000a). Next generation intrusion detection: Autonomous reinforcement learning of network attacks. In *Proceedings of 23rd National Information Systems Security Conference*. Academic Press.

Cannady, J. (2000b). Applying CMAC-based online learning to intrusion detection. *IEEE-INNS-ENNS International Joint Conference on Neural Networks, 5*, 405-410.

Dass, M., Cannady, J., & Potter, W. D. (2003). A blackboard-based learning intrusion detection system: A new approach. In *Developments in applied artificial intelligence* (pp. 359–378). Academic Press. doi:10.1007/3-540-45034-3_39

Debar, H., Dacier, M., & Wespi, A. (1999). Towards a taxonomy of intrusion-detection systems. *Computer Networks-The International Journal of Computer and Telecommunication Networking, 3*(8), 805–822.

Denning, D. E. (1987). An intrusion detection model. *IEEE Transactions on Software Engineering, 13*(2), 222–232. doi:10.1109/TSE.1987.232894

Eskin, E., Miller, M., Zhong, Z. D., Yi, G., Lee, W. A., & Stolfo, S. J. (2000). Adaptive model generation for intrusion detection systems. In *Proceedings of 7th ACM Conference on Computer Security*. Athens, Greece: ACM.

Honig, A., Howard, A., Eskin, E., & Stolfo, S. J. (2002). Adaptive model generation: An architecture for the deployment of data mining-based intrusion detection systems. In D. Barbara, & S. Jajodia (Eds.), *Applications of data mining in computer security*. Dordrecht, The Netherlands: Kluwer Academic Publishers. doi:10.1007/978-1-4615-0953-0_7

Hugh, J. M., Christie, A., & Allen, J. (2000). Defending yourself: The role of intrusion detection systems. *IEEE Software, 17*(5), 42–51. doi:10.1109/52.877859

Kayacik, H. G., Zincir-Heywood, A. N., & Heywood, M. I. (2005). Selecting features for intrusion detection: A feature relevance analysis on KDD 99 intrusion detection datasets. In *Proceedings of Third Annual Conference on Privacy, Security and Trust*. Academic Press.

KDD. (2013). Retrieved June 16, 2013, from http://kdd.ics.uci.edu/databases/kddcup99/kddcup99.html

Kumar, S., & Spafford, E. H. (1994). *An application of pattern matching in intrusion detection* (Technical Report CSD-TR-94-013). The COAST Project, Department of Computer Science, Perdue University.

Labib, K. (2004). Computer security and intrusion detection. *Crossroads, 11*(1), 2–2. doi:10.1145/1031859.1031861

Lacasse, A. (2006). *Approche algébrique pour la prévention d'intrusion. Mémoire de maîtrise en Informatique*. Québec, Canada: Faculté Des Etudes Supérieures de l'Université Laval.

Lappas, T., & Pelechrinis, K. (2007). *Data mining techniques for (network) intrusion detection systems* (White Paper). Department of Computer Science and Engineering, University of California Riverside.

Lazarevic, A., Kumar, V., & Srivastava, J. (2005). Intrusion detection: A survey. *Managing Cyber Threats, 5*, 19–78. doi:10.1007/0-387-24230-9_2

Lee, W., & Stolfo, S. J. (1998). Data mining approaches for intrusion detection. In *Proceedings of Seventh USENIX Security Symposium (SECURITY '98)*. San Antonio, TX: USENIX.

Lee, W., & Stolfo, S. J., & MoK, K. W. (2000). Adaptive intrusion detection: A data mining approach. *Artificial Intelligence Review, 14*(6), 533–567. doi:10.1023/A:1006624031083

Lee, W., Stolfo, S. J., Chan, P. K., Eskin, E., Fan, M., & Miller, M. (2001). Real time data mining-based intrusion detection. *DARPA Information Survivability Conference & Exposition II, 1*, 89–100.

Lee, W., Stolfo, S. J., & Molk, K. W. (1998). *A data mining framework for adaptive intrusion detection*. New York: Computer Science Department, Columbia University.

Liu, G., Yi, Z., & Yang, S. (2007). A hierarchical intrusion detection model based on the PCA neural networks. *Neurocomputing, 70*, 1561–1568. doi:10.1016/j.neucom.2006.10.146

Magnus, A., & Erland, J. (2004). Using active learning in intrusion detection. In *Proceedings of Computer Security Foundations Workshop*, (pp. 88-98). Academic Press.

McHugh, J. (2000). Testing intrusion detection systems: A critique of the 1998 and 1999 darpa intrusion detection system evaluations as performed by lincoln laboratory. *ACM Transactions on Information and System Security, 3*(4), 262–294. doi:10.1145/382912.382923

Mé, L. (1997). Un complément à l'approche formelle: La détection d'intrusion. Actes de la Journée CIDR97. Rennes, France.

Mé, L., Marrakchi, Z., Michel, C., Debar, H., & Cuppens, F. (2001). La détection d'intrusion: Les outils doivent coopérer. *Revue de l'Electricité et de l'Electronique, 5,* 50–55.

MIT. (2013). Retrieved June 16, 2013, from http://www.ll.mit.edu/mission/communications/cyber/CSTcorpora/ideval/data/

Mukkamala, S., Sung, A. H., & Abraham, A. (2005). Intrusion detection using an ensemble of intelligent paradigms. *Journal of Network and Computer Applications, 28*(2), 167–182. doi:10.1016/j.jnca.2004.01.003

NIST. (1995). An introduction to computer security. In The NIST handbook (Special publication 800-12). The National Institute of Standards and Technology (NIST).

Nobelis, N. (2004). Un modèle de case-based reasoning pour la detection d'iintrusion. Rapport de DEA Réseau et Système Distribué. Université Nice Sophia Antipolis, France, Septembre 2004.

Noel, S., Wijesekera, D., & Youman, C. (2002). Modern intrusion detection, data mining, and degrees of attack guilt. In D. Barbarà, & S. Jajodia (Eds.), *Applications of data mining in computer security* (pp. 1–31). Kluwer Academic Publisher. doi:10.1007/978-1-4615-0953-0_1

NSL. (2013). Retrieved June 16, 2013, from http://nsl.cs.unb.ca/NSL-KDD

Shafi, K., Abbass, H., & Zhu, W. (2006). An adaptive rule based intrusion detection architecture. In *Proceedings of Security Technology Conference, the 5th Homeland Security Summit,* (pp. 345-355). Canberra, Australia: Academic Press.

Singhal, A., & Jajodia, S. (2006). Data warehousing and data mining techniques for intrusion detection systems. *Distributed and Parallel Databases, 20*(2), 149–166. doi:10.1007/s10619-006-9496-5

Tavallaee, M., Bagheri, E., Lu, W., & Ghorbani, A. A. (2009). A detailed analysis of the KDD CUP 99 data set. In *Proceedings of IEEE Symposium on Computational Intelligence in Security and Defense Applications (CISDA 2009).* IEEE.

Xu, X. (2006). Adaptive intrusion detection based on machine learning: Feature extraction, classifier construction and sequential pattern prediction. *International Journal of Web Services Practices, 2*(1-2), 49–58.

Ye, N., Farley, T., & Lakshminarasimhan, D. (2006). An attack-norm separation approach for detecting cyber attacks. *Information Systems Frontiers, 8*(3), 163–177. doi:10.1007/s10796-006-8731-y

Zang, J., & Zulkernine, M. (2005). Network intrusion detection using random forests. In *Proceedings of Third Annual Conference on Privacy, Security and Trust,* (pp. 53-61). Academic Press.

Zhang, C., Jiang, J., & Kamel, M. (2005). Intrusion detection using hierarchical neural networks. *Pattern Recognition Letters, 26,* 779–79. doi:10.1016/j.patrec.2004.09.045

KEY TERMS AND DEFINITIONS

Adaptability: The ability of a system/agent to adjust itself to the permanent variations in a dynamic changing environment.

Alarm: An indication of security violation by sending a message in real time to notify the security administrator.

Anomaly: Unusual behaviour of a system/user/process which is considered as significant deviation with regard to the usual normal behaviour.

Attack: Illicit voluntary act which is led by an adversary called attacker against another adversary, called victim. It is a serial of consecutive events that has damaging consequences on the security of assets.

Audit: The mechanism of recording chronologically the events that occur during the activity of a system, process or application.

Incremental Learning: The capacity of system/agent to learn continuously in real time new learning examples by automatic mode.

Intrusion: Any deliberated tentative of violation of the logical security of a system in terms of confidentiality, availability, integrity and legitimate use.

Intrusion Detection: A security mechanism that constitutes the logical complement of the preventive security. It permits the permanent monitoring of system and network environments in order to identify intrusions and establish a response plan to these intrusions.

KDD: Standard benchmark which is available for the research community in intrusion detection field to carry on experimental evaluation of the proposed intrusion detection approaches.

Machine Learning: A branch of artificial intelligence focusing on the development of automatic learning techniques.

Related References

To continue our tradition of advancing information science and technology research, we have compiled a list of recommended IGI Global readings. These references will provide additional information and guidance to further enrich your knowledge and assist you with your own research and future publications.

Acharjya, D. P., & Mary, A. G. (2014). Privacy preservation in information system. In B. Tripathy, & D. Acharjya (Eds.) Advances in secure computing, internet services, and applications (pp. 49-72). Hershey, PA: Information Science Reference. doi: doi:10.4018/978-1-4666-4940-8.ch003

Agamba, J., & Keengwe, J. (2012). Pre-service teachers' perceptions of information assurance and cyber security. [IJICTE]. *International Journal of Information and Communication Technology Education, 8*(2), 94–101. doi:10.4018/jicte.2012040108

Aggarwal, R. (2013). Dispute settlement for cyber crimes in India: An analysis. In R. Khurana, & R. Aggarwal (Eds.), *Interdisciplinary perspectives on business convergence, computing, and legality* (pp. 160–171). Hershey, PA: Business Science Reference. doi:10.4018/978-1-4666-4209-6.ch015

Agwu, E. (2013). Cyber criminals on the internet super highways: A technical investigation of different shades and colours within the Nigerian cyber space. [IJOM]. *International Journal of Online Marketing, 3*(2), 56–74. doi:10.4018/ijom.2013040104

Ahmad, A. (2012). Security assessment of networks. In I. Management Association (Ed.), Wireless technologies: Concepts, methodologies, tools and applications (pp. 208-224). Hershey, PA: Information Science Reference. doi: doi:10.4018/978-1-61350-101-6.ch111

Ahmed, N., & Jensen, C. D. (2012). Security of dependable systems. In L. Petre, K. Sere, & E. Troubitsyna (Eds.), *Dependability and computer engineering: Concepts for software-intensive systems* (pp. 230–264). Hershey, PA: Engineering Science Reference.

Al, M., & Yoshigoe, K. (2012). Security and attacks in wireless sensor networks. In I. Management Association (Ed.), Wireless technologies: Concepts, methodologies, tools and applications (pp. 1811-1846). Hershey, PA: Information Science Reference. doi: doi:10.4018/978-1-61350-101-6.ch706

Al-Ahmad, W. (2011). Building secure software using XP. [IJSSE]. *International Journal of Secure Software Engineering, 2*(3), 63–76. doi:10.4018/jsse.2011070104

Al-Bayatti, A. H., & Al-Bayatti, H. M. (2012). Security management and simulation of mobile ad hoc networks (MANET). In H. Al-Bahadili (Ed.), *Simulation in computer network design and modeling: Use and analysis* (pp. 297–314). Hershey, PA: Information Science Reference. doi:10.4018/978-1-4666-0191-8.ch014

Al-Bayatti, A. H., Zedan, H., Cau, A., & Siewe, F. (2012). Security management for mobile ad hoc network of networks (MANoN). In I. Khalil, & E. Weippl (Eds.), *Advancing the next-generation of mobile computing: Emerging technologies* (pp. 1–18). Hershey, PA: Information Science Reference. doi:10.4018/978-1-4666-0119-2.ch001

Al-Hamdani, W. A. (2011). Three models to measure information security compliance. In H. Nemati (Ed.), *Security and privacy assurance in advancing technologies: New developments* (pp. 351–373). Hershey, PA: Information Science Reference.

Al-Hamdani, W. A. (2014). Secure e-learning and cryptography. In K. Sullivan, P. Czigler, & J. Sullivan Hellgren (Eds.), *Cases on professional distance education degree programs and practices: Successes, challenges, and issues* (pp. 331–369). Hershey, PA: Information Science Reference.

Al-Jaljouli, R., & Abawajy, J. H. (2012). Security framework for mobile agents-based applications. In A. Kumar, & H. Rahman (Eds.), *Mobile computing techniques in emerging markets: Systems, applications and services* (pp. 242–269). Hershey, PA: Information Science Reference. doi:10.4018/978-1-4666-0080-5.ch009

Al-Jaljouli, R., & Abawajy, J. H. (2014). Mobile agents security protocols. In I. Management Association (Ed.), Crisis management: Concepts, methodologies, tools and applications (pp. 166-202). Hershey, PA: Information Science Reference. doi: doi:10.4018/978-1-4666-4707-7.ch007

Al-Suqri, M. N., & Akomolafe-Fatuyi, E. (2012). Security and privacy in digital libraries: Challenges, opportunities and prospects. [IJDLS]. *International Journal of Digital Library Systems*, 3(4), 54–61. doi:10.4018/ijdls.2012100103

Alavi, R., Islam, S., Jahankhani, H., & Al-Nemrat, A. (2013). Analyzing human factors for an effective information security management system. [IJSSE]. *International Journal of Secure Software Engineering*, 4(1), 50–74. doi:10.4018/jsse.2013010104

Alazab, A., Abawajy, J. H., & Hobbs, M. (2013). Web malware that targets web applications. In L. Caviglione, M. Coccoli, & A. Merlo (Eds.), *Social network engineering for secure web data and services* (pp. 248–264). Hershey, PA: Information Science Reference. doi:10.4018/978-1-4666-3926-3.ch012

Alazab, A., Hobbs, M., Abawajy, J., & Khraisat, A. (2013). Malware detection and prevention system based on multi-stage rules. [IJISP]. *International Journal of Information Security and Privacy*, 7(2), 29–43. doi:10.4018/jisp.2013040102

Alazab, M., Venkatraman, S., Watters, P., & Alazab, M. (2013). Information security governance: The art of detecting hidden malware. In D. Mellado, L. Enrique Sánchez, E. Fernández-Medina, & M. Piattini (Eds.), *IT security governance innovations: Theory and research* (pp. 293–315). Hershey, PA: Information Science Reference.

Alhaj, A., Aljawarneh, S., Masadeh, S., & Abu-Taieh, E. (2013). A secure data transmission mechanism for cloud outsourced data. [IJCAC]. *International Journal of Cloud Applications and Computing*, 3(1), 34–43. doi:10.4018/ijcac.2013010104

Ali, M., & Jawandhiya, P. (2012). Security aware routing protocols for mobile ad hoc networks. In K. Lakhtaria (Ed.), *Technological advancements and applications in mobile ad-hoc networks: Research trends* (pp. 264–289). Hershey, PA: Information Science Reference. doi:10.4018/978-1-4666-0321-9.ch016

Ali, S. (2012). Practical web application security audit following industry standards and compliance. In J. Zubairi, & A. Mahboob (Eds.), *Cyber security standards, practices and industrial applications: Systems and methodologies* (pp. 259–279). Hershey, PA: Information Science Reference.

Aljawarneh, S. (2013). Cloud security engineering: Avoiding security threats the right way. In S. Aljawarneh (Ed.), *Cloud computing advancements in design, implementation, and technologies* (pp. 147–153). Hershey, PA: Information Science Reference.

Alshaer, H., Muhaidat, S., Shubair, R., & Shayegannia, M. (2014). Security and connectivity analysis in vehicular communication networks. In D. Rawat, B. Bista, & G. Yan (Eds.), *Security, privacy, trust, and resource management in mobile and wireless communications* (pp. 83–107). Hershey, PA: Information Science Reference.

Alzamil, Z. A. (2012). Information security awareness at Saudi Arabians' organizations: An information technology employee's perspective. [IJISP]. *International Journal of Information Security and Privacy, 6*(3), 38–55. doi:10.4018/jisp.2012070102

Anyiwo, D., & Sharma, S. (2011). Web services and e-business technologies: Security issues. In O. Bak, & N. Stair (Eds.), *Impact of e-business technologies on public and private organizations: Industry comparisons and perspectives* (pp. 249–261). Hershey, PA: Business Science Reference. doi:10.4018/978-1-60960-501-8.ch015

Apostolakis, I., Chryssanthou, A., & Varlamis, I. (2011). A holistic perspective of security in health related virtual communities. In I. Management Association (Ed.), *Virtual communities: Concepts, methodologies, tools and applications* (pp. 1190-1204). Hershey, PA: Information Science Reference. doi: doi:10.4018/978-1-60960-100-3.ch406

Arnett, K. P., Templeton, G. F., & Vance, D. A. (2011). Information security by words alone: The case for strong security policies. In H. Nemati (Ed.), *Security and privacy assurance in advancing technologies: New developments* (pp. 154–159). Hershey, PA: Information Science Reference.

Arogundade, O. T., Akinwale, A. T., Jin, Z., & Yang, X. G. (2011). A unified use-misuse case model for capturing and analysing safety and security requirements. [IJISP]. *International Journal of Information Security and Privacy, 5*(4), 8–30. doi:10.4018/jisp.2011100102

Arshad, J., Townend, P., Xu, J., & Jie, W. (2012). Cloud computing security: Opportunities and pitfalls. [IJGHPC]. *International Journal of Grid and High Performance Computing, 4*(1), 52–66. doi:10.4018/jghpc.2012010104

Asim, M., & Petkovic, M. (2012). Fundamental building blocks for security interoperability in e-business. In E. Kajan, F. Dorloff, & I. Bedini (Eds.), *Handbook of research on e-business standards and protocols: Documents, data and advanced web technologies* (pp. 269–292). Hershey, PA: Business Science Reference. doi:10.4018/978-1-4666-0146-8.ch013

Askary, S., Goodwin, D., & Lanis, R. (2012). Improvements in audit risks related to information technology frauds. [IJEIS]. *International Journal of Enterprise Information Systems, 8*(2), 52–63. doi:10.4018/jeis.2012040104

Aurigemma, S. (2013). A composite framework for behavioral compliance with information security policies. [JOEUC]. *Journal of Organizational and End User Computing, 25*(3), 32–51. doi:10.4018/joeuc.2013070103

Avalle, M., Pironti, A., Pozza, D., & Sisto, R. (2011). JavaSPI: A framework for security protocol implementation. [IJSSE]. *International Journal of Secure Software Engineering, 2*(4), 34–48. doi:10.4018/jsse.2011100103

Axelrod, C. W. (2012). A dynamic cyber security economic model: incorporating value functions for all involved parties. In M. Gupta, J. Walp, & R. Sharman (Eds.), *Threats, countermeasures, and advances in applied information security* (pp. 462–477). Hershey, PA: Information Science Reference. doi:10.4018/978-1-4666-0978-5.ch024

Ayanso, A., & Herath, T. (2012). Law and technology at crossroads in cyberspace: Where do we go from here? In A. Dudley, J. Braman, & G. Vincenti (Eds.), *Investigating cyber law and cyber ethics: Issues, impacts and practices* (pp. 57–77). Hershey, PA: Information Science Reference.

Baars, T., & Spruit, M. (2012). Designing a secure cloud architecture: The SeCA model. [IJISP]. *International Journal of Information Security and Privacy, 6*(1), 14–32. doi:10.4018/jisp.2012010102

Bachmann, M. (2011). Deciphering the hacker underground: First quantitative insights. In T. Holt, & B. Schell (Eds.), *Corporate hacking and technology-driven crime: Social dynamics and implications* (pp. 105–126). Hershey, PA: Information Science Reference. doi:10.4018/978-1-61350-323-2.ch112

Bachmann, M., & Smith, B. (2012). Internet fraud. In Z. Yan (Ed.), *Encyclopedia of cyber behavior* (pp. 931–943). Hershey, PA: Information Science Reference. doi:10.4018/978-1-4666-0315-8.ch077

Bai, Y., & Khan, K. M. (2011). Ell secure information system using modal logic technique. [IJSSE]. *International Journal of Secure Software Engineering*, 2(2), 65–76. doi:10.4018/jsse.2011040104

Bandeira, G. S. (2014). Criminal liability of organizations, corporations, legal persons, and similar entities on law of portuguese cybercrime: A brief discussion on the issue of crimes of "false information," the "damage on other programs or computer data," the "computer-software sabotage," the "illegitimate access," the "unlawful interception," and "illegitimate reproduction of the protected program". In I. Portela, & F. Almeida (Eds.), *Organizational, legal, and technological dimensions of information system administration* (pp. 96–107). Hershey, PA: Information Science Reference.

Barjis, J. (2012). Software engineering security based on business process modeling. In K. Khan (Ed.), *Security-aware systems applications and software development methods* (pp. 52–68). Hershey, PA: Information Science Reference. doi:10.4018/978-1-4666-1580-9.ch004

Bedi, P., Gandotra, V., & Singhal, A. (2013). Innovative strategies for secure software development. In H. Singh, & K. Kaur (Eds.), *Designing, engineering, and analyzing reliable and efficient software* (pp. 217–237). Hershey, PA: Information Science Reference. doi:10.4018/978-1-4666-2958-5.ch013

Belsis, P., Skourlas, C., & Gritzalis, S. (2011). Secure electronic healthcare records management in wireless environments. [JITR]. *Journal of Information Technology Research*, 4(4), 1–17. doi:10.4018/jitr.2011100101

Bernik, I. (2012). Internet study: Cyber threats and cybercrime awareness and fear. [IJCWT]. *International Journal of Cyber Warfare & Terrorism*, 2(3), 1–11. doi:10.4018/ijcwt.2012070101

Bhatia, M. S. (2011). World war III: The cyber war. [IJCWT]. *International Journal of Cyber Warfare & Terrorism*, 1(3), 59–69. doi:10.4018/ijcwt.2011070104

Blanco, C., Rosado, D., Gutiérrez, C., Rodríguez, A., Mellado, D., & Fernández-Medina, E. et al. (2011). Security over the information systems development cycle. In H. Mouratidis (Ed.), *Software engineering for secure systems: Industrial and research perspectives* (pp. 113–154). Hershey, PA: Information Science Reference.

Bobbert, Y., & Mulder, H. (2012). A research journey into maturing the business information security of mid market organizations. In W. Van Grembergen, & S. De Haes (Eds.), *Business strategy and applications in enterprise IT governance* (pp. 236–259). Hershey, PA: Business Science Reference. doi:10.4018/978-1-4666-1779-7.ch014

Boddington, R. (2011). Digital evidence. In D. Kerr, J. Gammack, & K. Bryant (Eds.), *Digital business security development: Management technologies* (pp. 37–72). Hershey, PA: Business Science Reference.

Bossler, A. M., & Burruss, G. W. (2011). The general theory of crime and computer hacking: Low self-control hackers? In T. Holt, & B. Schell (Eds.), *Corporate hacking and technology-driven crime: Social dynamics and implications* (pp. 38–67). Hershey, PA: Information Science Reference. doi:10.4018/978-1-61350-323-2.ch707

Bouras, C., & Stamos, K. (2011). Security issues for multi-domain resource reservation. In D. Kar, & M. Syed (Eds.), *Network security, administration and management: Advancing technology and practice* (pp. 38–50). Hershey, PA: Information Science Reference. doi:10.4018/978-1-60960-777-7.ch003

Bracci, F., Corradi, A., & Foschini, L. (2014). Cloud standards: Security and interoperability issues. In H. Mouftah, & B. Kantarci (Eds.), *Communication infrastructures for cloud computing* (pp. 465–495). Hershey, PA: Information Science Reference.

Brodsky, J., & Radvanovsky, R. (2011). Control systems security. In T. Holt, & B. Schell (Eds.), *Corporate hacking and technology-driven crime: Social dynamics and implications* (pp. 187–204). Hershey, PA: Information Science Reference.

Brooks, D. (2013). Security threats and risks of intelligent building systems: Protecting facilities from current and emerging vulnerabilities. In C. Laing, A. Badii, & P. Vickers (Eds.), *Securing critical infrastructures and critical control systems: Approaches for threat protection* (pp. 1–16). Hershey, PA: Information Science Reference.

Bülow, W., & Wester, M. (2012). The right to privacy and the protection of personal data in a digital era and the age of information. In C. Akrivopoulou, & N. Garipidis (Eds.), *Human rights and risks in the digital era: Globalization and the effects of information technologies* (pp. 34–45). Hershey, PA: Information Science Reference. doi:10.4018/978-1-4666-0891-7.ch004

Canongia, C., & Mandarino, R. (2014). Cybersecurity: The new challenge of the information society. In I. Management Association (Ed.), Crisis management: Concepts, methodologies, tools and applications (pp. 60-80). Hershey, PA: Information Science Reference. doi: doi:10.4018/978-1-4666-4707-7.ch003

Cao, X., & Lu, Y. (2011). The social network structure of a computer hacker community. In H. Nemati (Ed.), *Security and privacy assurance in advancing technologies: New developments* (pp. 160–173). Hershey, PA: Information Science Reference.

Cardholm, L. (2014). Identifying the business value of information security. In T. Tsiakis, T. Kargidis, & P. Katsaros (Eds.), *Approaches and processes for managing the economics of information systems* (pp. 157–180). Hershey, PA: Business Science Reference. doi:10.4018/978-1-4666-4983-5.ch010

Cardoso, R. C., & Gomes, A. (2012). Security issues in massively multiplayer online games. In M. Cruz-Cunha (Ed.), *Handbook of research on serious games as educational, business and research tools* (pp. 290–314). Hershey, PA: Information Science Reference. doi:10.4018/978-1-4666-0149-9.ch016

Carpen-Amarie, A., Costan, A., Leordeanu, C., Basescu, C., & Antoniu, G. (2012). Towards a generic security framework for cloud data management environments. [IJDST]. *International Journal of Distributed Systems and Technologies*, *3*(1), 17–34. doi:10.4018/jdst.2012010102

Caushaj, E., Fu, H., Sethi, I., Badih, H., Watson, D., Zhu, Y., & Leng, S. (2013). Theoretical analysis and experimental study: Monitoring data privacy in smartphone communications. [IJITN]. *International Journal of Interdisciplinary Telecommunications and Networking*, *5*(2), 66–82. doi:10.4018/jitn.2013040106

Cepheli, Ö., & Kurt, G. K. (2014). Physical layer security in wireless communication networks. In D. Rawat, B. Bista, & G. Yan (Eds.), *Security, privacy, trust, and resource management in mobile and wireless communications* (pp. 61–81). Hershey, PA: Information Science Reference.

Chakraborty, P., & Raghuraman, K. (2013). Trends in information security. In K. Buragga, & N. Zaman (Eds.), *Software development techniques for constructive information systems design* (pp. 354–376). Hershey, PA: Information Science Reference. doi:10.4018/978-1-4666-3679-8.ch020

Chandrakumar, T., & Parthasarathy, S. (2012). Enhancing data security in ERP projects using XML. [IJEIS]. *International Journal of Enterprise Information Systems*, *8*(1), 51–65. doi:10.4018/jeis.2012010104

Chapple, M. J., Striegel, A., & Crowell, C. R. (2011). Firewall rulebase management: Tools and techniques. In M. Quigley (Ed.), *ICT ethics and security in the 21st century: New developments and applications* (pp. 254–276). Hershey, PA: Information Science Reference. doi:10.4018/978-1-60960-573-5.ch013

Chen, L., Hu, W., Yang, M., & Zhang, L. (2011). Security and privacy issues in secure e-mail standards and services. In H. Nemati (Ed.), *Security and privacy assurance in advancing technologies: new developments* (pp. 174–185). Hershey, PA: Information Science Reference.

Chen, L., Varol, C., Liu, Q., & Zhou, B. (2014). Security in wireless metropolitan area networks: WiMAX and LTE. In D. Rawat, B. Bista, & G. Yan (Eds.), *Security, privacy, trust, and resource management in mobile and wireless communications* (pp. 11–27). Hershey, PA: Information Science Reference.

Cherdantseva, Y., & Hilton, J. (2014). Information security and information assurance: Discussion about the meaning, scope, and goals. In I. Portela, & F. Almeida (Eds.), *Organizational, legal, and technological dimensions of information system administration* (pp. 167–198). Hershey, PA: Information Science Reference.

Cherdantseva, Y., & Hilton, J. (2014). The 2011 survey of information security and information assurance professionals: Findings. In I. Portela, & F. Almeida (Eds.), *Organizational, legal, and technological dimensions of information system administration* (pp. 243–256). Hershey, PA: Information Science Reference.

Chowdhury, M. U., & Ray, B. R. (2013). Security risks/vulnerability in a RFID system and possible defenses. In N. Karmakar (Ed.), *Advanced RFID systems, security, and applications* (pp. 1–15). Hershey, PA: Information Science Reference. doi:10.4018/978-1-4666-4707-7.ch084

Cofta, P., Lacohée, H., & Hodgson, P. (2011). Incorporating social trust into design practices for secure systems. In H. Mouratidis (Ed.), *Software engineering for secure systems: Industrial and research perspectives* (pp. 260–284). Hershey, PA: Information Science Reference.

Conway, M. (2012). What is cyberterrorism and how real is the threat? A review of the academic literature, 1996 – 2009. In P. Reich, & E. Gelbstein (Eds.), *Law, policy, and technology: Cyberterrorism, information warfare, and internet immobilization* (pp. 279–307). Hershey, PA: Information Science Reference.

Corser, G. P., Arslanturk, S., Oluoch, J., Fu, H., & Corser, G. E. (2013). Knowing the enemy at the gates: Measuring attacker motivation. [IJITN]. *International Journal of Interdisciplinary Telecommunications and Networking*, *5*(2), 83–95. doi:10.4018/jitn.2013040107

Crosbie, M. (2013). Hack the cloud: Ethical hacking and cloud forensics. In K. Ruan (Ed.), *Cybercrime and cloud forensics: Applications for investigation processes* (pp. 42–58). Hershey, PA: Information Science Reference.

Curran, K., Carlin, S., & Adams, M. (2012). Security issues in cloud computing. In L. Chao (Ed.), *Cloud computing for teaching and learning: Strategies for design and implementation* (pp. 200–208). Hershey, PA: Information Science Reference. doi:10.4018/978-1-4666-0957-0.ch014

Czosseck, C., Ottis, R., & Talihärm, A. (2011). Estonia after the 2007 cyber attacks: Legal, strategic and organisational changes in cyber security. [IJCWT]. *International Journal of Cyber Warfare & Terrorism*, *1*(1), 24–34. doi:10.4018/ijcwt.2011010103

Czosseck, C., & Podins, K. (2012). A vulnerability-based model of cyber weapons and its implications for cyber conflict. [IJCWT]. *International Journal of Cyber Warfare & Terrorism*, *2*(1), 14–26. doi:10.4018/ijcwt.2012010102

da Silva, F. A., Moura, D. F., & Galdino, J. F. (2012). Classes of attacks for tactical software defined radios. [IJERTCS]. *International Journal of Embedded and Real-Time Communication Systems*, *3*(4), 57–82. doi:10.4018/jertcs.2012100104

Dabcevic, K., Marcenaro, L., & Regazzoni, C. S. (2013). Security in cognitive radio networks. In T. Lagkas, P. Sarigiannidis, M. Louta, & P. Chatzimisios (Eds.), *Evolution of cognitive networks and self-adaptive communication systems* (pp. 301–335). Hershey, PA: Information Science Reference. doi:10.4018/978-1-4666-4189-1.ch013

Dahbur, K., Mohammad, B., & Tarakji, A. B. (2013). Security issues in cloud computing: A survey of risks, threats and vulnerabilities. In S. Aljawarneh (Ed.), *Cloud computing advancements in design, implementation, and technologies* (pp. 154–165). Hershey, PA: Information Science Reference.

Dark, M. (2011). Data breach disclosure: A policy analysis. In M. Dark (Ed.), *Information assurance and security ethics in complex systems: Interdisciplinary perspectives* (pp. 226–252). Hershey, PA: Information Science Reference.

Das, S., Mukhopadhyay, A., & Bhasker, B. (2013). Today's action is better than tomorrow's cure - Evaluating information security at a premier indian business school. [JCIT]. *Journal of Cases on Information Technology*, *15*(3), 1–23. doi:10.4018/jcit.2013070101

Dasgupta, D., & Naseem, D. (2014). A framework for compliance and security coverage estimation for cloud services: A cloud insurance model. In S. Srinivasan (Ed.), *Security, trust, and regulatory aspects of cloud computing in business environments* (pp. 91–114). Hershey, PA: Information Science Reference. doi:10.4018/978-1-4666-5788-5.ch005

De Fuentes, J. M., González-Tablas, A. I., & Ribagorda, A. (2011). Overview of security issues in vehicular ad-hoc networks. In M. Cruz-Cunha, & F. Moreira (Eds.), *Handbook of research on mobility and computing: Evolving technologies and ubiquitous impacts* (pp. 894–911). Hershey, PA: Information Science Reference. doi:10.4018/978-1-60960-042-6.ch056

De Groef, W., Devriese, D., Reynaert, T., & Piessens, F. (2013). Security and privacy of online social network applications. In L. Caviglione, M. Coccoli, & A. Merlo (Eds.), *Social network engineering for secure web data and services* (pp. 206–221). Hershey, PA: Information Science Reference. doi:10.4018/978-1-4666-3926-3.ch010

Denning, D. E. (2011). Cyber conflict as an emergent social phenomenon. In T. Holt, & B. Schell (Eds.), *Corporate hacking and technology-driven crime: Social dynamics and implications* (pp. 170–186). Hershey, PA: Information Science Reference.

Desai, A. M., & Mock, K. (2013). Security in cloud computing. In A. Bento, & A. Aggarwal (Eds.), *Cloud computing service and deployment models: Layers and management* (pp. 208–221). Hershey, PA: Business Science Reference.

Dionysiou, I., & Ktoridou, D. (2012). Enhancing dynamic-content courses with student-oriented learning strategies: The case of computer security course. [IJCEE]. *International Journal of Cyber Ethics in Education*, 2(2), 24–33. doi:10.4018/ijcee.2012040103

Disterer, G. (2012). Attacks on IT systems: Categories of motives. In T. Chou (Ed.), *Information assurance and security technologies for risk assessment and threat management: Advances* (pp. 1–16). Hershey, PA: Information Science Reference.

Dougan, T., & Curran, K. (2012). Man in the browser attacks. [IJACI]. *International Journal of Ambient Computing and Intelligence*, 4(1), 29–39. doi:10.4018/jaci.2012010103

Dubey, R., Sharma, S., & Chouhan, L. (2013). Security for cognitive radio networks. In M. Ku, & J. Lin (Eds.), *Cognitive radio and interference management: Technology and strategy* (pp. 238–256). Hershey, PA: Information Science Reference.

Dunkels, E., Frånberg, G., & Hällgren, C. (2011). Young people and online risk. In E. Dunkels, G. Franberg, & C. Hallgren (Eds.), *Youth culture and net culture: Online social practices* (pp. 1–16). Hershey, PA: Information Science Reference.

Dunkerley, K., & Tejay, G. (2012). The development of a model for information systems security success. In Z. Belkhamza, & S. Azizi Wafa (Eds.), *Measuring organizational information systems success: New technologies and practices* (pp. 341–366). Hershey, PA: Business Science Reference. doi:10.4018/978-1-4666-0170-3.ch017

Dunkerley, K., & Tejay, G. (2012). Theorizing information security success: Towards secure e-government. In V. Weerakkody (Ed.), *Technology enabled transformation of the public sector: Advances in e-government* (pp. 224–235). Hershey, PA: Information Science Reference. doi:10.4018/978-1-4666-1776-6.ch014

Eisenga, A., Jones, T. L., & Rodriguez, W. (2012). Investing in IT security: How to determine the maximum threshold. [IJISP]. *International Journal of Information Security and Privacy*, 6(3), 75–87. doi:10.4018/jisp.2012070104

Eyitemi, M. (2012). Regulation of cybercafés in Nigeria. In I. Management Association (Ed.), *Cyber crime: Concepts, methodologies, tools and applications* (pp. 1305-1313). Hershey, PA: Information Science Reference. doi:doi:10.4018/978-1-61350-323-2.ch606

Ezumah, B., & Adekunle, S. O. (2012). A review of privacy, internet security threat, and legislation in Africa: A case study of Nigeria, South Africa, Egypt, and Kenya. In J. Abawajy, M. Pathan, M. Rahman, A. Pathan, & M. Deris (Eds.), *Internet and distributed computing advancements: Theoretical frameworks and practical applications* (pp. 115–136). Hershey, PA: Information Science Reference. doi:10.4018/978-1-4666-0161-1.ch005

Farooq-i-Azam, M., & Ayyaz, M. N. (2014). Embedded systems security. In I. Management Association (Ed.), *Software design and development: Concepts, methodologies, tools, and applications* (pp. 980-998). Hershey, PA: Information Science Reference. doi: doi:10.4018/978-1-4666-4301-7.ch047

Fauzi, A. H., & Taylor, H. (2013). Secure community trust stores for peer-to-peer e-commerce applications using cloud services. [IJEEI]. *International Journal of E-Entrepreneurship and Innovation*, *4*(1), 1–15. doi:10.4018/jeei.2013010101

Fenz, S. (2011). E-business and information security risk management: Challenges and potential solutions. In E. Kajan (Ed.), *Electronic business interoperability: Concepts, opportunities and challenges* (pp. 596–614). Hershey, PA: Business Science Reference. doi:10.4018/978-1-60960-485-1.ch024

Fernandez, E. B., Yoshioka, N., Washizaki, H., Jurjens, J., VanHilst, M., & Pernu, G. (2011). Using security patterns to develop secure systems. In H. Mouratidis (Ed.), *Software engineering for secure systems: Industrial and research perspectives* (pp. 16–31). Hershey, PA: Information Science Reference.

Flores, A. E., Win, K. T., & Susilo, W. (2011). Secure exchange of electronic health records. In A. Chryssanthou, I. Apostolakis, & I. Varlamis (Eds.), *Certification and security in health-related web applications: Concepts and solutions* (pp. 1–22). Hershey, PA: Medical Information Science Reference.

Fonseca, J., & Vieira, M. (2014). A survey on secure software development lifecycles. In I. Management Association (Ed.), Software design and development: Concepts, methodologies, tools, and applications (pp. 17-33). Hershey, PA: Information Science Reference. doi: doi:10.4018/978-1-4666-4301-7.ch002

Fournaris, A. P., Kitsos, P., & Sklavos, N. (2013). Security and cryptographic engineering in embedded systems. In M. Khalgui, O. Mosbahi, & A. Valentini (Eds.), *Embedded computing systems: Applications, optimization, and advanced design* (pp. 420–438). Hershey, PA: Information Science Reference. doi:10.4018/978-1-4666-3922-5.ch021

Franqueira, V. N., van Cleeff, A., van Eck, P., & Wieringa, R. J. (2013). Engineering security agreements against external insider threat. [IRMJ]. *Information Resources Management Journal*, *26*(4), 66–91. doi:10.4018/irmj.2013100104

French, T., Bessis, N., Maple, C., & Asimakopoulou, E. (2012). Trust issues on crowd-sourcing methods for urban environmental monitoring. [IJDST]. *International Journal of Distributed Systems and Technologies*, *3*(1), 35–47. doi:10.4018/jdst.2012010103

Fu, Y., Kulick, J., Yan, L. K., & Drager, S. (2013). Formal modeling and verification of security property in Handel C program. [IJSSE]. *International Journal of Secure Software Engineering*, *3*(3), 50–65. doi:10.4018/jsse.2012070103

Furnell, S., von Solms, R., & Phippen, A. (2011). Preventative actions for enhancing online protection and privacy. [IJITSA]. *International Journal of Information Technologies and Systems Approach*, *4*(2), 1–11. doi:10.4018/jitsa.2011070101

Gaivéo, J. (2011). SMEs e-business security issues. In M. Cruz-Cunha, & J. Varajão (Eds.), *Innovations in SMEs and conducting e-business: Technologies, trends and solutions* (pp. 317–337). Hershey, PA: Business Science Reference. doi:10.4018/978-1-60960-765-4.ch018

Gaivéo, J. M. (2013). Security of ICTs supporting healthcare activities. In M. Cruz-Cunha, I. Miranda, & P. Gonçalves (Eds.), *Handbook of research on ICTs for human-centered healthcare and social care services* (pp. 208–228). Hershey, PA: Medical Information Science Reference. doi:10.4018/978-1-4666-3986-7.ch011

Gelbstein, E. E. (2013). Designing a security audit plan for a critical information infrastructure (CII). In C. Laing, A. Badii, & P. Vickers (Eds.), *Securing critical infrastructures and critical control systems: Approaches for threat protection* (pp. 262–285). Hershey, PA: Information Science Reference.

Gódor, G., & Imre, S. (2012). Security aspects in radio frequency identification systems. In D. Saha, & V. Sridhar (Eds.), *Next generation data communication technologies: Emerging trends* (pp. 187–225). Hershey, PA: Information Science Reference.

Gogolin, G. (2011). Security and privacy concerns of virtual worlds. In B. Ciaramitaro (Ed.), *Virtual worlds and e-commerce: Technologies and applications for building customer relationships* (pp. 244–256). Hershey, PA: Business Science Reference.

Gogoulos, F. I., Antonakopoulou, A., Lioudakis, G. V., Kaklamani, D. I., & Venieris, I. S. (2014). Trust in an enterprise world: A survey. In M. Cruz-Cunha, F. Moreira, & J. Varajão (Eds.), *Handbook of research on enterprise 2.0: Technological, social, and organizational dimensions* (pp. 199–219). Hershey, PA: Business Science Reference.

Goldman, J. E., & Ahuja, S. (2011). Integration of COBIT, balanced scorecard and SSE-CMM as an organizational & strategic information security management (ISM) framework. In M. Quigley (Ed.), *ICT ethics and security in the 21st century: New developments and applications* (pp. 277–309). Hershey, PA: Information Science Reference. doi:10.4018/978-1-60960-573-5.ch014

Goldschmidt, C., Dark, M., & Chaudhry, H. (2011). Responsibility for the harm and risk of software security flaws. In M. Dark (Ed.), *Information assurance and security ethics in complex systems: Interdisciplinary perspectives* (pp. 104–131). Hershey, PA: Information Science Reference.

Grahn, K., Karlsson, J., & Pulkkis, G. (2011). Secure routing and mobility in future IP networks. In M. Cruz-Cunha, & F. Moreira (Eds.), *Handbook of research on mobility and computing: Evolving technologies and ubiquitous impacts* (pp. 952–972). Hershey, PA: Information Science Reference. doi:10.4018/978-1-60960-042-6.ch059

Greitzer, F. L., Frincke, D., & Zabriskie, M. (2011). Social/ethical issues in predictive insider threat monitoring. In M. Dark (Ed.), *Information assurance and security ethics in complex systems: Interdisciplinary perspectives* (pp. 132–161). Hershey, PA: Information Science Reference. doi:10.4018/978-1-61350-323-2.ch506

Grobler, M. (2012). The need for digital evidence standardisation. [IJDCF]. *International Journal of Digital Crime and Forensics, 4*(2), 1–12. doi:10.4018/jdcf.2012040101

Guo, J., Marshall, A., & Zhou, B. (2014). A multi-parameter trust framework for mobile ad hoc networks. In D. Rawat, B. Bista, & G. Yan (Eds.), *Security, privacy, trust, and resource management in mobile and wireless communications* (pp. 245–277). Hershey, PA: Information Science Reference.

Gururajan, R., & Hafeez-Baig, A. (2011). Wireless hand-held device and LAN security issues: A case study. In D. Kerr, J. Gammack, & K. Bryant (Eds.), *Digital business security development: Management technologies* (pp. 129–151). Hershey, PA: Business Science Reference. doi:10.4018/978-1-61350-101-6.ch402

Ha, H. (2012). Online security and consumer protection in ecommerce an Australian case. In K. Mohammed Rezaul (Ed.), *Strategic and pragmatic e-business: Implications for future business practices* (pp. 217–243). Hershey, PA: Business Science Reference. doi:10.4018/978-1-4666-1619-6.ch010

Hagen, J. M. (2012). The contributions of information security culture and human relations to the improvement of situational awareness. In C. Onwubiko, & T. Owens (Eds.), *Situational awareness in computer network defense: Principles, methods and applications* (pp. 10–28). Hershey, PA: Information Science Reference. doi:10.4018/978-1-4666-0104-8.ch002

Hai-Jew, S. (2011). The social design of 3D interactive spaces for security in higher education: A preliminary view. In A. Rea (Ed.), *Security in virtual worlds, 3D webs, and immersive environments: Models for development, interaction, and management* (pp. 72–96). Hershey, PA: Information Science Reference.

Halder, D., & Jaishankar, K. (2012). Cyber crime against women and regulations in Australia. In I. Management Association (Ed.), Cyber crime: Concepts, methodologies, tools and applications (pp. 757-764). Hershey, PA: Information Science Reference. doi: doi:10.4018/978-1-61350-323-2.ch404

Halder, D., & Jaishankar, K. (2012). Cyber victimization of women and cyber laws in India. In I. Management Association (Ed.), Cyber crime: Concepts, methodologies, tools and applications (pp. 742-756). Hershey, PA: Information Science Reference. doi: doi:10.4018/978-1-61350-323-2.ch403

Halder, D., & Jaishankar, K. (2012). Definition, typology and patterns of victimization. In I. Management Association (Ed.), Cyber crime: Concepts, methodologies, tools and applications (pp. 1016-1042). Hershey, PA: Information Science Reference. doi: doi:10.4018/978-1-61350-323-2.ch502

Hamlen, K., Kantarcioglu, M., Khan, L., & Thuraisingham, B. (2012). Security issues for cloud computing. In H. Nemati (Ed.), *Optimizing information security and advancing privacy assurance: New technologies* (pp. 150–162). Hershey, PA: Information Science Reference.

Harnesk, D. (2011). Convergence of information security in B2B networks. In E. Kajan (Ed.), *Electronic business interoperability: Concepts, opportunities and challenges* (pp. 571–595). Hershey, PA: Business Science Reference. doi:10.4018/978-1-60960-485-1.ch023

Harnesk, D., & Hartikainen, H. (2011). Multi-layers of information security in emergency response. [IJISCRAM]. *International Journal of Information Systems for Crisis Response and Management*, *3*(2), 1–17. doi:10.4018/jiscrm.2011040101

Hawrylak, P. J., Hale, J., & Papa, M. (2013). Security issues for ISO 18000-6 type C RFID: Identification and solutions. In I. Association (Ed.), *Supply chain management: Concepts, methodologies, tools, and applications* (pp. 1565–1581). Hershey, PA: Business Science Reference.

He, B., Tran, T. T., & Xie, B. (2014). Authentication and identity management for secure cloud businesses and services. In S. Srinivasan (Ed.), *Security, trust, and regulatory aspects of cloud computing in business environments* (pp. 180–201). Hershey, PA: Information Science Reference. doi:10.4018/978-1-4666-5788-5.ch011

Henrie, M. (2012). Cyber security in liquid petroleum pipelines. In J. Zubairi, & A. Mahboob (Eds.), *Cyber security standards, practices and industrial applications: Systems and methodologies* (pp. 200–222). Hershey, PA: Information Science Reference.

Herath, T., Rao, H. R., & Upadhyaya, S. (2012). Internet crime: How vulnerable are you? Do gender, social influence and education play a role in vulnerability? In I. Management Association (Ed.), Cyber crime: Concepts, methodologies, tools and applications (pp. 1-13). Hershey, PA: Information Science Reference. doi:doi:10.4018/978-1-61350-323-2.ch101

Hilmi, M. F., Pawanchik, S., Mustapha, Y., & Ali, H. M. (2013). Information security perspective of a learning management system: An exploratory study. [IJKSR]. *International Journal of Knowledge Society Research*, *4*(2), 9–18. doi:10.4018/jksr.2013040102

Hommel, W. (2012). Security and privacy management for learning management systems. In I. Management Association (Ed.), Virtual learning environments: Concepts, methodologies, tools and applications (pp. 1151-1170). Hershey, PA: Information Science Reference. doi:doi:10.4018/978-1-4666-0011-9.ch602

Hoops, D. S. (2012). Lost in cyberspace: Navigating the legal issues of e-commerce. [JECO]. *Journal of Electronic Commerce in Organizations*, *10*(1), 33–51. doi:10.4018/jeco.2012010103

Houmb, S., Georg, G., Petriu, D., Bordbar, B., Ray, I., Anastasakis, K., & France, R. (2011). Balancing security and performance properties during system architectural design. In H. Mouratidis (Ed.), *Software engineering for secure systems: Industrial and research perspectives* (pp. 155–191). Hershey, PA: Information Science Reference.

Huang, E., & Cheng, F. (2012). Online security cues and e-payment continuance intention. [IJEEI]. *International Journal of E-Entrepreneurship and Innovation*, *3*(1), 42–58. doi:10.4018/jeei.2012010104

Ifinedo, P. (2011). Relationships between information security concerns and national cultural dimensions: Findings in the global financial services industry. In H. Nemati (Ed.), *Security and privacy assurance in advancing technologies: New developments* (pp. 134–153). Hershey, PA: Information Science Reference.

Inden, U., Lioudakis, G., & Rückemann, C. (2013). Awareness-based security management for complex and internet-based operations management systems. In C. Rückemann (Ed.), *Integrated information and computing systems for natural, spatial, and social sciences* (pp. 43–73). Hershey, PA: Information Science Reference.

Islam, S., Mouratidis, H., Kalloniatis, C., Hudic, A., & Zechner, L. (2013). Model based process to support security and privacy requirements engineering. [IJSSE]. *International Journal of Secure Software Engineering*, *3*(3), 1–22. doi:10.4018/jsse.2012070101

Itani, W., Kayssi, A., & Chehab, A. (2012). Security and privacy in body sensor networks: Challenges, solutions, and research directions. In M. Watfa (Ed.), *E-healthcare systems and wireless communications: Current and future challenges* (pp. 100–127). Hershey, PA: Medical Information Science Reference.

Jansen van Vuuren, J., Grobler, M., & Zaaiman, J. (2012). Cyber security awareness as critical driver to national security. [IJCWT]. *International Journal of Cyber Warfare & Terrorism, 2*(1), 27–38. doi:10.4018/ijcwt.2012010103

Jansen van Vuuren, J., Leenen, L., Phahlamohlaka, J., & Zaaiman, J. (2012). An approach to governance of CyberSecurity in South Africa. [IJCWT]. *International Journal of Cyber Warfare & Terrorism, 2*(4), 13–27. doi:10.4018/ijcwt.2012100102

Jensen, J., & Groep, D. L. (2012). Security and trust in a global research infrastructure. In J. Leng, & W. Sharrock (Eds.), *Handbook of research on computational science and engineering: Theory and practice* (pp. 539–566). Hershey, PA: Engineering Science Reference.

Johnsen, S. O. (2014). Safety and security in SCADA systems must be improved through resilience based risk management. In I. Management Association (Ed.), Crisis management: Concepts, methodologies, tools and applications (pp. 1422-1436). Hershey, PA: Information Science Reference. doi: doi:10.4018/978-1-4666-4707-7.ch071

Johnston, A. C., Wech, B., & Jack, E. (2012). Engaging remote employees: The moderating role of "remote" status in determining employee information security policy awareness. [JOEUC]. *Journal of Organizational and End User Computing, 25*(1), 1–23. doi:10.4018/joeuc.2013010101

Jung, C., Rudolph, M., & Schwarz, R. (2013). Security evaluation of service-oriented systems using the SiSOA method. In K. Khan (Ed.), *Developing and evaluating security-aware software systems* (pp. 20–35). Hershey, PA: Information Science Reference.

Kaiya, H., Sakai, J., Ogata, S., & Kaijiri, K. (2013). Eliciting security requirements for an information system using asset flows and processor deployment. [IJSSE]. *International Journal of Secure Software Engineering, 4*(3), 42–63. doi:10.4018/jsse.2013070103

Kalloniatis, C., Kavakli, E., & Gritzalis, S. (2011). Designing privacy aware information systems. In H. Mouratidis (Ed.), *Software engineering for secure systems: Industrial and research perspectives* (pp. 212–231). Hershey, PA: Information Science Reference.

Kamoun, F., & Halaweh, M. (2012). User interface design and e-commerce security perception: An empirical study. [IJEBR]. *International Journal of E-Business Research, 8*(2), 15–32. doi:10.4018/jebr.2012040102

Kamruzzaman, J., Azad, A. K., Karmakar, N. C., Karmakar, G., & Srinivasan, B. (2013). Security and privacy in RFID systems. In N. Karmakar (Ed.), *Advanced RFID systems, security, and applications* (pp. 16–40). Hershey, PA: Information Science Reference.

Kaosar, M. G., & Yi, X. (2011). Privacy preserving data gathering in wireless sensor network. In D. Kar, & M. Syed (Eds.), *Network security, administration and management: Advancing technology and practice* (pp. 237–251). Hershey, PA: Information Science Reference. doi:10.4018/978-1-60960-777-7.ch012

Kar, D. C., Ngo, H. L., Mulkey, C. J., & Sanapala, G. (2011). Advances in security and privacy in wireless sensor networks. In H. Nemati (Ed.), *Security and privacy assurance in advancing technologies: New developments* (pp. 186–213). Hershey, PA: Information Science Reference. doi:10.4018/978-1-61350-101-6.ch810

Karadsheh, L., & Alhawari, S. (2011). Applying security policies in small business utilizing cloud computing technologies. [IJCAC]. *International Journal of Cloud Applications and Computing, 1*(2), 29–40. doi:10.4018/ijcac.2011040103

Karokola, G., Yngström, L., & Kowalski, S. (2012). Secure e-government services: A comparative analysis of e-government maturity models for the developing regions–The need for security services. [IJEGR]. *International Journal of Electronic Government Research, 8*(1), 1–25. doi:10.4018/jegr.2012010101

Kassim, N. M., & Ramayah, T. (2013). Security policy issues in internet banking in Malaysia. In I. Management Association (Ed.), IT policy and ethics: Concepts, methodologies, tools, and applications (pp. 1274-1293). Hershey, PA: Information Science Reference. doi: doi:10.4018/978-1-4666-2919-6.ch057

Kayem, A. V. (2013). Security in service oriented architectures: Standards and challenges. In I. Association (Ed.), *Digital rights management: Concepts, methodologies, tools, and applications* (pp. 50–73). Hershey, PA: Information Science Reference.

K.C, A., Forsgren, H., Grahn, K., Karvi, T., & Pulkkis, G. (2013). Security and trust of public key cryptography for HIP and HIP multicast. [IJDTIS]. *International Journal of Dependable and Trustworthy Information Systems*, 2(3), 17–35. doi: doi:10.4018/jdtis.2011070102

Kelarev, A. V., Brown, S., Watters, P., Wu, X., & Dazeley, R. (2011). Establishing reasoning communities of security experts for internet commerce security. In J. Yearwood, & A. Stranieri (Eds.), *Technologies for supporting reasoning communities and collaborative decision making: Cooperative approaches* (pp. 380–396). Hershey, PA: Information Science Reference.

Kerr, D., Gammack, J. G., & Boddington, R. (2011). Overview of digital business security issues. In D. Kerr, J. Gammack, & K. Bryant (Eds.), *Digital business security development: Management technologies* (pp. 1–36). Hershey, PA: Business Science Reference.

Khan, K. M. (2011). A decision support system for selecting secure web services. In I. Management Association (Ed.), Enterprise information systems: Concepts, methodologies, tools and applications (pp. 1113-1120). Hershey, PA: Business Science Reference. doi: doi:10.4018/978-1-61692-852-0.ch415

Khan, K. M. (2012). Software security engineering: Design and applications. [IJSSE]. *International Journal of Secure Software Engineering*, 3(1), 62–63. doi:10.4018/jsse.2012010104

Kilger, M. (2011). Social dynamics and the future of technology-driven crime. In T. Holt, & B. Schell (Eds.), *Corporate hacking and technology-driven crime: Social dynamics and implications* (pp. 205–227). Hershey, PA: Information Science Reference.

Kirwan, G., & Power, A. (2012). Hacking: Legal and ethical aspects of an ambiguous activity. In A. Dudley, J. Braman, & G. Vincenti (Eds.), *Investigating cyber law and cyber ethics: Issues, impacts and practices* (pp. 21–36). Hershey, PA: Information Science Reference.

Kline, D. M., He, L., & Yaylacicegi, U. (2011). User perceptions of security technologies. [IJISP]. *International Journal of Information Security and Privacy*, 5(2), 1–12. doi:10.4018/jisp.2011040101

Kolkowska, E., Hedström, K., & Karlsson, F. (2012). Analyzing information security goals. In M. Gupta, J. Walp, & R. Sharman (Eds.), *Threats, countermeasures, and advances in applied information security* (pp. 91–110). Hershey, PA: Information Science Reference. doi:10.4018/978-1-4666-0978-5.ch005

Korhonen, J. J., Hiekkanen, K., & Mykkänen, J. (2012). Information security governance. In M. Gupta, J. Walp, & R. Sharman (Eds.), *Strategic and practical approaches for information security governance: Technologies and applied solutions* (pp. 53–66). Hershey, PA: Information Science Reference. doi:10.4018/978-1-4666-0197-0.ch004

Korovessis, P. (2011). Information security awareness in academia. [IJKSR]. *International Journal of Knowledge Society Research*, 2(4), 1–17. doi:10.4018/jksr.2011100101

Koskosas, I., & Sariannidis, N. (2011). Project commitment in the context of information security. [IJITPM]. *International Journal of Information Technology Project Management*, 2(3), 17–29. doi:10.4018/jitpm.2011070102

Kotsonis, E., & Eliakis, S. (2013). Information security standards for health information systems: The implementer's approach. In I. Management Association (Ed.), User-driven healthcare: Concepts, methodologies, tools, and applications (pp. 225-257). Hershey, PA: Medical Information Science Reference. doi: doi:10.4018/978-1-4666-2770-3.ch013

Krishna, A. V. (2014). A randomized cloud library security environment. In S. Dhamdhere (Ed.), *Cloud computing and virtualization technologies in libraries* (pp. 278–296). Hershey, PA: Information Science Reference.

Kruck, S. E., & Teer, F. P. (2011). Computer security practices and perceptions of the next generation of corporate computer users. In H. Nemati (Ed.), *Pervasive information security and privacy developments: Trends and advancements* (pp. 255–265). Hershey, PA: Information Science Reference.

Kumar, M., Sareen, M., & Chhabra, S. (2011). Technology related trust issues in SME B2B E-Commerce. [IJICTHD]. *International Journal of Information Communication Technologies and Human Development*, 3(4), 31–46. doi:10.4018/jicthd.2011100103

Kumar, P., & Mittal, S. (2012). The perpetration and prevention of cyber crime: An analysis of cyber terrorism in India. [IJT]. *International Journal of Technoethics*, *3*(1), 43–52. doi:10.4018/jte.2012010104

Kumar, P. S., Ashok, M. S., & Subramanian, R. (2012). A publicly verifiable dynamic secret sharing protocol for secure and dependable data storage in cloud computing. [IJCAC]. *International Journal of Cloud Applications and Computing*, *2*(3), 1–25. doi:10.4018/ijcac.2012070101

Kumar, S., & Dutta, K. (2014). Security issues in mobile ad hoc networks: A survey. In D. Rawat, B. Bista, & G. Yan (Eds.), *Security, privacy, trust, and resource management in mobile and wireless communications* (pp. 176–221). Hershey, PA: Information Science Reference.

Lawson, S. (2013). Motivating cybersecurity: Assessing the status of critical infrastructure as an object of cyber threats. In C. Laing, A. Badii, & P. Vickers (Eds.), *Securing critical infrastructures and critical control systems: Approaches for threat protection* (pp. 168–189). Hershey, PA: Information Science Reference.

Leitch, S., & Warren, M. (2011). The ethics of security of personal information upon Facebook. In M. Quigley (Ed.), *ICT ethics and security in the 21st century: New developments and applications* (pp. 46–65). Hershey, PA: Information Science Reference. doi:10.4018/978-1-60960-573-5.ch003

Li, M. (2013). Security terminology. In A. Miri (Ed.), *Advanced security and privacy for RFID technologies* (pp. 1–13). Hershey, PA: Information Science Reference. doi:10.4018/978-1-4666-3685-9.ch001

Ligaarden, O. S., Refsdal, A., & Stølen, K. (2013). Using indicators to monitor security risk in systems of systems: How to capture and measure the impact of service dependencies on the security of provided services. In D. Mellado, L. Enrique Sánchez, E. Fernández-Medina, & M. Piattini (Eds.), *IT security governance innovations: Theory and research* (pp. 256–292). Hershey, PA: Information Science Reference.

Lim, J. S., Chang, S., Ahmad, A., & Maynard, S. (2012). Towards an organizational culture framework for information security practices. In M. Gupta, J. Walp, & R. Sharman (Eds.), *Strategic and practical approaches for information security governance: Technologies and applied solutions* (pp. 296–315). Hershey, PA: Information Science Reference. doi:10.4018/978-1-4666-0197-0.ch017

Lin, X., & Luppicini, R. (2011). Socio-technical influences of cyber espionage: A case study of the GhostNet system. [IJT]. *International Journal of Technoethics*, *2*(2), 65–77. doi:10.4018/jte.2011040105

Lindström, J., & Hanken, C. (2012). Security challenges and selected legal aspects for wearable computing. [JITR]. *Journal of Information Technology Research*, *5*(1), 68–87. doi:10.4018/jitr.2012010104

Maheshwari, H., Hyman, H., & Agrawal, M. (2012). A comparison of cyber-crime definitions in India and the United States. In I. Management Association (Ed.), Cyber crime: Concepts, methodologies, tools and applications (pp. 714-726). Hershey, PA: Information Science Reference. doi: doi:10.4018/978-1-61350-323-2.ch401

Malcolmson, J. (2014). The role of security culture. In I. Portela, & F. Almeida (Eds.), *Organizational, legal, and technological dimensions of information system administration* (pp. 225–242). Hershey, PA: Information Science Reference.

Mantas, G., Lymberopoulos, D., & Komninos, N. (2011). Security in smart home environment. In A. Lazakidou, K. Siassiakos, & K. Ioannou (Eds.), *Wireless technologies for ambient assisted living and healthcare: Systems and applications* (pp. 170–191). Hershey, PA: Medical Information Science Reference.

Maple, C., Short, E., Brown, A., Bryden, C., & Salter, M. (2012). Cyberstalking in the UK: Analysis and recommendations. [IJDST]. *International Journal of Distributed Systems and Technologies*, *3*(4), 34–51. doi:10.4018/jdst.2012100104

Maqousi, A., & Balikhina, T. (2011). Building security awareness culture to serve e-government initiative. In A. Al Ajeeli, & Y. Al-Bastaki (Eds.), *Handbook of research on e-services in the public sector: E-government strategies and advancements* (pp. 304–311). Hershey, PA: Information Science Reference.

Martin, N., & Rice, J. (2013). Spearing high net wealth individuals: The case of online fraud and mature age internet users. [IJISP]. *International Journal of Information Security and Privacy, 7*(1), 1–15. doi:10.4018/jisp.2013010101

Martino, L., & Bertino, E. (2012). Security for web services: Standards and research issues. In L. Jie-Zhang (Ed.), *Innovations, standards and practices of web services: Emerging research topics* (pp. 336–362). Hershey, PA: Information Science Reference.

Massonet, P., Michot, A., Naqvi, S., Villari, M., & Latanicki, J. (2013). Securing the external interfaces of a federated infrastructure cloud. In I. Management Association (Ed.), IT policy and ethics: Concepts, methodologies, tools, and applications (pp. 1876-1903). Hershey, PA: Information Science Reference. doi: doi:10.4018/978-1-4666-2919-6.ch082

Maumbe, B., & Owei, V. T. (2013). Understanding the information security landscape in South Africa: Implications for strategic collaboration and policy development. In B. Maumbe, & C. Patrikakis (Eds.), *E-agriculture and rural development: Global innovations and future prospects* (pp. 90–102). Hershey, PA: Information Science Reference.

Mazumdar, C. (2011). Enterprise information system security: A life-cycle approach. In I. Management Association (Ed.), Enterprise information systems: Concepts, methodologies, tools and applications (pp. 154-168). Hershey, PA: Business Science Reference. doi: doi:10.4018/978-1-61692-852-0.ch111

McCune, J., & Haworth, D. A. (2012). Securing America against cyber war. [IJCWT]. *International Journal of Cyber Warfare & Terrorism, 2*(1), 39–49. doi:10.4018/ijcwt.2012010104

Melvin, A. O., & Ayotunde, T. (2011). Spirituality in cybercrime (Yahoo Yahoo) activities among youths in south west Nigeria. In E. Dunkels, G. Franberg, & C. Hallgren (Eds.), *Youth culture and net culture: Online social practices* (pp. 357–380). Hershey, PA: Information Science Reference.

Miller, J. M., Higgins, G. E., & Lopez, K. M. (2013). Considering the role of e-government in cybercrime awareness and prevention: Toward a theoretical research program for the 21st century. In I. Association (Ed.), *Digital rights management: Concepts, methodologies, tools, and applications* (pp. 789–800). Hershey, PA: Information Science Reference.

Millman, C., Whitty, M., Winder, B., & Griffiths, M. D. (2012). Perceived criminality of cyber-harassing behaviors among undergraduate students in the United Kingdom. [IJCBPL]. *International Journal of Cyber Behavior, Psychology and Learning, 2*(4), 49–59. doi:10.4018/ijcbpl.2012100104

Minami, N. A. (2012). Employing dynamic models to enhance corporate IT security policy. [IJATS]. *International Journal of Agent Technologies and Systems, 4*(2), 42–59. doi:10.4018/jats.2012040103

Mirante, D. P., & Ammari, H. M. (2014). Wireless sensor network security attacks: A survey. In I. Management Association (Ed.), Crisis management: Concepts, methodologies, tools and applications (pp. 25-59). Hershey, PA: Information Science Reference. doi: doi:10.4018/978-1-4666-4707-7.ch002

Mishra, A., & Mishra, D. (2013). Cyber stalking: A challenge for web security. In J. Bishop (Ed.), *Examining the concepts, issues, and implications of internet trolling* (pp. 32–42). Hershey, PA: Information Science Reference. doi:10.4018/978-1-4666-2803-8.ch004

Mishra, S. (2011). Wireless sensor networks: Emerging applications and security solutions. In D. Kar, & M. Syed (Eds.), *Network security, administration and management: Advancing technology and practice* (pp. 217–236). Hershey, PA: Information Science Reference. doi:10.4018/978-1-60960-777-7.ch011

Mitra, S., & Padman, R. (2012). Privacy and security concerns in adopting social media for personal health management: A health plan case study. [JCIT]. *Journal of Cases on Information Technology, 14*(4), 12–26. doi:10.4018/jcit.2012100102

Modares, H., Lloret, J., Moravejosharieh, A., & Salleh, R. (2014). Security in mobile cloud computing. In J. Rodrigues, K. Lin, & J. Lloret (Eds.), *Mobile networks and cloud computing convergence for progressive services and applications* (pp. 79–91). Hershey, PA: Information Science Reference.

Mohammadi, S., Golara, S., & Mousavi, N. (2012). Selecting adequate security mechanisms in e-business processes using fuzzy TOPSIS. [IJFSA]. *International Journal of Fuzzy System Applications, 2*(1), 35–53. doi:10.4018/ijfsa.2012010103

Mohammed, L. A. (2012). ICT security policy: Challenges and potential remedies. In I. Management Association (Ed.), Cyber crime: Concepts, methodologies, tools and applications (pp. 999-1015). Hershey, PA: Information Science Reference. doi: doi:10.4018/978-1-61350-323-2.ch501

Molok, N. N., Ahmad, A., & Chang, S. (2012). Online social networking: A source of intelligence for advanced persistent threats. [IJCWT]. *International Journal of Cyber Warfare & Terrorism, 2*(1), 1–13. doi:10.4018/ijcwt.2012010101

Monteleone, S. (2011). Ambient intelligence: Legal challenges and possible directions for privacy protection. In C. Akrivopoulou, & A. Psygkas (Eds.), *Personal data privacy and protection in a surveillance era: Technologies and practices* (pp. 201–221). Hershey, PA: Information Science Reference.

Moralis, A., Pouli, V., Grammatikou, M., Kalogeras, D., & Maglaris, V. (2012). Security standards and issues for grid computing. In N. Preve (Ed.), *Computational and data grids: Principles, applications and design* (pp. 248–264). Hershey, PA: Information Science Reference. doi:10.4018/978-1-4666-0879-5.ch708

Mouratidis, H., & Kang, M. (2011). Secure by design: Developing secure software systems from the ground up. [IJSSE]. *International Journal of Secure Software Engineering, 2*(3), 23–41. doi:10.4018/jsse.2011070102

Murthy, A. S., Nagadevara, V., & De', R. (2012). Predictive models in cybercrime investigation: An application of data mining techniques. In J. Wang (Ed.), *Advancing the service sector with evolving technologies: Techniques and principles* (pp. 166–177). Hershey, PA: Business Science Reference. doi:10.4018/978-1-4666-0044-7.ch011

Nabi, S. I., Al-Ghmlas, G. S., & Alghathbar, K. (2012). Enterprise information security policies, standards, and procedures: A survey of available standards and guidelines. In M. Gupta, J. Walp, & R. Sharman (Eds.), *Strategic and practical approaches for information security governance: Technologies and applied solutions* (pp. 67–89). Hershey, PA: Information Science Reference. doi:10.4018/978-1-4666-0197-0.ch005

Nachtigal, S. (2011). E-business and security. In O. Bak, & N. Stair (Eds.), *Impact of e-business technologies on public and private organizations: Industry comparisons and perspectives* (pp. 262–277). Hershey, PA: Business Science Reference. doi:10.4018/978-1-60960-501-8.ch016

Namal, S., & Gurtov, A. (2012). Security and mobility aspects of femtocell networks. In R. Saeed, B. Chaudhari, & R. Mokhtar (Eds.), *Femtocell communications and technologies: Business opportunities and deployment challenges* (pp. 124–156). Hershey, PA: Information Science Reference. doi:10.4018/978-1-4666-0092-8.ch008

Naqvi, D. E. (2011). Designing efficient security services infrastructure for virtualization oriented architectures. In H. Nemati (Ed.), *Pervasive information security and privacy developments: Trends and advancements* (pp. 149–171). Hershey, PA: Information Science Reference.

Neto, A. A., & Vieira, M. (2011). Security gaps in databases: A comparison of alternative software products for web applications support. [IJSSE]. *International Journal of Secure Software Engineering, 2*(3), 42–62. doi:10.4018/jsse.2011070103

Ngugi, B., Mana, J., & Segal, L. (2011). Evaluating the quality and usefulness of data breach information systems. [IJISP]. *International Journal of Information Security and Privacy, 5*(4), 31–46. doi:10.4018/jisp.2011100103

Nhlabatsi, A., Bandara, A., Hayashi, S., Haley, C., Jurjens, J., & Kaiya, H. … Yu, Y. (2011). Security patterns: Comparing modeling approaches. In H. Mouratidis (Ed.), Software engineering for secure systems: Industrial and research perspectives (pp. 75-111). Hershey, PA: Information Science Reference. doi: doi:10.4018/978-1-61520-837-1.ch004

Nicho, M. (2013). An information governance model for information security management. In D. Mellado, L. Enrique Sánchez, E. Fernández-Medina, & M. Piattini (Eds.), *IT security governance innovations: Theory and research* (pp. 155–189). Hershey, PA: Information Science Reference.

Nicho, M., Fakhry, H., & Haiber, C. (2011). An integrated security governance framework for effective PCI DSS implementation. [IJISP]. *International Journal of Information Security and Privacy*, 5(3), 50–67. doi:10.4018/jisp.2011070104

Nobelis, N., Boudaoud, K., Delettre, C., & Riveill, M. (2012). Designing security properties-centric communication protocols using a component-based approach. [IJDST]. *International Journal of Distributed Systems and Technologies*, 3(1), 1–16. doi:10.4018/jdst.2012010101

Ohashi, M., & Hori, M. (2011). Security management services based on authentication roaming between different certificate authorities. In M. Cruz-Cunha, & J. Varajao (Eds.), *Enterprise information systems design, implementation and management: Organizational applications* (pp. 72–84). Hershey, PA: Information Science Reference.

Okubo, T., Kaiya, H., & Yoshioka, N. (2012). Analyzing impacts on software enhancement caused by security design alternatives with patterns. [IJSSE]. *International Journal of Secure Software Engineering*, 3(1), 37–61. doi:10.4018/jsse.2012010103

Oost, D., & Chew, E. K. (2012). Investigating the concept of information security culture. In M. Gupta, J. Walp, & R. Sharman (Eds.), *Strategic and practical approaches for information security governance: Technologies and applied solutions* (pp. 1–12). Hershey, PA: Information Science Reference. doi:10.4018/978-1-4666-0197-0.ch001

Otero, A. R., Ejnioui, A., Otero, C. E., & Tejay, G. (2013). Evaluation of information security controls in organizations by grey relational analysis. [IJDTIS]. *International Journal of Dependable and Trustworthy Information Systems*, 2(3), 36–54. doi:10.4018/jdtis.2011070103

Ouedraogo, M., Mouratidis, H., Dubois, E., & Khadraoui, D. (2011). Security assurance evaluation and IT systems' context of use security criticality. [IJHCR]. *International Journal of Handheld Computing Research*, 2(4), 59–81. doi:10.4018/jhcr.2011100104

Pal, S. (2013). Cloud computing: Security concerns and issues. In A. Bento, & A. Aggarwal (Eds.), *Cloud computing service and deployment models: Layers and management* (pp. 191–207). Hershey, PA: Business Science Reference.

Palanisamy, R., & Mukerji, B. (2012). Security and privacy issues in e-government. In M. Shareef, N. Archer, & S. Dutta (Eds.), *E-government service maturity and development: Cultural, organizational and technological perspectives* (pp. 236–248). Hershey, PA: Information Science Reference.

Pan, Y., Yuan, B., & Mishra, S. (2011). Network security auditing. In D. Kar, & M. Syed (Eds.), *Network security, administration and management: Advancing technology and practice* (pp. 131–157). Hershey, PA: Information Science Reference. doi:10.4018/978-1-60960-777-7.ch008

Patel, A., Taghavi, M., Júnior, J. C., Latih, R., & Zin, A. M. (2012). Safety measures for social computing in wiki learning environment. [IJISP]. *International Journal of Information Security and Privacy*, 6(2), 1–15. doi:10.4018/jisp.2012040101

Pathan, A. K. (2012). Security management in heterogeneous distributed sensor networks. In S. Bagchi (Ed.), *Ubiquitous multimedia and mobile agents: Models and implementations* (pp. 274–294). Hershey, PA: Information Science Reference.

Paul, C., & Porche, I. R. (2011). Toward a U.S. army cyber security culture. [IJCWT]. *International Journal of Cyber Warfare & Terrorism*, 1(3), 70–80. doi:10.4018/ijcwt.2011070105

Pavlidis, M., Mouratidis, H., & Islam, S. (2012). Modelling security using trust based concepts. [IJSSE]. *International Journal of Secure Software Engineering, 3*(2), 36–53. doi:10.4018/jsse.2012040102

Pendegraft, N., Rounds, M., & Stone, R. W. (2012). Factors influencing college students' use of computer security. In H. Nemati (Ed.), *Optimizing information security and advancing privacy assurance: New technologies* (pp. 225–234). Hershey, PA: Information Science Reference.

Petkovic, M., & Ibraimi, L. (2011). Privacy and security in e-health applications. In C. Röcker, & M. Ziefle (Eds.), *E-health, assistive technologies and applications for assisted living: Challenges and solutions* (pp. 23–48). Hershey, PA: Medical Information Science Reference. doi:10.4018/978-1-60960-469-1.ch002

Picazo-Sanchez, P., Ortiz-Martin, L., Peris-Lopez, P., & Hernandez-Castro, J. C. (2013). Security of EPC class-1. In P. Lopez, J. Hernandez-Castro, & T. Li (Eds.), *Security and trends in wireless identification and sensing platform tags: Advancements in RFID* (pp. 34–63). Hershey, PA: Information Science Reference.

Pieters, W., Probst, C. W., Lukszo, Z., & Montoya, L. (2014). Cost-effectiveness of security measures: A model-based framework. In T. Tsiakis, T. Kargidis, & P. Katsaros (Eds.), *Approaches and processes for managing the economics of information systems* (pp. 139–156). Hershey, PA: Business Science Reference. doi:10.4018/978-1-4666-4983-5.ch009

Pirim, T., James, T., Boswell, K., Reithel, B., & Barkhi, R. (2011). Examining an individual's perceived need for privacy and security: Construct and scale development. In H. Nemati (Ed.), *Pervasive information security and privacy developments: Trends and advancements* (pp. 1–13). Hershey, PA: Information Science Reference.

Podhradsky, A., Casey, C., & Ceretti, P. (2012). The bluetooth honeypot project: Measuring and managing bluetooth risks in the workplace. [IJITN]. *International Journal of Interdisciplinary Telecommunications and Networking, 4*(3), 1–22. doi:10.4018/jitn.2012070101

Pomponiu, V. (2011). Security in e-health applications. In C. Röcker, & M. Ziefle (Eds.), *E-health, assistive technologies and applications for assisted living: Challenges and solutions* (pp. 94–118). Hershey, PA: Medical Information Science Reference. doi:10.4018/978-1-60960-469-1.ch005

Pomponiu, V. (2014). Securing wireless ad hoc networks: State of the art and challenges. In I. Management Association (Ed.), Crisis management: Concepts, methodologies, tools and applications (pp. 81-101). Hershey, PA: Information Science Reference. doi: doi:10.4018/978-1-4666-4707-7.ch004

Pope, M. B., Warkentin, M., & Luo, X. R. (2012). Evolutionary malware: Mobile malware, botnets, and malware toolkits. [IJWNBT]. *International Journal of Wireless Networks and Broadband Technologies, 2*(3), 52–60. doi:10.4018/ijwnbt.2012070105

Prakash, S., Vaish, A., & Coul, N., G, S., Srinidhi, T., & Botsa, J. (2013). Child security in cyberspace through moral cognition. [IJISP]. *International Journal of Information Security and Privacy, 7*(1), 16–29. doi:10.4018/jisp.2013010102

Pye, G. (2011). Critical infrastructure systems: Security analysis and modelling approach. [IJCWT]. *International Journal of Cyber Warfare & Terrorism, 1*(3), 37–58. doi:10.4018/ijcwt.2011070103

Rahman, M. M., & Rezaul, K. M. (2012). Information security management: Awareness of threats in e-commerce. In M. Gupta, J. Walp, & R. Sharman (Eds.), *Threats, countermeasures, and advances in applied information security* (pp. 66–90). Hershey, PA: Information Science Reference. doi:10.4018/978-1-4666-0978-5.ch004

Rak, M., Ficco, M., Luna, J., Ghani, H., Suri, N., Panica, S., & Petcu, D. (2012). Security issues in cloud federations. In M. Villari, I. Brandic, & F. Tusa (Eds.), *Achieving federated and self-manageable cloud infrastructures: Theory and practice* (pp. 176–194). Hershey, PA: Business Science Reference. doi:10.4018/978-1-4666-1631-8.ch010

Ramachandran, M., & Mahmood, Z. (2011). A framework for internet security assessment and improvement process. In M. Ramachandran (Ed.), *Knowledge engineering for software development life cycles: Support technologies and applications* (pp. 244–255). Hershey, PA: Information Science Reference. doi:10.4018/978-1-60960-509-4.ch013

Ramachandran, S., Mundada, R., Bhattacharjee, A., Murthy, C., & Sharma, R. (2011). Classifying host anomalies: Using ontology in information security monitoring. In R. Santanam, M. Sethumadhavan, & M. Virendra (Eds.), *Cyber security, cyber crime and cyber forensics: Applications and perspectives* (pp. 70–86). Hershey, PA: Information Science Reference.

Ramamurthy, B. (2014). Securing business IT on the cloud. In S. Srinivasan (Ed.), *Security, trust, and regulatory aspects of cloud computing in business environments* (pp. 115–125). Hershey, PA: Information Science Reference. doi:10.4018/978-1-4666-5788-5.ch006

Raspotnig, C., & Opdahl, A. L. (2012). Improving security and safety modelling with failure sequence diagrams. [IJSSE]. *International Journal of Secure Software Engineering*, *3*(1), 20–36. doi:10.4018/jsse.2012010102

Reddy, A., & Prasad, G. V. (2012). Consumer perceptions on security, privacy, and trust on e-portals. [IJOM]. *International Journal of Online Marketing*, *2*(2), 10–24. doi:10.4018/ijom.2012040102

Richet, J. (2013). From young hackers to crackers. [IJTHI]. *International Journal of Technology and Human Interaction*, *9*(3), 53–62. doi:10.4018/jthi.2013070104

Rjaibi, N., Rabai, L. B., Ben Aissa, A., & Mili, A. (2013). Mean failure cost as a measurable value and evidence of cybersecurity: E-learning case study. [IJSSE]. *International Journal of Secure Software Engineering*, *4*(3), 64–81. doi:10.4018/jsse.2013070104

Roberts, L. D. (2012). Cyber identity theft. In I. Management Association (Ed.), Cyber crime: Concepts, methodologies, tools and applications (pp. 21-36). Hershey, PA: Information Science Reference. doi: doi:10.4018/978-1-61350-323-2.ch103

Rodríguez, J., Fernández-Medina, E., Piattini, M., & Mellado, D. (2011). A security requirements engineering tool for domain engineering in software product lines. In N. Milanovic (Ed.), *Non-functional properties in service oriented architecture: Requirements, models and methods* (pp. 73–92). Hershey, PA: Information Science Reference. doi:10.4018/978-1-60566-794-2.ch004

Roldan, M., & Rea, A. (2011). Individual privacy and security in virtual worlds. In A. Rea (Ed.), *Security in virtual worlds, 3D webs, and immersive environments: Models for development, interaction, and management* (pp. 1–19). Hershey, PA: Information Science Reference.

Rowe, N. C., Garfinkel, S. L., Beverly, R., & Yannakogeorgos, P. (2011). Challenges in monitoring cyber-arms compliance. [IJCWT]. *International Journal of Cyber Warfare & Terrorism*, *1*(2), 35–48. doi:10.4018/ijcwt.2011040104

Rwabutaza, A., Yang, M., & Bourbakis, N. (2012). A comparative survey on cryptology-based methodologies. [IJISP]. *International Journal of Information Security and Privacy*, *6*(3), 1–37. doi:10.4018/jisp.2012070101

Sadkhan, S. B., & Abbas, N. A. (2014). Privacy and security of wireless communication networks. In J. Rodrigues, K. Lin, & J. Lloret (Eds.), *Mobile networks and cloud computing convergence for progressive services and applications* (pp. 58–78). Hershey, PA: Information Science Reference.

Saedy, M., & Mojtahed, V. (2011). Machine-to-machine communications and security solution in cellular systems. [IJITN]. *International Journal of Interdisciplinary Telecommunications and Networking*, *3*(2), 66–75. doi:10.4018/jitn.2011040105

San Nicolas-Rocca, T., & Olfman, L. (2013). End user security training for identification and access management. [JOEUC]. *Journal of Organizational and End User Computing*, *25*(4), 75–103. doi:10.4018/joeuc.2013100104

Satoh, F., Nakamura, Y., Mukhi, N. K., Tatsubori, M., & Ono, K. (2011). Model-driven approach for end-to-end SOA security configurations. In N. Milanovic (Ed.), *Non-functional properties in service oriented architecture: Requirements, models and methods* (pp. 268–298). Hershey, PA: Information Science Reference. doi:10.4018/978-1-60566-794-2.ch012

Saucez, D., Iannone, L., & Bonaventure, O. (2014). The map-and-encap locator/identifier separation paradigm: A security analysis. In M. Boucadair, & D. Binet (Eds.), *Solutions for sustaining scalability in internet growth* (pp. 148–163). Hershey, PA: Information Science Reference.

Schell, B. H., & Holt, T. J. (2012). A profile of the demographics, psychological predispositions, and social/behavioral patterns of computer hacker insiders and outsiders. In I. Management Association (Ed.), Cyber crime: Concepts, methodologies, tools and applications (pp. 1461-1484). Hershey, PA: Information Science Reference. doi: doi:10.4018/978-1-61350-323-2.ch705

Schmidt, H. (2011). Threat and risk-driven security requirements engineering. [IJMCMC]. *International Journal of Mobile Computing and Multimedia Communications, 3*(1), 35–50. doi:10.4018/jmcmc.2011010103

Schmidt, H., Hatebur, D., & Heisel, M. (2011). A pattern-based method to develop secure software. In H. Mouratidis (Ed.), *Software engineering for secure systems: Industrial and research perspectives* (pp. 32–74). Hershey, PA: Information Science Reference.

Seale, R. O., & Hargiss, K. M. (2011). A proposed architecture for autonomous mobile agent intrusion prevention and malware defense in heterogeneous networks. [IJSITA]. *International Journal of Strategic Information Technology and Applications, 2*(4), 44–54. doi:10.4018/jsita.2011100104

Sen, J. (2013). Security and privacy challenges in cognitive wireless sensor networks. In N. Meghanathan, & Y. Reddy (Eds.), *Cognitive radio technology applications for wireless and mobile ad hoc networks* (pp. 194–232). Hershey, PA: Information Science Reference. doi:10.4018/978-1-4666-4221-8.ch011

Sen, J. (2014). Security and privacy issues in cloud computing. In A. Ruiz-Martinez, R. Marin-Lopez, & F. Pereniguez-Garcia (Eds.), *Architectures and protocols for secure information technology infrastructures* (pp. 1–45). Hershey, PA: Information Science Reference.

Sengupta, A., & Mazumdar, C. (2011). A mark-up language for the specification of information security governance requirements. [IJISP]. *International Journal of Information Security and Privacy, 5*(2), 33–53. doi:10.4018/jisp.2011040103

Shaqrah, A. A. (2011). The influence of internet security on e-business competence in Jordan: An empirical analysis. In I. Management Association (Ed.), Global business: Concepts, methodologies, tools and applications (pp. 1071-1086). Hershey, PA: Business Science Reference. doi: doi:10.4018/978-1-60960-587-2.ch413

Shareef, M. A., & Kumar, V. (2012). Prevent/control identity theft: Impact on trust and consumers' purchase intention in B2C EC. [IRMJ]. *Information Resources Management Journal, 25*(3), 30–60. doi:10.4018/irmj.2012070102

Sharma, K., & Singh, A. (2011). Biometric security in the e-world. In H. Nemati, & L. Yang (Eds.), *Applied cryptography for cyber security and defense: Information encryption and cyphering* (pp. 289–337). Hershey, PA: Information Science Reference.

Sharma, R. K. (2014). Physical layer security and its applications: A survey. In D. Rawat, B. Bista, & G. Yan (Eds.), *Security, Privacy, Trust, and Resource Management in Mobile and Wireless Communications* (pp. 29–60). Hershey, PA: Information Science Reference.

Shaw, R., Keh, H., & Huang, N. (2011). Information security awareness on-line materials design with knowledge maps. [IJDET]. *International Journal of Distance Education Technologies, 9*(4), 41–56. doi:10.4018/jdet.2011100104

Shebanow, A., Perez, R., & Howard, C. (2012). The effect of firewall testing types on cloud security policies. [IJSITA]. *International Journal of Strategic Information Technology and Applications, 3*(3), 60–68. doi:10.4018/jsita.2012070105

Shen, Y., Li, Y., Wu, L., Liu, S., & Wen, Q. (2014). Data protection in the cloud era. In Y. Shen, Y. Li, L. Wu, S. Liu, & Q. Wen (Eds.), *Enabling the new era of cloud computing: Data security, transfer, and management* (pp. 132–154). Hershey, PA: Information Science Reference.

Shen, Y., Li, Y., Wu, L., Liu, S., & Wen, Q. (2014). Enterprise security monitoring with the fusion center model. In Y. Shen, Y. Li, L. Wu, S. Liu, & Q. Wen (Eds.), *Enabling the new era of cloud computing: Data security, transfer, and management* (pp. 116–131). Hershey, PA: Information Science Reference.

Shore, M. (2011). Cyber security and anti-social networking. In I. Management Association (Ed.), *Virtual communities: Concepts, methodologies, tools and applications* (pp. 1286-1297). Hershey, PA: Information Science Reference. doi: doi:10.4018/978-1-60960-100-3.ch412

Siddiqi, J., Alqatawna, J., & Btoush, M. H. (2011). Do insecure systems increase global digital divide? In I. Management Association (Ed.), *Global business: Concepts, methodologies, tools and applications* (pp. 2102-2111). Hershey, PA: Business Science Reference. doi: doi:10.4018/978-1-60960-587-2.ch717

Simpson, J. J., Simpson, M. J., Endicott-Popovsky, B., & Popovsky, V. (2012). Secure software education: A contextual model-based approach. In K. Khan (Ed.), *Security-aware systems applications and software development methods* (pp. 286–312). Hershey, PA: Information Science Reference. doi:10.4018/978-1-4666-1580-9.ch016

Singh, S. (2012). Security threats and issues with MANET. In K. Lakhtaria (Ed.), *Technological advancements and applications in mobile ad-hoc networks: Research trends* (pp. 247–263). Hershey, PA: Information Science Reference. doi:10.4018/978-1-4666-0321-9.ch015

Sockel, H., & Falk, L. K. (2012). Online privacy, vulnerabilities, and threats: A manager's perspective. In I. Management Association (Ed.), *Cyber crime: Concepts, methodologies, tools and applications* (pp. 101-123). Hershey, PA: Information Science Reference. doi: doi:10.4018/978-1-61350-323-2.ch108

Spruit, M., & de Bruijn, W. (2012). CITS: The cost of IT security framework. [IJISP]. *International Journal of Information Security and Privacy*, 6(4), 94–116. doi:10.4018/jisp.2012100105

Srinivasan, C., Lakshmy, K., & Sethumadhavan, M. (2011). Complexity measures of cryptographically secure boolean functions. In R. Santanam, M. Sethumadhavan, & M. Virendra (Eds.), *Cyber security, cyber crime and cyber forensics: Applications and perspectives* (pp. 220–230). Hershey, PA: Information Science Reference.

Srivatsa, M., Agrawal, D., & McDonald, A. D. (2012). Security across disparate management domains in coalition MANETs. In I. Management Association (Ed.), *Wireless technologies: Concepts, methodologies, tools and applications* (pp. 1494-1518). Hershey, PA: Information Science Reference. doi: doi:10.4018/978-1-61350-101-6.ch521

Stojanovic, M. D., Acimovic-Raspopovic, V. S., & Rakas, S. B. (2013). Security management issues for open source ERP in the NGN environment. In I. Association (Ed.), *Enterprise resource planning: Concepts, methodologies, tools, and applications* (pp. 789–804). Hershey, PA: Business Science Reference. doi:10.4018/978-1-4666-4153-2.ch046

Stoll, M., & Breu, R. (2012). Information security governance and standard based management systems. In M. Gupta, J. Walp, & R. Sharman (Eds.), *Strategic and practical approaches for information security governance: Technologies and applied solutions* (pp. 261–282). Hershey, PA: Information Science Reference. doi:10.4018/978-1-4666-0197-0.ch015

Sundaresan, M., & Boopathy, D. (2014). Different perspectives of cloud security. In S. Srinivasan (Ed.), *Security, trust, and regulatory aspects of cloud computing in business environments* (pp. 73–90). Hershey, PA: Information Science Reference. doi:10.4018/978-1-4666-5788-5.ch004

Takabi, H., Joshi, J. B., & Ahn, G. (2013). Security and privacy in cloud computing: Towards a comprehensive framework. In X. Yang, & L. Liu (Eds.), *Principles, methodologies, and service-oriented approaches for cloud computing* (pp. 164–184). Hershey, PA: Business Science Reference. doi:10.4018/978-1-4666-2854-0.ch007

Takabi, H., Zargar, S. T., & Joshi, J. B. (2014). Mobile cloud computing and its security and privacy challenges. In D. Rawat, B. Bista, & G. Yan (Eds.), *Security, privacy, trust, and resource management in mobile and wireless communications* (pp. 384–407). Hershey, PA: Information Science Reference.

Takemura, T. (2014). Unethical information security behavior and organizational commitment. In T. Tsiakis, T. Kargidis, & P. Katsaros (Eds.), *Approaches and processes for managing the economics of information systems* (pp. 181–198). Hershey, PA: Business Science Reference. doi:10.4018/978-1-4666-4983-5.ch011

Talib, S., Clarke, N. L., & Furnell, S. M. (2011). Establishing a personalized information security culture. [IJM-CMC]. *International Journal of Mobile Computing and Multimedia Communications*, *3*(1), 63–79. doi:10.4018/jmcmc.2011010105

Talukder, A. K. (2011). Securing next generation internet services. In R. Santanam, M. Sethumadhavan, & M. Virendra (Eds.), *Cyber security, cyber crime and cyber forensics: Applications and perspectives* (pp. 87–105). Hershey, PA: Information Science Reference.

Tchepnda, C., Moustafa, H., Labiod, H., & Bourdon, G. (2011). Vehicular networks security: Attacks, requirements, challenges and current contributions. In K. Curran (Ed.), *Ubiquitous developments in ambient computing and intelligence: Human-centered applications* (pp. 43–55). Hershey, PA: Information Science Reference. doi:10.4018/978-1-60960-549-0.ch004

Tereshchenko, N. (2012). US foreign policy challenges of non-state actors' cyber terrorism against critical infrastructure. [IJCWT]. *International Journal of Cyber Warfare & Terrorism*, *2*(4), 28–48. doi:10.4018/ijcwt.2012100103

Thurimella, R., & Baird, L. C. (2011). Network security. In H. Nemati, & L. Yang (Eds.), *Applied cryptography for cyber security and defense: Information encryption and cyphering* (pp. 1–31). Hershey, PA: Information Science Reference.

Thurimella, R., & Mitchell, W. (2011). Cloak and dagger: Man-in-the-middle and other insidious attacks. In H. Nemati (Ed.), *Security and privacy assurance in advancing technologies: New developments* (pp. 252–270). Hershey, PA: Information Science Reference.

Tiwari, S., Singh, A., Singh, R. S., & Singh, S. K. (2013). Internet security using biometrics. In I. Management Association (Ed.), IT policy and ethics: Concepts, methodologies, tools, and applications (pp. 1680-1707). Hershey, PA: Information Science Reference. doi: doi:10.4018/978-1-4666-2919-6.ch074

Tomaiuolo, M. (2012). Trust enforcing and trust building, different technologies and visions. [IJCWT]. *International Journal of Cyber Warfare & Terrorism*, *2*(4), 49–66. doi:10.4018/ijcwt.2012100104

Tomaiuolo, M. (2014). Trust management and delegation for the administration of web services. In I. Portela, & F. Almeida (Eds.), *Organizational, legal, and technological dimensions of information system administration* (pp. 18–37). Hershey, PA: Information Science Reference.

Touhafi, A., Braeken, A., Cornetta, G., Mentens, N., & Steenhaut, K. (2011). Secure techniques for remote reconfiguration of wireless embedded systems. In M. Cruz-Cunha, & F. Moreira (Eds.), *Handbook of research on mobility and computing: Evolving technologies and ubiquitous impacts* (pp. 930–951). Hershey, PA: Information Science Reference. doi:10.4018/978-1-60960-042-6.ch058

Traore, I., & Woungang, I. (2013). Software security engineering – Part I: Security requirements and risk analysis. In K. Buragga, & N. Zaman (Eds.), *Software development techniques for constructive information systems design* (pp. 221–255). Hershey, PA: Information Science Reference. doi:10.4018/978-1-4666-3679-8.ch012

Tripathi, M., Gaur, M., & Laxmi, V. (2014). Security challenges in wireless sensor network. In D. Rawat, B. Bista, & G. Yan (Eds.), *Security, privacy, trust, and resource management in mobile and wireless communications* (pp. 334–359). Hershey, PA: Information Science Reference.

Trösterer, S., Beck, E., Dalpiaz, F., Paja, E., Giorgini, P., & Tscheligi, M. (2012). Formative user-centered evaluation of security modeling: Results from a case study. [IJSSE]. *International Journal of Secure Software Engineering*, *3*(1), 1–19. doi:10.4018/jsse.2012010101

Tsiakis, T. (2013). The role of information security and cryptography in digital democracy: (Human) rights and freedom. In C. Akrivopoulou, & N. Garipidis (Eds.), *Digital democracy and the impact of technology on governance and politics: New globalized practices* (pp. 158–174). Hershey, PA: Information Science Reference.

Tsiakis, T., Kargidis, T., & Chatzipoulidis, A. (2013). IT security governance in e-banking. In D. Mellado, L. Enrique Sánchez, E. Fernández-Medina, & M. Piattini (Eds.), *IT security governance innovations: Theory and research* (pp. 13–46). Hershey, PA: Information Science Reference.

Turgeman-Goldschmidt, O. (2011). Between hackers and white-collar offenders. In T. Holt, & B. Schell (Eds.), *Corporate hacking and technology-driven crime: Social dynamics and implications* (pp. 18–37). Hershey, PA: Information Science Reference.

Tvrdíková, M. (2012). Information system integrated security. In M. Gupta, J. Walp, & R. Sharman (Eds.), *Strategic and practical approaches for information security governance: Technologies and applied solutions* (pp. 158–169). Hershey, PA: Information Science Reference. doi:10.4018/978-1-4666-0197-0.ch009

Uffen, J., & Breitner, M. H. (2013). Management of technical security measures: An empirical examination of personality traits and behavioral intentions. [IJSODIT]. *International Journal of Social and Organizational Dynamics in IT, 3*(1), 14–31. doi:10.4018/ijsodit.2013010102

Vance, A., & Siponen, M. T. (2012). IS security policy violations: A rational choice perspective. [JOEUC]. *Journal of Organizational and End User Computing, 24*(1), 21–41. doi:10.4018/joeuc.2012010102

Veltsos, C. (2011). Mitigating the blended threat: Protecting data and educating users. In D. Kar, & M. Syed (Eds.), *Network security, administration and management: Advancing technology and practice* (pp. 20–37). Hershey, PA: Information Science Reference. doi:10.4018/978-1-60960-777-7.ch002

Venkataraman, R., Pushpalatha, M., & Rao, T. R. (2014). Trust management and modeling techniques in wireless communications. In D. Rawat, B. Bista, & G. Yan (Eds.), *Security, privacy, trust, and resource management in mobile and wireless communications* (pp. 278–294). Hershey, PA: Information Science Reference.

Venkataraman, R., & Rao, T. R. (2012). Security issues and models in mobile ad hoc networks. In K. Lakhtaria (Ed.), *Technological advancements and applications in mobile ad-hoc networks: Research trends* (pp. 219–227). Hershey, PA: Information Science Reference. doi:10.4018/978-1-4666-0321-9.ch013

Viney, D. (2011). Future trends in digital security. In D. Kerr, J. Gammack, & K. Bryant (Eds.), *Digital business security development: Management technologies* (pp. 173–190). Hershey, PA: Business Science Reference.

Vinod, P., Laxmi, V., & Gaur, M. (2011). Metamorphic malware analysis and detection methods. In R. Santanam, M. Sethumadhavan, & M. Virendra (Eds.), *Cyber security, cyber crime and cyber forensics: Applications and perspectives* (pp. 178–202). Hershey, PA: Information Science Reference.

von Solms, R., & Warren, M. (2011). Towards the human information security firewall. [IJCWT]. *International Journal of Cyber Warfare & Terrorism, 1*(2), 10–17. doi:10.4018/ijcwt.2011040102

Wall, D. S. (2011). Micro-frauds: Virtual robberies, stings and scams in the information age. In T. Holt, & B. Schell (Eds.), *Corporate hacking and technology-driven crime: Social dynamics and implications* (pp. 68–86). Hershey, PA: Information Science Reference.

Wang, H., Zhao, J. L., & Chen, G. (2012). Managing data security in e-markets through relationship driven access control. [JDM]. *Journal of Database Management, 23*(2), 1–21. doi:10.4018/jdm.2012040101

Warren, M., & Leitch, S. (2011). Protection of Australia in the cyber age. [IJCWT]. *International Journal of Cyber Warfare & Terrorism, 1*(1), 35–40. doi:10.4018/ijcwt.2011010104

Weber, S. G., & Gustiené, P. (2013). Crafting requirements for mobile and pervasive emergency response based on privacy and security by design principles. [IJISCRAM]. *International Journal of Information Systems for Crisis Response and Management, 5*(2), 1–18. doi:10.4018/jiscrm.2013040101

Wei, J., Lin, B., & Loho-Noya, M. (2013). Development of an e-healthcare information security risk assessment method. [JDM]. *Journal of Database Management, 24*(1), 36–57. doi:10.4018/jdm.2013010103

Weippl, E. R., & Riedl, B. (2012). Security, trust, and privacy on mobile devices and multimedia applications. In I. Management Association (Ed.), Cyber crime: Concepts, methodologies, tools and applications (pp. 228-244). Hershey, PA: Information Science Reference. doi: doi:10.4018/978-1-61350-323-2.ch202

White, G., & Long, J. (2012). Global information security factors. In H. Nemati (Ed.), *Optimizing information security and advancing privacy assurance: New technologies* (pp. 163–174). Hershey, PA: Information Science Reference.

White, S. C., Sedigh, S., & Hurson, A. R. (2013). Security concepts for cloud computing. In X. Yang, & L. Liu (Eds.), *Principles, methodologies, and service-oriented approaches for cloud computing* (pp. 116–142). Hershey, PA: Business Science Reference. doi:10.4018/978-1-4666-2854-0.ch005

Whyte, B., & Harrison, J. (2011). State of practice in secure software: Experts' views on best ways ahead. In H. Mouratidis (Ed.), *Software engineering for secure systems: Industrial and research perspectives* (pp. 1–14). Hershey, PA: Information Science Reference.

Wu, Y., & Saunders, C. S. (2011). Governing information security: Governance domains and decision rights allocation patterns. [IRMJ]. *Information Resources Management Journal, 24*(1), 28–45. doi:10.4018/irmj.2011010103

Yadav, S. B. (2011). SEACON: An integrated approach to the analysis and design of secure enterprise architecture–based computer networks. In H. Nemati (Ed.), *Pervasive information security and privacy developments: Trends and advancements* (pp. 309–331). Hershey, PA: Information Science Reference.

Yadav, S. B. (2012). A six-view perspective framework for system security: Issues, risks, and requirements. In H. Nemati (Ed.), *Optimizing information security and advancing privacy assurance: New technologies* (pp. 58–90). Hershey, PA: Information Science Reference.

Yamany, H. F., Allison, D. S., & Capretz, M. A. (2013). Developing proactive security dimensions for SOA. In I. Management Association (Ed.), IT policy and ethics: Concepts, methodologies, tools, and applications (pp. 900-922). Hershey, PA: Information Science Reference. doi: doi:10.4018/978-1-4666-2919-6.ch041

Yan, G., Rawat, D. B., Bista, B. B., & Chen, L. (2014). Location security in vehicular wireless networks. In D. Rawat, B. Bista, & G. Yan (Eds.), *Security, privacy, trust, and resource management in mobile and wireless communications* (pp. 108–133). Hershey, PA: Information Science Reference.

Yaokumah, W. (2013). Evaluating the effectiveness of information security governance practices in developing nations: A case of Ghana. [IJITBAG]. *International Journal of IT/Business Alignment and Governance, 4*(1), 27–43. doi:10.4018/jitbag.2013010103

Yates, D., & Harris, A. (2011). International ethical attitudes and behaviors: Implications for organizational information security policy. In M. Dark (Ed.), *Information assurance and security ethics in complex systems: Interdisciplinary perspectives* (pp. 55–80). Hershey, PA: Information Science Reference.

Yau, S. S., Yin, Y., & An, H. (2011). An adaptive approach to optimizing tradeoff between service performance and security in service-based systems. [IJWSR]. *International Journal of Web Services Research, 8*(2), 74–91. doi:10.4018/jwsr.2011040104

Zadig, S. M., & Tejay, G. (2012). Emerging cybercrime trends: Legal, ethical, and practical issues. In A. Dudley, J. Braman, & G. Vincenti (Eds.), *Investigating cyber law and cyber ethics: Issues, impacts and practices* (pp. 37–56). Hershey, PA: Information Science Reference.

Zafar, H., Ko, M., & Osei-Bryson, K. (2012). Financial impact of information security breaches on breached firms and their non-breached competitors. [IRMJ]. *Information Resources Management Journal, 25*(1), 21–37. doi:10.4018/irmj.2012010102

Zapata, B. C., & Alemán, J. L. (2013). Security risks in cloud computing: An analysis of the main vulnerabilities. In D. Rosado, D. Mellado, E. Fernandez-Medina, & M. Piattini (Eds.), *Security engineering for cloud computing: Approaches and tools* (pp. 55–71). Hershey, PA: Information Science Reference. doi:10.4018/978-1-4666-4301-7.ch045

Zboril, F., Horacek, J., Drahansky, M., & Hanacek, P. (2012). Security in wireless sensor networks with mobile codes. In M. Gupta, J. Walp, & R. Sharman (Eds.), *Threats, countermeasures, and advances in applied information security* (pp. 411–425). Hershey, PA: Information Science Reference. doi:10.4018/978-1-4666-0978-5.ch021

Zhang, J. (2012). Trust management for VANETs: Challenges, desired properties and future directions. [IJDST]. *International Journal of Distributed Systems and Technologies*, *3*(1), 48–62. doi:10.4018/jdst.2012010104

Zhang, Y., He, L., Shu, L., Hara, T., & Nishio, S. (2012). Security issues on outlier detection and countermeasure for distributed hierarchical wireless sensor networks. In A. Pathan, M. Pathan, & H. Lee (Eds.), *Advancements in distributed computing and internet technologies: Trends and issues* (pp. 182–210). Hershey, PA: Information Science Publishing.

Zheng, X., & Oleshchuk, V. (2012). Security enhancement of peer-to-peer session initiation. In M. Gupta, J. Walp, & R. Sharman (Eds.), *Threats, countermeasures, and advances in applied information security* (pp. 281–308). Hershey, PA: Information Science Reference. doi:10.4018/978-1-4666-0978-5.ch015

Zineddine, M. (2012). Is your automated healthcare information secure? In M. Watfa (Ed.), *E-healthcare systems and wireless communications: Current and future challenges* (pp. 128–142). Hershey, PA: Medical Information Science Reference.

Compilation of References

Abbasi, N. (2012). *Formal reliability analysis using theorem proving*. (PhD Thesis). Concordia University, Montreal, Canada.

Aboufadel, E., Olsen, J., & Windle, J. (2005). Breaking the holiday inn priority club CAPTCHA. *The College Mathematics Journal, 36*(2), 101–108. doi:10.2307/30044832

Abu Rajab, M., Zarfoss, J., Monrose, F., & Terzis, A. (2006). A multifaceted approach to understanding the botnet phenomenon. In IMC'06: Proceedings of the 6th ACM SIGCOMM Conference on internetInternet Measurement (pp. 41–52). New York, NY, USA: ACM.

Adam, N. R., & Wortman, J. C. (1989). Security control methods for statistical databases. *ACM Computing Surveys, 21*(4), 515–556. doi:10.1145/76894.76895

Agah, A., Das, S. K., & Basu, K. (2005). Enforcing security for prevention of DOS attack in wireless sensor networks using economical modeling. In *Proceedings of the 2nd IEEE International Conference on Mobile Ad-Hoc and Sensor Systems* (MASS). IEEE.

Agah, A., Das, S. K., & Basu, K. (2005). Preventing DOS attack in sensor and actor networks: A game theoretic approach. In *Proceedings of IEEE International Conferences on Communications* (ICC). IEEE.

Agah, A., Asadi, M., & Zimmerman, C. (2011). *Maximizing battery life: Applying game theory to wireless sensor networks*. The West Chester Research Consortium.

Aggarwal, C. C., & Yu, P. S. (2008). Privacy preserving data mining: Models and algorithms. *Advances in Database Systems, 34*(22), 513.

Agrawal & Srikant. (2000). Privacy preserving data mining. *Proceedings of the ACM SIGMOD Conference on Management of Data, 15* (3), 439–450.

Akiyama, M., Kawamoto, T., Shimamura, M., Yokoyama, T., Kadobayashi, Y., & Yamaguchi, S. (2007). A proposal of metrics for botnet detection based on its cooperative behavior. In Saint '07: Proceedings of the 2007 International Symposium on Applications and the internetInternet Workshops. Washington, DC, USA: IEEE Computer Society.

Akyildiz, I. F., & Vuran, M. C. (2010). *Wireless sensor networks*. Hoboken, NJ: John Wiley and Sons. doi:10.1002/9780470515181

Akyldiz, I. F., Sankarasubramaniam, Y., Su, W., & Cayirci, E. (2002). Wireless sensor networks: A survey. *Journal of Computer Networks, 38*.

Alazab, A., Alazab, M., Abawajy, J., & Hobbs, M. (2011). Web application protection against SQL injection attack. In *Proceedings of the 7th International Conference on Information Technology and Applications*. Academic Press.

Alazab, M., Monsamy, V., Batten, L., Lantz, P., & Tian, R. (2012). *Analysis of malicious and benign android applications*. Paper presented at the Distributed Computing Systems Workshops (ICDCSW). New York, NY.

Alazab, M., Venkataraman, S., & Watters, P. (2010). *Towards understanding malware behaviour by the extraction of API calls*. Paper presented at the Cybercrime and Trustworthy Computing Workshop (CTC). New York, NY.

Alazab, M., Ventatraman, S., Watters, P., Alazab, M., & Alazab, A. (2011). *Cybercrime: The case of obuscated malware*. Paper presented at the 7th International Conference on Global Security, Safety & Sustainability. Thessaloniki, Greece.

Al-Bayatti, A. H. (2009). *Security management for mobile ad hoc network of networks (MANoN).* (PhD Thesis). De Montfort University, Leicester, UK.

Al-Bayatti, A., Zedan, H., & Cau, A. (2009). Security solution for mobile ad hoc network of networks (manon). In *Proceedings of Networking and Services* (pp. 255–262). ICNS. doi:10.1109/ICNS.2009.30

Aldabbas, H., Alwada'n, T., Janicke, H., & Al-Bayatti, A. (2012). Data confidentiality in mobile ad hoc networks. *International Journal of Wireless and Mobile Networks,* 4(1), 225–236. doi:10.5121/ijwmn.2012.4117

Aldabbas, H., Janicke, H., AbuJassar, R., & Alwada'n, T. (2012). Ensuring data confidentiality and privacy in mobile ad hoc networks. In *Advances in computer science and information technology: Networks and communications* (pp. 490–499). Berlin: Springer. doi:10.1007/978-3-642-27299-8_51

Al-Hammadi, Y., & Aickelin, U. (2006). Detecting botnets through log correlation. Paper presented at In the Workshop on Monitoring, Attack Detection and Mitigation. New York, NY.

Al-Jaroodi, J. (2002). *Security issues at the network layer in wireless mobile ad hoc networks at the network layer (Technical Report).* Lincoln, NE: Faculty of Computer Science and Engineering, University of Nebraska-Lincoln.

Almomani, I. M. (2007). *Security solutions for wireless mobile ad hoc networks (WMANET).* (PhD Thesis). De Montfort University, Leicester, UK.

Almomani, I., & Zedan, H. (2007). *End-to-end security solution for wireless mobile ad hoc network (WMANET).* Academic Press.

Amine, A., Hamou, R. M., & Simonet, M. (2013). Detecting opinions in tweets. *International Journal of Data Mining and Emerging Technologies,* 3(1), 30–39. doi:10.5958/j.2249-3220.3.1.004

Anagnostakis, K. G., Sidiroglou, S., Akritidis, P., Xinidis, K., Markatos, E., & Keromytis, A. D. (2005). Detecting targeted attacks using shadow honeypots. In SSYM'05: Proceedings of the 14th Conference on USENIX Security Symposium. Berkeley, CA, USA: USENIX Association.

Anastasi, G., Falchi, A., Passarella, A., Conti, M., & Gregori, E. (2004). Performance measurements of motes sensor networks. In *Proceedings of the 7th ACM International Symposium on Modeling, Analysis and Simulation of Wireless and Mobile Systems* (pp. 174-181). New York, NY: ACM Press.

Anderson, J. P. (1980). *Computer security threat monitoring and surveillance (Technical Report).* Washington, PA: Academic Press.

Andrews, J. G., Ghosh, A., & Muhamed, R. (2007). *Fundamentals of WiMAX: Understanding broadband wireless networking.* Upper Saddle River, NJ: Prentice Hall.

Anestis, K., Brian, R., & David, H. (2007). Wide-scale botnet detection and characterization. In Hotbots'07: Proceedings of the First Conference on First Workshop on Hot Topics in Understanding Botnets. Berkeley, CA, USA: USENIX Association.

Anoop, M. (2007, May). *Elliptic curve cryptography: An implementation tutorial.* Retrieved August 30, 2012, from http://www.infosecwriters.com/text_resources/pdf/Elliptic_Curve_AnnopMS.pdf

Apache Foundation. (2012). *Apache rampart.* Apache Software Foundation. Retrieved May 2013 May 2013 from https://axis.apache.org/axis2/java/rampart/

Asadi, M., Zimmerman, C., & Agah, A. (2012). A quest for security in wireless sensor networks: A game theoretic model. In *Proceedings of the International Conference on Wireless Networks* (ICWN). ICWN.

Asadi, M., Zimmerman, C., & Agah, A. (2013). A game-theoretic approach to security and power conservation in wireless sensor networks. *International Journal of Network Security,* 15(1), 50–58.

Athanasopoulos, E., & Antonatos, S. (2006). Enhanced CAPTCHAs: Using animation to tell humans and computers apart. In *Proceedings of 10th IFIP International Conference on Communications and Multimedia Security (CMS 2006)* (pp. 97–108). IFIP.

Atwood, M. (2009). *OAuth core 1.0 revision A.* Retrieved May 2013 May 2013 from http://oauth.net/core/1.0a/

Austein, R. (2007). *DNS name server identifier (NSID) option.* IETF RFC 5001.

Axelsson, S. (2000). *Intrusion detection systems: A survey and taxonomy (Technical Report)*. Academic Press.

Bace, R., & Mell, P. (2001). *NIST special publication on intrusion detection. NIST Computer Security Division, National Institute of Standards and Technology*. NIST.

Baecher, P., Koetter, M., Holz, T., Dornseif, M., & Freiling, F. (2006). The nepenthes platform: An efficient approach to collect malware. Recent Advances in Intrusion Detection, 165–184.

Bai, F., & Krishnan, H. (2006). Reliability analysis of DSRC wireless communication for vehicle safety applications. In *Proceedings of Intelligent Transportation Systems Conference*, (pp. 355–362). IEEE.

Baier, C., Haverkort, B., Hermanns, H., & Katoen, J. (2003). Model checking algorithms for continuous time Markov chains. *IEEE Transactions on Software Engineering, 29*(4), 524–541. doi:10.1109/TSE.2003.1205180

Baird, H. S. (2002). The ability gap between human & machine reading systems. In *Proceedings of First Workshop on Human Interactive Proofs (HIP 2002)*. HIP.

Baird, H. S., & Bentley, J. L. (2005). Implicit CAPTCHAs. In *Proceedings of SPIE/IS&T Electronic Imaging, Document Recognition and Retrieval XII* (Vol. 5676, pp. 191–196). IEEE.

Baird, H. S., & Lopresti, D. P. (2005). Second international workshop on human interactive proofs - Preface. In *Proceedings of Second International Workshop on Human Interactive Proofs (HIP 2005)*. HIP.

Baird, H. S., & Luk, M. (2003). Protecting websites with reading-based CAPTCHAs. In *Proceedings of Second International Workshop on Web Document Analysis (WDA2003)*. WDA.

Baird, H. S., & Popat, K. (2002). Human interactive proofs and document image analysis. In *Proceedings of 5th IAPR International Workshop on Document Analysis Systems* (pp. 507–518). IAPR.

Baird, H. S., & Riopka, T. P. (2005). Scattertype: A reading CAPTCHA resistant to segmentation attack. In *Proceedings of SPIE/IS&T Electronic Imaging, Document Recognition and Retrieval XII* (pp. 197–207). SPIE.

Baird, H. S., Moll, M. A., & Wang, S. Y. (2005a). A highly legible CAPTCHA that resists segmentation attacks. In *Proceedings of Second International Workshop on Human Interactive Proofs (HIP 2005)* (pp. 27–41). HIP.

Baird, H. S., Moll, M. A., & Wang, S. Y. (2005b). Scattertype: A legible but hard-to-segment CAPTCHA. In *Proceedings of the 8th International Conference on Document Analysis and Recognition (ICDAR 05)* (Vol. 2, pp. 935–939). ICDAR.

Baird, H. S. (2006). Data complexity in pattern recognition. In M. Basu, & T. K. Ho (Eds.), *Complex image recognition and web security*. London: Springer-Verlag London Ltd.

Baird, H. S., Coates, A. L., & Fateman, R. J. (2003). Pessimalprint: A reverse turing test. *International Journal on Document Analysis and Recognition, 5*(2–3), 158–163. doi:10.1007/s10032-002-0089-1

Bandyopadhyay, S., & Coyle, E. (2003). *An energy efficient hierarchical clustering algorithm for wireless sensor networks*. INFOCOM.

Barbaro & Zeller. (2006). A face is exposed for AOL searcher no. 4417749. *New York Times, 42* (4), 248–263.

Barford, P., & Yegneswaran, V. (2007). *An inside look at botnets*. Academic Press.

Barnat, J., Brim, L., & Safranek, D. (2010). 05). High-performance analysis of biological systems dynamics with the DiVinE model checker. *Briefings in Bioinformatics, 11*(3), 301–312. doi:10.1093/bib/bbp074 PMID:20478855

Barreto, P., & Naehrig, M. (2006). Pairing-friendly elliptic curves of prime order. In *Proceedings of Selected Areas in Cryptography – SAC 2005* (pp. 319–331). Berlin: Springer.

Barth, A. (2011). *RFC 6265 - HTTP state management mechanism*. Internet Engineering Task Force (IETF). Retrieved May 2013 May 2013 from https://tools.ietf.org/html/rfc6265

Bellare, M., Canetti, R., & Krawczyk, H. (1996). Keying hash functions for message authentication. In *Proceedings of the 16th Annual International Cryptology Conference* (pp. 1-15). Santa Barbara, CA: Springer.

Bensefia, H., & Ahmed-Nacer, M. (2008). Towards an adaptive intrusion detection system: A critical and comparative study. In *Proceedings of International Conference on Computational Intelligence and Security*, (pp. 246-251). Academic Press.

Bentley, J., & Mallows, C. (2005). How much assurance does a PIN provide? In *Proceedings of Second International Workshop on Human Interactive Proofs (HIP 2005)* (pp. 111–126). HIP.

Bentley, J., & Mallows, C. (2006). CAPTCHA challenge strings: Problems and improvements. In *Proceedings of 18th SPIE/IS&T Electronic Imaging, Document Recognition and Retrieval XIII*. SPIE.

Bergmair, R., & Katzenbeisser, S. (2004). Towards human interactive proofs in the text-domain: Using the problem of sense-ambiguity for security. In *Proceedings of 7th International Information Security Conference (ISC 2004)* (pp. 257–267). ISC.

Berners–Lee, T., Fielding, R., & Masinter, L. (2005). *RFC 3986 - Uniform resource identifier (URI), generic syntax*. Network Working Group. Internet Engineering Task Force (IETF). Retrieved May 2013 from https://tools.ietf.org/html/rfc3986

Bertsche, B., & Ingenieure, V. D. (2008). *Reliability in automotive and mechanical engineering: Determination of component and system reliability*. Berlin: Springer.

Bethencourt, J., Franklin, J., & Vernon, M. (2005). Mapping internetinternet sensors with probe response attacks. In SSYM'05: Proceedings of the 14th Conference on USENIX Security Symposium. Berkeley, CA, USA: USENIX Association.

Beuchat, J.-L., López-Trejo, E., Martínez-Ramos, L., Mitsunari, S., & Rodríguez-Henríquez, F. (2009, December). Multi-core implementation of the tate pairing over supersingular elliptic curves. In *Proceedings of the 8th International Conference in Cryptology and Network Security*, (pp. 12-14). Academic Press.

Bharathidasan, A., & Ponduru, V. (2002). *Sensor networks: An overview (Technical Report)*. Davis, CA: Department of Computer Science, University of California.

Binkleyand, J. R., & Singh, S. (2006, 7 July 2006). An algorithm for anomaly- based botnet detection. In In Proceedings of 2nd Workshop on Steps to Reducing Unwanted Traffic on the internetInternet (p. (pp. 43-48). Berkeley, CA, USA: USENIX Association.

Binsalleeh, H., Ormerod, T., Boukhtouta, A., Sinha, P., Youssef, A., Debbabi, M., & Wang, L. (2010). *On the analysis of the zeus botnet crimeware toolkit*. Paper presented at the Privacy Security and Trust (PST). New York, NY.

Biondi, P. (2001). *Architecture expérimentale pour la détection d'intrusions dans un système informatique*.

Biswas, S., Tatchikou, R., & Dion, F. (2006). Vehicle-to-vehicle wireless communication protocols for enhancing highway traffic safety. *IEEE Communications Magazine*, *44*(1), 74–82. doi:10.1109/MCOM.2006.1580935

Blank, D. (2001). A practical turing test for detecting ad-bots. *Intelligence*, *12*(4), 6–7. doi:10.1145/376451.376458

Blaze, M., Feigenbaum, J., & Lacy, J. (1996). Decentralized trust management. In *Proceedings of the 1996 IEEE Symposium on Security and Privacy*. IEEE Computer Society Press.

Blum, M., von Ahn, L., & Langford, J. (2000). *The CAPTCHA project*. Retrieved from http://www.captcha.net/

Bohn, K. (2007). Teen questioned in computer hacking probe. Retrieved from http://www.cnn.com/2007/TECH/11/29/fbi.botnets/ index.html

Boneh, D., & Franklin, M. (2003). Identity-based encryption from the Weil pairing. *SIAM Journal on Computing*, *32*(3), 586–615. doi:10.1137/S0097539701398521

Botgraph: Large scale spamming botnet detection. In Nsdi'09: Pro- ceedings of the 6th USENIX Symposium on Networked Systems Design and Implementation (pp. 321–334). Berkeley, CA, USA: USENIX Association.

Boukerche, A. (2008). Algorithms and protocols for wireless sensor networks. Hoboken, NJ: A John Wiley and Sons.

Bray, T., Paoli, J., Sperberg-McQueen, C. M., Maler, E., & Yergeau, F. (2008). Extensible markup language (XML) 1.0 (5th ed.). W3C Recommendation.

Brelstaff, G., & Chessa, F. (2005). Practical application of visual illusions: Errare humanum est. In *Proceedings of the 2nd Symposium on Applied Perception in Graphics and Visualization (APGV 05)* (pp. 161). APGV.

Broder, A. (2002). Preventing bulk URL submission by robots in altavista. In *Proceedings of First Workshop on Human Interactive Proofs (HIP 2002)*. HIP.

Brown, D. R. (2010, January). *Sec 2: Recommended elliptic curve domain parameters*. Retrieved from www.secg.org/collateral/sec2_final.pdf

Brown, D. J., Suckow, B., & Wang, T. (2001). *A survey of intrusion detection systems*. San Diego, CA: Department of Computer Science, University of California.

Brugger, S. T. (2004). *Data mining methods for network intrusion detection* (UC Davis Dissertation Proposal). Davis, CA: Department of Computer Science, University of California.

Buchegger, S., & Boudec, J. L. (2002). Nodes bearing grudges: Toward routing security fairness and robustness in mobile ad hoc network. In *Proceedings of the 10th Euronicro Workshop on Parallel, Distributed and Network-Based Processing*. Academic Press.

Burbank, J., Chimento, P., Haberman, B., & Kasch, W. (2006). Key challenges of military tactical networking and the elusive promise of manet technology. *IEEE Communications Magazine, 44*(11), 39–45. doi:10.1109/COM-M.2006.248156

Caglayan, A., Toothaker, M., Drapeau, D., Burke, D., & Eaton, G. (2009). Real-time detection of fast flux service networks. In Proceedings Cybersecurity Applications and Technology Conference for Homeland Security, CATCH 2009, (pp. 285 — 292). Academic Press.

Cambridge University Press. (2012, June). *Cambridge dictionary online*. Retrieved May 2013 from http://dictionary.cambridge.org/

Campos-Nanez, E., Garcia, A., & Li, C. (2008). A game-theoretic approach to efficient power management in sensor networks. *Operations Research, 56*(3), 552–561. doi:10.1287/opre.1070.0435

Cannady, J. (2000a). Next generation intrusion detection: Autonomous reinforcement learning of network attacks. In *Proceedings of 23rd National Information Systems Security Conference*. Academic Press.

Cannady, J. (2000b). Applying CMAC-based on-line learning to intrusion detection. *IEEE-INNS-ENNS International Joint Conference on Neural Networks, 5*, 405-410.

Cantor, S., Kemp, J., Philpott, R., & Maler, E. (2005). *Assertions and protocols for the OASIS security assertion markup language (SAML) V2.0 (SAML core)*. OASIS Standard. Retrieved May 2013 from http://docs.oasis-open.org/security/saml/v2.0/saml-core-2.0-os.pdf

Cantor, S., Hirsch, F., Kemp, J., Philpott, R., & Maler, E. (2005). *Profiles for the OASIS security assertion markup language (SAML) V2.0*. OASIS Standard.

Cantor, S., Moreh, J., Philpott, R., & Maler, E. (2005). *Metadata for the OASIS security assertion markup language (SAML) V2.0*. OASIS Standard.

Capkun, S., Buttyán, L., & Hubaux, J. (2003). Self-organized public-key management for mobile ad hoc networks. *IEEE Transactions on Mobile Computing, 2*(1), 52–64. doi:10.1109/TMC.2003.1195151

Carcelle, X., Dangand, T., & Devic, C. (2006). Ad-hoc networking. In *Proceedings of IFIP International Federation for Information Processing*.

Carlisle, D. M., Rodrian, M. L., & Diamond, C. L. (2007). *California inpatient data reporting manual, medical information reporting for California* (5th ed.). Office of Statewide Health Planning and Development.

Carvalho, M. (2008). Security in mobile ad hoc networks. *IEEE Security Privacy, 6*(2), 72–75. doi:10.1109/MSP.2008.44

Chadha, R., & Kant, L. (2007). *Policy-driven mobile ad hoc network management*. Hoboken, NJ: Wiley-IEEE Press. doi:10.1002/9780470227718

Chan, N. (2002). Sound oriented CAPTCHA. In *Proceedings of First Workshop on Human Interactive Proofs (HIP 2002)*. HIP.

Chan, T. Y. (2003). Using a text-to-speech synthesizer to generate a reverse Turing test. In *Proceedings of the 15th IEEE International Conference on Tools with Artificial Intelligence (ICTAI 03)* (pp. 226–232). IEEE.

Chang, L., Zhan, J., & Matwin, S. (2005). Privacy preserving k-nearest neighbor classification. *International Journal of Network Security, 1*(1), 46–51.

Chau, C., Wahab, M. H., Qin, F., Wang, Y., & Tang, Y. (2009). *Battery recovery aware sensor networks.* Paper presented at the 7th International Symposium on Modeling and Optimization in Mobile, Ad Hoc and Wireless Networks (WiOpt). New York, NY.

Chellapilla, K., & Simard, P. (2004). Using machine learning to break visual human interaction proofs (HIPs). In *Proceedings of Advances in Neural Information Processing Systems (NIPS 2004)*. NIPS.

Chellapilla, K., Larson, K., Simard, P., & Czerwinski, M. (2005a). Building segmentation based human-friendly human interaction proofs (HIPs). In *Proceedings of Second International Workshop on Human Interactive Proofs (HIP 2005)* (pp. 1–26). HIP.

Chellapilla, K., Larson, K., Simard, P., & Czerwinski, M. (2005b). Computers beat humans at single character recognition in reading based human interaction proofs (HIPs). In *Proceedings of Second Conference on Email and Anti-Spam (CEAS 2005)*. CEAS.

Chellapilla, K., Larson, K., Simard, P., & Czerwinski, M. (2005c). Designing human friendly human interaction proofs (HIPs). In *Proceedings of the SIGCHI Conference on Human Factors in Computing Systems (CHI 05)* (pp. 711–720). ACM.

Chew, M., & Baird, H. S. (2003). Baffletext: A human interactive proof. In *Proceedings of SPIE/IS&T Electronic Imaging, Document Recognition and Retrieval X* (pp. 305–316). SPIE.

Chew, M., & Tygar, J. (2004). Image recognition CAPTCHAs. In *Proceedings of the 7th International Information Security Conference (ISC 2004)* (pp. 268–279). ISC.

Chew, M., & Tygar, J. (2005). Collaborative filtering CAPTCHAs. In *Proceedings of Second International Workshop on Human Interactive Proofs (HIP 2005)* (pp. 66–81). HIP.

Chiang, K., & Lloyd, L. (2007). A case study of the rustock rootkit and spam bot. In Hotbots'07: Proceedings of the First Conference on First Workshop on Hot Topics in Understanding Botnets. Berkeley, CA, USA: USENIX Association.

Chi, M., & Yang, Y. (2006). *Battery-aware routing for streaming data transmissions in wireless sensor networks.* Berlin: Springer Science and Business Media, LLC.

Chong, C., & Kumar, S. P. (2003). Sensor networks: Evolution, opportunities and challenge. *Proceedings of the IEEE, 91*(8).

Chua, J. P. (2013). *Whitehole exploit kit emerges.* Retrieved from http://blog.trendmicro.com/trendlabs-security-intelligence/whitehole-exploit-kit-emerges/

Ciocchetta, F., & Hillston, J. (2009). Bio-PEPA: A framework for the modelling and analysis of biological systems. *Theoretical Computer Science, 410*(33), 3065–3084. doi:10.1016/j.tcs.2009.02.037

Cisco. (2012). *Cisco networking academy.* Retrieved May 2013 from http://www.cisco.com/Web/learning/netacad/index.htm

Clark, C. F. (1978). The introduction of statistical noise to utility company data on a micro data tape with that data matched annual housing survey data. *Draft Project Report. Bureau of Census, 13*, 321–327.

Click Fraud Index. (2014). Retrieved from http://www.clickforensics.com/resources/click-fraud-index.html

Coates, A. L., Baird, H. S., & Fateman, R. J. (2001). Pessimal print: A reverse Turing test. In *Proceedings of the 6th International Conference on Document Analysis and Recognition (ICDAR 2001)* (pp. 1154–1158). ICDAR.

Comer, D. E. (2008). *Computer networks and internets* (5th ed.). Upper Saddle River, NJ: Prentice Hall.

Connolly, K. J. (2003). *Law of internet security and privacy.* Alphen aan den Rijn, The Netherlands: Aspen Publishers.

Cooper, G. F. (1990). The computational complexity of probabilistic inference using Bayesian belief networks. *Artificial Intelligence, 42*(2), 393–405. doi:10.1016/0004-3702(90)90060-D

Corporation., M. (2012). *Common vulnerabilities and exposures.* Retrieved from http://cve.mitre.org/

Corp, S. (2010). *Symantec global Internet security threat report: Trends for 2009.* Academic Press.

Cova, M., Kruegel, C., & Vigna, G. (2010). *Detection and analysis of drive-by-download attacks and malicious JavaScript code.* Academic Press. doi:10.1145/1772690.1772720

Crosby, G. V., Hester, L., & Pissinou, N. (2011). Location aware, trust-based detection and isolation of compromised nodes in wireless sensor networks. *International Journal of Network Security, 12*(2), 107–117.

Dagon, D., Gu, G., & Lee, C. (2008). A taxonomy of botnet structures. Botnet Detection, , 143–164.

Dailey, M., & Namprempre, C. (2004). A text-graphics character CAPTCHA for password authentication. In *Proceedings of 2004 IEEE Region 10 Conference (TENCON 2004)* (Vol. 2, pp. 45–48). IEEE.

Dalenius, T. (1986). Finding a needle in a haystack - Or identifying anonymous census record. *Journal of Official Statistics, 2*(3), 329–336.

Damiani, E., di Vimercati, S. D. C., & Samarati, P. (2005). *New paradigms for access control in open environments.* Paper presented at the Fifth IEEE International Symposium on Signal Processing and Information Technology. New York, NY.

Dass, M., Cannady, J., & Potter, W. D. (2003). A blackboard-based learning intrusion detection system: A new approach. In *Developments in applied artificial intelligence* (pp. 359–378). Academic Press. doi:10.1007/3-540-45034-3_39

Daswani, N., & Stoppelman, M. (2007). The anatomy of Clickbot.A. In Hotbots'07: Proceedings of the First Conference on First Workshop on Hot Topics in Understanding Botnets. Berkeley, CA, USA: USENIX Association.

Datta, R., Li, J., & Wang, J. Z. (2005). IMAGINATION: A robust image-based CAPTCHA generation system. In *Proceedings of the 13th Annual ACM International Conference on Multimedia (MULTIMEDIA 05)* (pp. 331–334). ACM.

Davi, J. (2014). Hackers take down the most wired country in Europe. Retrieved from http://www.wired.com/politics/security/ magazine/15-09/ff estonia

Davidson, B. (2008, November). *Web caching and content delivery resources.* Retrieved June 2013 from http://www.web-caching.com

Davis, P., Sakimura, N., Lindelsee, M., & Wachob, G. (2005). *Extensible resource identifier (XRI) syntax V2.0.* OASIS Committee Specification. Retrieved May 2013 from http://docs.oasis-open.org/xri/V2.0

Dean, S. (1938). Considerations involved in making system investments for improved service reliability. *EEI Bulletin,* (6), 491-496.

Debar, H., Dacier, M., & Wespi, A. (1999). Towards a taxonomy of intrusion-detection systems. *Computer Networks, 31*(8), 805–822. doi:10.1016/S1389-1286(98)00017-6

Debar, H., Dacier, M., & Wespi, A. (1999). Towards a taxonomy of intrusion-detection systems. *Computer Networks-The International Journal of Computer and Telecommunication Networking, 3*(8), 805–822.

Deian Stefan, D. Y. Chehai Wu, & Xu, G. (2009). A cryptographic provenance verification approach for host-based malware detection (Tech. Rep.). Rutgers University.

Denning, D. E., & Neumann, P. G. (1985). *Requirements and model for IDES—A real-time intrusion detection expert system* (Document A005). SRI International. Balasubramaniyan, J. S., Garcia-Fernandez, J. O., Isacoff, D., Spafford, E., & Zamboni, D. (1998). An architecture for intrusion detection using autonomous agents. In *Proceedings of Computer Security Applications Conference,* (pp. 13-24). IEEE.

Denning, D. E. (1987). An intrusion detection model. *IEEE Transactions on Software Engineering, 13*(2), 222–232. doi:10.1109/TSE.1987.232894

Desmedt, Y., & Frankel, Y. (1990). Threshold cryptosystems. In *Proceedings of Advances in Cryptology (CRYPTO'89)*. Springer.

Desmedt, Y. (1994). Threshold cryptography. *European Transactions on Telecommunications, 5*(4), 449–458. doi:10.1002/ett.4460050407

Dierks, T. (2008). *RFC 5246: The transport layer security (TLS) protocol version 1.2*. Retrieved May 2013 from http://tools.ietf.org/html/rfc5246

Dierks, T., & Allen, C. (1999). *TLS protocol (version 1.0) – RFC 2246*. Network Working Group. Retrieved May 2013 from http://www.ietf.org/rfc/rfc2246.txt

Dierks, T., & Rescorla, E. (2008). *The transport layer security (TLS) protocol, v. 1.2*. IETF RFC 5246.

Diffie, W., & Hellman, M. (1976). New directions in cryptography. *IEEE Transactions on Information Theory*, *22*(6), 644–654. doi:10.1109/TIT.1976.1055638

Digital Certificate.s (n.d.a). Retrieved from http://technet.microsoft.com/en-us/library/cc962029.aspx

Dittrich, D., & Dietrich, S. (2008). P2P as botnet command and control: A deeper insight. In In Proceedings of 3rd International Conference on Malicious and Unwanted Software (Malware) (p. (pp. 41-48). Piscataway, NJ: Academic Press., USA

Djenouri, D., Khelladi, L., & Badache, N. (2005). A survey of security issues in mobile ad hoc networks. *IEEE Communications Surveys, 7*(4).

Domingo-Ferrer, J., & Torra, V. (2001). Confidentiality, disclosure and data access: Theory and practical applications for statistical agencies. *Pre-Proceedings of ETK-NTTS, 179*(11), 1663–1677.

Donoho, D. L., Flesia, A. G., Shankar, U., Paxson, V., Coit, J., & Staniford, S. (2002). Multiscale stepping-stone detection: Detecting pairs of jittered interactive streams by exploiting maximum tolerable delay. In Proceedings (p. (pp. 17-35). Berlin, Germany: Springer- Verlag.

Dotzer, F. (2006). Privacy issues in vehicular ad hoc networks. In *Privacy enhancing technologies*. Springer. doi:10.1007/11767831_13

Dougherty, J., Kohavi, R., & Sahami, M. (1995). Supervised and unsupervised discretization of continuous features. In *Proceedings of ICML* (pp. 194-202). ICML.

Duda, R. O., Hart, P. E., & Stork, D. G. (2000). *Pattern classification and scene analysis: Pattern classification*. Academic Press.

Dumitru, C., Giurgiu, A., Kleef, A., & Timmers, N. (2010). *HTTPsig: HTTP response signing using DNSSEC*. Retrieved June 2013 from http://tnc2010.terena.org/schedule/posters/pdf/100511170332niek_tnc2010_poster.pdf

DVLabs. H. (2010). 2010 full year top cyber security risks report. Author.

Eastlake, D., & Jones, P. (2001). *US secure hash algorithm 1 (SHA1)*. IETF RFC 3174.

Eastlake, D., & Reagle, J. (2002). *XML encryption syntax and processing*. W3C Recommendation.

Eastlake, D., Reagle, J., Solo, D., Hirsch, F., & Roessler, T. (2008). XML signature syntax and processing (2nd ed.). W3C Recommendation.

Eaton, D. (n. d.). Diving into the 802.11i spec: A tutorial. *EETimes News and Analysis*. Retrieved August 30, 2012, from http://www.eetimes.com/electronics-news/4143367/Diving-into-the-802-11i-Spec-A-Tutorial

Ebeling, C. (1997). *An introduction to reliability and maintainability engineering*. Hoboken, NJ: McGraw Hill.

Eclipse Foundation. (2012). *Higgins project - Personal data service*. Retrieved May 2013 from http://eclipse.org/higgins/

Eidenbenz, S., Anderegg, L., & Wattenhofer, R. (2007). Incentives-compatible, energy-optimal, and efficient ad hoc networking in a selfish milieu. In *Proceedings of the 40th Hawaii International Conference on System Science (HICSS)*. ACM.

Eidenbenz, S., Kumar, V. S., & Zust, S. (2006). Topology control game for ad hoc networks. *ACM Mobile Networks and Application, 11*(2).

Eidenbenz, S., Resrta, G., & Santi, P. (2008). The commit protocol for truthful and cost-efficient routing in ad hoc networks with selfish nodes. *IEEE Transactions on Mobile Computing, 7*(1). doi:10.1109/TMC.2007.1069

Elson, J., Douceur, J. R., Howell, J., & Saul, J. (2007). ASIRRA: A CAPTCHA that exploits interest-aligned manual image categorization. In *Proceedings of the 14th ACM Conference on Computer and Communications Security (CCS 2007)* (pp. 366–374). ACM.

Eskin, E., Miller, M., Zhong, Z. D., Yi, G., Lee, W. A., & Stolfo, S. J. (2000). Adaptive model generation for intrusion detection systems. In *Proceedings of 7th ACM Conference on Computer Security*. Athens, Greece: ACM.

Esposito, F., Malerba, D., Semeraro, G., & Kay, J. (1997). A comparative analysis of methods for pruning decision trees. *IEEE Transactions on Pattern Analysis and Machine Intelligence*, *19*(5), 476–491. doi:10.1109/34.589207

Evan, C., Farnam, J., & Danny, M. (2005). The zombie roundup: Understanding, detecting, and disrupting botnets. In Sruti'05: Proceedings of the Steps to Reducing Unwanted Traffic on the internetInternet on Steps to Re-ducing Unwanted Traffic on the internetInternet Workshop. Berkeley, CA, USA: USENIX Association.

Facebook Developers. (2012). *Core concepts: Authentication*. Facebook Developers. Retrieved May 2013 from https://developers.facebook.com/docs/authentication/

Fayyad, U. M., & Irani, K. B. (1992). On the handling of continuous-valued attributes in decision tree generation. *Machine Learning*, *8*(1), 87–102. doi:10.1007/BF00994007

FBI. (2012). *DNSChanger malware*. Retrieved July, 2012, 2012, from http://www.fbi.gov/news/stories/2011/november/malware_110911/DNS-changer-malware.pdf

Fedor, S., & Collier, M. (2007). On the problem of energy efficiency of multi-hop vs one-hop routing in wireless sensor networks. In *Proceedings of the 21st International Conference on Advanced Information Networking and Applications Workshops* (pp. 380-385). Washington, DC: IEEE Computer Society.

Felegyhazi, M., Buttyan, L., & Hubaux, J. P. (2003). Equilibrium analysis of packet forwarding strategies in wireless ad hoc networks: The static case. In *Proceedings of Personal Wireless Communications*. Academic Press. doi:10.1007/978-3-540-39867-7_70

Felegyhazi, M., & Hubaux, J. P. (2007). *Game theory in wireless networks: A tutorial*. EPFL- Switzerland. LCA-REPORT.

Ferraiolo, D., Sandhu, R., Gavrila, S., Kuhn, D., & Chandramouli, R. (2001). Proposed NIST standard for role-based access control. *ACM Transactions on Information and System Security*, *4*(3), 224–274. doi:10.1145/501978.501980

Ferzli, R., Bazzi, R., & Karam, L. J. (2006). A CAPTCHA based on the human visual systems masking characteristics. In *Proceedings of 2006 IEEE International Conference on Multimedia and Expo (ICME 06)* (pp. 517–520). IEEE.

FIDES. (2012, April 30). *The FIDES methodology*. Retrieved from http://tinyurl.com/d5a2bn6

Financial Insights Evaluates Impact of Phishing on Retail Financial Institutions Worldwide. (2014). Retrieved from http://www.crm2day.com/ content/t6 librarynews 1.php?news id=EplAlZlEVFjAwhYlkt

Fiore, M., Harri, J., Filali, F., & Bonnet, C. (2007). Vehicular mobility simulation for VANETs. In *Proceedings of Simulation Symposium*. IEEE.

Franks, J., Hallam-Baker, P., Hostetler, J., Lawrence, S., Leach, P., Luotonen, A., & Stewart, L. (1999). *HTTP authentication: Basic and digest access authentication*. RFC 2617.

Freeman, D., Scott, M., & Teske, E. (2010). A taxonomy of pairing-friendly elliptic curves. *Journal of Cryptology*, *22*(2), 224–280. doi:10.1007/s00145-009-9048-z

Freier, A., Karlton, P., & Kocher, P. (2011). *Secure socket layer (SSL) protocol version 3.0 – RFC 6101*. Intenert Engineering Task Force (IETF). Retrieved May 2013 from http://tools.ietf.org/html/rfc6101

Freiling, F. C., Holz, T., & Wicherski, G. (2005). Botnet tracking: Exploring a root-cause methodology to prevent distributed denial-of- service attacks. In In Proceedings of 10th European Symposium on Research in Computer Security (LNCS), esorics 2005, september 12,2005 - september 14 (Vol. 3679 LNCS, pp. 319-335). Milan, Italy: Springer Verlag.

Freir, A. O., Karlton, P., & Kocher, P. C. (1996). *The SSL protocol version 3.0*. Netscape's Final SSL 3.0 Draft.

Friedman, N., & Goldszmidt, M. (1996). Building classifiers using Bayesian networks. In *Proceedings of the National Conference on Artificial Intelligence* (pp. 1277-1284). Academic Press.

Fuller. (1993). Masking procedures for microdata disclosure limitation. *Journal of Official Statistics, 9*(2), 383–406.

Fung, Wang, Chen, & Yu. (2010).Privacy-preserving data publishing: A survey of recent developments. *ACM Computing Surveys, 42*(4). doi:10.1145/1749603.1749605

Fürnkranz, J. (1997). Pruning algorithms for rule learning. *Machine Learning, 27*(2), 139–172. doi:10.1023/A:1007329424533

Ganeriwl, S., & Srivastava, M. B. (2004). *Reputation based framework for high integrity sensor networks*. Paper presented at the ACM Workshop on Security of Ad hoc and Sensor Networks. New York, NY.

Garfinkel, S. (1994). *PGP: Pretty good privacy*. Sebastopol, CA: O'Reilly.

Gast, M. (2005). *802.11 wireless networks: The definitive guide*. Sebastopol, CA: O'Reilly Media.

Gerard, M. (2008). *Smart sensor systems*. Hoboken, NJ: John Wiley & Sons Inc.

Gerlach, M., & Guttler, F. (2007). Privacy in VANETs using changing pseudonyms-ideal and real. In *Proceedings of Vehicular Technology Conference*. IEEE.

Ghosh, A., Wolter, D., Andrews, J., & Chen, R. (2005). Broadband wireless access with wimax/802.16: Current performance benchmarks and future potential. *IEEE Communications Magazine, 43*(2), 129–136. doi:10.1109/MCOM.2005.1391513

Giroire, F., Chandrashekar, J., Taft, N., Schooler, E., & Papagiannaki, D. (2009). Exploiting temporal persistence to detect covert botnet channels. In In Proceedings of the 12th International Symposium on Recent Advances in Intrusion Detection (RAID'09). RAID.

Gitanjali, J., Banu, Mary, Indumathi, & Uma, G.V. (2007). An agent based burgeoning framework for privacy preserving information harvesting systems. *Computer Science and Network Security, 7*(11), 268–276.

GlassFish Metro Project. (2012). Retrieved May 2013 from http://metro.java.net/

Godfrey, P. B. (2002). Text-based CAPTCHA algorithms. In *Proceedings of First Workshop on Human Interactiv Proofs (HIP 2002)*. HIP.

Golle, P. (2008). Machine learning attacks against the ASIRRA CAPTCHA. In *Proceedings of the 15th ACM Conference on Computer and Communications Security (CCS '08)* (pp. 535–542). ACM.

Goodman, J., & Rounthwaite, R. (2004). Stopping outgoing spam. In *Proceedings of the 5th ACM Conference on Electronic Commerce* (pp. 30–39). ACM.

Goodrich, M. T. (2002). Efficient packet marking for large-scale IP traceback. In Proceedings of the 9th ACM Conference on Computer and Communications Security, November 18,2002 - November 22 (p.(pp. 117-126). Washington, DC, United states: Association for Computing Ma- chinery.

Google Developers. (2012). *SAML single sign-on (SSO) service for Google Apps*. Retrieved May 2013 from https://developers.google.com/google-apps/sso/saml_reference_implementation

Google. (2012). *Federated login for Google account users*. Google Developers. Retrieved May 2013 from https://developers.google.com/accounts/docs/OpenID

Gordon, M., & Melham, T. (1993). *Introduction to HOL: A theorem proving environment for higher-order logic*. Cambridge, UK: Cambridge University Press.

Govil, A. (1983). *Reliability engineering*. Hoboken, NJ: TATA McGraw-Hill Publishing Company.

Grabher, P., Groszschaedl, J., & Page, D. (2008). On software parallel implementation of cryptographic pairing. In *Selected areas in cryptology* (pp. 35–50). Berlin: Springer-Verlag.

Greenberg, B. (1990). Disclosure avoidance research at the census bureau. In *Proceedings of Census Bureau Annual Research Conference*. Washington, DC: US Government.

Grizzard, J. B., Sharma, V., Nunnery, C., Kang, B. B., & Dagon, D. (2007). Peer-to-peer botnets: Overview and case study. In Hotbots'07: Proceedings of the First Conference on First Workshop on Hot Topics in Understanding Botnets. Berkeley, CA, USA: USENIX Association.

Gu, G., Porras, P., Yegneswaran, V., Fong, M., & Lee, W. (2007). Bothunter: Detecting malware infection through ids-driven dialog correlation. In SS'07: Proceedings of 16th USENIX Security Symposium on USENIX Security symposium (pp. 1–16). Berkeley, CA, USA: USENIX Association.

Gu, G., Zhang, J., & Lee, W. (2008, February). Botsniffer: Detecting botnet command and control channels in network traffic. In Proceedings of the 15th Annual Network and Distributed System Security Symposium (NDSS'08). NDSS.

Gudgin, M., Hadley, M., Mendelsohn, N., Moreau, J., Frystyk, H., Karmarkar, A., & Lafon, Y. (2007). SOAP version 1.2 part 1: Messaging framework (2nd ed.). W3C Recommendation.

GummadiR.BalakrishnanH.ManiatisP.RatnasamyS. (2009).

Guofei, G., Roberto, P., Junjie, Z., & Wenke, L. (2008). Botminer: Clustering analysis of network traffic for protocol and structure-independent botnet detection. In SS'08: Proceedings of the 17th Conference on Security Symposium (p. (pp. 139-154). Berkeley, CA, USA: USENIX Association.

Haenggi, M. (2004). Twelve reasons not to route over many short hops. In *Proceedings of 60th Vehicular Technology Conference* (pp. 3130-3134). Piscataway, NJ: IEEE Computer Society.

Haenggi, M., & Puccinelli, D. (2005). Routing in ad hoc networks: A case for long hops. *IEEE Communications Magazine*, 93–101. doi:10.1109/MCOM.2005.1522131

Hammer, E. (2010). *Introducing OAuth 2.0*. Hueniverse Blog. Retrieved May 2013 from http://hueniverse.com/2010/05/introducing-oauth-2-0

Hammer-Lahav, E. (2010). *RFC 5849 - The OAuth 1.0 protocol*. Internet Engineering Task Force (IETF). Retrieved May 2013 from http://tools.ietf.org/html/rfc5849

Hamou, R. M., Amine, A., Lokbani, A. C., & Simonet, M. (2012). *Visualization and clustering by 3D cellular automata: Application to unstructured data.* arXiv preprint arXiv:1211.5766

Hamou, R. M., Amine, A., & Boudia, A. (2013). A new meta-heuristic based on social bees for detection and filtering of spam. *International Journal of Applied Metaheuristic Computing*, *4*(3), 15–33. doi:10.4018/ijamc.2013070102

Hamou, R. M., Amine, A., & Rahmani, M. (2012). A new biomimetic approach based on social spiders for clustering of text. In *Proceedings of Software Engineering Research, Management and Applications 2012* (pp. 17–30). Berlin: Springer. doi:10.1007/978-3-642-30460-6_2

Hamou, R. M., Lehireche, A., Lokbani, A. C., & Rahmani, M. (2010). Representation of textual documents by the approach wordnet and n-grams for the unsupervised classification (clustering) with 2D cellular automata: A comparative study. *Computer and Information Science*, *3*(3), 240–255.

Hardt, D. (2012). *The OAuth 2.0 authorization framework*. Internet Engineering Task Force (IETF). Retrieved May 2013 from http://tools.ietf.org/html/rfc6749

Hardt, D., Bufu, J., & Hoyt, J. (2007). *OpenID attribute exchange 1.0*. OpenID.net. Retrieved May 2013 from https://openid.net/specs/openid-attribute-exchange-1_0.html

Harkins, D., & Carrel, D. (1998). *The internet key exchange (IKE)*. IETF RFC 2409.

Harris, S. (2007). *CISSP all-in-one exam guide*. New York: McGraw-Hill Osborne Media.

Hasan, O. (2008). *Formal probabilistic analysis using theorem proving*. (PhD Thesis). Concordia University, Montreal, Canada.

Hasan, O., & Tahar, S. (2008). Performance analysis of ARQ protocols using a theorem prover. In *Proceedings of the International Symposium on Performance Analysis of Systems and Software* (pp. 85-94). IEEE Computer Society.

Hasan, O., Tahar, S., & Abbasi, N. (2010). Formal reliability analysis using theorem proving. *IEEE Transactions on Computers*, *59*(5), 579–592. doi:10.1109/TC.2009.165

He, L., & Liu, H. (2005). Shape context for image understanding. In *Proceedings of the 5th WSEAS International Conference on Signal, Speech and Image Processing* (pp. 276–281). WSEAS.

Heidemann, J., Ye, W., & Estrin, D. (2002). *An energy efficient mac protocol for wireless sensor networks*. Paper presented at IEEE INFOCOM. New York, NY.

Heinzelman, W. R., Chandrakasan, A., & Balakrishnan, H. (2000). Energy-efficient communication protocol for wireless microsensor networks. In *Proceedings of the 33rd Hawaii International Conference on System Sciences* (pp. 3005-3014). Washington, DC: IEEE Computer Society.

Hogben, G., Plohmann, D., Gerhards-Padilla, E., & Leder, F. (2011). *Botnets: Detection, measurement, disinfection and defence. European Network and Information Security Agency*. ENISA.

Holman, J., Lazar, J., Feng, J. H., & D'Arcy, J. (2007). Developing usable captchas for blind users. In *Proceedings of the 9th International ACM SIGACCESS Conference on Computers and Accessibility (ASSETS '07)* (pp. 245–246). ACM.

Holz, T., & Raynal, F. (2005). Detecting honeypots and other suspicious environments. In (Vol. 2005, p. 29 - 36). West Point, NY: United statesAcademic Press.

Holz, T., Gorecki, C., Rieck, K., & Freiling, F. C. (2008). Measuring and detecting fast-flux service networks. In Proceedings of the 15th Annual Network and Distributed System Security Symposium (NDSS'08). NDSS.

Holz, T., Steiner, M., Dahl, F., Biersack, E., & Freiling, F. (2008). Measurements and mitigation of peer-to-peer-based botnets: A case study on storm worm. In LEET'08: Proceedings of the 1st USENIX Workshop on Large-Scale Exploits and Emergent Threats (pp. 1–9). Berkeley, CA, USA: USENIX Association.

Honig, A., Howard, A., Eskin, E., & Stolfo, S. J. (2002). Adaptive model generation: An architecture for the deployment of data mining-based intrusion detection systems. In D. Barbara, & S. Jajodia (Eds.), *Applications of data mining in computer security*. Dordrecht, The Netherlands: Kluwer Academic Publishers. doi:10.1007/978-1-4615-0953-0_7

Hopper, N. (2002). Security and complexity aspects of human interactive proofs. In *Proceedings of First Workshop on Human Interactive Proofs (HIP 2002)*. HIP.

Hoque, M. E., Russomanno, D. J., & Yeasin, M. (2006). 2D CAPTCHAs from 3D models.[IEEE.]. *Proceedings of the IEEE SouthEastCon, 2006*, 165–170.

Howard, F. (2012). *Exploring the blackhole exploit kit*. Retrieved from http://nakedsecurity.sophos.com/exploring-the-blackhole-exploit-kit-3/

Hu, X., Knysz, M., & Shin, K. G. (2009). RB-seeker auto-detection of redirection botnets. In In Proceedings of 16th Annual Network & Distributed System Security Symposium (NDSS'09). NDSS.

Hubaux, J., Buttyán, L., & Capkun, S. (2001). The quest for security in mobile ad hoc networks. In *Proceedings of the 2nd ACM International Symposium on Mobile Ad Hoc Networking & Computing*. ACM.

Hughes, J., Cantor, S., Hirsch, F., Mishra, P., Philpott, R., & Maler, E. (2005). *Bindings for the OASIS security assertion markup language (SAML) V2.0*. OASIS Standard. Retrieved May 2013 from ttp://docs.oasis-open.org/security/saml/v2.0/saml-profiles-2.0-os.pdf

Hugh, J. M., Christie, A., & Allen, J. (2000). Defending yourself: The role of intrusion detection systems. *IEEE Software, 17*(5), 42–51. doi:10.1109/52.877859

Hunt, R. (2001). PKI and digital certification infrastructure. In *Proceedings of Networks*. IEEE.

Hurd, J. (2002). *Formal verification of probabilistic algorithms*. (PhD Thesis). University of Cambridge, Cambridge, UK.

Hurd, J., McIver, A., & Morgan, C. (2005). Probabilistic guarded commands mechanized in HOL. *Theoretical Computer Science, 346*(1), 96–112. doi:10.1016/j.tcs.2005.08.005

Ilgun, K., Kemmerer, R. A., & Porras, P. A. (1995). Probability propagation. *IEEE Transactions on Software Engineering, 21*(3), 181–199. doi:10.1109/32.372146

Imad, M., & Mohammed, I. (2005). *Handbook of sensor networks: Compact wireless and wired sensing systems*. New York, NY: CRC Press.

Indumathi, J., & Uma, G. V. (2008c). A novel framework for optimized privacy preserving data mining using the innovative desultory technique. *International Journal of Computer Applications in Technology, 35*(2/3/4), 194 – 203.

Indumathi, J., & Uma, G. V. (2007a). Customized privacy preservation using unknowns to stymie unearthing of association rules. *Journal of Computer Science, 3*(12), 874–881.

Indumathi, J., & Uma, G. V. (2007b). Using privacy preserving techniques to accomplish a secure accord. *Computer Scienceand Network Security, 7*(8), 258–266.

Indumathi, J., & Uma, G. V. (2008a). An aggrandized framework for genetic privacy preserving pattern analysis using cryptography and contravening-conscious knowledge management systems. *Molecular Medicine and Advance Sciences, 4*(1), 33–40.

Indumathi, J., & Uma, G. V. (2008b). A new flustering approach for privacy preserving data fishing in tele-health care systems. *International Journal of Healthcare Technology and Management, 9*(5), 495–516. doi:10.1504/IJHTM.2008.020201

Indumathi, J., & Uma, G. V. (2008d). A Panglossian solitary-skim sanitization for privacy preserving data archaeology. *International Journal of Electrical and Power Engineering, 2*(3), 154–165.

Institute of Electrical and Electronics Engineers. (1998). *IEEE standard reliability program for the development and production of electronic systems and equipment.* IEEE.

Jan, G., & Thorsten, H. (2007). Rishi: Identify bot contaminated hosts by IRC nickname evaluation. In Hotbots'07: Proceedings of the First Conference on First Workshop on Hot Topics in Understanding Botnets. Berkeley, CA, USA: USENIX Association.

Janicke, H., Sarrab, M., & Aldabbas, H. (2012). Controlling data dissemination. In *Data privacy management and autonomous spontaneus security.* Springer. doi:10.1007/978-3-642-28879-1_21

Jiang, D., Taliwal, V., Meier, A., Holfelder, W., & Herrtwich, R. (2006). Design of 5.9 GHz DSRC-based vehicular safety communication. *IEEE Wireless Communications, 13*(5), 36–43. doi:10.1109/WC-M.2006.250356

John, J. P., Moshchuk, A., Gribble, S. D., & Krishnamurthy, A. (2009). Studying spamming botnets using botlab. In NSDI'09: Proceedings of the 6th USENIX Symposium on Networked Systems Design and Implementation (pp. 291–306). Berkeley, CA, USA: USENIX Association.

Jones, J. (2012). *State of web exploit kits.* Paper presented at the BlackHat USA 2012. Las Vegas, NV. Retrieved from http://media.blackhat.com/bh-us-12/Briefings/Jones/BH_US_12_Jones_State_Web_Exploits_WP.pdf

Jones, M., & Hardt, D. (2012). *The OAuth 2.0 authorization protocol: Bearer tokens usage.* Internet Engineering Task Force (IETF). Retrieved May 2013 from http://tools.ietf.org/html/rfc6750

Jueles, A. (2002). At the juncture of cryptography and humanity. In *Proceedings of First Workshop on Human Interactive Proofs (HIP 2002).* HIP.

Kafeine. (2012). *Cool exploit kit - A new browser exploit pack on the battlefield with a Duqu like font drop.* Retrieved from http://malware.dontneedcoffee.com/2012/10/newcoolek.html

Kar, D. C., Ngo, H. L., & Mulkey, C. J. (2011). Applied cryptography in wireless sensor networks. In Nemati & Yang (Eds.), Applied cryptography for cyber security and defense: Information encryption and cyphering, (pp. 146-167). Hershey, PA: IGI Global.

Karlof, C., & Wagner, D. (2003). *Secure routing in wireless sensor networks: Attacks and countermeasures.* Paper presented at the 1st IEEE International Workshop on Sensor Network Protocols and Applications (SPNA). New York, NY.

Kaspersky. (2012). *Kaspersky security bulletin 2012: The overall statistics for 2012.* Retrieved 21 June, 2012, from https://www.securelist.com/en/analysis/204792255/Kaspersky_Security_Bulletin_2012_The_overall_statistics_for_2012

Katz, J., & Lindell, Y. (2008). *Introduction to modern cryptography.* London: Chapman & Hall.

Kayacik, H. G., Zincir-Heywood, A. N., & Heywood, M. I. (2005). Selecting features for intrusion detection: A feature relevance analysis on KDD 99 intrusion detection datasets. In *Proceedings of Third Annual Conference on Privacy, Security and Trust.* Academic Press.

KDD. (2013). Retrieved June 16, 2013, from http://kdd. ics.uci.edu/databases/kddcup99/kddcup99.html

Kent, S., & Atkinson, R. (1998a). *Security architecture for the internet protocol*. IETF RFC 2401.

Kent, S., & Atkinson, R. (1998b). *IP authentication header*. IETF RFC 2402.

Kent, S., & Atkinson, R. (1998c). *IP encapsulating security (ESP)*. IETF RFC 2406.

Killat, M., Schmidt-Eisenlohr, F., Hartenstein, H., Rossel, C., Vortisch, P., Assenmacher, S., & Busch, F. (2007). Enabling efficient and accurate large-scale simulations of vanets for vehicular traffic management. In *Proceedings of the Fourth ACM International Workshop on Vehicular Ad Hoc Networks*. ACM. http://doi.acm.org/10.1145/1287748.1287754

Kim & Winkler. (1995). Masking microdata files. In *Survey Research Methods Section* (pp. 114–119). American Statistical Association.

Kindsight. (2012). *Malware report*. Author.

Klosgen, W. (1995). Anonymization techniques for knowledge discovery in databases. In *Proceedings of the First International Conference on Knowledge and Discovery in Data Mining*, (pp. 186-191). Academic Press.

Know Your Enemy. (2014). *Fast-Flux Service Networks*. Retrieved from. http://www.honeynet.org/papers/ff/

Kochanski, G., Lopresti, D., & Shih, C. (2002). A reverse turing test using speech. In *Proceedings of the 7ᵗʰ International Conference on Spoken Language Processing (ICSLP 2002)* (pp. 1357–1360). ICSLP.

Kolupaev, A., & Ogijenko, J. (2008). CAPTCHAs: Humans vs. bots. *IEEE Security & Privacy, 6*(1), 68–70. doi:10.1109/MSP.2008.6

Krebs, B. (2014). Storm worm dwarfs world's top supercomputers. Retrieved from http://blog.washingtonpost.com/securityfix/2007/08/storm worm dwarfs worlds top s 1.html

Krebsonsecurity. (2013). *Crimeware author funds exploit buying spree*. Retrieved from http://krebsonsecurity.com/2013/01/crimeware-author-funds-exploit-buying-spree/

Kumar, S., & Spafford, E. H. (1994). *An application of pattern matching in intrusion detection* (Technical Report CSD-TR-94-013). The COAST Project, Department of Computer Science, Perdue University.

Kurose, J. F., & Ross, K. W. (2008). The link layer and local area networks. In *Computer networking: A top-down approach* (4th ed.). Upper Saddle River, NJ: Pearson Education Inc.

Kwiatkowska, M., Norman, G., Segala, R., & Sproston, J. (2002). Automatic verification of real-time systems with discrete probability distributions. *Theoretical Computer Science, 282*(1), 101–150. doi:10.1016/S0304-3975(01)00046-9

Labadi, K., Saggadi, S., & Amodeo, L. (2009). PSA-SPN - A parameter sensitivity analysis method using stochastic petri nets: Application to a production line system. *AIP Conference Proceedings, 1107*(1), 263–268. doi:10.1063/1.3106483

Labib, K. (2004). Computer security and intrusion detection. *Crossroads, 11*(1), 2–2. doi:10.1145/1031859.1031861

Lacasse, A. (2006). *Approche algébrique pour la prévention d'intrusion. Mémoire de maîtrise en Informatique*. Québec, Canada: Faculté Des Etudes Supérieures de l'Université Laval.

Langford, J. (2006). *Logistics: Principles and applications*. Hoboken, NJ: SOLE Press/McGraw-Hill.

Lappas, T., & Pelechrinis, K. (2007). *Data mining techniques for (network) intrusion detection systems* (White Paper). Department of Computer Science and Engineering, University of California Riverside.

Larsen, C. (2012). *Forbidden fruit: The sweet orange exploit kit*. Retrieved from http://www.bluecoat.com/security-blog/2012-12-17/forbidden-fruit-sweet-orange-exploit-kit

Lashkari, A., Danesh, M., & Samadi, B. (2009). A survey on wireless security protocols (WEP, WPA, and WPA2/802.11i). In *Proceedings of Second IEEE International Conference on, Computer Science and Information Technology (ICCSIT)*, (pp. 48-52). IEEE.

Lashkari, A. H., Ghalebandi, S. G., & Reza Moradhaseli, M. (2011). A wide survey on botnet. In *Digital information and communication technology and its applications* (pp. 445–454). Academic Press. doi:10.1007/978-3-642-21984-9_38

Lawrence, K., & Kaler, C. (2006a). *Web services security: SAML token profile 1.1.* OASIS Web Services Security (WSS) TC. Retrieved May 2013 from http://docs.oasis-open.org/wss/v1.1/wss-v1.1-spec-errata-os-SAMLTokenProfile.pdf

Lawrence, K., & Kaler, C. (2006b). *Web services security: Kerberos token profile 1.1.* Web Services Security (WSS). Retrieved May 2013 from http://docs.oasis-open.org/wss/v1.1/wss-v1.1-spec-errata-os-KerberosTokenProfile.pdf

Lawrence, K., & Kaler, C. (2006c). *Web services security: X.509 certificate token profile 1.1.* Web Services Security (WSS). Retrieved May 2013 from http://docs.oasis-open.org/wss/v1.1/wss-v1.1-spec-errata-os-x509TokenProfile.pdf

Lawrence, K., & Kaler, C. (2007a). *WS-SecureConversation 1.3.* OASIS Web Services Secure Exchange TC. Retrieved May 2013 from http://docs.oasis-open.org/ws-sx/ws-secureconversation/200512/ws-secureconversation-1.3-os.html

Lawrence, K., & Kaler, C. (2007b). *WS-SecurityPolicy 1.2.* OASIS Web Services Secure Exchange TC. Retrieved May 2013 from http://docs.oasis-open.org/ws-sx/ws-securitypolicy/200702/ws-securitypolicy-1.2-spec-os.html

Lawrence, K., & Kaler, K. (2006d). *Web services security: SOAP message security 1.1 (WS-Security 2004).* OASIS Standard. Retrieved May 2013 from http://docs.oasis-open.org/wss/v1.1/wss-v1.1-spec-errata-os-SOAPMessageSecurity.pdf

Lazarevic, A., Kumar, V., & Srivastava, J. (2005). Intrusion detection: A survey. *Managing Cyber Threats, 5,* 19–78. doi:10.1007/0-387-24230-9_2

Lee, C. D. D. Wenke; & Wang. (Ed.). (2008). Botnet detection: Countering the largest security threat (Vol. 36). New York: Springer-Verlag New York.

Lee, W., & Stolfo, S. J. (1998). Data mining approaches for intrusion detection. In *Proceedings of Seventh USENIX Security Symposium (SECURITY '98).* San Antonio, TX: USENIX.

Lee, W., & Stolfo, S. J., & MoK, K. W. (2000). Adaptive intrusion detection: A data mining approach. *Artificial Intelligence Review, 14*(6), 533–567. doi:10.1023/A:1006624031083

Lee, W., Stolfo, S. J., Chan, P. K., Eskin, E., Fan, M., & Miller, M. et al. (2001). Real time data mining-based intrusion detection. *DARPA Information Survivability Conference & Exposition II, 1,* 89–100.

Lee, W., Stolfo, S. J., & Molk, K. W. (1998). *A data mining framework for adaptive intrusion detection.* New York: Computer Science Department, Columbia University.

LeFevre. DeWitt, & Ramakrishnan. (2005). Incognito: Efficient full-domain k-anonymity. In *Proceedings of the 2005 ACM SIGMOD International Conference on Management of Data (SIGMOD'05).* Baltimore, MD: ACM.

Lehr, W., & McKnight, L. (2003). Wireless Internet access: 3G vs. WiFi. *Telecommunications Policy, 27*(5-6), 351–370. doi:10.1016/S0308-5961(03)00004-1

Lemos, R. (2014). *Bot software looks to improve peerage.* Retrieved from. http://www.securityfocus.com/news/11390

Levin, D. (2006). *Punishment in selfish wireless networks: A game theoretic analysis.* Paper presented at the Workshop on the Economics of Networked Systems. New York, NY.

Li, J., Sung, M., Xu, J., & Li, L. (2004). Large-scale IP traceback in high-speed internetinternet: Practical techniques and theoretical foundation. In Proceedings - 2004 IEEE Symposium on Security and Privacy, May 09,2004 - May 12 (pVol. 2004, p. 115-129). Berkeley, CA, United states: IEEE Computer Society.

Li, S., & Wang, X. (n.d.). *Enhanced security design for threshold cryptography in ad hoc network.* Academic Press.

Liao, W. H. (2006). A CAPTCHA mechanism by exchange image blocks. In *Proceedings of the 18th International Conference on Pattern Recognition (ICPR 06)* (pp. 1179–1183). ICPR.

Liao, W. H., & Chang, C. C. (2004). Embedding information within dynamic visual patterns. In *Proceedings of the 2004 IEEE International Conference on Multimedia and Expo (ICME 04)* (Vol. 2, pp. 895–898). IEEE.

Li, F., & Wang, Y. (2008). Routing in vehicular ad hoc networks: A survey. *IEEE Vehicular Technology Magazine*, 2(2), 12–22. doi:10.1109/MVT.2007.912927

Liu, A., & Ning, P. (2008). TinyECC: A configurable library for elliptic curve cryptography in wireless sensor networks. In *Proceedings of the 7th International Conference on Information Processing in Sensor Networks,* (pp. 245-256). Academic Press.

Liu, L., Chen, S., Yan, G., & Zhang, Z. (2008). Bottracer: Execution-based bot-like malware detection. Information Security, , 97–113.

Liu, Y., & Yang, Y. R. (2003). Reputation propagation and agreement in mobile ad-hoc networks. In *Proceedings of IEEE Wireless Communications and Networking Conference* (WCNC). IEEE.

Liu, G., Yi, Z., & Yang, S. (2007). A hierarchical intrusion detection model based on the PCA neural networks. *Neurocomputing*, 70, 1561–1568. doi:10.1016/j.neucom.2006.10.146

Livadas, C., Walsh, R., Lapsley, D., & Strayer, W. T. (2006). Using ma- chine learning techniques to identify botnet traffic. In In Proceedings of 31st Annual IEEE Conference on Local Computer Networks, November 14,2006 - November 16 (p.(pp. 967-974). Tampa, FL, United states: IEEE Computer Society.

Li, W., & Joshi, A. (2004). Security issues in mobile ad hoc networks-a survey. *White House Papers Graduate Research in Informatics at Sussex, 17*, 1–23.

Lockhart, H., & Campbell, B. (2008). *Security assertion markup language (SAML) V2.0 technical overview*. OASIS Committee Draft. Retrieved May 2013 from https://www.oasis-open.org/committees/download.php/27819/sstc-saml-tech-overview-2.0-cd-02.pdf

Lockhart, H., Andersen, S., Bohren, J., et al. (2006). *Web services federation language (WSFederation)*. OASIS Standard. Retrieved May 2013 from http://download.boulder.ibm.com/ibmdl/pub/software/dw/specs/ws-fed/WS-Federation-V1-1B.pdf

Lopresti, D. (2005). Leveraging the CAPTCHA problem. In *Proceedings of Second International Workshop on Human Interactive Proofs (HIP 2005)* (pp. 97–110). HIP.

Lopresti, D., & Shih, C. (2002). Human interactive proofs for spoken language interface. In *Proceedings of First Workshop on Human Interactive Proofs (HIP 2002)*. HIP.

Lorincz, K. et al. (2004). Sensor networks for emergency response: Challenges and opportunities. *IEEE Pervasive Computing / IEEE Computer Society [and] IEEE Communications Society*, 3(4), 16–23. doi:10.1109/MPRV.2004.18

Lu, W., Tavallaee, M., & Ghorbani, A. (2009). Automatic discovery of botnet communities on large-scale communication networks. In Asia CCS'09: Proceedings of the 4th International Symposium on Information, Computer, and Communications Security (pp. 1–10). New York, NY, USA: ACM.

Lu, W., Tavallaee, M., Rammidi, G., & Ghorbani, A. (2009). Botcop: An online botnet traffic classifier. In CNSR '09: Proceedings of the 2009 Seventh Annual Communication Networks and Services Research Conference (pp. 70–77). Washington, DC, USA: IEEE Computer Society.

Lunt, T. F., Javitz, H., Tamaru, A., & Valdes, A. (1995). *Detecting unusual program behavior using the statistical component of the next-generation intrusion detection expert system (NIDES). SRI International.* Computer Science Laboratory.

Määttänen, T. (2002). *Single sign-on systems*. Helsinki University of Technology.

Machado, R., & Tekinay, S. (2008). A survey of game theoretic approaches in wireless sensor networks. *Elsevier Computer Networks Journal, 52.*

Maclean's J. Gatehouse V. (2005). *You are exposed (Canadian Ed.*, pp. 26–29). Maclean's.

MacMichael, J. L. (n.d.). Auditing wi-fi protected access (WPA) pre-shared key mode. *Linux Journal, 137.*

Magnini, G. (2005, September). *Introduction to SSL.* Retrieved June 2013 from https://developer.mozilla.org/en/Introduction_to_SSL

Magnus, A., & Erland, J. (2004). Using active learning in intrusion detection. In *Proceedings of Computer Security Foundations Workshop*, (pp. 88-98). Academic Press.

Malekzadeh, M., Abdul Ghani, A. A., Subramaniam, S., & Desa, J. (2011). Validating reliability of omnet++ in wireless networks DOS attacks: Simulation vs. test-bed. *International Journal of Network Security, 123*(1), 13–21.

MalwareIntelligence. (2010). *Phoenix exploit's kit from the mythology to a criminal business.* Author.

Manui, S., & Kakkasageri, M. (2008). Issues in mobile ad hoc networks for vehicular communication. *IETE Technical Review, 25*(2), 59.

Mario, N., Joern, P., & Klaus, K. (2006). Evaluation of energy costs for single hop vs. multi hop with respect to topology parameters. In *Proceedings of IEEE International Workshop on Factory Communication Systems*, (pp. 175-182). IEEE.

Markkola, A., & Lindqvist, J. (2008). Accessible voice captchas for internet telephony. In *Proceedings of the 4th Symposium on Usable Privacy and Security (SOUPS '08).* SOUPS.

Markovic, M. (2007). Data protection techniques, cryptographic protocols and PKI systems in modern computer networks. In *Proceedings of 14th International Workshop on Systems, Signals, and Image Processing and 6th EURASIP Conference focused on Speech and Image Processing, Multimedia Communications, and Services*, (pp. 13-24). EURASIP.

Martignoni, L., Stinson, E., Fredrikson, M., Jha, S., & Mitchell, J. (2008). A layered architecture for detecting malicious behaviors. Recent Advances in Intrusion Detection, , 78–97.

Masud, M. M., Al-Khaleeb, T., Khan, L., Thuraisinghatn, B., & Hamlcn, K. W. (2008). Flow-based identification of botnet traffic by mining multiple log files. In (p.In Proceedings (pp. 200 - 206). Penang, Malaysia: Academic Press.

Maughan, D., Schertler, M., Schneider, M., & Turner, J. (1998). *Internet security association and key management protocol (ISAKMP).* IETF RFC 2408.

McHugh, J. (2000). Testing intrusion detection systems: A critique of the 1998 and 1999 darpa intrusion detection system evaluations as performed by lincoln laboratory. *ACM Transactions on Information and System Security, 3*(4), 262–294. doi:10.1145/382912.382923

Mé, L. (1997). Un complément à l'approche formelle: La détection d'intrusion. Actes de la Journée CIDR97. Rennes, France.

Mehul, E., & Limaye, V. (2009). Security in mobile ad hoc networks. In *Handbook of research in mobile business: Technical, methodological and social perspectives.* Hershey, PA: IGI Global.

Mé, L., Marrakchi, Z., Michel, C., Debar, H., & Cuppens, F. (2001). La détection d'intrusion: Les outils doivent coopérer. *Revue de l'Electricité et de l'Electronique, 5,* 50–55.

MEMSIC Inc. (n.d.). *Micaz wireless measurement system.* Retrieved from http://www.memsic.com

Menezes, A., Van Oorschot, P., & Vanstone, S. (1997). *Handbook of applied cryptography.* Boca Raton, FL: CRC.

Michiardi, P., & Molva, R. (2002)a. *Core: A collaborative reputation mechanism to enforce node cooperation in mobile ad hoc networks.* Paper presented at the Communications and Multimedia Security Conference. New York, NY.

Michiardi, P., & Molva, R. (2002d). *Simulation based analysis of security exposures in mobile ad hoc networks.* Paper presented at the European Wireless 2002: Next Generation Wireless Networks: Technologies, Protocols, Services and Applications. New York, NY.

Michiardi, P., & Molva, R. (2002b). *Game theoretic analysis of security in mobile ad hoc networks (Research Report).* Institute Eurecom.

Michiardi, P., & Molva, R. (2002c). *Prevention of denial of service attack and selfishness in mobile ad hoc networks (Research Report).* Institute Eurecom.

Microsoft. (2007). *ASIRRA (animal species image recognition for restricting access).* Retrieved from http://research.microsoft.com/asirra/

Mishra, A., & Nadkarni, K. (2003). Security in wireless ad hoc networks. In *The handbook of ad hoc wireless networks*. Boca Raton, FL: CRC Press, Inc.

Misra, D., & Gaj, K. (2006). Face recognition CAPTCHAs. In *Proceedings of the Advanced International Conference on Telecommunications and International Conference on Internet and Web Applications and Services (AICT-ICIW 06)* (pp. 122). AICT-ICIW.

Misra, S., Woungang, I., & Misra, S. C. (2009). *Guide to wireless ad hoc networks*. New York: Springer-Verlag New York Inc. doi:10.1007/978-1-84800-328-6

MIT. (2013). Retrieved June 16, 2013, from http://www.ll.mit.edu/mission/communications/cyber/CSTcorpora/ideval/data/

Mockapetris, P. (1987, November). Domain names - Implementation and specification (Tech. Rep.). RFC 1035.

Mogul, J., & Van Hoff, A. (2002, January). *Instance digests in HTTP*. Retrieved June 2013 from http://tools.ietf.org/html/rfc3230

Mollin, R. (2007). *An introduction to cryptography*. Boca Raton, FL: CRC Press.

Moore, D., Shannon, C., Brown, D. J., Voelker, G. M., & Savage, S. (2006). Inferring internetinternet denial-of-service activity. *ACM Transactions on Computer Systems*, *24*(2), 115–139. doi:10.1145/1132026.1132027

Moore, R. A. Jr. (1996). *Controlled data-swapping techniques for masking public use microdata sets*. Washington, DC: US Bureau of Census.

Mori, G., & Malik, J. (2003). Recognizing objects in adversarial clutter: Breaking a visual CAPTCHA. In *Proceedings of 2003 IEEE Conference on Computer Vision and Pattern Recognition (CVPR 03)* (Vol. 1, pp. 134–141). IEEE.

Mori, G., Belongie, S., & Malik, J. (2005). Efficient shape matching using shape contexts. *IEEE Transactions on Pattern Analysis and Machine Intelligence*, *27*(11), 1832–1837. doi:10.1109/TPAMI.2005.220 PMID:16285381

Moses, T. (2005). *eXtensible access control markup language (XACML) version 2.0*. OASIS Standard. Retrieved May 2013 from http://docs.oasis-open.org/xacml/2.0/access_control-xacml-2.0-core-spec-os.pdf

Moy, G., Jones, N., Harkless, C., & Potter, R. (2004). Distortion estimation techniques in solving visual CAPTCHAs. In *Proceedings of 2004 IEEE Conference on Computer Vision and Pattern Recognition (CVPR 04)* (Vol. 2, pp. 23–28). IEEE.

Mozilla. (2011, February). *Intercepting page loads - MDC docs*. Retrieved June 2013 from https://developer.mozilla.org/en/XUL_School/Intercepting_Page_Loads

Mukkamala, S., Sung, A. H., & Abraham, A. (2005). Intrusion detection using an ensemble of intelligent paradigms. *Journal of Network and Computer Applications*, *28*(2), 167–182. doi:10.1016/j.jnca.2004.01.003

Murthy, C. S. R., & Manoj, B. (2004). *Ad hoc wireless networks: Architectures and protocols*. Upper Saddle River, NJ: Prentice Hall PTR.

Myers, R. H., & Ball, L. W. (1964). *Reliability engineering for electronic systems*. Hoboken, NJ: J. Wiley.

MySpace Developer Team. (2012). *MySpace developers platform*. Author.

Nadalin, A. (2009). *WS-trust 1.4*. OASIS Standard. Retrieved May 2013 from http://docs.oasis-open.org/ws-sx/ws-trust/v1.4/os/ws-trust-1.4-spec-os.pdf

Naunheimer, H., Bertsche, B., Ryborz, J., Novak, W., & Kuchle, A. (2010). *Automotive transmissions: Fundamentals, selection, design and application*. Berlin: Springer.

Nazario, J., & Holz, T. (2008). As the net churns: Fast-flux botnet observations. In In Proceedings of MALWARE 2008. 3rd International Conference on In Malicious and Unwanted Software, (pp. 24-31)., Alexandria, VA: Academic Press, United states.

Nazario, J. (2007). *Blackenergy ddos bot analysis (Tech. Rep.)*. Arbor Networks.

Neuman, B. C., & Tso, T. (1994). Kerberos: An authentication service for computer networks. *IEEE Communications*, *32*(9), 33–38. doi:10.1109/35.312841

Niels, P., Panayiotis, M., Abu, R. M., & Fabian, M. (2008). All your iframes point to us. In SS'08: Proceedings of the 17th Conference on Security Symposium (p. (pp. 1-15). Berkeley, CA, USA: USENIX Association.

NIST. (1995). An introduction to computer security. In The NIST handbook (Special publication 800-12). The National Institute of Standards and Technology (NIST).

NIST. (2007, March). *Recommendation for key management - Part 1: General*. National Institute of Standards and Technology (NIST). Retrieved August 30, 2012, from http://csrc.nist.gov/publications/nistpubs/800-57/sp800-57-Part1-revised2_Mar08-2007.pdf

Nobelis, N. (2004). Un modèle de case-based reasoning pour la detection d'iintrusion. Rapport de DEA Réseau et Système Distribué. Université Nice Sophia Antipolis, France, Septembre 2004.

Noel, S., Wijesekera, D., & Youman, C. (2002). Modern intrusion detection, data mining, and degrees of attack guilt. In D. Barbarà, & S. Jajodia (Eds.), *Applications of data mining in computer security* (pp. 1–31). Kluwer Academic Publisher. doi:10.1007/978-1-4615-0953-0_1

Norton. (2012). *2012 Norton cybercrime report*. Norton.

Not-a-bot (NAB):), improving service availability in the face of botnet attacks. In Paper presented at NSDI 2009. Boston, MA.

NSL. (2013). Retrieved June 16, 2013, from http://nsl.cs.unb.ca/NSL-KDD

Nurmi, P. (2006). *Modeling energy constrained routing in selfish ad hoc networks*. Paper presented at the International Conference on Game Theory for Networks (GameNets). New York, NY.

OASIS Security Services (SAML) Technical Committee. (2012). Retrieved May 2013 from https://www.oasis-open.org/committees/tc_home.php?wg_abbrev=security

OASIS Web Services Security (WSS) TC. (2006). Retrieved May 2013 from https://www.oasis-open.org/committees/tc_home.php?wg_abbrev=wss

Oates, J. (2011). *Toyota and Microsoft ink e-car deal in a cloud of telematics*. Retrieved from http://www.theregister.co.uk/2011/04/07/microsoft_toyota/

OAuth 2.0. (2012). *Microsoft MSDN*. Retrieved May 2013 from http://msdn.microsoft.com/en-us/library/live/hh243647.aspx

Odvarko, J. (2008, September). *NsITraceableChannel intercept HTTP traffic*. Retrieved June 2013 from http://www.softwareishard.com/blog/firebug/nsitraceablechannel-intercept-http-traffic

OECD. (2014). Malicious software (malware):): A security threat to the internetinternet economy (Tech. Rep.). (2014). Organization for economic cooperation and development (OECD). Retrieved from http://www.oecd.org/dataoecd/53/34/40724457.pdf

Olariu, S., & Weigle, M. (2009). *Vehicular networks from theory to practice*. New York: Chapman & Hall. doi:10.1201/9781420085891

Oliveira, L., Aranha, D., Morais, E., Daguano, F., Lopez, J., & Dahab, R. (2007). Tinytate: Computing the tate pairing in resource-constrained sensor nodes. In *Proceedings of Sixth IEEE International Symposium on Network Computing and Applications (NCA)*, (pp. 318-323). IEEE.

OpenID Authentication 2.0. (2007). Retrieved from OpenID.net

Oracle Group. (2010). *Understanding login authentication*. Retrieved May 2013 from http://docs.oracle.com/javaee/1.4/tutorial/doc/Security5.html

Osborne, M., & Rubinstein, A. (1994). *A course in game theory*. Cambridge, MA: The MIT Press.

Owen, G. (2001). *Game theory*. New York: Academic Press.

Pairing. (n.d.). *The pairing based crypto lounge*. Retrieved August 30, 2012, from http://www.larc.usp.br/~pbarreto/pblounge.html

Palomar, E., Tapiador, J., Hernández-Castro, J., & Ribagorda, A. (2009). 17 cooperative security in peer-to-peer and mobile ad hoc networks. In *Cooperative wireless communications*. Academic Press. doi:10.1201/9781420064704.ch17

Papadimitratos, P., & Haas, Z. J. (2003). *Securing mobile ad hoc networks*. Boca Raton, FL: CRC Press, Inc. Retrieved from http://dl.acm.org/citation.cfm?id=989711.989743

Park, C., Lahiri, K., & Raghunathan, A. (2005). *Battery discharge characteristic of wireless sensor nodes: An experimental analysis*. IEEE SECON.

Passerini, E., Paleari, R., Martignoni, L., & Bruschi, D. (2008, July). FluXOR. Detecting and monitoring fast-flux service networks. In Proceedings of the 5th Conference on Detection of Intrusions and Malware & Vulnerability Assessment., DIMVA, Paris, France. Springer.

Patcha, A., & Park, J. M. (2007). An overview of anomaly detection techniques: Existing solutions and latest technological trends. *Computer Networks*, *51*(12), 3448–3470. doi:10.1016/j.comnet.2007.02.001

Paul Bcher, M. K. G. W. Thorsten & Holz. (2014). Know your enemy: Tracking botnets. Retrieved from http://www.honeynet.org/papers/ bots/

Pearson, S., & Casassa-Mont, M. (2011). Sticky policies: An approach for privacy management across multiple parties. *Computers & Society*, *1*(99), 60–68. doi:10.1109/MC.2011.225

Pesovie, U. M., Mohorko, J. J., & Karl, B. Z. F. (2010). Single-hop vs. multi-hop energy efficiency analysis in wireless sensor networks. In *Proceedings of Telekomunikacioni forum TELFOR, Srbija*, (pp. 23-25). TELFOR.

Peter Loscocco, N. (2001). Integrating flexible support for security policies into the Linux operating system. In *Proceedings of the FREENIX Track: 2001 USENIX Annual Technical Conference*. Boston: USENIX Association.

Pfleeger, C. (2006). *Security in computing* (4th ed.). Upper Saddle River, NJ: Prentice Hall.

Ponec, M. (2006). Visual reverse turing tests: A false sense of security. In *Proceedings of the 2006 IEEE Workshop on Information Assurance* (pp. 305–311). IEEE.

Ponemon, I. (2012). *Cost of cyber crime study*. United States: Academic Press.

Pope, C., & Kaur, K. (2005). Is it human or computer? Defending e-commerce with captchas. *IT Professional*, *7*(2), 43–49. doi:10.1109/MITP.2005.37

Porras, P., Sadi, H., & Yegneswaran, V. (2007). A multi-perspective analysis of the storm (peacomm) worm (Tech. Rep.). Computer Science Laboratory, SRI International.

Postel, J. (1981). *Internet control message protocol*. IETF RFC 792.

Postel, J. (1983). *Character generator protocol*. IETF RFC 864.

Postel, J., & Reynolds, J. (1983). *TELNET protocol specification*. IETD RFC 854.

President Information Technology Advisory Committee. (2004). *Revolutionizing health care through information technology*. Washington, DC: Executive Office of the President of the United States.

Przydatek, B. (2002). On the (im)possibility of a text-only CAPTCHA. In *Proceedings of First Workshop on Human Interactive Proofs (HIP 2002)*. Palo Alto, CA: HIP.

Ragen, S. (2011, January). *Tunisian government harvesting usernames and passwords*. Retrieved June 2013 from http://www.thetechherald.com/article.php/201101/6651/Tunisian-government-harvesting-usernames-and-passwords

Rajab, M. A., Zarfoss, J., Monrose, F., & Terzis, A. (2007). My botnet is bigger than yours (maybe, better than yours):), why size estimates remain challenging. In Hotbots'07: Proceedings of the First Conference on First Workshop on Hot Topics in Understanding Botnets. Berkeley, CA, USA: USENIX Association.

Ramachandran, A., Feamster, N., & Dagon, D. (2006). Revealing botnet membership using DNSBL counter-intelligence. In In Proceedings of 2nd Workshop on Steps to Reducing Unwanted Traffic on the internetInternet (p. (pp. 49-54). Berkeley, CA, USA: USENIX Association.

Ramachandran, A., & Feamster, N. (2006). Understanding the network-level behavior of spammers. *SIGCOMM Comput. Commun. Rev.*, *36*(4), 291–302. doi:10.1145/1151659.1159947

Ramsbrock, D., Wang, X., & Jiang, X. (2008). A first step towards live botmaster traceback. In In Proceedings of Recent Advances in Intrusion Detection - 11th International Symposium (LNCS), raid 2008, proceedings, september 15,2008 - september 17 (Vol. 5230 LNCS, pp. 59-77). Cambridge, MA, United states: Springer Verlag.

Ramsdell, B. (1999). *S/MIME version 3 message specification*. IETF RFC 2633.

Rappaport, T. S. (2002). *Wireless communications: Principles and practice*. Upper Saddle River, NJ: Prentice Hall.

Raya, M., & Hubaux, J.-P. (2005). The security of vehicular ad hoc networks. In K. P. Laberteaux, H. Hartenstein, D. B. Johnson & R. Sengupta (Eds.), *Vehicular ad hoc networks*, (pp. 93-94). ACM. Retrieved from http://dblp.uni-trier.de/db/conf/mobicom/vanet2005.html#RayaH05

Raya, M., & Hubaux, J.-P. (2007). Securing vehicular ad hoc networks. *Journal of Computer Security, 15*(1), 39–68.

Raya, M., Papadimitratos, P., & Hubaux, J.-P. (2006). Securing vehicular communications. *IEEE Wireless Communications, 13*(5), 8–15. doi:10.1109/WC-M.2006.250352

Resnick, P., Kuwabarra, K., Zeckauser, R., & Friedman, E. (2000). Reputation systems: Facilitating trust in e-commerce systems. *Communications of the ACM, 43*(12). doi:10.1145/355112.355122

Richardson, L., & Ruby, S. (2007). *RESTful web services: Web services for the real world.* Sebastopol, CA: O'Reilly Media.

Rivest, R. L., Shamir, A., & Adleman, L. (1978). A method for obtaining digital signatures and public-key cryptosystems. *Communications of the ACM, 21*, 120–126. http://doi.acm.org/10.1145/359340.359342 doi:10.1145/359340.359342

Robles, R., & Choi, M. (2009). Symmetric-key encryption for wireless Internet scada. *Security Technology*, 289–297.

Rui, Y., & Liu, Z. (2003a). *ARTIFACIAL: Automated reverse turing test using facial features* (Tech. Rep. No. MSR-TR-2003-48). Microsoft.

Rui, Y., & Liu, Z. (2003b). Excuse me, but are you human? In *Proceedings of the 11th ACM International Conference on Multimedia (MULTIMEDIA 03)* (pp. 462–463). ACM.

Rui, Y., Liu, Z., Kallin, S., Janke, G., & Paya, C. (2005). Characters or faces: A user study on ease of use for HIPs. In *Proceedings of Second International Workshop on Human Interactive Proofs (HIP 2005)* (pp. 53–65). HIP.

Russell, R., Kaminsky, D., Puppy, R. F., Grand, J., Ahmad, D., & Flynn, H. … Permeh, R. (2002). Hack proofing your network (2nd Ed.). Amsterdam: Syngress.

Rusu, A. (2006). *Exploiting the gap in human and machine abilities in handwriting recognition for web security applications.* (Doctoral dissertation). University of New York at Buffalo, Buffalo, NY.

Rusu, A., & Govindaraju, V. (2004). Handwritten CAPTCHA: Using the difference in the abilities of humans and machines in reading handwritten words. In *Proceedings of the 9th International Workshop on Frontiers in Handwriting Recognition (IWFHR 04)* (pp. 226–231). IWFHR.

Rusu, A., & Govindaraju, V. (2005a). A human interactive proof algorithm using handwriting recognition. In *Proceedings of the 8th International Conference on Document Analysis and Recognition (ICDAR 05)* (Vol. 2, pp. 967–971). ICDAR.

Rusu, A., & Govindaraju, V. (2005b). Visual CAPTCHA with handwritten image analysis. In *Proceedings of Second International Workshop on Human Interactive Proofs (HIP 2005)* (pp. 42–52). HIP.

Rutten, J., Kwaiatkowska, M., Normal, G., & Parker, D. (2004). *Mathematical techniques for analyzing concurrent and probabilisitc systems* (Vol. 23). American Mathematical Society.

Saad, S., Traore, I., Ghorbani, A., Sayed, B., Zhao, D., Lu, W., & Hakimian, P. (2011). *Detecting P2P botnets through network behavior analysis and machine learning.* Paper presented at the Privacy, Security and Trust (PST). New York, NY.

Sakai, R., & Kasahara, M. (2003). Id based cryptosystems with pairing on elliptic curve. *Cryptology ePrint Archive, Report 2003/054.* Retrieved August 8, 2012, from http://eprint.iacr.org/2003/054

Sakimura, N., Bradley, J., Jones, M., de Medeiros, B., & Jay, E. (2013, June). *OpenID connect standard 1.0 - draft 21.* OpenID.net Working Group.

Sakimura, N., Bradley, J., Jones, M., de Medeiros, B., Mortimore, C., & Jay, E. (2013a, June). *OpenID connect implicit client profile 1.0 - Draft 11.* OpenID.net Working Group.

Sakimura, N., Bradley, J., Jones, M., de Medeiros, B., Mortimore, C., & Jay, E. (2013b, June). *OpenID connect messages 1.0 - draft 20.* OpenID.net Working Group.

Sampigethaya, K., Huang, L., Li, M., Poovendran, R., Matsuura, K., & Sezaki, K. (2005). Caravan: Providing location privacy for vanet. In Embedded security in cars (ESCAR). Citeseer.

Sampigethaya, K., Li, M., Huang, L., & Poovendran, R. (2007). Amoeba: Robust location privacy scheme for vanet. *IEEE Journal on Selected Areas in Communications*, 25(8), 1569–1589. doi:10.1109/JSAC.2007.071007

Sandhu, R., & Munawer, Q. (1998). How to do discretionary access control using roles. In *Proceedings of the Third ACM Workshop on Role-Based Access Control*. ACM. http://doi.acm.org/10.1145/286884.286893

Sarkar, S. K., Basavaraju, T. G., & Puttamadappa, C. (2007). *Ad hoc mobile wireless networks: Principles, protocols and applications*. Boston: Auerbach Publications. doi:10.1201/9781420062229

Sauer, G., Hochheiser, H., Feng, J., & Lazar, J. (2008). Towards a universally usable captcha. In *Proceedings of the 4th Symposium on Usable Privacy and Security (SOUPS'08)*. SOUPS.

Savage, S., Wetherall, D., Karlin, A., & Anderson, T. (2000). Practical network support for IP traceback. SIGCOMM Comput. Commun. Rev30(4), 295–306.

Schneier, B. (1996). *Applied cryptography* (2nd ed.). Hoboken, NJ: John Wiley and Sons.

Sengupta, S., Chatterjee, M., & Kwiat, K. (2010). A game theoretic framework for power control in wireless sensor networks. *IEEE Transactions on Computers*, 59(2). doi:10.1109/TC.2009.82

Senie, D. (1999). *Changing the default for directed broadcasts in routers*. IETF RFC 2644.

Shafi, K., Abbass, H., & Zhu, W. (2006). An adaptive rule based intrusion detection architecture. In *Proceedings of Security Technology Conference, the 5th Homeland Security Summit*, (pp. 345-355). Canberra, Australia: Academic Press.

Shamir, A. (1984). Identity based cryptosystems and signatures. In *Proceedings of Cryptology* (pp. 47–53). Berlin: Springer-Verlag.

Shirali-Shahreza, M. (2008). Highlighting CAPTCHA. In *Proceedings of the Conference on Human System Interaction (HSI2008)* (pp. 247–250). HSI.

Shirali-Shahreza, M. H., & Shirali-Shahreza, M. (2007e). Localized CAPTCHA for illiterate people. In *Proceedings of the International Conference on Intelligent & Advanced Systems (ICIAS 2007)*. ICIAS.

Shirali-Shahreza, M. H., & Shirali-Shahreza, M. (2007f). Multilingual CAPTCHA. In *Proceedings of 5th IEEE International Conference on Computational Cybernetics (ICCC 2007)* (pp. 135–139). IEEE.

Shirali-Shahreza, M., & Shirali-Shahreza, M. H. (2008a). Online PIX CAPTCHA. In *Proceedings of the IEEE International Conference on Signal Processing, Communications and Networking (ICSCN 2008)* (pp. 582–585). IEEE.

Shirali-Shahreza, M., & Shirali-Shahreza, S. (2006a). Drawing CAPTCHA. In *Proceedings of 28th International Conference on Information Technology Interfaces (ITI 2006)* (pp. 475–480). ITI.

Shirali-Shahreza, M., & Shirali-Shahreza, S. (2007a). CAPTCHA for blind people. In *Proceedings of the 7th IEEE International Symposium on Signal Processing and Information Technology (ISSPIT 2007)* (pp. 995–998). IEEE.

Shirali-Shahreza, M., & Shirali-Shahreza, S. (2007b). Collage CAPTCHA. In *Proceedings of the 20th IEEE International Symposium Signal Processing and Application (ISSPA 2007)*. IEEE.

Shirali-Shahreza, M., & Shirali-Shahreza, S. (2007c). Online collage CAPTCHA. In *Proceedings of the 8th International Workshop on Image Analysis for Multimedia Interactive Services (WIAMIS 2007)* (pp. 58). WIAMIS.

Shirali-Shahreza, M., & Shirali-Shahreza, S. (2007d). Question-based CAPTCHA. In *Proceedings of the International Conference on Computational Intelligence and Multimedia Applications (ICCIMA 2007)* (Vol. 4, pp. 54–58). ICCIMA.

Shirali-Shahreza, M., & Shirali-Shahreza, S. (2008b). CAPTCHA systems for disabled people. In *Proceedings of the IEEE Intelligent Computer Communication and Processing 2008 (ICCP 2008)* (pp. 319-322). IEEE.

Shirali-Shahreza, M., & Shirali-Shahreza, S. (2008c). Motion CAPTCHA. In *Proceedings of the Conference on Human System Interaction (HSI 2008)* (pp. 1042–1044). HSI.

Shirali-Shahreza, S., & Shirali-Shahreza, M. (2008d). Bibliography of works done on CAPTCHA. In *Proceedings of the 3rd International Conference on Intelligent System & Knowledge Engineering (ISKE 2008)*. ISKE.

Shirali-Shahreza, S., & Shirali-Shahreza, M. (2008e). CAPTCHA for children. In *Proceedings of 3rd International Conference on System of Systems Engineering (SoSE 2008)*. SoSE.

Shirali-Shahreza, S., & Shirali-Shahreza, M. (2008f). A new human interactive proofs system for deaf persons. In *Proceedings of the 5th International Conference on Information Technology: New Generations (ITNG 2008)* (pp. 807–810). ITNG.

Shirali-Shahreza, S., Shirali-Shahreza, M., & Movaghar, A. (2007). Exam HIP. In *Proceedings of the 2007 IEEE International Workshop on Anti-Counterfeiting, Security, Identification (ASID 2007)* (pp. 415–418). IEEE.

Shirali-Shahreza, M. H., & Shirali-Shahreza, M. (2006b). Persian/Arabic baffletext CAPTCHA. *Journal of Universal Computer Science*, *12*(12), 1783–1796.

Shirali-Shahreza, M. H., & Shirali-Shahreza, M. (2006c). Persian/Arabic CAPTCHA. *IADIS International Journal on Computer Science and Information Systems*, *1*(2), 63–75.

Shirali-Shahreza, M. H., & Shirali-Shahreza, M. (2007g). Nastaliq CAPTCHA. *Iranian Journal of Electrical and Computer Engineering*, *5*(2), 109–114.

Shirley, B., & Mano, C. (2008). A model for covert botnet communication in a private subnet. In Proceedings of NETWORKING 2008 Ad Hoc and Sensor Networks, Wireless Networks, Next Generation Internet, (pp. 624–632). Academic Press.

Simard, P. Y., Szeliski, R., Benaloh, J., Couvreur, J., & Calinov, I. (2003). Using character recognition and segmentation to tell computer from humans. In *Proceedings of the 7th International Conference on Document Analysis and Recognition (ICDAR 03)* (Vol. 1, pp. 418–423). ICDAR.

Simon, G., Maroti, M., Lèdeczi, A., & Balogh, G. (2004). Sensor network-based countersniper system. In *Proceedings of the 2nd International Conference on Embedded Networked Sensor Systems* (pp. 1-12). New York, NY: ACM Press.

Simon, H. A. (1996). *The sciences of the artificial*. Cambridge, MA: MIT Press.

Simpson, W. (1995). *IP in IP tunneling*. IETF RFC 1853.

Singh, S., Woo, M., & Raghavendra, C. S. (1998). Power-aware routing in mobile ad hoc networks. In *Proceedings of the 4th Annual ACM/IEEE International Conference on Mobile Computing and Networking* (pp. 181-190). ACM/IEEE. doi: 10.1145/288235.288286

Singhal, A., & Jajodia, S. (2006). Data warehousing and data mining techniques for intrusion detection systems. *Distributed and Parallel Databases*, *20*(2), 149–166. doi:10.1007/s10619-006-9496-5

Sirois, K., & Kent, S. (1997). Securing the nimrod routing architecture. In *SNDSS*. IEEE.

Snedecor, G. W., & Cochran, W. (1989). Statistical methods (No. v. 276). Iowa State University Press.

Snoeren, A. C., Partridge, C., Sanchez, L. A., Jones, C. E., Tchakountio, F., Kent, S. T., & Strayer, W. T. (2001). 10). Hash-based IP traceback. In *Applications, technologies, architectures, and protocols for computer communications* (Vol. 31, pp. 3–14). USA: ACM.

Sohraby, K., Minoli, D., & Znati, T. F. (2007). *Wireless sensor networks: Technology, protocols, and applications*. Hoboken, NJ: Wiley-Interscience. doi:10.1002/047011276X

Sood, A. K., & Enbody, R. J. (2013). Crimeware-as-a-service—A survey of commoditized crimeware in the underground market. *International Journal of Critical Infrastructure Protection*, *6*(1), 28-38. doi: http://dx.doi.org/10.1016/j.ijcip.2013.01.002

Spitz, A. L. (2002). A feeble classifier relying on strong context. In *Proceedings of First Workshop on Human Interactive Proofs (HIP 2002)*. HIP.

Stallings, W. (2005). *Cryptography and network security: Principles and practice* (4th ed.). New York: Pearson Education.

Stallings, W. (2005). *Wireless communications and networks* (2nd ed.). Upper Saddle River, NJ: Pearson Education Inc.

Staniford, S., Hoagland, J. A., & McAlerney, J. M. (2002). Practical auomated detection of stealthy portscans. *J. Comput. Secur.*, *10*(1-2), 105–136.

Starnberger, G., Kruegel, C., & Kirda, E. (2008). Overbot: A botnet protocol based on kademlia. In Securecomm '08: Proceedings of the 4th International Conference on Security and Privacy in Communication NetowrksNetworks (pp. 1–9). New York, NY, USA: ACM.

Steven Malby, R. M. Holterhof, Brown, Kascherus, & Ignatuschtschenko. (2013). Comprehensive study on cybercrime. Academic Press.

Stevens, W. R. (1994). *TCP/IP illustrated: The protocols* (Vol. 1). Boston: Addison-Wesley Professional.

Stewart, J. (2014). Bobax trojan analysis. Retrieved from http www.secureworks.com/research/threats/bobax/?threat=bobax

Stinson, E., & Mitchell, J. C. (2007). Characterizing bots' remote control behavior. In In Proceedings of 4th GI International Conference on Detection of Intrusions and Malware, and Vulnerability Assessment (LNCS), DIMVA 2007, July 12,2007 - July 13 (Vol. 4579 LNCS, pp. 89-108). Lucerne, Switzerland: Springer Verlag.

Stone-Gross, B., Cova, M., Cavallaro, L., Gilbert, B., Szydlowski, M., Kemmerer, R., & Vigna, G. (2009). *Your botnet is my botnet: Analysis of a botnet takeover*. Academic Press. doi:10.1145/1653662.1653738

Strayer, W., Lapsely, D., Walsh, R., & Livadas, C. (2008). Botnet detection based on network behavior. Botnet Detection, , 1–24.

Strayer, W. T., Walsh, R., Livadas, C., & Lapsley, D. (2006). Detecting botnets with tight command and control. In In Proceedings of 31st Annual IEEE Conference on Local Computer Networks, LCN 2006, november 14,2006 - november 16 (p.(pp. 195-202). Tampa, FL, United states: IEEE Computer Society.

Sweeney. (2002). k-Anonymity: A model for protecting privacy. International Journal on Uncertainty, Fuzziness and Knowledge-Based Systems, 10(5), 557-570.

Symantec. (2010). *Symantec report on attack kits and malicious websites*. Author.

Symantec. (2011). *Internet security threat report*. Author.

Szczechowiak, P., & Collier, M. (2009). Tinyibe: Identity-based encryption for heterogeneous sensor networks. In *Proceedings of Fifth International Conference on Intelligent Sensors, Sensor Networks, and Information Processing (ISSNIP)* (pp. 319-354). ISSNIP.

Szczechowiak, P., Kargl, A., Scott, M., & Collier, M. (2009). On the application of pairing based cryptography to wireless sensor networks. In *Proceedings of the Second ACM Conference on Wireless Network Security*. ACM.

Takemori, K., Fujinaga, M., Sayama, T., & Nishigaki, M. (2009). Host-based traceback; tracking bot and C&C server. In Icuimc '09: Proceedings of the 3rd International Conference on Ubiquitous Information Management and Communication (pp. 400–405). New York, NY, USA: ACM.

Tam, J., Simsa, J., Huggins-Daines, D., von Ahn, L., & Blum, M. (2008). Improving audio CAPTCHAs. In *Proceedings of the 4th Symposium on Usability, Privacy and Security (SOUPS '08)*. SOUPS.

Tang, L., & Hong, X. (n.d.). *Protecting location privacy by camouflaging movements*. Academic Press.

Tate Pairing. (2009). *Multi-core implementation of the tate pairing over supersingular elliptic curves (source code)*. Retrieved May 7, 2011, from: http://delta.cs.cinvestav.mx/~francisco/temp/Page-TatePairing2009/TatePairing-2009.html

Tavallaee, M., Bagheri, E., Lu, W., & Ghorbani, A. A. (2009). A detailed analysis of the KDD CUP 99 data set. In *Proceedings of IEEE Symposium on Computational Intelligence in Security and Defense Applications (CISDA 2009)*. IEEE.

Thayananthan, A., Stenger, B., Torr, P., & Cipolla, R. (2003). Shape context and chamfer matching in cluttered scenes. In *Proceedings of 2003 IEEE Conference on Computer Vision and Pattern Recognition (CVPR 03)* (Vol. 1, pp. 127–133). IEEE.

Thing, V., Lee, H., & Sloman, M. (2005). Traffic redirection attack protection system. In *Proceedings of the 20th International Information Security Conference* (pp. 309-325). Chiba, Japan: IFIP.

Tiny, O. S. (n.d.). *Tinyos documentation*. Retrieved from http://docs.tinyos.net

Toh, C. (2001). Maximum battery life routing to support ubiquitous mobile computing in wireless ad hoc networks. *IEEE Communications Magazine*, *39*(6), 138–147. doi:10.1109/35.925682

Topolski, R. M. (2008, June). *NebuAd and partner ISPs: Wiretapping, forgery and browser hijacking*. Retrieved June 2013 from http://www.freepress.net/files/NebuAd_Report.pdf

Trustwave. (2012). *Simple solutions to your complex security and compliance challenges*. Retrieved November, 2012, from https://www.trustwave.com/

Turing, A. M. (1950). Computing machinery and intelligence. *Mind*, *59*(236), 433–460. doi:10.1093/mind/LIX.236.433

Twitter Developers. (2012). *Authentication & authorization*. Twitter Developers. Retrieved May 2013 from https://dev.twitter.com/docs/auth

US Department of Defence. (1991). *Reliability prediction of electronic equipment, military handbook (MIL-HDBK-217F)*. Washington, DC: US Department of Defence.

US Department of Defense. (1998). *Reliability-centered maintenance (RCM) requirements for naval aircraft, weapon systems, and support equipment (MIL-HDBK-2173)*. Washington, DC: US Department of Defense.

Vijayan, J. (2014). Teen used botnets to push adware to hundreds of thousands of pcs. Retrieved from http://www.computerworld.com/s/ article/9062839/Teen used botnets to push adware to hundreds of thousands of PCs

Vogt, R., Aycock, J., Michael, J., & Jacobson, J. (2007). Army of bot- nets. In In Proceedings of 14th Annual Network and Distributed System Security Symposium (p. (pp. 111-123). Academic Press.

von Ahn, L. (2005). *Human computation*. (Doctoral dissertation). Carnegie Mellon University, Pittsburgh, PA.

von Ahn, L., Blum, M., Hopper, N. J., & Langford, J. (2003). CAPTCHA: Using hard AI problems for security. In *Proceedings of International Conference on the Theory and Applications of Cryptographic Techniques (EUROCRYPT 2003)* (pp. 294–311). Springer.

von Ahn, L., Blum, M., & Langford, J. (2004). Telling humans and computers apart automatically. *Communications of the ACM*, *47*(2), 56–60. doi:10.1145/966389.966390

von Ahn, L., Maurer, B., McMillen, C., Abraham, D., & Blum, M. (2008). reCAPTCHA: Human-based character recognition via web security measures. *Science*, *321*(5895), 1465–1468. doi:10.1126/science.1160379 PMID:18703711

Voth, D. (2003). The paradox of CAPTCHAs. *IEEE Intelligent Systems*, *18*(2), 6–7. doi:10.1109/MIS.2003.1234761

W3C. (2005). *Inaccessibility of CAPTCHA* (W3C Working Group Note No. 23 November 2005). Retrieved from http://www.w3.org/TR/2005/NOTE-turingtest-20051123/

W3C. (2008). *Web content accessibility guidelines (WCAG) 2.0* (W3C Proposed Recommendation). Retrieved from http://www.w3.org/TR/2008/PR-WCAG20-20081103/

Wall, D. (2007). *Cybercrime: The transformation of crime in the information age* (Vol. 4). Cambridge, MA: Polity.

Wang, P., Sparks, S., & Zou, C. C. (2007). An advanced hybrid peer-to-peer botnet. In Hotbots'07: Proceedings of the First Conference on First Workshop on Hot Topics in Understanding Botnets. Berkeley, CA, USA: USENIX Association.

Wang, S. Y., & Bentley, J. L. (2006). CAPTCHA challenge tradeoffs: Familiarity of strings versus degradation of images. In *Proceedings of the 18th International Conference on Pattern Recognition (ICPR 06)* (pp. 164–167). ICPR.

Wang, X., & Reeves, D. S. (2003). Robust correlation of encrypted attack traffic through stepping stones by manipulation of interpacket delays. In Proceedings of the 10th ACM Conference on Computer and Communications Security, ccs 2003, October 27,2003 - October 31 (p.(pp. 20-29). Washington, DC, United states: Association for Computing Machinery.

Wang, X., Chen, S., & Jajodia, S. (2005). Tracking anonymous peer- to-peer VoIP on the internetinternet. In CCS 2005 -In Proceedings of 12th ACM Conference on Computer and Communications Security, November 07,2005 – November 11 (p.(pp. 81-91). Alexandria, VA, United states: Association for Computing Machinery.

Wang, X., Chen, S., & Jajodia, S. (2007). Network flow watermarking attack on low-latency anonymous communication systems. In Proceedings of IEEE Symposium on Security and Privacy, SP'07, May 20,2007 - May 23 (p.(pp. 116-130). Berkeley, CA, United states: Institute of Electrical and Electronics Engineers Inc.

Wang, X., Reeves, D. S., & Wu, S. F. (2002, 14-16 Oct. 2002). Inter-packet delay based correlation for tracing encrypted connections through step- ping stones. In Proceedings (p. (pp. 244-263). Berlin, Germany: Springer- Verlag.

Ward, M. (2014). *More than 95% of e-mail is ''junk.* Retrieved from.

Weber, T. (2014). *Criminals 'may overwhelm the webweb.* Retrieved from.

Werner-Allen, G., Lorincz, K., Welsh, M., Marcillo, O., Johnson, J., Ruiz, M., & Lees, J. (2006). *Deploying a wireless sensor network on an active volcano* (2nd ed., Vol. 10, pp. 18–25). Piscataway, NJ: IEEE Educational Activities Department.

Wikipedia. (2010, December). *SSL with virtual hosts using SNI.* Retrieved June 2013 from https://wiki.apache.org/httpd/NameBasedSSLVHostsWithSNI

Williams, D. (1991). *Probability with martingales.* Cambridge, UK: Cambridge University Press. doi:10.1017/CBO9780511813658

Windows Communication Foundation Security Benefits. (2012). *MSDN Microsoft.* Retrieved May 2013 from http://msdn.microsoft.com/en-us/library/ms735093.aspx

Windows Identity Foundation. (2012). *MSDN Microsoft.* Retrieved May 2013 from http://msdn.microsoft.com/en-us/library/ee517276.aspx

Wireshirk. (n.d.). *Wireshark network protocol analyzer.* Retrieved August 30, 2012, from www.wireshark.org

Wisitpongphan, N., Bai, F., Mudalige, P., & Tonguz, O. (2007). On the routing problem in disconnected vehicular ad-hoc networks. In *Proceedings of 26th IEEE International Conference on Computer Communications.* IEEE.

Wright, C. V., Monrose, F., & Masson, G. M. (2006). On inferring application protocol behaviors in encrypted network traffic. *Journal of Machine Learning Research, 7,* 2745–2769.

Wu, T. (2009, September). *RSA and ECC in JavaScript.* Retrieved June 2013 from http://www-cs-students.stanford.edu/~tjw/jsbn/

Wu, B., Chen, J., Wu, J., & Cardei, M. (2007). A survey of attacks and countermeasures in mobile ad hoc networks. In *Wireless network security* (pp. 103–135). Academic Press. doi:10.1007/978-0-387-33112-6_5

Wurzinger, P., Bilge, L., Holz, T., Goebel, J., Kruegel, C., & Kirda, E. (2009). Automatically generating models for botnet detection. In *Proceedings of Computer Security ESORICS 2009* (pp. 232–249). Academic Press. doi:10.1007/978-3-642-04444-1_15

X.commerce. (2012). *Standard OpenID integration for PayPal access getting started guide.* Author.

Xie Y. Yu F. Achan K. Panigrahy R. Hulten G. Osipkov I. (2008). Spamming botnets: Signatures and characteristics. SIGCOMM Com- put.Communication Review, 38(4), 171–182.

Ximenes, P., dos Santos, A., Fernandez, M., & Celestino, J. (2006). A CAPTCHA in the text domain. In *Proceedings of Workshops on the Move to Meaningful Internet Systems 2006 (OTM 2006)* (pp. 605–615). OTM.

Xing, F., & Wang, W. (2007). Understanding dynamic denial of service attacks in mobile ad hoc networks. In *Proceedings of Military Communications Conference.* IEEE.

Xiong, X., Wong, D., & Deng, X. (2010). Tinypairing: A fast and lightweight pairing-based cryptographic library for wireless sensor networks. In *Proceedings of IEEE Wireless Communications and Networking Conference (WCNC).* IEEE.

Xu, J., Essa, I. A., & Lipton, R. J. (2000). *Hello, are you human?* (Tech. Rep. No. GIT-CC-00-28). Atlanta, GA: Georgia Institute of Technology.

Xu, S., Lau, F. C. M., Cheung, W. K., & Pan, Y. (2005). Automatic generation of artistic Chinese calligraphy. *IEEE Intelligent Systems, 20*(3), 32–39. doi:10.1109/MIS.2005.41

Xu, X. (2006). Adaptive intrusion detection based on machine learning: Feature extraction, classifier construction and sequential pattern prediction. *International Journal of Web Services Practices, 2*(1-2), 49–58.

Yahoo. (2012). *Yahoo! meets OpenID*. Yahoo Inc. Retrieved May 2013 from http://openid.yahoo.com/

Yan, J., & Ahmad, A. S. E. (2007). Breaking visual CAPTCHAs with naive pattern recognition algorithms. In *Proceedings of 23ʳᵈ Annual Computer Security Applications Conference (ACSAC 2007)* (pp. 279–291). ACSAC.

Yan, J., & Ahmad, A. S. E. (2008a). A low-cost attack on a Microsoft CAPTCHA. In *Proceedings of the 15ᵗʰ ACM Conference on Computer and Communications Security (CCS '08)* (pp. 543–554). ACM.

Yan, J., & Ahmad, A. S. E. (2008b). Usability of CAPTCHA or usability issues in CAPTCHA design. In *Proceedings of the 4ᵗʰ Symposium on Usable Privacy and Security (SOUPS '08)*. SOUPS.

Yan, Z., & Chen, Y. (2010). Adcontrep: A privacy enhanced reputation system for MANET content services. In Ubiquitous intelligence and computing (pp. 414–429). Academic Press.

Yang, K. (2002). Issues for Chinese CAPTCHA. In *Proceedings of First Workshop on Human Interactive Proofs (HIP 2002)*. HIP.

Yang, H., Luo, H., Ye, F., Lu, S., & Zhang, L. (2004). Security in mobile ad hoc networks: Challenges and solutions. *IEEE Wireless Communications, 11*(1), 38–47. doi:10.1109/MWC.2004.1269716

Yen, T.-F., & Reiter, M. K. (2008). Traffic aggregation for malware detection. In In Proceedings of 5th International Conference on Detection of Intrusions and Malware, and Vulnerability Assessment (LNCS), DIMVA 2008, July 10,2008 - July 11 (Vol. 5137 LNCS, pp. 207-227). Paris, France: Springer-Verlag.

Ye, N., Farley, T., & Lakshminarasimhan, D. (2006). An attack-norm separation approach for detecting cyber attacks. *Information Systems Frontiers, 8*(3), 163–177. doi:10.1007/s10796-006-8731-y

Yen, T.-F., Huang, X., Monrose, F., & Reiter, M. (2009). Browser fingerprinting from coarse traffic summaries: Techniques and implications. In *Detection of intrusions and malware, and vulnerability assessment* (pp. 157–175). Academic Press. doi:10.1007/978-3-642-02918-9_10

Yick, J., Mukherjee, B., & Ghosal, D. (2008). Wireless sensor network survey. *Computer Networks, 52*(12), 2292–2330. doi:10.1016/j.comnet.2008.04.002

Yin, B., Shi, H., & Shang, Y. (2005). A two-level strategy for topology control in wireless sensor networks. In *Proceedings of the 11th International Conference on Parallel and Distributed Systems – Workshops* (pp. 358-362). Washington, DC: IEEE Computer Society.

Ylonen, T. (2006). *The secure shell (SSH) authentication protocol*. IETF RFC 4252.

Yoda, K., & Etoh, H. (2000). Finding a connection chain for tracing intruders. In In Proceedings of 6th European Symposium on Research in Computer Security (p. (pp. 191-205). Berlin, Germany: Springer-Verlag.

Yousefi, S., Bastani, S., & Fathy, M. (2007). On the performance of safety message dissemination in vehicular ad hoc networks. In *Proceedings of 4th European Conference on Universal Multiservice Networks* (pp. 377–390). ECUMN.

Zang, J., & Zulkernine, M. (2005). Network intrusion detection using random forests. In *Proceedings of Third Annual Conference on Privacy, Security and Trust,* (pp. 53-61). Academic Press.

Zayatz, L. (2007). Disclosure avoidance practices and research at the U.S. census bureau: An update. *Journal of Official Statistics, 23*(2), 253–265.

Zhang, Y., & Paxson, V. (2000, 14-17 Aug. 2000). Detecting stepping stones. In Proceedings of 9th USENIX Security Symposium (p. (pp. 171-183). Berkeley, CA, USA: USENIX Assoc.

Zhang, Z., Rui, Y., Huang, T., & Paya, C. (2004). Breaking the clock face HIP. In *Proceedings of 2004 IEEE International Conference on Multimedia and Expo (ICME 04)* (Vol. 3, pp. 2167–2170). IEEE.

Zhang, C., Jiang, J., & Kamel, M. (2005). Intrusion detection using hierarchical neural networks. *Pattern Recognition Letters, 26,* 779–79. doi:10.1016/j.patrec.2004.09.045

Zhang, Y., & Lee, W. (2005). Security in mobile ad-hoc networks. In *Ad hoc networks* (pp. 249–268). Academic Press. doi:10.1007/0-387-22690-7_9

Zhang, Z., Ando, R., & Kadobayashi, Y. (2009). Hardening botnet by a rational botmaster. In *Information security and cryptology* (pp. 348–369). Academic Press. doi:10.1007/978-3-642-01440-6_27

Zhao Y. Xie Y. Yu F. Ke Q. Yu Y. Chen Y. Gillum E. (2009).

Zhou, L., & Haas, Z. (1999). Securing ad hoc networks. *IEEE Network*, *13*(6), 24–30. doi:10.1109/65.806983

Zhuang, L., Dunagan, J., Simon, D. R., Wang, H. J., & Tygar, J. D. (2008). Characterizing botnets from email spam records. In Leet'08: Proceedings of the 1st USENIX Workshop on Large-Scale Exploits and Emergent Threats (pp. 1–9). Berkeley, CA, USA: USENIX Association.

Zimmerman, C., Agah, A., & Asadi, M. (2011). *Applying economical modeling to wireless sensor networks for maximizing the battery life*. Paper presented at the 26th Pennsylvania Computer and Information Science Educators (PACISE) Conference. Philadelphia, PA.

Zimmerman, C., Agah, A., & Asadi, M. (2011). *Incorporating economical modeling to extend battery life in wireless sensor networks*. Paper presented at the Graduate Research and Creative Projects Symposium. New York, NY.

Zimmermann, H. (1980). OSI reference model - The ISO model of architecture for open systems interconnection. *IEEE Transactions on Communications*, *28*(4), 425–432. doi:10.1109/TCOM.1980.1094702

About the Contributors

Abdelmalek Amine received an engineering degree in Computer Science from the Computer Science department of Djillali Liabes University of Sidi-Belabbes-Algeria, received the Magister diploma in Computational Science and PhD from Djillali Liabes University in collaboration with Joseph Fourier University of Grenoble. His research interests include data mining, text mining, ontology, classification, clustering, neural networks, and biomimetic optimization methods. He participates in the program committees of several international conferences and on the editorial boards of international journals. Dr. Amine is the head of GeCoDe-knowledge management and complex data-laboratory at UTM University of Saida, Algeria; he also collaborates with the "knowledge base and database" team of TIMC laboratory at Joseph Fourier University of Grenoble.

Otmane Ait Mohamed received his Ph.D. (1996) in Computer Science from Université Henri Poincaré, Nancy 1. Before his arrival at Concordia in 2002, he worked as a Postdoctoral Fellow at Université de Montréal, a Research Scientist at Cistel, and a Senior Verification Engineer at Nortel Networks in Ottawa. Dr. Otmane Ait Mohamed was promoted to Associate Professor in the Department of Electrical and Computer Engineering in June 2008. Dr. Ait Mohamed has been working on formal verification for hardware and communication protocol since 1992. He contributed to the development of the MDG tool, a formal verification tool developed at the University of Montreal from 1996-1998. He joined Cistel Technology, then Nortel Networks, where he introduced the use of formal method techniques in the hardware design flow to identify critical issues in the protocols used in Nortel's Virtual Processor Subsystems. His work with the verification team consisted of verifying four different ASICs used in the communication data switch. His main research areas include hardware model checking, assertion-based verification, automatic test generations, and FPGA-based design and verification. Since joining Concordia, Dr. Ait Mohamed has published more than 80 papers in refereed conference proceedings and 30 journal papers. He is the principal or co-investigator of several team grants from agencies such as NATEQ, MDEIE, and various companies. Dr. Ait Mohamed has supervised or co-supervised to completion 25 M.A.Sc. students, 4 Ph.D. students, and 2 postdoctoral Fellows. Dr. Ait Mohamed also served as a reviewer for several related conferences and journals, and he maintains collaborations with AMD, ST, Synopsys, Texas Instruments, and Qualcomm. Dr. Ait Mohamed was the program co-chair for the prestigious 21st TPHOLs conference in 2008. He is a registered professional engineer with the *Ordre des ingénieurs du Québec*, member of IEEE, and member of ACM.

Boualem Benatallah received a PhD degree from Grenoble 1 University (France). He is professor and research group leader at the School of Computer Science (CSE), University of New South Wales (UNSW, Sydney, Australia). His main research interests are developing fundamental concepts and techniques in service composition, integration, and business processes management. He has published more than 170 refereed papers, including more than 40 journal papers. He has a very strong international track record demonstrated by the high citations of his work, some of which are considered seminal in the field of services composition. He also has strong collaboration with Industry including projects, consultancy, and patents. Boualem has been PC co-chair of number of international conferences (BPM'05, ICSOC'05, WISE'07, ICWE'2010, IEEE/ACM WI'11, IEEE SOCA'11). He is member of the steering committee of BPM and ICSOC. He is member of the editorial board of numerous international journals and series including Springer Series on Services Science. He is member of the steering committees of ICSOC and BPM. His recent work focuses is on digital services engineering and innovation.

* * *

Jemal Abawajy is a faculty member at Deakin University and has published more than 100 articles in refereed journals and conferences as well as a number of technical reports. He is on the editorial board of several international journals and edited several international journals and conference proceedings. He has also been a member of the organizing committee for over 60 international conferences and workshops serving in various capacities including best paper award chair, general co-chair, publication chair, vice-chair, and program committee.

Naeem Abbasi received the BSc degree from the University of Engineering and Technology, Lahore, Pakistan, in 1991. He received the MSEE degree from Columbia University in New York in 1995. He received his PhD degree from Concordia University, Montreal, Quebec, Canada in 2012. He is a Senior Formal Verification Engineer at Qualcomm Technologies Inc. in San Diego, California. His research interests include formal methods, functional equivalence checking, model checking, higher order logic theorem proving, formal statistical analysis of circuits, low power VLSI design verification and fast algorithms and architectures for DSP systems.

Rahmoun Abdellatif is a PhD in computer science since 1998. He has been teaching as an assistant professor at The University of Sidi Bel-Abbes up to 2001. He has been enrolled at King Faisal University (Saudi Arabia) as an Associate Professor for eight years. In 2009, he went back to the University of Sidi Bel-Abbes in Algeria, where he got his degree of professor in 2012, and where he is still working. He has been and still being involved in several teaching and research activities in the area of artificial intelligence such as: artificial genetics, neural networks, fuzzy logic and fuzzy systems, hybrid intelligent systems, genetic programming.... His works are published in several international research journals as well as presented in conferences all around the world.

Mai Abu Baqar received her B.Sc. degree in Computer Engineering from Al-Balqa'a Applied University- in Jordan, and a M.Sc degree in New York Institute Of Technology (NYIT). Currently, she is a lecturer in Al-Balqa'a Applied University at the Faculty of Engineering in Jordan.

Afrand Agah's scholarly interests include security in wireless sensor networks, economical modeling of security protocols, and security and trust in pervasive computing. She is PI for a grant from National Science Foundation for a proposal on security in Wireless Sensor Networks and security in mobile ad-hoc networks. Dr. Agah is recipient of several grants from the West Chester University College of Arts and Sciences, Office of Multicultural Faculty, and Faculty Development Committee at West Chester University. She is also Co-PI for a grant from Hewlett Packard for "Active Collaborative Learning Community Using HP Tablet PCs." She also served as a reviewer for a number of journals such as the *Journal of Mobile Communication, Computation and Information*; the *International Journal of Network Security*. She has also contributed as a reviewer for *Handbook of Information Security, and the Internet Encyclopedia*, by John Wiley and Sons.

Ammar Alazab is a researcher at the Deakin University in the school of Information technology, Australia, with thesis title "Malware Prevention and Detection." He received his Bachelor degree in Computer Science from Al-Balqa Applied University in 2001. He worked as a researcher in Jordan and Australia. His research interests are in the area of computer malware, mobile digital forensic, internet security, host and network intrusion detection system. He has published research papers in different well-known international conferences and journals.

Hamza Aldabbas obtained his PhD in Computer Science and Software Engineering from School of Technology - De Montfort University, UK, and a M.Sc degree in Computer Science from Al-Balqa'a Applied University, Jordan, and B.Sc. degree in Computer Information System from the same university. His research interests are in Mobile Ad Hoc Networks (MANETs), Wireless Sensor Networks (WSNs), Vehicular Ad-Hoc Networks (VANETS), policy-based management systems, and human-computer interaction and e-commerce. Currently, he is a lecturer at Al Balqa'a Applied University, with responsibility for teaching and project supervision.

Mai Alfawair obtained his PhD in Software Engineering from School of Technology - De Montfort University, UK, and B.Sc. degree in Computer Information System from Al Balqa'a Applied University. Her research interest is in grid computing. Currently, she is a lecturer at Al Balqa'a Applied University.

Tareq Alwadan obtained his PhD in Computer Science from School of Technology - De Montfort University, UK. His main research interest is in grid computing. Currently, he is a lecturer at The World Islamic Sciences and Education University, Jordan.

Subrata Acharya is an Assistant Professor in the CIS Department at Towson University with over a decade of research, teaching, and mentoring experience in the area of Computer Security. Before joining Towson, she completed her Ph.D. in Computer Science (Major: Security) from University of Pittsburgh (2008). She has collaborated on various cutting edge research projects with AT&T, Symantec, and IBM Research Laboratories. Her research interests are in the areas of cyber security, privacy, compliance, health information security, and trust-worthy computing. She has contributed to projects such as S-CITI project, NSF; Securing-NGI, NSF; Healthcare Security, HSS.gov; security education, MHEC-BRAC, DoD IASP, etc. Her research has been published in various peer reviewed international conferences and journals. She has published numerous book chapters in the area of Network Security and Healthcare Information Security. She has served as NSF panel review member on Trustworthy Computing, Cyber Physical Systems and various Cross Cutting Programs.

Mehran Asadi obtained his Ph.D. degree in Computer Science from the University of Texas at Arlington. Dr. Asadi's scholarly interests include machine learning, in particular hierarchical reinforcement learning and security in mobile ad-hoc networks. Dr. Asadi has presented his research at several national and international conferences. Dr. Asadi is recipient of several grants from college of Arts and Sciences and office of multicultural faculty at West Chester University of Pennsylvania. He is also PI for a grant from Hewlett Packard for "Active Collaborative Learning Community Using HP Tablet PCs" and Co-PI for a grant from National Science Foundation in Wireless Sensor Networks and security in mobile ad-hoc networks. Dr. Asadi is currently a member of ACM; he has been program committee member of several national and international conferences. He has been reviewer for the journal of information science and in addition, he has contributed as a reviewer for handbook of computer networks by John Wiley and Sons.

Ahmad Azab received his Bachelor degree in Computer Engineering from Jordan University of Science and Technology in 2008 and then worked for 5 years as a network security specialist for different large projects to plan, secure and maintain their network infrastructure. He attained different network certificates from Cisco as Cisco Certified Network Associate (CCNA) and Cisco Certified Security Professional (CCSP). Currently, he is studying his PhD degree in information security at Internet Commerce Security Laboratory (ICSL), Federation University Australia. His research focuses in identifying cybercrime activities from computer devices by monitoring their network traffic, classifying them and identified the used application using packets statistical features values and machine learning approaches.

Hassina Bensefia is an assistant professor in computer science department of Elbachir Elibrahimi University of Bordj Bou Arreridj, Algeria and a permanent researcher at Networks and Systems Laboratory of Badji Mokhtar University of Annaba, Algeria, since 2011. Before, she was a research assistant at the CEntre of Research in Scientific and Technical Information (CERIST) of Algiers, Algeria. She graduated from Algerian universities and obtained the computer science engineer degree, in 1994, from Mentouri University of Constantine, the specialized post-graduation diploma in computer security, in 2002, from CERIST, and the magister degree in artificial intelligence, in 2009, from Badji Mokhtar University of Annaba. Her research interests include artificial intelligence, network security, intrusion detection, firewalls, cryptography, and computer network forensics.

Hamad Binsalleeh is currently a PhD candidate at Concordia University in Computer Science and Software Engineering department. He received his B.S degree in Computer Science from King Saud University at Saudi Arabia, and master degree from Concordia University at Canada. He has been active in Intrusion detection systems research for the last 8 years. Currently, he is focusing on botnet analysis and detection using automatic behavioral analysis and network traffic analysis. Also, he is working on identifying the abuse of DNS by malicious networks.

Nassira Ghoualmi-Zine is currently a full Professor at the computer science department of Badji Mokhtar University of Annaba, Algeria. She is director of Networks and Systems Laboratory and head of Master and Doctoral Option entitled Network and Computer Security. She graduated from Algerian universities and obtained the engineer degree, magister degree, and the doctorate degree in computer science mention network. She is a lecturer in the department of Computer Science of Badji Mokhtar University of Annaba, Algeria since 1985. Her research interests include wireless and sensors networks, distributed multimedia applications, quality of service, security in protocol, and optimization in networks.

325

Reda Mohamed Hamou received an engineering degree in computer Science from the Computer Science Department of Djillali Liabes University of Sidi-Belabbes-Algeria and PhD (Artificial Intelligence) from the same university. He has several publications in the field of BioInspired and Metaheuristic. His research interests include data mining, text mining, classification, clustering, computational intelligence, neural networks, evolutionary computation, and biomimetic optimization method. Dr. Hamou is an Associate Professor in Science and Technology faculty in UTMS University of Saida-Algeria.

Osman Hasan received the BEng (Hons) degree from the N-W.F.P University of Engineering and Technology, Pakistan, in 1997, and the MEng and PhD degrees from Concordia University, Montreal, Quebec, Canada, in 2001 and 2008, respectively. He worked as a postdoctoral fellow at the Hardware Verification Group (HVG) of Concordia University for one year until August 2009. Currently, he is an assistant professor with the School of Electrical Engineering and Computer Science, National University of Science and Technology, Islamabad, Pakistan. His current research interests include formal methods, higher order logic theorem proving, probabilistic analysis, and real-time systems.

Michael Hobbs is a faculty member at Deakin University and has published more than 100 articles in refereed journals and conferences as well as a number of technical reports.

J. Indumathi received her Ph.D. from Anna University, Chennai, India. Here research interests include software testing, network security, internet programming, project management, and software engineering. She has authored more than 12 books and 200 scientific papers published in reputed publications. She has carried out quite a lot of edification programmes, enduring education programmes, all designed to congregate the precise skill set essential by the functioning professionals of industries and students. She has given several guest lecturers in Government I.A.S coaching centre for S.C and S.T, backward classes.

Helge Janicke is working as a Senior Lecturer in Computer Security at De Montfort University. He is located in the Software Technology Research Laboratory (STRL), which is part of the Faculty of Technology. His main research interests are in computer security/forensic, policy-based management, formal methods, and software quality assurance.

Dulal C. Kar received the B.Sc.Engg. and the M.Sc.Engg. degrees from Bangladesh University of Engineering and Technology, Dhaka, Bangladesh, and the MS and the Ph.D. degrees from North Dakota State University, Fargo, North Dakota. Currently, he is working as an associate professor in the School of Engineering and Computing Sciences at Texas A&M University – Corpus Christi, Texas. Previously, he was a faculty in the Department of Computer Science at Virginia Polytechnic Institute and State University, Virginia; Mountain State University, West Virginia; and Bangladesh University of Engineering and Technology, Bangladesh. He is an editor of the *International Journal of Network and Computer Applications*, a publication of Elsevier and the lead editor of the book, *Network Security, Administration, and Management: Advancing Technology and Practice*, published by IGI Global. His research interests include network and information security, wireless sensor networks, signal and image processing algorithms, network architecture, and network performance measurement.

Mekkaoui Kheireddine received an engineering degree in computer science from the computer science department at the University of Sidi-bel-Abbes, Algeria, in 2001 and received, in 2009, the magister diploma in industrial computer science from the computer science at the university of Mascara, Algeria. He has been and still being involved in several teaching and research activities.

Ansam Khresiat is a master research student at the Balllart University in the School of Information Technology, Australia. She received her Bachelor degree in Computer science from Al-Balqa Applied University in 2006. She has published more than 5 articles in refereed journals and conferences as well as a number of technical reports.

Ahmed Lehireche completed his ING Diploma from ESI of Algiers (1981) with the final curriculum project at the IMAG (France), M. Sc from USTOran (1993), and Ph.D. from UDL Sidi bel Abbes (2005). He is working as a Director of research, head of the knowledge engineering team at the EEDIS laboratory and A. Professor at the computer science department of UDL Sidi bel Abbes. His research interest includes AI, computer science theory, and semantics in IT.

Ahmed Chaouki Lokbani received an engineering degree in computer Science from the Computer Science Department of Djillali Liabes University of Sidi-Belabbes-Algeria and Magister degree from UTMS University of Saida, Algeria. His research interests include data mining, text mining, information security, cryptography, and network. He is teacher in Computer Science Department of UTMS University of Saida-Algeria.

Natarajan Meghanathan is a tenured Associate Professor of Computer Science at Jackson State University, Jackson, MS. He graduated with a Ph.D. in Computer Science from The University of Texas at Dallas in May 2005. Dr. Meghanathan has published more than 150 peer-reviewed articles (more than half of them being journal publications). He has also received federal education and research grants from the U.S. National Science Foundation, Army Research Lab and Air Force Research Lab. Dr. Meghanathan has been serving in the editorial board of several international journals and in the Technical Program Committees and Organization Committees of several international conferences. His research interests are Wireless Ad hoc Networks and Sensor Networks, Graph Theory, Network and Software Security, Bioinformatics and Computational Biology. For more information visit http://www.jsums.edu/cms/nmeghanathan.

Gabriel López Millán is a full time lecturer in the Department of Information and Communications Engineering of the University of Murcia. His research interests include network security, PKI, identity management, authentication, and authorization. He received his MS and PhD in computer science from the University of Murcia.

Clifton J. Mulkey graduated from Eastern New Mexico University in 2009 with a double major Bachelor's degree in Computer Science and Mathematics. He graduated from Texas A&M University – Corpus Christi in 2011 with a Master's degree in Computer Science and an emphasis in computer/network security and cryptography. Clifton currently works with a consulting firm, assisting clients with cyber threat and vulnerability management.

Mohammad Hassan Shirali-Shahreza is an assistant professor in the Center for E-Learning of Amirkabir University of Technology (Tehran Polytechnic), Tehran, Iran. He was educated at Isfahan University of Technology, Isfahan, Iran (B.Sc., Computer Hardware Engineering, 1986), Sharif University of Technology, Tehran, Iran (M.Sc., Computer Hardware Engineering, 1988), and Amirkabir University of Technology (Tehran Polytechnic), Tehran, Iran (Ph.D. Computer Hardware Engineering, 1996). In 1994, he was a visiting research scholar in the Electrical Engineering Department, Southern Methodist University (SMU), Dallas, Texas, USA. His interesting fields are Neural Networks, OCR (Optical Character Recognition), Steganography, CAPTCHA, and Pattern Recognition. He is a member of Iranian Computer Society, Iranian Society of Cryptology, Association for Computing Machinery (ACM), and a senior member of Institute of Electrical and Electronics Engineers (IEEE).

Sajad Shirali-Shahreza received Bachelor of Science and Master of Science in Software Engineering from Computer Engineering Department of Sharif University of Technology, Tehran, Iran, in 2006 and 2007. Currently, he is a PhD student at Department of Computer Science, University of Toronto. His research interests are Human Computer Interaction, Computer Networks, and Computer Security. He ranked second in the 2006 Iranian Scientific Olympiad in Computer Engineering and also has the silver medal of 2002 National Iranian Olympiad in Informatics. He was the only student who finished B.Sc in computer engineering in 3 years among 200 undergraduate students of his department in 2007. He is the first student in the history of Computer Engineering Department of Sharif University who finished MSc in 1 year. He published 10 journal and 74 conference papers. He is a member of IEEE Computer Society, IEEE Signal Processing and ACM.

Sofiène Tahar received the diploma degree in computer engineering from the University of Darmstadt, Germany, in 1990, and the PhD degree with distinction in computer science from the University of Karlsruhe, Germany, in 1994. Currently, he is a professor with the Department of Electrical and Computer Engineering, Concordia University, Montreal, Quebec, Canada. His research interests include formal hardware verification, microprocessor and system-on-chip verification, analog and mixed signal circuits verification, and probabilistic, statistical, and reliability analysis of systems. Prof. Tahar is founder and director of the Hardware Verification Group (HVG) at Concordia University, and currently holds a senior Concordia University Research Chair in Formal Verification of System-on-Chip.

Elena Torroglosa is a researcher in the Department of Information and Communications Engineering of the University of Murcia since 2008, where she received her B.S. degree on Computer Science and the M.S. degree on New Technologies in Computer Science in 2012. She participated in Secure Widespread Identities for Federated Telecommunications (SWIFT) as part of the 7th Framework Program. Currently, she is a PH.D. candidate at the University of Murcia and is involved in the GEMBus Project, as part of the GN3+ (FP7-2013-2015). Her research interests include network security and identity management.

Christopher Zimmerman has received his Master of Science degree in Computer Science from West Chester University of Pennsylvania.

Index